Turbo C®++ for Windows Programming for Beginners

Turbo C® ++ for Windows Programming for Beginners

Paul Perry

A Division of Macmillan Computer Publishing
201 West 103rd Street, Indianapolis, Indiana 46290USA

Dedicated to one of the early pioneers in electronics, Thomas Edison, who had more than 1000 inventions to his credit including the incandescent light bulb, the phonograph, and motion pictures.

FIRST EDITION

International Standard Book Number: 0-672-30229-2

Library of Congress Catalog Card Number: 92-83923

96 95 94 4 3 2

Interpretation of the printing code: the rightmost double-digit number is the year of the book's printing; the rightmost single-digit, the number of the book's printing. For example, a printing code of 93-1 shows that the first printing of the book occurred in 1993.

Composed in Palatino and MCPdigital by Prentice Hall Computer Publishing

Printed in the United States of America

Publisher
Richard K. Swadley

Acquisitions Manager
Jordan Gold

Acquisitions Editor
Gregory Croy

Development and Technical Editor
Bruce Graves

Editors
Fran Hatton
Melba Hopper
Michael Cunningham
Erik Dafforn
Dean Miller
Rebecca S. Freeman

Editorial Coordinators
Rebecca S. Freeman
Bill Whitmer

Editorial Assistants
Rosemarie Graham

Cover Designer
Jean Bisesi

Director of Production and Manufacturing
Jeff Valler

Production Manager
Corinne Walls

Imprint Manager
Matthew Morrill

Book Designer
Michele Laseau

Production Analyst
Mary Beth Wakefield

Proofreading/Indexing Coordinator
Joelynn Gifford

Graphics Image Specialists
Jerry Ellis
Dennis Sheehan
Susan Vandewalle

Production
Debra Adams, Lisa Daugherty, Terri Edwards, Dennis Hager, Howard Jones, John Kane, Sean Medlock, Roger Morgan, Juli Pavey, Angela Pozdol, Linda Quigley, Michelle Self, Susan Shepard, Greg Simsic, Angie Trzepacz

Indexers
John Sleeva, Suzanne G. Snyder

OVERVIEW

Part III Advanced Windows Programming

Appendixes

CONTENTS

FOREWORD

At Borland we are extremely proud of the Turbo C++ success story. Turbo C++ for Windows provides a Windows development system capable of creating fast and powerful Windows applications. As Director of Developer Relations at Borland, I know that many professional and novice programmers embrace Borland programming tools every day to create top-notch applications. At Borland we have moved our entire development efforts over to object-oriented programming to deliver world-class product features and user benefits to our customers.

In *Turbo C++ for Windows Programming for Beginners,* Paul clearly and logically shows that you can build exciting new Windows applications using our tools and your programming skills. In my travels around the world talking with programmers, most have told me that they need more C++ and Windows examples. In response to the demand, this book is loaded with detailed program examples and descriptions. Furthermore, you will learn how to master the Windows Application Programming Interface (API) and use C++ and our ObjectWindows Library to greatly simplify Windows programming.

I think you'll find this an appealing book, regardless of how much (or how little) exposure you've had to programming graphical user interfaces. Paul has done an exceptional job of covering the basics of Windows programming in a way that programmers new to Windows can begin writing programs and quickly move to more complex projects.

I know that you'll be successful in your programming efforts.

David Intersimone

Director, Developer Relations

Borland International

ACKNOWLEDGMENTS

As always, thanks to the fantastic crew at Sams Publishing, including Gregory Croy, Michael Cunningham, Fran Hatton, Melba Hopper, Dean Miller, Becky Freeman, Erik Dafforn, and all the others behind the scenes. You are always great to work with.

Thanks to my colleagues at work, including Bruneau for always being willing to help out, Dave S. for answering hard to answer questions, Mike R. for making the workplace an interesting environment, Bill D. for such a good attitude, Dave W. for giving a helping hand whenever necessary, Jeff P. for being the ultimate hacker, Tom O. for being overly helpful, Gary J. for coming up with challenging ideas for new projects, Shea for teaching me about the Advisor line, Bob B. for being a mentor when no one else was around, Shawn for always having code almost written for yet another fantastic program, Matt A. for getting me interested in MIDI, Greg M. for a good sense of humor, Kevin K. for being the very first person I ever knew in the group, and Tommy H. for being able to debug nasty pointer problems. Also thanks to Xavier and Rich for putting up with my constant work schedule.

ABOUT THE AUTHOR

Paul J. Perry is a technical support engineer at Borland, where he handles enhanced technical support issues relating to the Advisor line. His specialty is Windows programming. Mr. Perry is the author of *Do It Yourself Turbo C++* (Sams), *Using Turbo Pascal for Windows* (Que), and *Crash Course in C* (Que). If he's not writing or programming, you will find him on his bicycle, riding 15 to 20 miles per day.

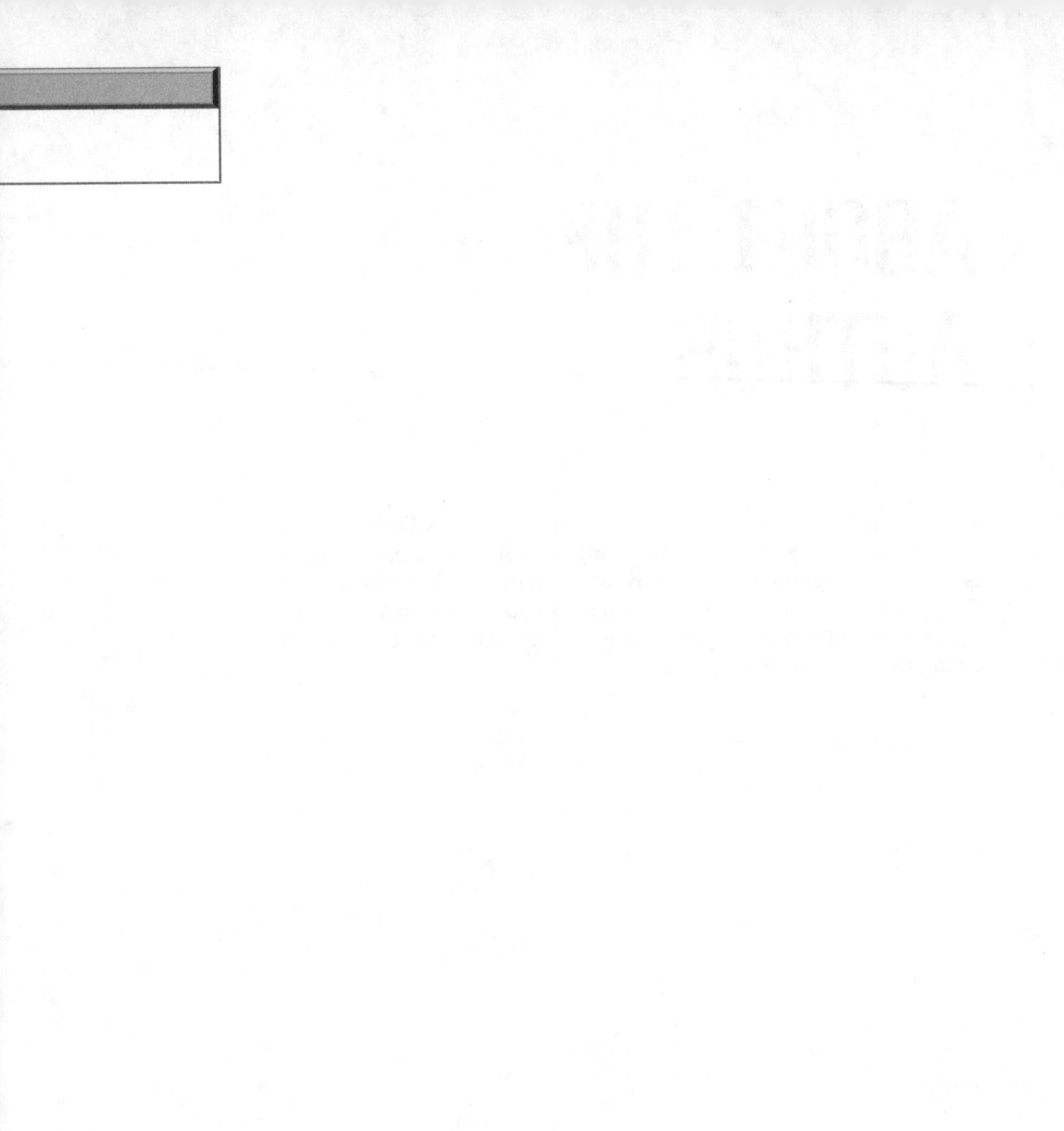

INTRODUCTION

Who Should Use This Book?

Turbo C++ for Windows Programming for Beginners is for anyone interested in programming Windows using the Turbo C++ for Windows compiler from Borland International. This book begins with the basics of programming for an event-driven environment like Windows. It continues to teach the important fundamentals of programming Windows 3.0 and 3.1 with Turbo C++ for Windows. You learn how to create windows, use custom resources, display graphical output, use the ObjectWindows Library (OWL), create dialog boxes, and program data exchange.

By the end of this book, you will be able to program the specialties of Windows, including: icons, cursors, menus, accelerator keys, and dialog boxes. You will understand dynamic linking. You will know how to make programs that use the Borland windows custom controls—also called the "look of chiseled steel"—and how to use interprocess communication, including the clipboard and dynamic data exchange.

Although you may not know these terms now, you will by the end of the book. With its discussion of Windows programming, this book describes the inner workings of Windows. This makes it easier for you to understand how Windows works.

Besides saving you the frustration of typing example programs, this book's companion diskette gets you up and running quickly. Use the diskette and book together—all the programs are on the diskette.

Beyond the Windows programming fundamentals, you learn how to use the powerful Turbo C++ for Windows package tools. These include the Integrated Development Environment, the Resource Workshop, the Turbo Debugger for Windows, the WinSpector, and the Import Librarian. You also find tips and techniques to help you create excellent Windows programs.

What You Should Know to Use This Book

Programming for the Windows environment requires special knowledge.

First, you must be accustomed to Windows. Although you find information about the user interface in this book, you do not learn how to use Windows. This is a programmer's book, not a user's.

Windows is easy to use, but as a programmer, you must know the fine points of the common user interface. You must provide a certain feel users expect with their programs. If you know how to use Windows, your programs can have the look and feel of other Windows applications.

Turbo C++ for Windows Programming for Beginners is for the programmer who has a good working knowledge of programming with C and C++, but wants to understand how to program for Windows. You, therefore, must be familiar with the C and C++ programming language. You need a basic understanding of object-oriented programming principles.

If you need more help with C and C++ programming, you might refer to my book, *Do It Yourself Turbo C++* (Sams Publishing, 1992). It gives a firm introduction to the fundamentals in C and C++ programming and includes many examples and hints.

What You Need to Use This Book

As the title suggests, this book is for the programmer who already owns Turbo C++ for Windows. If you own the Borland C++ package, you possess a Windows-hosted environment that enables you to take full advantage of this book (except installation instructions in Chapter 1, "Getting Started with Turbo C++ for Windows").

This book, therefore, is for the programmer who uses Turbo C++ for Windows 3.1 or Borland C++ 3.1 with Application Frameworks. If you use Microsoft C with the Windows Software Development Kit (SDK), much of the information about Windows programming is still valid. However, the

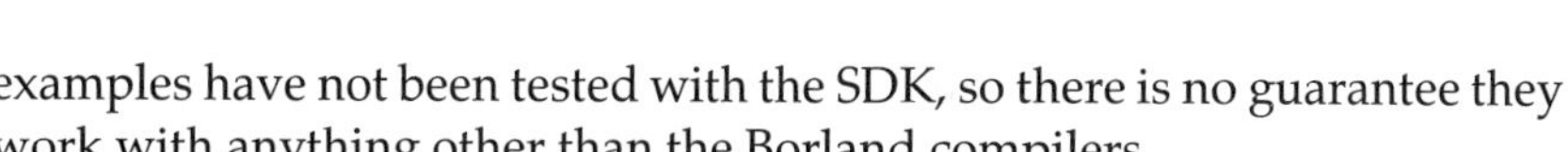

examples have not been tested with the SDK, so there is no guarantee they work with anything other than the Borland compilers.

Organization of This Book

You learn by example with this book. Each chapter focuses on a specific element of programming for Windows. The book progresses in logical order, starting with program installation and moving to more advanced topics such as window creation, the graphics device interface, dialog boxes, the use of multiple document interface, clipboard transfers, and the dynamic data-exchange management library.

Turbo C++ for Windows Programming for Beginners is in three sections. Essentially, they provide an introduction to the Turbo C++ for Windows programming environment, explain how to write Windows programs, and explain advanced Windows programming concepts. You find practical example programs in each section.

Part I, "The Turbo C++ for Windows Programming Environment," introduces the Turbo C++ for Windows Integrated Development Environment.

- Chapter 1, "Getting Started with Turbo C++ for Windows," discusses general information about programming for Windows and then leads you through the stages of installing the compiler.
- Chapter 2, "Programming Environment," gives detailed information about using the Integrated Development Environment. You learn how to use the menus and dialog boxes. You master the editor and understand the modes in which these resources are available. You also learn how to take advantage of the essential information in the online help system.
- Chapter 3, "Getting Started in Windows," covers the methods of programming with Turbo C++ for Windows, as well as Windows principles and methodology, including basic input and output.

You start creating and understanding Windows programs in Part II, "Windows Programming with Turbo C++." You learn about message handling concepts, multitasking aspects, object-oriented programming with Windows, and the use of resources. You gain a sound understanding of the internal structures and concepts of Windows application design in this section.

- Chapter 4, "Writing Windows Programs," introduces the specifics of an event-driven user interface. You learn how to create an actual Windows program that uses the Windows API and how to compile, link, and run the program with project files.
- Chapter 5, "Using the ObjectWindows Library," demonstrates how to use object-oriented programming principles with the OWL. You learn how to create a unique derived class of your application and a main program window. You also learn how to use the ObjectBrowser to view C++ class hierarchies.
- Chapter 6, "Working with Windows," explains the differences in window styles and demonstrates the many types of windows available. You learn about child windows and how they are created.
- Chapter 7, "A First Look at Resources," examines what a resource is and starts your work with the Resource Workshop to create icons and custom cursors for use in your own programs.
- Chapter 8, "Adding Menus to Your Program," shows you how to add a menu to your program and respond to selecting a menu choice. This chapter includes details about how to customize menus by showing how to add checkmarks to menus and how to disable menus.
- Chapter 9, "Using Scroll Bars," gives two methods of adding scroll bars to your main window. You learn how to process the window scroll bar messages in a traditional C program, as well as how to integrate the window scroll bars with the OWL.
- Chapter 10, "Getting Input from the User," describes the two primary forms of user input: the keyboard and the mouse. In Windows, you must consider these input devices, and this chapter shows you how to harness the power of input.
- Chapter 11, "Working with the GDI," is an introduction to the powerful library of graphics functions Windows uses to display graphical output.

- Chapter 12, "Turbo C++ for Windows Programming Tools," takes a break from Windows programming concepts and focuses on the tools included with Turbo C++ for Windows. You learn how to debug code with Turbo Debugger for Windows. You also learn about the mighty WinSpector and discover how to use it to debug your programs.

- Chapter 13, "Using Dialog Boxes," returns to Windows programming concepts and explains the basics of dialog boxes. You learn the difference between modal and modeless dialog boxes, as well as what a dialog box control is and what types are available. You learn how to use the dialog boxes that come with Turbo C++ for Windows and are standard in Windows 3.1.

- Chapter 14, "More About Dialog Boxes," continues the discussion of dialog boxes, showing Resource Workshop tricks to create dialog boxes and ways to use the Borland Windows Custom Controls in a program.

Part III, "Advanced Windows Programming," shows you how to use the more advanced features of Windows programming. It covers dynamic link libraries, advanced GDI functions, and data interchange.

- Chapter 15, "Dynamic Link Libraries," discusses the special nature of Windows DLLs and how to use them in your own programs. You learn what an import library is and how to create one.

- Chapter 16, "Even More GDI," describes some of the more advanced GDI functions. It includes information about using metafiles to create screen displays, displaying text in different fonts, and using bitmaps in your programs.

- Chapter 17, "Using the Multiple Document Interface," explains what MDI is and shows you how to use the OWL to create applications that conform to the MDI specification.

- Chapter 18, "Using the Clipboard," introduces the primary way to exchange data in the Windows environment. You learn what the clipboard is, where it stores its contents, and how you access the clipboard to store text bitmaps and metafiles.

- Chapter 19, "Dynamic Data Exchange," covers another form of interprocess communications known as DDE. You learn the message protocol. The chapter ends with the dynamic data exchange management library, which greatly simplifies DDE transfers.
- Chapter 20, "Putting It All Together," puts the concepts you have learned in the book to practical use to create a useful utility for displaying the Windows desktop.

You use the appendixes as a quick reference to Windows virtual key codes, ASCII codes, and the Windows API reference. By the end of this book, you are comfortable with Windows Programming conventions. The book can continue to be a ready reference with useful code for creating custom applications.

Notation and Conventions

To gain full benefit, you must understand the design of this book. The chapters contain bold text, italicized text, bulleted lists, numbered lists, figures, program listings, code fragments, and tables of information. All these design features help you understand the material.

Characters you are asked to type appear in `monospace`. In lines you must type, characters that hold the place of a drive or filename (such as *C:*)—or anything else you must substitute—are in *`monospace italics`*.

Italic type emphasizes an important word or phrase. Pay close attention to italicized text. It also introduces new technical terms. A definition or an explanation usually follows an italicized term.

Bulleted lists have the following characteristics:

- A shadowed box (the bullet) precedes each item in a bulleted list. The bullet is a special flag that draws your attention to important material.
- The order of items in a bulleted list is not mandatory. That is, the items represent related points you must understand, but not in a special sequence.

- The text for items in a bulleted list is often longer than the text you see in other kinds of lists. Items in bulleted lists contain explanations, not simple actions.

Numbered lists contain actions you perform, or lists of items that must be in a particular sequence. When you see a numbered list, you do the following:

1. Start at the beginning of the list. Don't skip ahead to later items in the list; order is important.
2. Be sure you completely understand each item as you encounter it.
3. Read all the items in the list. Don't skip any of them—each item is important.

Figures are pictures or graphics that help you understand the text. Each figure has a number in the form *c.n. c* is the chapter with the figure, and *n* is the number of the figure in a sequence within the chapter.

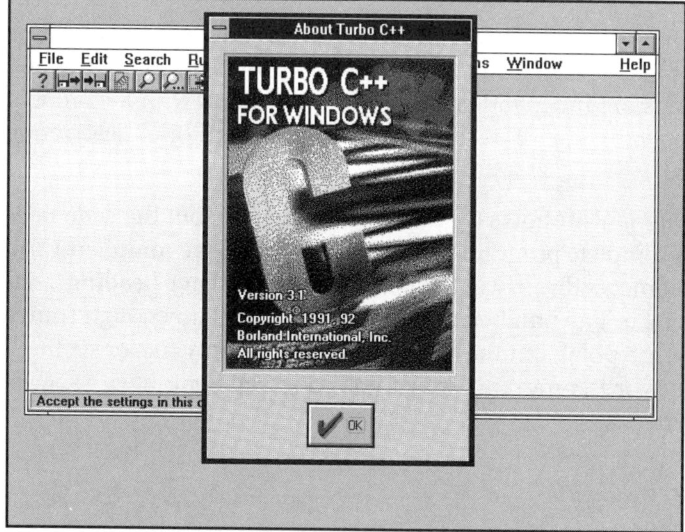

Figure 0.1.
A sample illustration.

Listings give the C and C++ source code for a complete program, or perhaps for a program module. In either case, you can compile source code shown in a listing. Listing 0.1, for example, shows the source code for a complete program. (Most complete programs are much longer than this sample.)

Listing 0.1. START.C. A sample program listing.

```
// START.C - Sample C Program Listing
//
// Programming Windows with Turbo C++ for Windows
// by Paul J. Perry

#include <stdio.h>

void main()
{

  printf("hello, world\n");

}
```

As shown in Listing 0.1, program listings, like figures, have numbers (see header for Listing 0.1). However, the reference numbers for figures and program listings are independent. Each program starts with a comment section that instantly identifies the program and gives a brief description of its purpose.

A *code fragment* also shows C and C++ source code, but the code does not make up a complete program. (The fragment cannot be compiled.) You insert code fragments directly in the text. They do not have headings, reference numbers, or line numbers. Code fragments contain enough source code to illustrate a point, but they are short—usually only five or six lines. Notice that keywords, program listings, and code fragments have a special monospace typeface.

TIP

Tip boxes like this one provide useful or insightful tips. You find information such as programming tips, tricks, and shortcuts in a tip box.

NOTE

Note boxes hold convenient notes that help you learn to program with Turbo C++ for Windows. A note box includes a brief statement to remind you about important facts about programming.

WARNING

Warning boxes give important warnings about problems or possible unwanted side effects that might occur in your code, as well as important cautions.

Tables appear when lists and columns of information are suitable. Tables have their own headings and reference numbers—independent of the numbers for figures and program listings. Table 0.1 shows how a table appears in this book.

Table 0.1. The Formatting Conventions Used in This Book.

Format Convention	*Use*
Italic	An eye-catching type style that emphasizes important words or phrases.
Bulleted lists	A list of items with a bullet flagging each item; the sequence of items is usually not important.
Numbered lists	A list of items with numbers flagging each item; sequence is important.
Program listings	Complete programs that you can compile.

continues

Table 0.1. continued

Format Convention	*Use*
Code fragments	A small number of source code lines that illustrate a point; you cannot compile code fragments apart from other code.
Tip boxes	Boxed text that gives you programming tips, tricks, and shortcuts.
Note boxes	Notes about programming.
Warning boxes	Important warnings of problems that might occur.
Tables	Information shown in columnar format; tables may or may not contain explanations or descriptions.

A Note on Programming

You probably already know: to learn to program, you must program.

Remember an important point about learning programming: it is impossible to learn without writing code, compiling your programs, and observing the way they do or do not work.

Because practicing Windows programming is essential to learning Windows programming, the book gives you many example programs to use. However, try different things in your own programs. It is important to experiment to learn how a program works.

TURBO C++ FOR WINDOWS PROGRAMMING ENVIRONMENT

1

GETTING STARTED WITH TURBO C++ FOR WINDOWS

IN THIS CHAPTER

■

Items in the Turbo C++ for Windows package.

■

False rumors about programming for Windows.

■

A history of the Windows graphical user interface, as well as a look into the future of Windows.

■

Benefits of programming for Windows from the perspectives of both the developer and the user.

■

Installation of Turbo C++ for Windows.

About the Turbo C++ for Windows Package

Turbo C++ for Windows is the first C++ programming tool with a Windows-hosted Integrated Development Environment (IDE) for Microsoft Windows. When Windows was first introduced, all programming tools were DOS-based. As a programmer, you worked from the DOS command line with a text-based editor. You started Windows only when you were ready to test your software. Mostly, you were forced to work from the command line.

This all changed with Turbo C++ for Windows. With a Windows-hosted IDE, Turbo C++ for Windows gets you up and running faster because you can develop programs inside Windows.

The Turbo C++ for Windows package includes much more than a built-in compiler and editor. Windows is a special environment that uses special memory management and resources such as icons, cursors, and bitmaps. Turbo C++ for Windows enables you to employ these fully.

The tools in the Turbo C++ for Windows package include the following:

- A full Integrated Development Environment (IDE). This enables you to edit, compile, and link your programs while running Windows. This book focuses on program development with the IDE.
- Turbo Debugger for Windows (TDW). This is the complete version of Borland's professional debugger, with extensions designed especially for tracking the messages critical to Windows operation.
- The Resource Workshop. This is a visual tool kit that enables you to quickly design and manage your custom resources, including icons, cursors, bitmaps, menus, dialog boxes, menu accelerator keys, and string resources.
- The ObjectWindows Library (OWL). This complete object-oriented C++ programming library is a framework to rapid development of Windows applications.

- Full rights to use and distribute the Borland Windows Custom Controls (BWCC). These custom controls give your programs an impressive look of chiseled steel—the look of all Borland's Windows products and the one you want for your programs.

- Valuable utilities for programming in Windows. These include WinSpector, for tracking nasty program errors, and the graphical Import Librarian, for accessing routines in dynamic link libraries (DLLs).

- Extensive online documentation to the entire Windows 3.1 Applications Programming Interface (API). This is all available at the press of a single key. Because the documentation is based on the Windows help engine, you instantly can search for any topic and use advanced hypertext technology to move among subjects.

Users often wonder how Turbo C++ for Windows compares to Borland's other language products. The Turbo C++ for Windows package is an excellent beginner's tool for programming with Windows in C and C++. It, however, creates only Windows applications: you cannot create DOS programs with this package.

Turbo C++ (for DOS) is the beginner's programming tool that enables you to write DOS programs in both C and C++. It creates only DOS programs and does not include the extensive tools in Borland C++.

About Borland C++

Borland C++ is the professional package that enables you to create DOS and Windows applications. Most important, it includes compiler optimizations that help you create more efficient code. This makes it attractive to professional developers. The package has extensive programming tools, including Turbo Assembler, two versions of Turbo Debugger, and two versions of Turbo Profiler (one for DOS and one for Windows). It also includes other programming tools that make creating advanced applications easier.

You can purchase Borland C++ with the Application Frameworks. This package has two object-oriented user interface libraries: Turbo Vision (for creating DOS programs) and the ObjectWindows Library. The Application Frameworks also includes complete source code for the C runtime library, as well as the source code for Turbo Vision and the OWL.

The remainder of this chapter helps get you quickly up and running with Turbo C++ for Windows. In later sections of the book, you will learn to use each aspect of the Turbo C++ for Windows package.

Rumors About Windows Programming

You probably have heard some wicked stories about programming for Windows. It's certainly true that programming Windows is different from programming for DOS. Part of the steep learning curve involves learning new concepts related to event-driven programming.

This learning curve is necessary with any advanced multitasking windowing system under any environment. Windows is easy for the user to adapt to; however, the programmer bears the burden of making it easy. You, therefore, have much to consider when you program for Windows—or when you program for any multitasking graphical user interface.

Remember, however, Turbo C++ for Windows offers some of the industry's finest development tools. With the OWL and object-oriented programming technology, you can make Windows programming much easier.

NOTE

Windows does not use C++ code. About 70 percent of Windows was written in the C programming language. The other 30 percent was written in low-level 80x86 assembly language. The parts written in assembly language include routines that require extra speed, such as device drivers.

Which Version of Windows?

Although Windows has gained recent popularity, earlier versions have been available since 1985. Microsoft began work with Windows in 1983 and released Version 1.1 in November, 1985. This version was designed for a two-floppy, 8088-based system with a CGA graphics adapter. Windows 1.1 was not an instant success, mainly because it was announced about two years before its release, and even then, it didn't meet expectations.

In 1987, Microsoft released Version 2.0 with a new user interface that supported overlapping windows. A major advantage to Windows 2.0 was the improved use of memory. Soon, Version 2.1 was released with bug fixes and minor upgrades. Microsoft later released Windows/286 and Windows/386: both took advantage of the microprocessors that bear their names. Users were sometimes confused about which version to use because the advantages of each were not evident. Finally, the only available application was PageMaker (a desktop publishing package). Many used Windows solely to run PageMaker.

Windows 3.0

Version 3.0 of Windows, however, caught on. Fanfare from the Microsoft marketing machine accompanied its release in May 1990. It had an improved user interface. It also had an automatic capacity to detect the microprocessor running it (80866/88, 80286, or 80386) and then to adjust and work optimally under that processor.

Windows 3.0 improved support for running DOS applications. Additionally, when run on an 80386 or 80486 machine, 16M of memory can be addressed. At the time, if you wanted to program for Windows, you had to buy the Microsoft C compiler and the costly software development kit (SDK).

The requirement for expensive programming tools changed when Borland announced its programming tools for Windows. You didn't have an extra charge to program Windows. The entire Windows API was available when you purchased the compiler. As a result, the Borland tools are respected industry-wide as the standard for developing Windows applications. Many major applications on the market—Aldus, Lotus, and others—are written with Borland language products.

Windows 3.1

Windows 3.1 was announced in June 1992 and is what 3.0 should have been. It is a mature version of Windows 3.0. It runs faster, and it contains better protection for programs that run amok. It includes about 200 more API functions for features and operations—such as common dialog boxes, drag and drop operations, tool help libraries, data compression support, dynamic data exchange, and object linking and embedding.

Shortly after the announcement of Windows 3.1, Borland updated its language products and released Version 3.1 of its programming tools which take full advantage of Windows 3.1.

Windows NT

The current industry hype is Windows NT (which stands for New Technology). Microsoft has made some exciting claims about this newest version of Windows. Although Windows NT looks similar to the Windows you run now, Microsoft claims it's a vastly improved operating system.

Windows is actually an operating environment; that is, it runs on top of DOS, which is an operating system. Windows NT will replace DOS and Windows, giving you all you need to run your computer. When you start your computer, Windows NT will be the first thing to start up.

Windows NT will not run under the limitations of DOS, which was first designed more than ten years ago. When Microsoft committed to Windows NT, it recruited some of the world's best operating system designers from mainframe computer manufacturers. Thus, Windows NT has advanced features you only dream about when operating a system on a PC.

Windows NT will not be for everybody. At about $500 and with expensive upgrades, not everybody will want to move to NT immediately. Also, Windows NT will require a minimum of 16M of memory to run and a CD-ROM drive to install. This means an additional investment in hardware for many users.

The Windows NT Application Programming Interface (the Win32 specification) is in a prerelease form (Win32 Application Programming Interface Prerelease Volume 1 and Volume 2, 1992, Microsoft Press). Although only a privileged few can test prerelease versions of Windows NT, anyone can purchase the set of books and learn about the future plans. The prerelease specification helps you gear up for Windows NT software development. All programs in this book follow the rules set forth by Microsoft for upward mobility to NT. Therefore, when NT is available, you should be able, with minimal changes, to recompile all these programs and run them under Windows NT.

As you learn about Windows programming, you find ways your program will be compatible with NT and what Microsoft has on the horizon for you.

Why Program for Windows?

Although many might still wonder if its justified, Windows has created a big fuss in the computer industry. In this section, you learn the advantages users and developers gain with the Windows operating environment, as well as special aspects of the windows interface.

NOTE

Throughout this book, Windows (with an uppercase W) refers to the Microsoft Windows operating environment. The word windows (with a lowercase w) refers to the more general term for a rectangular area on the screen.

User Advantages of Windows

Most users agree graphical-oriented user environments are much easier to use than their nongraphical counterparts. The graphical interface provides a visual environment that speeds communications between users and computers. A common user interface is an interface that is similar regardless of the program being executed. The basic operational concepts in Windows always remain the same, so the user can use new programs productively with little training.

Certain elements of the environment are defined by Microsoft to make communication between programs easy. You can design Windows application programs that enable a user to copy data to a system clipboard memory area. The data then is pasted from the clipboard to another program. For example, you can use the Windows Paint program to create pictures and copy those pictures into the Windows Write word processing program.

With Windows you can execute two or more programs at the same time. This process, called nonpreemptive multitasking, allows several programs to operate at the same time through a system of messages passed between the program's windows.

The Dynamic Data Exchange (DDE) protocol allows applications to share data on either a one-time or dynamic ongoing basis. A word processor can import a graph from a spreadsheet, and when the data changes in the spreadsheet, the graph in the word processor is updated to show the new data.

Developer Advantages

Writing a program in Windows ensures compatibility with a large number of input and output devices. More than 280 printer drivers, ranging from a nine-pin dot matrix printer to a Postscript laser printer, are available. More than 24 display drivers are accessible, for everything from a Hercules monochrome adapter to a Super VGA color display with resolutions of 1024 by 768 and a display of 256 colors.

This selection of drivers means you don't have to create multiple device drivers so your program can be run on as many machines as possible. Instead, you use your time and energy producing an excellent product.

Regarding accessible memory, your application no longer has the DOS 640K limit when you program in Windows. Your programs can access all installed memory and any available virtual memory (memory swapped to disk). Windows automatically performs the memory management, including virtual memory management.

You no longer have to write and debug complex graphics routines: these are part of Windows. Microsoft defines many core graphics features, which enables you to develop complex graphical displays with minimum effort.

Programming in a graphics-based environment is different than you might expect. However, these differences should be for the better. If this is your first time programming in graphics, you are about to discover many nice features in Windows programming, but you might need time to adjust to them.

Aspects of the Windows Interface

Programming for Windows has many aspects. Although most features in Windows are familiar to computing professionals, you must recognize the elements of programming in Windows.

The most striking feature of Windows is the graphical user interface. This is what you first see when you use the environment. Windows has a rich variety of user interface objects. A user interface object is a method for the Windows user to interact with the computing environment. Some of the interface objects are the following:

- *Windows.* The window (for which the environment is named) is the basic element of the interface. Although you can think of a window as a specific running application, a single program can have an unlimited number of windows. All the interface objects (command buttons, menus, dialog boxes, and so on) are windows.
- *Menus.* Displayed along the top row of a program, the menu bar lists the options in a program. Most applications use a menu to interact with the user.

- *Dialog boxes.* The dialog box gives your program a way to request and provide information for the user. You complete a dialog box by supplying information. A dialog box consists of dialog box controls, including command buttons, listboxes, drop-down lists, option buttons, and checkboxes.
- *A consistent user interface.* After you learn to use one program, you easily can learn to use another because they look and feel the same. If you have ever worked in DOS and switched between programs (for example, between WordPerfect and Lotus 1-2-3), you know the user interface is different for each program. Windows programs all act and feel similar.
- *Device independent graphical output.* The Windows graphics device interface (GDI) enables you to create graphics that work on a multitude of output devices. Many of the disks that come with Windows are drivers to support a great number of output devices.
- *Multiple instances.* The capacity to run many instances of a program and share the same code for each instance. (See Figure 1.1 for an example of Notepad.)

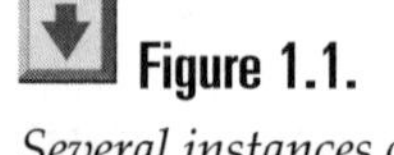

Figure 1.1.

Several instances of the same program.

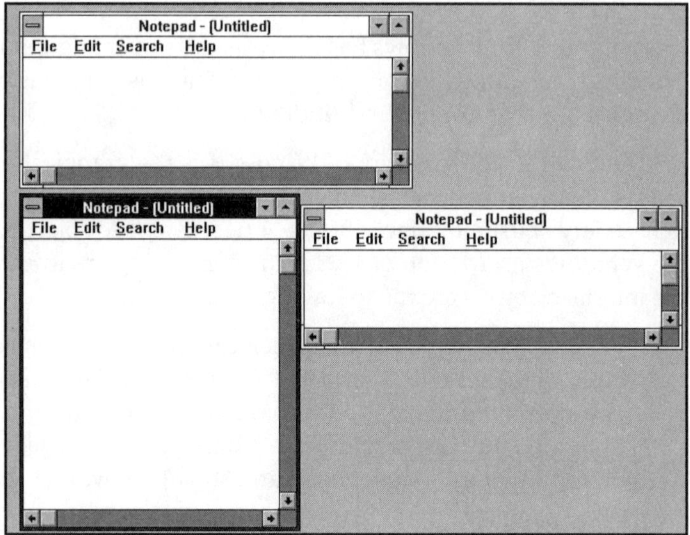

- *Message-driven programming.* In Windows, think of each program as a function called by Windows. A given application communicates with Windows (and vice versa) by sending messages within themselves. A message is a number that tells your program an event has happened. If you are using the Windows Paint program and switch to Program Manager, a message is sent to Paint indicating it is no longer the main application in use. At the same time, Program Manager receives a message indicating it has the full focus of the user.

- *Multitasking.* Running more than one program at a time accomplishes more (see Figure 1.2). If you load Microsoft Excel and Windows Paint at the same time, you easily can switch between the two. No longer must you save the file you are working on in one program, exit the program, load the other program, and then repeat the process. When multitasking, special considerations must be taken because all the computing resources are being shared. For example, your program can write only in its designated area.

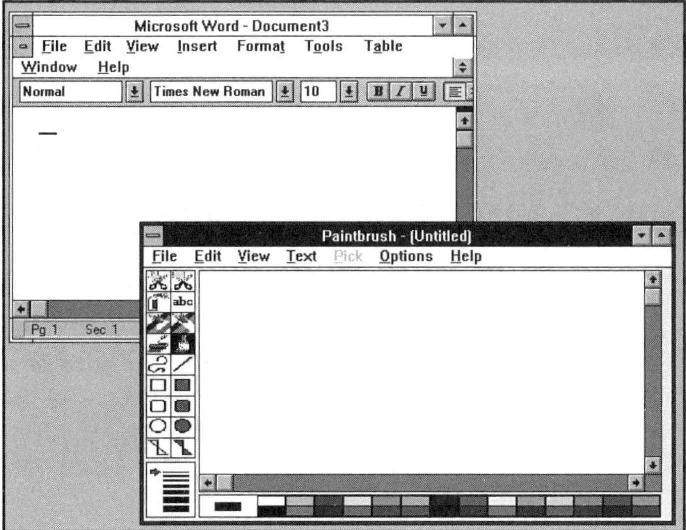

Figure 1.2.
Multitasking in Windows.

- *Data interchange.* Windows has a built-in clipboard (see Figure 1.3), which is an area of memory set aside to store specific information. You can transfer the clipboard information to a different program for use there. Another form of data interchange is Dynamic Data Exchange, which lets one program automatically update the information another program requests.

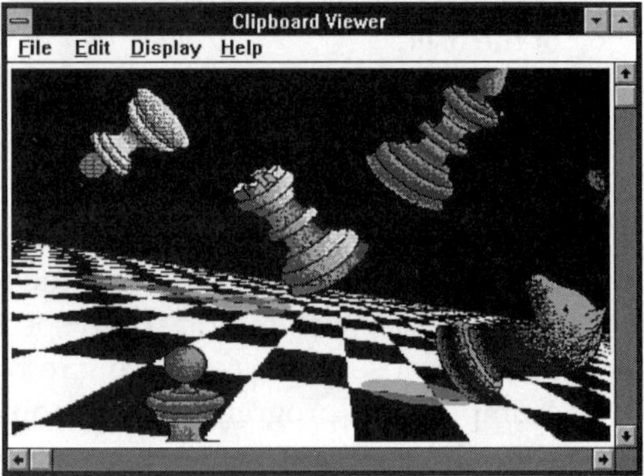

Figure 1.3.
The Windows Clipboard.

In later chapters, you will learn to use the special aspects of Windows to create practical software tools.

Installation of Turbo C++ for Windows

Borland's excellent installation utility makes installing Turbo C++ for Windows an easy task. All you do is tell the INSTALL program which subdirectory of the hard drive should receive the program. Then, load each disk when prompted. After specifying a couple of options, the rest of the work is done for you. This section discusses available options.

System Requirements

The minimum software and hardware requirements your computer system needs to run Turbo C++ for Windows successfully are as follows:

- Microsoft Windows 3.0 or 3.1. (Version 3.1 is preferred.)
- MS-DOS or PC-DOS. I suggest version 3.1 or later. (DOS 5.0 is best.)
- A personal computer with an 80286 processor. (I recommend an 80386 or better for improved performance.)
- A system with at least 2M of RAM. (4M is better, 8M is preferred.)
- A hard disk drive with about 26M free disk space and at least one floppy disk drive. Although you can accomplish a partial install of the product—which requires less hard disk space—I recommend you either free up the space necessary or buy a new hard drive. You might think this is plenty of disk space (it was just several years ago when computers came standard with a single 20M hard drive), but you'll want the amenities that come with the product's full installation.
- An EGA, VGA, or Hercules video adapter. As an option, you can use two video monitors (one color, one monochrome) to debug your programs. With this setup, you will see Windows and the debugger on separate screens.
- A mouse pointing device.

NOTE

Sometimes readers are curious about the author's system. When writing this book, I used a 40MHz 486 clone—actually a 33MHz chip being pushed at 40MHz—with a 220M hard disk, 8M of memory, an Orchid ProDesigner IIs graphics board, a NEC MultiSync 4FG monitor, and a Microsoft mouse. I used Microsoft Word for Windows 2.0 to write the manuscript and did my printing on a Hewlett-Packard LaserJet III printer.

With an understanding of the basic system necessary to run Turbo C++ for Windows, you are ready to install the package.

Running the Installation Program

To begin the installation process, put your disk labeled "INSTALL DISK" in a floppy drive and type:

```
WIN n:INSTALL
```

where *n*: is the floppy drive with the INSTALL DISK. This loads Windows and starts the automated installation procedure.

If you are already running Windows, switch to Program Manager and choose the Run option from the File menu. On the screen, you will see the Run dialog box (see Figure 1.4). In the edit box provided, type:

```
n:INSTALL
```

and choose OK or press Enter.

Figure 1.4.

The Program Manager Run dialog box.

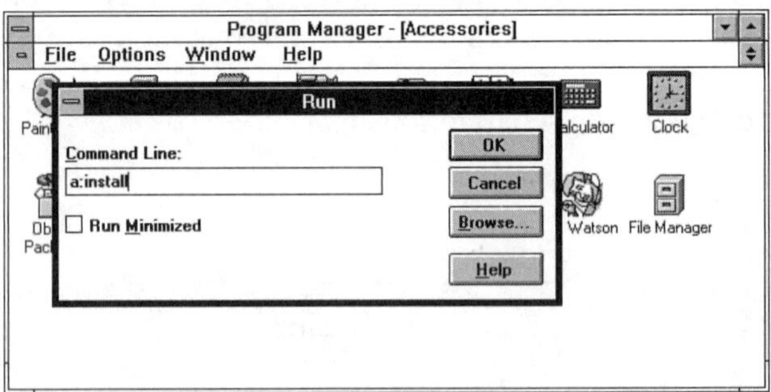

When the installation program starts, it displays a dialog box that enables you to specify which directory location to use for different groups of files found in the Turbo C++ for Windows package (see Figure 1.5). Several buttons enable you to modify installation options.

The first button, Turbo C++ Base Directory (see Figure 1.6), enables you to change the root directory in which the package is installed. The default is TCWIN. You probably want to leave this setting as is.

The second button, Installation Options (see Figure 1.7), enables you to specify the parts of the package you want to install.

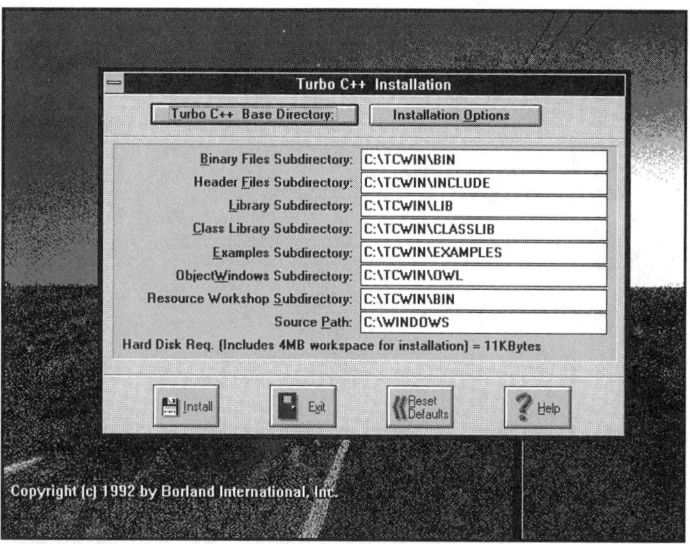

Figure 1.5.
Turbo C++ for Windows Installation dialog box.

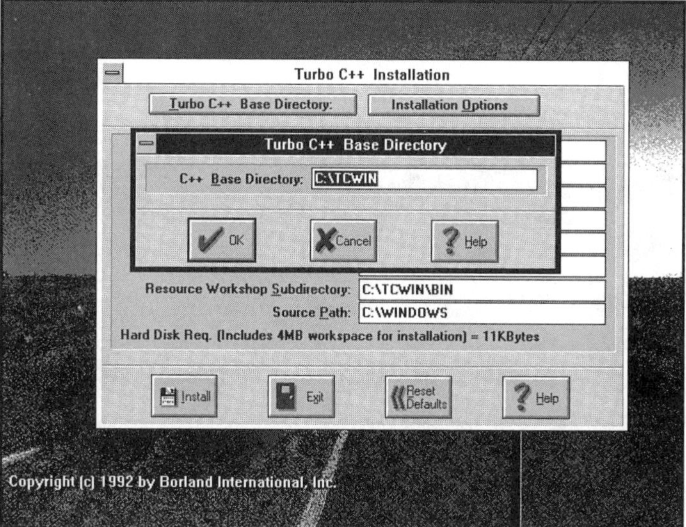

Figure 1.6.
The Turbo C++ Base Directory dialog box.

Figure 1.7.

The Turbo C++ Installation Options dialog box.

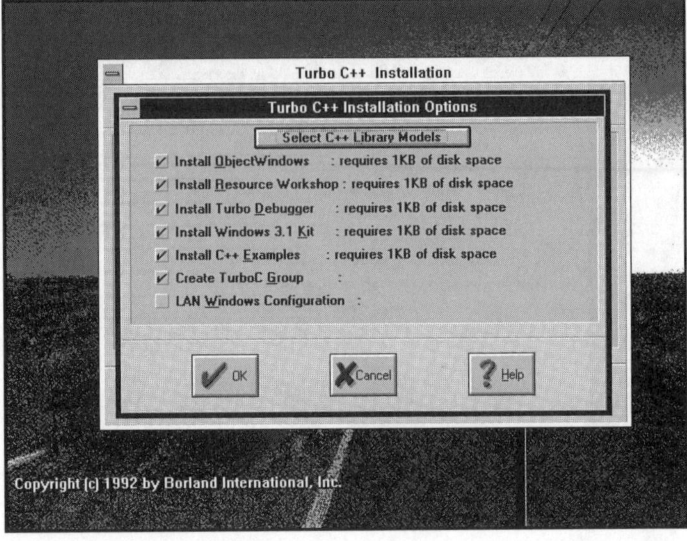

Clicking the first button, Select C++ Library Models (see Figure 1.8), enables you to select the Memory Model libraries you want to install. Memory models need further explanation.

Figure 1.8.

The C++ Library Model Selection dialog box.

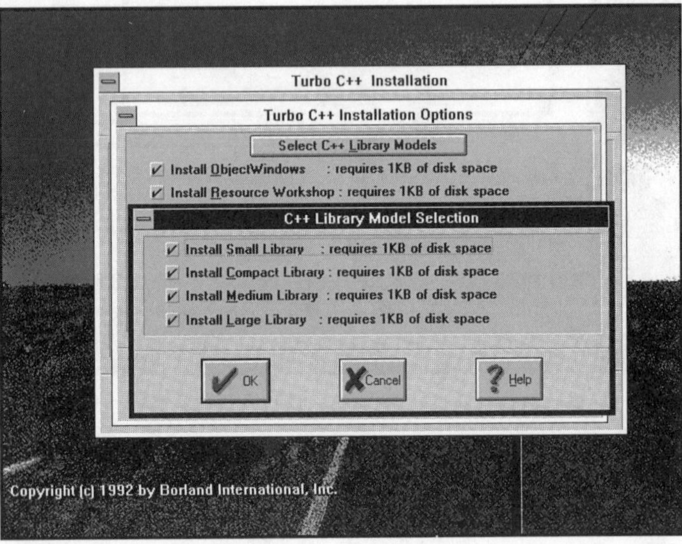

When the dialog box is displayed, it asks which memory models you want to use. This question relates to the segmented architecture of the 80286, 386, and 486 microprocessors. A program consists of both code and data. You quickly can access code and data that fit in a single segment. However, when it exceeds the size of a segment—64K—the process is slower because you must access it differently internally.

Depending on the type of application being developed, the programmer must select a memory model large enough to accommodate the program—but to keep a speedy execution, not unnecessarily large. (See Table 1.1 while specifying the memory model to install.) If you're not sure which memory model to install, use the large memory model. You can safely use it with almost every program you write.

Table 1.1. Memory model specification.

Memory Model	*Meaning*
Small	All code and data must reside in a single 64K segment.
Compact	Your code has 64K available to it, and your data has 64K (minus some overhead) available to it.
Medium	1M is available to your code, and 64K is available to your data.
Large	Your code has 1M available to it, and your data has 1M available to it.

C, C++, and the OWL use library routines to perform input, output, math, and other operations. Each group of library routines comes in three different versions to match each available memory model (small and compact use the same one). To build a program under a specific memory model, you must have the library routines for that model. To use the ObjectWindows Library, you must have the small, medium, or large memory model. Regular C programs can use any memory model.

The other installation options in Figure 1.3 are listed in Table 1.2.

Table 1.2. Installation Options dialog box items.

Option	*Description*
Install ObjectWindows	This installs the ObjectWindows Library.
Install Resource Workshop	This installs Resource Workshop editor.
Install Turbo Debugger	This installs Turbo Debugger for Windows.
Install Windows 3.1 kit	This installs Windows 3.1. It has specific information, including example programs and libraries for using all the Windows 3.1 specific features such as True Type fonts, dynamic data exchange management library, common dialog boxes, and more.
Install C++ examples	Installs OWL example programs.
Create TurboC group	Installs automatically a program group titled "Turbo C++ 3.1" to Program Manager.
LAN Windows configuration	Use only when installing on a network. This tells the INSTALL program to copy specific files to the local workstation.

To accept the default settings, click OK or press Enter.

Finally, you return to the Turbo C++ installation dialog box in Figure 1.5. This dialog box enables you to specify which directory location to use for different groups of files in the Turbo C++ for Windows package. To modify an item on the installation dialog box, press Tab to move the focus to the next item (the focus moves top to bottom and left to right).

Clicking the mouse cursor on an item gives it the focus immediately. The fields you type information in are text boxes.

Table 1.3 lists the groups of files and their uses in the installation program dialog box. Again, I recommend installing the files in the default directory on the drive with your programming tools.

Table 1.3. Installation directories.

Install Directory	*Description*
Binary files	This is the directory for executable files (TCW, TDW, IMPLIBW, and others).
Header files	This is the location for the C and C++ header files.
Library	This is the location for the C and C++ library files.
Class Library	This is the location for the C++ class libraries.
Examples	This is the location for the example C source code.
ObjectWindows	This is the location for the ObjectWindows Libraries; files, examples, and source code.
Resource Workshop	This is the location for the Resource Workshop files.
Source path	This is the drive you are installing from (usually a: or b:).

After all options are set correctly, highlight the Install button on the lower-left corner of the dialog box and press Enter, or click the button with the mouse. The installation program will start running and it will display a visual clock showing the time required to install the files to your hard disk as well as the disk space being consumed by the new files (see Figure 1.9).

Figure 1.9.

The Installation screen.

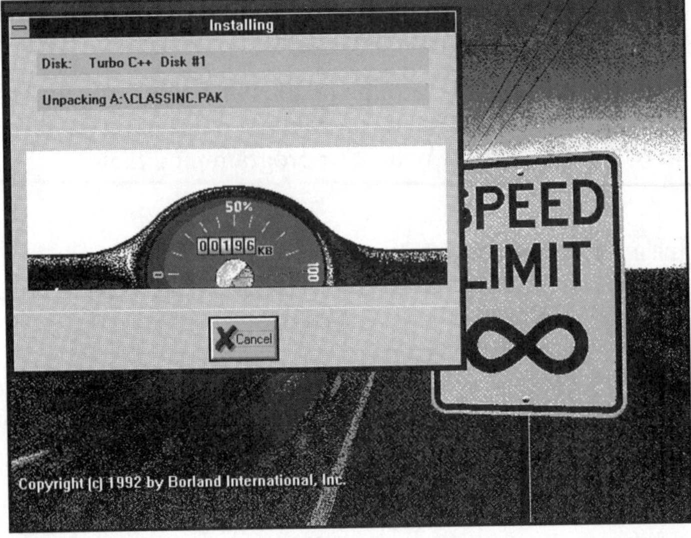

After the installation program is finished, the required files are on your hard drive in the specified directory. You also should find a group created in Program Manager (see Figure 1.10).

Figure 1.10.

The program groups created in Program Manager.

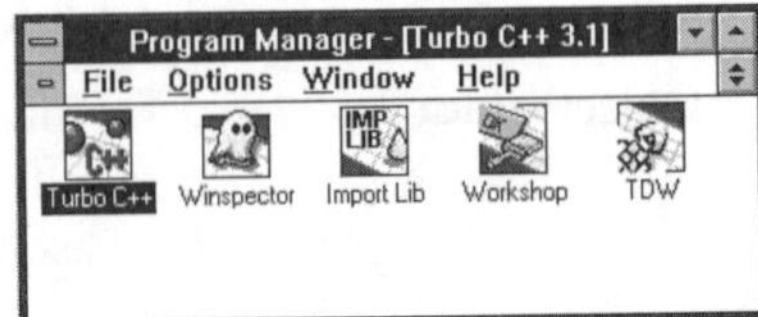

TIP

Glance through the files in the C:\TCWIN\DOC subdirectory. You will find valuable last-minute documentation for using Turbo C++ for Windows. The important files include HELPME!.DOC, WIN31.DOC, and BWCCAPI.RW. If you have a printer, you might want these three files on hard copy.

Installing the Book Disk

Switch to Program Manager to install the programs accompanying this book. Then choose the Run option from the File menu. On the screen, you will see the Run dialog box. In the edit box provided, type:

```
n:setup
```

and insert the disk in drive `n:`. Choose the OK button or press Enter to start the setup program. Type the destination directory where you want the programs installed. The setup program checks whether your hard disk has enough space to install the program.

For organization, the programs have a directory for each chapter with the appropriate programs installed beneath it. Program groups are added to the Program Manager to enable you to run programs immediately.

With the compiler and the book disks installed, you are ready to start coding. In the next chapter, you will learn to use the Integrated Development Environment.

What You Have Learned

In this chapter, you toured the Turbo C++ for Windows installation process. You learned some advantages of Windows to the user and the programmer. These important points were covered:

- The Turbo C++ for Windows package includes more than a compiler. Besides the Integrated Development Environment (IDE), the package comes with Turbo Debugger for Windows, the Resource Workshop, the ObjectWindows Library, Borland Windows Custom Controls, WinSpector, IMPLIBW, and complete online help.
- Most information in this book is applicable to the Borland C++ for Windows compiler. Although the title of this book denotes Turbo C++ for Windows, you also can apply most information to the Borland C++ for Windows compiler as well.
- Programming for Windows requires rethinking of old programming concepts. After programming in DOS for some time, Windows is a change. It's not that Windows programming is difficult,

but that you must handle many operations and adjust to a new way of thinking. Windows programming, however, is greatly simplified by the Turbo C++ for Windows compiler.

- Windows 3.0 is not a new environment. Even though Windows 3.0 made Windows popular, earlier releases date back to 1985 when it was first introduced.
- Windows NT is the next generation of Windows. Although Windows NT is not yet available, programs you write now can conform to specifications already set and you should be able to use these programs in Windows NT with minor changes.
- The advantages and disadvantages of Windows are numerous. You gain many benefits, for yourself and your users, by taking on the challenge of programming for Windows.
- Installing Turbo C++ for Windows and its companion products is accomplished with the INSTALL program that comes with the package.
- Installing the diskette for this book is accomplished with the SETUP program on the disk.

Getting Started with Turbo C++ for Windows

CHAPTER

1

2 PROGRAMMING ENVIRONMENT

IN THIS CHAPTER

- How to start the Integrated Development Environment.
- The main features of the IDE.
- How to use the menu system and purposes of the main menu options.
- How to use the IDE editor window system.
- The SpeedBars and how to use them.
- The status line and how to use it.
- The features of an editor window and how to use them.
- How to use the built-in search and the search and replace functions.
- Methods for customizing the built-in editor.
- Syntax highlighting and how to customize colors with your system.
- How to set preferences for the editor and purpose of each preference.
- Type of help available and how to access it.

Using the Integrated Development Environment

With the IDE you do your programming work in one convenient environment. The IDE integrates all the tools you need so you can be a productive and efficient programmer. This section introduces you to the IDE and helps you start using its features immediately.

Starting the IDE

It's easy to start the Turbo C++ for Windows IDE. In Program Manager, choose the Turbo C++ 3.1 program group and double-click the Turbo C++ icon (see Figure 2.1).

Figure 2.1.
The Turbo C++ for Windows icon.

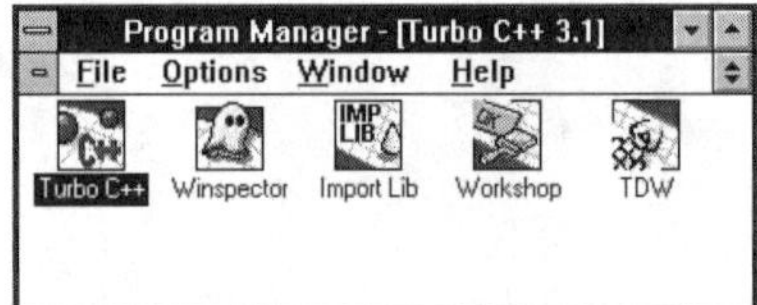

When you invoke the IDE, a graphical image is displayed, giving a copyright message. This is a splash screen. (You learn to create your own splash screen in Chapter 16, "Even More GDI.") After a few seconds, the splash screen disappears, and the program loads. The screen should display the empty Turbo C++ for Windows desktop. Welcome to the IDE!

Before you start writing a program, look at the IDE's menus and editor window system. With the information about the IDE in this chapter, you can start writing a program in Chapter 3, "Getting Started in Windows."

The menu bar at the top of the window serves as a gateway to the features in the Turbo C++ for Windows IDE. Figure 2.2 shows the main parts of the Turbo C++ for Windows desktop.

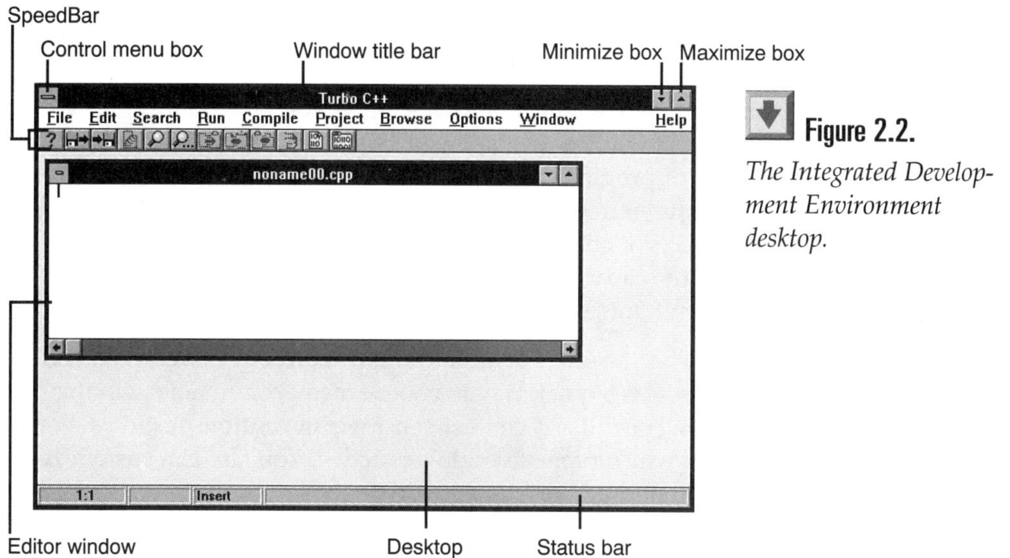

Figure 2.2.

The Integrated Development Environment desktop.

The Turbo C++ for Windows desktop contains the following features:

- *Window title bar.* The title bar, located at the top of the window, shows the name of the application the window belongs to. If more than one window is open, the color of the title bar for the active window (the one you're working in) is different from the others.
- *Menu bar.* The second line of the window lists the available menus.
- *Control menu box.* Located in the upper-left corner of each window, the control menu (also called the system menu) enables you to resize, move, maximize, minimize, and close windows. It also enables you to switch to the task list. Press Alt-Space to display the system menu, and click the small rectangle in the upper-left corner of the window.
- *Maximize and minimize buttons.* Located in the upper-right corner of each window, these buttons enlarge the active application window to fill the entire desktop or shrink the window to an icon. After you enlarge a window, Maximize changes to Restore. Use Restore to return the window to its previous size.

- *Desktop.* The desktop takes up a large part of the IDE screen. You use the desktop to open editor windows.
- *Edit window.* When you create or open the source code to a program, an edit window is displayed, enabling you to view and modify your program code. You can open multiple edit windows and view the source code for several different programs at once. Many aspects of an edit window are similar to a main window, including the capacity to move and resize the window, the maximize and minimize buttons, and the control menu.
- *SpeedBar.* The SpeedBar default location is directly under the menu bar. It is used as a quick way to choose menu commands with the mouse. The SpeedBar is context-sensitive: the buttons it shows depend on which type of window is active. You also can customize the location of the SpeedBar.
- *Status line.* Located at the bottom of the window, the status line displays information about the edit window. It shows the line and column location of the cursor, whether the window has been modified, and whether the editor is in overwrite or insert mode. The right side of the status line gives a message describing a selected menu option's purpose.

Take a look at the individual elements of the IDE. This gives you an idea about each feature and how to use it.

The Menu System

The menu system has the features you need to manage your programming tasks efficiently. In the menu system, you find utilities and features for handling files and for editing, running, and compiling your programs. You can enter the menu system in one of three ways (the first two with the keyboard and the third with the mouse):

- Press F10. This moves the highlight to the menu bar. Then press the right or left arrow to move the highlight to the menu you want to open. Finally, press Enter or the down arrow to display the menu.

- Press Alt and the first letter of the command on the menu you want to select. The first letter of each menu title on the menu bar is underlined.
- Click the menu you want to open.

Some menu commands are context-sensitive. Depending on the state of your work, certain menu options are available, but others are not. Those not available are shown in gray.

Often a command in the main level of the menus leads to another option. Each menu command followed by a series of ellipsis marks (...) displays a dialog box. With the dialog box, you set additional options. Dialog boxes appear, enabling you to make several choices about the command you have selected (see Figure 2.3).

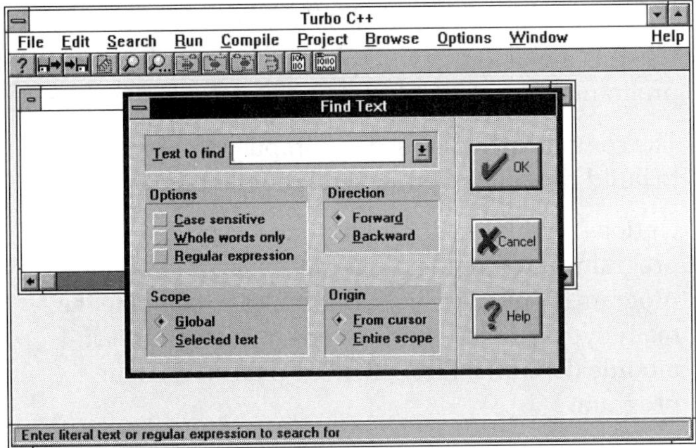

Figure 2.3.
A typical dialog box.

An arrow ← follows some menu commands, leading to another pop-up menu. You can make further selections from that menu which, in turn, often lead to a dialog box.

If a dialog box has a title bar, you can move it around the screen. Often, you must move within a dialog box to make several selections. Your current option is either highlighted or shown with a dotted rectangle. To move to an option or group within a dialog box, click it. You also can press Tab to move forward and Shift-Tab to move in the opposite direction. You can press Esc at any time to hide a menu.

No menu selection method is best: you quickly will develop your own habits. In Windows, a single procedure can be done several ways. Users choose the most convenient method, although the best method can be a combination of the procedures.

Now, let's review the main menu options:

File — This menu enables you to open, save, create, and print program files. Select Exit in the menu to exit the IDE.

Edit — Use this menu to cut, copy, paste, and clear text in the edit windows. Use it also to restore (undo) deleted text or to redo the previous undone editor operation.

Search — This menu has powerful tools that enable you to search and replace text in the edit windows. With the search menu, you also can find compile-time errors and jump to specific line numbers in your file.

Run — Use this menu to run your program and to debug programs using Turbo Debugger for Windows.

Compile — The compile menu is used to compile your programs or to build programs from several different files.

Project — Options on this menu enable you to manage multifile programs through the project make facility. Windows programs commonly use Project files to combine the many types of files—source code, resource files, and module definition files—that are part of the final program.

Browse — This invokes the ObjectBrowser utility, which enables you to view class hierarchies in C++ programs. Use it to see graphically how your programs are organized.

Options — This menu enables you to change directories used by Turbo C++ for Windows and various default settings in the package's compiler and linker. Because the default settings are adequate for most programming tasks, for now, accept them. As you use the environment, you will learn how to customize it.

Window — The Window menu options enable you to manage the various edit windows. This menu is especially helpful if you don't use a mouse. Options enable you to select which editor window to make active, to arrange edit windows on the desktop, and to close all open windows.

Help — This contains a powerful online help system. You can find help for every aspect of the Turbo C++ for Windows programming environment, including the C and C++ programming languages, the Windows API (application program interface) functions, and the ObjectWindows Library (OWL).

The Window System

When you use Turbo C++, you will do most of your work inside a window. The IDE is based on the concept of windows. A window is a specific portion of the screen. Although all windows share similar characteristics, several kinds are available. They provide areas where you can write programs, see program output, debug problem code, and display status information. Figure 2.4 shows a typical editor window.

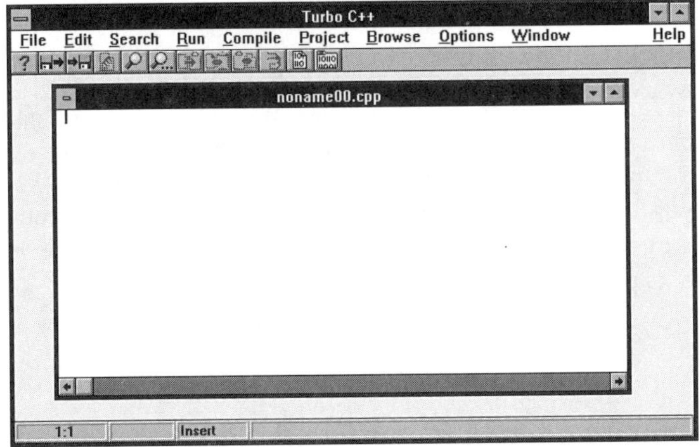

Figure 2.4.

Features of a typical editor window.

You can open any number of editor windows on the desktop at once—you are limited only by your computer's memory. Your current working window is the active window. The active window appears on top of all other windows and has a highlighted title bar and border.

When multiple editor windows are open, you can move among windows with either the mouse or the keyboard. To make a window active with the mouse, click anywhere in the other window. Using the keyboard, select the Window menu and choose the number of the window you want to make active. If more than nine windows are open, you can choose 0 and select the window to make active from a dialog box.

An editor window has the following elements:

- *Title bar.* The title bar, located at the top of the window, describes how you use the window. Editor windows contain the name of the file being edited in the window. To move a window with the mouse, go to the top border of the window. Press and hold the left button and drag the window to its new location. A window enlarged to fill the entire desktop cannot be moved.
- *Control menu.* The control menu is at the upper-left corner of each window. For the IDE, use the keyboard with the control menu. With control-menu commands, you can resize, move, maximize, minimize, and close windows. To access the control menu of editor windows, press and hold Alt, then press the hyphen (-) key, and then release both keys.
- *Minimize button.* Use the minimize button with the mouse to reduce the window to an icon.
- *Maximize button.* Located in the upper-right corner of the editor window, the maximize button consists of an up-arrow. Use it to enlarge a window. After an enlarged window fills the desktop, the zoom box appears as a double-sided arrow. Click it to reduce the window to its previous size.

- *Scroll bars.* Vertical and horizontal scroll bars enable you to scroll text in a window with the mouse. Click the up- or down-arrows to move vertical scroll bars one line at a time. A slider box moves along the scroll bar, indicating the relative position in the file. Click the scroll bar, and the text in the window moves up or down depending on which side of the scroll bar you clicked.
- *Resizable window corners.* Drag any corner to change the size of the window.

You should check these options for yourself. If an editor window is not already displayed, go to the File menu and select New. Experiment with the editor window that now appears. You soon will be able to use the editor window options like a pro.

Using Multiple Windows

The Turbo C++ for Windows IDE offers a multiple-document interface (MDI) to display several editor windows at the same time. You can open more than one editor window to view the same file or different files. You might load two programs into multiple windows and use one program's information to write statements in another.

When you open the same program in two windows and change it in one window, the program in the other window is automatically updated (see Figure 2.5). The filename in the title bar for each window is followed by a colon (:) and the number of the instance which the file is loaded.

Click the new window to switch quickly from one window to the next. You also can use the Window menu and type the number of the edit window you want.

The Window menu offers several other options for working with multiple editor windows. If you choose the Tile option, Turbo C++ for Windows arranges all open editor windows so you can see them at the same time. The Cascade option rearranges the editor windows so only the window title bar is displayed and the windows overlap on the desktop.

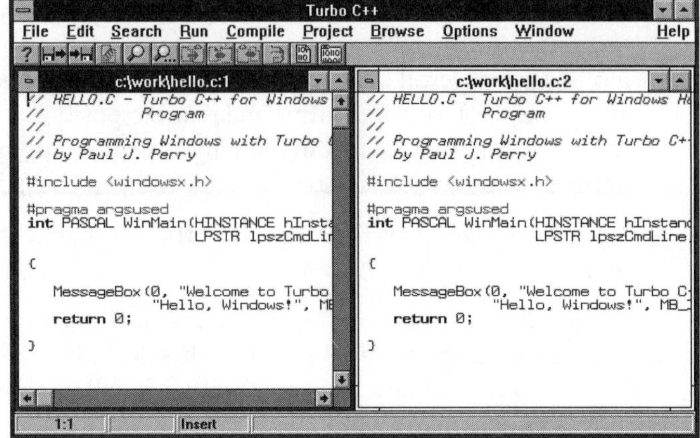

Figure 2.5.

The same file in two editor windows.

Using SpeedBars

The SpeedBar is a quick way to choose commonly used menu commands with the mouse. This handy device pops up in many new Windows programs. The SpeedBar is initially displayed under the menu bar as a horizontal group of buttons. To use the SpeedBar, move the cursor to the appropriate button and click.

The SpeedBar is context-sensitive. The buttons that appear on it—and whether they are disabled—depend on the IDE's state. If the clipboard is empty, Paste is dim, which means the button's command is not currently available.

Some buttons always will be displayed in the SpeedBar. These include Help, Open File, and Make. Other buttons depend on which window is active. Now that you know about editor windows, it's time to learn about project and message windows. Figure 2.6 shows the buttons active in an editor window. Table 2.1 summarizes which buttons are active in which window.

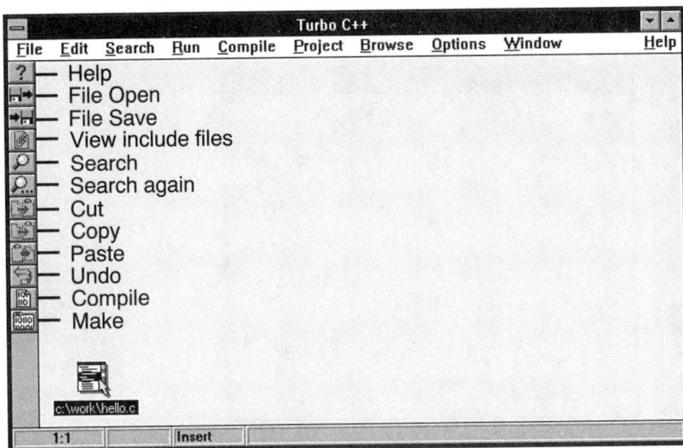

Figure 2.6.

Vertical SpeedBar buttons available in an editor window.

Table 2.1. Active SpeedBar buttons in various windows.

Active Window	*Active Buttons*
Doesn't matter	Help, File Open, Make.
Editor	File Save, Search, Search Again, Cut, Copy, Paste, Undo, Compile, View Include Files.
Project	Compile, Edit, View Include Files, Add Project Item, Delete Project Item.
Message	Compile, Edit, View Error.
None	Exit IDE.

You can change the location and position of the SpeedBar to suit your needs. It can be moved as a vertical bar on the left side of the window or as a pop-up tool palette, which you can move to any location on the Turbo C++ for Windows desktop. To change the location of the SpeedBar, go to Options, select Environment and choose Desktop. The Desktop Preferences dialog box is displayed, giving you the following options: to disable the SpeedBar, to make it a pop-up palette, to keep it as a horizontal bar, or to display it as a vertical bar (see Figure 2.7).

Figure 2.7.

The Desktop Preferences dialog box.

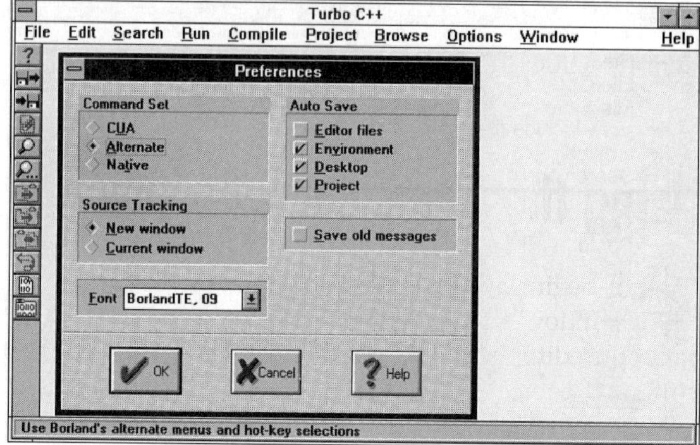

The Status Line

The line at the bottom of the screen is the status line. It displays a short comment about your current task. The status line changes as you switch windows or change activities.

When you select a menu command, the status line displays a summary of the function for the selected menu item. For example, if you select File menu option (press F10 to check this), the status line displays the following text:

```
File-management commands (Open, Save, Print, etc.)
```

The information on the status line gives you a visual understanding of the current focus of the IDE.

You see one of the most common status lines in an editor window. It includes the following text:

```
1:1     Modified       Insert
```

At the extreme left, you find the current line and column position of the cursor. If a file has been modified, the word "Modified" will appear as the next item in the status bar. If no modifications have been made, the space will be empty. You also see the current status of the editor—either insert or overwrite mode. (You are about to learn more about editor modes.)

If you ever wonder what to do next, look at the status line as you move through menu options. Often, it gives you the clue you need to sail in the right direction.

Using the Editor

When it begins executing, the IDE creates an active editor window. An editor window enables you to type and modify program code. The title bar of the editor window contains the name of the file being edited. When you start the IDE, an editor window is created with the filename NONAME00.CPP. Before you exit, choose the File menu and select Save As and give the file a new name.

An active editor window with no current activity is ready to accept input. Before typing the text, place the cursor in the upper-left corner of the editor window. As you start to type, the text appears in the editor window at the cursor.

The editor begins in insert mode. As you type, the text inserts at the cursor. Another mode is overwrite mode. It enables you to type over existing text. To toggle between the two modes, press Insert.

The editor is intuitive and easy to use. Your type appears on the screen at the cursor. Press Enter to insert a new line and move the cursor to the start of the next line. Backspace deletes the character to the left of the cursor. Delete removes the character directly at the cursor.

Press PageUp or PageDown to scroll the window up or down one screen at a time. To move through text quickly, you can combine the action of several keys with Ctrl. Press Ctrl-Left Arrow or Ctrl-Right Arrow to move the cursor to the beginning of the previous or next word, respectively. Press Ctrl-PageUp to move the cursor to the beginning of the file. Ctrl-PageDown moves the cursor to the end of the file. Table 2.2 summarizes the commonly used editing commands.

Table 2.2. Important cursor keyboard commands.

Key	*Description*
Arrow Keys	Moves cursor one unit in appropriate direction.
PageUp	Scrolls window one screen up.
PageDown	Scrolls window one screen down.
Home	Moves cursor to beginning of line.
End	Moves cursor to last character of line.
Enter	Inserts line, moves to beginning of next line.
BackSpace	Removes character to the left of cursor.
Delete	Removes character under the cursor.
Insert	Toggles between insert and overwrite mode.
Ctrl-Left Arrow	Repositions cursor left one word.
Ctrl-Right Arrow	Repositions cursor right one word.
Ctrl-PageUp	Moves to beginning of file.
Ctrl-PageDown	Moves to end of file.
Ctrl-Y	Deletes current line.

Now, to work with the editor, first be sure an editor window is active (choose the File menu and select New) and then type. If you make a mistake, use the previously mentioned keys to correct it. Try inserting a line of text. Remember to put the editor in insert mode and press Enter. Then, type the text you want to insert. Don't worry about saving the file at this point.

The Clipboard Commands

The editor enables you to manipulate a block of text. After you select a block of text, you can easily copy it to a new location, move it, or delete it. The Edit menu gives you access to the set of options, enabling you to work on blocks of text.

There are several ways to mark a block of text. The easiest method is to move the cursor to the beginning of your work area and pressing Shift move the cursor. At the end of that text, release Shift. The highlighted text is now the selected block. To select text with the mouse, move the cursor to the beginning of the text you want and then press and hold down the left mouse button. Move the cursor to the end of that text and release the mouse button. This operation, called dragging, highlights the block.

At this time, several options on the Edit menu become active (see Figure 2.8). Cut removes the text from the cursor location and stores it in the clipboard. The clipboard temporarily stores a block of text. Copy duplicates the highlighted text and stores it in the clipboard. Clear deletes the currently selected text, but does not store it in memory.

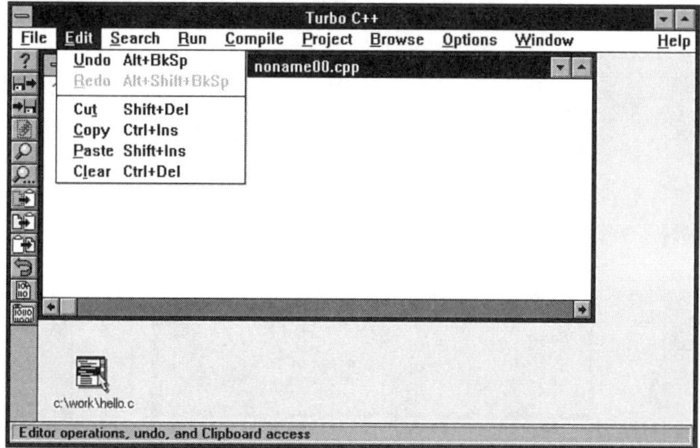

Figure 2.8.

The Edit menu.

To insert the text currently in the clipboard, you choose Paste on the Edit menu. This copies the contents of the clipboard and inserts them at the cursor in the active editor window. Because the text remains in the clipboard, you can continue to repeat this command.

Use Cut on the Edit menu to remove highlighted text from an editor window and place it on the clipboard. Use this if you want to move rather than copy text.

When copying large amounts of text to the clipboard, you may want to clear it before continuing your editing operation to give your program more memory. You can select and copy a single character, such as a space, to the clipboard. This quickly removes the clipboard's previous contents.

Searching Operations

To find a specific sequence of characters, use Find on the Search menu. You receive a prompt from the dialog box (see Figure 2.9). Type the string you want to search for and specify any of the various search options. Notice the combo box lists a history of your current text (text typed during the current editor session). The default settings start the search at the cursor and then move the search forward. The search is treated as case-sensitive.

Figure 2.9.

Find Text dialog box.

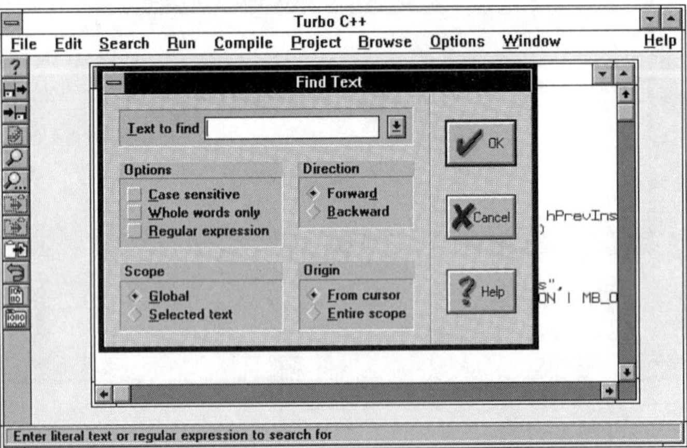

You select the backward option to move the search in the opposite direction. To start the search at the beginning of the file, choose Entire scope. A case-sensitive search treats uppercase and lowercase characters separately. However, you might want to do a case-insensitive search. If so, do not select Case sensitive.

If you select the Whole words only option, the editor searches for a character that is not part of a full word. The editor makes distinctions between strings contained in other strings. If, for example, you check this option and your searching string is Rem, the editor finds the string when it is alone in text, but not when it is inside another string, such as Rembrandt.

With the Regular Expression box, you can use wild-card characters in your searches. To confine the search to a currently selected block, use the Selected text option.

After you have entered your text and selected appropriate options, choose OK to search. This highlights the text and places you at the appropriate place in the editor window. If the text is not found, you receive a message relating that.

Choose Search Again from the Search menu to repeat a search. You can press F3, however, for a simpler method. This is a quick way to search a file for a string with multiple copies.

To do a search and replace operation, choose Replace on the Search menu (see Figure 2.10). Its options are similar to the Search dialog box. Along with the text you are searching for, enter the new replacement text.

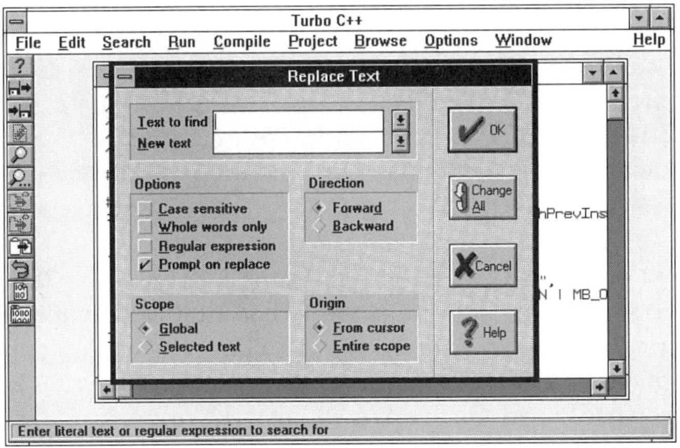

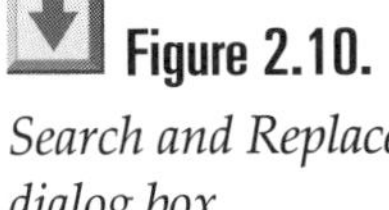

Figure 2.10.

Search and Replace dialog box.

The editor will prompt you before carrying out a search and replace operation. To stop this option, turn off Prompt on replace. Change All then does the search and replace operation for every instance of the search string, without prompting you for verification. This handy option makes many changes quickly.

Customizing the Editor

You probably used certain keys to accomplish specific tasks as you started the IDE. An editor must receive commands to act upon them. With Turbo C++ for Windows, you can change many aspects of the IDE. First, you can customize the way an editor window operates.

Turbo C++ for Windows has two sets of editor commands. The Common User Access (CUA) command set makes the editor behave similarly to other Windows editors—such as Notepad. The Alternate command set is handy if you are familiar with Borland programming language: it mimics the editor in the Borland language products.

TIP

If you are proficient with the Turbo C++ or the Borland C++ (or even the Turbo Pascal) IDEs, use the Alternate command set. It makes the Windows-based editor much easier to use.

When you first start Turbo C++ for Windows, the editor uses the CUA command set. To use the Alternate command set, choose the Options menu and select Preferences. Select the Alternative radio button from the command set group and choose OK. Changing the active command set changes the commands you use to perform various editing tasks.

Notice there are three command set options in the dialog box. At this time, the Native command set is exactly the same as the CUA set. The Native option is for future editor modifications.

Tables 2.3, 2.4, and 2.5 show various editor keystrokes you use in each editor mode. This quick reference makes the editor windows easier to use.

Table 2.3. Menu command hot keys for both command sets.

Keystroke	*Description*
Ctrl-Esc	Displays task list of programs to transfer control to.
Ctrl-F4	Closes the active editor window.
Ctrl-Tab	Displays next open editor window.
Alt-Backspace	Reverses (or undoes) the last editing operation.
Shift-Del	Removes the currently selected text and puts it on the clipboard.
Ctrl-Ins	Copies the currently selected text on the clipboard.
Shift-Ins	Pastes the current clipboard contents in the active editor window.
Ctrl-F9	Compiles and runs the program in the current editor window.
Alt-F9	Compiles the file in the current editor window.
F9	Compiles only the files that need updating.
Shift-F5	Tiles multiple editor windows so each one is displayed at the same time.
Shift-F4	Cascades multiple editor windows so only the title is displayed for each one.

Table 2.4. Menu command hot keys for CUA command set.

Keystroke	*Description*
Alt-F4	Exits the IDE.
F3	Repeats the last find or replace command.
Ctrl-E	Moves to top of editor window.
Ctrl-X	Moves to end of editor window.
Ctrl-Home	Moves to top of file.
Ctrl-End	Moves to end of file.

Table 2.5. Menu command hot keys for Alternate command set.

Keystroke	*Description*
Alt-X	Exits the IDE.
F2	Saves the file in the active editor window.
F3	Opens a new file from disk.
Ctrl-Q E	Moves to top of editor window.
Ctrl-Q X	Moves to end of editor window.
Ctrl-PageUp	Moves to top of file.
Ctrl-PageDown	Moves to end of file.

You should find the information in these three tables helpful when typing your programs. Notice the Alternate command set uses many editor commands from the once famous Wordstar editor.

Color Syntax Highlighting

Although you may have heard the term syntax highlighting, you might not know what it means. While typing programs in the IDE, notice how different keywords are displayed in different colors. This is syntax highlighting. It enables you to see the different elements of your code. The syntax elements you can alter are listed in Table 2.6.

Table 2.6. Syntax highlighting elements.

Element	*Description*
Whitespace	Spaces, tabs, and newline characters.
Comment	Text that annotates your code.
Reserved word	C and C++ keywords reserved for special purposes.
Identifier	Variable or function names.
Symbol	Operators and other miscellaneous characters.
String	String constants in double quotes.
Integer	Integer numbers.
Float	Floating point numbers with a decimal point.
Octal	Octal (base eight) numbers.
Hex	Hexadecimal (base 16) numbers.
Character	Single characters.
Preprocessor	Preprocessor directives.
Illegal character	Incorrect characters.

To change the color of code elements, choose Options menu, select Environment, and then choose Highlight. The Highlighting dialog box appears (see Figure 2.11). The listbox on the left side of the dialog box lists the elements of C and C++ code. At the upper-right, the dialog box shows the colors you can choose for the syntax highlighting. At the bottom of the dialog box, you can preview an example of your code.

Figure 2.11.

The Highlighting dialog box.

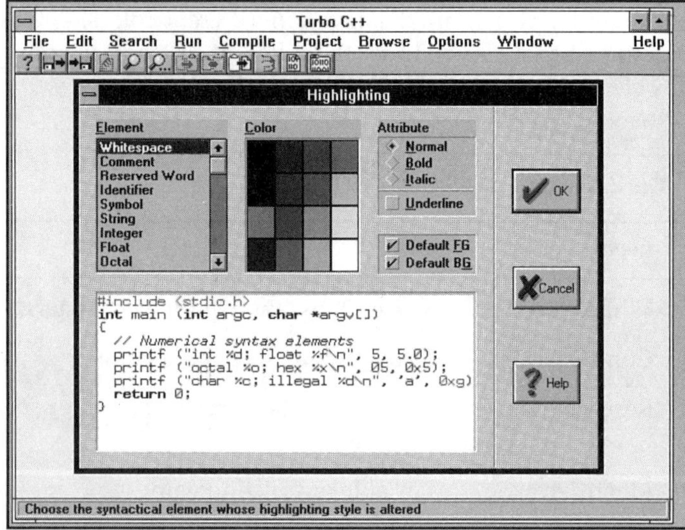

To modify the color of an element, select the element you want to change—either select it from the listbox or click that element in the sample code. Then select the colors for the syntax element. You will see the letters FG in the color square, which denote the foreground color, and BG, which denote the background of the current syntax element. If the foreground and background colors are the same, the letters FB will be displayed in the color square.

To choose the foreground color with the mouse, use the left mouse button to select the appropriate color in the color square. To choose it with the keyboard, press Tab to activate the color square. Then, use the arrow keys to move within the color matrix. After you have selected the color you want to use for the foreground, press F.

To select a background color with the mouse, click the appropriate color with the right mouse button. For the keyboard, use the previous actions, except press B to select the background color. You can change the attribute of the syntax element (either normal, bold, or italic). You also can choose whether to underline the element and whether to use options in the dialog box. When the appropriate colors are set, click OK.

TIP

You must use the BorlandTE font to modify the attributes for syntax highlighting. You select this in the Preferences dialog box: choose Options, select Environment, and then Preferences. If you don't select the BorlandTE font, you cannot choose normal, bold, or italic as syntax highlighting characteristics. It automatically defaults to normal if you don't use the BorlandTE font.

Setting Preferences

The Preferences option on the Options main menu displays a dialog box that enables you to change various functions in the IDE. Use the check boxes in the Editor options group to tell Turbo C++ for Windows how to control editor window action (see Figure 2.12). The default settings for Editor options are on.

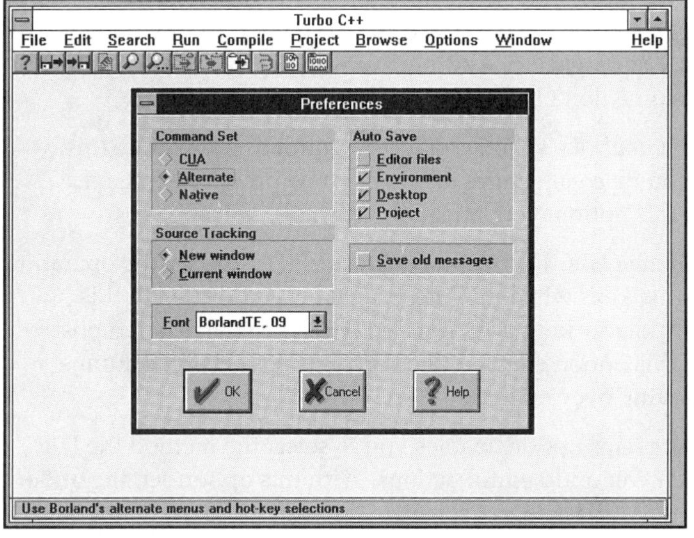

Figure 2.12.

The Preferences dialog box.

The Editor options on the Preferences dialog box are the following:

- *Create backup file.* With this option checked, the Integrated Development Environment automatically will create a backup of the source file in the active editor window when you save it. The backup file always receives the extension .BAK.
- *Insert mode.* This option tells the IDE to start the editor in Insert mode. Without this option, the editor mode always starts in Overwrite mode. You still can use the Insert key to switch between modes.
- *Auto indent mode.* With this option, press Enter in an edit window to move the cursor under the first character in the previous line that is not blank.
- *Use tab character.* The IDE saves C++ source code as ASCII files. If this option is checked, when the IDE saves a file, it will include the tab character. If this option is not checked, all tabs are converted into spaces, according to the number of spaces set for a tab.
- *Optimal fill.* Check this option to begin every line with the minimum number of characters possible using tabs and spaces. When this option is checked, lines have fewer characters.
- *Syntax highlighting.* This option enables you to choose whether to use syntax highlighting. Although most users like syntax highlighting, some don't because it gives them a headache.
- *Backspace unindents.* When you use an editor window with this option, you delete an entire tab position by pressing backspace. Without this option, you delete only a single space.
- *Cursor through tabs.* This option enables you to specify the operation of the arrow keys when moving in an edit window. With this option, the arrow keys will move the cursor to the next tab position. Without this option enabled, the cursor jumps several columns when moving over multiple tabs.
- *Group undo.* This option enables you to select the method the IDE uses when you undo editor actions. With this option set, the undo command (Alt-Backspace) reverses a group of actions in one step;

otherwise it only restores a single keystroke. If you type pprogram (you meant to type program), delete it, and then choose Undo from the Edit menu with Group undo checked, the entire word will be displayed; without Group undo checked, only a single character is restored.

- *Persistent blocks.* Persistent blocks relates to cut and paste operations with the clipboard. With this option enabled, if you move the cursor while you are highlighting a block, the block stays highlighted; without this option, that block becomes inactive.
- *Overwrite blocks.* When a block of text is marked and this option is checked, typing a letter will replace the marked block with the typed letter.

Besides these previous options, you can set other preferences. The Tab size edit box controls the number of columns the cursor moves for each tab. The Default Extension drop down box enables you to choose the default file extension for editor files—either C (for regular C files) or CPP (for C++ files).

When you have selected the appropriate options, set focus to OK and press Enter or click OK. This sets the default values for future editing sessions.

TIP

To regain the factory default settings for all the options in the IDE, exit Turbo C++ for Windows, go to a DOS box, and type the following command:

```
del C:\BORLANDC\BIN\TCDEFW.*
```

This erases the configuration files, and when Turbo C++ for Windows is restarted, it creates new configuration files with default values.

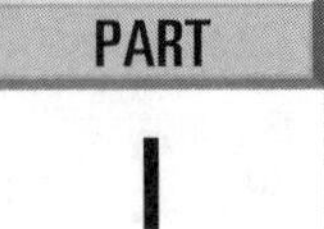

Getting Online Help

The IDE of Turbo C++ for Windows takes full advantage of the Windows help system. It employs advanced hypertext technology to implement online help. It includes online reference for the predefined C and C++ language definitions, OWL, Windows API function calls, and more.

To access the help system, press F1. The Help program automatically loads and gives information about the IDE editor (see Figure 2.13). Use the scroll bars in the Help window or arrow keys to see topics not currently visible. You also can resize the Help window to see more or less information.

Figure 2.13.

A sample online Help window.

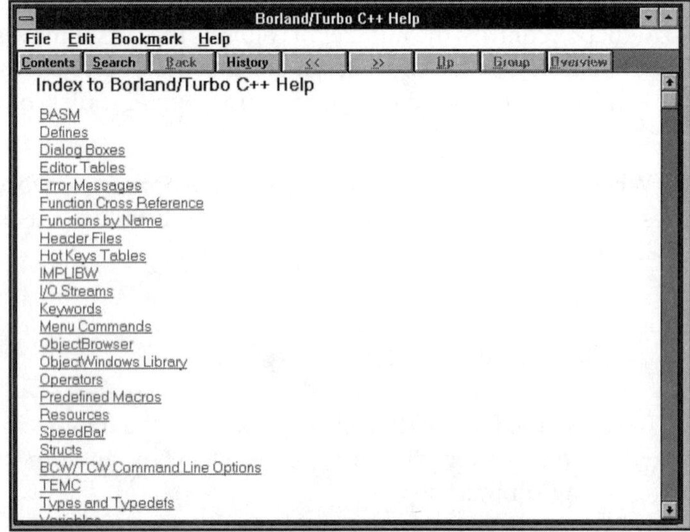

Click the Contents button to access a list of help topics. If you know what you need, choose Search. A dialog box displays, requesting you to enter a keyword. As you type the keyword, the Help system searches its database and locates and displays the keyword most closely matching the one you entered.

Choose the File option and select Exit to exit the help system. You also can leave the help program resident—to load quicker next time you need help—and switch to Turbo C++ for Windows by pressing Ctrl-Esc to display the task list and then select the appropriate program from the list.

When using IDE, if you need specific information on a keyword, use the hypertext help system. Turbo C++ for Windows uses a hypertext-based system—also called a context-sensitive help system—that gives immediate access to help files. While in an editor window, move the cursor to any keyword character and press Ctrl-F1. This method displays the required information instantly, without searching the menu system (see Figure 2.14).

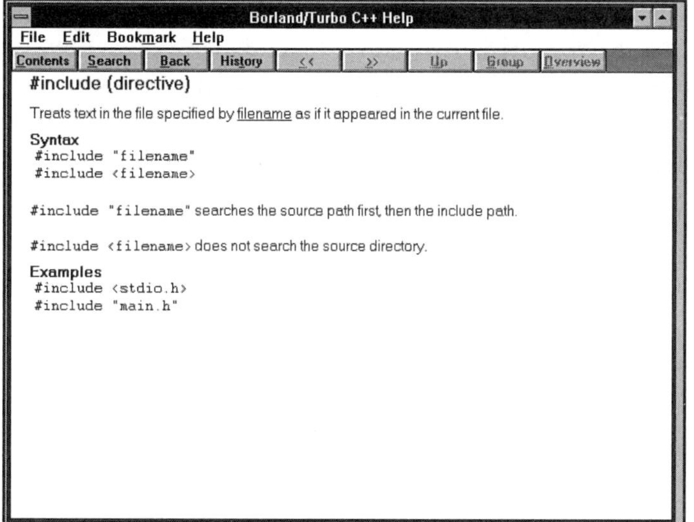

Figure 2.14.

A context-sensitive Help screen.

The package's copious online documentation needs ample disk space. The help system contains nearly the entire text of the Turbo C++ for Windows manuals. It also documents the entire Windows API functions (more than 700). You don't find this documentation in hard copy with Turbo C++ for Windows. It is available only through online help.

To exit the help system, choose the File menu and select Exit. This will return you to the IDE. To exit the Turbo C++ for Windows IDE, choose the File menu and select Exit (or, if you are using the alternate editor command set, press Alt-X). You should return to Program Manager.

What You Have Learned

This chapter took a close look at using the Integrated Development Environment, part of Turbo C++ for Windows. The following important points were covered:

- To start the IDE, double click the Turbo C++ for Windows icon from Program Manager.
- The IDE consists of the title bar, menu bar, control menu, maximize and minimize buttons, desktop, edit windows, SpeedBar, and status line.
- You can select a menu option with either the mouse or the keyboard. With the keyboard, press either Alt and the first letter of the menu selection or F10 to highlight the menu bar. Then use the arrow keys or Enter to select a menu item.
- The main menu across the top of the IDE has all the options you need to interact with the Turbo C++ for Windows package.
- The IDE can work on more than one file at a time. It uses multiple edit windows to enable you to switch among several documents.
- The SpeedBar gives the user a quick way to choose commonly used menu commands. It is context-sensitive: different buttons appear on it depending on the state of the IDE.
- The Status line gives additional help for menu commands and information about the current editor window.
- You can use Find on the Search menu to locate a specific string of text in an editor window. Replace searches for a string and replaces another string with it.
- The editor has two editor command sets: the CUA command set and the Alternate command set. The one you choose depends on your preferences.

- Color Syntax highlighting displays different code elements in different colors. To modify the colors and attributes for different syntax elements, go to the Options menu and select Environment and choose Highlighting.
- To receive online context-sensitive help about any aspect of programming in Turbo C++ for Windows, press F1 at any time. This brings up the help system.

3 GETTING STARTED IN WINDOWS

IN THIS CHAPTER

- How to load, compile, link, and run a Windows program.
- The three types of Turbo C++ for Windows programming styles.
- Why programs written in straight C code are referred to as traditional Windows programs.
- How encapsulation makes writing programs with the ObjectWindows Library (OWL) easier.
- How the three styles of programming Windows differ.
- How to use the EasyWin library in C or C++ programs.
- The special functions available with the EasyWin library.
- How to call Windows Application Program Interface (API) routines in an EasyWin program.

This chapter gets you started using the Integrated Development Environment (IDE). First, you compile, link, and execute an example program. You then learn about program styles you can write with Turbo C++ for Windows and look at an example program for each style. Finally, you take an in-depth look at the EasyWin library.

Getting Started

To begin your hands-on practice, start the IDE as described in Chapter 2, "Programming Environment." Go to the File menu and select Open. Type the appropriate drive and directory followed by HELLO.C. The program appears in Listing 1.1. Make sure you load the correct file from the disk.

Listing 3.1. HELLO.C. Hello Windows program.

```
// HELLO.C - Turbo C++ for Windows Hello Windows
//          program
//
// Programming Windows with Turbo C++ for Windows
// by Paul J. Perry

#include <windowsx.h>

#pragma argsused
int PASCAL WinMain(HINSTANCE hInstance, HINSTANCE hPrevInstance,
                   LPSTR lpszCmdLine, int cmdShow)

{

   MessageBox(0, "Welcome to Turbo C++ for Windows",
             "Hello, Windows!", MB_ICONEXCLAMATION ¦ MB_OK);
   return 0;

}
```

Next, you must compile and link the program. With Turbo C++ for Windows, you do this with just one keystroke. Press F9 or select the

Compile menu and choose Make. The Compile Status dialog box is displayed as you compile and link the program (see Figure 3.1).

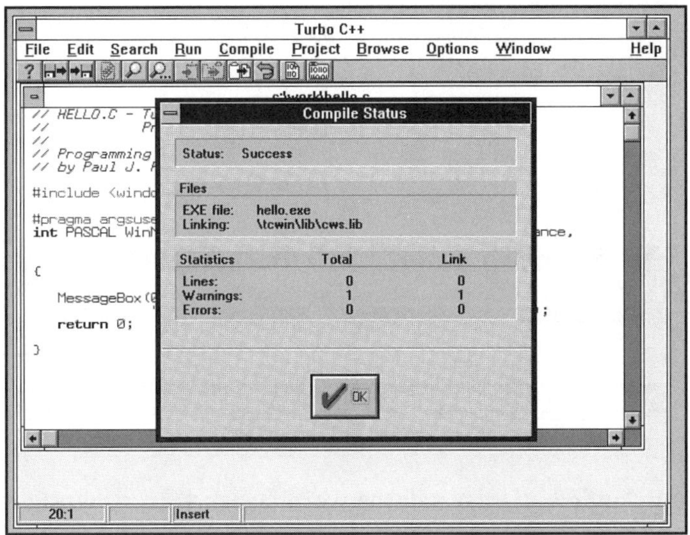

Figure 3.1.
Compile Status dialog box.

As you compile and link your program, this dialog box reports your program's progress. Notice processing the header files takes the majority of time—especially windows.h. These files provide function prototypes and data declarations that are required the majority of the time you program for Windows. Choose OK when the Status box reports the process is complete.

When the compiler is finished and after you choose OK, a different type of window opens in the IDE. It is a Message window entitled "Message" (see Figure 3.2). It should be the active window, but you can always select it from the Window menu.

Although no errors should be reported, you receive a linker warning—"Linker Warning: No module definition file specified: using defaults." Don't worry about this. For this simple program you don't need custom module definition files, and the defaults work just fine. (You learn all about custom module definition files in coming chapters).

Figure 3.2.

A Message window.

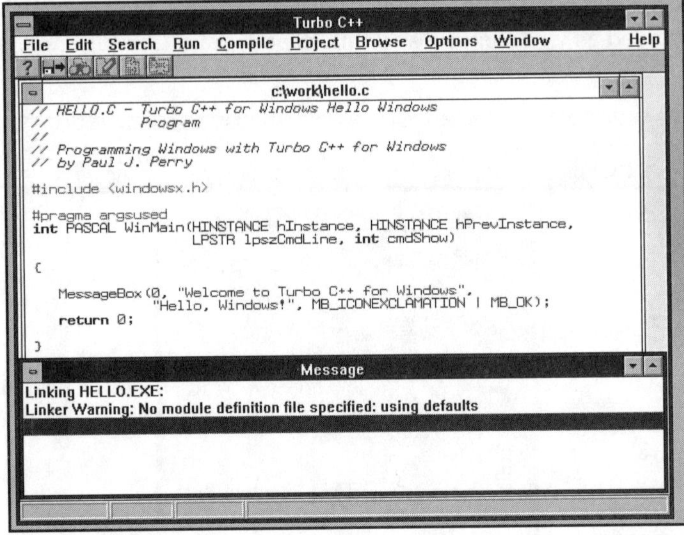

The Message window displays all the warnings and error messages generated during the compile and link cycle. If there were any errors, you could move the bar cursor to the message and press Enter. The appropriate source code file becomes active in an editor window. The cursor then is positioned where the compiler found the problem.

Execute the program by pressing Ctrl-F9 (or by choosing the Run main menu option and selecting Run again). A message box is displayed on the Windows desktop (see Figure 3.3). It may seem incredible that you were able to create a complete graphical window like this in only a few lines of code.

Figure 3.3.

The Hello Windows program.

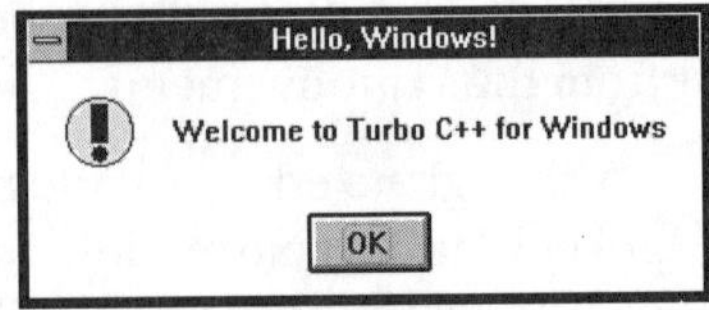

Programs for Windows usually require more code than a text-based application. However, your Windows program also does more than a comparable DOS-based program. The HELLO.C program uses a predefined Windows dialog box, called a message box, to accomplish quite a bit in just a few lines of code. Notice the following features of the program:

- A graphical window is in the center of the screen.
- The window is given a title bar with text in it.
- Text is printed in a special font, the system font, in the window.
- A graphical image (called an icon) is displayed in the window.
- A special user-interface feature called a command button is displayed.
- Keyboard input is processed so the program can respond to the Enter key, as well as bring up the control menu using Alt-Spacebar.
- A mouse cursor is displayed. This cursor tracks mouse movement and responds when you click over the command button, the control menu, or within the title bar.
- It includes mouse support that enables you to drag the window to a new position on the screen.
- The program operates on many computer systems. You don't need to write special code for it to run on a CGA, EGA, VGA, or even Super VGA display adapter.

Now that you know Windows handles many details, you are ready to look at the methods—or styles—you can use to program Windows with Turbo C++ for Windows.

Types of Turbo C++ for Windows Programs

There are three ways to program using Turbo C++ for Windows. Before examining each one in detail, however, generally consider the look and feel of the three styles.

- Programs that use the EasyWin library.
- Programs that use the C programming language, often called traditional Windows programs.
- Programs that use the OWL. This library implements an object-oriented framework to make Windows programming easier.

In this book, you use all three methods to create Windows applications. Look at each method now.

The EasyWin Library

By including certain statements in your Turbo C++ for Windows programs, you can write Windows applications that use the same input and output statements (using `stdin` and `stdout`) used in standard C programs. Listing 3.2 is an example. See Figure 3.4 for an example of the program's output.

Listing 3.2. Program using the EasyWin library.

```
// EZWIN.C - Example EasyWin program
//
// Programming Windows with Turbo C++ for Windows
// by Paul J. Perry

#include <stdio.h>

void main()
{

   printf("Example Program Using the EasyWin programmers
library\n");

}
```

When you use the EasyWin library, you don't have to access the special Windows API functions. The EasyWin library enables you to create "quick and dirty" Windows programs. On the downside, the EasyWin library does not make much use of the Windows environment, other than to create a window that can be scrolled. It does not use any special features of Windows, such as menus, dialog boxes, cursors, or icons.

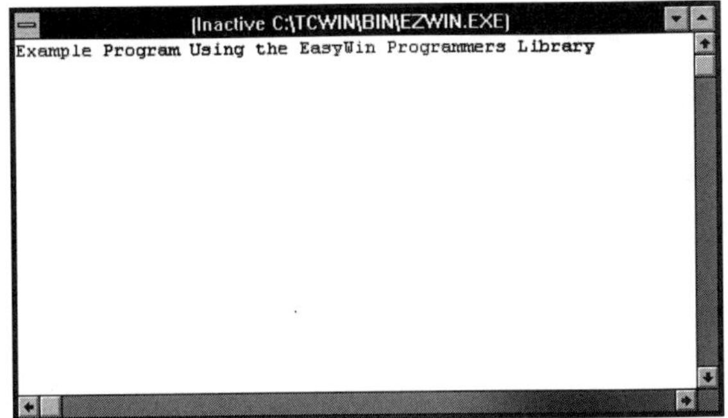

Figure 3.4.

Output of program written with the EasyWin library.

With the EasyWin library, you can quickly bring programs originally written for a text-mode environment (such as DOS) into Windows. Although the EasyWin library is handy, it's rarely used. It works only on the simplest programs, and the programs you write for it don't use any of the special features of Windows.

The last part of this chapter covers the use of the EasyWin library. Although you won't use this library after this chapter, it helps you learn the basic concepts of programming.

Traditional C Programs

Originally, the only compilers for programming in Windows were C compilers, so all program development for Windows traditionally was done with straight C code. Those programs don't use the C++ language features. They do have characteristics that set them apart from most other programs.

Traditional C programs usually require many lines of code to accomplish a simple task. Characteristics of traditional C programs include data registration, windows procedures, and a `switch` statement for message processing.

Listing 3.3 shows an example of a program written in straight C code (also see Figure 3.5). Look quickly through the code. In Chapter 4, "Writing Windows Programs," you discover how C programs work in Windows.

Listing 3.3. Program written in straight C code.

```
// TRADIT.C - Traditional Windows C Program
//
// Programming Windows with Turbo C++ for Windows
// by Paul J. Perry

#define STRICT

#include <windowsx.h>


// Function Prototypes
LRESULT CALLBACK MainWndProc(HWND hWnd, UINT message,
                             WPARAM wParam, LPARAM lParam);

/****************************************/
#pragma argsused
int PASCAL WinMain(HINSTANCE hInstance, HINSTANCE hPrevInstance,
                   LPSTR lpCmdParam, int nCmdShow)
{
   char        ProgName[] = "Traditional Windows C Program";
   HWND        hWnd;
   MSG         msg;


   if (!hPrevInstance)
   {
      WNDCLASS    wndclass;

      wndclass.style         = CS_VREDRAW ¦ CS_HREDRAW;
      wndclass.lpfnWndProc   = (WNDPROC) MainWndProc;
      wndclass.hInstance     = hInstance;
      wndclass.hIcon         = LoadIcon(NULL, IDI_APPLICATION);
      wndclass.hCursor       = LoadCursor(NULL, IDC_ARROW);
      wndclass.hbrBackground = (HBRUSH) (COLOR_WINDOW + 1);
      wndclass.lpszMenuName  = NULL;
      wndclass.cbClsExtra    = 0;
      wndclass.cbWndExtra    = 0;
      wndclass.lpszClassName = ProgName;

      RegisterClass(&wndclass);
   }
```

```
   hWnd = CreateWindow(ProgName,"Traditional Windows C Program",
                       WS_OVERLAPPEDWINDOW,
                       CW_USEDEFAULT, CW_USEDEFAULT,
                       CW_USEDEFAULT, CW_USEDEFAULT,
                       NULL, NULL, hInstance, NULL);

   ShowWindow(hWnd, nCmdShow);
   UpdateWindow(hWnd);

   while (GetMessage(&msg, NULL, 0, 0))
   {
      TranslateMessage(&msg);
      DispatchMessage(&msg);
   }
   return msg.wParam;
}

/*******************************************/
LRESULT CALLBACK MainWndProc(HWND hWnd, UINT message,
                             WPARAM wParam, LPARAM lParam)
{
   switch (message)
   {
      case WM_PAINT :
      {
         HDC         PaintDC;
         PAINTSTRUCT ps;

         PaintDC = BeginPaint(hWnd, &ps);

         TextOut(PaintDC, 1, 1,
                 "Hello From a Traditional Windows C Program", 42);

         EndPaint(hWnd, &ps);
         return 0;
      }

      case WM_DESTROY :
      {
         PostQuitMessage(0);
         return 0;
      }
   }
   return DefWindowProc (hWnd, message, wParam, lParam);
}
```

Figure 3.5.

Output of program written in straight C code.

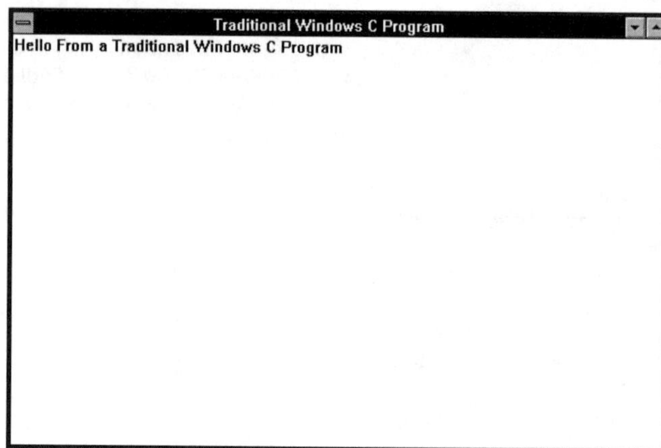

The ObjectWindows Library

The OWL is a C++ class hierarchy that can make program development in Windows easier and more efficient. Much of a traditional C program for Windows is duplicated in every program you write. With the OWL, you inherit the base functionality of a window for your own program and you can avoid rewriting identical code in most programs.

Listing 3.4 shows a program based on the OWL (see Figure 3.6 for program output). Notice the length of this program is about one-third of the one in Listing 3.3.

Listing 3.4. Program based on the ObjectWindows Library.

```
// OWLPROG.CPP - Example ObjectWindows Library Program
//
// Programming Windows with Turbo C++ for Windows
// by Paul J. Perry

#define WIN31
#define STRICT

#include <owl.h>
#include <windowsx.h>

// Class Declarations
```

```
/********************************************/
class TOwlApp : public TApplication
{
   public :
      TOwlApp (LPSTR AName, HINSTANCE hInstance,
          HINSTANCE hPrevInstance, LPSTR CmdLine, int CmdShow) :
          TApplication(AName, hInstance, hPrevInstance,
            CmdLine, CmdShow) { } ;

   virtual void InitMainWindow();
};


/********************************************/
class TMainWindow : public TWindow
{
   public :
      TMainWindow(PTWindowsObject AParent, LPSTR ATitle)
                      : TWindow(AParent, ATitle) { };
      virtual void Paint(HDC PaintDC, PAINTSTRUCT &PaintInfo);

};

// Class Member Functions

/********************************************/
void TOwlApp::InitMainWindow()
{
   MainWindow = new TMainWindow(NULL, Name);
}


/********************************************/
#pragma argsused
void TMainWindow::Paint(HDC PaintDC, PAINTSTRUCT &PaintInfo)
{

   TextOut(PaintDC, 1, 1,
           "Hello From an ObjectWindows Library Program", 43);

}

/********************************************/
int PASCAL WinMain(HINSTANCE hInstance, HINSTANCE hPrevInstance,
                   LPSTR lpCmdLine, int nCmdShow)
{
```

continues

Listing 3.4. continued

```
    TOwlApp ThisApp("ObjectWindows Library Program", hInstance,
                    hPrevInstance, lpCmdLine, nCmdShow);
    ThisApp.Run();
    return ThisApp.Status;
}
```

Figure 3.6.

Output of program written with the ObjectWindows Library.

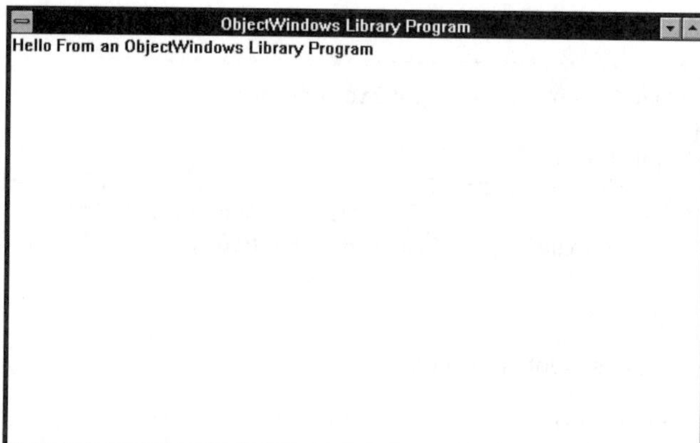

Chapter 5, "Using the ObjectWindows Library," covers the OWL in detail. With it, you learn the benefits of using object-oriented programming methods to code. Because a basic program's functionality is largely in the class hierarchy, you significantly reduce program development time with the OWL.

Which Method Is for You?

Each method has its advantages and disadvantages. Throughout this book, you learn special features about each Windows programming style.

Notice in the last three listings, each program basically does the same task. The output is almost identical, but the code for each is different. Some differences are major. You learn about these differences in the next two chapters.

In this chapter, you learn to use the EasyWin library and its special features. You also learn to make EasyWin programs that call Windows API functions.

Using the EasyWin Library

As you know, in a C program written for a conventional environment, the program entry point is the `main()` function. This is where program execution begins. Notice the traditional C and OWL programs previously listed don't use `main()`. That is because Windows programs use `WinMain()` as their main entry point.

The Turbo C++ for Windows compiler is smart enough to notice whether a program has a `main()` or `WinMain()` function. If it finds `main()`, it implements the EasyWin library and links the appropriate library files with your program. If it finds `WinMain()`, it recognizes a traditional C or OWL program. Notice you cannot have both `main()` and `WinMain()`. The compiler cannot handle this situation and reports an error.

Using EasyWin does not require special compiler options. To use EasyWin, just be sure your program uses `main()` rather than `WinMain()`. Beyond this, the compiler links the correct libraries.

Although you can use the EasyWin library with both C and C++ programs, you must include the appropriate header files (stdio.h, stdlib.h, and so on) in your program. This provides necessary prototypes for the functions your program may call.

Listing 3.5 (GETNAME.C) shows a C program with user interaction. The program uses standard input and output and relies on EasyWin. The program receives the user's name and displays it in a window (see Figure 3.7).

Listing 3.5. C Program using standard input and output.

```
// GETNAME.C - Shows use of standard I/O in C
//
// Programming Windows with Turbo C++ for Windows
// by Paul J. Perry


#include <stdio.h>

void main()
{

   char buffer[255];

   printf("Hello There\n\n");
   printf("Please enter your name and press the ENTER key : \n");

   scanf("%s", &buffer);

   printf("Hey %s, thanks for trying EasyWin!\n", buffer);

}
```

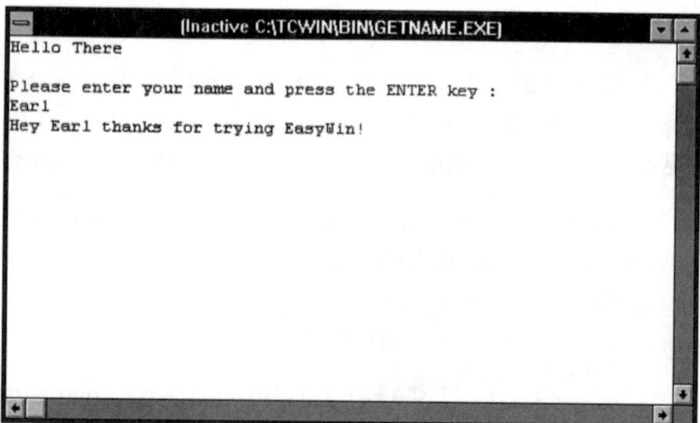

Figure 3.7. *Output of the GETNAME.C program.*

As you see, this program uses the standard `printf()` and `scanf()` library functions to receive and display data. The program's window appears on the screen without you performing special actions. Although you don't have much control over it, you can control where it displays, its color, the text in the title bar, and the icon that appears when you minimize the program.

The window has a title bar that contains the drive, path, and filename of the program. After the program executes, the title bar changes to include the text "inactive." This tells the user that the program has come to the end of `main()` and is no longer running.

The scroll bars are at the lower-right side of the window. These scroll bars enable you to view the window's contents. The standard input and output routines rely on a teletype screen for their I/O. The EasyWin library emulates a teletype screen by providing a window that displays 25 rows by 80 columns. If you try to resize the window—either with the system menu or with the mouse dragging the corners of the window—you cannot view the entire contents of the window. The scroll bars enable you to select and view a certain portion of the output screen.

To get an idea of how the EasyWin library works in C++, try running Listing 3.6. It does the same thing as Listing 3.5, except it uses the IOSTREAM C++ I/O routines. Notice how this uses the C++ `cin` and `cout` stream functions to output text and receive input.

Listing 3.6. C++ program using standard input and output.

```
// GETNAME.CPP - Shows use of standard I/O
//
// Programming Windows with Turbo C++ for Windows
// by Paul J. Perry

#include <iostream.h>

void main()
{

  char buffer[255];

  cout << "Hello There" << endl << endl;
  cout << "Please enter your name and press the ENTER key : ";
  cout << endl;

  cin >> buffer;

  cout << "Hey " << buffer;
  cout << " thanks for trying EasyWin!" << endl;

}
```

More Advanced Examples

The previous two programs should give you an idea of how the EasyWin library works. You might wonder whether other regular C runtime library functions can be called in a Windows program. You can call most of them, but check before you use them.

To be sure, consult the online help system. If you don't find a function usually called in DOS, you have an instant clue it can't be used in Windows. The context-sensitive help system (press Ctrl-F1 for this) helps you find information about library functions' availability in Windows.

Listing 3.7 shows a program that uses the regular C runtime library functions. It gives information about your computer system (see Figure 3.8). Run it to discover what it displays.

Listing 3.7. System Information program.

```
// SYSINFO.C - System Information using BIOS calls
//
// Programming Windows with Turbo C++ for Windows
// by Paul J. Perry

#include <stdio.h>
#include <bios.h>
#include <dos.h>
#include <conio.h>

#define MATH_PROCESSOR_MASK 2

void main()
{

   int memorysize, equipment;

   clrscr();
   printf("System Information\n");
   printf("------------------\n\n");

   printf("DOS version : %d\n", _version);
   printf("  major version is : %d\n", _osmajor);
   printf("  minor version is : %d\n", _osminor);

   memorysize = biosmemory();  /* Get memory available */
```

```
    printf("Amount of conventional RAM available : %dK\n",
           memorysize);

    equipment = biosequip();  /* Get bios settings  */
    if (equipment & MATH_PROCESSOR_MASK)
       printf("Math coprocessor is installed\n");
    else
       printf("No math coprocessor installed\n");

    printf("Number of printer ports : %d \n",
          ((unsigned)equipment) >> 14);

}
```

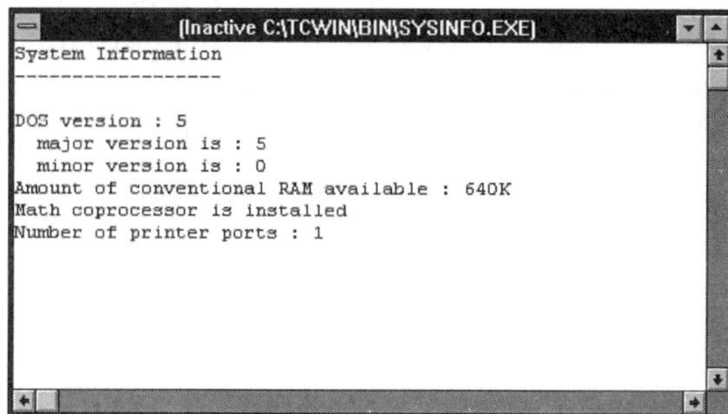

Figure 3.8.

System Information window.

The first three pieces of information are predefined constants available to all programs compiled with Borland products. To request the amount of available memory, the program uses the `biosmemory()` function. To return the presence of a math coprocessor and the number of printer ports, the program uses the `biosequip()` function. Both functions are declared in the bios.h header file.

NOTE

If you use the DOS version of Turbo C++, you might think you can create nice graphical output in Windows using the Borland Graphics Interface (BGI) routines. You might expect to include the graphics.h header file, use the appropriate functions, and

> let the linker take care of the rest. However, because the BGI routines are available only to DOS programs (EasyWin does not provide emulation for them), this trick will not work. Don't despair! You learn about even better graphical output in Chapter 11, "Working with the Graphics Device Interface."

Added Functionality

EasyWin also has several additional functions that enable you to specify coordinates for input and output. You already used the `clrscr()` routine in the SYSINFO.C program to clear the contents of the window. The other special functions receive and set the position of the cursor in a window.

DOS programmers know the `clrscr()` function clears the screen. Your EasyWin program defines this function to clear the current window. Table 3.1. lists the functions with special meaning in the EasyWin library.

Table 3.1. Special EasyWin functions.

Function	*Description*
`clreol()`	Clears to end of current line.
`clrscr()`	Clears contents of window and moves cursor to upper-left corner of window.
`gotoxy()`	Moves cursor to specified x and y locations within window.
`wherex()`	Returns x coordinate of cursor within window.
`wherey()`	Returns y coordinate of cursor within window.

To use the functions in Table 3.1, you must include the conio.h header file at the beginning of your program. Listing 3.8 shows how the functions are used.

Listing 3.8. Using the special functions in EasyWin.

```
// CONIO.C - How to Use Special EasyWin functions
//
// Programming Windows with Turbo C++ for Windows
// by Paul J. Perry

#include <stdio.h>
#include <conio.h>

void main()
{

   printf("This is a test.  It is only a test\n");
   printf("Testing 1...2...3...");
   printf("Current cursor location is X=%d, Y=%d\n",
          wherex(), wherey());

   gotoxy(1,10);
   printf("Current cursor location is X=%d, Y=%d\n",
          wherex(), wherey());
   gotoxy(8,10);
   clreol();

   printf("Press ENTER to clear contents of window\n");
   getch();
   clrscr();

}
```

The functions are easy to use. The table and the example program explain the functions clearly. All x coordinates are from 1 to 80. All y coordinates are from 1 to 25. The upper-left corner of the window is `1,1`, and the numbers increase from left to right and from top to bottom.

Calling API Routines

Because the EasyWin library includes a Windows header file—for function prototypes—you can call regular Windows API routines. Examine Listing 3.9 and then compile and run it.

Listing 3.9. Number guessing game.

```
// GUESS.C - Guess the Number Game
//
// Programming Windows with Turbo C++ for Windows
// by Paul J. Perry


#include <stdlib.h>
#include <stdio.h>
#include <conio.h>

#include <windows.h>

void main()
{

   const int secretnumber = 9;
   int number;

   _InitEasyWin();
   SetWindowText(GetFocus(), "Guess That Number Game");

   printf("Enter a number (between 1 and 10) and try to guess\n");
   printf("the one I am thinking of: ");

   scanf("%d", &number);
   printf("\n");

   if(number == secretnumber)
      printf("You guessed it!\n");
   else
      printf("Sorry, you didn't guess it\n");

   printf("\n\nPress any key to exit the program\n");
   getch();

   PostQuitMessage(0);

}
```

Figure 3.9 shows the output of the program. From the users perspective, notice the title bar no longer shows the unappealing drive, path, and filename of the program. You now see "Guess That Number Game." This is the first improvement. After you guess a number, the program tells you it is about to exit. You press any key to indicate you are done, and the window disappears from the screen, almost like magic.

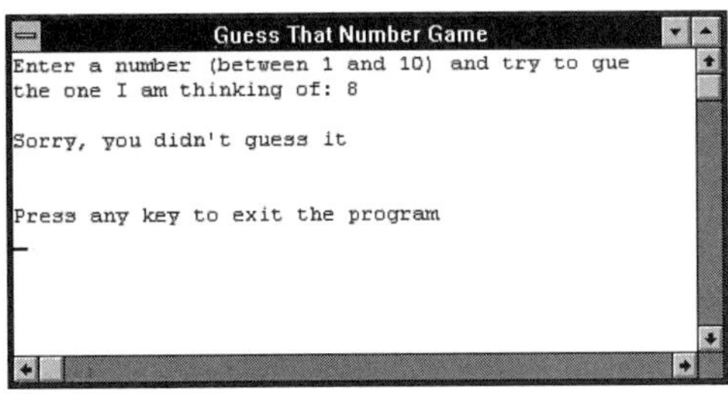

Figure 3.9.

Number guessing game window.

Accomplishing these tasks is tricky. In the code, the windows.h file is included at the beginning of the program. Recall, this header file provides prototypes for the entire set of Windows functions, as well as data types and structures functions rely on.

First, your program calls `_InitEasyWin()`. This is a special EasyWin function. With it, you can create and display an EasyWin window. Usually when you call `printf()`, the EasyWin library checks whether a window has been created. If not, it will call `_InitEasyWin()`. Because you have not used input or output functions in your program yet, you must call the initialization routine directly. This creates and displays your EasyWin window. You want to initialize the window to change its title.

The following line uses Windows API functions:

```
SetWindowText(GetFocus(), "Guess That Number Game");
```

The function name `SetWindowText()` is self-explanatory. `SetWindowText()` enables you to set the text displayed in the window title bar—the string you are passing to it as the second parameter. You also call `GetFocus()`. This function returns a number that identifies the window and passes it to `SetWindowText()`. With a handle—a number that identifies the window you refer to—Windows recognizes different interface elements. This is one way you identify different windows on the screen.

If you think about it, this is a logical concept. People call me Paul all the time. I call my boss Don. The difference in Windows is you use character strings: Windows calls a window 23459. If you think about it, it is really a simple concept.

The main body of the program where you ask the user to guess a secret number is self-explanatory: it is at the end of the program, when you make a call to another Windows API routine—`PostQuitMessage()`. This function tells Windows your program execution is complete. Windows closes the window and clears evidence the program ever existed.

Although `PostQuitMessage()` sounds strange, messages are the basis of Windows. That is why you must send a message to Windows when you exit and why a Windows program must notify the operating environment when it is done executing.

To spruce up the guessing game even more, modify it to make use of message boxes. Try Listing 3.10.

Listing 3.10. Enhanced Guess the Number Game.

```
// GUESS2.C - Enhanced Guess the Number Game
//
// Programming Windows with Turbo C++ for Windows
// by Paul J. Perry


#include <stdlib.h>
#include <stdio.h>
#include <conio.h>

#include <windows.h>

void main()
{

   const int secretnumber = 9;
   int number;

   _InitEasyWin();
   SetWindowText(GetFocus(), "More Guess The Number");

   printf("Enter a number (between 1 and 10) and try to guess\n");
   printf("the one I am thinking of: ");

   scanf("%d", &number);
   printf("\n");
```

```
    if(number == secretnumber)
       MessageBox(GetFocus(), "You Guessed It!",
                  "RESULT", MB_ICONEXCLAMATION | MB_OK);
    else
       MessageBox(GetFocus(), "Sorry You Did Not Guess It",
                  "RESULT", MB_ICONSTOP | MB_OK);

    MessageBox(GetFocus(), "Goodbye", "About to Exit", MB_OK);

    PostQuitMessage(0);

}
```

In response to the user's question, rather than using `printf()` to display a string, use `MessageBox()` to display a dialog box. The dialog box (more accurately, the message box) is the same one you used in your Hello Windows program.

`MessageBox()` gives you flexibility and makes EasyWin more functional. It enables you to display a variety of icons and to specify text and a title bar.

The Final Word on EasyWin

As you see, the EasyWin library provides a quick way to create Windows programs; however, it is limited. It is not the answer to every user interface problem. It does enable you to get a program up and running quickly.

This chapter has most of the EasyWin library programs that this book covers. The next chapter covers the use of the OWL.

What You Have Learned

This chapter got you up and running with several Windows programs. You learned about the three styles of Windows programs and the EasyWin library. This chapter covered the following material:

- To execute a program that you write in the Integrated Development Environment (IDE), you must load the source code and choose Run from the Run menu. The program is then compiled, linked, and executed.
- If any error or warning messages occur during the compile and link process, a Message window is opened in Turbo C++ for Windows that lists each message. To view the error's location, move the bar cursor to the message and press Enter. The editor window with the bad source code becomes active, and the cursor moves to the location where the message occurred.
- The three styles of programs you can write in Turbo C++ for Windows include those that rely on the EasyWin library, those that use straight C code, and those that are object-oriented and rely on the ObjectWindows Library.
- The EasyWin library is the simplest method to use, but also produces the simplest results. Programs that rely on the EasyWin library usually don't take full advantage of the Windows user interface. The EasyWin library, however, is a quick way to adapt a program that uses standard I/O to work under Windows.
- Traditional C programs use only C and are easy to spot because they usually include data registration, window procedures, and lengthy switch statements.
- To make Windows programming easier, you can write your programs with the ObjectWindows Library (OWL). The OWL is an object-oriented hierarchy of classes that allows your Windows program to inherit much of the functionality of a Windows program, without having to rewrite similar code.
- The entry point for programs based on the EasyWin library is the `main()` function. The program entry point for all other types of programs is the `WinMain()` function.
- Five DOS-based functions are redefined in an EasyWin program to clear the screen and to get and change the location of the cursor in a window.

- To call a Windows Application Program Interface (API) routine from an EasyWin program, you must include the windows.h header file at the beginning of your program.

II

WINDOWS PROGRAMMING WITH TURBO C++

4 WRITING WINDOWS PROGRAMS

IN THIS CHAPTER

- What project files are and how to create them.
- The purpose of a module definition file.
- The structure of a traditional Windows C program.
- The two parts of a minimum Windows C program.
- What Hungarian notation is, and why it's used.
- The four important variables passed to the WinMain function.
- What a window class is and how to register one in your own programs.
- How to create a window and display it on the Windows desktop.
- What a Windows procedure is and when in your program it is called.
- The role of messages in your Windows programs.
- The messages processed by the default window procedure.
- How to terminate a Windows program.
- The statements used in a module definition file.

In Chapter 3,"Getting Started in Windows," you learned the three program styles you can use in Turbo C++ for Windows. Using the EasyWin library, you also wrote simple programs that created a window and displayed text. You gained a basic feel for how the compiler works and how to compile, link, and execute a program.

This chapter discusses a traditional Windows C program and the logic required to write a C program for the Windows environment. You learn about the two parts of a Windows program written in C. You find how Windows classes affect the look of a window. You learn about working in a multitasking environment and see how Windows programs multitask by communicating with messages.

Designing Windows Programs

To make a C program work with Windows, you must include a number of statements that call Windows routines. Necessary tasks in all C programs include registering a window class, creating the main window, setting up a message loop, and providing window procedures to handle incoming messages.

As you become acquainted with programming for Windows, you find that besides being a programmer, you must develop artistic skills. Windows is a graphical interface and relies on visual clues. The way your Windows program is presented to the user is more important than if you were programming in a regular text-based environment.

The programs in this chapter serve as the basis for all C programs in this book based on traditional Windows programming techniques. Figure 4.1 shows the window your C program creates. You can move, resize, close, and minimize or maximize the window. It has a control menu that enables you to perform these tasks with either the keyboard or the mouse. The window has all the functionality of a normal Windows program. It displays "Hello from a Traditional Windows C Program" inside the center of the window.

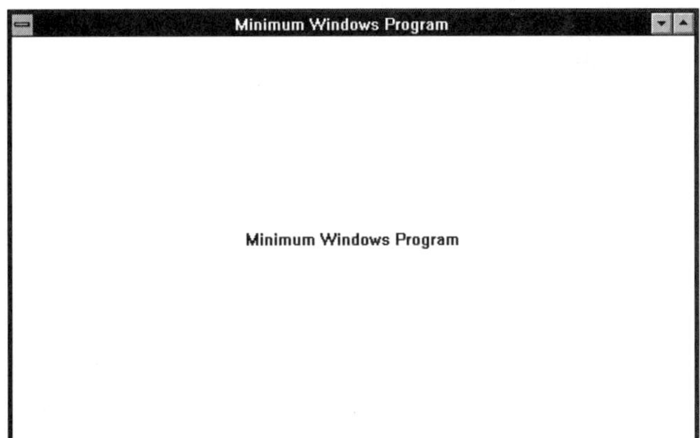

Figure 4.1.

A window created from a traditional Windows C program.

You might not be enthusiastic about the source code required to create this program. The program has more than 90 lines and requires 2 files to be compiled. The size represents the work a program must do to tap into the Windows user interface. Most of the code is overhead and repeats in every program.

Working with Project Files

Although you can run and compile the program presented in this chapter without a project file, now is a good time to introduce the concepts behind a project file.

For most C compilers, you can combine several source files into one executable program two ways. You can do this step by step—by typing DOS command-line directives to compile each source file and then linking them together—or you can use a project file. Many compilers also have a make utility that accomplishes the same task.

The integrated project make facility of Turbo C++ for Windows automates the compiling and linking process. It combines multiple files and then links them into an executable file. Most Windows programs consist of several files, and programs with several source files require project files. You, therefore, often use the project make facility when programming for Windows. Without the project facility, you would have to compile each one and then manually link the resulting files to create an .EXE file.

When you change a single source file in your program, you must recompile and relink it with the rest of the files in your program. However, you don't have to recompile every source file. You recompile only those files that changed, and then you relink the program. This makes the compile and link cycle quicker. With several files, it's difficult to keep track of which ones have been compiled since the last time the program was linked.

That's where project files come in handy. You tell the integrated make facility the name of the source files, and it keeps track of which source files must be recompiled to produce a final .EXE file. It also automates the compile and link process, so one command performs all the steps necessary to generate the final .EXE program.

Windows programs usually include source code, module definition files, and files describing icons, cursors, dialog boxes, and other interface elements. To use several files, you must create a project file. The project file keeps track of combining the source code and creating the final executable program for you.

Using Project Files

Project files are easy to use. To create a new project file, go to the Project menu and select Open. An Open Project File dialog box is displayed. It enables you to type the name of your project. After you enter the project name, a project window is created on the desktop (see Figure 4.2). To insert a source file into the project, press Insert or choose the Project menu item and select Add item.

A dialog box is displayed that enables you to select filenames. You can enter files that have already been created, or you can enter new filenames. Each time you select a file and press Enter, you add that file to the project. The Add to Project List dialog box is displayed, enabling you to enter another filename. When you enter all filenames, press Esc to close the dialog box.

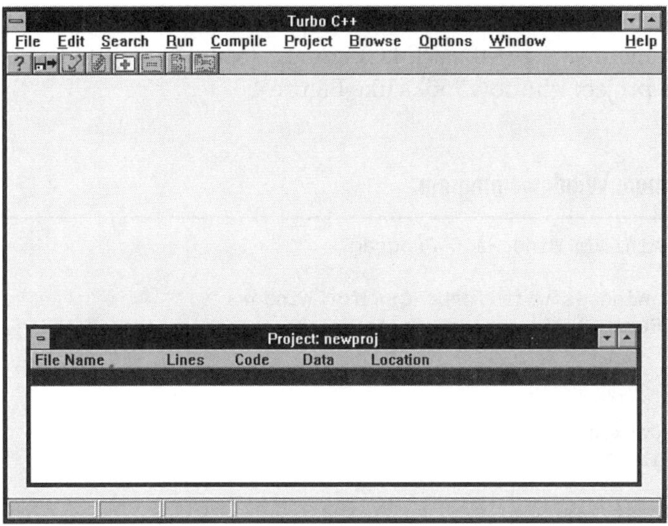

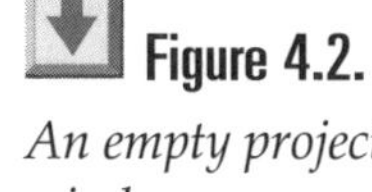

Figure 4.2.

An empty project window.

You then see the Project window filled with information, including the filenames you just entered, the number of lines in the code and data, and the location of the files (if they are in a drive or directory different from the project's original one).

WARNING

Never put header files (which have the extension .h) in a project file. Header files are meant to be included in your code with the `#include preprocessor` directive and should not appear in a project. For now, you put only .C or .CPP source code files or .DEF module definition files in your projects. As you learn about other types of files, you learn which ones you can include in your project files.

When a project file is loaded, the program you compile always receives the same base filename as your project filename, along with the .EXE extension. If you try to compile a complete stand-alone single file program active in an editor window with an active project file, the project file is compiled.

To begin a project file, create and name your project MINWIN.PRJ. Then, add the files in Listings 4.1 (MINWIN.C) and 4.2 (MINWIN.DEF) to the project file. The project Window looks like Figure 4.3.

Listing 4.1. Minimum Windows program.

```
// MINWIN.C - Minimum Windows C Program
//
// Programming Windows with Turbo C++ for Windows
// by Paul J. Perry

#define STRICT

#include <windowsx.h>
#include <stdlib.h>

// Function Prototypes
LRESULT CALLBACK MainWndProc(HWND hWnd, UINT message,
                             WPARAM wParam, LPARAM lParam);

/*******************************************/
#pragma argsused
int PASCAL WinMain(HINSTANCE hInstance, HINSTANCE hPrevInstance,
                   LPSTR lpCmdParam, int nCmdShow)
{
   char        ProgName[] = "Minimum Windows C Program";
   HWND        hWnd;
   MSG         msg;


   if (!hPrevInstance)
   {
      WNDCLASS    wndclass;

      wndclass.lpszClassName = ProgName;
      wndclass.lpfnWndProc   = (WNDPROC) MainWndProc;
      wndclass.cbClsExtra    = 0;
      wndclass.cbWndExtra    = 0;
      wndclass.hInstance     = hInstance;
      wndclass.hIcon         = LoadIcon(NULL, IDI_APPLICATION);
      wndclass.hCursor       = LoadCursor(NULL, IDC_ARROW);
      wndclass.hbrBackground = (HBRUSH) (COLOR_WINDOW + 1);
      wndclass.lpszMenuName  = NULL;
      wndclass.style         = CS_VREDRAW | CS_HREDRAW;

      if (!RegisterClass(&wndclass)) exit(0);;
   }
```

```
    hWnd = CreateWindow(ProgName,"Minimum Windows C Program",
                        WS_OVERLAPPEDWINDOW,
                        CW_USEDEFAULT, CW_USEDEFAULT,
                        CW_USEDEFAULT, CW_USEDEFAULT,
                        NULL, NULL, hInstance, NULL);

    ShowWindow(hWnd, nCmdShow);
    UpdateWindow(hWnd);

    while (GetMessage(&msg, NULL, 0, 0))
    {
       TranslateMessage(&msg);
       DispatchMessage(&msg);
    }
    return msg.wParam;
}

/*******************************************/
LRESULT CALLBACK _export MainWndProc(HWND hWnd, UINT message,
                                     WPARAM wParam, LPARAM lParam)
{
   switch (message)
   {
      case WM_PAINT :
      {
         HDC         PaintDC;
         RECT        rect;
         PAINTSTRUCT ps;

         PaintDC = BeginPaint(hWnd, &ps);
         GetClientRect(hWnd, &rect);

         DrawText(PaintDC, "Minimum Windows Program",
                  -1, &rect, DT_SINGLELINE | DT_CENTER | DT_VCENTER);

         EndPaint(hWnd, &ps);
         return 0;
      }

      case WM_DESTROY :
      {
         PostQuitMessage(0);
         return 0;
      }
   }
   return DefWindowProc (hWnd, message, wParam, lParam);
}
```

Listing 4.2. Module definition file for minimum Windows program.

```
;
; MINWIN.DEF module definition file
;

DESCRIPTION    'Minimum Windows C Program'
NAME           TRADITIONAL
EXETYPE        WINDOWS
STUB           'WINSTUB.EXE'
HEAPSIZE       1024
STACKSIZE      8192
CODE           PRELOAD MOVEABLE DISCARDABLE
DATA           PRELOAD MOVEABLE MULTIPLE
```

Figure 4.3.

Project window for MINWIN program.

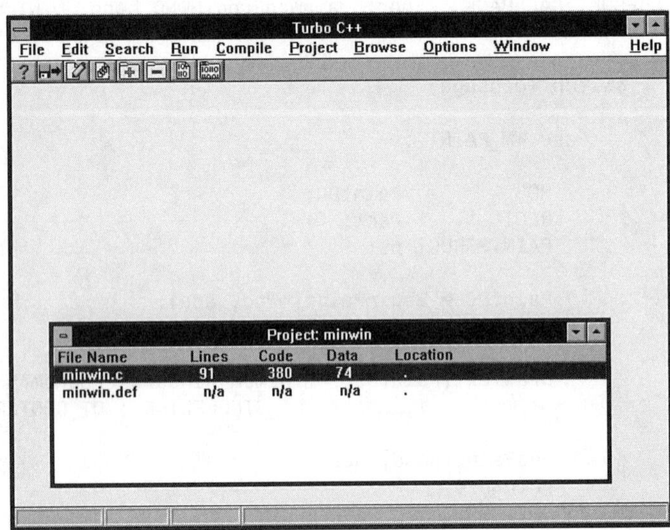

If you recall, the SIMPLE.C program in Chapter 3 produced a linker warning message "No module definition file specified: using defaults." The file added to the project, MINWIN.DEF, is a module definition and satisfies the linker warning message for a module definition file.

All module definition files have the extension .DEF. These files help the linker create the .EXE file by specifying characteristics about the program's code, its data, and so on. Recall, the MINWIN program could have been compiled without an additional module definition file (you receive the same warning message). Whenever possible, however, avoid compiler warning messages. By supplying your own .DEF file, you can better control the resulting program. You read about module definition files at the end of this chapter.

Now, you start digging into the code for Listings 4.1 and 4.2. The rest of this chapter covers what the program statements do and how you use them.

Preprocessor Directives

Listing 4.1 has two preprocessor directives. The first preprocessor directive,

```
#define STRICT
```

provides stricter type checking for your Windows programs. This helps you find type mismatch errors quickly. This directive is new to Windows 3.1 programming and was meant to let the compiler warn when incorrect variables are assigned values of different types.

Strict compile-time checking helps you find programming errors when you compile your application—rather than at runtime, with UAEs that cause your program to crash. The `STRICT` keyword is a real benefit, especially with code under development, because it helps you catch bugs right away when you compile your code, rather than having to track them down at runtime with a debugger. By catching bugs when you compile, you reduce the chance of shipping your applications with bugs not encountered when testing.

`STRICT` will help you more easily migrate your code to the 32-bit Windows NT platform in the future. It helps you locate and deal with type incompatibilities that arise when migrating to 32 bits.

The next preprocessor directive,

```
#include <windowsx.h>
```

provides the function prototypes, structure declarations, and symbol name identifiers for programming in Windows.

The windowsx.h header file is new with Windows 3.1 program development. It contains several new API functions and compiler macros. Generally, these make your code easier to read and write and can reduce typing. Most important, all these macros are portable to Windows NT.

The include file, windows.h, has defined Windows functions and definitions. You still can use windows.h. The windowsx.h header file includes windows.h (you can tell by looking at the compile status dialog box as the program is being compiled). Because of its compatibility with future versions of Windows and the added macros, windowsx.h header file is used throughout this book.

Structure of a Windows Program

The minimum Windows program has two main parts—the `WinMain` entry point and the `MainWndProc` function.

You already know `WinMain` is the main entry point for the application. In most Windows applications, `WinMain` does the following tasks:

- Calls initialization functions that register Windows classes.
- Creates and displays a window.
- Enters a message loop to process messages from the Windows application queue.
- Terminates the application.

`MainWndProc` responds to input and window-management messages received from Windows. These can be input messages sent by the main initialization function or Windows management messages that come directly from Windows. The window procedure must examine each message and carry out a specific action based on that message.

You examine `WinMain` and `MainWndProc` and their uses later in this chapter. For now, look at some of the other elements of the minimum Windows program.

The Windows API

The Windows Application Program Interface (API) includes more than 600 functions. The MINWIN program uses 14 Windows functions. The following list shows these functions in the order they occur in MINWIN.C.

- `LoadIcon`—Loads an icon for use by the program.
- `LoadCursor`—Loads a cursor for use by the program.
- `RegisterClass`—Registers a window class for the main window program.
- `CreateWindow`—Creates a window based on the specified class.
- `ShowWindow`—Displays the window on the desktop.
- `UpdateWindow`—Instructs the program's window to display itself.
- `TranslateMessage`—Translates keyboard input into messages.
- `DispatchMessage`—Sends a message to `MainWndProc`.
- `BeginPaint`—Asks for permission to start painting inside the window.
- `GetClientRect`—Returns the dimensions of the window.
- `DrawText`—Displays centered text in the window.
- `EndPaint`—Tells Windows your program is finished painting text.
- `PostQuitMessage`—Notifies Windows that the program is ready to terminate.
- `DefWindowProc`—Performs default processing of Windows messages.

NOTE

API routines refer to the large body of functions that are part of the Windows operating environment. Your program can call any of these functions at any time, although, usually, you use only a small subset of these functions. DOS does not have an API. However, DOS does use interrupts which act like API functions, but at a much lower level.

For a complete overview of these functions, you use the context-sensitive help system. You find information about each function as you examine the MINWIN.C program.

Hungarian Notation

You may have noticed that many of the variables and fields inside structures in the program have strange names. Consider `wndclass.hIcon`. Many Windows programmers use a variable-naming convention called Hungarian notation.

Hungarian notation got its name from the nationality of its creator, Charles Simonyi. In Hungarian notation, variable names are created by putting a short prefix before a longer, more descriptive name. The prefix indicates the type of data referenced by the variable. The `h` prefix in `hIcon` stands for a *handle,* or, more specifically, a handle to an icon. The `h` prefix in `hCursor` stands for a handle to a cursor.

Some of the prefixes can be used in combination. The `lpsz` prefix in the `wndcls` structure is one example. The variable `lpszClassName` stands for *l*ong *p*ointer to a *s*tring terminated by *z*ero (or an ASCIIZ string). The `lpfn` in `wndclass.lpfnWndProc` stands for a *l*ong *p*ointer to a *f*unction *n*ame.

Usually the prefixes are in lowercase, and the long names are in upper- and lowercase. Because C and C++ are case-sensitive languages, you must use the same case when you refer to a variable, or you will have errors when you try to compile and link the program. Hungarian notation is a convention to be used for your benefit as a programmer. It enables you to understand the lines of code in your program and to recognize the type of variables being referenced in specific locations of a program.

The trick to learning Hungarian notation is to learn the prefixes. Table 4.1 lists the more common prefixes in Windows programming.

In Turbo C++ for Windows, Hungarian notation is used mostly for variable names or structure field names. The notation enables you to assign variables properly. When you know the name of a variable is `hBrush`, and you know a certain function returns a handle to a brush, you don't have to think about what type of value a function returns. This frees you to focus on how your application works.

Table 4.1. Hungarian notation prefixes.

Prefix	*Description*
b	Boolean (BOOL) variable type.
by	Byte (BYTE) variable type.
c	Character (char) variable type.
cb	Count of bytes variable.
cx, cy	Integer used as width variables.
fn	Function name.
h	Handle type.
i	Integer (int) variable.
l	Long (LONG) variable.
lp	Long pointer variable type.
n	Short or integer value.
sz	ASCIIZ string (string terminated with a zero byte).
w	Word (WORD) value.
x, y	Integer used as x or y coordinates.

Global Program Variables

In Chapter 3, you learned that the entry point for all Windows programs is the `WinMain` function. You might have noticed several variables which were passed to that function. Look at them again, now. `WinMain` is declared in the listing as follows:

```
int PASCAL WinMain(HINSTANCE hInstance, HINSTANCE hPrevInstance,
                   LPSTR lpCmdParam, int nCmdShow)
```

This function uses the `PASCAL` calling convention and returns an integer. The `PASCAL` calling convention is used frequently in Windows programming because it passes variables between functions more efficiently.

`WinMain` has four parameters passed to it. The `hInstance` variable is a number that uniquely identifies the program when it is running under Windows. Your Windows program can have several copies of the function running at each time. Each copy uses the same code, but has its own data. Each executing copy of the program is called an instance and has a different instance handle.

You can think of it as a name given to the window by the operating system. The Windows operating environment gives a unique number to each instance of a program. Other Windows functions in the program use `hInstance` to differentiate which copy of the program is being executed.

The `hPrevInstance` variable is the handle to the instance of the most recent running copy of the program. If there are no other running programs, `hPrevInstance` is set to `0`. A program is notified of its previous instance so that information can be shared between programs. When running multiple programs, memory is conserved because, as mentioned, Windows shares the code between each running program. The memory required for data is duplicated in memory. This method allows more than one executing copy of a program to use much less memory.

The third parameter, `lpCmdParam`, points to a string that contains the command-line parameters passed to the program. You can run a Windows program with a command line by typing the program name and the parameters in the Run dialog box (either in Program Manager or File Manager—see Figure 4.4—or by entering it as part of the DOS command line when starting Windows). The line

```
win minwin one two three
```

typed from the DOS prompt starts Windows, executes the MINWIN.EXE program, and passes the string "`one two three`" to the program through the `lpCmdParam` variable.

The last variable, `nCmdShow`, is an integer describing how the window is to be initially displayed on the Windows desktop. This is determined by how you execute the program. If you start the application from the Program Manager and press Enter—or double-click the icon—the program is run and displayed full-screen. If you press Shift-Enter—or Shift-double-click the icon—the program loads as an icon. `nCmdShow` tells your program how it should be displayed.

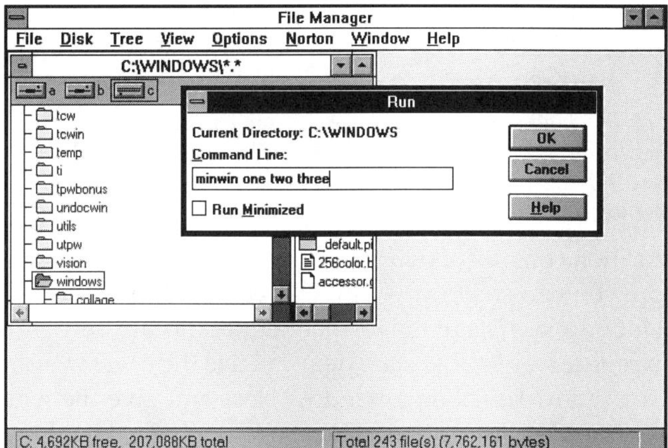

Figure 4.4.

The File Manager Run dialog box.

Now that you understand the four main parameters passed to your program from `WinMain`, you can look at the initialization required by your minimum Windows program.

Program Initialization

`WinMain` contains the following program initialization statements from Listing 4.1:

```
if (!hPrevInstance)
{
   WNDCLASS    wndclass;

   wndclass.lpszClassName = ProgName;
   wndclass.lpfnWndProc   = (WNDPROC) MainWndProc;
   wndclass.cbClsExtra    = 0;
   wndclass.cbWndExtra    = 0;
   wndclass.hInstance     = hInstance;
   wndclass.hIcon         = LoadIcon(NULL, IDI_APPLICATION);
   wndclass.hCursor       = LoadCursor(NULL, IDC_ARROW);
   wndclass.hbrBackground = (HBRUSH) (COLOR_WINDOW + 1);
   wndclass.lpszMenuName  = NULL;
   wndclass.style         = CS_VREDRAW | CS_HREDRAW;

   if (!RegisterClass(&wndclass)) exit(0);;
}
```

```
hWnd = CreateWindow(ProgName,"Minimum Windows C Program",
                    WS_OVERLAPPEDWINDOW,
                    CW_USEDEFAULT, CW_USEDEFAULT,
                    CW_USEDEFAULT, CW_USEDEFAULT,
                    NULL, NULL, hInstance, NULL);

ShowWindow(hWnd, nCmdShow);
UpdateWindow(hWnd);
```

Program initialization consists of two parts: class registration and window creation. Before you can create any window, you must first create a window class. A window class is a template that defines the attributes of a window. After you register a window class, you can use the `CreateWindow` function to create a window based on a window class and give the window specific attributes and styles.

Window Classes

Only the first instance of a program must register a window class. The window class is automatically available to subsequent instances of the program. In the sample program, first check the `hPrevInstance` variable to see whether it is equal to `0`. If so, you are executing the first instance of the program.

Use `RegisterClass` to create a window class. `RegisterClass` takes a single variable: a pointer to a structure of type `WNDCLASS`. windows.h defines `WNDCLASS` as follows:

```
typedef struct tagWNDCLASS
{
    UINT          style;
    WNDPROC       lpfnWndProc;
    int           cbClsExtra;
    int           cbWndExtra;
    HINSTANCE     hInstance;
    HICON         hIcon;
    HCURSOR       hCursor;
    HBRUSH        hbrBackground;
    LPCSTR        lpszMenuName;
    LPCSTR        lpszClassName;
} WNDCLASS;
```

In the block of code, you define a structure of type WNDCLASS as follows:

```
WNDCLASS    wndclass;
```

The program then initializes the fields of the structure and registers the class.

The WNDCLASS structure has 10 fields. You specify the information for a window class in these fields and RegisterClass copies the information to the Windows list of window classes. The fields describe characteristics of all windows based on the window class. The information includes the following:

```
wndclass.style = CS_VREDRAW ¦ CS_HREDRAW;
```

- Assigns a class style using the C or (¦) operator to combine individual style settings.
- These two class style identifiers tell the operating environment that all windows based on this class should be redrawn automatically if the window is resized or moved by the user. The windows.h header file defines the valid class styles that can be used to register a class. A list of valid class types appears in Table 4.2.

Table 4.2. Class styles declared in windows.h.

Style	*Description*
CS_VREDRAW	Forces entire window to be redisplayed if vertical size changes.
CS_HREDRAW	Forces entire window to be redisplayed if horizontal size changes.
CS_DBLCLKS	Sends double-click messages to window.
CS_OWNDC	Forces each window to have its own display context.
CS_CLASSDC	Gives window class its own display context.

continues

Table 4.2. continued

Style	*Description*
CS_PARENTDC	Gives parent window display context to window class.
CS_NOCLOSE	Disables the Close option on control menu for windows created with this class.
CS_SAVEBITS	Objects covered by this window will be saved as bitmaps. This is usually used for small windows that are displayed only for a short while.
CS_BYTEALIGNCLIENT	Aligns window's client area on the byte boundary.
CS_BYTEALIGNWINDOW	Aligns a window on the byte boundary.
CS_GLOBALCLASS	Makes window class system global.

- `wndclass.lpfnWndProc = (WNDPROC) MainWndProc;` This field informs Windows the address of the function to be used as the main window procedure. When the window receives a request or notice of an event, the window procedure is called and passed a message describing the event that occurred or the service that needs to be performed. The typecast tells the compiler you are passing the address of a window procedure (`WNDPROC`). After your program starts running, this routine actually becomes a function that Windows calls itself.

- `wndclass.hInstance = hInstance;` This informs Windows which instance of the program owns the window class. It is used by Windows so that the class may be automatically discarded when the program terminates.

- `wndclass.hIcon = LoadIcon(NULL, IDI_APPLICATION);` This specifies an icon to be used by the program when it is in the minimized state. For this program, ask with `LoadIcon` for a handle to a predefined icon. With the first parameter set to `NULL`, the second parameter is an identifier to a constant defined in windows.h. The `IDI_APPLICATION` icon shows the Windows flag (see Figure 4.5).

Figure 4.5.

The IDI_APPLICATION default icon.

- `wndclass.hCursor = LoadCursor(NULL, IDC_ARROW);` This loads a predefined mouse cursor. When the mouse cursor appears over the client area of a Window, based on this window class, the cursor becomes the specified cursor shape. In this case, you use the predefined arrow cursor that is so common in Windows programs.
- `wndclass.hbrBackground = (HBRUSH) (COLOR_WINDOW + 1);` This field assigns the background color of the client area of windows created with this windows class. `(COLOR_WINDOW+1)` tells Windows to use the background color that the user has currently set up from Control Panel. The typecast tells the compiler you are passing a handle to a brush as the parameter. The default background color is usually white.
- `wndclass.lpszMenuName = NULL;` For any application that has a top-level, pull-down menu you specify the name of it in this field. All windows created based on this class have the specified menu. The example program does not use a menu, so its value is set to `NULL`.
- `wndclass.cbClsExtra = 0;` This tells Windows how many extra bytes to allocate for the class structure. It is used to reserve extra space in the class structure for program data. The minimum Windows program does not make use of this, so it is set to `0`.
- `wndclass.cbWndExtra = 0;` Like the previous field, this one allocates extra bytes for use by the programmer. The `cbWndExtra` bytes are

allocated for each window created from the class. No extra window bytes are used in this program.

- `wndclass.lpszClassName = ProgName;` Finally, you must give each class a name. This is the lookup value that identifies a class entry. In this example, `ProgName` is a string constant set to the name of the program.

When all fields of the window class have been set, MINWIN.C registers the Window class by calling the `RegisterClass` function.

Creating the Window

After you register a window class, you can create as many windows of that class as you like, using the `CreateWindow` function. The parameters to `CreateWindow` include information unique to each instance of the window, including the window title, the parent window, the window position and its size, a window menu, and the window style.

`CreateWindow` takes 11 parameters. This is how it is called in the MINWIN program:

```
hWnd = CreateWindow(ProgName,"Minimum Windows C Program",
                    WS_OVERLAPPEDWINDOW,
                    CW_USEDEFAULT, CW_USEDEFAULT,
                    CW_USEDEFAULT, CW_USEDEFAULT,
                    NULL, NULL, hInstance, NULL);
```

As you might expect, the first parameter to `CreateWindow` specifies the name of the Window class on which this window is based. The name must be the window class which was previously registered with the `RegisterClass` function. If the class is not valid, `CreateWindow` returns a NULL value.

The second parameter is the title of the window. The window title is displayed both in the title bar at the top of the window and also as text in the icon when the window is minimized.

The window created by this code is a normal overlapped window with a title bar, a system menu, minimize and maximize buttons, and a thick border for resizing. You specify this style in the third parameter to `CreateWindow`. `WS_OVERLAPPEDWINDOW` is the standard style used by many Windows programs. Table 4.3 lists other available window styles.

Table 4.3. Window styles declared in windows.h.

Window Style	*Description*
WS_OVERLAPPEDWINDOW	Specifies a default overlapped window type.
WS_OVERLAPPED	Creates an overlapped window.
WS_POPUP	Specifies a pop-up window.
WS_CHILD	Specifies that a window is a child window.
WS_MINIMIZEBOX	Includes Minimize button.
WS_MAXIMIZEBOX	Includes Maximize button.
WS_CAPTION	Includes title bar for window.
WS_BORDER	Includes border around window.
WS_VISIBLE	Forces window to be visible initially.
WS_DISABLED	Forces window to be disabled initially.
WS_CLIPSIBLINGS	Clips child windows relative to each other.
WS_CLIPCHILDREN	Doesn't paint in area occupied by child windows.
WS_DLGFRAME	Creates window with double border but no title bar.
WS_VSCROLL	Includes vertical scroll bar on window.
WS_HSCROLL	Includes horizontal scroll bar on window.
WS_SYSMENU	Includes system menu on window.
WS_THICKFRAME	Includes thick window border that can be resized.

The next four arguments are passed the constant `CW_USEDEFAULT`. The parameters specify the starting x and y position of the window and the initial width and height of the window. The identifier `CW_USEDEFAULT` tells Windows to use default values for these parameters. The default values are passed from the operating environment to the program. If you run several instances of the program, you find the operating environment automatically cascades the windows (see Figure 4.6).

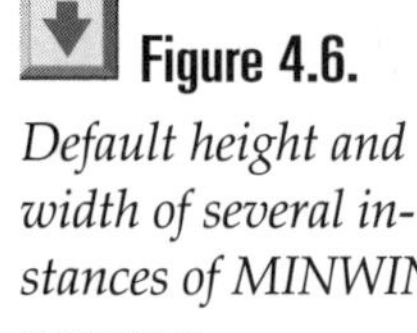

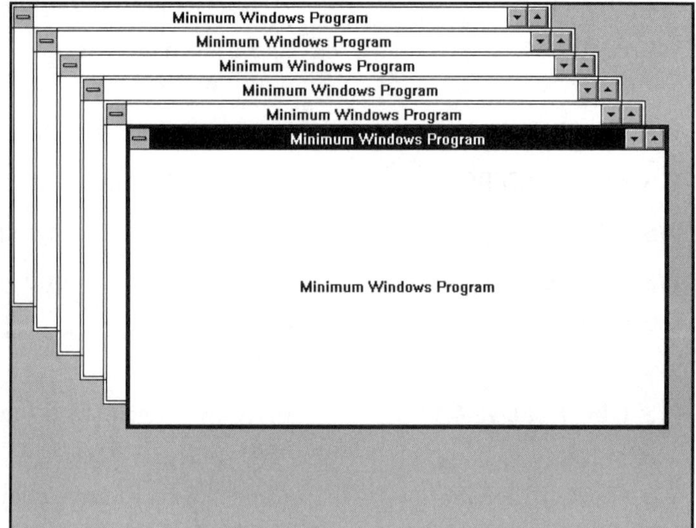

Figure 4.6.
Default height and width of several instances of MINWIN program.

You can pass integer values for these four parameters to force the window at a starting x and y location and to specify the beginning width and height. Most programs just use the defaults as passed by Windows.

The final line in the program's call to `CreateWindow` includes several important variables that specify window characteristics. The seventh parameter, which is set to 0, specifies that the program has no parent window. Parent windows are an important concept. When a window has a parent window, the window always stays inside its parent window location. Child windows have many uses. In a dialog box, for example, each command button—and every other control—is a separate window. It is thought of as a child window of the dialog box.

The eighth parameter, `NULL`, specifies not to use a menu for this specific window. If a menu is used, it overrides the menu specified in a window class declaration. In the ninth parameter, the function takes the `hInstance` variable (from `WinMain`). This is used to identify the instance of the program creating the window. Finally, the last parameter is set to `NULL` because the class definition does not ask to reserve any extra bytes of memory for your programs.

After `CreateWindow` returns a number, Windows has all the internal information needed to display and process a window.

Displaying the Window

Although `CreateWindow` creates a window, it does not automatically display the window on the desktop. You do that with `ShowWindow` as follows:

```
ShowWindow(hWnd, nCmdShow);
```

`ShowWindow` tells Windows to display the new window. The function takes as the first parameter the handle to the window, which was returned by the `CreateWindow` function.

The second parameter to `ShowWindow` is the global variable `nCmdShow`. This determines how the window is to initially be displayed on the screen. Usually your program should display its main application window, using the value supplied in `nCmdShow` passed from `WinMain`. However, you can ignore the `nCmdShow` parameter and display the window any way you want by passing a different value to `ShowWindow`. You can pass any of the values in Table 4.4.

Table 4.4. ShowWindow states.

Value	*Description*
SW_HIDE	Hides the window and activates another window.
SW_MINIMIZE	Minimizes the window and activates another window.

continues

Table 4.4. continued

Value	*Description*
SW_SHOW	Activates a window and displays it in its current size and position.
SW_SHOWMAXIMIZED	Activates a window and displays it as a maximized window.
SW_SHOWMINIMIZED	Activates a window and displays it as iconic.
SW_SHOWMINNOACTIVE	Displays a window as an icon without activating it.
SW_SHOWNA	Displays a window in its current state without activating it.
SW_SHOWNOACTIVATE	Displays a window in its most recent size and position without activating it.
SW_SHOWNORMAL	Activates and displays a window. If the window is minimized or maximized, Windows restores it to its original size and position.

By passing your own value for `nCmdShow` to the `ShowWindow` function your program has more control over how it's main window will be displayed.

With the window displayed on the Windows desktop, the background is erased with the background brush specified in the window class. The function call:

```
UpdateWindow(hWnd);
```

causes the client area to be painted. Windows causes the `WM_PAINT` message to be issued to the window procedure.

The `WM_PAINT` message is important for applications because it notifies the window procedure to display the graphical element in the client area of the program. You soon examine how the window procedure deals with this message.

Windows programs differentiate parts of the window. The *client area* is the entire inside area of a window and is usually painted the background color. The *nonclient area* is all parts outside the main window, such as the border, title bar, control menu, and any part of the window not located inside the main window.

The Message Loop

In Chapter 1,"Getting Started with Turbo C++ for Windows," you learned that one of the benefits of running Windows is that it is a multitasking environment. It enables you to execute more than one program at the same time. To accomplish this, the system must run and manage several programs at the same time with a single processor.

Many operating environments—such as DESQview—use a method that alots each executing program a certain amount of the microprocessor's time. After the designated time has passed, the next program receives a specific amount of time, and the process continues. This is *preemptive* multitasking.

A second method gives complete control of the processor to a program. When that program finishes a task, it returns control of the microprocessor to the environment. Then, the environment can pass the microprocessor to the next program. Windows uses this *nonpreemptive* approach.

Windows programs rely on messages to receive input from the user and from interface objects. Some messages are hardware related, for example the press of a key or the click of a mouse. Other messages are only for interaction between programs.

What About Messages?

You might wonder how a message relates to Windows. You know what a message is in the broadest sense: "John called, give him a call at 123-8088" is an example of a message in human terms. Messages in Windows function in much the same way.

Your minimum Windows program defines a message structure as type MSG. Look inside windows.h to discover the fields:

```
typedef struct tagMSG
{
    HWND        hwnd;
    UINT        message;
    WPARAM      wParam;
    LPARAM      lParam;
    DWORD       time;
    POINT       pt;
} MSG;
```

A Windows message has six elements. Take a look at each element in this record:

- hwnd contains a handle to the window to which the message is being directed. Messages are directed only to a single window. In the MINWIN program, the handle to the window is the same value returned from a call to the CreateWindow function.
- message contains the actual message. Rather than a string of characters, a message is a 16-bit value that corresponds to a constant defined in windows.h. All messages have the prefix WM_, which stands for *W*indows *M*essage.
- wParam is a 16-bit message parameter. Its meaning and value depend on the particular message being sent.
- lParam is a 32-bit message parameter. Again, the meaning and value of this depends on the particular message being sent. You can think of the wParam and lParam values as extra information that comes with a message.
- time holds the time that the message was generated.
- pt holds the coordinates of the mouse cursor when the message was created.

In the earlier example, "John called, give him a call at 123-8088," the message value would be an identifier that says John_Called and the lParam parameter might be the phone number. The time and pt values would each have a value, but they would not be useful in this context, because they do not relate to what the original message was.

Getting Messages

Every program has a message loop that allows it to poll continuously for messages from the operating environment. With this method, each program can receive messages and act appropriately. The message processing system for each program has two parts. A *message loop* receives messages from the operating environment, translates them as necessary, and sends them to the window procedure. The *window procedure* is the code that acts on the messages.

Here is the message loop from MINWIN:

```
while (GetMessage(&msg, NULL, 0, 0))
{
   TranslateMessage(&msg);
   DispatchMessage(&msg);
}
return msg.wParam;
```

The loop runs continuously for as long as the MINWIN program is running. The call to `GetMessage` indicates to the compiler to fill the `msg` structure with the appropriate message information. The second parameter is set to `NULL`. This tells Windows to process all windows created by this program. The third and fourth parameters are set to `0`. This indicates the program wants all messages for all windows created by the program.

If the message field is equal to the `WM_QUIT` constant, `GetMessage` returns a `0` value. At this point, the `while` loop is exited and the program is exited with a return statement.

The second routine in the loop is a call to `TranslateMessage`. This routine converts raw keystroke messages to usable ASCII values. This makes it easy for a Windows program to know when a specific key has been pressed. It removes the need to interpret two messages: one, that the key has been pressed; and two, that the key has been released.

The final part of the message loop, the call to `DispatchMessage`, sends the window message to the window procedure. It is then the job of the window procedure to act on the message.

Looking at the Window Procedure

Everything you have learned so far is really only initialization code. The real action occurs in the program's window procedure. Although named a procedure, the code is actually a function and does return a value. Somehow, the function received the name *procedure* and it has stuck with Windows programmers ever since.

The window procedure determines how a program acts. A window procedure can receive many messages quickly. Probably, your program does not need to act on most messages.

From a structural point, a window procedure is usually a case statement that responds to the many window messages dispatched from the operating environment. The window procedure for your MINWIN program looks like this:

```
LRESULT CALLBACK _export MainWndProc(HWND hWnd, UINT message,
                                     WPARAM wParam, LPARAM lParam)
{
   switch (message)
   {
      case WM_PAINT :
      {
         HDC         PaintDC;
         RECT        rect;
         PAINTSTRUCT ps;

         PaintDC = BeginPaint(hWnd, &ps);
         GetClientRect(hWnd, &rect);

         DrawText(PaintDC, "Minimum Windows Program",
               -1, &rect, DT_SINGLELINE ¦ DT_CENTER ¦ DT_VCENTER);

         EndPaint(hWnd, &ps);
         return 0;
      }

      case WM_DESTROY :
      {
         PostQuitMessage(0);
         return 0;
      }
   }
   return DefWindowProc (hWnd, message, wParam, lParam);
}
```

The first line contains the definition of the window procedure. Every window procedure has exactly four parameters defined as follows:

```
LRESULT CALLBACK _export MainWndProc(HWND hWnd, UINT message,
                                      WPARAM wParam, LPARAM lParam)
```

If you are familiar with creating DOS-based programs, you probably are not accustomed to the environment calling your program. In DOS, a program makes calls to the operating system, but not the other way around. Because of the complex design of Windows, the operating environment actually calls the functions and procedures inside your program.

The return type of `LRESULT CALLBACK _export` informs the compiler to add the required code that allows Windows to call your function. This directive makes a procedure or function exportable. You must specify this for all window procedures.

Notice that the first four parameters passed to the window procedure are identical to the first four fields of the `MSG` structure. The handle to a window, `hWnd`, identifies the window associated with the message. This is important because a single program can have any number of windows displayed on the desktop. The second parameter, `message`, is a number that identifies the message being sent. The last two parameters, `wParam` and `lParam`, provide more information about the message. As described earlier, the meaning of `wParam` and `lParam` are specific to the message being sent.

The WM_PAINT Message

The first message the window procedure processes is `WM_PAINT`. This message notifies the program that it must redisplay the elements inside its window. This might sound like a strange thing. You might think when something is written over a window, Windows should save the image that is there and then redisplay it when it needs to be displayed? The answer is No!

Storing high-resolution graphics requires a great amount of memory. With the memory requirements of Windows already high, the designers made a decision: when a window's area must be redisplayed, a message is sent to its window procedure. Then it is displayed as though for the first time.

When a window is obstructed, it becomes *invalid*. When another program writes over the window of your program, it becomes invalidated. When your program receives focus again, the operating environment sends the window procedure a WM_PAINT message to redisplay the window's contents.

The window is also invalid when you first create it. UpdateWindow actually sends a WM_PAINT message to the window procedure. The window procedure then knows to redisplay the window's client area.

Because CS_HREDRAW and CS_VREDRAW are the specified class styles, Windows sends a WM_PAINT message when the window's size changes. If you do not specify these style types, the text in the window does not change when the window is resized.

Displaying Text

When your MINWIN program knows it is time to display the contents of its window area, several lines of code are used to display the message "Minimum Windows C Program." The code is as follows:

```
case WM_PAINT :
{
   HDC         PaintDC;
   RECT        rect;
   PAINTSTRUCT ps;

   PaintDC = BeginPaint(hWnd, &ps);
   GetClientRect(hWnd, &rect);

   DrawText(PaintDC, "Minimum Windows Program",
            -1, &rect, DT_SINGLELINE ¦ DT_CENTER ¦
            DT_VCENTER);

   EndPaint(hWnd, &ps);
   return 0;
}
```

Remember with the EasyWin library, you code a statement similar to the following:

```
printf("Minimum Windows Program");
```

With this routine, you have no control of where the text is displayed and what color it is. Programming explicitly for Windows is different. When processing the `WM_PAINT` message, a program must always make a call to the `BeginPaint` routine and end with a call to the `EndPaint` routine. In both cases, the first parameter is a handle to the window and the second is a variable of type `PAINTSTRUCT`. The paint structure contains information for painting in a window.

`BeginPaint` returns a handle to a device context. A device context is required when you write to a window. The device context specifies characteristics about what is to be painted. In a text-based environment, the only items that can be displayed are text or text-based boxes. While displaying these the only characteristic is the color of the text. You have no choice in size, drawing mode, brush type, pen type, and so on.

Because displaying text is actually displaying graphics in Windows, the device context specifies the characteristics of what you want to display. When you request a display context with `BeginPaint`, you borrow the display context from the system—because it has so many attributes for displaying text or objects. Each display context requires about 640 bytes of memory. When you are done using it, you must return the display context to Windows with the `EndPaint` function.

Table 4.5. lists the default drawing attributes of a display context.

Table 4.5. Default attributes of the display context.

Attribute	*Default Value*
Background color	White
Background mode	Opaque
Bitmap	none
Brush	White_Brush
Brush origin	(0,0)
Clipping region	Entire client area

continues

Table 4.5. continued

Attribute	*Default Value*
Color palette	Default_Palette
Current pen position	(0,0)
Device origin	Upper-left center of client area
Drawing mode	R2_CopyPen
Font	System_Font
Intercharacter spacing	0
Mapping mode	mm_Text
Pen	Black_Pen
Polygon-filling mode	Alternate
Relative or absolute display	Absolute
Stretching mode	BlackOnWhite
Text color	Black
Viewport extent	(1,1)
Viewport origin	(0,0)
Window extents	(1,1)
Window origin	(0,0)

Notice, you don't use every attribute for every drawing routine. Each drawing routine takes the attributes it needs from the display context.

The second routine called in the program is `GetClientRect`. The first parameter is a handle to the window. The second parameter is the address of a structure of type `RECT`. The definition for `RECT` looks like this in windows.h:

```
typedef struct tagRECT
{
    int left;
    int top;
    int right;
    int bottom;
} RECT;
```

`Rect` is a rectangular structure. It has four integer fields that specify the left, top, right, and bottom area coordinates of a rectangle. The `GetClientRect` function returns the size of the client area in this structure. Remember, the client area does not include the extra elements—the title bar, border, and system menu—but only the main part of the window.

The coordinates of the rectangle are passed to the `DrawText` routine. `DrawText` displays text in a window. The first parameter is a handle to the device context that was returned from `BeginPaint`. The second parameter is the text to display, and the third parameter is `-1`, which tells the routine the text is an ASCIIZ string.

The last parameter is a series of flags defined in windows.h. The flags indicate that the text should be displayed as a single line centered within the rectangle specified by the fourth parameter. `DrawText` actually displays the message in the center of the window.

When the rectangle becomes invalid—that is, when it is written over or the size changes—Windows erases the window's background. The background changes to that specified in the window class, and the window procedure receives another `WM_PAINT` message.

The last statement called for processing `WM_PAINT` is `EndPaint`. Recall, you must return a display context to Windows. `EndPaint` returns the display context to Windows. If the display context is not returned to the system, the memory is wasted, and system resources diminish quickly.

Program Termination

The second part of the case statement processes when a window is to be closed and the corresponding program is to stop executing. The program receives the message `WM_DESTROY`. This tells the program that Windows is in the process of destroying the window based on a command from the user.

The message can be a result of the user choosing the close option on the system menu , by pressing Alt-F4, or by exiting windows completely. When you exit Windows, each program that is currently being executed receives a `WM_DESTROY` message. You can use this feature to good advantage, for example, to remind a user to save text in a word processor.

In response to the message, the MINWIN program executes the `PostQuitMessage` function. This function sends a `WM_QUIT` message to the program's main message loop which, as discussed earlier, forces the program out of the message loop.

Default Message Processing

Wait a moment. If you have been following along closely you might remember that I said every window receives many Windows messages. A program, however, does not use every message it receives. With so many messages, actions in response to a message often are the same for every program, no matter what program you are using.

To account for this, Windows provides a routine called `DefWindowProc`. This routine provides default responses for a number of messages.

In your window procedure, if the case falls through and the message is not `WM_PAINT` or `WM_DESTROY`, control is passed to the default window procedure as follows:

```
return DefWindowProc (hWnd, message, wParam, lParam);
```

This processes the default window messages and returns the result to the window procedure, which in turn returns the result to the operating environment. Table 4.6. is a list of the messages processed by the default window procedure.

Table 4.6. Messages responded to by the default window procedure.

Message	*Message*
WM_NCACTIVATE	WM_ERASEBKGND
WM_NCHITTEST	WM_QUERYOPEN

Message	Message
WM_NCCALCSIZE	WM_QUERYENDSESSION
WM_NCLBUTTONDOWN	WM_SYSCOMMAND
WM_NCMOUSEMOVE	WM_KEYUP
WM_NCLBUTTONUP	WM_SYSCHAR
WM_NCLBUTTONDBLCLK	WM_CHARTOITEM
WM_CANCELMODE	WM_VKEYTOITEM
WM_NCCREATE	WM_ACTIVATE
WM_NCDESTROY	WM_SETREDRAW
WM_NCPAINT	WM_SHOWWINDOW
WM_SETTEXT	WM_CTRLCOLOR
WM_GETTEXT	WM_SETCURSOR
WM_GETTEXTLENGTH	WM_MOUSEACTIVATE
WM_CLOSE	WM_DRAWITEM
WM_PAINT	WM_SYSKEYDOWN
WM_PAINTICON	WM_SYSKEYUP
WM_ICONERASEBKGNE	

The Module Definition File

To compile the program, recall that you include two files in the project: MINWIN.C and MINWIN.DEF. The MINWIN.DEF module definition file describes the structure and organization of a program to the linker. MINWIN.DEF provides additional information that is needed with linking Windows programs.

The first line of the module definition file is:

```
DESCRIPTION   'Minimum Windows C Program'
```

This statement inserts text into the resulting executable file. You usually use this for program or copyright information.

The NAME statement designates the program as a program (rather than a dynamic link library (DLL)) and assigns it a module name. NAME is sometimes, but not always, the same name given to the executable (.EXE).

```
NAME          TRADITIONAL
```

The EXETYPE line tells the linker that this program is meant to run under Windows. This field is left over from the OS/2 days. OS/2 was the first operating system to have module definition files. The idea was to allow the linker to create executables for either DOS or OS/2 by changing a line in the module definition file. The only statement you can use when working with Turbo C++ for Windows is WINDOWS.

```
EXETYPE       WINDOWS
```

STUB is a regular DOS program that is inserted inside the .EXE file of the Windows program. This program is run when someone attempts to run the program directly from the DOS command line. The WINSTUB.EXE program included with Turbo C++ for Windows simply displays the message "This program requires Microsoft Windows" and returns the command line.

If you have a DOS compiler—such as Borland C++ or Turbo C++ 3.0—you could write your own stub program and insert its name in the module definition file. You could then create a more customized version of STUB that displays a message to help the users of your program get up to speed.

```
STUB          'WINSTUB.EXE'
```

The HEAPSIZE line specifies the amount of available local heap memory that will be available for memory allocation. This value is not critical, because Windows can expand a program's local heap.

```
HEAPSIZE      1024
```

The STACKSIZE statement assigns the size of the stack. With a larger program, you definitely want to increase the number specified.

```
STACKSIZE     8192
```

The CODE statement gives an idea about memory management under Windows. It means the program's code will always be loaded at the time the program starts executing (PRELOAD), that it can be swapped around in memory (MOVEABLE), and that if memory is needed for something else, it can be temporarily moved out of memory (DISCARDABLE).

```
CODE           PRELOAD MOVEABLE DISCARDABLE
```

You can specify attributes about the data in your program similar to the way you specify attributes about the code. The DATA statement indicates that you want the data segment to be preloaded, to be moveable in memory, and to allow for more than one data area (for multiple instances of a program to run).

```
DATA           PRELOAD MOVEABLE MULTIPLE
```

As other important topics about module definition files come up, you learn about them. For now, the only items that change are the DESCRIPTION and NAME of the program.

Wrapping It Up

This chapter started by describing what project files are and how to use them. It then took a close look at a minimum Windows C program. You learned about the WinMain function, program initialization, and the windows procedure. The end of the chapter covered the items in a module definition file and their uses.

With a basic understanding of a Windows program, you are ready to continue your study of programming for Windows. In Chapter 5, "Using the ObjectWindows Library," you find a detailed discussion about OWL.

What You Have Learned

Because this chapter introduced some of the main concepts in programming for Windows, it is a starting point for the rest of the chapters in this book's close examination of other aspects of programming for Windows.

Before continuing, review the following points about writing traditional Windows programs:

- You use project files to combine multiple modules that result in a complete program. Project files are commonly used with Windows programs, because several files are usually required to compile the program, including multiple source code files, a module definition file, and a resource file.
- You never insert header files in a project file. They are only included in your source code with the `#include preprocessor` directive.
- Windows programs are composed of two parts: the initialization section and the window procedure.
- Hungarian notation is a technique for naming variables that prefixes the variable name with letters that tell the programmer what type the variable is. Some of the more common prefixes are `b` (BOOL), `w` (WORD), `fn` (function), `sz` (an ASCIIZ string), and `lp` (long pointer).
- A Windows program has four global variables: `hInstance`, `hPrevInstance`, `lpCmdParam`, and `nCmdShow`. The handle to the instance of this program is `hInstance`. `hPrevInstance` is a handle to the previous running instance of the program. `lpCmdLine` is the command line passed to the program, and `nCmdShow` specifies how the program should initially be displayed.
- Program initialization includes registering a window class and creating a window.
- A window class defines the fundamental behavior of a window. There are 10 fields to the window class. `RegisterClass` is the function that registers a class with the environment.
- The `CreateWindow` function creates windows. It takes nine parameters that specify the title of the window, the window type, the beginning location, the height, and the width of the window.
- Multitasking in Windows is based on a method called non-preemptive multitasking. In this method, the microprocessor gives complete attention to an executing program until that program gives up control.

- To implement multitasking, Windows relies on messages sent between programs and the operating environment. A message is a record type with six fields. The fields include a handle to the window that the message belongs to, a code relating to the message, two parameters that specify additional message information, a parameter that tells when the message was created, and the coordinates of the mouse cursor when the message was created.
- Messages are passed from the main program's message loop to the program's window procedure.
- The `WM_PAINT` message is generated every time a window needs its client area to be displayed. When a window needs to be redisplayed, it becomes invalid.
- You must always respond to a `WM_PAINT` message with the `BeginPaint` routine. As you finish processing `WM_PAINT`, always use the `EndPaint` function to free the display context.
- A display context defines many attributes for displaying text or graphics in a window.
- When a program has access to a display context, the program actually borrows the display context from the system. When finished with the display context, your program must return it to the system.
- The `GetClientRect` routine returns the current size of the window's client area.
- The `DrawText` routine displays text in the window's client area.
- Always use the `BeginPaint` and `EndPaint` routines as a pair, or serious memory corruption problems result.
- The `DefWindowProc` routine provides default processing of more than 30 Windows messages.

5

USING THE OBJECTWINDOWS LIBRARY

IN THIS CHAPTER

- What the OWL is, how to use it, and why you use it.

- The three statements that compose the WinMain of every OWL program.

- How to use the TApplication class to inherit application level functions in your programs based on the OWL.

- How to inherit from the `TWindows` class to create a main program window.

- What message response functions are and how to use them in your programs.

- How to use the ObjectBrowser built into the Turbo C++ for Windows Integrated Development Environment (IDE).

The ObjectWindows Library (OWL) is an object-oriented class library that incorporates the advantages of inheritance, polymorphism, and encapsulation to make programming Windows applications easier. Because the OWL is based on object-oriented programming concepts, all its programs are written in C++.

Using an Object Hierarchy

In the last several years, the computer industry has created a great deal of hype about object-oriented programming (Borland International is no exception). The result is a wide acceptance of C++ and object-oriented versions of Turbo Pascal. It seems like object-oriented programming is starting to pop up everywhere. Object-oriented programming techniques have even been starting to show up in one form or another in some of the newest forms of BASIC.

To exploit the object-oriented features of C++ while programming Windows, you need an object hierarchy of classes. You could develop your own class hierarchy; however, this requires a great deal of time and effort. The easiest way to program with objects is to use a predefined set of object-oriented classes.

Rather than develop a complete object hierarchy, use the OWL included with Turbo C++ for Windows. The OWL handles many complex issues of Windows programming. It takes care of most overhead associated with class registration, message loops, and Windows procedures that you learned about in Chapter 4, "Writing Windows Programs."

Because the OWL takes care of most application overhead in Windows programming, you now can put your time and energy into developing great applications, rather than dealing with the tedious exercise of registering Windows classes. However, first you must know about object-oriented programming. To learn how the OWL works, you will create a minimum program based on the OWL, which you use as you work through this book.

NOTE

Because the OWL provides so much functionality, the resulting executable file of programs based on OWL is usually larger than the executable file from a comparable program based on traditional C programming methods (as described in Chapter 4). This difference is because additional code in the OWL is linked into your program. If program size is an issue, you might program your application with traditional C methods, rather than with C++ and the OWL.

It also usually takes longer to compile programs based on the OWL. Again, additional header files must be processed and the OWL libraries must be linked with your program to create the final executable program.

Creating an ObjectWindows Program

All programs based on the OWL contain a `WinMain` entry point, just like in traditional Windows C programs. The body of the `WinMain` function typically contains three statements. First, you create an instance of the application, then you execute the program, and finally the program returns its final status.

Take a look at some code. Listing 5.1 contains a program that uses default Windows characteristics of the OWL. Listing 5.2 contains the module definition file for the program. You will create a project (as described in Chapter 4) that includes these two files. Figure 5.1 shows the resulting window.

WARNING

To compile your programs based on the OWL, you must set a couple of compiler options.

First, select the Options menu and then select Linker and choose Libraries. Be sure all three libraries are set to static. Press OK when these are set.

Second, set the program's memory model to Large by selecting the Options menu, choosing Compiler, and selecting Code Generation. In the dialog box, choose the radio button for the Large Memory Model.

Listing 5.1. ObjectWindows program using default window attributes.

```
// MINOWL1.CPP - Using the abstract TApplication type
//
// Programming Windows with Turbo C++ for Windows
// by Paul J. Perry


#define WIN31
#define STRICT

#include <owl.h>
#include <windowsx.h>


/*********************************************/
int PASCAL WinMain(HINSTANCE hInstance, HINSTANCE hPrevInstance,
                      LPSTR lpCmdLine, int nCmdShow)
{

   TApplication ThisApp("ObjectWindows Library Program #1",
                         hInstance, hPrevInstance, lpCmdLine,
                         nCmdShow);
   ThisApp.Run();
   return ThisApp.Status;

}
```

Listing 5.2. MINOWL module definition file.

```
;
;  MINOWL.DEF module definition file
;

DESCRIPTION    'Minimum ObjectWindows Library Program'
NAME           MINOWL
EXETYPE        WINDOWS
STUB           'WINSTUB.EXE'
HEAPSIZE       4096
STACKSIZE      5120
CODE           PRELOAD MOVEABLE DISCARDABLE
DATA           PRELOAD MOVEABLE MULTIPLE
```

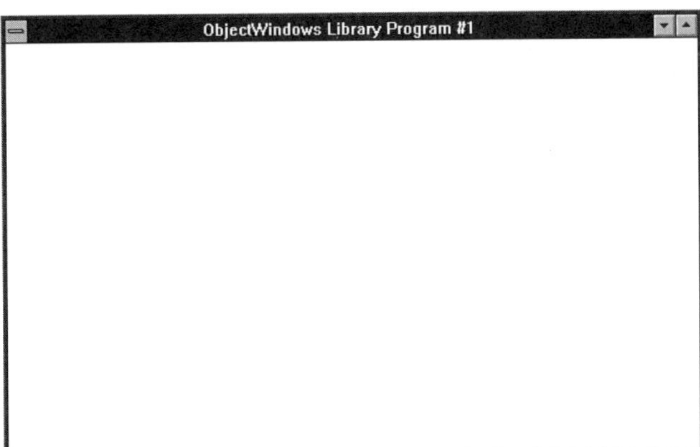

Figure 5.1.

Window created by MINOWL1 program.

TIP

To compile programs based on the OWL, you must specify appropriate pathnames for the default include files and libraries. The ones you must use for OWL programming are not included as default values. You must set them. To do this, choose the Options menu and select Directories. The Directories dialog box appears (see Figure 5.2).

Figure 5.2.

Directories dialog box.

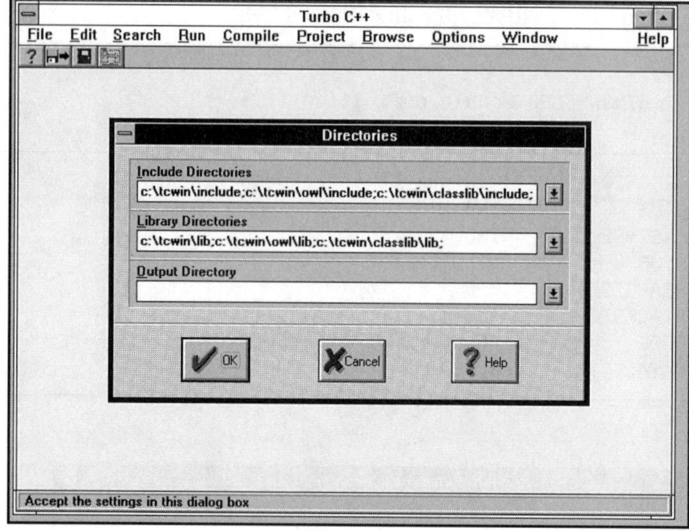

Be sure the Include files section has the following directories separated by semicolons:

C:\TCWIN\OWL\INCLUDE;C:\TCWIN\CLASSLIB\INCLUDE;C:\TCWIN\INCLUDE;

The Libraries section must include the following subdirectories:

C:\TCWIN\OWL\LIB;C:\TCWIN\CLASSLIB\LIB;C:\TCWIN\LIB;

Obviously, if you change the default location where you installed the compiler—or if you are using the Borland C++ Windows-based IDE—the first subdirectory (\TCWIN\) changes.

All ObjectWindows programs in this book use the STRICT preprocessor directive, as well as the windowsx.h header file you saw in the minimum C program. You will find two additional preprocessor directives in Listing 5.1. The definition for WIN31 targets the version of Windows your program will run under. If you declare WIN31, the program runs only under Windows 3.1. If you declare WIN30, the program runs under either Windows 3.0 or 3.1. You must declare either WIN30 or WIN31 for the program to compile correctly. If not, the compiler displays an error message.

The `#include` preprocessor directive includes the owl.h header file in the program. This header file includes the prototypes for the classes that compose the OWL hierarchy. You must include owl.h for all programs based on the OWL.

The declaration of the `WinMain` appears as it did in Chapter 4. The main body of `WinMain` contains only three lines. They appear as follows:

```
TApplication ThisApp("ObjectWindows Library Program #1",
                     hInstance, hPrevInstance, lpCmdLine, nCmdShow);
ThisApp.Run();
return ThisApp.Status;
```

The first statement calls the constructor of `TApplication` to construct the application object that initializes the data members of the class. Most applications usually inherit features from the `TApplication` class. The constructor receives five parameters: the window title and four values, including `hInstance` (the handle to the instance), `hPrevInstance` (the handle to the previous instance), `lpCmdLine` (the command line string), and `nCmdShow` (a value indicating how the window displays).

The OWL follows some of the Hungarian naming conventions in Chapter 4. It also adds some of its own. The OWL classes use an uppercase T to identify class names. The T stands for "type" and differentiates class types from other symbols. From the declaration of the `ThisApp` class instance, you see that it is class type `TApplication`. Throughout the OWL libraries, you find the T prefix, so it makes good sense to follow it.

The second statement calls the `run()` member function for the instance of the class you just declared. Besides initializing the application and the instance of the program, `run()` internally calls the `MessageLoop` functions that process Windows messages—which you saw in Chapter 4. This allows your program to receive and process Windows messages.

The third statement returns the final status of the application. A `0` return value is usually a normal return value. A nonzero value indicates an error.

The three statements that are the body of `WinMain` are in every program based on the OWL. The following takes place:

- Application initialization
- Application execution
- Application termination

This is basically a program to create a window with three lines of code. Unfortunately, as Figure 5.1 shows, it is a generic window. The program neither displays anything in its client area, nor does much more than appear. To give the program more functionality, declare new classes that inherit characteristics from those in the base OWL program in Listing 5.1.

Creating an Application Instance

To add more functionality to the program, declare a new instance of `TApplication`. The new class provides custom application level processing of your Windows programs. Take a look at Listing 5.3 for an example of how this is done. Figure 5.3 shows the resulting program window.

To compile the program, use the module definition file from Listing 5.2. Remember to set the directories appropriately, as mentioned in the earlier sidebar.

Listing 5.3. ObjectWindows program with new TApplication class.

```
// MINOWL2.CPP - Using our own descendant of TApplication
//
// Programming Windows with Turbo C++ for Windows
// by Paul J. Perry


#define WIN31
#define STRICT

#include <owl.h>
#include <windowsx.h>


// Class Declarations
```

```
/*******************************************/
class TOwlApp : public TApplication
{
   public :
      TOwlApp (LPSTR AName, HINSTANCE hInstance,
               HINSTANCE hPrevInstance,
          LPSTR CmdLine, int CmdShow) :
           TApplication(AName, hInstance, hPrevInstance,
            CmdLine, CmdShow) { } ;

};


/*******************************************/
int PASCAL WinMain(HINSTANCE hInstance, HINSTANCE hPrevInstance,
                       LPSTR lpCmdLine, int nCmdShow)
{

   TOwlApp ThisApp("ObjectWindows Library Program #2", hInstance,
                    hPrevInstance, lpCmdLine, nCmdShow);
   ThisApp.Run();
   return ThisApp.Status;

}
```

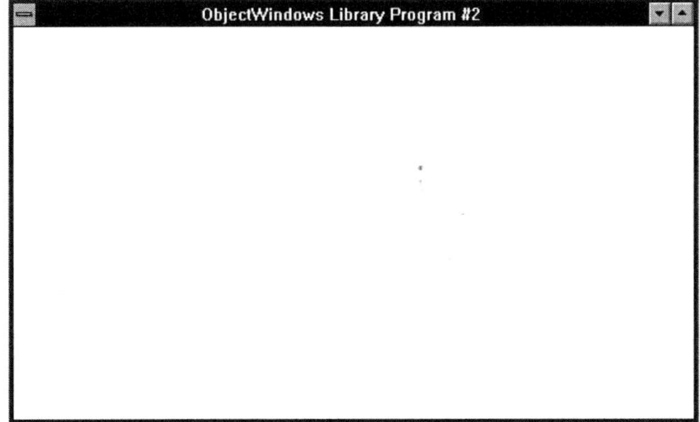

Figure 5.3.

Minimum OWL program.

You find that `WinMain` looks similar to Listing 5.1 except the first initialization statement is different. The constructor to the class actually creates an instance of a new type of class, called `TOwlApp` rather than `TApplication`.

WARNING

Notice the ending semicolon on the class declaration. The newest specification for the C++ language requires each class declaration to have an ending semicolon. Because this requirement is new, earlier versions of the Borland compilers didn't mind whether you had the semicolon.

Turbo C++ for Windows requires the ending semicolon. If it is not there, the compiler gives a warning. The message that displays does not always show clearly what is happening. The message sometimes appears as an unrelated problem. For a beginning C++ programmer, this can cause confusion.

`TOwlApp` is a class declared in the program as follows:

```
class TOwlApp : public TApplication
{
   public :
      TOwlApp (LPSTR AName, HINSTANCE hInstance, HINSTANCE
               hPrevInstance, LPSTR CmdLine, int CmdShow) :
               TApplication(AName, hInstance, hPrevInstance,
               CmdLine, CmdShow) { };
```

The class is derived publicly from `TApplication`. Therefore, your class has all the functionality of `TApplication`, and you can give it new functionality (which you see in the next program). The declaration of the constructor only calls the base class constructor.

You must always define constructors in classes derived from the OWL classes. In most cases, you call the derived class constructor. The derived applications constructor is an inline function, although you can separate the class declaration and member function declaration as follows:

```
class TOwlApp : public TApplication
{
   public :
      TOwlApp (LPSTR AName, HINSTANCE hInstance,
               HINSTANCE hPrevInstance,
          LPSTR CmdLine, int CmdShow);
};


TOwlApp::TOwlApp(LPSTR AName, HINSTANCE hInstance, HINSTANCE
                 hPrevInstance,   LPSTR CmdLine, int CmdShow) :
                 TApplication(AName, hInstance, hPrevInstance,
                 CmdLine, CmdShow)
{
   // The class inherits all of its functionality from base class
}
```

You declare a new class based on `TApplication` to give new functionality to the program. Because you want to display text in the main window, you must attach an instance of `TWindow` to the application class. You do this next.

Creating a Windows Instance

Most OWL programs have at least two classes defined. One is derived from `TApplication`, which provides application level functionality; and the other from `TWindow`, which deals with displaying and interacting with the window. Listing 5.4 allows an OWL program to display text in its main window (see Figure 5.4). You can use the module definition file specified in Listing 5.2 for this program.

Listing 5.4. ObjectWindows program with new TWindow class.

```
// MINOWL3.CPP - Minimum ObjectWindows Program
//
// Programming Windows with Turbo C++ for Windows
// by Paul J. Perry
```

continues

Listing 5.4. continued

```
#define WIN31
#define STRICT

#include <owl.h>
#include <windowsx.h>


// Class Declarations

/*******************************************/
class TOwlApp : public TApplication
{
   public :
      TOwlApp (LPSTR AName, HINSTANCE hInstance, HINSTANCE
               hPrevInstance, LPSTR CmdLine, int CmdShow) :
               TApplication(AName, hInstance, hPrevInstance,
               CmdLine, CmdShow) { } ;

   virtual void InitMainWindow();
};


/*******************************************/
class TMainWindow : public TWindow
{
   public :
      TMainWindow(PTWindowsObject AParent, LPSTR ATitle)
                    : TWindow(AParent, ATitle) { };
      virtual void Paint(HDC PaintDC, PAINTSTRUCT &PaintInfo);

};



// Class Member Functions

/*******************************************/
void TOwlApp::InitMainWindow()
{
   MainWindow = new TMainWindow(NULL, Name);
}


/*******************************************/
#pragma argsused
```

```
void TMainWindow::Paint(HDC PaintDC, PAINTSTRUCT &PaintInfo)
{
   RECT rect;

   GetClientRect(HWindow, &rect);

   DrawText(PaintDC, "Minimum ObjectWindows Program", -1, &rect,
            DT_SINGLELINE | DT_CENTER | DT_VCENTER);

}


/*******************************************/
int PASCAL WinMain(HINSTANCE hInstance, HINSTANCE hPrevInstance,
                   LPSTR lpCmdLine, int nCmdShow)
{

   TOwlApp ThisApp("Minimum ObjectWindows Library Program #3",
                    hInstance, hPrevInstance, lpCmdLine, nCmdShow);
   ThisApp.Run();
   return ThisApp.Status;

}
```

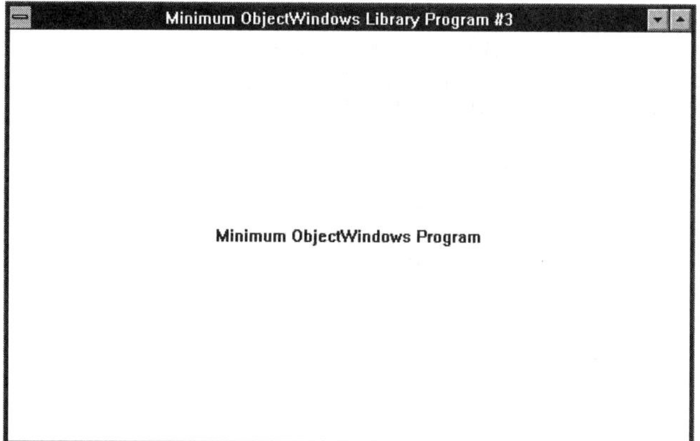

Figure 5.4.

Minimum ObjectWindows program.

Notice the similarity between Listings 5.4 and 5.3. Each program builds upon the previous one. MINOWL3 uses the same `WinMain` program entry point and `TOwlApp` class as Listing 5.3.

The TOwlApp class declares a new member function called InitMainWindow, as follows:

```
virtual void InitMainWindow();
```

InitMainWindow creates an instance of the window that becomes attached to the main application class. InitMainWindow has only one line. It creates an instance of a Window class using the new operator to return a pointer to the class. It looks like this:

```
void TOwlApp::InitMainWindow()
{
   MainWindow = new TMainWindow(NULL, Name);
}
```

TMainWindow is a new class that declares in the beginning of the program. The first parameter is passed a NULL value, as a pointer to a window object. This is used when working with child windows (which you see in Chapter 6, "Working with Windows"). The second parameter is global, and it holds the name of the application module.

The TMainWindow class is derived from TWindow. The declaration looks like this:

```
class TMainWindow : public TWindow
{
   public :
      TMainWindow(PTWindowsObject AParent, LPSTR ATitle)
                       : TWindow(AParent, ATitle) { };
      virtual void Paint(HDC PaintDC, PAINTSTRUCT &PaintInfo);

};
```

Two member functions are declared. The constructor TMainWindow calls the base class constructor. The Paint function replaces the processing of the WM_PAINT message in traditional C programs. Everything that shows up in a Window for programs based on the OWL is in the Paint function.

Processing the WM_PAINT Message

The Paint member function follows next:

```
#pragma argsused
void TMainWindow::Paint(HDC PaintDC, PAINTSTRUCT &PaintInfo)
```

```
{
   RECT rect;

   GetClientRect(HWindow, &rect);

   DrawText(PaintDC, "Minimum ObjectWindows Program", -1, &rect,
           DT_SINGLELINE ¦ DT_CENTER ¦ DT_VCENTER);

}
```

The preprocessor directive `#pragma argsused` is used to suppress the warning message "Parameter PaintInfo not used." In Windows programs, often values are passed to a function and are not used. The compiler wants to warn to that effect; however, many times you don't have to use the variables. Because I hate it when the compiler issues any type of message (be it warning or error message), I like to use the `#pragma argsused` directive to suppress the warning. The preprocessor directive tells the compiler that you know the argument is not used, but you don't want the warning message to display.

In the `Paint` member function, the `GetClientRect` function is called to return the coordinates of the client area of the window. You pass the `HWindow` class variable and a pointer to a `RECT` structure. The `HWindow` variable is the handle to the window. You can use it in classes derived from `TWindow`.

The `DrawText` function is used to display text in the window. The OWL program does not have to call the `BeginPaint` and `EndPaint` functions when responding to `WM_PAINT` messages. Part of the beauty of the OWL is that it handles much of the overhead for programming Windows. For the `Paint` member function, `BeginPaint` and `EndPaint` are called internally to the program.

Message Response Functions

You might wonder how your programs respond to Windows messages. In the traditional C program, you add a case statement for each message you want to process yourself. However, your OWL program does not have an apparent place to process messages.

The OWL enables you to declare special functions that are automatically called when the program receives the specific message. These functions are called *message response functions*.

NOTE

Message response functions are implemented through a mechanism known as dynamic dispatch virtual tables (DDVTs), available only in Turbo C++ for Windows or Borland C++). When you declare a message response function, you specify a dispatch index value (which happens to be the Window message). Although Windows messages are given descriptive names like `WM_PAINT`, each one is actually an integer value.

The OWL program responds to the Windows messages and automatically calls the appropriate member function. You no longer have to create large case statements like you would usually do in a C program. Instead, you create independent functions that contain the code to process a single message.

`Paint` is actually a predefined function that responds to the `WM_PAINT` message. You can declare your message response functions using special notation. In the class declaration, you must add special notation to the member function declaration. In a nutshell, to declare a message response function, you should tell the compiler which message your function should respond to.

Look at an example. A Windows program receives a `WM_LBUTTONDOWN` message anytime you click the left mouse button. To declare a function that is called every time the message is passed to the program, use notation like this in your class:

```
virtual void WMLButtonDown(TMessage &msg) =
   [WM_FIRST + WM_LBUTTONDOWN];
```

Message response functions are usually named after the message they respond to, but it's not necessary. Each message response function is passed a parameter of type `TMessage`. `TMessage` is a structure that stores the `lParam` and `wParam` values that usually are passed to a window procedure.

WM_FIRST is a predefined constant in the owl.h header file. It tells the compiler this is a message response function for Windows messages—those starting with WM_. You add the WM_FIRST to the message you want to respond to (after all, the messages are just defined with the #define preprocessor directive) as numbers.

The function appears as follows:

```
void TMainWindow::WMLButtonDown(TMessage &msg)
{
   // Message processing goes here

}
```

Let's take a look at an example program which makes use of message response functions. The next program, MCLICKS.CPP (in Listing 5.5), uses message response functions to respond to the press of the left and right mouse buttons. In the project file, you can use the module definition file in Listing 5.2. Figure 5.5 shows the output of the program.

Listing 5.5. Responding to mouse messages in an OWL program.

```
// MCLICKS.CPP - Using Message Respond functions to respond
//               to mouse clicks
//
// Programming Windows with Turbo C++ for Windows
// by Paul J. Perry

#define WIN31
#define STRICT

#include <owl.h>
#include <windowsx.h>


// Class Declarations

/*******************************************/
class TOwlApp : public TApplication
{
   public :
      TOwlApp (LPSTR AName, HINSTANCE hInstance,
               HINSTANCE hPrevInstance,
```

continues

Listing 5.5. continued

```
          LPSTR CmdLine, int CmdShow) :
          TApplication(AName, hInstance, hPrevInstance,
            CmdLine, CmdShow) { } ;

   virtual void InitMainWindow();
};


/*******************************************/
class TMainWindow : public TWindow
{
   public :
      TMainWindow(PTWindowsObject AParent, LPSTR ATitle)
                      : TWindow(AParent, ATitle) { };
      virtual void Paint(HDC PaintDC, PAINTSTRUCT &PaintInfo);
      virtual void WMLButtonDown(TMessage &msg) =
         [WM_FIRST + WM_LBUTTONDOWN];
      virtual void WMRButtonDown(TMessage &msg) =
         [WM_FIRST + WM_RBUTTONDOWN];

};

// Class Member Functions

/*******************************************/
void TOwlApp::InitMainWindow()
{
   MainWindow = new TMainWindow(NULL, Name);
}


/*******************************************/
#pragma argsused
void TMainWindow::Paint(HDC PaintDC, PAINTSTRUCT &PaintInfo)
{
   RECT rect;

   GetClientRect(HWindow, &rect);
```

```
   DrawText(PaintDC, "Click either mouse button", -1, &rect,
            DT_SINGLELINE ¦ DT_CENTER ¦ DT_VCENTER);

}

/*******************************************/
void TMainWindow::WMLButtonDown(TMessage &msg)
{
   HDC hDC;

   hDC = GetDC(HWindow);
   TextOut(hDC, LOWORD(msg.LParam), HIWORD(msg.LParam),
           "Left Mouse Button Pressed", 25);
   ReleaseDC(HWindow, hDC);

}


/*******************************************/
void TMainWindow::WMRButtonDown(TMessage &msg)
{
   HDC hDC;

   hDC = GetDC(HWindow);
   TextOut(hDC, LOWORD(msg.LParam), HIWORD(msg.LParam),
           "Right Mouse Button Pressed", 26);
   ReleaseDC(HWindow, hDC);

}


/*******************************************/
int PASCAL WinMain(HINSTANCE hInstance, HINSTANCE hPrevInstance,
                   LPSTR lpCmdLine, int nCmdShow)
{

   TOwlApp ThisApp("Minimum ObjectWindows Library Program #3",
                   hInstance, hPrevInstance, lpCmdLine, nCmdShow);
   ThisApp.Run();
   return ThisApp.Status;

}
```

Figure 5.5.

Window created with MCLICKS program.

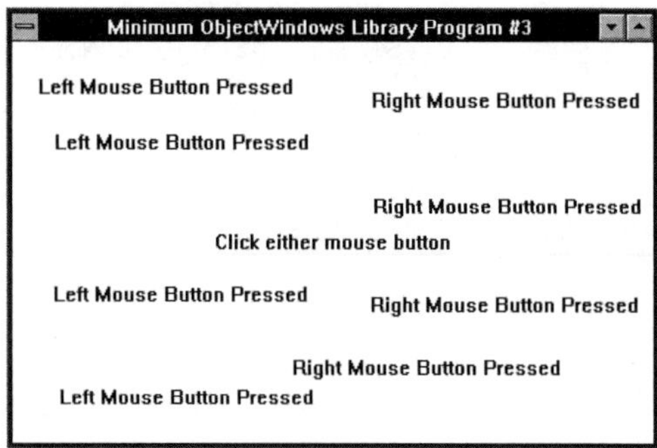

The program declares two message response functions that process the `WM_LBUTTONDOWN` and `WM_RBUTTONDOWN` messages. Each function displays a message when you click it.

The `WMLButtonDown` function looks like this:

```
HDC hDC;

hDC = GetDC(HWindow);
TextOut(hDC, LOWORD(msg.LParam), HIWORD(msg.LParam),
        "Left Mouse Button Pressed", 25);
ReleaseDC(HWindow, hDC);
```

The `TextOut` function is self-explanatory: it displays text in the window. You must call to the `GetDC` routine to return a handle to a display context. Then, it is passed to the `TextOut`. When you finish with `hDC`, you must return it to Windows, using the `ReleaseDC` function. If you do not release it, system resources quickly deplete.

The `WMRButtonDown` function is similar in functionality to `WMLButtonDown`. If you iconize or resize the program, you lose all the text generated with the mouse. The reason for this is that the only function called when the window needs to be updated is the `Paint` function. Unless you don't redisplay what you want in this function, it does not display when the window needs updating. Although not a serious limitation, consider it when designing larger programs. Any text or graphics you want to display must be displayed in the `Paint` member function.

You now have the step-by-step instructions to create an OWL program. Next, you look at one tool built into the IDE that helps you see the structure of object-oriented programs.

Using the Class Browser

The ObjectBrowser enables you to visually browse through your class hierarchies, member functions, and member variables. To use the ObjectBrowser, your program must be compiled. This puts the necessary browsing information in your program.

All ObjectBrowser options are selected from the Browse main menu item. The following items are displayed on the menu:

Classes	Creates a window that contains a graphical class hierarchy for all the classes in your application. If the entire hierarchy does not fit in the window, you can use the scroll bars on the right and bottom sides of the window to view the hidden sections.
Functions	Displays an alphabetical list of all the functions that are part of your program.
Variables	Displays an alphabetical list of all global variables that are part of your program.
Symbol at Cursor	Displays the class hierarchy for the symbol the cursor is currently positioned over in the IDE.

The other selections on the menu (separated by a bar) are available only after an ObjectBrowser window has been opened. These commands mimic keyboard equivalents as well as command buttons you will find shortly. The other commands as follows:

Rewind	Displays or rewinds the window to display the previous view.
Overview	Goes up the class hierarchy to display a summary of classes, functions, or variables—depending on what is currently being viewed.
Inspect	Displays specific details of a selected item.
Goto	Takes you to the source code for the specified class. If the file the class is declared in is not loaded, the file is opened automatically and the cursor is positioned at the beginning of the class declaration.

The remainder of this section shows you how to use the ObjectBrowser to view class hierarchies, functions, member functions, and global variables.

Looking at the ObjectBrowser

To display the class hierarchy for an application, first be sure it is compiled. Then, choose Browse and select Classes. This creates a window that displays all the classes in your application. A horizontal tree displays, branching from left to right. This tree enables you to visualize the relationship among classes.

Figure 5.6 shows the window you created when you selected the Class browser for the MINOWL3.CPP program. You might not recognize all the classes in the window; your program inherits much functionality from base classes in both the class libraries and the OWL libraries.

Figure 5.6.

The Class Browser window for the MINOWL3.CPP program.

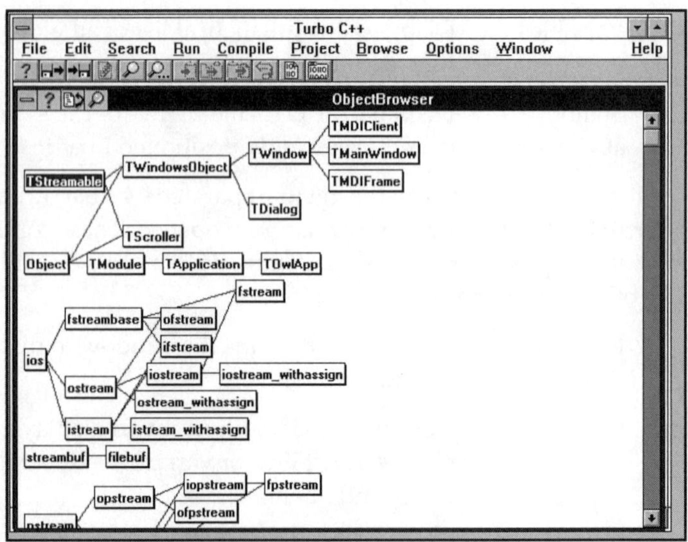

In Figure 5.6, the `TMainWindow` class is in the window's upper-right corner. Also, notice the `TOwlApp` class, down one level from the `TMainWindow` class. Examine the classes from which they inherit and how they interrelate.

The `TStreamable` class contains a highlight bar. You can use the arrow keys or the mouse to move through the class structure. If you press Enter over a class or double-click it, the window is resized and changes to show the member functions for the class. Figure 5.7 shows what happens when you select `TMainWindow`.

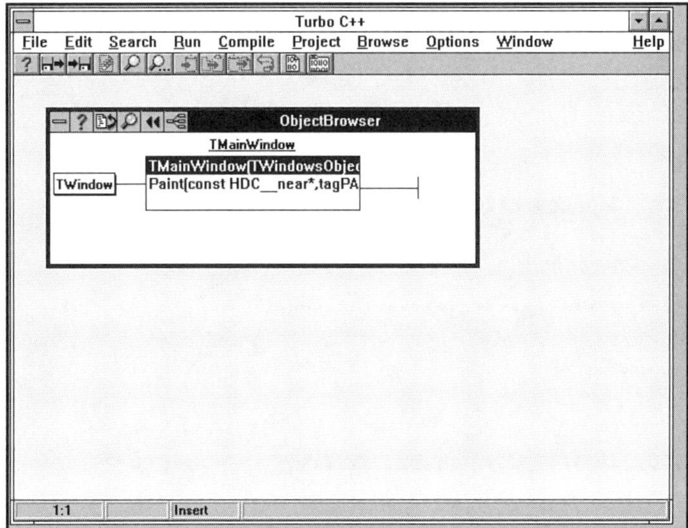

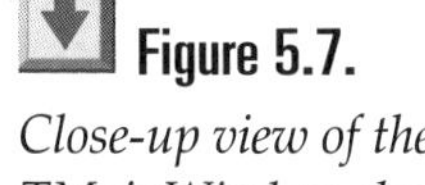

Figure 5.7.

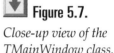

Close-up view of the TMainWindow class.

The title bar of the ObjectBrowser window has special buttons that enable you to quickly select certain menu options with the mouse.

To get you learning the ObjectBrowser, let's take a look at a class hierarchy that is not so complex. Start with Listing 5.6, which shows an EasyWin program that declares several classes. It then creates instances of those classes in the main part of the program. The program does not create a window or display output. EasyWin enables you to view the class hierarchy without being overburdened with classes such as seen in Figure 5.7.

For now, load the program into the IDE. Be sure the program compiles. (You don't need a module definition file for this one.) Then follow the step-by-step demonstration for using the ObjectBrowser. The program does nothing fabulous; mainly, you're interested in learning about the ObjectBrowser, rather than programming in C++.

Listing 5.6. Example program for using the ObjectBrowser.

```
// CLASSES.CPP - Example program for using the ObjectBrowser
//
// Programming Windows with Turbo C++ for Windows
// by Paul J. Perry


#include<stdio.h>
#include<string.h>
#include<conio.h>


// Glboal Variables
int global;
char AppName[] = "Classes Example";


// function
/*******************************************/
void ClearWindow()
{
   clrscr();
}

/*******************************************/
class TPerson
{
   public :
      char name[255];
      int age;

      TPerson(char aname[255], int anage)  // constructor #1
      {
         strcpy(name, aname);
              age = anage;
      }

      TPerson()                            // constructor #2
      {
              strcpy(name, "");
              age = 0;
      }

      void SetName(char aname[255])        // Member function to
                                           // set name
      {
```

```
            strcpy(name, aname);
        }

        void SetAge(int anage)              // Member function to set
                                            // age
        {
            age = anage;
        }
};


/*******************************************/
class TEmployee : public TPerson
{
    public :
        float payrate;

        TEmployee(char aname[255], int anage, float apayrate)
                // constructor
        {
            TPerson::TPerson(aname, anage);
          payrate = apayrate;
        }

        TEmployee()
        {
            TPerson::TPerson();
            payrate = 0;
        }

        void SetPayrate(float apayrate)
        {
            payrate = apayrate;
        }

};


/*******************************************/
class THourly : public TEmployee
{
    public :
        int hours;

        THourly(char aname[255], int anage, float apayrate,
            int NumHours)
        {
```

continues

Listing 5.6. continued

```
            TEmployee::TEmployee(aname, anage, apayrate);
            hours = NumHours;
    }

    THourly()
    {
            TEmployee::TEmployee();
            hours = 0;
    }

    void SetHoursWorked(int NumHours)
    {
            hours = NumHours;
    }

};


/*******************************************/
void main()
{
   // Instances of TPerson class
   TPerson man("Alex", 25);
   TPerson woman;

   woman.SetName("Amy");
   woman.SetAge(22);

   // Instances of TEmployee class
   TEmployee worker("Sam", 33, 9.99);
   TEmployee typist;

   typist.SetName("Bill");
   typist.SetAge(28);
   typist.SetPayrate(4.45);

   // Instances of THourly class
   THourly Clerk("Cindy", 18, 5.34, 20);
   THourly Checker;

   Checker.SetName("Jim");
   Checker.SetAge(55);
   Checker.SetPayrate(27.66);
   Checker.SetHoursWorked(40);

}
```

Displaying a Class Hierarchy

To display the class hierarchy for the CLASSES.CPP program, choose Browse on the main menu and select Classes (see Figure 5.8). A window is displayed that shows a tree of classes used in the program.

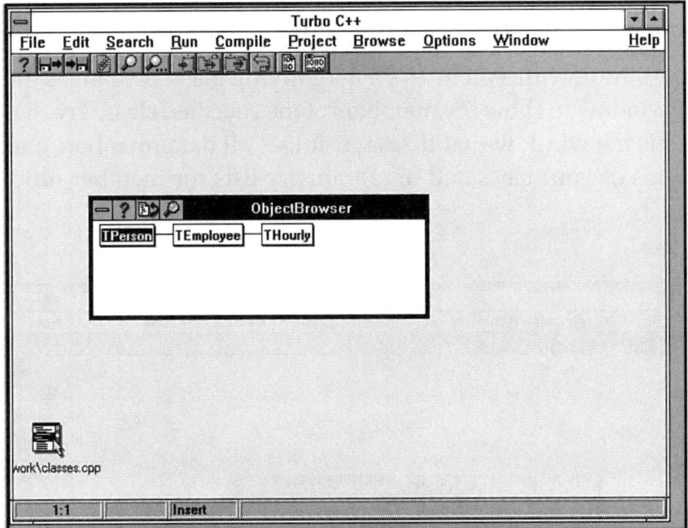

Figure 5.8.

Browsing the classes in the CLASSES.CPP program.

The program declares the following three classes: `TPerson`, `TEmployee`, and `THourly`. The second class inherits from the first class, and the third class inherits from the second class. The lines in the figure are connecting to show this relationship among the classes.

The ObjectBrowser window's title bar contains several buttons. To select these, click them with the left mouse button. They enable you to receive help and to move quickly through your class hierarchy.

The left-most button—the one with a question mark—is the Help button. It is equivalent to the F1 key. When you click this button, the Windows Help system displays and it gives you information about using the ObjectBrowser.

The next button is Goto, which contains a paper page with an arrow pointing around it. With this button, you locate the position in your code where the selected class is declared. If you choose this button, the ObjectBrowser window closes, and you enter an editor window of the IDE at the location your class was selected. In order to use the Goto button, you must make sure your program is compiled with ObjectBrowser information turned on. To do this, select the Options | Compiler | Advanced Code generation menu and make sure "Browser Info" box is checked.

Inspect is the button with a picture of a magnifying glass. It changes the ObjectBrowser window to show the members of the specified class. Try that now. Figure 5.9 is the window that displays. It lists all data members and member functions of your class and all parameter lists for member functions.

Figure 5.9.

ObjectBrowser window showing members of TPerson class.

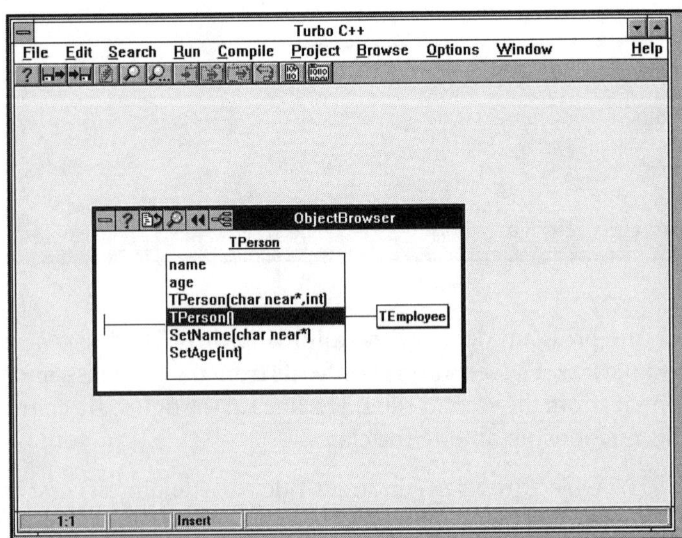

Several new buttons now appear on the button bar. Click the button with two black arrows pointing west. It rewinds the ObjectBrowser to show the previous view.

The Overview button has a mini-hierarchy icon. It brings you back to an overview of the entire class hierarchy for the program. At this point, you still can use the Help, Goto, and Inspect buttons to carry out their associated tasks.

If you aren't using a mouse, use keyboard commands to do these functions. Table 5.1 lists the icon names and keyboard commands that do the same tasks.

Table 5.1. Keyboard equivalents of ObjectBrowser buttons.

Icon Name	*Description*	*Key*
Goto	Displays source code for selected item	Ctrl-G
Help	Brings up context-sensitive help	F1
Inspect	Views details of selected item	Ctrl-I
Overview	Shows overview of entire class hierarchy	Ctrl-O
Rewind	Displays previous view	Ctrl-R

As you see, the ObjectBrowser's main feature is that it visually inspects the class hierarchy of a program, but it does more. The next sections show you how to view the functions and variables declared in your program.

Viewing Functions

To display an alphabetical list of the functions in your program, select Browse and choose the Functions option (see Figure 5.10). The ObjectBrowser window changes to an alphabetical list of every function in your program. The list shows class member functions and regular C functions. It lists Class member functions by their class, followed by the scope-resolution operator and their name (`class::functionname`).

You can scroll through the list to view each function. In addition, you can start typing the function you are searching for. As you type, the functions in the listbox change to match the characters you type. This is a handy feature for finding functions quickly.

The title bar of the ObjectBrowser window has the Help, Goto, and Inspect icons, which carry out their functions as described earlier.

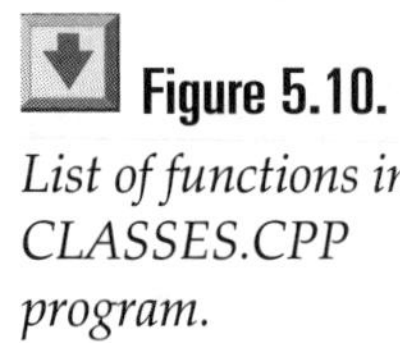

Figure 5.10.

List of functions in CLASSES.CPP program.

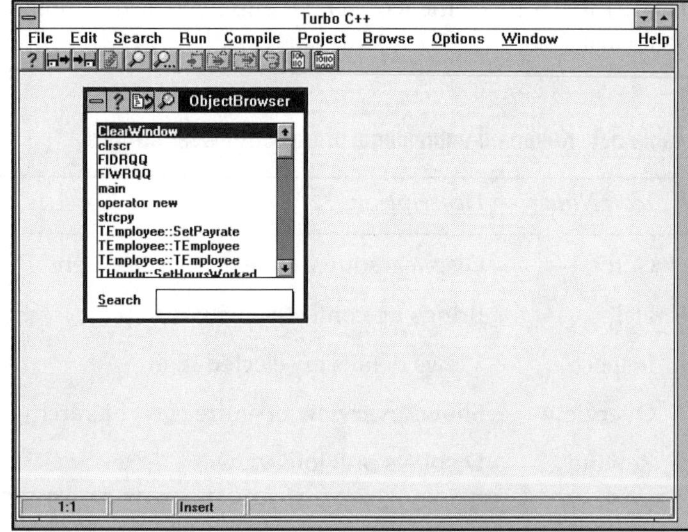

Displaying Global Variables

If you choose Browser and select Variables, the ObjectBrowser window shows an alphabetical list of every global variable declared in your program (see Figure 5.11). To find a variable quickly, start typing its name. The selections in the list change to match the characters you are typing.

The title bar shows the buttons for Help, Goto, and Inspect. Use these as described earlier. To close the ObjectBrowser window, either press Alt-F4 or double-click the control menu.

This wraps up the discussion of the ObjectBrowser tool. As you program, you will use it to view the relationship among the classes you create. It is even more useful when you view code written by someone else.

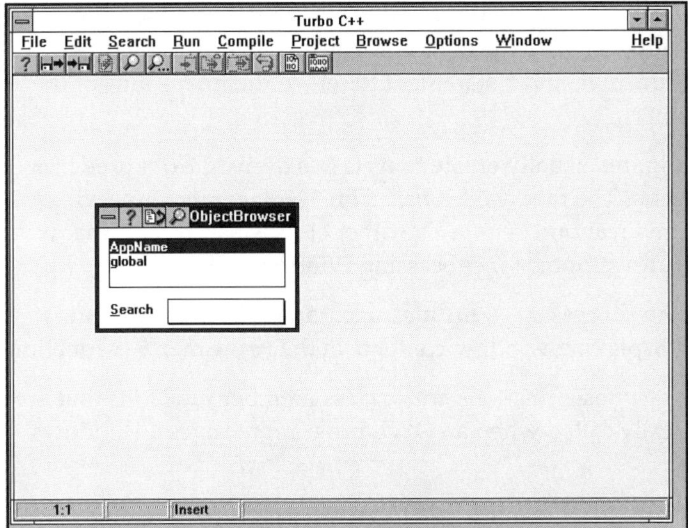

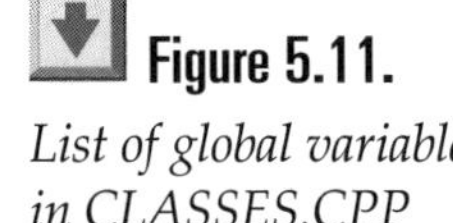

Figure 5.11.

List of global variables in CLASSES.CPP program.

What You Have Learned

This chapter has covered much ground. You learned how a basic program based on the OWL is written. You began with a generic window. You added your own functionality to it by creating your own classes that inherited features from the default values.

You also learned how to use the ObjectBrowser tool to view a graphical representation of classes in your program. In particular, the following points were covered:

- The OWL provides a class hierarchy of functions from which your program can inherit features. By putting all the functionality in the class libraries, your programs are shorter and easier to understand.

- All OWL programs have three statements in their `WinMain` function. These include a call to the class constructor, a call to the `run()` member function, and a statement to return the final status of the application.
- OWL programs usually create two classes derived from predefined OWL classes. The first class is based on `TApplication`. It provides application level processing. The other class is based on `TWindows` and provides support for processing Windows messages.
- Rather than process `WM_PAINT` messages, an OWL program puts code for displaying window contents in the `Paint` member function.
- Message response functions create class member functions that are automatically called when an OWL program receives a Windows message.
- The ObjectBrowser enables you to view a graphical tree that represents the class hierarchy of your program. You choose its features from the Browse menu selection.
- The ObjectBrowser is a useful tool for understanding the order of a C++ program. It especially is useful for understanding how other programmers have arranged their code.

Using the ObjectWindows Library

CHAPTER

5

6

WORKING WITH WINDOWS

IN THIS CHAPTER

- The two-step window creation process.
- The three scopes of window classes: system global, application global, and application local.
- The fields in the `WNDCLASS` structure.
- The class style types declared in windows.h.
- The parameters to the `CreateWindow` routine.
- The relationship between parent and child windows.
- Predefined window classes.
- Modification of class and window attributes in an ObjectWindows Library (OWL) program.

In previous chapters, you read how to create minimum Windows programs using C and C++ programming models. The example programs demonstrated how to initialize a window class and create and display a window. The minimum ObjectWindows library (OWL) program also showed how to create message response functions.

This chapter looks closely at window classes and styles. You learn about the different types of windows and the many types of attributes you can assign to them.

Working with Windows Classes

You know creating a window is a two-step process. You first must register a window class with the environment, using the `RegisterClass` routine. The window then is created based on a specified class with the `CreateWindow` routine.

You initialize a window class to create many windows based on one class with little overhead required for each window. You already know the first instance of a program usually registers its Windows class. In the example program in the Chapter 5, "Using the ObjectWindows Library," you registered a class with code like this:

```
if (!hPrevInstance)
{
   WNDCLASS    wndclass;

   wndclass.style         = CS_VREDRAW ¦ CS_HREDRAW;
   wndclass.lpfnWndProc   = (WNDPROC) MainWndProc;
   wndclass.hInstance     = hInstance;
   wndclass.hIcon         = LoadIcon(NULL, IDI_APPLICATION);
   wndclass.hCursor       = LoadCursor(NULL, IDC_ARROW);
   wndclass.hbrBackground = (HBRUSH) (COLOR_WINDOW + 1);
   wndclass.lpszMenuName  = NULL;
   wndclass.cbClsExtra    = 0;
   wndclass.cbWndExtra    = 0;
   wndclass.lpszClassName = ProgName;

   RegisterClass(&wndclass);
}
```

WNDCLASS defines the attributes of a window class. With a window class defined, you register a class with the RegisterClass API function. If there is a problem registering the class, the function returns a false value.

Types of Classes

There are three types of window classes: system global, application global, and application local.

System global classes are registered by Windows when you first start the environment. Windows defines all the attributes for these classes. The system global classes are available to any program running while Windows is active. You can create system global classes by specifying a certain style flag during class registration. The class also must be defined in a dynamic link library (DLL). (Chapter 15, "Dynamic Link Libraries," discusses DLLs in detail.)

Application global classes are registered by an application program. This means the classes created are active only while the program runs. However, after a class is registered, any other program can create a window based on the class.

Application local classes are registered by your program for its sole use. Other applications cannot create windows based on application local classes. These classes are available from the time they are registered until they are unregistered, or until the program that registered them terminates. When you register a class in your program, it is, by default, an application local class.

Because of the different scope of classes, it's possible for different applications to register window classes with the same name. When an application is creating a window, Windows first tries to match the class name with local application classes. If a matching local class is not found, Windows searches for an application global class. If an application global class is not found, Windows searches the system global classes.

Now that you know the scope of different window classes, take a close look at each element of WNDCLASS.

WNDCLASS Elements

The `lpszClassName` field defines a string that refers to the class. Later, when you create the window, you must use the class name to refer to the string. Generally, you want to make the class name unique. Windows already predefines seven class types. They are registered by the operating environment even before Program Manager is loaded.

Because every interface object in Windows is a window, you soon see the predefined classes refer to interface objects.

The `lpfnWndProc` field identifies the code that processes messages for windows based on the specified class. A single window procedure can support several windows. This is because each window accessing the window procedure has a unique window handle. Therefore, the messages delivered to a window procedure allow the code to operate on a specific window.

The `cbClsExtra` field refers to class extra bytes. They are bytes added at the end of the class definition as reserved data. Programs can use this data to store additional information. Special API routines (see Table 6.1) enable you to change the values in the class extra bytes. It is important to notice class extra bytes are reserved only once for each class.

Table 6.1. Functions to access class extra bytes.

Routine	*Description*
SetClassWord	Changes word value in class extra bytes.
GetClassWord	Retrieves word value in class extra bytes.
SetClassLong	Changes long value in class extra bytes.
GetClassLong	Retrieves long value in class extra bytes.

Every window created from the class definition can access the same bytes. If you don't plan to use the class extra bytes, be sure to set the `cbClsExtra` field to `0`. If you don't initialize it to `0`, it might randomly be set high and waste precious memory.

The `cbWndExtra` field is similar to the class extra bytes. It is the window extra bytes and refers to a certain amount of memory reserved for each window in the class. The routines to access the window extra bytes are in Table 6.2.

Table 6.2. Functions to access window extra bytes.

Routine	*Description*
SetWindowWord	Changes word value in window extra bytes.
GetWindowWord	Retrieves word value in window extra bytes.
SetWindowLong	Changes long value in window extra bytes.
GetWindowLong	Retrieves long value in window extra bytes.

The `hInstance` field is the instance handle of the program. You always set this to the global variable `hInstance` (which is passed from `WinMain`). The field identifies which program created the window class, so when all instances of the program can terminate, Windows automatically unregisters each class created by the program.

The `hIcon` field points to the icon's handle to display when the window based on this window class is minimized. An icon is a small visual window. In Windows, icons are known as a resource. Resources always are defined outside the source code in a resource script.

You use the Resource Workshop to create custom icons. In your example program, you used a predefined icon the color of the Windows marketing flag (you've seen it: it usually has "Microsoft Windows Compatible" beneath it). You used `LoadIcon` to return a handle to the icon. It's sometimes easy to use the Windows predefined icon `IDI_APPLICATION` when developing an application. After programming, you can do the artwork necessary to create a custom icon that relates better to your program's purpose.

The cursor is another type of resource. The `hCursor` field is a handle to the cursor Windows displays when the mouse cursor is over a window created from this class.

In Windows, when you move the mouse cursor across the screen over different windows, the cursor changes from an arrow to a large cross hair and to arrows pointing in different directions when resizing a window. Windows handles all the logic necessary to change the cursor when the user moves it across the desktop. Your program doesn't have to do any processing to change the cursor (unless you want to).

A program also can change the cursor as a program runs. This feature usually is used during a file-load operation, when the program displays an hourglass to notify the user a lengthy operation is taking place. In Chapter 7, "First Look at Resources," you examine cursors in more detail.

The `LoadCursor` routine returns a handle to the specified cursor. In your program, you used one of the predefined cursors made available by the operating environment. If you set `hIcon` to `0`, you can display information in the icon's window. You learn how to do this in Chapter 7.

The `hbrBackground` field specifies how to display the client area's background color. It can contain the handle of a brush that displays the background of the window. An alternative is to typecast the field equal to (`COLOR_WINDOW + 1`). Using this value obtains the default color set by the user from the Control Panel. This is a nice feature, because it allows your program to take advantage of the preferences the user already has set. It is also part of the common user-interface theme prevalent in Windows.

To use a specific pattern as the background color, pass a handle to the brush. Use the `GetStockBrush` function along with one of the constants in Table 6.3. The table lists the seven predefined brushes your program can use. You also can create your own brush, as you learn in Chapter 11, "Working with the Graphics Device Interface."

Table 6.3. Predefined brushes.

Brush Type	*Description*
BLACK_BRUSH	Black background color.
DKGRAY_BRUSH	Dark gray background color.
GRAY_BRUSH	Gray background color.
HOLLOW_BRUSH	Hollow background color (looks white).

Brush Type	*Description*
LTGRAY_BRUSH	Light gray background color.
NULL_BRUSH	Null brush.
WHITE_BRUSH	White background color.

The `lpszMenuName` field specifies the name of the menu to use when creating windows based on this class. Menus are another type of resource you create and modify in the Resource Workshop.

When you specify a menu for a window class, all windows based on that class include the regular pull-down menu at the top of the window under the title bar. The operating environment displays the menu and responds to the user's mouse clicks and keystrokes. To use the menus, you must respond to messages sent to the window procedure of your program.

The style field contains a set of flags that identifies how windows based on this window class act. You take a close look at the many available class styles next.

Class Styles

The style field of `WNDCLASS` specifies some behavioral aspects of windows based on the class. The flags are defined in windows.h. Table 6.4. gives an overview of the 11 valid style flags. All class style constants are prefaced with the `CS_ IDENTIFIER`, which stands for class style.

Table 6.4. Class styles declared in windows.h.

Style	*Description*
CS_VREDRAW	Forces window contents to redisplay if vertical size changes.
CS_HREDRAW	Forces window contents to redisplay if horizontal size changes.

continues

Table 6.4. continued

Style	*Description*
CS_DBLCLKS	Sends double-click messages to window.
CS_OWNDC	Forces each window to have its own display context.
CS_CLASSDC	Gives window class its own display context.
CS_PARENTDC	Gives parent window display context to window class.
CS_NOCLOSE	Disables the Close option on system menu for windows created with this class.
CS_SAVEBITS	Saves portion of window covered by other objects as a bitmap.
CS_BYTEALIGNCLIENT	Aligns window's client area on the byte boundary.
CS_BYTEALIGNWINDOW	Aligns a window on the byte boundary.
CS_GLOBALCLASS	Makes window class system global.

You often use class style bites in combination with others by employing the C or (¦) operator. For example, the statement

```
wndclass.style = CS_VREDRAW ¦ CS_HREDRAW;
```

assigns the attributes of the two styles, `CS_VREDRAW` and `CS_HREDRAW`, to the window class. You'll frequently combine window styles.

The `CS_VREDRAW` and `CS_HREDRAW` styles tell the window procedure to redisplay the contents of the client area any time the user resizes window. When this happens, Windows invalidates the client area and sends a `WM_PAINT` message to the window procedure associated with the window class.

CS_VREDRAW tells the window procedure to redisplay its client area if the user changes the vertical size of the window. CS_HREDRAW tells the window procedure to redisplay its client area if the user changes the horizontal size of the window.

CS_DBLCLICKS tells Windows to send mouse double-click messages to the window procedure. A mouse double-click is two clicks of the mouse button in quick succession.

Windows automatically checks to be sure the time interval between the mouse clicks is appropriate as set by the user in the Control Panel. If you include the CS_DBLCLICKS style flag, Table 6.5 lists the messages your program can receive for mouse double-click actions.

Table 6.5. Mouse double-click messages.

Message	*Description*
WM_LBUTTONDBLCLK	Left mouse button double-clicks.
WM_MBUTTONDBLCLK	Middle mouse button double-clicks.
WM_RBUTTONDBLCLK	Right mouse button double-clicks.

If you don't include CS_DBLCLICKS and the user tries to double-click the mouse buttons, your program receives a group of messages that indicates the mouse button was clicked and released once, clicked and released twice, and so on. You can't easily differentiate the type of mouse clicks for the program, unless you include CS_DBLCLICKS.

The next group of style flags deals with windows and their corresponding device context. The device context is what every program must receive before it can display items in the client area. As you learned in Chapter 4, "Writing Windows Programs," the entire system has a limited number of device contexts, and you must borrow a device context when you output or paint to the screen.

The previous statement is only partly true. By using flags discussed in this section, you can get around this rule.

You can specify that a window based on a certain class have its own display context or a display context for all windows based on the class. You also can specify that child windows use their parent window's display context.

The `CS_OWNDC` flag provides a private device context for each window in the window class. This way, each window has its own device context. This might seem like the easiest method of programming for Windows, because you don't worry continuously about obtaining the display context. However, a private display context requires about 640 bytes of extra memory for each window. This is expensive memory consumption compared to consumption in the system display context.

If your program uses graphics intensively, you can use `CS_OWNDC` to increase performance. Examples in which a private display context improves performance of a program include a CAD application, a word processing application, or a desktop publishing application. Notice, each of these applications is graphics intensive.

Programs that use a private display context still must utilize the `BEGINPAINT` and `ENDPAINT` routines when responding to a `WM_PAINT` message. Using the pair of routines tells Windows you did respond to the message. The routines are capable of returning the private display context for your program's window.

The `CS_CLASSDC` flag gives all windows based on a specific window class their own display context. The advantage to a class that displays context is the display context attributes are not reset after every call to get a display context. This improves speed and uses less memory than a private display context.

`CS_PARENTDC` improves system performance when the program draws in a window. The flag is used to give a parent window's display context to the window class. This tells the window to repaint the area in both a parent and child window. This also can improve performance for certain applications.

You already know a normal overlapped window contains a system menu. The `CS_NOCLOSE` field removes the Close menu item from the system menu. Be careful when you remove this option, because it might leave the user no way to exit your program. It's best to include the Close option on the system menu because then the user always can shut down the application.

A group of flags helps optimize the feel of a program and makes it run more efficiently. CS_SAVEBITS saves the portion of a window covered by other objects.

When menus are displayed (these are also windows), they use CS_SAVEBITS. Menus display quickly and then the area underneath redisplays rapidly. The downfall is CS_SAVEBITS requires a great deal of memory to save a window area. If you think it's worth the memory and your program's performance benefits, you might want to use the flag. Otherwise, it's not recommended.

Two flags help align the window's client area on the screen. To speed programs, use CS_BYTEALIGNCLIENT to align a window's client area on the byte boundary. This affects the width of a window. The flag forces the x-axis to align on a byte boundary. This improves performance for certain graphics operations.

The other flag that affects alignment on the screen is CS_BYTEALIGNWINDOW. It aligns a window on the byte boundary in the x-direction. Again, this can improve system performance.

Generally, the byte alignment flags affect performance only on displays that use multiple-plane color and monochrome monitors. If you expect your program's users to employ one of these types of monitors, consider utilizing the flags to increase performance—otherwise, there is no increase.

The final flag is CS_GLOBALCLASS. It makes a window class system global. Recall, by specifying the window class as system global, you tell Windows the class is available to any program running the entire time Windows is active. If you run a group of related programs at once, use this class so the programs can share the window class.

Predefined Windows Classes

With this discussion of window class styles, you now look at a program that uses a predefined window class. Table 6.6 lists the predefined window classes.

Table 6.6. Predefined window classes.

Class	*Description*
BUTTON	Command button interface object.
COMBOBOX	Combination box interface object.
EDIT	Edit box interface object.
LISTBOX	Listbox interface object.
MDICLIENT	MDI Client window.
SCROLLBAR	Scroll bar interface object (not attached to a window).
STATIC	Object constantly the same.

Before you study the window classes, look at a program that uses one of them. Listing 6.1 creates a window using the Button window class. Listing 6.2. is the module definition file for the program. Figure 6.1 shows the window created by the BUTWIN.C program.

Listing 6.1. BUTWIN.C program.

```
// BUTWIN.C - Program showing the use of predefined window
//            classes
//
// Programming Windows with Turbo C++ for Windows
// by Paul J. Perry

#define STRICT

#define BUTTON1_ID 10
#define BUTTON2_ID 20

#include <windowsx.h>
#include <string.h>
#include <stdlib.h>

// Function Prototypes
LRESULT CALLBACK _export MainWndProc(HWND hWnd, UINT message,
                                     WPARAM wParam, LPARAM lParam);
```

```
// Global Variables
HINSTANCE hInst;

/*******************************************/
#pragma argsused
int PASCAL WinMain(HINSTANCE hInstance, HINSTANCE hPrevInstance,
                   LPSTR lpCmdParam, int nCmdShow)
{
   char        ProgName[] = "Window with Buttons";
   HWND        hWnd;
   MSG         msg;


   hInst = hInstance;   // Initialize Global Variable

   if (!hPrevInstance)
   {
      WNDCLASS    wndclass;

      wndclass.lpszClassName = ProgName;
      wndclass.lpfnWndProc   = (WNDPROC) MainWndProc;
      wndclass.cbClsExtra    = 0;
      wndclass.cbWndExtra    = 0;
      wndclass.hInstance     = hInstance;
      wndclass.hIcon         = LoadIcon(NULL, IDI_APPLICATION);
      wndclass.hCursor       = LoadCursor(NULL, IDC_ARROW);
      wndclass.hbrBackground = (HBRUSH) (COLOR_WINDOW + 1);
      wndclass.lpszMenuName  = NULL;
      wndclass.style         = CS_VREDRAW ¦ CS_HREDRAW;

      if (!RegisterClass(&wndclass)) exit(0);

   }

   hWnd = CreateWindow(ProgName,"Window With Buttons",
                       WS_OVERLAPPEDWINDOW,
                       CW_USEDEFAULT, CW_USEDEFAULT,
                       270, 125,
                       NULL, NULL, hInstance, NULL);

   ShowWindow(hWnd, nCmdShow);
   UpdateWindow(hWnd);

   while (GetMessage(&msg, NULL, 0, 0))
   {
      TranslateMessage(&msg);
      DispatchMessage(&msg);
```

continues

Listing 6.1. continued

```
   }
   return msg.wParam;
}

/******************************************/
LRESULT CALLBACK _export MainWndProc(HWND hWnd, UINT message,
                                     WPARAM wParam, LPARAM lParam)
{
   static HWND hButton1;
   static HWND hButton2;

   switch (message)
   {
      case WM_CREATE :
      {
         hButton1 = CreateWindow("BUTTON", "Exit", WS_CHILD ¦
                                 WS_VISIBLE ¦ BS_PUSHBUTTON,
                                 10, 50, 100, 30, hWnd,
                                 (HMENU) BUTTON1_ID,
                                 hInst, NULL);
         ShowWindow(hButton1, SW_SHOW);

         hButton2 = CreateWindow("BUTTON", "Message Box", WS_CHILD ¦
                                  WS_VISIBLE ¦ BS_PUSHBUTTON,
                                  150, 50, 100, 30, hWnd,
                                  (HMENU) BUTTON2_ID,
                                  hInst, NULL);
         ShowWindow(hButton2, SW_SHOW);

      }

      case WM_COMMAND :
      {
         switch(wParam)
         {
            case BUTTON1_ID :
            {
               PostQuitMessage(0);
            }

            case BUTTON2_ID :
            {
               MessageBox(hWnd, "Button #2 Pressed",
                          "Message", MB_OK);
            }
```

```
      }
   }

   case WM_PAINT :
   {
      HDC         PaintDC;
      PAINTSTRUCT ps;
      char        string[] = "Click on a button:";

      PaintDC = BeginPaint(hWnd, &ps);

      TextOut(PaintDC, 90, 10, string , strlen(string));

      EndPaint(hWnd, &ps);
      return 0;
   }

   case WM_DESTROY :
   {
      PostQuitMessage(0);
      return 0;
   }
 }
 return DefWindowProc (hWnd, message, wParam, lParam);
}
```

Listing 6.2. BUTWIN.DEF module definition file.

```
;
; BUTWIN.DEF module definition file
;

DESCRIPTION    'Button Window'
NAME           BUTWIN
EXETYPE        WINDOWS
STUB           'WINSTUB.EXE'
HEAPSIZE       1024
STACKSIZE      8192
CODE           PRELOAD MOVEABLE DISCARDABLE
DATA           PRELOAD MOVEABLE MULTIPLE
```

This sample program creates a main overlapped window. Inside the window, it creates two command buttons. Each command button is treated as a separate window, using the `CreateWindow` and `ShowWindow` functions to create and display them. The method is similar to the one that first created the main window.

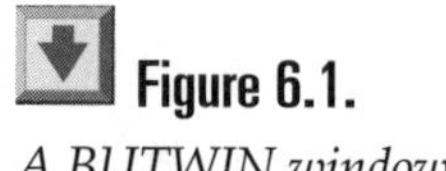

Figure 6.1.
A BUTWIN window.

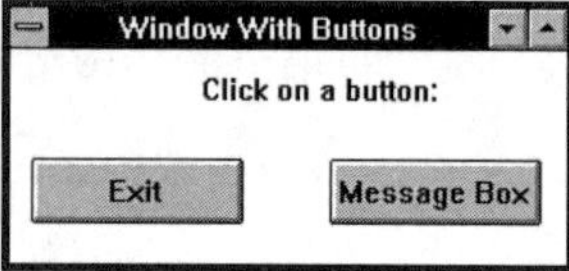

If you click the command buttons, the buttons respond. The Exit button quits the program by executing `PostQuitMessage`. This function is similar to the `exit()` function in DOS programs. `PostQuitMessage` tells the program to shut itself down.

When you click the other button, Message Box, it displays a message box in the middle of the desktop. Although the message box may look like a dialog box, dialog boxes can do much more. You usually don't create a dialog box with multiple calls to the `CreateWindow` function—that's too tedious.

As you soon see, all aspects of Windows are smaller windows themselves. The main overlapped window is the basic element of a program. Each button, listbox, and edit box is a window inside a window.

The interface objects can also be set up as child windows in a program. Child windows are used to divide other windows into smaller functional areas. A child window has a parent because it is usually inside another window. The parent of a window is passed to the window during creation as one of the parameters of `CreateWindow`.

A main program window has a parent window—although it is not specified. That window is the window's desktop. It is important to remember a child window is visible only when positioned in the parent window area.

You nearly always use the predefined window classes for creating controls in dialog boxes, but you don't generally use them in a program. It's interesting, however, to know you can create windows based on them.

Types of Windows

You saw the `CreateWindow` routine create a window in Chapter 5. Windows has many window creation options and two routines to create windows—`CreateWindow` and `CreateWindowEx`.

Listing 6.3., the MULWIN.C program, shows how to create more than one window in a program. Listing 6.4 is the module definition file for the program. It creates four different windows with different styles to demonstrate versatility of the Windows' window creation routine.

Listing 6.3. MULWIN.C program to open multiple windows.

```
// MULWIN.C - Open multiple styles of Windows in a Program
//
// Programming Windows with Turbo C++ for Windows
// by Paul J. Perry

#define STRICT

#include <windowsx.h>
#include <stdlib.h>

// Function Prototypes
LRESULT CALLBACK _export FirstWndProc(HWND hWnd, UINT message,
                                     WPARAM wParam,
                                     LPARAM lParam);

LRESULT CALLBACK _export SecondWndProc(HWND hWnd, UINT message,
                                      WPARAM wParam,
                                      LPARAM lParam);

/*******************************************/
#pragma argsused
int PASCAL WinMain(HINSTANCE hInstance, HINSTANCE hPrevInstance,
                   LPSTR lpCmdParam, int nCmdShow)
{
   HWND         hWnd1, hWnd2, hWnd3, hWnd4;
   MSG          msg;


   if (!hPrevInstance)
```

continues

Listing 6.3. continued

```
{
   WNDCLASS    wndclass;

   wndclass.lpszClassName = "First";
   wndclass.lpfnWndProc   = (WNDPROC) FirstWndProc;
   wndclass.cbClsExtra    = 0;
   wndclass.cbWndExtra    = 0;
   wndclass.hInstance     = hInstance;
   wndclass.hIcon         = LoadIcon(NULL, IDI_APPLICATION);
   wndclass.hCursor       = LoadCursor(NULL, IDC_CROSS);
   wndclass.hbrBackground = GetStockBrush(BLACK_BRUSH);
   wndclass.lpszMenuName  = NULL;
   wndclass.style         = CS_VREDRAW ¦ CS_HREDRAW;

   // Register first class type
   if (!RegisterClass(&wndclass)) exit(0);;

   wndclass.lpszClassName = "Second";
   wndclass.lpfnWndProc   = (WNDPROC) SecondWndProc;
   wndclass.cbClsExtra    = 0;
   wndclass.cbWndExtra    = 0;
   wndclass.hInstance     = hInstance;
   wndclass.hIcon         = LoadIcon(NULL, IDI_APPLICATION);
   wndclass.hCursor       = LoadCursor(NULL, IDC_ICON);
   wndclass.hbrBackground = GetStockBrush(GRAY_BRUSH);
   wndclass.lpszMenuName  = NULL;
   wndclass.style         = CS_VREDRAW ¦ CS_HREDRAW;

   // Register second class type
   if (!RegisterClass(&wndclass)) exit(0);
}

hWnd1 = CreateWindow("First", "Window #1",
                     WS_OVERLAPPEDWINDOW,
                     5, 5, 200, 100,
                     NULL, NULL, hInstance, NULL);

hWnd2 = CreateWindow("First", "Window #1",
                     WS_MINIMIZEBOX ¦ WS_MAXIMIZEBOX,
                     300, 5, 200, 100,
                     NULL, NULL, hInstance, NULL);


hWnd3 = CreateWindow("Second", "Window #3",
                     WS_DLGFRAME,
                     5, 150, 200, 100,
                     NULL, NULL, hInstance, NULL);
```

```
    hWnd4 = CreateWindow("Second", "Window #4",
                        WS_SYSMENU | WS_THICKFRAME,
                        300, 150, 200, 100,
                        NULL, NULL, hInstance, NULL);

    ShowWindow(hWnd1, SW_SHOW);
    ShowWindow(hWnd2, SW_SHOW);
    ShowWindow(hWnd3, SW_SHOW);
    ShowWindow(hWnd4, SW_SHOW);



    UpdateWindow(hWnd1);
    UpdateWindow(hWnd2);
    UpdateWindow(hWnd3);
    UpdateWindow(hWnd4);


    while (GetMessage(&msg, NULL, 0, 0))
    {
       TranslateMessage(&msg);
       DispatchMessage(&msg);
    }
    return msg.wParam;
}

/*******************************************/
LRESULT CALLBACK _export FirstWndProc(HWND hWnd, UINT message,
                                      WPARAM wParam, LPARAM lParam)
{
   switch (message)
   {
      case WM_PAINT :
      {
         HDC         PaintDC;
         RECT        rect;
         PAINTSTRUCT ps;

         PaintDC = BeginPaint(hWnd, &ps);
         GetClientRect(hWnd, &rect);

         DrawText(PaintDC, "Class Type #1", -1, &rect,
                  DT_SINGLELINE | DT_CENTER | DT_VCENTER);

         EndPaint(hWnd, &ps);
```

continues

Listing 6.3. continued

```
         return 0;
      }

      case WM_DESTROY :
      {
         PostQuitMessage(0);
         return 0;
      }
   }
   return DefWindowProc (hWnd, message, wParam, lParam);
}


/*********************************************/
LRESULT CALLBACK _export SecondWndProc(HWND hWnd, UINT message,
                                        WPARAM wParam,
                                        LPARAM lParam)
{
   switch (message)
   {
      case WM_PAINT :
      {
         HDC         PaintDC;
         RECT        rect;
         PAINTSTRUCT ps;

         PaintDC = BeginPaint(hWnd, &ps);
         GetClientRect(hWnd, &rect);

         DrawText(PaintDC, "Class Type #2", -1, &rect,
                  DT_SINGLELINE | DT_CENTER | DT_VCENTER);

         EndPaint(hWnd, &ps);
         return 0;
      }

      case WM_DESTROY :
      {
         PostQuitMessage(0);
         return 0;
      }
   }
   return DefWindowProc (hWnd, message, wParam, lParam);
}
```

Listing 6.4. MULWIN.DEF module definition file.

```
;
; MULWIN.DEF module definition file
;

DESCRIPTION   'Multiple Windows'
NAME          MULWIN
EXETYPE       WINDOWS
STUB          'WINSTUB.EXE'
HEAPSIZE      1024
STACKSIZE     8192
CODE          PRELOAD MOVEABLE DISCARDABLE
DATA          PRELOAD MOVEABLE MULTIPLE
```

Notice, this program uses two window classes for its four main windows. They are both registered once in the initialization section of the program. Window #2 and Window #3 are displayed without a sizable window frame. The other windows have a resizeable frame. See Figure 6.2 to find what the Windows desktop looks like after you run the MULWIN program.

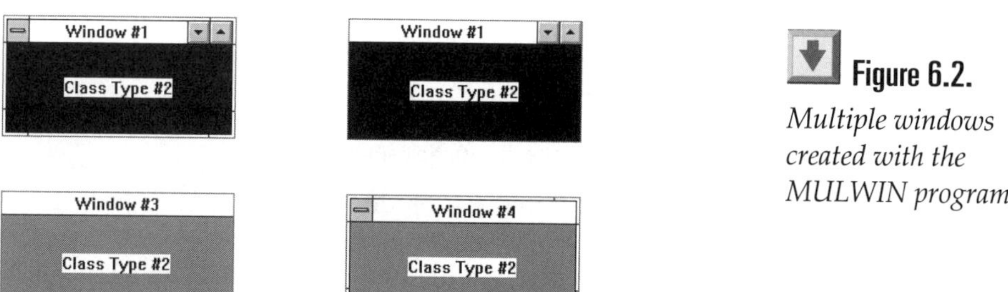

Figure 6.2. *Multiple windows created with the MULWIN program.*

The second class definition is interesting. You use the `GRAY_BRUSH` constant as the background color. When you display the contents of the client area, you don't change the text's background color. Therefore, the text displays as black on white. Because the background color is different, you can see the rectangular area the text occupies.

With an idea about the different window styles, you now look at the window creation routines and learn about each parameter associated with them.

Creating Windows

The two window creation routines defined in the Windows API are `CreateWindow` and `CreateWindowEx`. The second routine is an extended version of the first. It does everything the first does, and more.

In its early days, Windows' designers started with `CreateWindow`. When the routine ran out of styles that could be passed to the it, designers created a second routine that accepts more style parameters.

The routines are as follows:

```
HWND CreateWindow(LPCSTR lpszClassName, LPCSTR lpszWindowName,
                  DWORD dwStyle, int x, int y, int nWidth, int
nHeight,
                  HWND hwndParent, HMENU hmenu, HINSTANCE hinst,
                  void FAR* lpvParam);

HWND CreateWindowEx(DWORD dwExStyle, LPCSTR lpszClassName,
                    LPCSTR lpszWindowName,DWORD dwStyle,
                    int x, int y, int nWidth, int nHeight,
                    HWND hwndParent, HMENU hmenu, HINSTANCE hinst,
                    void FAR* lpvCreateParams)
```

The only difference between the extended functions is the addition of an extra parameter, `dwExStyle`. `CreateWindow` is used most often. Employ `CreateWindowEx` to create specialized dialog box window elements and to take advantage of special features in Windows 3.1.

Rather than use a data structure as `RegisterClass` does, `CreateWindow` requires all the information to pass as parameters to the function. Next, you take a closer look at each parameter passed to `CreateWindow`.

CreateWindow Parameters

`ClassName`, the first parameter to `CreateWindow`, is a string that holds the class name on which to base the window being created. The class name can be any name registered earlier with `RegisterClass` or any of the predefined control-class names specified in Table 6.6.

The second parameter, `WindowName`, is a string that is the name to display in the title bar of the window. Not all windows have title bars, so `WindowName` is not always used. Sometimes, as with the command button class, the parameter is used for the text inside the button.

The `Style` field identifies the style to use when creating the window. Table 6.7 gives an overview of available window creation styles.

Table 6.7. Window creation styles summary.

Window Style	*Description*
WS_MINIMIZEBOX	Includes minimize button.
WS_MAXIMIZEBOX	Includes maximize button.
WS_CAPTION	Includes title bar for window.
WS_BORDER	Includes border around window.
WS_SYSMENU	Includes system menu on window.
WS_VISIBLE	Forces window initially to be visible.
WS_DISABLED	Forces window initially to be disabled.
WS_CLIPSIBLINGS	Clips child windows relative to each other.
WS_CLIPCHILDREN	Specifies not to paint in area occupied by child windows.
WS_DLGFRAME	Creates window with double border but no title bar.
WS_THICKFRAME	Includes thick window border that can be resized.

continues

Table 6.7. continued

Window Style	*Description*
WS_VSCROLL	Includes vertical scroll bar on window.
WS_HSCROLL	Includes horizontal scroll bar on window.
WS_OVERLAPPED	Specifies a default overlapped window type.
WS_POPUP	Specifies a pop-up window.
WS_CHILD	Specifies window is a child window.

The fourth and fifth parameters to the function are the x- and y-coordinates of the window on the screen. The default coordinate system is pixels. On a VGA display, 640 pixels are across the screen and 480 pixels are top to bottom. The point in the upper-left corner of the client area is 0,0. The numbers increase, starting from left to right and from top to bottom (a little different from a regular Cartesian coordinate system).

The `Width` and `Height` parameters specify width and height of the window. Again, these are specified in pixel units. Remember, when you make these specifications, they are for the entire window, including the nonclient area.

These four parameters (`x`, `y`, `Width`, and `Height`) can be set to the identifier `CW_USEDEFAULT`, in which case Windows assigns default values for the starting position and the size of the window. The usual effect is to cascade windows on the Windows desktop.

The `WndParent` parameter specifies the parent window or owner of the window being created. A valid window handle must be specified when creating a child window. A child window must also have the `WS_CHILD` value in the style parameter. If the window does not have a parent or is not owned by another window, set this parameter to `0`.

The `hMenu` field receives a handle to a menu. Recall how you specify a menu to belong to a window during the window class definition. If you specify a window here, it overrides the window specified for the class. You must use the `LoadMenu` routine to return a handle to a menu located in a resource file. You set this parameter to `0` if you don't want a menu to be associated with the window.

The `Instance` field identifies the instance of the module associated with the window. You always set this to the `hInstance` variable passed from the `WinMain` function.

The `Param` field is an extra value passed to the window through the `CreateStruct` data structure. You generally employ this parameter only for programs that utilize the multiple document interface (MDI). As a result, most programs don't use it.

The `CreateWindowEx` routine adds one more parameter (the first parameter passed to it), `dwExStyle`. This is the extended style parameter of the window being created. This parameter currently has five extended style settings, as shown in Table 6.8. Undoubtedly, more styles will appear in future versions of Windows.

Table 6.8. Extended style types.

Window Style	*Description*
WS_EX_ACCEPTFILES	Specifies the window created can accept, drag, and drop files.
WS_EX_DLGMODALFRAME	Specifies window with a double border, created optionally with a title bar by designating the WS_CAPTION style flag.
WS_EX_NOPARENTNOTIFY	Specifies child window created with this style does not notify its parent window when the child window is created or destroyed.
WS_EX_TOPMOST	Specifies the window is placed as the top window on the desktop. No other window can display on top of this window.
WS_EX_TRANSPARENT	Specifies the window is transparent. Anything beneath the window displays.

Window Creation Styles

Now, look closely at the window creation styles. First, notice all the flags Tables 6.7 and 6.8 summarize. All window style constants are prefaced with the identifier `WS_`, which stands for window style.

The first group of window creation styles specifies different aspects of the window. The `WS_MINIMIZEBOX` flag includes a minimize button in the upper-right corner of the window. Likewise, you can specify `WS_MAXIMIZEBOX` to include a maximize button in the window. When you maximize a window, the maximize button changes to a restore button. If this button is pushed, the window returns to its previous size and to its location before being maximized.

The `WS_CAPTION` style tells the program to include a caption bar or title bar at the top of the window. Not all windows have a title bar, so this style isn't always used. If you specify a title caption and the window doesn't use it, the parameter is ignored.

The `WS_BORDER` style tells the program to create a window with a border. The border is thick and similar to the type on a main overlapped window.

To include a system menu in the window you create, be sure to specify the `WS_SYSMENU` flag. This ensures the system menu displays and processes automatically. With this flag, users conveniently can manipulate with the keyboard those windows your program lets them close.

Two flags force the state of a window when you first create it. `WS_VISIBLE` makes the window visible at its creation. If it's a top-level window, you still must call the `ShowWindow` routine. You find the flag useful when creating a child window in another window.

By using the `WS_DISABLED` style, you initially disable a window. This means mouse and keyboard input isn't sent to the window procedure associated with the window. When users click a disabled window with the mouse, a warning beep generates to notify them about the window's state.

Two flags determine how windows are clipped. *Clipping* is the process that automatically separates output from different windows. Clipping creates borders around a window that force the graphics output routines to write only in a window. If you write a long string in a client area that doesn't have enough space for the string, the text is automatically cut or clipped.

Figure 6.3 shows an example of clipping with the clock and solitaire programs that come with Windows.

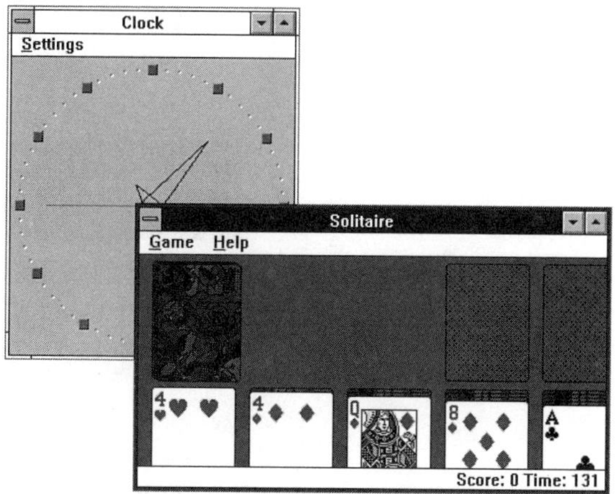

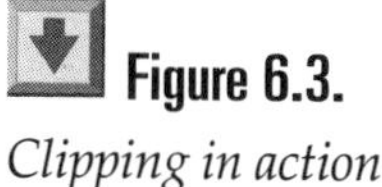

Figure 6.3.
Clipping in action.

Notice, as you run the solitaire program, the clock still runs in the background. The clock's hands still move. However, the clock program never writes in Solitaire's client area.

Clipping is shown in Solitaire too. If familiar with it, you know you need enough screen space to view all the cards. Notice in the figure, only several of the cards are displaying because the window is resized. However, the program's output routines still write all the cards to the window. It is the clipping mechanism that displays only part of the window when it is resized.

The `WS_CLIPSIBLINGS` flag clips child windows relative to each other. This flag excludes the area occupied by child windows when drawing in the parent window. This flag is used only when creating the children windows.

The `WS_CLIPCHILDREN` flag clips child windows relative to each other. When a particular child window receives a paint message, `WS_CLIPSIBLINGS` clips all other overlapped child windows out of the region of the child window to be updated. If this flag isn't given and the child windows overlap, it's possible to draw in the client area of a neighboring child window when drawing in the client area of one child window. As you might expect, you use this flag only with `WS_CHILD`.

Two flags control the border of the window. WS_DLGFRAME creates a window with double borders (see Figure 6.4). The WS_THICKFRAME flag includes a thick window border for the window (see Figure 6.5). The thick frame border is the type you know as the main window for programs that can be resized.

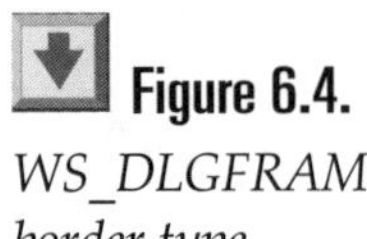
Figure 6.4.
WS_DLGFRAME border type.

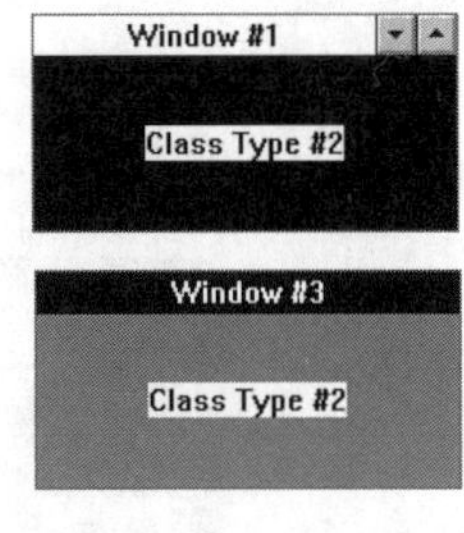

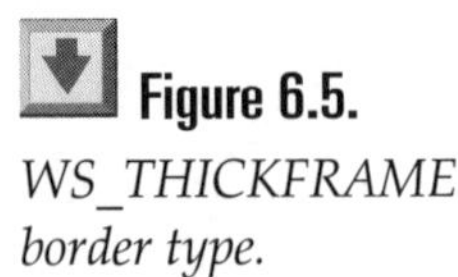
Figure 6.5.
WS_THICKFRAME border type.

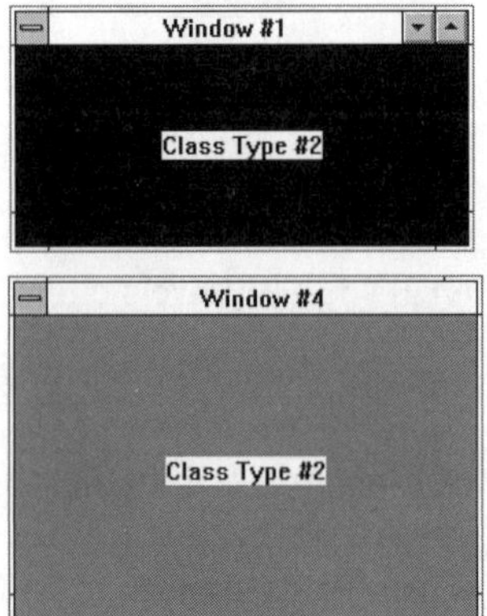

Sometimes a window isn't large enough to hold all the information you work with, even if you maximize the window. For example, if you use a word processor, you might not have space to view a whole document that's more than about 30 lines. Windows provides a solution with its scroll bar.

The WS_VSCROLL style adds a scroll bar at the right side of the window. The WS_HSCROLL style adds a horizontal scroll bar at the window's bottom edge. You can add both types of scroll bars to a window by combining them with the C or (¦) operator as in Figure 6.6. Windows displays the scroll bar for you. You only respond to window messages (big surprise). You learn about window scroll bars and how to make them work in your programs in Chapter 9, "Using Windows Scroll Bars."

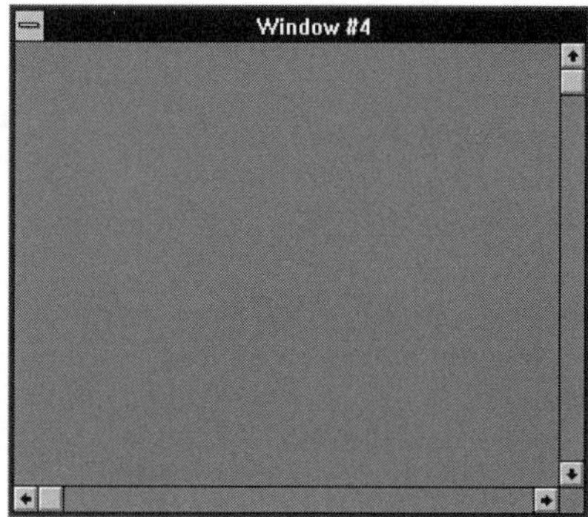

Figure 6.6.
Window scroll bars.

The WS_OVERLAPPED style allows the creation of an overlapped window. The overlapped window has a title bar and a window. The WS_POPUP style is a floating window. This window can be moved about the screen and is intended to be used as a dialog box. The WS_CHILD style bit tells Windows the window is a child window.

Utilize the WS_OVERLAPPEDWINDOW style to define a window used as the top-level main window for a program. This style includes the characteristics of several window styles already shown. The definition of WS_OVERLAPPEDWINDOW looks like this:

```
#define WS_OVERLAPPEDWINDOW (WS_OVERLAPPED ¦ WS_CAPTION ¦
                             WS_SYSMENU ¦ WS_THICKFRAME ¦
                             WS_MINIMIZEBOX ¦ WS_MAXIMIZEBOX)
```

You have information about creating a window. Now, you look at another program that creates windows. The program in Listing 6.5 (and related module definition file in Listing 6.6) creates a child window. Examine the listing and remember to create a project that contains the two files.

Listing 6.5. Child window creation program.

```
// CHILD.C - Example program using child windows
//
// Programming Windows with Turbo C++ for Windows
// by Paul J. Perry

#define STRICT

#include <windowsx.h>
#include <stdlib.h>


// Function Prototypes
LRESULT CALLBACK _export FirstWndProc(HWND hWnd, UINT message,
                                      WPARAM wParam, LPARAM

lParam);

LRESULT CALLBACK _export SecondWndProc(HWND hWnd, UINT message,
                                       WPARAM wParam, LPARAM

lParam);

/*******************************************/
#pragma argsused
int PASCAL WinMain(HINSTANCE hInstance, HINSTANCE hPrevInstance,
                   LPSTR lpCmdParam, int nCmdShow)
{
   HWND        hWndParent, hWndChild;
   MSG         msg;


   if (!hPrevInstance)
   {
      WNDCLASS    wndclass;

      wndclass.lpszClassName = "Parent";
      wndclass.lpfnWndProc   = (WNDPROC) FirstWndProc;
      wndclass.cbClsExtra    = 0;
      wndclass.cbWndExtra    = 0;
      wndclass.hInstance     = hInstance;
      wndclass.hIcon         = LoadIcon(NULL, IDI_APPLICATION);
      wndclass.hCursor       = LoadCursor(NULL, IDC_ARROW);
      wndclass.hbrBackground = (HBRUSH) (COLOR_WINDOW + 1);
      wndclass.lpszMenuName  = NULL;
      wndclass.style         = CS_VREDRAW | CS_HREDRAW;

      if (!RegisterClass(&wndclass)) exit(0);
```

```
      wndclass.lpszClassName = "Child";
      wndclass.lpfnWndProc   = (WNDPROC) SecondWndProc;
      wndclass.cbClsExtra    = 0;
      wndclass.cbWndExtra    = 0;
      wndclass.hInstance     = hInstance;
      wndclass.hIcon         = LoadIcon(NULL, IDI_APPLICATION);
      wndclass.hCursor       = LoadCursor(NULL, IDC_ARROW);
      wndclass.hbrBackground = GetStockBrush(GRAY_BRUSH);
      wndclass.lpszMenuName  = NULL;
      wndclass.style         = CS_VREDRAW ¦ CS_HREDRAW;

      if (!RegisterClass(&wndclass)) exit(0);;

   }

   hWndParent = CreateWindow("Parent","Parent Window",
                             WS_OVERLAPPEDWINDOW, 5, 5,
                             CW_USEDEFAULT, CW_USEDEFAULT,
                             NULL, NULL, hInstance, NULL);


   hWndChild = CreateWindow("Child", "Child Window",
                            WS_CHILD, 300, 250, 200, 200,
                            hWndParent, NULL, hInstance, NULL);


   ShowWindow(hWndParent, nCmdShow);
   ShowWindow(hWndChild, SW_SHOW);

   UpdateWindow(hWndParent);
   UpdateWindow(hWndChild);

   while (GetMessage(&msg, NULL, 0, 0))
   {
      TranslateMessage(&msg);
      DispatchMessage(&msg);
   }
   return msg.wParam;
}

/*******************************************/
LRESULT CALLBACK _export FirstWndProc(HWND hWnd, UINT message,
                                      WPARAM wParam, LPARAM lParam)
{
   switch (message)
   {
      case WM_PAINT :
```

continues

Listing 6.5. continued

```
      {
         HDC         PaintDC;
         RECT        rect;
         PAINTSTRUCT ps;

         PaintDC = BeginPaint(hWnd, &ps);
         GetClientRect(hWnd, &rect);

         DrawText(PaintDC, "Inside Parent Window", -1, &rect,
                  DT_SINGLELINE ¦ DT_CENTER ¦ DT_VCENTER);

         EndPaint(hWnd, &ps);
         return 0;
      }

      case WM_DESTROY :
      {
         PostQuitMessage(0);
         return 0;
      }
   }
   return DefWindowProc (hWnd, message, wParam, lParam);
}


/*******************************************/
LRESULT CALLBACK _export SecondWndProc(HWND hWnd, UINT message,
                                       WPARAM wParam, LPARAM
lParam)
{
   switch (message)
   {
      case WM_PAINT :
      {
         HDC         PaintDC;
         RECT        rect;
         PAINTSTRUCT ps;

         PaintDC = BeginPaint(hWnd, &ps);
         GetClientRect(hWnd, &rect);
         SetBkColor(PaintDC, RGB(127, 127, 127));

         DrawText(PaintDC, "Inside Child Window", -1, &rect,
                  DT_SINGLELINE ¦ DT_CENTER ¦ DT_VCENTER);

         EndPaint(hWnd, &ps);
```

```
            return 0;
        }

        case WM_DESTROY :
        {
            PostQuitMessage(0);
            return 0;
        }
    }
    return DefWindowProc (hWnd, message, wParam, lParam);
}
```

Listing 6.6. Module definition file.

```
;
; CHILD.DEF module definition file
;

DESCRIPTION    'Child Window Creation'
NAME           CHILD
EXETYPE        WINDOWS
STUB           'WINSTUB.EXE'
HEAPSIZE       1024
STACKSIZE      8192
CODE           PRELOAD MOVEABLE DISCARDABLE
DATA           PRELOAD MOVEABLE MULTIPLE
```

The program in Listing 6.5 creates two windows. The parent window is the main overlapped window and the other window is defined as the child window (see Figure 6.7). Each window has its own window procedure to demonstrate features of child windows and clipping.

Notice, if you change the size of the parent window so only part of the child window is visible, the child window is clipped, and you cannot see all of it (see Figure 6.8).

Finally, if you resize the parent window so the area where the child window usually displays is not visible (see Figure 6.9), you cannot see the child window at all. The program thinks it's still outputting to the window; however, Windows handles all the logic necessary so the window text does not display.

Figure 6.7.

Child window creation program displayed maximized.

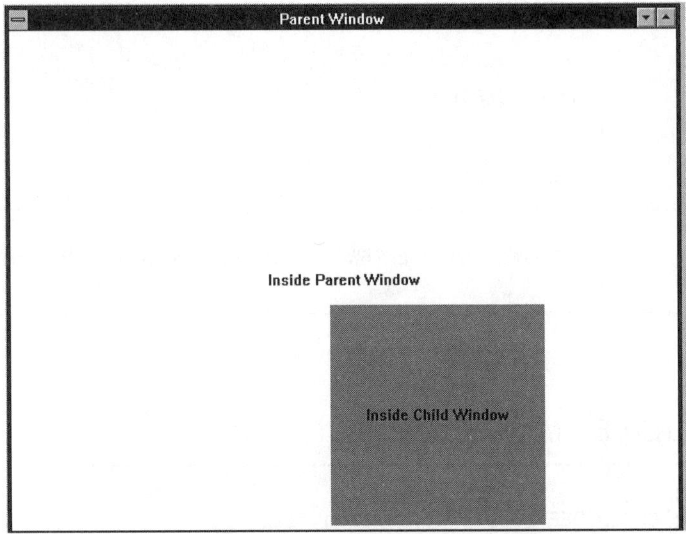

Figure 6.8.

Child window with clipping in action.

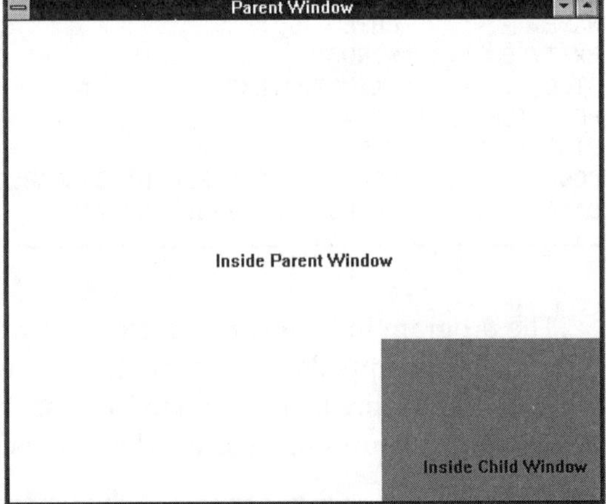

Window class registration and creation is one of the fundamental elements of programming with Windows. In the next section, you learn how to change these important class styles in programs based on the OWL.

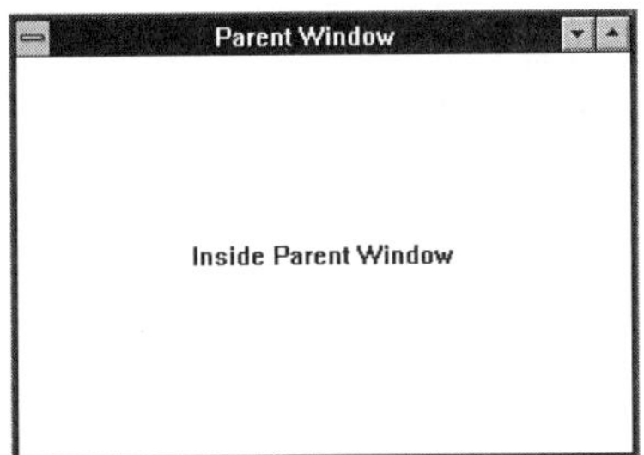

Figure 6.9.
Child window is not visible.

Windows Classes in OWL Programs

Because of the concepts of encapsulation, the OWL hides the task of registering a window class. In the OWL programs in Chapter 5, the library registers a class for you. The class is registered with the `TWindowClass::RegisterClass` member function. It looks like this:

```
void TWindow::GetWindowClass(WNDCLASS& AWndClass)
{
  AWndClass.cbClsExtra         = 0;
  AWndClass.cbWndExtra         = 0;
  AWndClass.hInstance          = hInstance;
  AWndClass.hIcon              = LoadIcon(0, IDI_APPLICATION);
  AWndClass.hCursor            = LoadCursor(0, IDC_ARROW);
  AWndClass.hbrBackground      = (HBRUSH)(COLOR_WINDOW + 1);
  AWndClass.lpszMenuName       = NULL;
  AWndClass.lpszClassName      = GetClassName();
  AWndClass.style              = CS_HREDRAW ¦ CS_VREDRAW;
  AWndClass.lpfnWndProc        = InitWndProc;
}
```

To customize, in any way, a program based on the OWL, you must enable the program to override the `GetWindowClass` member function. Listing 6.7 is a program that modifies the window class an OWL program uses. Listing 6.8 is the module definition file.

NOTE

When referring to a class, I mean a C++ class. When referring to a Window class, I mean a class contained in a `WNDCLASS` structure and registered with the `RegisterClass` function.

Listing 6.7. OWL program that uses custom classes.

```
// OWLWC.CPP - Using Window Classes with ObjectWindows
//             Library Programs.
//
// Programming Windows with Turbo C++ for Windows
// by Paul J. Perry


#define WIN31
#define STRICT

#include <owl.h>
#include <windowsx.h>


// Class Declarations

/*******************************************/
class TOwlApp : public TApplication
{
   public :
      TOwlApp (LPSTR AName, HINSTANCE hInstance,
               HINSTANCE hPrevInstance,
               LPSTR CmdLine, int CmdShow) :
               TApplication(AName, hInstance, hPrevInstance,
               CmdLine, CmdShow) { } ;

   virtual void InitMainWindow();
};


/*******************************************/
class TMainWindow : public TWindow
{
   public :
```

```
      TMainWindow(PTWindowsObject AParent, LPSTR ATitle);
      virtual void GetWindowClass(WNDCLASS& wndclass);
      virtual LPSTR GetClassName();
      virtual void Paint(HDC PaintDC, PAINTSTRUCT &PaintInfo);
};


// Class Member Functions

/*******************************************/
void TOwlApp::InitMainWindow()
{
   MainWindow = new TMainWindow(NULL, Name);
}


/*******************************************/
TMainWindow::TMainWindow(PTWindowsObject AParent, LPSTR ATitle)
                    : TWindow(AParent, ATitle)
{
   Attr.W = 400;  // Set initial window width
   Attr.H = 400;  // Set initial window height
}


/*******************************************/
void TMainWindow::GetWindowClass(WNDCLASS& wndclass)
{
   TWindow::GetWindowClass(wndclass);

   wndclass.hIcon = LoadIcon(0, IDI_QUESTION);
   wndclass.hCursor = LoadCursor(0, IDC_CROSS);
   wndclass.style = CS_HREDRAW | CS_VREDRAW | CS_CLASSDC;
   wndclass.hbrBackground = GetStockBrush(LTGRAY_BRUSH);
}


/*******************************************/
LPSTR TMainWindow::GetClassName()
{
   return "UniqueWindowClassName";
}


/*******************************************/
#pragma argsused
```

continues

Listing 6.7. continued

```
void TMainWindow::Paint(HDC PaintDC, PAINTSTRUCT &PaintInfo)
{
   RECT rect;

   GetClientRect(HWindow, &rect);

   DrawText(PaintDC, "Custom Windows Classes With the ObjectWindows
                     Library",
-1, &rect,
            DT_SINGLELINE ¦ DT_CENTER ¦ DT_VCENTER);

}


/*******************************************/
int PASCAL WinMain(HINSTANCE hInstance, HINSTANCE hPrevInstance,
                    LPSTR lpCmdLine, int nCmdShow)
{

   TOwlApp ThisApp("Custom ObjectWindows Library Window Classes",
                   hInstance, hPrevInstance, lpCmdLine, nCmdShow);
   ThisApp.Run();
   return ThisApp.Status;

}
```

Listing 6.8. Module definition file.

```
;
; OWLWC.DEF module definition file
;

DESCRIPTION    'OWL Window Classes'
NAME           OWLWC
EXETYPE        WINDOWS
STUB           'WINSTUB.EXE'
HEAPSIZE       1024
STACKSIZE      8192
CODE           PRELOAD MOVEABLE DISCARDABLE
DATA           PRELOAD MOVEABLE MULTIPLE
```

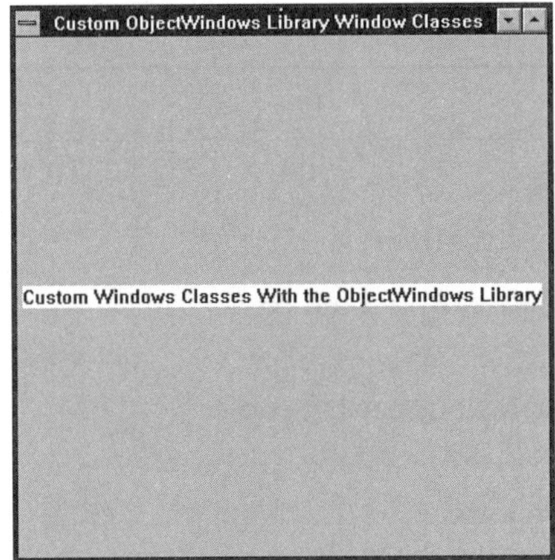

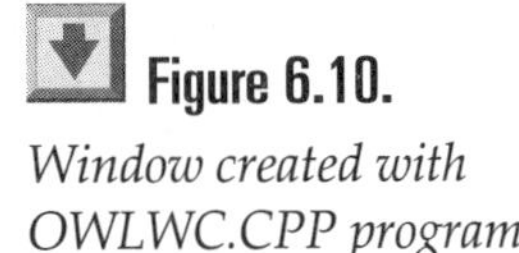

Figure 6.10.

Window created with OWLWC.CPP program.

OWLWC.CPP overrides `GetWindowClass`. Notice, OWLWC.CPP first calls `GetWindowClass` from the base class. The program modifies the class style, icon, cursor, and background fields. In your programs, you can override any element in the `WNDCLASS` data structure. Programmers commonly modify the ones changed in OWLWC.CPP.

To return a new name for the class, OWLWC.CPP includes a `GetClassName` member function. The sole purpose of this function is to return a string containing the new window's class name. If you use `GetWindowClass`, you always must create a `GetClassName` function in order to use the new class definition.

Creating a Custom Window

Although your OWL programs don't make explicit calls to `CreateWindow`, you still can create windows with various attributes and windows styles. The attributes are stored in the `TWindow::Attr` structure.

Table 6.9 lists some window creation attributes you might change in your program.

Table 6.9. Window styles used in TWindow::Attr data item.

Element	*Description*
Style	Window style flags.
ExStyle	Extended window style flags.
X	Starting x coordinate of upper-left corner of window.
Y	Starting y coordinate of upper-left corner of window.
W	Starting window width.
H	Starting window height.

The OWLWC.CPP program specifies a starting window width and height using the following statements:

```
Attr.W = 400;  // Set initial window width
Attr.H = 400;  // Set initial window height
```

These are found in the constructor for the window. You always put them in the constructor so they take effect before your window is constructed.

Because you know about the `WNDCLASS` data structure elements and the window class (`WC_`) and class style (`CS_`) flags, you know the flags you can access. You use these for similar purposes in OWL programs as you do in traditional C programs. Throughout this book, you find uses for many of the window and style flags shown in this chapter.

What You Have Learned

This chapter offers a detailed description about creating windows for Microsoft Windows. You learn about the following topics:

- *The Windows classes that are the basis for creating windows.*

- *The three different scopes for window classes.* These are system global, application global, and application local. Most programs create application local window classes.
- *Registering a window class.* This defines the class name, window procedure, instance of the program that owns the window class, background color for windows based on the window class, and extra bytes you store with the window class.
- *The resources a window class defines.* Resources the window class defines include the icon, menu, and cursor type.
- *The window class style.* This defines how a window acts. Currently, 11 different window class styles are defined in `WinTypes`.
- *Windows, seven predefined window classes that compose the interface objects.*
- *A single program can create multiple windows of the same class.*
- *Creating a window.* You must define the class that the window is defined on, the coordinates of the window, and parent window (if it's a child window).
- *The two routines used to create windows.* These are `CreateWindow` and `CreateWindowEx`.
- *The 13 window styles that define how a window looks.* Some of the styles are compound styles; that is, they are combinations of the other styles.
- *Child windows.* These windows are connected to another window (the parent) and reside in the area occupied by their parent window.
- *Clipping.* This forces windows to write in their own program screen area, without infringing on the territory of another window.
- *Registering your Window class in an OWL program.* You must override the `GetWindowClass` and `GetClassName` `TWindow` member functions.
- *Modifying attributes of a window in an OWL program.* You specify the elements in the `TWindow::Attr` data element in the constructor for the window object.

7

A FIRST LOOK AT RESOURCES

IN THIS CHAPTER

- The definition of a resource and the seven types of predefined resources available in Windows.
- Creating a dynamic icon that changes while a program is running.
- Starting and using the Resource Workshop.
- Using the icon editor in the Resource Workshop.
- Using the cursor editor in the Resource Workshop.
- Using custom icons and cursors in a program based on the ObjectWindows Library (OWL).

This chapter introduces you to Windows resources. You learn what these are and the types Windows offers. You then learn how to use the Resource Workshop that comes with Turbo C++ for Windows to create your own resources. You also learn about using custom icons and designing specialized cursors. In the process, you learn what a resource script file is.

What Is a Resource?

You use resources every time you run Windows. Resources are the parts of your program users interact with. The seven types of predefined resources are accelerator keys, bitmaps, cursors, dialog boxes, icons, menus, and resource strings.

Resources are created separately from your program's source code. Although resources usually reside in the .EXE file of your program, Windows controls when these are loaded. Resources are not always loaded immediately when you execute a program. You might have noticed this if you've tried to display a dialog box and have seen the light on your hard drive flicker as Windows went to the drive for information relating to the resource.

A resource script is an ASCII text file that defines the attributes of a resource. The easiest way to create a resource is to use the Resource Workshop; however, the resource script is a good way to convey what a resource is when trying to describe it in English.

The Resource Workshop is divided into separate editors. This enables you to create and modify the resources in your program. All editors are integrated into a single program. The Resource Workshop's design makes creating resources easy.

Types of Windows Resources

You might be familiar with some of the seven types of resources. You might recognize a resource—such as accelerator keys—but not be sure how it's referred to in a program. The following sections take a closer look at resources.

Accelerator Keys

Accelerator keys, also called keyboard accelerators, are keys that mimic menu functions. In the Integrated Development Environment (IDE), the F3 key is an accelerator for the File Open menu selection—when using the alternate menu structure.

Other common accelerator keys include Shift-Del, which almost always cuts the current selection to the Windows clipboard; Ctrl-Ins, which copies the current selection to the clipboard; and Shift-Ins, which pastes the current contents of the clipboard to the application being used.

Usually, the accelerator key is listed next to the menu selection in the menu tree, so the user knows which key corresponds to which menu selection. See Figure 7.1 for an example of accelerator keys.

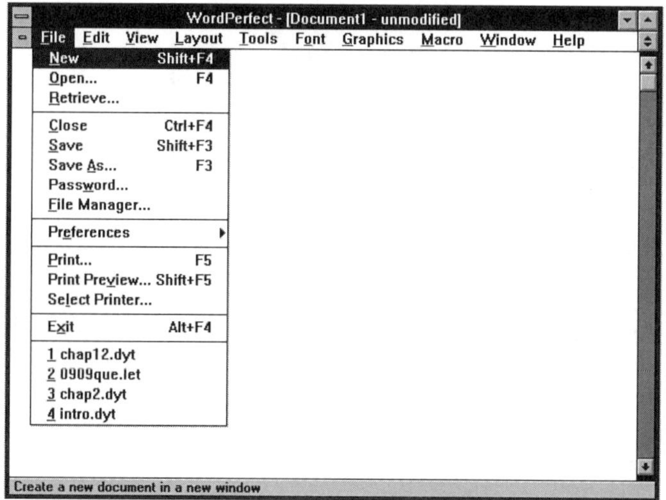

Figure 7.1.

Accelerator keys in WordPerfect for Windows.

Accelerator keys are important to Windows users because many power users do not always want to employ the mouse or press several keys to make a menu selection. An accelerator key is a quick way to make a menu selection.

Bitmaps

Bitmaps are graphical images you can use in your program. A bitmap is an image formed by a pattern of bits—for example, the picture displayed when you first run the IDE. You can use a graphical image to dress up your programs (see Figure 7.2).

Figure 7.2.
Bitmap displayed in an About box.

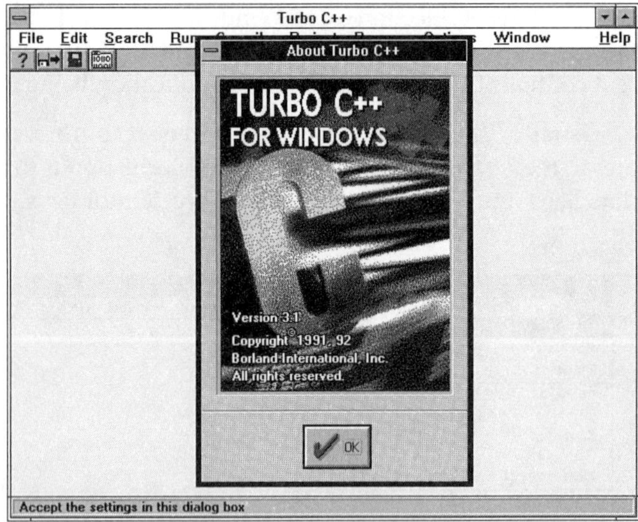

Your program also can create bitmaps. Windows Paintbrush (which comes with Windows) enables you to create and edit bitmaps. However, generally only the artistic person who wants an etch-a-sketch program to play with utilizes this. Professional programmers require more control of the size and attributes of the resulting bitmap.

Cursors

A cursor is a special bitmap that shows the user the location of the mouse on the screen. After you have created a cursor in the Resource Workshop cursor editor, you tell Windows the name of the cursor when you register a class. Then, Windows automatically updates the location of the cursor on the screen.

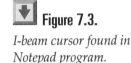

The most popular cursor is the pointed arrow. However, you saw the crosshair used in Chapter 6 and you probably have seen the I-beam used in an edit box (see Figure 7.3).

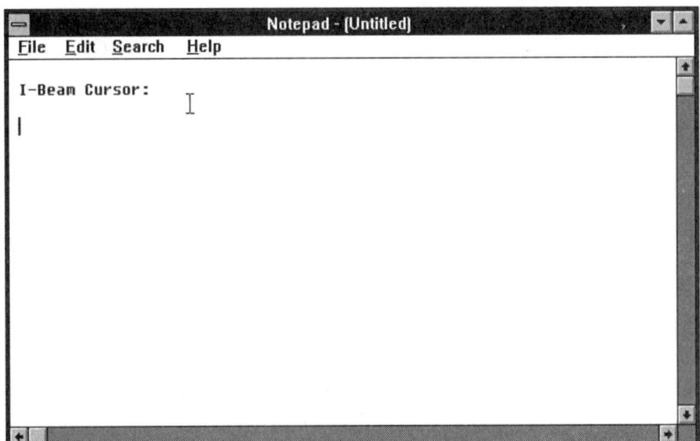

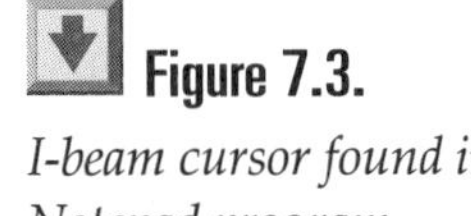

Figure 7.3.

I-beam cursor found in Notepad program.

Dialog Boxes

Dialog boxes are the most striking elements of Windows programming. Dialog boxes are pop-up windows that contain one or (usually) more interface objects the user interacts with.

Dialog boxes can also be used to display information. Generally, dialog boxes are displayed after the user makes a selection from a program's top-level menu. With the dialog box displayed, the user can make intelligent selections.

One of the most common dialog boxes is File Open. This box specifies a file that can be loaded by your application (see Figure 7.4). The user can interact with dialog boxes using both the keyboard and the mouse.

You create dialog boxes with the dialog editor. You can specify the controls and exactly how you want them displayed. Creating dialog boxes is an advanced technique covered in Chapter 13, "Dialog Boxes," and Chapter 14, "More About Dialog Boxes."

Figure 7.4.

A File Open dialog box from Cardfile.

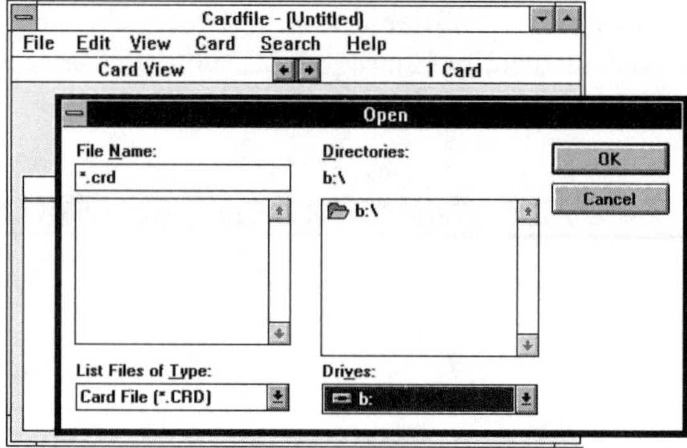

Icons

Icons are probably the features most people connect with graphical user interfaces. Although an icon can be displayed in a window as well as a dialog box, icons usually represent a Windows application when it has been minimized (see Figure 7.5).

Figure 7.5.

The Windows desktop with programs displayed as icons.

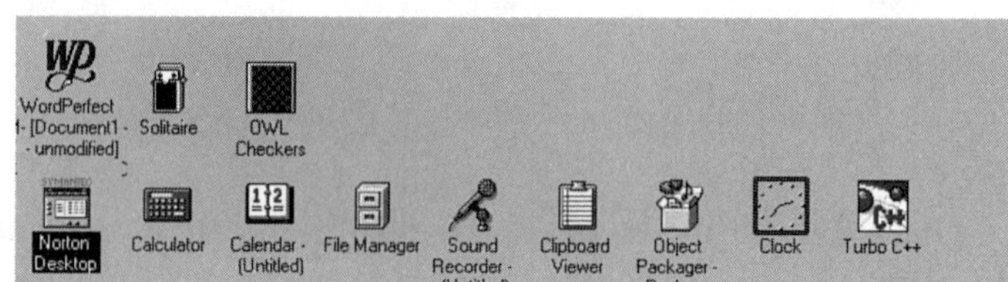

Similar to a cursor, an icon is a type of bitmap. Each icon has a predetermined size, is easier to work with than a normal bitmap, and serves a different purpose from a cursor. The icon editor is used to create and modify icons.

Windows comes with several predefined icons you can utilize in your program. You saw some of them employed with the `MessageBox` routine.

Menus

You might be surprised that menus are considered resources. You create menus outside a program and use them inside the program by specifying the name, either while registering the class or creating the window.

The menus in Windows are hierarchical; that is, they are pull-down menus (see Figure 7.6). Today, this is rather common; users expect most programs, even compilers, to have pull-down menus. Most text-based applications written for DOS have pull-down menus too. However, they are limited as compared to those offered by Windows.

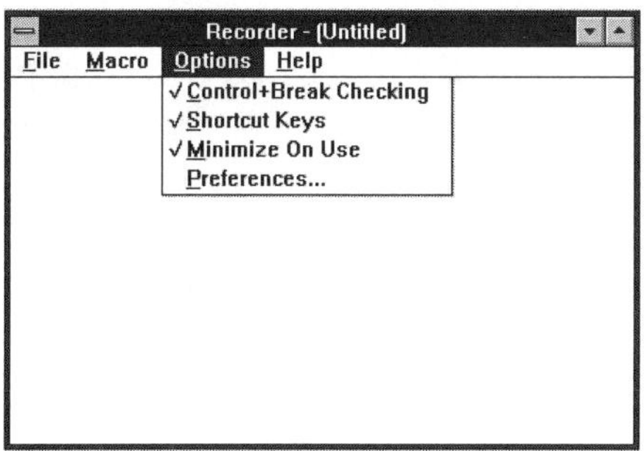

Figure 7.6.

Menus used in the window recorder program.

The menus supported by Windows make using the interface easier. As you begin to work with menus, you see some available features.

Strings

When I say strings are resources, I'm not talking about a character array. String resources are sections of text stored outside your program. This conserves memory because the string resource is loaded only when needed. Also, program messages can be changed easily because the text is outside the program.

Error messages usually are stored as strings. Then, when a program is sold on the international market, loading the string editor and changing the English strings to their foreign language counterparts is easy.

Looking at Icons

Now that you are familiar with the different types of resources in Windows, you can learn to use custom icons in your programs. Recall, to employ icons in a program, you specify the name of the icon to the WNDCLASS structure in the hIcon field before you apply the RegisterClass function as follows:

```
wndclass.hIcon = LoadIcon(0, IDI_APPLICATION);
```

This example utilizes the stock icon included with Windows. After you create a custom icon, employ a line similar to the following:

```
wndclass.hIcon = LoadIcon(hInstance, "IconName");
```

IconName refers to a unique name you give the icon in a resource script file. To include the resource script in your program, you must insert the filename of the resource file into your project.

Before you go further, look at dynamic icons.

Always an Icon

Notice, when some programs are displayed as icons, the icon changes. An example is the clock program. When it is minimized, the icon has the image of a clock that keeps time. How do you modify the icon like this, on the fly?

By specifying a zero value to the hIcon field to the window class, you give a special code that tells Windows not to display an icon; rather, the program displays images in the icon area.

This way, your program continues to receive WM_PAINT messages while in the icon state. Remember, you no longer have a large window to display output. You can display anything in the small area the icon occupies, just as you can display anything in your program's client area.

Listing 7.1, MEM.C, is an example program that lives as an icon. Listing 7.2 is the MEM.DEF module definition file.

Listing 7.1. MEM.C program displays memory information to an icon.

```
// MEM.C - Program which stays an icon and dynamically reports
//         the amount of memory available to Windows Program
//
// Programming Windows with Turbo C++ for Windows
// by Paul J. Perry

#define STRICT

#include <windowsx.h>
#include <stdlib.h>
#include <stdio.h>
#include <string.h>

#define ID_UPDATE 10


// Function Prototypes
LRESULT CALLBACK _export MainWndProc(HWND hWnd, UINT message,
                                     WPARAM wParam, LPARAM lParam);

/*******************************************/
#pragma argsused
int PASCAL WinMain(HINSTANCE hInstance, HINSTANCE hPrevInstance,
                   LPSTR lpCmdParam, int nCmdShow)
{
   char        ProgName[] = "Memory Status";
   HWND        hWnd;
   MSG         msg;
   WNDCLASS    wndclass;



   // Allow only ONE instance of program to be executed
   if (hPrevInstance)
      return FALSE;

   wndclass.lpszClassName = ProgName;
   wndclass.lpfnWndProc   = (WNDPROC) MainWndProc;
   wndclass.cbClsExtra    = 0;
   wndclass.cbWndExtra    = 0;
   wndclass.hInstance     = hInstance;

   // Tells Windows you want to paint your own icon
   wndclass.hIcon         = 0;

   wndclass.hCursor       = LoadCursor(NULL, IDC_ARROW);
```

continues

Listing 7.1. continued

```
   // Change background to be gray
   wndclass.hbrBackground = GetStockBrush(DKGRAY_BRUSH);

   wndclass.lpszMenuName  = NULL;
   wndclass.style         = CS_VREDRAW ¦ CS_HREDRAW;

   if (!RegisterClass(&wndclass)) exit(0);

   // Use extended window creation routine so you can make icon
   // always be displayed, even when another program is active
   hWnd = CreateWindowEx(WS_EX_TOPMOST, ProgName,"Memory Status",
                         WS_OVERLAPPEDWINDOW,
                         CW_USEDEFAULT, CW_USEDEFAULT,
                         CW_USEDEFAULT, CW_USEDEFAULT,
                         NULL, NULL, hInstance, NULL);


   // Create timer
   SetTimer(hWnd, ID_UPDATE, 1000, NULL);

   ShowWindow(hWnd, SW_SHOWMINIMIZED);
   UpdateWindow(hWnd);

   while (GetMessage(&msg, NULL, 0, 0))
   {
      TranslateMessage(&msg);
      DispatchMessage(&msg);
   }
   return msg.wParam;
}

/*******************************************/
LRESULT CALLBACK _export MainWndProc(HWND hWnd, UINT message,
                                     WPARAM wParam, LPARAM lParam)
{

   UINT  SysRes;
   DWORD FreeSpace;


   switch (message)
   {
      case WM_PAINT :
      {
         HDC         PaintDC;
         PAINTSTRUCT ps;
         char        buffer[25];
```

```
            PaintDC = BeginPaint(hWnd, &ps);

            // Set mode to transparent
            SetBkMode(PaintDC, TRANSPARENT);

            SysRes = GetFreeSystemResources(GFSR_SYSTEMRESOURCES);
            FreeSpace = GetFreeSpace(0);

            // GetFreeSpace returns the number of bytes.
            // Therefore, you have to
            // convert it to the number of megabytes of space
            // available!

            // Display Memory Information
            sprintf(buffer, "%f", FreeSpace / 1024.0 / 1024.0);
            TextOut(PaintDC, 1, 1,buffer, strlen(buffer));

            // Display Resource Information
            sprintf(buffer, "%d %%", SysRes);
            TextOut(PaintDC, 1, 18,buffer, strlen(buffer));

            EndPaint(hWnd, &ps);
            return 0;
        }

        case WM_QUERYOPEN :
        {
            // Show only as an icon.  Do not allow it to be maximized.
            return 0;
        }

        case WM_TIMER :
        {
            // Re-paint icon area
            InvalidateRect(hWnd, NULL, TRUE);
            return 0;
        }

        case WM_DESTROY :
        {
            KillTimer(hWnd, ID_UPDATE);
            PostQuitMessage(0);
            return 0;
        }
    }
    return DefWindowProc (hWnd, message, wParam, lParam);
}
```

Listing 7.2. MEM.DEF module definition file.

```
;
; MEM.DEF module definition file
;

DESCRIPTION    'Shows Memory Information'
NAME           MEM
EXETYPE        WINDOWS
STUB           'WINSTUB.EXE'
HEAPSIZE       1024
STACKSIZE      8192
CODE           PRELOAD MOVEABLE DISCARDABLE
DATA           PRELOAD MOVEABLE MULTIPLE
```

MEM.C shows a continually updated display of the amount of memory and the percentage of system resources available to Windows. The program calls the Windows API `GetFreeSpace` and `GetFreeSystemResources` functions to return the amount of free global memory and free system resources. Program Manager uses these same functions to display this information in its About box.

The program utilizes the extended window creation function (`CreateWindowEx`) to specify the `WS_EX_TOPMOST` style. This allows the icon to be visible, even if another program has the focus. After you have executed the program, it sits at the bottom line of your screen (see Figure 7.7) and reports the information commonly reported by Program Manager. The top line displays the amount of available memory, and the bottom line lists the amount of available system resources.

If you load another program (which takes its toll on system memory), the MEM.C program automatically is updated with the new amount of available memory. The program performs these updates by setting up a Windows timer. The timer is initialized after the window is created in the `WinMain` function.

Figure 7.7.
MEM.C shows free memory and system resources.

Windows Timers

After a timer is initialized, the program receives a `WM_TIMER` message in the interval specified in the call to the `SetTimer` function. For MEM.C, the interval is set to 1,000 milliseconds.

Every time the program receives a `WM_TIMER` message, the program sends itself a `WM_PAINT` message by calling the `InvalidateRect` function to invalidate the area. With the client area invalidated, the `WM_PAINT` case operates, and the area in the icon is redisplayed.

The background color is shown in dark gray because of the value set in the `hbrBackground` of the `wndclass` structure. Also, in the `WM_PAINT` processing, you tell Windows you want to display text without overwriting the background. This is done by setting the background mode (`SetBkMode`) to `TRANSPARENT`.

Windows has only 30 available timers. They are a limited resource. If Windows runs out of timers, the `SetTimer` function returns `FALSE`, and your program doesn't receive any `WM_TIMER` messages. If you are using several timers in a program, check the return value of `SetTimer` to be sure the call was carried out.

Finally, the MEM.C program does not allow itself to be opened or displayed as a regular window. Whenever a program wants to open an icon in a window, Windows sends a `WM_QUERYOPEN` message to the program's window procedure. The default window procedure normally processes the `WM_QUERYOPEN` message. In MEM.C, however, you catch the message and return a `0` value. This, in effect, tells Windows you do not want your icon to be displayed as a regular window.

You are almost ready to look at creating custom icons. First, though, you must know how to use the Resource Workshop.

Using the Resource Workshop

The Resource Workshop is the application you use to create and modify resources. It is a Windows application, so it works side by side with Turbo C++ for Windows. The Resource Workshop is included with all of Borland's Windows language products. Resource Workshop is probably the best resource editor available. Although I might be biased, if you examine the other resource editing tools on the market, you'll probably agree Resource Workshop is the best.

The Resource Workshop is an integrated package that enables you to work on and modify many types of resources.

Starting the Workshop

The Resource Workshop is started like most other Windows applications. You double-click the Workshop icon in program manager, or if you are outside Windows in DOS and want to load the Resource Workshop when Windows starts, type the following:

```
win workshop
```

As the program loads, the splash screen is displayed. After the program loads, the main menu is displayed (see Figure 7.8).

Figure 7.8.

Resource Workshop main menu.

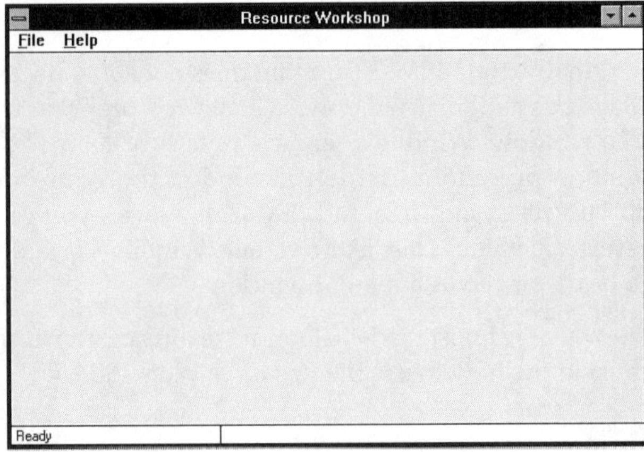

NOTE

If you examine the Resource Workshop splash screen (or choose the Help menu item and select About), you will see a globe with shapes around it. Take a closer look in the upper-left corner of the picture. Notice the constellation that forms the outline of a hat. This hat honors the creator of Resource Workshop. The author wears a hat that looks exactly like the one in the picture.

Using the Workshop

With the main menu displayed, you should notice only two main-level menu options. After you load a file, other menu options appear that enable you to work on your resources.

You choose the File menu and select the New Project menu option to start the resource editor. To use the resource editor on resources already started, choose the File menu and select Open Project. When you specify a filename, you can view and change all the resources for that program. If you change the type of the file (you learn about file types later), you can view resources from different types of files.

Check some resources now. Follow these steps to view the resources in the IDE of Turbo C++ for Windows:

1. Choose the File menu and select the Open Project option.
2. When the File Open dialog box is displayed, specify the drive and directory where Turbo C++ for Windows is installed along with the name of the executable file. For example, type C:\TCWIN\BIN\TCW.EXE.
3. When the file is loaded, a window is created that enables you to scroll through the types of resources available in the specified file.
4. Find the main heading for BITMAPS.

5. Underneath the heading for BITMAPS is a list of numbers, or identifiers, that identifies the resource to the program (see Figure 7.9). The identifiers in this box don't tell you much, but they do indicate interesting resources.

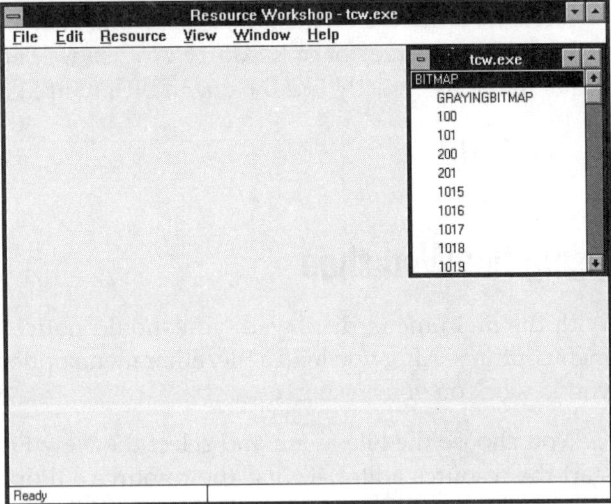

Figure 7.9. *Resource Workshop with bitmap resources in TCW.EXE.*

6. Double click 100. The bitmap editor displays for the associated bitmap (see Figure 7.10).
7. You can use the Resource Workshop to view resources in other Windows programs. Try digging into copies of other commercial programs you have to see what they are really made of.

Getting Help

Anytime you use the Resource Workshop, you can receive context-sensitive help by pressing F1 (as in the IDE).

When the Resource Workshop's main menu is displayed, choose the Help menu item. Different selections are available, depending on the kind of help you need. The Windows help engine displays additional information to facilitate use of the program (see Figure 7.11).

Figure 7.10.

The bitmap editor with familiar graphical image.

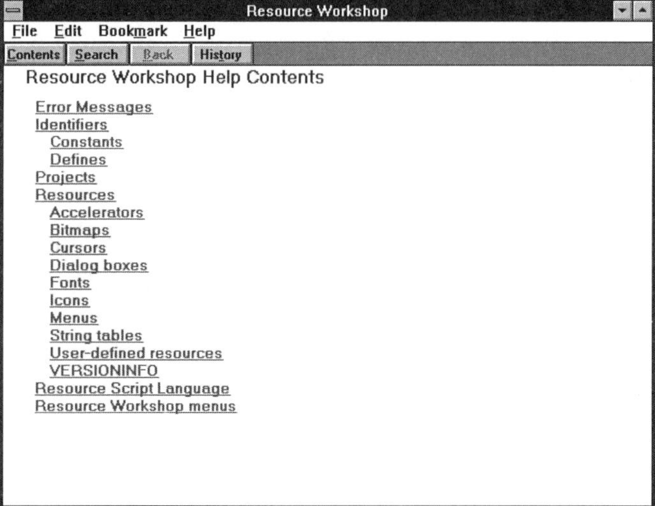

Figure 7.11.

Getting help using the resource Workshop.

File Types

When you open a file with the File Open command, you see it's different from most Windows programs' File Open dialog boxes. File type contains a drop-down combo box that lists a number of different file types the Resource Workshop can employ, including the following:

- BMP—Bitmap file. You can save only a single bitmap resource in this file type.
- CUR—Cursor file. You can save only a single cursor resource in this file type.
- DLG—Contains the ASCII description for a dialog box.
- DLL—Dynamic link library.
- DRV—A Windows device driver.
- EXE—Executable program file.
- FNT—Single font description.
- FON—Groups of font descriptions.
- ICO—Icon file. You can save only a single icon resource in this file type.
- RES—Compiled binary resource file.
- RC—Resource script files. These are uncompiled ASCII text files you cannot use directly. The resource compiler must compile them before you can use them in your program.

The various resource editors can load and save files in all the file formats applicable to that resource. For example, you cannot save a bitmap in an ICO file, because files with the extension ICO are for icons only.

Now that you know how to start and utilize the Resource Workshop, examine the use of the icon editor.

The Workshop Icon Editor

To start the icon editor, open the File menu and choose the New Project menu option. Then, specify the type of file you want. Go ahead and choose the ICO icon file type.

A dialog box is displayed that enables you to choose the resolution of the icon you want to create. It asks for the type of display device for which you plan to create the icon. Because Windows supports many types of video adapters, you can create several types of icons.

Windows' history is the reason for the different resolutions of icons. When designers first conceived icons in the Windows environment, color CGA displays were considered top of the line. Today, most people run Windows with at least a VGA monitor, and CGA is a distant memory of hackers.

The different resolutions of icons are targeted for different display devices. Each resolution of icons comes with the resource. When a program is executed, Windows chooses the appropriate resolution of icon to use at the time the program runs. If you want to support the largest number of users for your program and you include icons for every resolution, the result is proper-looking icons, no matter what type of display the user employs—even with Windows on an 80286 with 2M of memory and a trusty old CGA adapter.

TIP

When developing programs, you might prefer to use a single icon resolution. When it's time to distribute your program, and you have made the decision to support multiple display adapters, include icons that support the greatest number of resolutions possible.

I recommend using the default icon resolution. This is generally the highest resolution your video adapter can support creation of. This is usually a 32x32 icon. At least make the icon look good on your system!

After you select the icon resolution, the icon editor displays its main editing screen (see Figure 7.12).

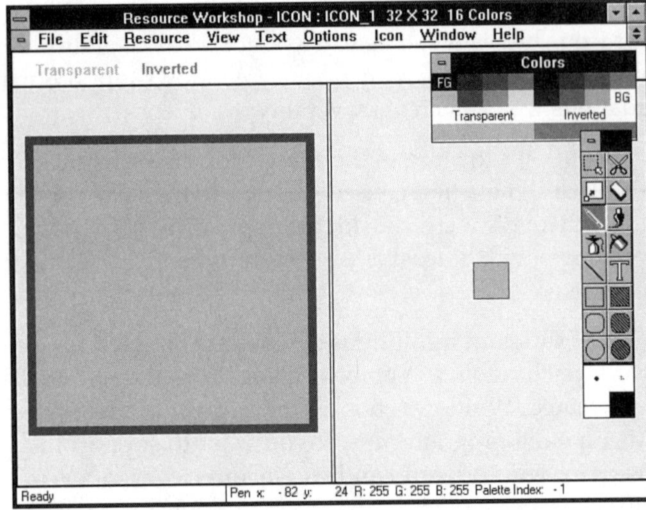

Figure 7.12.
Icon Editor window.

With the resolution specified, the icon editor screen clears. The icon editor window consists of the following parts:

- The movable *Toolbar*. It contains buttons you can select to carry out common operations quickly.
- The movable *Color Palette*. It begins on the right side of the screen.
- The *cursor editing area*. It is on the left side of the window.
- The *Menu bar*. It is at the top of the window under the title bar.
- *Graphics tools*. They are on the right and under the menu bar. The graphics tools mimic menu commands.
- The icon you are creating is displayed in actual size on the right side of the window.

An Icon Example

Are you annoyed by that nagging little question the Program Manager asks you each time you try to exit Windows: "Are you sure you want to exit?" I was, so I wrote a program that enables me to bypass that question.

The next program, STOP.C, is probably the shortest Windows program you'll ever write. Listing 7.3 contains the C source code for the program. Listing 7.4. contains the module definition file, and Listing 7.5 is the resource script. All three files should be included in a project file.

Listing 7.3. STOP.C program.

```
// STOP.C - Exit Windows without questions from Program Manager
//
// Programming Windows with Turbo C++ for Windows
// by Paul J. Perry

#include <windows.h>


/*******************************************/
#pragma argsused
int PASCAL WinMain(HINSTANCE hInstance, HINSTANCE hPrevInstance,
                   LPSTR lpCmdParam, int nCmdShow)
{
   ExitWindows(FALSE, 0);
   return (0);
}
```

Listing 7.4. STOP.DEF module definition file.

```
;
; STOP.DEF module definition file
;

DESCRIPTION   'Exit Windows'
NAME          STOP
EXETYPE       WINDOWS
STUB          'WINSTUB.EXE'
HEAPSIZE      1024
STACKSIZE     8192
CODE          PRELOAD MOVEABLE DISCARDABLE
DATA          PRELOAD MOVEABLE MULTIPLE
```

Listing 7.5. STOP.RC resource script file.

```
//
// STOP.RC resource script file
//

STOPICON ICON "stop.ico"
```

The source code for the program includes one API routine that automatically shuts down the system and exits to DOS. The `ExitWindows` function sends a `WM_QUERYENDSESSION` message to notify all currently running applications that the user is about to exit Windows.

Listing 7.5 contains the resource script for the program. It associates a symbolic name (`STOPICON`) with a disk filename (STOP.ICO). The line

```
STOPICON ICON "stop.ico"
```

instructs the compiler to include the specified icon resource file in the executable file of the program.

For the program to compile, you need a disk file with the icon resource. The ICO file to include is a fire-engine red stop sign that enables you to locate the icon quickly. The file is on the disk (see Figure 7.13), or you can try making a new one.

Figure 7.13.

The STOP icon.

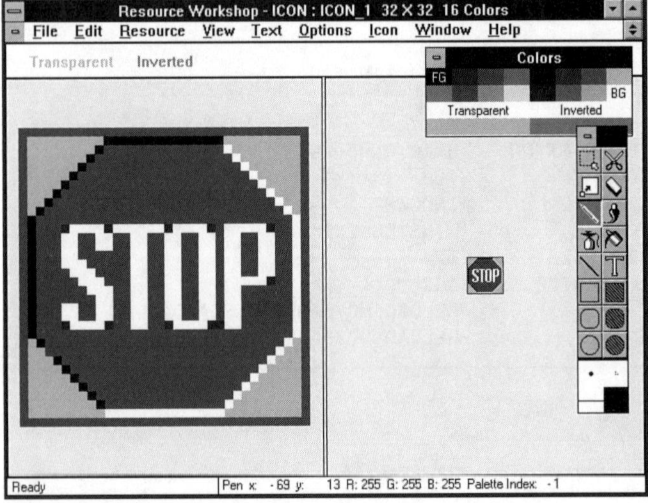

After you have all the files, compile the program by pressing F9. Don't execute it directly from the IDE, because you will be dropped out of Windows. Rather, add the program to a Program Manager group.

Notice, the icon is not associated with a window or referenced in the program. The Program Manager automatically associates the icon with the program when you create a program item (see Figure 7.14).

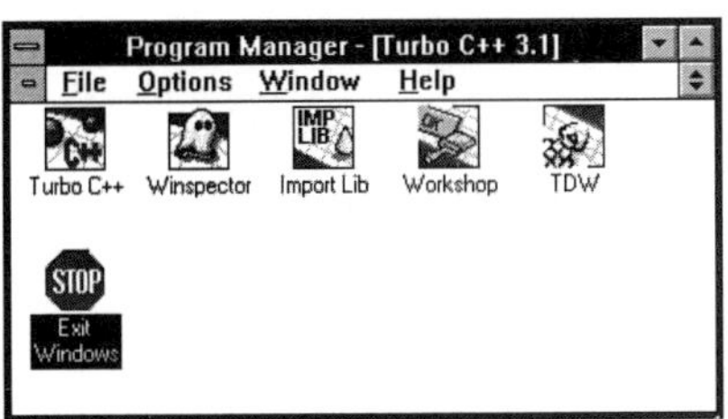

Figure 7.14.

The Program Manager group with the STOP program displayed.

Icons Attached to Windows

The STOP.C program associates an icon with a program. However, the icon name was never used in the program. The next program (Listings 7.6, 7.7, and 7.8) associates a window to the icon with the `LoadIcon` call while initializing the `WNDCLASS` structure type.

Listing 7.6. CUSTICO.C program that associates a window with a custom icon.

```
// CUSTICO.C - Windows program with an icon
//
// Programming Windows with Turbo C++ for Windows
// by Paul J. Perry

#define STRICT

#include <windowsx.h>
#include <stdlib.h>

// Function Prototypes
LRESULT CALLBACK _export MainWndProc(HWND hWnd, UINT message,
                                     WPARAM wParam, LPARAM lParam);
```

continues

Listing 7.6. continued

```
/*******************************************/
#pragma argsused
int PASCAL WinMain(HINSTANCE hInstance, HINSTANCE hPrevInstance,
                   LPSTR lpCmdParam, int nCmdShow)
{
   char        ProgName[] = "Window with an Icon";
   HWND        hWnd;
   MSG         msg;

   if (!hPrevInstance)
   {
      WNDCLASS    wndclass;

      wndclass.lpszClassName = ProgName;
      wndclass.lpfnWndProc   = (WNDPROC) MainWndProc;
      wndclass.cbClsExtra    = 0;
      wndclass.cbWndExtra    = 0;
      wndclass.hInstance     = hInstance;

      // Specify the name of cursor to the Window class
      wndclass.hIcon         = LoadIcon(hInstance, "NEWICON");

      wndclass.hCursor       = LoadCursor(NULL, IDC_ARROW);
      wndclass.hbrBackground = (HBRUSH) (COLOR_WINDOW + 1);
      wndclass.lpszMenuName  = NULL;
      wndclass.style         = CS_VREDRAW ¦ CS_HREDRAW;

      if (!RegisterClass(&wndclass)) exit(0);
   }

   hWnd = CreateWindow(ProgName,"Window with an Icon",
                       WS_OVERLAPPEDWINDOW,
                       CW_USEDEFAULT, CW_USEDEFAULT,
                       CW_USEDEFAULT, CW_USEDEFAULT,
                       NULL, NULL, hInstance, NULL);

   // Show the window as initially minimized
   ShowWindow(hWnd, SW_SHOWMINIMIZED);
   UpdateWindow(hWnd);

   while (GetMessage(&msg, NULL, 0, 0))
   {
      TranslateMessage(&msg);
      DispatchMessage(&msg);
   }
```

```
   return msg.wParam;
}

/*******************************************/
LRESULT CALLBACK _export MainWndProc(HWND hWnd, UINT message,
                                      WPARAM wParam, LPARAM lParam)
{
   switch (message)
   {
      case WM_PAINT :
      {
         HDC         PaintDC;
         RECT        rect;
         PAINTSTRUCT ps;

         PaintDC = BeginPaint(hWnd, &ps);
         GetClientRect(hWnd, &rect);

         DrawText(PaintDC, "Minimize Window to See Icon",
                  -1, &rect, DT_SINGLELINE | DT_CENTER | DT_VCENTER);

         EndPaint(hWnd, &ps);
         return 0;
      }

      case WM_DESTROY :
      {
         PostQuitMessage(0);
         return 0;
      }
   }
   return DefWindowProc (hWnd, message, wParam, lParam);
}
```

Listing 7.7. CUSTICO.DEF module definition file.

```
;
; CUSTICO.DEF module definition file
;

DESCRIPTION   'Window with a minimized icon'
NAME          CUSTICO
EXETYPE       WINDOWS
```

continues

Listing 7.7. continued

```
STUB            'WINSTUB.EXE'
HEAPSIZE        1024
STACKSIZE       8192
CODE            PRELOAD MOVEABLE DISCARDABLE
DATA            PRELOAD MOVEABLE MULTIPLE
```

Listing 7.8. CUSTICO.RC resource script file.

```
//
// CUSTICO.RC resource script
//

NEWICON ICON "custico.ico"
```

The CUSTICO.C program initially is displayed as an icon with the use of the `ShowWindow` call, as follows:

```
ShowWindow(hWnd, SW_SHOWMINIMIZED);
```

The `SW_SHOWMINIMIZED` constant forces the window to be displayed as an icon. However, you can restore the window. If you do, a message tells you how to view the icon.

The CUSTICO.RC resource script file contains the line

```
NEWICON ICON "custico.ico"
```

which associates the filename CUSTICO.ICO with the name NEWICON. In the source code, reference the NEWICON name with the LoadIcon call as follows:

```
wndclass.hIcon          = LoadIcon(hInstance, "NEWICON");
```

You pass the handle of the instance of the program and then the identifier in quotes. The icon has the shape of an umbrella (see Figure 7.15).

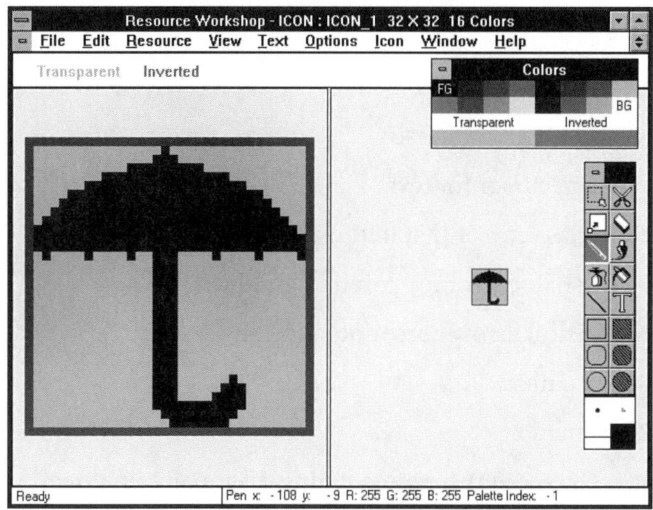

Figure 7.15.
The CUSTICO.C program icon.

Looking at Cursors

The next type of resource you look at is cursors. In a DOS text mode program, the cursor shows the location for the keyboard input. In Windows, cursors track the mouse location.

Cursors are bitmap images displayed on the screen. The cursor is nondestructive; that is, when the cursor moves, it leaves no trail.

Cursors are different from icons: they contain a hot-spot. The hot spot is the point that defines the active location of the cursor.

Cursors are specified similarly to icons in a window class. You use the `LoadCursor` command to return a handle to a cursor that is given to the `hCursor` field of the window class, as follows:

```
wndclass.hCursor = LoadCursor(hInstance, "CursorName");
```

With the cursor specified in the window class for a window, when the cursor moves across that window, the operating environment automatically loads the cursor from the EXE file and displays it at the appropriate location on the screen.

System Cursors

Windows comes with 11 predefined cursors:

- IDC_ARROW—Standard arrow cursor.
- IDC_IBEAM—I-beam cursor for text.
- IDC_WAIT—Hourglass cursor that tells user to wait.
- IDC_CROSS—Crosshair cursor for painting graphics.
- IDC_UPARROW—Vertical arrow cursor pointing straight up.
- IDC_SIZE—Sizing cursor.
- IDC_ICON—Blank cursor.
- IDC_SIZENWSE—Cursor with arrow pointing diagonally (in directions northwest and southeast), used to resize window.
- IDC_SIZENESW—Cursor with arrow pointing diagonally (in directions northeast and southwest), used to resize window.
- IDC_SIZEWE—Double arrow cursor pointing horizontally, used to resize window.
- IDC_SIZENS—Double arrow cursor pointing vertically, used to resize window.

You probably are familiar with most of the cursors if you use Windows at all. To employ a predefined cursor, set the instance parameter to 0 and utilize the previously listed predefined identifier as the name of the cursor, as follows:

```
wndclass.hCursor = LoadCursor(0, IDC_IBEAM);
```

This tells Windows to use the I-beam cursor when the cursor is moved over the window that is based on this class.

The Workshop Cursor Editor

The cursor editor is similar to the icon editor. When you start it, you must define the cursor resolution. The same principles apply for cursors as for icons. Windows uses the best resolution for the display it is running on. Again, I recommend using the highest resolution you can create on your system.

With the cursor editor displayed, the same highlights of the icon editor are displayed on the screen (see Figure 7.16). The big difference is you have a menu option for selecting the cursor hot spot. To access the Set hot spot dialog box, choose the Cursor Menu option and then select Set Hot Spot. The dialog box enables you to enter the x- and y-pixel coordinates of the cursor hot spot.

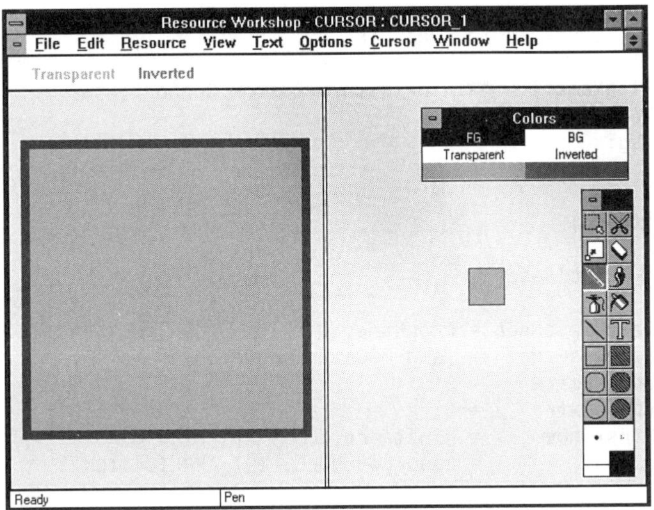

Figure 7.16.

The Resource Workshop cursor editor.

As an example, the next program, CUSTCUR.C in Listing 7.9, uses a custom cursor for its window class. Listing 7.10 contains the CUSTCUR.DEF module definition file, and Listing 7.11 contains the CUSTCUR.RC resource script file. Include these three files in your project file.

Listing 7.9. CUSTCUR.C program with a custom cursor.

```
// CUSTCUR.C - Windows with its own custom cursor
//
// Programming Windows with Turbo C++ for Windows
// by Paul J. Perry
```

continues

Listing 7.9. continued

```
#define STRICT

#include <windowsx.h>
#include <stdlib.h>

// Function Prototypes
LRESULT CALLBACK _export MainWndProc(HWND hWnd, UINT message,
                                    WPARAM wParam, LPARAM lParam);

/*******************************************/
#pragma argsused
int PASCAL WinMain(HINSTANCE hInstance, HINSTANCE hPrevInstance,
                   LPSTR lpCmdParam, int nCmdShow)
{
   char        ProgName[] = "Window With a Custom Cursor";
   HWND        hWnd;
   MSG         msg;


   if (!hPrevInstance)
   {
      WNDCLASS    wndclass;

      wndclass.lpszClassName = ProgName;
      wndclass.lpfnWndProc   = (WNDPROC) MainWndProc;
      wndclass.cbClsExtra    = 0;
      wndclass.cbWndExtra    = 0;
      wndclass.hInstance     = hInstance;
      wndclass.hIcon         = LoadIcon(NULL, IDI_APPLICATION);

      // Specify custom cursor to the window class
      wndclass.hCursor       = LoadCursor(hInstance, "NEWCUR");

      wndclass.hbrBackground = (HBRUSH) (COLOR_WINDOW + 1);
      wndclass.lpszMenuName  = NULL;
      wndclass.style         = CS_VREDRAW | CS_HREDRAW;

      if (!RegisterClass(&wndclass)) exit(0);
   }

   hWnd = CreateWindow(ProgName,"Window With a Custom Cursor",
                       WS_OVERLAPPEDWINDOW,
                       CW_USEDEFAULT, CW_USEDEFAULT,
                       CW_USEDEFAULT, CW_USEDEFAULT,
                       NULL, NULL, hInstance, NULL);
```

```
   ShowWindow(hWnd, SW_SHOWMAXIMIZED);
   UpdateWindow(hWnd);

   while (GetMessage(&msg, NULL, 0, 0))
   {
      TranslateMessage(&msg);
      DispatchMessage(&msg);
   }
   return msg.wParam;
}

/*********************************************/
LRESULT CALLBACK _export MainWndProc(HWND hWnd, UINT message,
                                     WPARAM wParam, LPARAM lParam)
{
   switch (message)
   {
      case WM_PAINT :
      {
         HDC         PaintDC;
         RECT        rect;
         PAINTSTRUCT ps;

         PaintDC = BeginPaint(hWnd, &ps);
         GetClientRect(hWnd, &rect);

         DrawText(PaintDC, "Move Mouse to Locate Custom Cursor",
                  -1, &rect, DT_SINGLELINE | DT_CENTER |
                  DT_VCENTER);

         EndPaint(hWnd, &ps);
         return 0;
      }

      case WM_DESTROY :
      {
         PostQuitMessage(0);
         return 0;
      }
   }
   return DefWindowProc (hWnd, message, wParam, lParam);
}
```

Listing 7.10. CUSTCUR.DEF module definition file.

```
;
; CUSTCUR.DEF module definition file
;

DESCRIPTION    'Window With a Custom Cursor'
NAME           CUSTCUR
EXETYPE        WINDOWS
STUB           'WINSTUB.EXE'
HEAPSIZE       1024
STACKSIZE      8192
CODE           PRELOAD MOVEABLE DISCARDABLE
DATA           PRELOAD MOVEABLE MULTIPLE
```

Listing 7.11. CUSTCUR.RC resource script file.

```
//
// CUSTCUR.RC resource script file
//

NEWCUR CURSOR "custcur.cur"
```

The window initially is displayed as maximized by passing the `SW_SHOWMAXIMIZED` constant to the `ShowWindow` function. You still can restore the window to a smaller size and then resize it.

Observe how the cursor is specified in the resource script file:

```
NEWCUR CURSOR "custcur.cur"
```

The keyword `CURSOR` tells the compiler that you associated a disk filename (CUSTCUR.CUR) with an identifier (`NEWCUR`).

Reference the identifier in the LoadCursor function, as follows:

```
wndclass.hCursor = LoadCursor(hInstance, "NEWCUR");
```

Again, you pass the handle to the instance of the program and the identifier specified in the resource script file. You must have a copy of CUSTCUR.CUR available. The one I created is a curved arrow (see Figure 7.17).

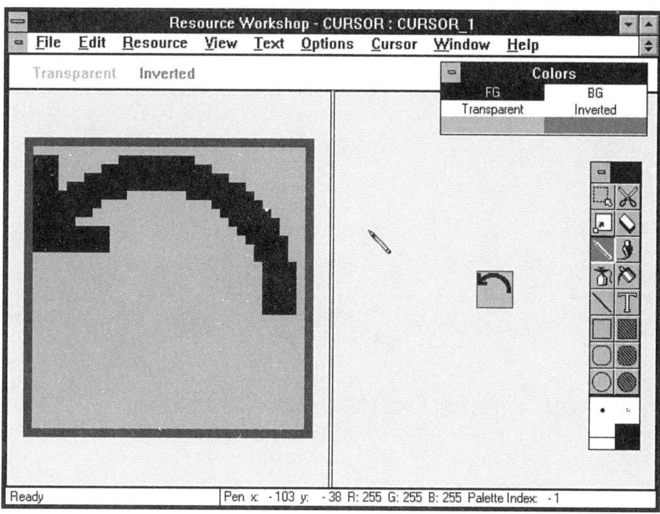

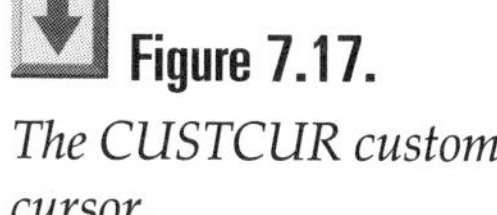
Figure 7.17.
The CUSTCUR custom cursor.

As you can see, it's easy to add your custom cursor or icon to your program's window. Now that you have seen this done in traditional C programs, examine doing it in a program based on the OWL.

Using Cursors and Icons in an OWL Program

To specify the new icons and cursors to the `WNDCLASS` structure, you must override the `GetClassName` and `GetWindowClass` member functions. The next program, ICOCUR.CPP, shows how to do this. Listing 7.12 contains the ICOCUR.CPP source code, Listing 7.13 contains the ICOCUR.DEF module definition file, and Listing 7.14 contains the ICOCUR.RC resource script file.

Listing 7.12. ICOCUR.CPP ObjectWindows Library program with custom icons and cursors.

```
// ICOCUR.CPP - Program based on ObjectWindows Library which
//              contains its own custom icon and cursor
//
// Programming Windows with Turbo C++ for Windows
// by Paul J. Perry

#define WIN31
#define STRICT

#include <owl.h>
#include <windowsx.h>

// Class Declarations

/*******************************************/
class TOwlApp : public TApplication
{
   public :
      TOwlApp (LPSTR AName, HINSTANCE hInstance, HINSTANCE
               hPrevInstance,  LPSTR CmdLine, int CmdShow) :
               TApplication(AName, hInstance, hPrevInstance,
               CmdLine, CmdShow) { } ;

   virtual void InitMainWindow();
};


/*******************************************/
class TMainWindow : public TWindow
{
   public :
      TMainWindow(PTWindowsObject AParent, LPSTR ATitle)
                        : TWindow(AParent, ATitle) { };
      virtual void GetWindowClass(WNDCLASS& wndclass);
      virtual LPSTR GetClassName();
      virtual void Paint(HDC PaintDC, PAINTSTRUCT &PaintInfo);
};


// Class Member Functions

/*******************************************/
void TMainWindow::GetWindowClass(WNDCLASS& wndclass)
```

```
{
   TWindow::GetWindowClass(wndclass);

   wndclass.hIcon = LoadIcon(GetApplication()->hInstance,
                             "NEWICO");
   wndclass.hCursor = LoadCursor(GetApplication()->hInstance,
                                 "NEWCUR");

}

/*******************************************/
LPSTR TMainWindow::GetClassName()
{
   return "New_ICO_CUR_Class";
}

/*******************************************/
void TOwlApp::InitMainWindow()
{
   MainWindow = new TMainWindow(NULL, Name);
}

/*******************************************/
#pragma argsused
void TMainWindow::Paint(HDC PaintDC, PAINTSTRUCT &PaintInfo)
{
   RECT rect;

   GetClientRect(HWindow, &rect);

   DrawText(PaintDC, "Custom Icons and Cursors in an OWL program",
            -1, &rect,
            DT_SINGLELINE | DT_CENTER | DT_VCENTER);

}

/*******************************************/
int PASCAL WinMain(HINSTANCE hInstance, HINSTANCE hPrevInstance,
                   LPSTR lpCmdLine, int nCmdShow)
{

   TOwlApp ThisApp("OWL Program with Custom Icons and Cursors",
                   hInstance, hPrevInstance, lpCmdLine, nCmdShow);
   ThisApp.Run();
   return ThisApp.Status;

}
```

Listing 7.13. ICOCUR.DEF module definition file.

```
;
; ICOCUR.DEF module definition file
;

DESCRIPTION    'OWL Program With Custom Icon and Cursor'
NAME           ICOCUR
EXETYPE        WINDOWS
STUB           'WINSTUB.EXE'
HEAPSIZE       1024
STACKSIZE      8192
CODE           PRELOAD MOVEABLE DISCARDABLE
DATA           PRELOAD MOVEABLE MULTIPLE
```

Listing 7.14. ICOCUR.RC resource script file.

```
//
// ICOCUR.RC resource script file
//

NEWICO ICON "CUSTICO.ICO"
NEWCUR CURSOR "CUSTCUR.CUR"
```

For simplicity, the ICOCUR.CPP program uses the CUSTICO.ICO icon (from CUSTICO.C) and the CUSTCUR.CUR cursor (from CUSTCUR.C).

The `GetWindowClass` member function first calls the base class member function. It then reassigns the `hIcon` and `hCursor` fields of the `wndclass` structure, as follows:

```
wndclass.hIcon = LoadIcon(GetApplication()->hInstance, "NEWICO");
wndclass.hCursor = LoadCursor(GetApplication()->hInstance,
"NEWCUR");
```

To get a copy of the handle to the instance, you must use the `GetApplication` function call. (The `hInstance` value is part of `TApplication` and available only to it.) It's part of the encapsulation that the OWL handles.

The ICOCUR.RC resource script file has two lines that reference the identifiers for the new icon and the new cursor. It looks like this:

```
NEWICO ICON "CUSTICO.ICO"
NEWCUR CURSOR "CUSTCUR.CUR"
```

When you load this file in Resource Workshop, it tells you the two resources available and enables you to edit them. In some ways, it's nice to let Resource Workshop manage writing the files for you; however, you must understand the behind-the-scenes activities.

When the ICOCUR.EXE program executes, it is displayed as a regular window. You can move the cursor and see how it looks. If you move the cursor outside the client area, the cursor changes as it's defined for the other window. When you minimize the program, you see it as an icon.

What You Have Learned

This chapter has covered valuable information about resources. You examined how to utilize custom icons and cursors in a program. You learned how to use the Resource Workshop to create cursors and icons. You saw how to associate an icon and a cursor with a window. You also learned how to use custom icons and cursors in a program based on the OWL.

This chapter examined the following important points:

- Resources are elements that users employ to interact with Windows. These are defined outside a program's source code and are created and modified with the Resource Workshop.
- The seven types of Windows resources are accelerator keys, bitmaps, cursors, dialog boxes, icons, menus, and strings.
- To include a resource script in your program, you must add the RC file to your program's project file. The resource script usually contains lines that reference other types of resource files.
- To utilize a custom icon in your program, specify the icon name in the window class before you register it. You use the `LoadIcon` routine to return a handle to the icon.

- Cursors are similar to icons, except that they have a hot spot that identifies the current location of the cursor. You use the `LoadCursor` routine to return a handle to a cursor.
- To utilize your custom icons or cursors in a program based on the ObjectWindows library, you must override the `GetClassName` and `GetWindowClass` member functions. In the `GetClassName` function, you return a unique name that's used as the new window class name. In the `GetWindowClass` function, you modify fields found in the `wndclass` data structure.

A First Look at Resources

CHAPTER

7

8 ADDING MENUS TO YOUR PROGRAM

IN THIS CHAPTER

- How menus are implemented in a Windows program, and how to add them to your program.
- What is required to create a menu resource using the Resource Workshop menu editor.
- How to process menu selections in traditional C programs that use message crackers.
- What you have to do to define message response functions in programs based on the ObjectWindows library so that class member functions are called automatically when a menu selection is made.
- What an accelerator key is and how it is implemented in C and C++ programs.
- How to use the Resource Workshop accelerator editor to create customized accelerator keys for your program.

This chapter covers the use of menus in your programs. You learn how menus are implemented and how your program has to work to have a menu and process menu commands.

Using Menus in Programs

Menus are the key method used by most Windows programs to receive commands from the user. A menu belonging to a window is displayed immediately under the title bar (see Figure 8.1). The menu bar is usually called the program's "main menu."

Figure 8.1.

Turbo C++ for Window's main menu with the File menu selected.

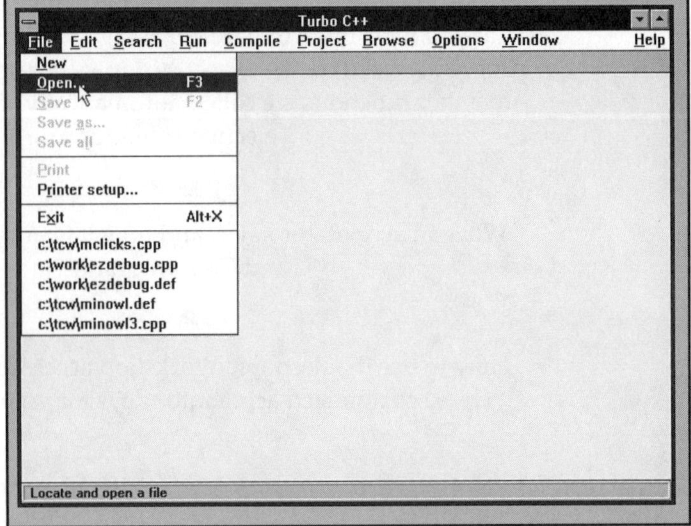

When you make a selection from the main menu, a drop-down submenu (or pop-up menu) is usually displayed. Windows takes care of processing mouse actions while selecting menu items and moving the menu highlight bar to the appropriate selection. A menu can be layered so that several pop-up menus are displayed. You want to limit the use of menu layering in your programs; when the menu structure goes too deep, it's hard for the user to access menu options. Also, a dialog box is a better way to request information when many layers are introduced into a menu tree.

Menu items usually have a single, underlined letter for each menu item. The key designated by the menu letter can be pressed by the user to select the menu item. If the menu item is a main menu, the user presses the Alt key in combination with the menu letter. If the menu is a pop-up menu, the user presses the letter of the key identified with the menu selection.

Menus may also have *separator bars* that divide menu items into logical groups of commands. A program can also make use of a checkmark that is displayed next to the menu item. The checkmark usually acts as a toggle between when an option is selected and when it is not.

Programs that use the default window procedure already have a menu. The *system menu* is located at the far left of the title bar. This is actually a pop-up menu that Windows controls for your program. The system menu enables the user to resize the window, close the window, and switch to a different program using the Task Manager. A program can also add custom items to the system menu.

Menus contain visual clues that tell the user the result of a menu selection. Usually, an ellipsis (...) appears when the menu item leads to a dialog box. An Arrow indicates that a menu item leads to a nested menu, in which case there are several layers of menu items.

Adding a menu to a program is easy. You specify the menu name when specifying the window class `hMenuName` field, as follows:

```
wndcls.lpszMenuName   =   "MenuName";
```

If you want to specify a menu for a single window in a class, you specify the menu when creating the menu, using the `LoadMenu` command to return a handle to the menu, as follows:

```
hWnd = CreateWindow(AppName, "Window Name",
                    WS_OVERLAPPEDWINDOW,
                    CW_USEDEFAULT, CW_USEDEFAULT,
                    CW_USEDEFAULT, CW_USEDEFAULT,
// This is the line you want to be aware of:
                    0, LoadMenu(hInstance, "MenuName"),

                    hInstance, NULL);
```

Programs that use ObjectWindows process menus differently. You learn how they work later in this chapter.

Once you have added the menus to the Window class or in the call to `CreateWindow`, they automatically are displayed under the window title bar for your program. Your program then must respond appropriately to the menu items.

To respond to a menu item, you associate a menu item with an integer number. When the user selects a menu, your program's window procedure receives a message notifying it that a menu item has been selected. Your program then processes the menu item by displaying a dialog box, setting the value of a variable, or by carrying out some task.

Using menus in your program is a two-step process. First, you separately create the menu in the Resource Workshop menu editor. After the menu is created, you modify your source code to respond to menu message commands. Because menus are resources, you use the Resource Workshop menu editor and include a description of the menu inside an RC resource script file. Then (as with other types of resources) you include the resource file in your program's project file.

Resource Scripts

Menus are the first type of resource you have examined closely that can actually be described and specified by a resource script file. Chapter 7, "A First Look at Resources," only deals with referring to a cursor or icon file name in the resource file. It's difficult to describe how an icon looks with text. In this chapter, you learn how to describe the entire menu structure in an RC resource script (rather than just a reference to a binary file that contains the menu). Remember, the resource script file always has the extension .RC. It is an ASCII text file that specifies how the resource appears.

Although you can create your entire resource script in an ASCII text editor, it's easier to create menus in the Resource Workshop menu editor. The Resource Workshop menu editor enables you to test interactively how the menu works. You often use the Resource Workshop menu editor to come up with the basic idea of the menu, and then use a regular text editor (like an IDE editor window) to make small adjustments to the menu description.

Turbo C++ for Windows includes an integrated resource compiler, which is part of the Integrated Development Environment. The Resource Workshop also compiles an RC script file into a RES binary resource file. However, it's more convenient to use the IDE for the entire compile and link process.

TIP

In Version 3.0 of Turbo C++ for Windows, you have to use a command line resource compiler called RC.EXE to compile resource scripts into binary resource files (.RES extension). This is not necessary in Version 3.1. The integrated resource compiler (inside the IDE) takes a resource script included in a project (with the extension RC) and compiles it into a binary resource file (.RES extension).

As an alternate method, rather than include the RC script file in a project, you can include the .RES binary form of the script. If you work with the RES file directly in Resource Workshop, the resources never have to be compiled because they are saved in binary format. However, in relaying the structure of the menu, I use the RC text file in this book, because the binary versions of the resources would be inconvenient to include.

Finally, there is another trick for users of Turbo C++ for Windows Version 3.0. Go into Resource Workshop, open the RC file, then choose the Preferences option from the File menu. In the Preferences dialog box, put a checkmark next to the RES option (see Figure 8.2). Now whenever you save your project, Resource Workshop always saves two versions of the file. It saves the text version of the RC script and the binary RES form of that same file.

NOTE

In the next section, you take a look at creating your own custom menus using the menu editor.

Figure 8.2.

Resource Workshop Preferences dialog box.

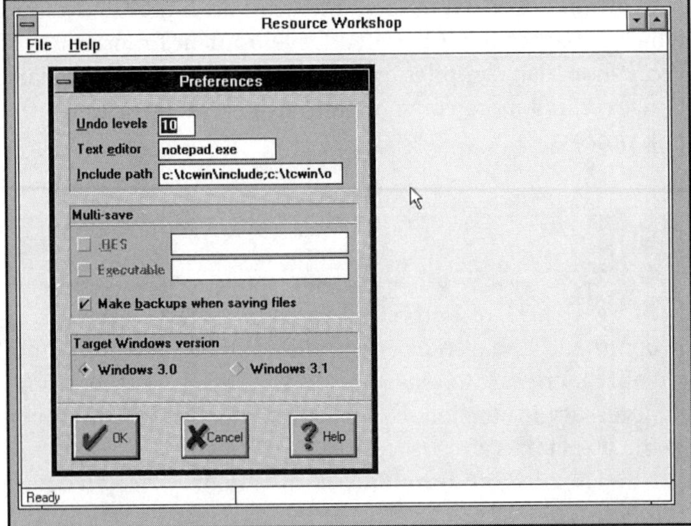

The Workshop Menu Editor

Use the menu editor by starting Resource Workshop, and then beginning a new resource script by selecting the File menu and choosing the New Project menu option. To demonstrate some of the Resource Workshop features, we will walk through a sample session next. The New Project dialog box is displayed, which enables you to select the type of file you want to work with (see Figure 8.3). Choose a file type of RC.

Give the project a name by selecting the File menu and selecting the Save Project menu option. At this point, you can give it any name.

I mentioned earlier that each menu item (for example, the Copy option under the Edit menu) is identified by a unique integer number. In your Window Procedure, check the identifier of a menu item to see which menu selection the user chose.

Although you can refer to a menu item as number 9, most programmers use features of the C programming language to make identifying the number easier. Programs that rely on menu commands contain a header file with `#define` statements that relate the number 9 with an identifier, such as `IDM_EDITCOPY`. After all, it's easier to remember what `IDM_EDITCOPY` refers to

(IDM_ stands for *i*dentification of a *m*enu *i*tem) rather than what the number 9 refers to. Therefore, you first want to add a header file to your resource project. Go to the File menu and select Add to Project. The Add file to project dialog box is displayed (see Figure 8.4). You want to specify the name of a header file (with the .h file extension) that automatically is added to the project. If the header file is not already present, Resource Workshop checks to see whether you want to create the file.

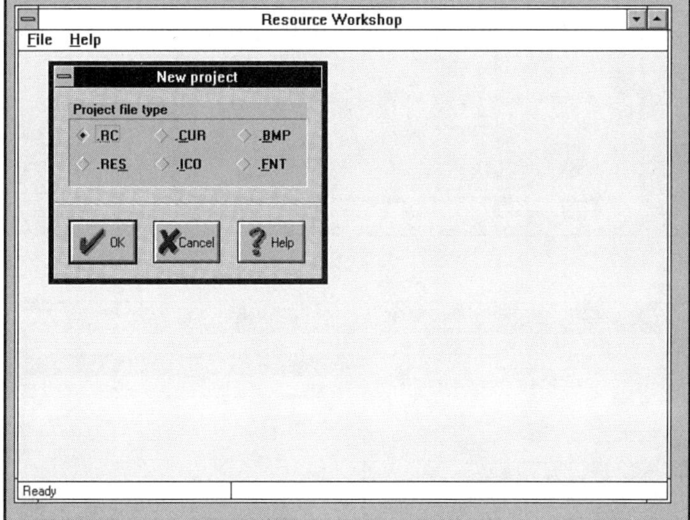

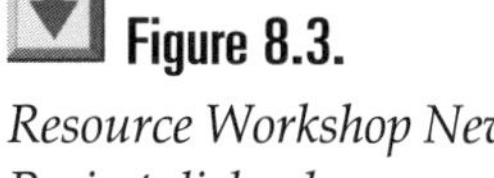

Figure 8.3.

Resource Workshop New Project dialog box.

Adding a header file to the resource file is an important step. A header file enables you to identify menu items with a text identifier, and Resource Workshop takes care of the actual integer values. You later include this header file in your source code so that you can use the same identifiers you defined here.

To start the menu editor from Resource Workshop, choose the Resource option and select New. When you choose the Menu option from the listbox, the menu editor is loaded and displayed (see Figure 8.5).

Figure 8.4.

The Add file to project dialog box.

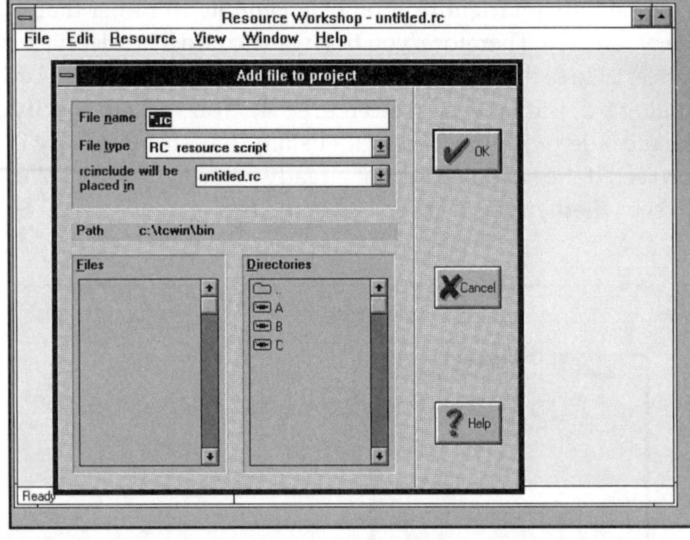

Figure 8.5.

The menu editor window.

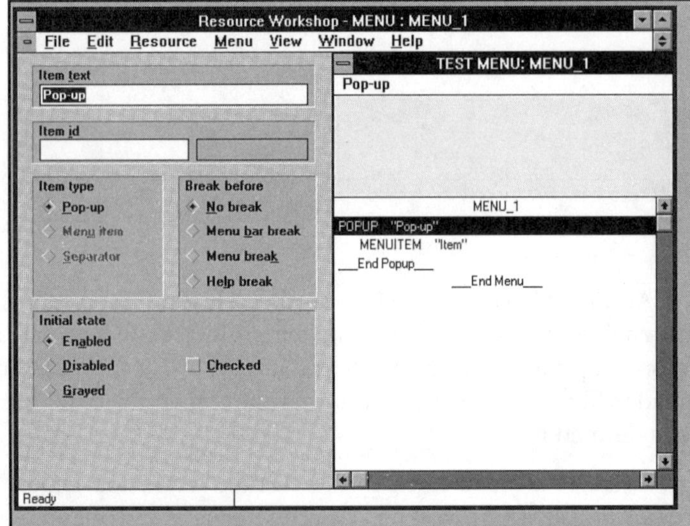

The menu editor is made up of three parts. The left side of the window enables you to enter information about the current menu selection, including the name and the identifier. The upper-right side of the window creates a sample menu that you use to test the menu you're creating. The lower-right side of the screen shows what the resource script for the menu looks like.

As you create your menu, you can switch to the TEST MENU window and dynamically test how your program's menu acts. It is one of the most convenient features of the menu editor.

When the menu editor starts out, it creates a default menu with the word *pop-up* in the menu bar and *item* as the first pull-down menu item. You start by modifying these values, and then you usually add more menu items to the menu.

Remember that there are two main parts to a menu item. The first is the menu text, and the second is the menu identifier. The identifier is an integer value that is used by your program to tell when the menu has been selected. In your case, you are going to assign an uppercase identifier to the integer value and store that in your header file.

To start a menu resource, begin typing the name of the menu item in the 'Item text' edit box. This item is going to be top level. The top-level menu items are usually called pop-up menu items; they are identified by the word *POPUP* in the resource script. The POPUP menus almost always have a pull-down menu, from which you actually choose your menu items. Because the POPUP menu item leads to a lower-level menu, it does not have an identifier associated with it.

To move to the next menu item, highlight the item in the resource script and then click the Item text edit box. You can type a new string for the first item of the pull-down menu item. This time, press the Tab key and enter the text description of the identifier in the Item id edit box. You can type something like `IDM_MYMENU` and press Enter. The Resource Workshop asks whether you want to create a new identifier (see Figure 8.6).

Choose Yes, and then a New Identifier dialog box is displayed (see Figure 8.7). Unless you require a special id value (there is no reason you should), you can choose OK and accept the default integer value. You then are returned to the menu editor.

Using this method, you can continue typing the text and id of menu items in the dialog box. However, you might want to add some new menu items to the menu.

Figure 8.6.

Creating a new identifier.

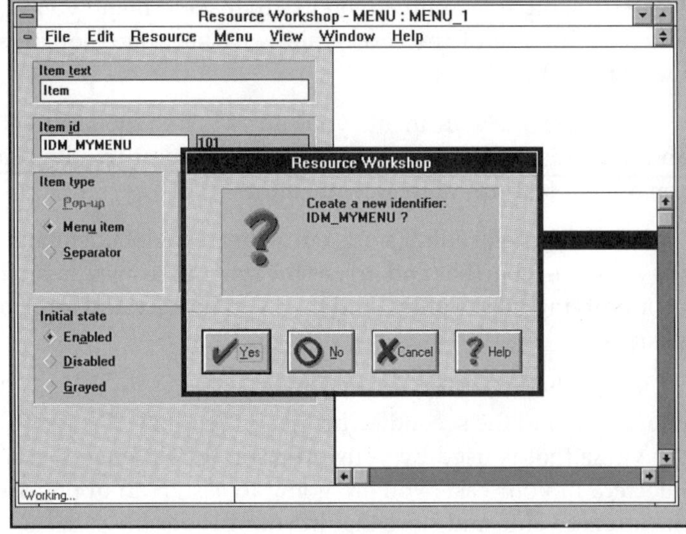

Figure 8.7.

The New Identifier dialog box.

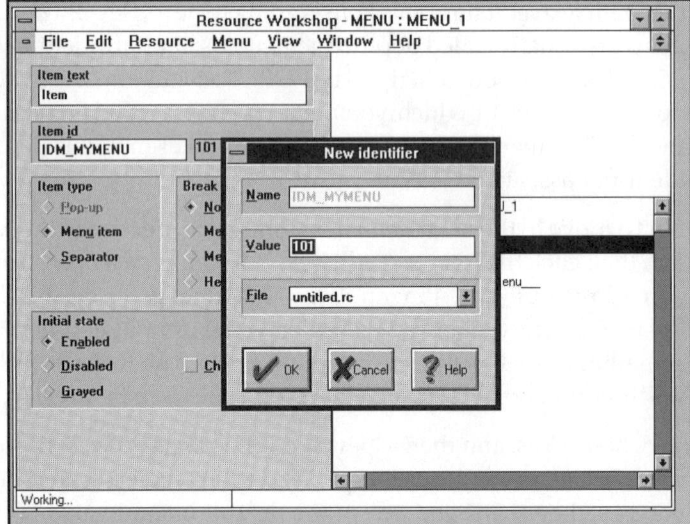

Adding Menu Items

To create a new pop-up menu item, choose the New Menu Item on the Menu option of the Resource Workshop's main menu bar. To add a new pull-down menu item, select the New Menu Item from the Menu selection; this indents the menu text. With several entries in the item text box, switch to the test menu to see how your menu looks (see Figure 8.8).

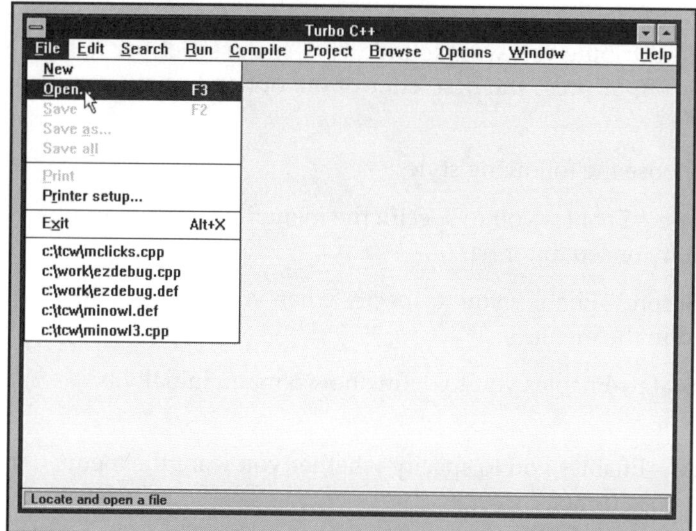

Figure 8.8.

The menu editor with test resource.

Several hot keys are defined to help you use the menu editor. The Insert key adds a new menu item within the tree structure. To add a new pop-up menu to the tree, choose the Menu option and select the New Popup... command (or press Ctrl-P).

To specify the key that the user presses to access the menu item, precede the letter of the item's text with the & character. For example, in the 'Item Text' box, you type

```
&File
```

to specify that the user can access the File menu by pressing F. To insert a tab character in the menu text, use the `\t` character combination. The tab usually is used to separate a menu item's text from its accelerator key. For example

```
Paste\tShift+Ins.
```

correctly aligns the menu so that the accelerator key is displayed on the right side of the menu.

Below the item text and item id options in the dialog box, several options enable you to define different styles and attributes of the menu items. To define styles, move the cursor over the item to modify. Click the mouse cursor over the attribute you want to modify. Use the space bar to toggle the item on or off, or press the first letter of the option to how you want it set.

You can choose the following styles:

- **Item Type**—Enables you to specify the menu item type: pop-up, menu item, or separator bar.
- **Break Before**—Enables you to specify when you want a break included in the menu.
- **Initial State**—Enables you to define how a menu initially is displayed.
- **Checked**—Enables you to specify whether you want the menu item checked or not.

To change the resource name of the menu, choose the Resource menu and select the Resource Name option. You then can type a new filename to be used. The resource name is the one that you specify to the window class `lpszMenuName` field. You also use the resource name in the `LoadMenu` routine to specify the menu.

When you finish defining a menu, choose the File menu option in the menu editor and select Save As.

Now that you understand how to create menus, you're ready to look at the second part of using menus—processing the menus inside your program.

A Menu Example

Like most other elements of a Windows application, your program's window procedure receives messages when menu items have been selected by the user. When the user chooses a command in a menu, Windows sends a WM_COMMAND message to the window procedure of your program. The message contains the menu ID of the command in its wParam parameter.

Program Listing 8.1 is a C example program that uses a menu. Listing 8.2 is the associated resource file, Listing 8.3 is the header file, and Listing 8.4 is the module definition file. (Wow! Now you know why a disk is included with this book.) Insert all four files into a project. Then you can compile, link, and run the resulting program.

Listing 8.1. Example C program using menus.

```
// MENUS.C - Sample C Program which processes menus
//
// Programming Windows with Turbo C++ for Windows
// by Paul J. Perry

#define STRICT

#include <windowsx.h>
#include <stdlib.h>

#include "menus.h"

// Function Prototypes
LRESULT CALLBACK _export MainWndProc(HWND hWnd, UINT message,
                                     WPARAM wParam, LPARAM lParam);

void WMCommand_Handler(HWND hWnd, int id, HWND hWndCtl, UINT
codeNotify);


/*******************************************/
#pragma argsused
int PASCAL WinMain(HINSTANCE hInstance, HINSTANCE hPrevInstance,
                   LPSTR lpCmdParam, int nCmdShow)
{
```

continues

Listing 8.1. continued

```
   char         ProgName[] = "Window with a menu";
   HWND         hWnd;
   MSG          msg;


   if (!hPrevInstance)
   {
      WNDCLASS    wndclass;

      wndclass.lpszClassName = ProgName;
      wndclass.lpfnWndProc   = (WNDPROC) MainWndProc;
      wndclass.cbClsExtra    = 0;
      wndclass.cbWndExtra    = 0;
      wndclass.hInstance     = hInstance;
      wndclass.hIcon         = LoadIcon(NULL, IDI_APPLICATION);
      wndclass.hCursor       = LoadCursor(NULL, IDC_ARROW);
      wndclass.hbrBackground = (HBRUSH) (COLOR_WINDOW + 1);

// Notice the lpszMenuName structure member points to
//   name of menu resource
      wndclass.lpszMenuName  = "MAINMENU";

      wndclass.style         = CS_VREDRAW ¦ CS_HREDRAW;

      if (!RegisterClass(&wndclass)) exit(0);;
   }

   hWnd = CreateWindow(ProgName,"C Program With a Main Menu",
                       WS_OVERLAPPEDWINDOW,
                       CW_USEDEFAULT, CW_USEDEFAULT,
                       CW_USEDEFAULT, CW_USEDEFAULT,
                       NULL, NULL, hInstance, NULL);

   ShowWindow(hWnd, nCmdShow);
   UpdateWindow(hWnd);

   while (GetMessage(&msg, NULL, 0, 0))
   {
      TranslateMessage(&msg);
      DispatchMessage(&msg);
   }
   return msg.wParam;
}


/*******************************************/
```

```
#pragma argsused
void WMCommand_Handler(HWND hWnd, int id, HWND hWndCtl, UINT
                       codeNotify)
{
   switch (id)
   {
      case IDM_NEW :
      {
         MessageBox(hWnd, "File New Option Selected",
                    "MENUS Program", MB_ICONEXCLAMATION ¦ MB_OK);
         break;

      }

      case IDM_OPEN :
      {
         MessageBox(hWnd, "File Open Option Selected",
                    "MENUS Program", MB_ICONEXCLAMATION ¦ MB_OK);
         break;

      }

      case IDM_ASCIITEXT :
      case IDM_PERFECTWORD :
      case IDM_SUPERWORD :
      case IDM_REVIEW :
      case IDM_INDEX :
      {
         MessageBox(hWnd, "Feature Not Implemented",
                    "MENUS Program", MB_ICONSTOP ¦ MB_OK);
         break;
      }

      case IDM_EXIT :
      {
         PostQuitMessage(0);
         break;
      }

      case IDM_ABOUT :
      {
      // Strange indending of following lines is so it will line up
      //   in message box
         MessageBox(hWnd, "Programming Windows with Turbo C++ for
                    Windows \n \ MENUS.C Program \n \
                           by Paul J. Perry", "About Box",
                           MB_ICONINFORMATION ¦ MB_OK);
```

continues

Listing 8.1. continued

```
         break;

      }

   }
}


/*******************************************/
LRESULT CALLBACK _export MainWndProc(HWND hWnd, UINT message,
                                     WPARAM wParam, LPARAM lParam)
{
   switch (message)
   {
      case WM_COMMAND :
      {
         return HANDLE_WM_COMMAND(hWnd, wParam, lParam,
                                  WMCommand_Handler);

      }

      case WM_PAINT :
      {
         HDC         PaintDC;
         RECT        rect;
         PAINTSTRUCT ps;

         PaintDC = BeginPaint(hWnd, &ps);
         GetClientRect(hWnd, &rect);

         DrawText(PaintDC, "Choose a menu selection",
                  -1, &rect, DT_SINGLELINE | DT_CENTER |
                  DT_VCENTER);

         EndPaint(hWnd, &ps);
         return 0;
      }

      case WM_DESTROY :
      {
         PostQuitMessage(0);
         return 0;
      }
   }
   return DefWindowProc (hWnd, message, wParam, lParam);
}
```

Listing 8.2. Resource script for MENUS program.

```
#include "menus.h"

MAINMENU MENU
BEGIN
     POPUP "&File"
     BEGIN
          MENUITEM "&New", IDM_NEW
          MENUITEM "&Open", IDM_OPEN
          MENUITEM SEPARATOR
          POPUP "&Import"
          BEGIN
               MENUITEM "&ASCII Text", IDM_ASCIITEXT
               MENUITEM "&PerfectWord", IDM_PERFECTWORD
               MENUITEM "&SuperWord", IDM_SUPERWORD
          END

          MENUITEM "E&xit", IDM_EXIT
     END

     POPUP "&Messages"
     BEGIN
          MENUITEM "&Review", IDM_REVIEW
     END

     POPUP "\a&Help"
     BEGIN
          MENUITEM "&Index", IDM_INDEX
          MENUITEM "&About", IDM_ABOUT
     END

END
```

Listing 8.3. Header file for MENUS program.

```
//
// MENUS.H Header file
//
#define IDM_NEW          100
#define IDM_OPEN         110
#define IDM_ASCIITEXT    120
```

continues

Listing 8.3. continued

```
#define IDM_PERFECTWORD  130
#define IDM_SUPERWORD    140
#define IDM_EXIT         150
#define IDM_REVIEW       160
#define IDM_INDEX        170
#define IDM_ABOUT        180
```

Listing 8.4. Module Definition file for MENUS program.

```
;
; MENUS.DEF module definition file
;


DESCRIPTION    'Windows Program with a Menu'
NAME           MENUS
EXETYPE        WINDOWS
STUB           'WINSTUB.EXE'
HEAPSIZE       1024
STACKSIZE      8192
CODE           PRELOAD MOVEABLE DISCARDABLE
DATA           PRELOAD MOVEABLE MULTIPLE
```

Figure 8.9 contains the window created with the MENUS program.

You can see that when the window class is set up at the beginning of the program, the wndclass.lpszMenuName structure member points to the name of the menu as declared in the resource file. The Resource Workshop defaults to naming a menu MENU_1. You had to manually rename it to MAINMENU by selecting the Resource menu and choosing Rename.

Menu items are processed in the window procedure. You trap the `WM_COMMAND` message in the main switch statement. Rather than processing the menu items inside the main window procedure, you have defined another function that takes care of menu processing. It is called `WMCommand_Handler`.

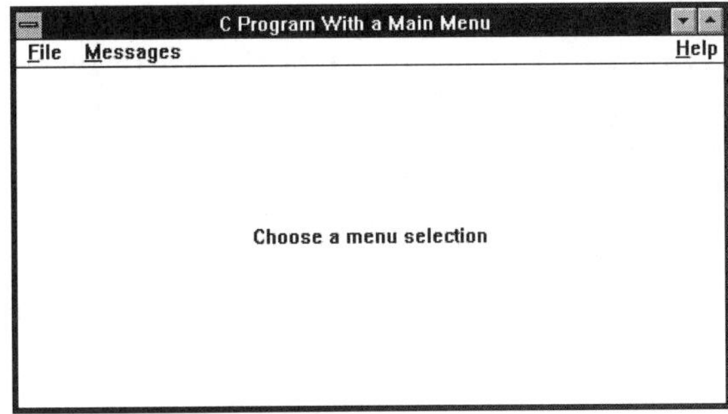

Figure 8.9.
Window created from MENUS program.

Let's examine how this works for a moment. Inside the main `switch()` statement for the window procedure, you catch `WM_COMMAND`, like this:

```
case WM_COMMAND :
{
   return HANDLE_WM_COMMAND(hWnd, wParam, lParam,
                            WMCommand_Handler);

}
```

You then return the value of the `HANDLE_WM_COMMAND` function. However, that is not the name of the function that takes care of the menu processing (it is called `WMCommand_Handler`). The function name only shows up as the last parameter to this other function. So what is going on here?

The `HANDLE_WM_COMMAND` identifier is a C macro declared inside windowsx.h. It takes care of calling your menu command processing function. It also passes the `hWnd`, `wParam`, and `lParam` to the `WMCommand_Handler` function.

However, the `WMCommand_Handler` function is declared like this:

```
void WMCommand_Handler(HWND hWnd, int id, HWND hWndCtl, UINT
                       codeNotify);
```

You can see the `hWnd` being passed along, but where do the id, `hWndCtrl`, and `codeNotify` parameters come from? What happens is that the `HANDLE_WM_COMMAND` macro converts the appropriate low and high words of `lParam` and `wParam` directly into values that you can use. The idea is to make the message handling more flexible. Most importantly, there is compatibility to programming in Windows on different platforms, which may use different sizes of wParam and `lParam` values.

The end result is that it provides future compatibility with programming for Windows NT. Because Windows NT runs in 32 bits, the size of `wParam` and `lParam` changes. If you rely on using the high and low values of these numbers, your code is not easily transportable to Windows NT.

The `HANDLE_WM_COMMAND` macro is used through a system called *message crackers*. The system got its name because the macro cracks the values of the message down to variables that you can use directly—both now and in the future. It then automatically calls your message handler function.

Anyway, once you have handled the `WM_COMMAND` message, your `WMCommand_Handler` function is called. The function looks like this:

```
void WMCommand_Handler(HWND hWnd, int id, HWND hWndCtl, UINT
                        codeNotify)
{
   switch (id)
   {
      case IDM_NEW :
      {
         MessageBox(hWnd, "File New Option Selected",
                    "MENUS Program", MB_ICONEXCLAMATION | MB_OK);
         break;

      }

      case IDM_OPEN :
      {
         MessageBox(hWnd, "File Open Option Selected",
                    "MENUS Program", MB_ICONEXCLAMATION | MB_OK);
         break;

      }

      case IDM_ASCIITEXT :
      case IDM_PERFECTWORD :
      case IDM_SUPERWORD :
      case IDM_REVIEW :
      case IDM_INDEX :
      {
         MessageBox(hWnd, "Feature Not Implemented",
                    "MENUS Program", MB_ICONSTOP | MB_OK);
         break;
      }

      case IDM_EXIT :
      {
```

```
            PostQuitMessage(0);
            break;
        }

        case IDM_ABOUT :
        {
        // Strange indending of following lines is so it will line up
        //    in message box
            MessageBox(hWnd, "Programming Windows with Turbo C++ for
                       Windows \n \ MENUS.C Program \n \
                            by Paul J. Perry", "About Box",
                            MB_ICONINFORMATION ¦ MB_OK);
            break;

        }

    }
}
```

Basically, it's one long `switch()` statement that checks for the id of the menu item, and then responds based on the menu item. In most cases, you call `MessageBox` to display a message about the menu option. However, in a full program you process each menu item as appropriate.

So far, I've talked about how to use a menu in a traditional C program. The ObjectWindows library uses a different method to program for Windows. Next, you learn how this is done.

ObjectWindows and Menus

Because of the way ObjectWindows programs are designed, there is a different method for using menus. Of the two steps in using menus that I discussed earlier, you still create your menu in Resource Workshop. What's different is the way the messages are processed in the source code.

Remember that the ObjectWindows library uses message response functions that are automatically called when a message is sent to your program. After learning how to process menus in your C program, you probably think that you can create a message response function for `WM_COMMAND` and then use a `switch()` statement to trap each menu identifier.

Well, ObjectWindows works even better than that. It enables you to create a message response function for each menu item. Program Listing 8.5 (OWLMENU.CPP) is the source code demonstrating how to use menus in an ObjectWindows library program. Program Listing 8.6 is the resource script that goes with the program, Listing 8.7 is the header file, and Listing 8.8 is the module definition file. Remember each one of these must be inserted into a project file when you compile and run the program.

Listing 8.5. ObjectWindows based program that uses a main menu.

```
// OWLMENU.CPP - Menu program using ObjectWindows library
//
// Programming Windows with Turbo C++ for Windows
// by Paul J. Perry

#define WIN31
#define STRICT

#include <owl.h>
#include <windowsx.h>

#include "owlmenu.h"

// Class Declarations

/********************************************/
class TOwlApp : public TApplication
{
   public :
      TOwlApp (LPSTR AName, HINSTANCE hInstance, HINSTANCE
               hPrevInstance,
               LPSTR CmdLine, int CmdShow) :
          TApplication(AName, hInstance, hPrevInstance,
                       CmdLine, CmdShow) { } ;

   virtual void InitMainWindow();
};


/********************************************/
class TMainWindow : public TWindow
{
   public :
      TMainWindow(PTWindowsObject AParent, LPSTR ATitle)
                : TWindow(AParent, ATitle) { };
```

```
      virtual void Paint(HDC PaintDC, PAINTSTRUCT &PaintInfo);
      virtual void GetWindowClass(WNDCLASS& wndclass);

      virtual void ViewInfoIcon(TMessage& msg)
         = [CM_FIRST + IDM_INFO];
      virtual void ViewExclamationIcon(TMessage& msg)
         = [CM_FIRST + IDM_EXCLAMATION];
      virtual void ViewStopIcon(TMessage& msg)
         = [CM_FIRST + IDM_STOP];
      virtual void ViewQuestionIcon(TMessage& msg)
         = [CM_FIRST + IDM_QUESTION];
      virtual void ExitProgram(TMessage& msg)
         = [CM_FIRST + IDM_EXIT];
};


// Class Member Functions

/*******************************************/
void TOwlApp::InitMainWindow()
{
   MainWindow = new TMainWindow(NULL, Name);
}

/*******************************************/
void TMainWindow::GetWindowClass(WNDCLASS& wndclass)
{
   TWindow::GetWindowClass(wndclass);

 // Specify the name of the menu resource
   wndclass.lpszMenuName = "MAINMENU";

}

/*******************************************/
#pragma argsused
void TMainWindow::ViewInfoIcon(TMessage& msg)
{
   MessageBox(HWindow, "Information Icon", "OWLMENU Program",
              MB_ICONINFORMATION ¦ MB_OK);

}


/*******************************************/
#pragma argsused
```

continues

Listing 8.5. continued

```
void TMainWindow::ViewExclamationIcon(TMessage& msg)
{
   MessageBox(HWindow, "Exclamation Icon", "OWLMENU Program",
              MB_ICONEXCLAMATION ¦ MB_OK);
}


/*******************************************/
#pragma argsused
void TMainWindow::ViewStopIcon(TMessage& msg)
{
   MessageBox(HWindow, "Stop Icon", "OWLMENU Program",
              MB_ICONSTOP ¦ MB_OK);

}


/*******************************************/
#pragma argsused
void TMainWindow::ViewQuestionIcon(TMessage& msg)
{
   MessageBox(HWindow, "Question Mark Icon", "OWLMENU Program",
              MB_ICONQUESTION ¦ MB_OK);
}

/*******************************************/
#pragma argsused
void TMainWindow::ExitProgram(TMessage& msg)
{
   PostQuitMessage(0);
}


/*******************************************/
#pragma argsused
void TMainWindow::Paint(HDC PaintDC, PAINTSTRUCT &PaintInfo)
{
   RECT rect;

   GetClientRect(HWindow, &rect);

   DrawText(PaintDC, "Make a Menu Selection", -1, &rect,
            DT_SINGLELINE ¦ DT_CENTER ¦ DT_VCENTER);

}
```

```
/*********************************************/
int PASCAL WinMain(HINSTANCE hInstance, HINSTANCE hPrevInstance,
                   LPSTR lpCmdLine, int nCmdShow)
{

   TOwlApp ThisApp("ObjectWindows Library Program with a Menu",
                   hInstance, hPrevInstance, lpCmdLine, nCmdShow);
   ThisApp.Run();
   return ThisApp.Status;

}
```

Listing 8.6. OWLMENU resource script file.

```
#include "owlmenu.h"

MAINMENU MENU
BEGIN
     POPUP "&View"
     BEGIN
          MENUITEM "&Information Icon", IDM_INFO
          MENUITEM "&Exclamation Icon", IDM_EXCLAMATION
          MENUITEM "&Stop Icon", IDM_STOP
          MENUITEM "&Question Mark Icon", IDM_QUESTION
          MENUITEM SEPARATOR
          MENUITEM "E&xit", IDM_EXIT
     END

END
```

Listing 8.7. OWLMENU header file.

```
//
// OWLMENU.H header file
//

#define IDM_INFO     101
#define IDM_EXCLAMATION     102
```

continues

Listing 8.7. continued

```
#define IDM_STOP      103
#define IDM_QUESTION      104
#define IDM_EXIT      105
```

Listing 8.8. Module definition file for OWLMENU program.

```
;
; OWLMENU.DEF module definition file
;

DESCRIPTION    'ObjectWindows Program with a Menu'
NAME           OWLMENU
EXETYPE        WINDOWS
STUB           'WINSTUB.EXE'
HEAPSIZE       1024
STACKSIZE      8192
CODE           PRELOAD MOVEABLE DISCARDABLE
DATA           PRELOAD MOVEABLE MULTIPLE
```

The example program displays a menu that enables you to choose the built-in windows icon you want to see within the message box. After you make a selection, a message box is displayed with the appropriate icon inside it (see Figure 8.10).

Figure 8.10.

OwlMenu demonstration menu program.

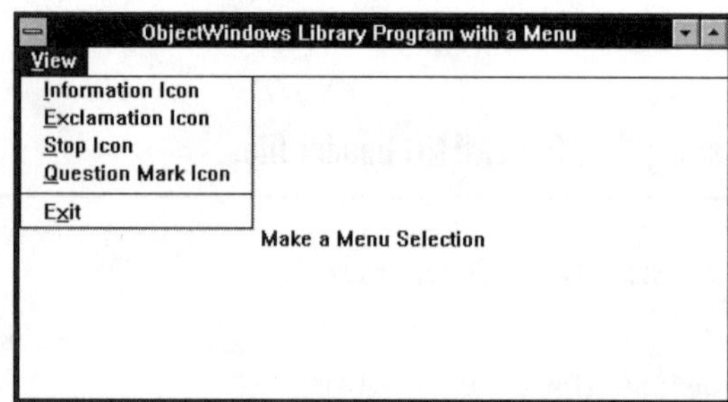

To respond to a menu, you must specify the menu handle to the `lpszMenuName` field of `wndclass`. This is done in the `GetWindowClass` member function for the window, as follows:

```
void TMainWindow::GetWindowClass(WNDCLASS& wndclass)
{
   TWindow::GetWindowClass(wndclass);

   wndclass.lpszMenuName = "MAINMENU";
}
```

Rather than setting up a message loop, an ObjectWindows library creates a special type of message response methods. These methods are called every time the program receives a window message corresponding to menu selections. The method that responds to a menu command has a special definition, as follows:

```
virtual void MenuItem(TMessage& msg)
  = [CM_FIRST + IDM_MENUITEM];
```

This definition allows the program to respond to the appropriate menu ID, as you specified in the resource script. By adding the `CM_FIRST` identifier with the identifier of the menu item, the compiler knows that you are creating a message response function for a menu item rather than for a windows message, which looks like:

```
virtual void WMFunctionName(TMessage &msg)
   = [WM_FIRST + WM_MESSAGENAME];
```

Notice the different use of the `WM_FIRST` identifier rather than `CM_FIRST`.

When a window message is passed to an ObjectWindows program, the appropriate message response function is automatically executed. All processing for each menu command is found in a separate function with names similar to the menu command (to make things easy to understand).

A typical message response function is declared like this:

```
void TMainWindow::ViewQuestionIcon(TMessage& msg)
{
   MessageBox(HWindow, "Question Mark Icon", "OWLMENU Program",
              MB_ICONQUESTION ¦ MB_OK);
}
```

This function pops up a simple `MessageBox` with the appropriate icon displayed.

Besides learning how menus are used in an ObjectWindows program, you can view the types of icons that can be used inside a message box.

So far, you have looked at how to process menu items in both a traditional C program and with the ObjectWindows library. The next topic you learn about is accelerator keys. These are closely related to menus, so it seems like an appropriate time to discuss them.

The following section shows how to define and use accelerator keys in your programs.

Accelerator Keys

Accelerator keys are keystroke combinations that carry out a menu option. In a DOS program, they might be called hot keys. Consider this example of an accelerator key. Most programs that have an Edit Paste menu option also enable you to press the Shift-Insert key combination (or the newer Ctrl-V keystroke) to carry out the same command. Basically, an accelerator key is a shortcut to a menu command.

Keyboard support is an important part of Windows. Many old computing diehards who use DOS applications feel silly going to a graphical user interface because they have to use a mouse to make menu selections. Accelerator keys are an important part of Windows programming; they make your program more attractive to a greater number of people.

The common user interface guidelines set forth by Microsoft even recommend certain keyboard accelerators that should be common between applications. You probably are familiar with those keys used in the clipboard. However, besides the clipboard-related accelerator keys, there are no other guidelines for accelerator key definitions.

Accelerator keys are a combination of an ASCII key and either the Shift key or Ctrl key. You cannot use the Alt key in an accelerator key combination because it is used to pull down top-level menus. Accelerator keys are a type of resource. They are declared inside the accelerator key editor with Resource Workshop and accessed from your program.

To allow the user to have access to accelerator keys, you add processing information to your program. You must first get a handle to the accelerator key resource in the initialization section of your program with the LoadAccelerators routine, as follows:

```
HACCEL   hAccelerators;

hAccelerators = LoadAccelerators(hInstance,
                                 "ACCELERATORNAME");
```

To use the keys, you use the TranslateAccelerator function in your main window loop. For example, to use accelerator keys, the main window loop of your C programs now looks like this:

```
while (GetMessage(&msg, NULL, 0, 0))
{
   if (!TranslateAccelerator(hWnd, hAccelerators, &msg))
   {
      TranslateMessage(&msg);
      DispatchMessage(&msg);
   }
}
return msg.wParam;
```

The call to `TranslateAccelerator` actually converts the window message for the keystroke to an appropriate menu response message. When your program responds to a keyboard accelerator, it doesn't know that a keyboard accelerator is a special keypress. The program thinks that the menu is selected as it's normally selected; the program has no knowledge of the "hot key."

The Resource Workshop Accelerator Editor

The accelerator editor is selected by choosing the Resource menu option, and then selecting the New... menu command and selecting the Accelerator option from the dialog box. As soon as the editor is loaded, a table is displayed that you use to define the accelerator keys (see Figure 8.11). The dialog box on the left enables you to select the accelerator keys as well as specify different attributes about each accelerator key.

The left side of the window contains a list of the accelerator keys as you create them. The list initially starts out empty. As you create accelerator keys, they are added to the list.

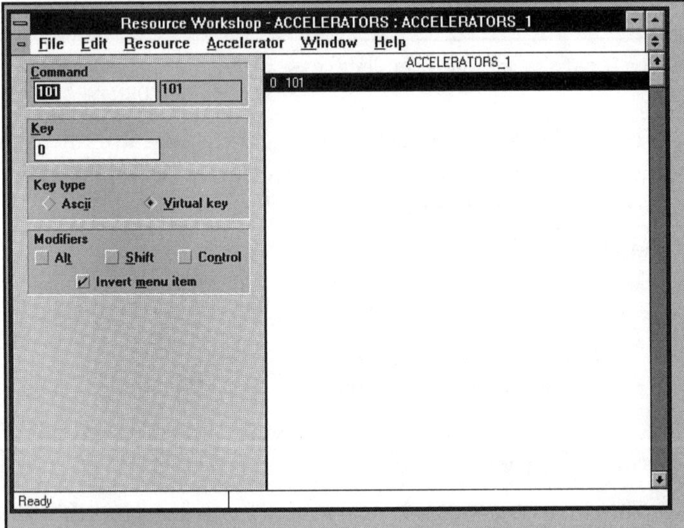

Figure 8.11.

The Resource Workshop accelerator key editor.

To use the accelerator editor, use the tab keys to move through the dialog box and specify the associated items. To insert a new row in the table, press the Ins key.

The following list gives information about each item in the dialog box on the left of the accelerator editor window:

- **Command**—This integer value defines the ID number associated with the virtual key. It should correspond to the value specified when defining a menu command identifier.
- **Key**—Represents the actual key you want as the accelerator key. You must press the keystroke, followed by Alt-Esc, to tell Resource Workshop which key you want to use.
- **Key Type**—Specifies whether the key is a virtual key code or an ASCII character.

- **Modifiers**—Tells the program which keys modify the target keystroke. Choose one of three: Alt, Shift, or Ctrl.
- **Invert Menu Item**—Set to either yes or no, this field indicates whether the menu tree should flash when the user presses the key.

Program Listing 8.9 is a modified version of the MENUS program you saw earlier. It is called ACCMENU.C and loads an accelerator table. It then uses the `TranslateAccelerator` routine in its message loop to process accelerator keys. Listing 8.10 is the resource script, Listing 8.11 is the header file, and Listing 8.12 is the module definition file.

Listing 8.9. Menu Program With Accelerators.

```
// ACCMENU.C - Sample C Program which processes menus
//            and contains accelerator keys
//
// Programming Windows with Turbo C++ for Windows
// by Paul J. Perry

#define STRICT

#include <windowsx.h>
#include <stdlib.h>

#include "accmenu.h"

// Function Prototypes
LRESULT CALLBACK _export MainWndProc(HWND hWnd, UINT message,
                                     WPARAM wParam, LPARAM lParam);

void WMCOmmand_Handler(HWND hWnd, int id, HWND hWndCtl, UINT
                       codeNotify);


/********************************************/
#pragma argsused
int PASCAL WinMain(HINSTANCE hInstance, HINSTANCE hPrevInstance,
                   LPSTR lpCmdParam, int nCmdShow)
{
   char        ProgName[] = "Menus with Accelerators";
   HWND        hWnd;
   MSG         msg;
   HACCEL      hAccelerators;
```

continues

Listing 8.9. continued

```
   if (!hPrevInstance)
   {
      WNDCLASS    wndclass;

      wndclass.lpszClassName = ProgName;
      wndclass.lpfnWndProc   = (WNDPROC) MainWndProc;
      wndclass.cbClsExtra    = 0;
      wndclass.cbWndExtra    = 0;
      wndclass.hInstance     = hInstance;
      wndclass.hIcon         = LoadIcon(NULL, IDI_APPLICATION);
      wndclass.hCursor       = LoadCursor(NULL, IDC_ARROW);
      wndclass.hbrBackground = (HBRUSH) (COLOR_WINDOW + 1);

// Notice the lpszMenuName structure member points
//   to name of menu resource
      wndclass.lpszMenuName  = "MAINMENU";

      wndclass.style         = CS_VREDRAW | CS_HREDRAW;

      if (!RegisterClass(&wndclass)) exit(0);
   }


// Load accelerator resource
   hAccelerators = LoadAccelerators(hInstance, "MENUACCS");

   hWnd = CreateWindow(ProgName,"Main Menu with Accelerators",
                       WS_OVERLAPPEDWINDOW,
                       CW_USEDEFAULT, CW_USEDEFAULT,
                       CW_USEDEFAULT, CW_USEDEFAULT,
                       NULL, NULL, hInstance, NULL);

   ShowWindow(hWnd, nCmdShow);
   UpdateWindow(hWnd);

// Notice the ALL NEW message loop.  The TranslateAccelerator call
//   has been added
   while (GetMessage(&msg, NULL, 0, 0))
   {
      if (!TranslateAccelerator(hWnd, hAccelerators, &msg))
      {
         TranslateMessage(&msg);
         DispatchMessage(&msg);
      }
   }
   return msg.wParam;
}
```

```
/*******************************************/
#pragma argsused
void WMCommand_Handler(HWND hWnd, int id, HWND hWndCtl, UINT
codeNotify)
{
   switch (id)
   {
      case IDM_OPEN :
      {
         MessageBox(hWnd, "File Open Option Selected",
                    "MENUS Program", MB_ICONEXCLAMATION ¦ MB_OK);
         break;

      }

      case IDM_SAVE :
      case IDM_SAVEAS :
      {
         MessageBox(hWnd, "File Save/As Option Selected",
                    "MENUS Program", MB_ICONEXCLAMATION ¦ MB_OK);
         break;

      }

      case IDM_EXIT :
      {
         PostQuitMessage(0);
         break;
      }

      case IDM_CUT :
      {
         MessageBox(hWnd, "Edit Cut Option Selected",
                    "MENUS Program", MB_ICONEXCLAMATION ¦ MB_OK);
         break;

      }

      case IDM_COPY :
      {
         MessageBox(hWnd, "Edit Copy Option Selected",
                    "MENUS Program", MB_ICONEXCLAMATION ¦ MB_OK);
         break;

      }

      case IDM_PASTE :
```

continues

Listing 8.9. continued

```
      {
         MessageBox(hWnd, "Edit Paste Option Selected",
                    "MENUS Program", MB_ICONEXCLAMATION ¦ MB_OK);
         break;

      }


   }
}


/*******************************************/
LRESULT CALLBACK _export MainWndProc(HWND hWnd, UINT message,
                                     WPARAM wParam, LPARAM lParam)
{
   switch (message)
   {
      case WM_COMMAND :
      {
         return HANDLE_WM_COMMAND(hWnd, wParam, lParam,
                                  WMCommand_Handler);

      }

      case WM_PAINT :
      {
         HDC         PaintDC;
         RECT        rect;
         PAINTSTRUCT ps;

         PaintDC = BeginPaint(hWnd, &ps);
         GetClientRect(hWnd, &rect);

         DrawText(PaintDC, "Choose a menu selection",
                  -1, &rect, DT_SINGLELINE ¦ DT_CENTER ¦
                  DT_VCENTER);

         EndPaint(hWnd, &ps);
         return 0;
      }

      case WM_DESTROY :
      {
```

```
            PostQuitMessage(0);
            return 0;
         }
      }
      return DefWindowProc (hWnd, message, wParam, lParam);
}
```

Listing 8.10. Resource Script for modified menu program.

```
#include "accmenu.h"
MAINMENU MENU
BEGIN
     POPUP "&File"
     BEGIN
          MENUITEM "&Open\tCtrl+O", IDM_OPEN
          MENUITEM "&Save\tCtrl+S", IDM_SAVE
          MENUITEM "Save &As...\tCtrl+A", IDM_SAVEAS
          MENUITEM "Exit\tAlt+X", IDM_EXIT
     END

     POPUP "&Edit"
     BEGIN
          MENUITEM "Cu&t\tShift+Del", IDM_CUT
          MENUITEM "&Copy\tCtrl+Ins", IDM_COPY
          MENUITEM "&Paste\tShift+Ins", IDM_PASTE
     END

END

MENUACCS ACCELERATORS
BEGIN
     "^O", 101
     "^S", 102
     "^A", 103
     "x", 104, ASCII, ALT
     VK_DELETE, 105, VIRTKEY, SHIFT
     VK_INSERT, 106, VIRTKEY, CONTROL
     VK_INSERT, 107, VIRTKEY, SHIFT
END
```

Listing 8.11. ACCMENU header file.

```
//
// ACCMENU.H header file
//

#define IDM_OPEN     101
#define IDM_SAVE     102
#define IDM_SAVEAS   103
#define IDM_EXIT     104
#define IDM_CUT      105
#define IDM_COPY     106
#define IDM_PASTE    107
```

Listing 8.12. ACCMENU module definition file.

```
;
; ACCMENU.DEF module definition file
;

DESCRIPTION    'Menu with Accelerator Keys'
NAME           ACCMENU
EXETYPE        WINDOWS
STUB           'WINSTUB.EXE'
HEAPSIZE       1024
STACKSIZE      8192
CODE           PRELOAD MOVEABLE DISCARDABLE
DATA           PRELOAD MOVEABLE MULTIPLE
```

Accelerator keys aren't hard to use. Once the resources script is created to define the accelerator keys, it's mostly a matter of letting Windows process the commands.

However, one of the aesthetic features changed in the program was the definition of the menus to include the accelerator keys (see Figure 8.12). Although I probably overdid it by adding an accelerator key to every menu item (the menu starts to become crowded), you can tastefully use accelerator keys in your own program.

The accelerator editor window for ACCMENU is shown in Figure 8.13.

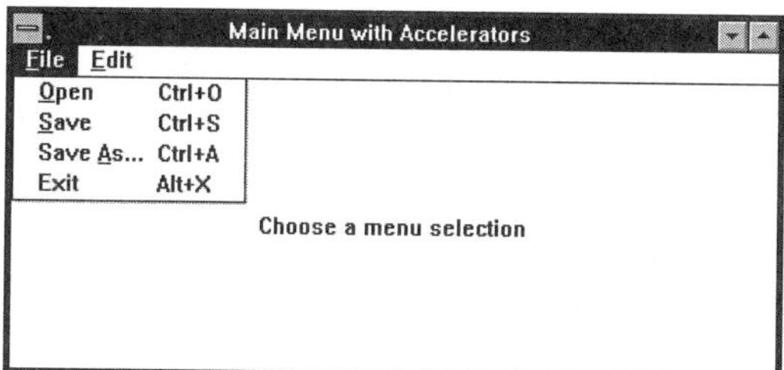

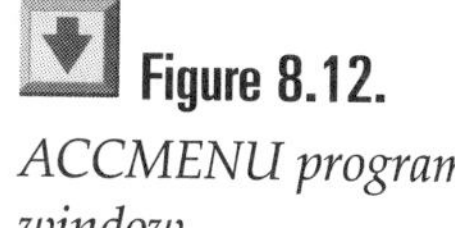

Figure 8.12.

ACCMENU program window.

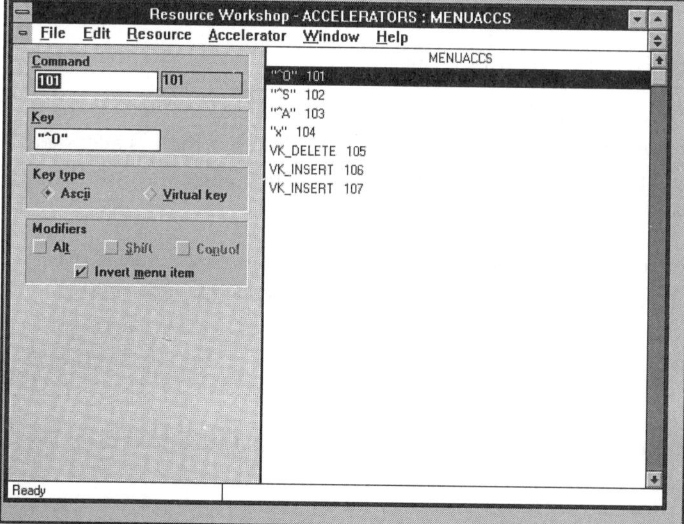

Figure 8.13.

Accelerator editor with ACCMENU accelerator editor.

ObjectWindows Library and Accelerators

Using Accelerator keys in the ObjectWindows library is even easier then when you were writing with C. You must create an inherited `InitInstance` method that loads the accelerator table. Other than that, ObjectWindows takes care of the rest. Here's an example of the overridden method that you should use:

```
void TMainWindow::InitInstance()
{
   TApplication::InitInstance();
   HAccTable = LoadAccelerator(GetApplication()-> hInstance,
                               "ACCELERATORNAME");
}
```

Once the accelerators are loaded, ObjectWindows takes care of using them for you. You don't have to make any other modifications.

What You Have Learned

In this chapter, you learned about using menus and accelerator keys in your C and C++ programs. In the next chapter, you take a look at using scroll bars attached to a window.

This chapter covered the following topics:

- Menus provide a straight-forward method of making selections in all Windows programs. A menu has a top level, which is accessed with the **Alt** key along with the key associated with an underlined letter in the menu item text.
- Main menu selections usually are pulled down to display more menu selections. Windows takes care of processing mouse and keyboard actions when related to using menus, therefore your program does not have to do any of the work of displaying the menus.
- Menus are created in the Resource Workshop and stored as resources.
- To specify a menu in your program, you must pass the resource name to the `lpszMenuName` member of the `wndclass` structure.
- RC resource scripts are used to store a textual description of menus. RES resource scripts are binary forms of the same files. RC files usually are used to describe the menu because they are easy to modify with a text editor.
- The Resource Workshop enables you to create and modify menus interactively—that is, it enables you to layout the structure of a menu and then immediately test it for usability.
- Message crackers are implemented through C macros that convert `wParam` and `lParam` values into identifiable values and then call a

separate function to process the message. The benefit of using message crackers is in creating an easier port of your program over to Windows NT.

- To process menus in an ObjectWindows program, you write message response functions identified by adding `CM_FIRST` to the identifier (`IDM_`) of the menu item in the class declaration.
- Accelerator keys convert key combinations into menu commands.
- To create an accelerator key, you use Resource Workshop to create an accelerator key resource that defines which key is pressed and which menu item it carries out.
- To process accelerator keys in a C program, you must first load the accelerator key resource with the `LoadAccelerator` function. You also have to modify the main message loop to call `TranslateAccelerator` in order to process the accelerator keys.
- Programs based on the ObjectWindows library process accelerators by assigning the handle of the accelerator table to the `HAccTable` variable in the `InitInstance` member function.

9 USING SCROLL BARS

IN THIS CHAPTER

■

The statements necessary to add scroll bars to a program.

■

How scroll bars send and receive messages.

■

What must be done to process scroll bars in a C program.

■

How message crackers help respond to scroll bar messages.

■

How object-oriented programming can make programming scroll bars easy.

■

How to use an ObjectWindows object to process scroll bar messages automatically.

Scroll bars provide an intuitive method for adjusting the view inside a window. Many programs use scroll bars, including graphics editors (Windows Paintbrush), text editors (Notepad), and program editors (the Turbo C++ for Windows Integrated Development Environment). This chapter shows how to add scroll bars to the main window of your program.

Scroll Bars

One difficult aspect of programming for a graphical user interface like Windows is you have little control over the window's size. The user can resize most main overlapped windows in a program. Therefore, when designing your program, you don't know how much of the window you will actually be able to write to.

Safely assume that everything you want to fit in the window can't fit. The window scroll bar is the mechanism Windows provides to enable the user to see a much larger area of the screen. The window is a viewport to a portion of a larger display surface. Scroll bars enable the user to move between different portions of your program's output.

Recall from Chapter 6, "Working with Windows," you can add scroll bars to your program by specifying the `WS_VSCROLL` and `WS_HSCROLL` window style creation flags. After scroll bars are added to your program, its window procedure acts on messages sent to it that help interact with the scroll bars.

Many Windows programs utilize scroll bars attached to their main window to enable the user to move between different portions of a client area. For example, you can use the Notepad program to display a text file; using the mouse, you also can use the scroll bars to scroll the text in the client area of the window (see Figure 9.1).

After a scroll bar is added to a window, use the mouse to click either the arrows at each end of the scroll bar or the area between the arrows. The scroll bar thumb is the square box between the arrows. The scroll thumb moves across the length of the scroll bar. It gives feedback about the approximate location of the material shown in the window in the larger viewport. You also can use the mouse cursor to drag the scroll bar thumb to move to a specific location.

Scroll bars are controls you can apply only with a mouse. For the keyboard to be able to control scroll bars, the keyboard controls must be written into your code. (You examine keyboard input in Chapter 10, "Getting Input from the User.")

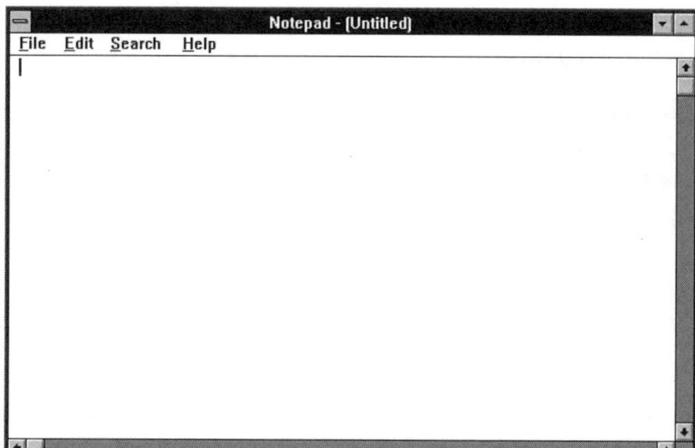

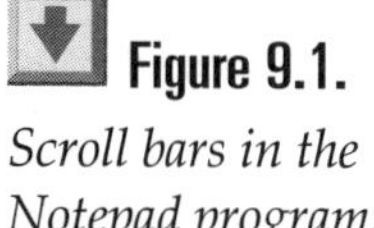

Figure 9.1.
Scroll bars in the Notepad program.

Scrolling Basics

You must keep track of three values while using scroll bars. The minimum value occurs when the scroll bar thumb rests at the top of the scroll bar. The maximum value occurs when the scroll bar thumb rests at the bottom of the scroll bar. The current position is the one represented by the scroll bar thumb between the minimum and maximum values. Horizontal scroll bars have similar values.

To add the scroll bars to the window, you change the `CreateWindow` function call to specify the styles `WS_VSCROLL` and `WS_HSCROLL`, as follows:

```
hWnd = CreateWindow(ProgName,"Window Title",
// Notice our new window styles:
                    WS_OVERLAPPEDWINDOW ¦ WS_VSCROLL ¦ WS_HSCROLL,
```

```
CW_USEDEFAULT, CW_USEDEFAULT,
CW_USEDEFAULT, CW_USEDEFAULT,
NULL, NULL, hInstance, NULL);
```

After the scroll bars are attached to a window with the WS_VSCROLL and WS_HSCROLL window style flags, the user's actions are relayed to your program through window messages. Vertical scroll bars send WM_VSCROLL messages, and horizontal scroll bars send WM_HSCROLL messages. Each message includes other values in the wParam and lParam window procedure parameters that indicate the portion of the scroll bar the user has clicked. You can use message crackers to break the scroll bar values into usable values (more about message crackers in a moment).

All aspects of the scroll bar send a single message in the wParam parameter (see Figure 9.2). The exception is when the user drags the scroll bar thumb. The SB_THUMBTRACK message is sent while the thumb is dragged. Then, the SB_THUMBPOSITION message is received when the dragging is completed. Table 9.1 lists the scroll bar messages for horizontal scroll bars, and Table 9.2 lists the scroll bar messages for vertical scroll bars.

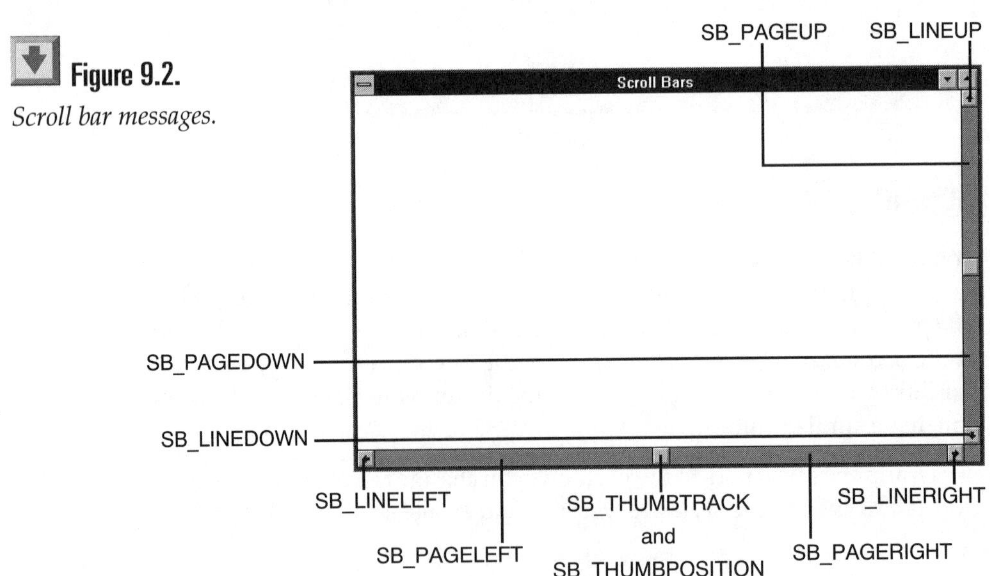

Figure 9.2.
Scroll bar messages.

Table 9.1. Horizontal scroll bar messages.

Message	*Description*
SB_LINELEFT	User clicked the left arrow.
SB_LINERIGHT	User clicked the right arrow.
SB_PAGELEFT	User clicked area between the left arrow and the scroll bar thumb.
SB_PAGERIGHT	User clicked area between the scroll bar thumb and the right arrow.
SB_THUMBTRACK	User is dragging the scroll bar thumb.
SB_THUMBPOSITION	User dropped the scroll bar thumb.

Table 9.2. Vertical scroll bar messages.

Message	*Description*
SB_LINDOWN	User clicked top arrow.
SB_LINEUP	User clicked bottom arrow.
SB_PAGEDOWN	User clicked area between thumb and bottom arrow.
SB_PAGEUP	User clicked area between thumb and top arrow.
SB_THUMBTRACK	User is dragging the scroll bar thumb.
SB_THUMBPOSITION	User dropped the scroll bar thumb.

Scroll Bar Routines

Several Windows API routines are defined to help you implement the use of scroll bars in your program.

The SetScrollRange routine enables you set the minimum and maximum position values for a scroll bar. The default value is 0 to 100. The function is defined as follows:

```
void SetScrollRange(HWND hWnd, int Scrollbar,
                    int Min, int Max, BOOL Redisplay);
```

You pass the function the handle to the window, along with the type of scroll bar. The type of scroll bar is set as the Scrollbar value and is either the constant SB_HORZ or the constant SB_VERT. These constants specify which scroll bar you set the range for. The Min value represents the minimum value the scroll bar holds, and the Max value holds the maximum value. You set Redisplay equal to TRUE to repaint the scroll bar; otherwise, the scroll bar is not redisplayed.

After you set the range of the scroll bar, the position of the thumb is always an integer value between the range. For example, a scroll bar with a range 0 through 9 has 10 thumb positions.

The converse of the SetScrollRange function is GetScrollRange. It returns information about the scroll bars in your program. It is declared like this:

```
void GetScrollRange(HWND hWnd, int Scrollbar,
                    int FAR * Min, int FAR * Max);
```

This routines takes similar values as the SetScrollRange routine, but it returns the Max and Min values of the scroll bars. Sometimes it's useful to find the minimum and maximum value of the scroll bars. Do that with GetScrollRange function.

The SetScrollPos routine sets the current position of the scroll bar thumb as specified by the Pos parameter. As before, you also can specify to redraw the scroll bar to reflect the new values. WINDOWS.H defines SetScrollPos as follows:

```
int SetScrollPos(HWND hWnd, int ScrollBar, int Position,
                 BOOL Redisplay);
```

The SetScrollPos routine moves the thumb within the scroll bar. It takes the handle to the window, to the minimum value, to the SB_HORZ or SB_VERT to specify which scroll bar to set, to the position in the scroll bar, and then to a boolean value specifying whether to update the scroll bar.

The SetScrollPos routine has a counterpart, GetScrollPos, which obtains information about the scroll bar position. Declare it as follows:

```
int GetScrollPos(HWNDhWnd, int ScrollBar);
```

The GetScrollPos function returns the integer position of the scroll bar when it receives the handle to the window and the SB_HORZ or SB_VERT to specify which scroll bar to get information for.

Another routine that is helpful when processing scroll bar messages is the ScrollWindow routine. This routine scrolls a window by moving the contents of the window's client area the number of units specified by an {XAmount} and {YAmount} parameter. It is defined as follows:

```
void ScrollWindow(HWND hWnd, int XAmount, int YAmount,
                  RECT rect, RECT ClipRect);
```

Besides the handle to the window, you pass the XAmount and YAmount you want to scroll and the rectangle you want to move.

Using Scroll Bars

You must work with Windows to provide support for scroll bars in your program. It is the responsibility of your program to do the following:

- Initialize the scroll bar range.
- Process scroll bar messages.
- Update the position of the scroll bar thumb (using SetScrollPos).

Windows handles the graphical processing of scroll bars as well as the processing of mouse messages related to the scroll bars. You never have to display the scroll bar elements or even to "flash" the scroll bar area when the user clicks an area between the arrows and the scroll bar thumb.

Let's get down and dirty to find out how scroll bars are used in a program. Program Listing 9.1 creates a window with attached scroll bars. It displays a list of football teams and enables you to use the scroll bars to see the whole list. Listing 9.2 contains the module definition file. Figure 9.3 contains the output of the program.

Figure 9.3.
Output of FOOTBALL.C program.

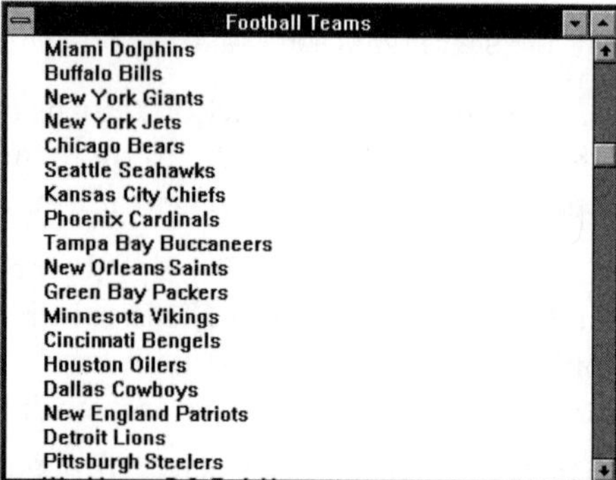

Listing 9.1. Program that uses scroll bars.

```
// FOOTBALL.C - C Program showing processing of scroll bars
//
// Programming Windows with Turbo C++ for Windows
// by Paul J. Perry

#define STRICT

#define  MAXNUMB 28
#define  NAMELEN 30

#include <windowsx.h>
#include <stdlib.h>
#include <string.h>

// Function Prototypes
LRESULT CALLBACK _export MainWndProc(HWND hWnd, UINT message,
                                     WPARAM wParam, LPARAM lParam);

void WMVScroll_Handler(HWND hWnd, HWND hwndCtl, UINT code,
                       int pos);
```

```
void WMSize_Handler(HWND hwnd, UINT state, int cx, int cy);


// Global Data
int CharHeight;     // The height (in pixels) of each character
int LinesInWindow; // The number of lines which can currently be
                    // displayed in the window
int Item=0;         // The item (in the array) that we want to
                    // display at the top-left corner of window

char Names[MAXNUMB][NAMELEN] =
{
   "San Francisco Forty Niners",
   "L.A. Raiders",
   "Indianapolis Colts",
   "Cleveland Browns",
   "L.A. Rams",
   "San Diego Chargers",
   "Miami Dolphins",
   "Buffalo Bills",
   "New York Giants",
   "New York Jets",
   "Chicago Bears",
   "Seatle Seahawks",
   "Kansas City Chiefs",
   "Phoenix Cardinals",
   "Tampa Bay Buccaneers",
   "New Orlean Saints",
   "Green Bay Packers",
   "Minnesota Vikings",
   "Cincinatti Bengals",
   "Houghston Oilers",
   "Dallas Cowboys",
   "New England Patriots",
   "Detroit Lions",
   "Pittsburg Steelers",
   "Washington D.C. Redskins",
   "Denver Broncos",
   "Philadelphia Eagles",
   "Atlanta Falcons"
};


/*******************************************/
#pragma argsused
```

continues

Listing 9.1. continued

```
int PASCAL WinMain(HINSTANCE hInstance, HINSTANCE hPrevInstance,
                   LPSTR lpCmdParam, int nCmdShow)
{
   char         ProgName[] = "Football Teams";
   HWND         hWnd;
   MSG          msg;


   if (!hPrevInstance)
   {
      WNDCLASS    wndclass;

      wndclass.lpszClassName = ProgName;
      wndclass.lpfnWndProc   = (WNDPROC) MainWndProc;
      wndclass.cbClsExtra    = 0;
      wndclass.cbWndExtra    = 0;
      wndclass.hInstance     = hInstance;
      wndclass.hIcon         = LoadIcon(NULL, IDI_APPLICATION);
      wndclass.hCursor       = LoadCursor(NULL, IDC_ARROW);
      wndclass.hbrBackground = (HBRUSH) (COLOR_WINDOW + 1);
      wndclass.lpszMenuName  = NULL;
      wndclass.style         = CS_VREDRAW ¦ CS_HREDRAW;

      if (!RegisterClass(&wndclass)) exit(0);
   }

   // Create window with scroll bars.
   // Notice the new window style passed to CreateWindow
   // We only add vertical scroll bars.  To add horizontal
   // scroll bars, you would use the WS_HSCROLL type.
   hWnd = CreateWindow(ProgName,"Football Teams",
                       WS_OVERLAPPEDWINDOW ¦ WS_VSCROLL,
                       CW_USEDEFAULT, CW_USEDEFAULT,
                       CW_USEDEFAULT, CW_USEDEFAULT,
                       NULL, NULL, hInstance, NULL);

   ShowWindow(hWnd, nCmdShow);
   UpdateWindow(hWnd);

   while (GetMessage(&msg, NULL, 0, 0))
   {
      TranslateMessage(&msg);
      DispatchMessage(&msg);
   }
   return msg.wParam;
```

```
}

/*******************************************/
#pragma argsused
void WMVScroll_Handler(HWND hWnd, HWND hwndCtl, UINT code, int pos)
{
   switch(code)
   {
      case SB_LINEUP :
      {
         // User clicked on top scroll bar arrow.
         // We will move one line up the page.
         // To do this, we decrement Item.
         Item -= 1;
         break;

      }

      case SB_LINEDOWN :
      {
         // User clicked on bottom scroll bar arrow.
         // We will move one line down the page.
         // To do this, we increment the Item.
         Item += 1;
         break;
      }

      case SB_PAGEUP :
      {
         // User clicked on upper portion of scroll bar,
         // we will move down one page.
         // This would be like pressing the PageUp key.
         Item -= LinesInWindow;
         break;
      }

      case SB_PAGEDOWN :
      {
         // User clicked on lower portion of scroll bar,
         // we will move up one page.
         // This would be like pressing the PageDown key.
         Item += LinesInWindow;
         break;
      }

      case SB_THUMBTRACK :
      {
```

continues

Listing 9.1. continued

```
            // User is moving the scroll bar thumb.
            // We can redisplay the text, as the user
            // moves the thumb.
            Item = pos;
            break;
         }
   }

   // Check for bounds
   Item = max(Item, 0);
   Item = min(MAXNUMB, Item);

   // Adjust scroll bar position and repaint window
   SetScrollPos(hWnd, SB_VERT, Item, TRUE);
   InvalidateRect(hWnd, NULL, TRUE);

}

/*******************************************/
#pragma argsused
void WMSize_Handler(HWND hWnd, UINT state, int cx, int cy)
{
    // Calculates the actual text lines which will fit in the
    // window.
    LinesInWindow = cy/CharHeight;

    // If the number of lines can be displayed in the window
    // all at once, then make the scroll bar disappear.
    // It is not needed and takes space away from the client area.
    //
    // Otherwise, if they are still needed, we display them.
    if (LinesInWindow > MAXNUMB)
       ShowScrollBar(hWnd, SB_VERT, FALSE);
    else
       ShowScrollBar(hWnd, SB_VERT, TRUE);
}

/*******************************************/
LRESULT CALLBACK _export MainWndProc(HWND hWnd, UINT message,
                                      WPARAM wParam, LPARAM lParam)
{
   switch (message)
   {
      // Catch vertical scroll bar messages.
      // To catch the horizontal scroll bar messages,
```

```
// you would use a case WM_HSCROLL statement.
case WM_VSCROLL :
{
   return HANDLE_WM_VSCROLL(hWnd, wParam,
                            lParam, WMVScroll_Handler);

}

case WM_CREATE :
{
   HDC         hDC;
   TEXTMETRIC  tm;

   // Get the character height
   hDC = GetDC(hWnd);
   GetTextMetrics(hDC, &tm);
   CharHeight = tm.tmHeight + tm.tmExternalLeading;
   ReleaseDC(hWnd, hDC);

   // Set scroll bar ranges so range goes from 0 to MAXNUMB
   // The default is from 0 to 100.
   SetScrollRange(hWnd, SB_VERT, 0 , MAXNUMB, TRUE);
   return 0;

}

case WM_SIZE :
{
   return HANDLE_WM_SIZE(hWnd, wParam, lParam,
                         WMSize_Handler);
}

case WM_PAINT :
{
   HDC         PaintDC;
   PAINTSTRUCT ps;
   int         i;

   PaintDC = BeginPaint(hWnd, &ps);

   for(i=0; i<(MAXNUMB-Item); i++)
   {
      TextOut(PaintDC, 25, CharHeight*i, &Names[Item+i][0],
              strlen(&Names[Item+i][0]));
   }

   EndPaint(hWnd, &ps);
```

continues

Listing 9.1. continued

```
            return 0;
         }

         case WM_DESTROY :
         {
            PostQuitMessage(0);
            return 0;
         }
      }
      return DefWindowProc (hWnd, message, wParam, lParam);
}
```

Listing 9.2. Module definition file for FOOTBALL.C program.

```
;
; FOOTBALL.DEF module definition file
;

DESCRIPTION    'Windows Program with Scrollbars'
NAME           FOOTBALL
EXETYPE        WINDOWS
STUB           'WINSTUB.EXE'
HEAPSIZE       1024
STACKSIZE      8192
CODE           PRELOAD MOVEABLE DISCARDABLE
DATA           PRELOAD MOVEABLE MULTIPLE
```

For simplicity, the program only processes vertical scroll bar messages. Therefore, you only see a scroll bar on the right side of the window. After you work with the program, you will notice the program is smart enough to know the size of the window and how it relates to the text that is going to be displayed. If the client area of the window is large enough, the scroll bar is removed. Afterwards, if the window is resized so the entire list is no longer visible, the scroll bar reappears.

Main Window Creation

The first message sent to your program's window procedure is WM_CREATE. This is sent when the window is created with the CreateWindow function. In FOOTBALL.C you catch the message and do some preliminary processing, as follows:

```
case WM_CREATE :
{
   HDC         hDC;
   TEXTMETRIC  tm;

   hDC = GetDC(hWnd);
   GetTextMetrics(hDC, &tm);
   CharHeight = tm.tmHeight + tm.tmExternalLeading;
   ReleaseDC(hWnd, hDC);

   SetScrollRange(hWnd, SB_VERT, 0 , MAXNUMB, TRUE);
   return 0;

}
```

The first part of the code calculates the height of the font that displays characters. You get this information from the GetTextMetrics function. It is passed in the TEXTMETRIC structure as the tm.tmheight and tm.tmExternalLeading fields. The character height value is the height of the character in pixels. By getting the height of the font currently used, your program still operates correctly if the system font changes.

Second, you set the scroll bar range with the SetScrollRange function. Set it to go from 0 to the number of lines you want to display in the window (in this case MAXNUMB or 28).

Sizing the Window

When the program's window is resized, the window procedure receives a WM_SIZE message. You use a message cracker to call the WMSize_Handler function.

```
void WMSize_Handler(HWND hWnd, UINT state, int cx, int cy)
{
    LinesInWindow = cy/CharHeight;
```

```
    if (LinesInWindow > MAXNUMB)
        ShowScrollBar(hWnd, SB_VERT, FALSE);
    else
        ShowScrollBar(hWnd, SB_VERT, TRUE);
}
```

In `WMSize_Handler`, you first calculate the number of lines that can fit in the window. The `cy` value is the height of the window in pixels. By dividing it by the height of characters, you discover that the number of lines fit in the window. This is important later, when you display the text inside the client area. Also remember, the `LinesInWindow` value changes every time the window is resized.

You also check whether the number of lines in the window is greater than the number of lines you want to display. If so, hide the scroll bar with a call to `ShowScrollBar` function.

More About Message Crackers

You saw in Chapter 8, "Adding Menus to Your Program," how to use message crackers to respond to `WM_COMMAND` messages. The FOOTBALL.C program uses a message cracker to respond to the `WM_SIZE` message. You might wonder how you go from

```
case WM_SIZE :
{
    return HANDLE_WM_SIZE(hWnd, wParam, lParam, WMSize_Handler);
}
```

to calling a function with the prototype

```
void WMSize_Handler(HWND hwnd, UINT state, int cx, int cy);
```

In the `WMSize_Handler` function you receive a handle to the window and three other parameters: `state`, `cx`, and `cy`.

Remember, `HANDLE_WM_SIZE` is a C macro. Somehow you go from variables of `wParam` and `lParam` to variables of `state`, `cx`, and `cy`. What's happening here?

Essentially, the macro converts the `wParam` and `lParam` message parameters to and from explicitly typed parameters and invokes the function. The

HANDLE_WM_SIZE message calls the supplied function (WMSize_Handler) with the parameters supplied to the macro. The macro looks like this:

```
#define HANDLE_WM_SIZE(hwnd, wParam, lParam, fn) \
    ((fn)((hwnd), (UINT)(wParam), (int)LOWORD(lParam),
    (int)HIWORD(lParam)), 0L)
```

Although you might comprehend the idea of message crackers, you may wonder why to use them. The following reasons apply:

- They make the code easier to read and understand; rather than using statements such as

  ```
  state = wParam;
  cx = LOWORD(lParam);
  cy=HIWORD(lParam);
  ```

  you can use directly the variables state, cx, and cy.

- Message crackers move code into functions, rather than incorporating all the code in a huge switch() statement. This improves code readability.

- Allows for portability to Windows NT. The size of the wParam and lParam values are changing in Windows NT. Message crackers convert message types from wParam and lParam to the type that the function expects. If you rely on LOWORD() and HIWORD(), your code is not directly transportable, and this might cause you future grief.

NOTE

Unfortunately, not much documentation is found about message crackers. About the best you find is in online text files. Check out C:\TCWIN\DOC\WIN31.DOC for information about message crackers. To find message crackers that actually exist and how to declare the functions the message cracker calls, consult the WINDOWSX.H header file.

Responding to Scroll Bars

The WMVScroll_Handler function handles all details of responding to the WM_VSCROLL message. The function (minus comments) looks like this:

```
void WMVScroll_Handler(HWND hWnd, HWND hwndCtl, UINT code, int pos)
{
   switch(code)
   {
      case SB_LINEUP :
      {
         Item -= 1;
         break;

      }

      case SB_LINEDOWN :
      {
         Item += 1;
         break;
      }

      case SB_PAGEUP :
      {
         Item -= LinesInWindow;
         break;
      }

      case SB_PAGEDOWN :
      {
         Item += LinesInWindow;
         break;
      }

      case SB_THUMBTRACK :
      {
         Item = pos;
         break;
      }
   }

   Item = max(Item, 0);
   Item = min(MAXNUMB, Item);

   SetScrollPos(hWnd, SB_VERT, Item, TRUE);
   InvalidateRect(hWnd, NULL, TRUE);

}
```

Basically, the function checks the type of action the user performs on the scroll bar and then sets a variable accordingly. The Item variable specifies which name in the array should be displayed as the top line in the window. It originally starts out as `0`. As the user clicks parts of the scroll bar, it is incremented or decremented appropriately.

After the `Item` value is changed, you use the `max()` and `min()` macros to be sure the value is not less than `0` or greater than the maximum number of items (`MAXNUMB` or `28`).

Finally, you update the location of the thumb in the scroll bar, using the `SetScrollPos` function. The `InvalidateRect` function sends a `WM_PAINT` message to the window procedure, which results in the window repainting itself.

Displaying the Items

Your `WM_PAINT` message handling is tricky because you must display the correct items in the window area. The code looks like this:

```
case WM_PAINT :
{
   HDC         PaintDC;
   PAINTSTRUCT ps;
   int         i;

   PaintDC = BeginPaint(hWnd, &ps);

   for(i=0; i<(MAXNUMB-Item); i++)
   {
      TextOut(PaintDC, 25, CharHeight*i, Names[Item+i],
              strlen(&Names[Item+i][0]));
   }

   EndPaint(hWnd, &ps);
   return 0;
```

As can you see, after you get a handle to the display context with a call to `BeginPaint`, you set up a loop that goes from `0` to the maximum number of items minus the top item value (`MAXNUMB-Item`). The loop displays the array elements to the screen.

The end of the WM_PAINT message handling calls EndPaint to return the handle to the display context back to Windows.

To process the scroll bar messages, you first must plan the project. Although planning the project is not hard, it's tedious, because you must respond to each message and then redisplay the client area appropriately.

Now that you know how to process scroll bars in a C program, observe how it's done inside the ObjectWindows Library (OWL). You'll probably like this.

Letting the ObjectWindows Library Handle Scroll Bars

TScroller is the ObjectWindows object that provides processing of scroll bars in a TWindow object. It provides an automated way to scroll both text and graphics that you display in a window.

The TScroller object implements another method of changing the scroll bar range: auto-scrolling. When the user clicks the client area and then drags the mouse cursor outside a window's client area, the scrolling action takes place.

One useful feature of auto-scrolling is that the further you move the mouse out of a window's client area, the faster the window scrolls. Although this is a useful feature, most Windows programs don't provide it, and it is not mentioned in Microsoft's Windows user-interface guidelines *The Windows Interface,* (copyright 1987, 1992). It certainly does no harm to have auto-scrolling in your program. However, unless you document it, most users won't know it exists.

Using TScroller

To add the physical scroll bars to your program, you must specify the WS_HSCROLL and WS_VSCROLL types to the Attr.Style parameter, as follows:

```
Attr.Style |= WS_VSCROLL | WS_HSCROLL;
```

It's best to put this code in the constructor of your window class.

The `TScroller` object is created in the constructor of your `TMainWindow` class. To create a new instance of `TScroller`, you use code like this:

```
Scroller = new TScroller(this, 10, 15, 100, 100);
```

This line creates the `TScroller` object. This sets up both horizontal and vertical scroll bars. The first parameter is a pointer to a window's object. The next two parameters are the number of units for the horizontal scroll bar and the number of units for the vertical scroll bar. The final parameters are the scroll bar ranges.

After you give your window a scroll bar with the `TScroller` object, you can change the default values by using member functions as necessary (see Table 9.3).

Table 9.3. TScroller member variables.

Member Function	*Description*
ScrollBy	Scrolls window specified amount.
ScrollTo	Scrolls to a specified location.
SetPageSize	Sets size of page.
SetRange	Sets X and Y scroll bar range.
SetUnits	Sets new units for the scroll bar.
XRangeValue	Converts horizontal scroll bar range value.
XScrollValue	Converts between horizontal scroll values.
YRangeValue	Converts vertical scroll bar range value.
YScrollValue	Converts between vertical scroll values.

Once the window is displayed, you can use the mouse to scroll the contents of the client area. The only thing your program must do is include a paint method that draws the information in the window. It doesn't have to know that scrolling is taking place. Listing 9.3 shows how to use the `TScroller` object.

Listing 9.3. Displays list of United States presidents.

```
// PRESID.CPP - Use scrollbars in an OWL program to display
//              list of U.S. Presidents in client area
//
// Programming Windows with Turbo C++ for Windows
// by Paul J. Perry

#define WIN31
#define STRICT

#include <owl.h>
#include <windowsx.h>
#include <string.h>

#define MAXNUMB 42
#define NAMELEN 25


// Class Declarations

/*********************************************/
class TOwlApp : public TApplication
{
   public :
      TOwlApp (LPSTR AName, HINSTANCE hInstance, HINSTANCE
               hPrevInstance,
            LPSTR CmdLine, int CmdShow) :
            TApplication(AName, hInstance, hPrevInstance,
                         CmdLine, CmdShow) { } ;
   virtual void InitMainWindow();
};


/*********************************************/
class TMainWindow : public TWindow
{
   public :
      TMainWindow(LPSTR ATitle);
```

```
      virtual void Paint(HDC PaintDC, PAINTSTRUCT &PaintInfo);

};


// Class Member Functions

/*******************************************/
void TOwlApp::InitMainWindow()
{
   MainWindow = new TMainWindow(Name);
}


/*******************************************/
TMainWindow::TMainWindow(LPSTR ATitle)
                         : TWindow(NULL, ATitle)
{

//  Add physical scrollbars to the window
   Attr.Style |= WS_VSCROLL | WS_HSCROLL;

//  Create instance of TScroller object
   Scroller = new TScroller(this, 10, 15, 100, 100);

}

/*******************************************/
#pragma argsused
void TMainWindow::Paint(HDC PaintDC, PAINTSTRUCT &PaintInfo)
{

   static char PresidentNames[MAXNUMB][NAMELEN] =
   {
      "George Washington",       "John Adams",
      "Thomas Jefferson",        "James Madison",
      "James Monroe",            "John Quincy Adams",
      "Andrew Jackson",          "Martin Van Buren",
      "William Henry Harrison", "John Tyler",
      "James Knox Polk",         "Zachary Taylor",
      "Millard Fillmore",        "Franklin Pierce",
      "James Buchanan",          "Abraham Lincoln",
      "Andrew Johnson",          "Ulysses S. Grant",
      "Rutherford B. Hayes",     "James Garfield",
      "Chester Alan Arthur",     "Grover Cleveland",
      "Benjamin Harrison",       "William McKinley",
      "Theodore Roosevelt",      "William Howard Taft",
```

continues

Listing 9.3. continued

```
      "Woodrow Wilson",           "Warren G. Harding",
      "Calvin Coolidge",          "Herbert Hoover",
      "Franklin D. Roosevelt",    "Harry S. Truman",
      "Dwight D. Eisenhower",     "John F. Kennedy",
      "Lyndon Baines Johnson",    "Richard Nixon",
      "Gerald Ford",              "Jimmy Carter",
      "Ronald Reagan",            "George Bush"
   };

   int         i, Spacing;
   TEXTMETRIC  tm;


   GetTextMetrics(PaintDC, &tm);
   Spacing = tm.tmHeight + tm.tmExternalLeading + 1;

   for (i=0; i<MAXNUMB; i++)
   {
      TextOut(PaintDC, 20, Spacing*i, &PresidentNames[i][0],
              strlen(&PresidentNames[i][0]) );
   }

}


/*******************************************/
int PASCAL WinMain(HINSTANCE hInstance, HINSTANCE hPrevInstance,
                        LPSTR lpCmdLine, int nCmdShow)
{

   TOwlApp ThisApp("U.S. Presidents, with Scrollbars", hInstance,
                   hPrevInstance, lpCmdLine, nCmdShow);
   ThisApp.Run();
   return ThisApp.Status;

}
```

Listing 9.4. Module definition file for PRESID.CPP.

```
;
; PRESID.DEF module definition file
;
```

```
DESCRIPTION    'OWL Program Using Scrollbars'
NAME           PRESID
EXETYPE        WINDOWS
STUB           'WINSTUB.EXE'
HEAPSIZE       1024
STACKSIZE      8192
CODE           PRELOAD MOVEABLE DISCARDABLE
DATA           PRELOAD MOVEABLE MULTIPLE
```

The PRESID.CPP program creates a top-level window that lists 40 United States presidents in the client area. As you might expect, there's not enough space to list all the names vertically, so scroll bars are implemented that enable the user to see all the names (see Figure 9.4).

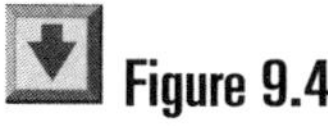

Figure 9.4.
Presidents of the United States.

The presidents' names are stored in a character array. The `TMainWindow` constructor adds the `WS_HSCROLL` and `WS_VSCROLL` window styles and also creates the `TScroller` method. This is all that's necessary to process scroll bars.

In the `Paint` member function, you display the entire array at one time. The `TScroller` object controls what is displayed, according to the current status of the scroll bars.

Hopefully, you see how helpful the OWL is. The two programs in this chapter show a radical difference between how scroll bars are processed. In the C program, you constantly attend to updating scroll bar positions, incrementing and decrementing variables, and displaying certain sections of text. In the C++ program, you initialize the scroller, and the object handles the work.

What You Have Learned

In this chapter, you examined how to process scroll bar messages in a Windows program. You learned the messages your program receives and how to respond to the messages in a C program. You also learned how to use the `TScroller` object in an OWL program to process scroll bar messages automatically.

Specifically, the following topics were covered in this chapter:

- The main window of a program is, in effect, a viewport to a portion of a larger display surface. Scroll bars provide an intuitive method for adjusting the view in a window. They enable the user to move between views of your program's output.
- To add scroll bars to a window, specify the `WS_VSCROLL` and `WS_HSCROLL` window style creation flags when you call `CreateWindow`.
- Scroll bars send messages to your window procedure that describe how the user employs the scroll bar.
- Three values are associated with scroll bars: the minimum value (when the scroll bar thumb rests at one end of the scroll bar), the maximum value (when the scroll bar rests at the opposite end of the scroll bar), and the current position (represented by the location of the scroll bar thumb).
- Your program usually sets the scroll bar range with a call to `SetScrollRange` and specifies the maximum and minimum values the scroll bar represents. The default values are `0` and `100`.
- After you set the range of the scroll bar, the position of the thumb is always an integer value between the minimum and maximum values.

- Your C program is responsible for initializing the scroll bar range, processing the scroll bar messages, and updating the position of the scroll bar thumb.
- Message crackers help respond to window messages by converting the `wParam` and `lParam` message parameters to explicitly typed parameters that invoke a separate function.
- The benefits of message crackers include making your code easier to understand, breaking your code into smaller functions, and allowing future portability to Windows NT.
- To process scroll bar messages in a program based on the OWL, use the `TScroller` class. It handles all scroll bar message processing.
- To add scroll bars to the main window of a program based on the OWL, you modify the `Attr.Style` value to include `WS_HSCROLL` and `WS_VSCROLL`.
- `TScroller`'s constructor takes parameters that enable you to define the number of units and the range of both a vertical and horizontal scroll bar.
- After the `TScroller` object is created, you can write your `Paint` member function to display your program's output all at once. It's almost as though your screen size is unlimited and you can display on that entire area. `TScroller` handles displaying the appropriate part in the window.

10

GETTING INPUT FROM THE USER

IN THIS CHAPTER

- What happens when the user presses a key and how the keystroke information is sent to your program through (you guessed it) messages.

- The basic methods Windows provides for using keyboard input in a program.

- Keyboard messages and how a program's main message loop translates key presses.

- How the Windows keyboard driver helps provide a device-independent operating environment.

- Virtual key codes and why they are used in Windows.

- What character codes are and how they are used in your program.

- How to process mouse messages in a program.

- How to get the coordinates of the mouse cursor during program execution.

- A way to change the mouse cursor during a program's execution.

- The different types of keyboards available for IBM PC-compatible computers and how they work with Windows.

In Chapter 9, "Using Scroll Bars," you examined using scroll bars to enable the user to interact with your program. Now, you explore the way Windows handles other types of user input.

The keyboard is the primary method of gaining input from the user on most computers, regardless of the operating system. Windows is no exception. Windows also relies heavily on the mouse as a pointing device. Therefore, it's important to know how your programs interact with these user input devices. In this chapter, you gain a fundamental understanding about how to get input from the user through the keyboard and from the mouse.

Keyboard Basics

The original IBM XT computer was shipped with an 83-key keyboard. When the AT (80286-based) computer was announced, a new keyboard was introduced that moved a few keys around and added the SysReq key for a total of 84 keys.

With the current line of PS/2 computers, another keyboard is adapted—the enhanced 101/102-key keyboard. This keyboard adds two function keys (F11 and F12) and duplicates some keys already present on the older keyboards.

Other third-party companies created extended keyboards, such as the popular Northgate OmniKey series. However, most third-party keyboards only rearrange the keyboard or give the keys a different tactile feeling. They don't add new keys or radically change the way keys are processed internally.

Although most Americans haven't seen them, keyboards also are specially designed for the international market. For example, special keyboards that add diacritic marks to the basic keyboard layout are used in Europe. Other parts of the world modify the keyboard for their languages as well.

Although a keyboard is a keyboard, you probably believe deep down that there are differences. There are, and Windows is designed to support the greatest number of computer systems available. As a result, it must support all types of keyboards—or as many as possible.

The basic operation of all keyboards is the same. You press a key, and a code is sent to the computer with information about what you type. However, this description sounds much simpler than the operation is.

A keyboard has a built-in microprocessor that controls operations. The press of a key creates a signal that converts to a *scan code* that's sent to the computer. A scan code is a number sent from the keyboard to the computer that represents a certain keyboard character. Each key has a unique scan code.

On receiving the scan code, the computer usually converts it to an ASCII (American Standard Code for Information Interchange) code. The ASCII code is a universal code compatible with most computers, regardless of the operating system, manufacturer, or program.

Then, your program must use the keystroke appropriately. Sometimes a program is interested in a certain keystroke, such as Esc, or a string of characters—when it prompts a user to type a name, for example.

Often, Windows responds to keyboard input. You rarely must write specialized code to respond to the keyboard. For example, Windows automatically handles the following uses of the keyboard for you:

- Most main windows contain a control menu, for which Windows processes the keyboard keystrokes. You don't have to write any code to process the control menu.
- While users engage a menu, if a letter is prefaced with the & character in its resource file (as in Chapter 8, "Adding Menus to Your Program"), Windows automatically makes keyboard allowances for those menu commands and responds appropriately.
- Accelerator keys allow for duplication of menu commands. When you add a couple of lines to your program (as in Chapter 8) and add the correct resource file, Windows processes the keys for you, without much additional programming.
- Dialog boxes enable users to use Tab, Shift-Tab, Space bar, and Enter keys to duplicate mouse operations, with Windows processing the keys for you.
- You can create an edit box interface object that allows keyboard input and uses editing features generally associated with a professional editor.

Even though Windows appears to do all the work for you, in certain instances you may want to use the keyboard directly. It also helps to understand how keyboard input is processed internally so that you know how your program can utilize keyboard input more efficiently. Even if you don't use the keyboard directly, you should know about certain conventions that Windows has adapted to enable users to operate older keyboards—and to use new keyboards in the future.

The Windows Keyboard Driver

During Windows initialization, a Windows keyboard driver is installed, according to your specifications (see Figure 10.1). The keyboard driver always is active and converts keyboard characters to Windows key code messages. The keyboard driver is the start of device-independent keyboard processing in Windows.

Figure 10.1.

Specifying a keyboard driver.

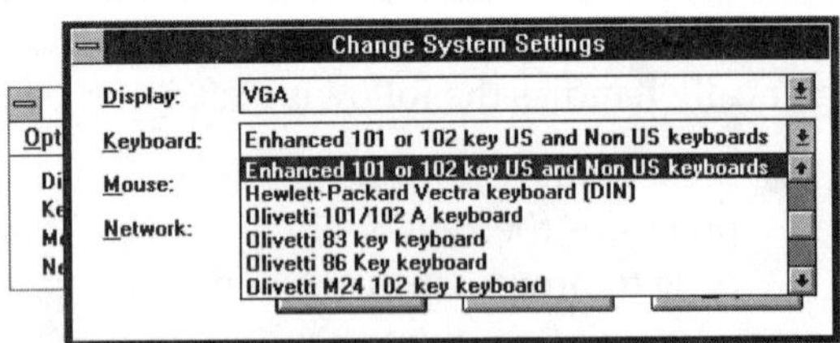

Getting Keyboard Input

With the EasyWin Library you can use a short program such as

```
#include <stdio.h>

void main()
{
   char str[80];

   gets(str);   // input string
   puts(str);   // display string

}
```

to accept keyboard input, store it in a variable named `str` and display it to the user in the window. This is relatively easy; however, if you need to check for an extended keyboard character such as F2, you have no way doing it.

As you probably realize, pure Windows programs process keyboard input much differently than the previous example.

Keyboard input arrives to a window procedure as keyboard messages, with several messages generated for each key pressed. With the `gets()` function, your program only receives input if you specifically ask for it (by using the statement in your program). In a Windows program, keyboard messages are always coming to your program. Even if your program doesn't ask for a keystroke, when one is pressed, a message describing it is sent to your program's window procedure.

You generally do not have to respond to keyboard messages. However, when you want to use keyboard input, you must modify your code. Using the ObjectWindows Library (OWL), you can create a message-response function. With a traditional Windows program, you must intercept the keyboard message in the main window procedure and then (preferably) utilize a message cracker to call a handler function that processes the keyboard input.

Two types of keystroke messages can be passed to your program. Windows differentiates between system keys and regular keys. Table 10.1 lists the keystroke messages that your program can receive. Usually, the keystroke messages occur in pairs. *System keystroke* messages refer to the keystrokes more important for using Windows than for running the application. The system keystrokes generally are associated with the system menu. Most often, you do not have to worry about intercepting the system keystroke messages because the default window procedure processes them.

Table 10.1. Keystroke messages.

Message	*Description*
WM_KEYDOWN	Keystroke pressed.
WM_KEYUP	Keystroke released.
WM_SYSKEYDOWN	System key pressed.
WM_SYSKEYUP	System key released.

For each keystroke message, the lParam parameter of the window procedure contains specific information about the key pressed. This information is divided into bit fields in the lParam value. They are divided into six parts: repeat count, OEM scan code, extended key flag, context code, previous key state, and transition states. Examine these fields one at a time.

- **Repeat Count.** If a key is held down, the repeat count is incremented. In doing so, several WM_KEYDOWN messages are combined into a single message. A repeat count greater than 1 indicates that keyboard events are occurring faster than your program can process them.
- **OEM Scan Code.** This contains the value of the scan code as it was sent from the keyboard. Although you might be tempted to use this scan code value to check for specific key presses, it's best not to. Using this value sets up a device-dependent nature to your program. One advantage of using Windows is it can support the greatest number of computers available in a device-independent nature.
- **Extended Key Flag.** This contains an extension of the scan code. If the extended key flag is 1, it results from the use of one of the additional keys on the IBM extended keyboard. Again, this value is ignored for the same reason the OEM scan code is ignored.
- **Context Code.** This flag is set to 1 when the user presses Alt. Therefore, it is always 1 for system keystroke messages and for when the user makes a menu selection with the keyboard. At any other time, it has a value of 0.
- **Previous Key State.** This helps process messages with a repeat count greater than one. This field has a value of 1 if the previous state of the key pressed was down and a value of 0 if the previous state of the key was up.
- **Transition States.** The value of this field is 0 if the key is being pressed and 1 if the key is being released. It always is set to 1 for WM_KEYUP or WM_SYSKEYUP messages and to 0 for WM_KEYDOWN or wm_SYSKEYDOWN messages.

With these fields, you might think Windows supplies a great deal of information about the key being pressed. However, I already advised you not to use the scan code value to check for keys. To check for a keystroke, a

Windows program tests the `wParam` value of the message that contains the Windows virtual key code for the keystroke.

The Windows virtual key codes (see Appendix A) define a standard set of keys for all keyboards currently available, as well as a set of keys that might be on keyboards in the future. Each key code has a symbolic name, as defined in WINDOWS.H. Each virtual key code identifier starts with `VK_`, which stands for virtual key code. Examples of virtual keys include:

`VK_RETURN`	Enter key pressed.
`VK_SNAPSHOT`	Print Screen key pressed.
`VK_F1`	F1 function key pressed.
`VK_P`	Alphabetic P key pressed.
`VK_PRIOR`	Page Up.
`VK_NEXT`	Page Down.

The virtual key codes define keyboard keys in a device-independent nature. For this reason, certain virtual key codes are defined that currently don't have corresponding keys on the IBM keyboard. It's possible that Windows will be available for non-IBM-compatible computers some day.

If you are using message crackers, the correct values are automatically passed to your handler function, and you do not have to work with `lParam` and `wParam` values.

Character Codes

Virtual key codes give keyboards a device-independent nature. You can test for any key by checking for its virtual key code. However, you still might find a need for ASCII character codes in your programs.

Windows automatically translates virtual key codes into character codes. You have seen the main message loop in a C program (programs based on the OWL have the same processing, but it is done behind the scenes):

```
while (GetMessage(&msg, NULL, 0, 0))
{
   TranslateMessage(&msg);
   DispatchMessage(&msg);
}
```

The `GetMessage` function retrieves the message from Windows. The `DispatchMessage` routine sends the message to your program's window procedure.

The `TranslateMessage` function converts keystroke messages into character messages. The character messages are passed to your window procedure just like other messages. The message names for character codes are in Table 10.2.

Table 10.2. Character messages.

Message	*Description*
WM_CHAR	Character.
WM_SYSCHAR	System character.
WM_DEADCHAR	Dead character.
WM_SYSDEADCHAR	System dead character.

It is important to remember that the regular keyboard messages still are sent to your window procedure, so you, in effect, have the character code slipped between other keystroke messages. For example,

`WM_KEYDOWN`	Virtual key P
`WM_CHAR`	Character code P
`WM_KEYUP`	Virtual key P

are sent to your window procedure when the user presses the P key.

Dead Characters

Earlier, you read that Windows includes support for many countries (see Figure 10.2). Dead characters are certain keys that have been defined on non-U.S. keyboards which work in conjunction with other keys. For example, on a Spanish keyboard, an accent mark ´ is usually combined with an *a* key to provide for an accented letter *a*. To type this, the user types *a* and then the accent key. The keys work in combination.

Windows sends a WM_DEADCHAR message with a keyboard character to be combined with other keys. When developing a Windows program, consider the capacity for international support of your program.

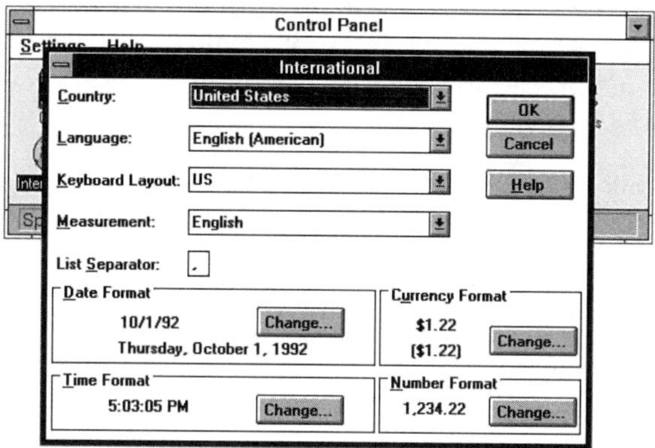

Figure 10.2.
Control Panel international setup.

You might not use the feature at first; however, when you sell your programs worldwide, it's important to support dead keys for the international market.

An Example

Listing 10.1 (GETKEY.C) shows how to use character codes and virtual key codes in your program. Listing 10.2 contains the module definition file.

TIP

You might want to implement an undocumented keyboard function in your program to display copyright information.

For example, in Windows 3.1, to go to the About Box of Program Manager, choose the Help menu option and then select About. When the About dialog box is displayed, hold down the Ctrl and Shift keys and double-click the icon in the upper-left corner with the left mouse button. Click OK to close the dialog box. Choose the dialog box again and follow the same procedure—pressing the Ctrl-Shift keyboard combination and double-clicking the icon. Surprise! You see a waving flag that dedicates Windows to all the hard-working people on the Windows development team. Click OK to close the dialog box. Now, choose the About dialog box once again and follow the same procedure. You see a scrolling list of the actual people who worked on Windows.

If you have Windows 3.0, you can get a similar hidden screen, although it is not as fancy. To see it, go to the Windows desktop and type **WIN3** while pressing F3. Release F3 and press backspace once. The Windows desktop lists the e-mail names of the people who created Windows. With the mouse, click the desktop to return it to its previous state.

Listing 10.1. GETKEY program.

```
// GETKEY.C - Example of processing keyboard messages
//            Uses message crackers to ease message
//            processing.
//
// Programming Windows with Turbo C++ for Windows
// by Paul J. Perry

#define STRICT

#include <windowsx.h>
#include <stdlib.h>

#include "menus.h"

#define BUFLENGTH 50          // Buffer Length


// Global Variables
char Buffer[BUFLENGTH];       // Character buffer
int  BufferPosition = 0;      // Current position in buffer

// Function Prototypes
LRESULT CALLBACK _export MainWndProc(HWND hWnd, UINT message,
                                   WPARAM wParam, LPARAM lParam);
```

```
void WMKeydown_Handler(HWND hWnd, UINT vk, BOOL fDown,
                       int cRepeat, UINT flags);

void WMChar_Handler(HWND hWnd, UINT ch, int cRepeat);

/*******************************************/
#pragma argsused
int PASCAL WinMain(HINSTANCE hInstance, HINSTANCE hPrevInstance,
                   LPSTR lpCmdParam, int nCmdShow)
{
   char        ProgName[] = "Get Keyboard Keystrokes";
   HWND        hWnd;
   MSG         msg;


   if (!hPrevInstance)
   {
      WNDCLASS    wndclass;

      wndclass.lpszClassName = ProgName;
      wndclass.lpfnWndProc   = (WNDPROC) MainWndProc;
      wndclass.cbClsExtra    = 0;
      wndclass.cbWndExtra    = 0;
      wndclass.hInstance     = hInstance;
      wndclass.hIcon         = LoadIcon(NULL, IDI_APPLICATION);
      wndclass.hCursor       = LoadCursor(NULL, IDC_ARROW);
      wndclass.hbrBackground = (HBRUSH) (COLOR_WINDOW + 1);
      wndclass.lpszMenuName  = "";
      wndclass.style         = CS_VREDRAW | CS_HREDRAW;

      if (!RegisterClass(&wndclass)) exit(0);
   }

   hWnd = CreateWindow(ProgName,"Keyboard Processing Program",
                       WS_CAPTION | WS_SYSMENU | WS_MINIMIZEBOX,
                       CW_USEDEFAULT, CW_USEDEFAULT,
                       400, 200, NULL, NULL, hInstance, NULL);

   ShowWindow(hWnd, nCmdShow);
   UpdateWindow(hWnd);

   while (GetMessage(&msg, NULL, 0, 0))
   {
      TranslateMessage(&msg);
      DispatchMessage(&msg);
   }
   return msg.wParam;
```

continues

Listing 10.1. continued

```
}

/*******************************************/
#pragma argsused
void WMChar_Handler(HWND hWnd, UINT ch, int cRepeat)
{
/*
 *  The ch value passed to this function is actually the virtual
 *  key (VK_...) code!
 */

   // Trap BACKSPACE and ENTER key.
   // We don't want to add them to buffer
   if ( (ch == VK_BACK) || (ch == VK_RETURN) )
      return;

   // If we are past buffer length, then leave
   // We must take into account terminating zero
   if(BufferPosition > BUFLENGTH-1)
      return;

   // Add entered keystroke (ch) to buffer
   Buffer[BufferPosition++] = ch;
   Buffer[BufferPosition+1] = 0;


   // Redisplay client area
   InvalidateRect(hWnd, NULL, TRUE);

}

/*******************************************/
#pragma argsused
void WMKeydown_Handler(HWND hWnd, UINT vk,
                       BOOL fDown, int cRepeat, UINT flags)
{
   switch (vk)
   {
      case VK_HOME :     // HOME key pressed
      {
         BufferPosition = 0;
         Buffer[0] = 0;
         break;
      }

      case VK_LEFT :     // LEFT ARROW key pressed
```

```
      case VK_BACK :      // BACKSPACE key pressed
      {
         if (BufferPosition == 0)
         {
            MessageBeep(0);
            Buffer[0] = 0;
            break;
         }

         BufferPosition--;
         Buffer[BufferPosition+1] = 0;  // Make sure we
                                        // add terminating 0
         break;
      }

      case VK_SHIFT :     // SHIFT key pressed
      {                   // we want to let this go through
         break;           // in order to process U/C and special
      }                   // characters

      default :           // ANY OTHER KEY pressed
      {                   // by catching this, the display
         return;          // is not updated as often, and
      }                   // therefore not as "flashy"

   }

   InvalidateRect(hWnd, NULL, TRUE);

}


/*********************************************/
LRESULT CALLBACK _export MainWndProc(HWND hWnd, UINT message,
                                     WPARAM wParam, LPARAM lParam)
{
   switch (message)
   {
      case WM_CREATE :
      {
         TEXTMETRIC tm;
         HDC        hDC;

         // Create and show caret
         // base the width and height on the current font

         hDC = GetDC(hWnd);
```

continues

Listing 10.1. continued

```
         GetTextMetrics(hDC, &tm);

         CreateCaret(hWnd, NULL,
                     tm.tmAveCharWidth,  // width of current font
                     tm.tmHeight);       // height of current font
         ShowCaret(hWnd);

         ReleaseDC(hWnd, hDC);
         return 0;
      }

      case WM_CHAR :
      {
         return HANDLE_WM_CHAR(hWnd, wParam, lParam,
WMChar_Handler);
      }

      case WM_KEYDOWN :
      {
         return HANDLE_WM_KEYDOWN(hWnd, wParam, lParam,
WMKeydown_Handler);
      }

      case WM_PAINT :
      {
         HDC         PaintDC;
         PAINTSTRUCT ps;

         PaintDC = BeginPaint(hWnd, &ps);

         // set location of caret
         SetCaretPos(5+LOWORD(GetTextExtent(PaintDC, Buffer,
BufferPosition)),
                     5);

         // display current line
         TextOut(PaintDC, 5, 5, Buffer, BufferPosition);

         EndPaint(hWnd, &ps);
         return 0;
      }

      case WM_DESTROY :
      {
         // When program is done and closed down,
```

```
        // we will display text to user ala MessageBox
        MessageBox(0, Buffer, "String Entered:", MB_OK);
        PostQuitMessage(0);
        return 0;
      }
   }
   return DefWindowProc (hWnd, message, wParam, lParam);
}
```

Listing 10.2. Module definition file for GETKEY program.

```
;
; GETKEY.DEF module definition file
;

DESCRIPTION    'Get Keyboard Information'
NAME           GETKEY
EXETYPE        WINDOWS
STUB           'WINSTUB.EXE'
HEAPSIZE       1024
STACKSIZE      8192
CODE           PRELOAD MOVEABLE DISCARDABLE
DATA           PRELOAD MOVEABLE MULTIPLE
```

Program GETKEY (see Figure 10.3) is a C program that uses message crackers to process keyboard messages. The program displays a nonresizeable window with a specific starting size and enables the user to type characters in a line of text. The program does processing for Enter, Home, BackSpace, and Left Arrow. When you close the program by pressing Alt-F4 or choosing Close on the control menu, a message box is displayed that shows the string the user entered.

The input string is stored in a character buffer. The program keeps track of the current position within the string in the `BufferPosition` variable. As the user types keystrokes, the characters are added to the string buffer. Each time the string changes, it is redisplayed by calling the `InvalidateRect` routine, which, in turn, sends the program a `WM_PAINT` message to redisplay the client area of the program.

Figure 10.3.

The GETKEY program.

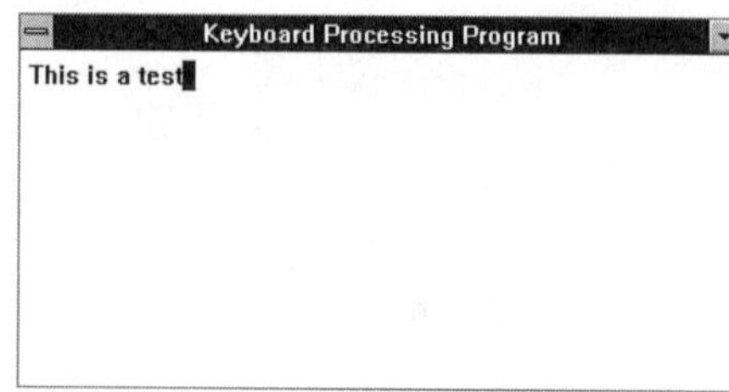

To process keyboard messages, the program traps two messages: `WM_KEYDOWN` and `WM_CHAR`. A message cracker is used to call a function for each Windows message defined. The `WMKeydown_Handler` function processes special keystrokes: the left arrow key, Backspace, Enter, and Home. The `WMChar_Handler` function takes care of catching all other characters as they are typed and puts the key entered to the string buffer. The `TextOut` function is used in `WM_PAINT` to display the new status of the client area.

When you run the program, notice the flashing cursor. It displays where keyboard entry currently starts. In Windows, this cursor is called a caret. The term *cursor* is reserved for the mouse cursor.

The caret does not appear automatically. You must create the caret and then display it. You also must keep track of where the caret should be displayed, and call a function every time the caret should be moved. Windows takes care of forcing the caret to flash.

To use a caret in GETKEY, the program processes the `WM_CREATE` function as follows:

```
case WM_CREATE :
{
   TEXTMETRIC tm;
   HDC        hDC;

   // Create and show caret
   // base the width and height on the current font

   hDC = GetDC(hWnd);
   GetTextMetrics(hDC, &tm);

   CreateCaret(hWnd, NULL,
               tm.tmAveCharWidth,   // width of current font
               tm.tmHeight);        // height of current font
   ShowCaret(hWnd);
```

```
   ReleaseDC(hWnd, hDC);
   return 0;
}
```

To use the caret, you first create it with a call to `CreateCaret`. You specify the handle to the window it belongs to, a handle to a bitmap you can use for the caret (you utilize the default caret), and the width and the height of the caret.

In GETKEY, you call `GetTextMetrics` to find the average width and height of the characters for the current font. Although you can pass arbitrary values, if the size of the font ever changes, the size of the cursor won't appear correct. Always be aware of device independence.

To force the caret to be displayed, you call the `ShowCaret` function. This displays the caret in the current caret position in the window, if the window has focus.

The caret is a shared system resource, and there can be only one caret displayed on-screen at one time. This is because you cannot type text into two different programs at once. Therefore, the `ShowCaret` function checks to make sure the window is active before displaying it.

To change the caret position, you call `SetCaretPos` in the code that processes the `WM_PAINT` message. The call looks like this:

```
SetCaretPos(5+LOWORD(GetTextExtent(PaintDC, Buffer,
BufferPosition)), 5);
```

`SetCaretPos` takes the `x` and `y` location (in pixels) of where to display the caret. However, in your program you don't necessarily know where this is. Therefore, you call the `GetTextExtent` function. `LOWORD` contains the number of pixels equivalent to a string's width, and `hiword` contains the height of the string. The routine takes into account the current font, so you always receive a correct value—even if the font changes.

When your program is done executing and if your caret does nothing fancy—such as use a bitmap as the caret—Windows discards the caret. Therefore, you don't have to add to the `WM_DESTROY` message-processing code to deal with the caret.

Enhancing Scroll Bars with Keyboard Input

In Chapter 9, you learned how to process scroll bar messages. Recall, the FOOTBALL.C program enabled the user to click the scroll bar to display new text in the window's client area. The program required a mouse. If the user doesn't have a mouse, she is just plain out of luck. If you add a keyboard interface, you have more prospective users than you would have without the keyboard interface.

An obvious way to add keyboard control to the program is to catch the keyboard keys and then duplicate the logic used for the scroll bars. This method works, but what if you change the scroll bar logic? Then, you must change the same code twice—once for the scroll bar messages and once for the keyboard messages. That's a hassle.

A better way to add a keyboard interface is to force the keyboard commands to evoke the function that handles the scroll bar logic. The best way to do this is through nothing other than messages. The Windows API provides a mechanism for a program to send a message to itself. This is done with the `SendMessage` function.

Look at how it's done. Listing 10.3 shows the program, KBSCROLL.C, and Listing 10.4 contains the module definition file. The program is a superset of the FOOTBALL.C program from Chapter 9. For variety, the window displays different types of fruit rather than football teams.

Listing 10.3. KBSCROLL.C program.

```
// KBSCROLL.C - C Program showing processing of scroll bars
//              Modification of FOOTBALL.C program.
//              This version adds a keyboard interface
//
// Programming Windows with Turbo C++ for Windows
// by Paul J. Perry

#define STRICT
```

```
#define  MAXNUMB 28
#define  NAMELEN 50

#include <windowsx.h>
#include <stdlib.h>
#include <string.h>

// Function Prototypes
LRESULT CALLBACK _export MainWndProc(HWND hWnd, UINT message,
                                     WPARAM wParam, LPARAM lParam);

void WMVScroll_Handler(HWND hWnd, HWND hwndCtl, UINT code, int
pos);

void WMSize_Handler(HWND hwnd, UINT state, int cx, int cy);

void WMKeydown_Handler(HWND hWnd, UINT vk, BOOL fDown,
                       int cRepeat, UINT flags);

// Global Data
int CharHeight;     // The height (in pixels) of each character
int LinesInWindow;  // The number of lines which can currently be
                    // displayed in the window
int Item=0;         // The item (in the array) that we want to
                    // display at the top-left corner of window

char Names[MAXNUMB][NAMELEN] =
{
   // The definition of fruit is courtesy of
   // Websters New World Dictionary, Second College Edition
   "Fruit - 'A sweet and edible plant",
   "         structure, consisting of a fruit",
   "         or of a flowering plant usually eaten",
   "         raw or as a dessert'",
   "----------------------------------------------",
   "Watermelon",          "Apple",
   "Pear",                "Grape",
   "Peach",               "Strawberry",
   "Guava",               "Kiwi",
   "Honeydew",            "Cantaloupe",
   "Plum",                "Nectarine",
   "Pineapple",           "Blackberry",
   "Raspberry",           "Apricot",
   "Oranges",             "Papayas",
   "Bananas",             "Coconut",
   "Lemons",              "Cherries",
   "Blueberries"
};
```

continues

Listing 10.3. continued

```
/*******************************************/
#pragma argsused
int PASCAL WinMain(HINSTANCE hInstance, HINSTANCE hPrevInstance,
                   LPSTR lpCmdParam, int nCmdShow)
{
   char        ProgName[] = "Fruits";
   HWND        hWnd;
   MSG         msg;


   if (!hPrevInstance)
   {
      WNDCLASS    wndclass;

      wndclass.lpszClassName = ProgName;
      wndclass.lpfnWndProc   = (WNDPROC) MainWndProc;
      wndclass.cbClsExtra    = 0;
      wndclass.cbWndExtra    = 0;
      wndclass.hInstance     = hInstance;
      wndclass.hIcon         = LoadIcon(NULL, IDI_APPLICATION);
      wndclass.hCursor       = LoadCursor(NULL, IDC_ARROW);
      wndclass.hbrBackground = (HBRUSH) (COLOR_WINDOW + 1);
      wndclass.lpszMenuName  = NULL;
      wndclass.style         = CS_VREDRAW | CS_HREDRAW;

      if (!RegisterClass(&wndclass)) exit(0);
   }

   // Create window with scrollbars
   // notice the new window style passed to CreateWindow
   // We only add vertical scroll bars.  To add horizontal
   // scroll bars, you would use the WS_HSCROLL type
   hWnd = CreateWindow(ProgName,"Scroll Bars With Keyboard
                       Processing",
                       WS_OVERLAPPEDWINDOW | WS_VSCROLL,
                       CW_USEDEFAULT, CW_USEDEFAULT,
                       CW_USEDEFAULT, CW_USEDEFAULT,
                       NULL, NULL, hInstance, NULL);

   ShowWindow(hWnd, nCmdShow);
   UpdateWindow(hWnd);

   while (GetMessage(&msg, NULL, 0, 0))
   {
      TranslateMessage(&msg);
      DispatchMessage(&msg);
```

```
   }
   return msg.wParam;
}

/*******************************************/
#pragma argsused
void WMVScroll_Handler(HWND hWnd, HWND hwndCtl, UINT code, int pos)
{
   switch(code)
   {
      case SB_LINEUP :
      {
         // User clicked on top scroll bar arrow
         // we will move one line up the page.
         // To do this, we decrement Item.
         Item -= 1;
         break;

      }

      case SB_LINEDOWN :
      {
         // User clicked on bottom scroll bar arrow
         // we will move one line down the page.
         // To do this, we increment the Item.
         Item += 1;
         break;
      }

      case SB_PAGEUP :
      {
         // User clicked on upper portion of scroll bar,
         // we will move down one page.
         // This would be like pressing the PageUp key.
         Item -= LinesInWindow;
         break;
      }

      case SB_PAGEDOWN :
      {
         // User clicked on lower portion of scroll bar,
         // we will move up one page.
         // This would be like pressing the PageDown key.
         Item += LinesInWindow;
         break;
      }
```

continues

Listing 10.3. continued

```
      case SB_THUMBTRACK :
      {
         // User is moving the scroll bar thumb.
         // We can redisplay the text, as the user
         // moves the thumb.
         Item = pos;
         break;
      }
   }

   // Check for bounds
   Item = max(Item, 0);
   Item = min(MAXNUMB, Item);

   // Adjust scroll bar position and repaint window
   SetScrollPos(hWnd, SB_VERT, Item, TRUE);
   InvalidateRect(hWnd, NULL, TRUE);

}

/********************************************/
#pragma argsused
void WMSize_Handler(HWND hWnd, UINT state, int cx, int cy)
{
    // Calculates the actual text lines which will fit in the
    // window
    LinesInWindow = cy/CharHeight;

    // If the number of lines can be displayed in the window
    // all at once, then make the scroll bar disappear.
    // It is not needed and takes space away from the client area.
    // Otherwise, if they are still needed, we display them
    if (LinesInWindow > MAXNUMB)
       ShowScrollBar(hWnd, SB_VERT, FALSE);
    else
       ShowScrollBar(hWnd, SB_VERT, TRUE);
}

/********************************************/
#pragma argsused
void WMKeydown_Handler(HWND hWnd, UINT vk,
                       BOOL fDown, int cRepeat, UINT flags)
{
   switch(vk)
   {
      case VK_UP :        // UP ARROW key pressed
```

```
        {
           SendMessage(hWnd, WM_VSCROLL, SB_LINEUP, 0L);
           break;
        }

        case VK_DOWN :       // DOWN ARROW key pressed
        {
           SendMessage(hWnd, WM_VSCROLL, SB_LINEDOWN, 0L);
           break;
        }

        case VK_PRIOR :      // PAGE UP key pressed
        {
           SendMessage(hWnd, WM_VSCROLL, SB_PAGEUP, 0L);
           break;
        }

        case VK_NEXT :       // PAGE DOWN key pressed
        {
           SendMessage(hWnd, WM_VSCROLL, SB_PAGEDOWN, 0L);
           break;
        }

     }

     return;

}

/*******************************************/
LRESULT CALLBACK _export MainWndProc(HWND hWnd, UINT message,
                                     WPARAM wParam, LPARAM lParam)
{
   switch (message)
   {
      // Catch vertical scroll bar messages.
      // To catch the horizontal scroll bar messages,
      // you would use a case WM_HSCROLL statement.
      case WM_VSCROLL :
      {
         return HANDLE_WM_VSCROLL(hWnd, wParam,
                                  lParam, WMVScroll_Handler);
      }

      case WM_CREATE :
      {
         HDC          hDC;
```

continues

Listing 10.3. continued

```
         TEXTMETRIC  tm;

         // Get the character height
         hDC = GetDC(hWnd);
         GetTextMetrics(hDC, &tm);
         CharHeight = tm.tmHeight + tm.tmExternalLeading;
         ReleaseDC(hWnd, hDC);

         // Set scroll bar ranges so range goes from 0 to MAXNUMB
         // The default is from 0 to 100.
         SetScrollRange(hWnd, SB_VERT, 0 , MAXNUMB, TRUE);
         return 0;

      }

      case WM_SIZE :
      {
         return HANDLE_WM_SIZE(hWnd, wParam, lParam,
                               WMSize_Handler);
      }

      case WM_PAINT :
      {
         HDC         PaintDC;
         PAINTSTRUCT ps;
         int         i;

         PaintDC = BeginPaint(hWnd, &ps);

         for(i=0; i<(MAXNUMB-Item); i++)
         {
            TextOut(PaintDC, 25, CharHeight*i, &Names[Item+i][0],
                    strlen(&Names[Item+i][0]));
         }

         EndPaint(hWnd, &ps);
         return 0;
      }

      case WM_KEYDOWN :
      {
         return HANDLE_WM_KEYDOWN(hWnd, wParam, lParam,
                                  WMKeydown_Handler);
```

```
        case WM_DESTROY :
        {
            PostQuitMessage(0);
            return 0;
        }
    }
    return DefWindowProc (hWnd, message, wParam, lParam);
}
```

Listing 10.4. KBSCROLL module definition file.

```
;
; KBSCROLL.DEF module definition file
;

DESCRIPTION    'Scrollbars That Process Keyboard Input'
NAME           KBSCROLL
EXETYPE        WINDOWS
STUB           'WINSTUB.EXE'
HEAPSIZE       1024
STACKSIZE      8192
CODE           PRELOAD MOVEABLE DISCARDABLE
DATA           PRELOAD MOVEABLE MULTIPLE
```

The new code sets up a message cracker for processing the keyboard messages. Figure 10.4 contains program output.

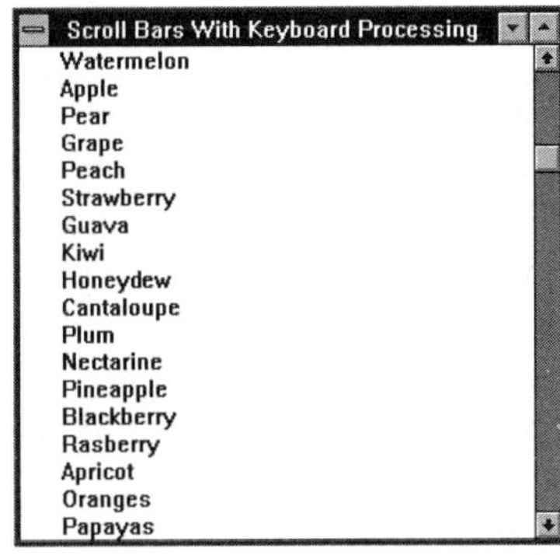

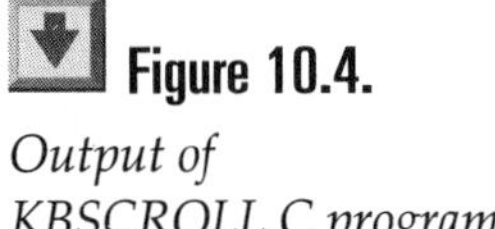

Figure 10.4.

Output of KBSCROLL.C program.

The handler function has statements that look like this:

```
case VK_UP :          // UP ARROW key pressed
{
   SendMessage(hWnd, WM_VSCROLL, SB_LINEUP, 0L);
   break;
}
```

Each virtual key you trap calls the `SendMessage` function to allow your program to process the keyboard messages. The `SendMessage` function is declared like this:

```
LRESULT SendMessage(HWND hWnd, UINT msg, WPARAM wParam, LPARAM
lParam);
```

You must specify which window you want to send the message to. The `hWnd` parameter specifies the window. You can send a message to the window procedure of your own program or to that of other programs that are running—but remember, you must have a handle to that window. The `msg` parameter specifies which message you want to send. Finally, the `wParam` and `lParam` values specify the word and long parameter you want to send as part of the message.

By sending a message to the window procedure of your program, you simplify the necessary code. You also enable your program to be modified easily. Now that you have examined keyboard processing, look briefly at a related topic, character sets.

Character Sets

A character set is a group of characters used to output information. You probably are familiar with the ASCII character set. It defines the character codes for 0 through 127 decimal (see Appendix B). IBM-compatible computers use an extended ASCII character set, which defines additional characters above 127. Most text-based applications make use of the extended characters while displaying boxes. Greek and international characters are included in the extended ASCII character set as well as the box drawing characters.

Windows uses the ASCII character set too. However, because of the graphical nature of Windows, the extended character set is not really needed. Thus, Windows supports several character sets. Windows calls the IBM-extended character set the OEM character set. It is included mainly for compatibility with DOS applications.

Windows uses an ANSI (American National Standards Institute) character set for most of its operations. During input of text in an edit box, the user can press and hold down the Alt key and type the three characters of the OEM character set. The character is displayed in the edit box and converted internally to an ANSI character code.

Sometimes a conversion problem occurs when using different character sets. Therefore, Windows provides several routines to convert between character sets. Table 10.3 lists the routines and what they do.

Table 10.3. Character set conversion routines.

Routine	*Description*
AnsiToOem	Converts from ANSI to OEM characters.
AnsiToOemBuff	Converts from ANSI to OEM characters, specifying buffer size.
OemToAnsi	Converts from OEM to ANSI characters.
OemToAnsiBuff	Converts from OEM to ANSI characters, specifying buffer size.

If you share your data between DOS and Windows programs, you might need to use the character set conversion routines. If your program doesn't share data with other types of applications, you may not need to use these routines much.

Mouse Basics

The mouse (not the crawly type) first gained popularity when the Macintosh computer was announced. With its graphical user environment, the Macintosh made special use of the mouse for almost all input. At first, some users were frustrated with the Macintosh. Because a mouse was required to do most everything, users accustomed to using a keyboard could not carry out common operations quickly. Apple Computer Corporation did update the operating system to add support for keyboard shortcuts in later revisions of the operating system to satisfy these people.

Clearly, the designers of Windows watched the evolution of the Macintosh, because they provided mouse and keyboard input. You know how the keyboard can be used. The rest of this chapter explores utilizing the mouse.

On the PC, the mouse didn't become a popular input device immediately. First of all, most software didn't support the mouse; second, users didn't perceive it as a real input device. Well, times have changed. Today, most PC software users expect to have a mouse user interface.

Not until programs such as Windows 3 came out did users find the mouse a useful and helpful input device. The cursor tracks the physical movement of the mouse on the screen. As the user moves the mouse down, the cursor moves down the screen. The shape of the cursor helps give feedback to the user about certain operations that are taking place. You probably have seen the cursor change to an hourglass during a lengthy file operation. This enables the user to know exactly what is happening when the machine seems to be in idle mode.

The mouse is an important input device for Windows. You have already seen how to specify a custom cursor in a window when defining a window class. This section of the book shows you how to change the cursor on-the-fly and how to respond to mouse messages.

Mouse Messages

As you might guess, all mouse activity is sent to a window's window procedure as a message. Most mice contain only two buttons, whereas some others contain three buttons. Windows supports up to three buttons (although, interestingly enough, Microsoft's own mouse contains only two buttons). Table 10.4 summarizes the mouse messages your program can receive.

Table 10.4. Mouse messages.

Message	*Description*
WM_LBUTTONDBLCLK	Left button double-clicked.
WM_LBUTTONDOWN	Left button pressed.
WM_LBUTTONUP	Left button released.
WM_MBUTTONDBLCLK	Middle button double-clicked.
WM_MBUTTONDOWN	Middle button pressed.
WM_MBUTTONUP	Middle button released.
WM_RBUTTONDBLCLK	Right button double-clicked.
WM_RBUTTONDOWN	Right button pressed.
WM_RBUTTONUP	Right button released.
WM_MOUSEMOVE	User moved the mouse.

A double-click is the quick-clicking of the mouse button. To receive mouse double-click messages, you must set a flag in the `WNDCLASS` data structure in the style field at class registration time. You can do this with the following:

```
wndcls.style = CS_DBLCLKS;
```

As usual, the style field probably is combined with other styles. If you specify the `CS_DBLCLKS` class style, when a mouse click is sent to a window, an internal timer is created. If the user presses the mouse again within the time set in the Windows Control Panel, the double-click message is sent to the window procedure of your application.

Changing the Cursor

So far, you have seen the use of the `LoadCursor` routine used to load a predefined cursor or a custom cursor created in the Resource Workshop. You can use this routine at any time to retrieve a handle to a cursor. Listing 10.5 shows a program (WAIT.CPP) that displays the wait cursor when the left mouse button is pressed in the client area. The cursor then changes back to the arrow cursor when the user releases the mouse button (see Figure 10.5). Listing 10.6 contains the module definition file.

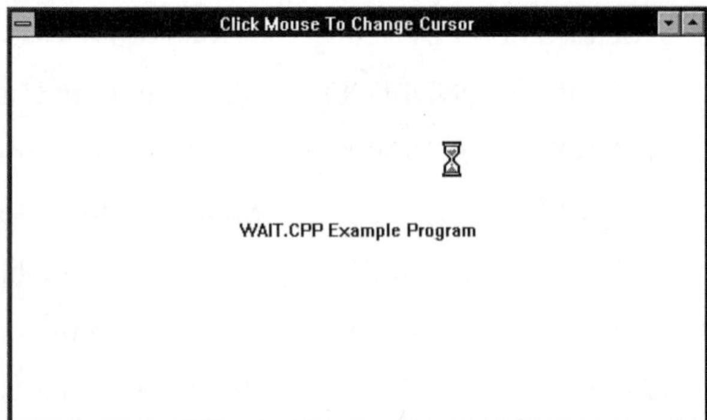

Figure 10.5.
The WAIT program.

Listing 10.5. WAIT.CPP program.

```
// WAIT.CPP - Program which controls mouse cursor
//
// Programming Windows with Turbo C++ for Windows
// by Paul J. Perry

#define WIN31
#define STRICT

#include <owl.h>
#include <windowsx.h>
```

```
// Class Declarations

/*******************************************/
class TOwlApp : public TApplication
{
   public :
      TOwlApp (LPSTR AName, HINSTANCE hInstance, HINSTANCE
               hPrevInstance,
               LPSTR CmdLine, int CmdShow) :
         TApplication(AName, hInstance, hPrevInstance,
            CmdLine, CmdShow) { } ;

   virtual void InitMainWindow();
};


/*******************************************/
class TMainWindow : public TWindow
{
   public :
      TMainWindow(PTWindowsObject AParent, LPSTR ATitle)
                  : TWindow(AParent, ATitle) { };
      virtual void Paint(HDC PaintDC, PAINTSTRUCT &PaintInfo);
      virtual void GetWindowClass(WNDCLASS& wndclass);
      virtual LPSTR GetClassName();
      virtual void SetupWindow();
      virtual void WMLButtonDown(TMessage& Msg)
         = [WM_FIRST + WM_LBUTTONDOWN];
      virtual void WMLButtonUp(TMessage& Msg)
         = [WM_FIRST + WM_LBUTTONUP];
};



// Class Member Functions

/*******************************************/
void TOwlApp::InitMainWindow()
{
   MainWindow = new TMainWindow(NULL, Name);
}


/*******************************************/
void TMainWindow::GetWindowClass(WNDCLASS& wndclass)
{
   TWindow::GetWindowClass(wndclass);
```

continues

Listing 10.5. continued

```
   // Set handle of icon to zero
   wndclass.hCursor = 0;
}


/********************************************/
LPSTR TMainWindow::GetClassName()
{
   return "Wait Class";

}

/********************************************/
void TMainWindow::SetupWindow()
{
   SetCursor(LoadCursor(0, IDC_ARROW));
}


/********************************************/
#pragma argsused
void TMainWindow::WMLButtonDown(TMessage& Msg)
{
   SetCursor(LoadCursor(0, IDC_WAIT));
}

/********************************************/
#pragma argsused
void TMainWindow::WMLButtonUp(TMessage& Msg)
{
   SetCursor(LoadCursor(0,IDC_ARROW));
}


/********************************************/
#pragma argsused
void TMainWindow::Paint(HDC PaintDC, PAINTSTRUCT &PaintInfo)
{
   RECT rect;

   GetClientRect(HWindow, &rect);

   DrawText(PaintDC, "WAIT.CPP Example Program", -1, &rect,
            DT_SINGLELINE ¦ DT_CENTER ¦ DT_VCENTER);

}
```

```
/*******************************************/
int PASCAL WinMain(HINSTANCE hInstance, HINSTANCE hPrevInstance,
                   LPSTR lpCmdLine, int nCmdShow)
{

   TOwlApp ThisApp("Click Mouse To Change Cursor", hInstance,
                   hPrevInstance, lpCmdLine, nCmdShow);
   ThisApp.Run();
   return ThisApp.Status;

}
```

Listing 10.6. WAIT.DEF module definition file.

```
; WAIT.DEF module definition file
;

DESCRIPTION   'Change the Mouse Cursor'
NAME          WAIT
EXETYPE       WINDOWS
STUB          'WINSTUB.EXE'
HEAPSIZE      1024
STACKSIZE     8192
CODE          PRELOAD MOVEABLE DISCARDABLE
DATA          PRELOAD MOVEABLE MULTIPLE
```

The WAIT.CPP program is based on the OWL. Hopefully, by now you can see the similarities between regular C programs and programs based on the OWL. Previous chapters compared similar programs in C and in C++ with those based on the OWL. In the second half of this book, you focus on learning new concepts about Windows, applicable to both C and C++.

The `LoadCursor` routine is used in conjunction with the `SetCursor` routine. `SetCursor` changes the current cursor to the handle of one specified. Because predefined stock cursors are used, a statement like

```
SetCursor(LoadCursor(0,IDC_WAIT));
```

retrieves a handle to the cursor and changes the cursor at one time.

If you were to write this program in straight C, you would create a case statement for the WM_LBUTTONDOWN and WM_LBUTTONUP messages and respond appropriately. You might take that up as an exercise for yourself, in converting WAIT.CPP to a traditional Windows program. It would be an excellent learning experience. In the meantime, you can study more material relating to the mouse.

Mouse Coordinates

Your program can get the coordinates of the mouse cursor at any time. Remember, each message contains the time and cursor coordinates. The next demonstration program in Listing 10.7 shows you how to display the mouse coordinates in a program. Listing 10.8 contains the module definition file.

Listing 10.7. Program shows the mouse coordinates.

```
// CURPOS.CPP - Program shows the current
//              position of the mouse
//
// Programming Windows with Turbo C++ for Windows
// by Paul J. Perry

#define WIN31
#define STRICT

#include <owl.h>
#include <windowsx.h>

#include <stdio.h>      // for sprintf() function


// Class Declarations

/*******************************************/
class TOwlApp : public TApplication
{
   public :
      TOwlApp (LPSTR AName, HINSTANCE hInstance, HINSTANCE
               hPrevInstance,
               LPSTR CmdLine, int CmdShow) :
         TApplication(AName, hInstance, hPrevInstance,
```

```
            CmdLine, CmdShow) { } ;

   virtual void InitMainWindow();
};

/*******************************************/
class TMainWindow : public TWindow
{
   public :
      POINT CurrPt;

      TMainWindow(PTWindowsObject AParent, LPSTR ATitle)
                     : TWindow(AParent, ATitle) { };
      virtual void Paint(HDC PaintDC, PAINTSTRUCT &PaintInfo);
      virtual void WMMouseMove(TMessage& Msg)
         = [WM_FIRST + WM_MOUSEMOVE];
};

// Class Member Functions

/*******************************************/
void TOwlApp::InitMainWindow()
{
   MainWindow = new TMainWindow(NULL, Name);
}

/*******************************************/
#pragma argsused
void TMainWindow::WMMouseMove(TMessage& Msg)
{
   RECT rect;

   // Get the current mouse cursor coordinates

   // What follows stands for the loword of
   //   the lParam of the message
   CurrPt.x = Msg.LP.Lo;

   // The next one stands for the hiword of
   // the lParam of the message
   CurrPt.y = Msg.LP.Hi;

   // Repaint cursor coordinates in client area
   // We only want to repaint upper left corner of
   // the client area.  Therefore we can specify
   // an "update" region by passing the coordinates
   // in the second parameter to the function.
```

continues

Listing 10.7. continued

```
   // By specifying the update area, the screen window
   //  does not flicker as much.

   rect.left    = 0;
   rect.top     = 0;
   rect.right   = 150;
   rect.bottom  = 60;
   InvalidateRect(HWindow, &rect, TRUE);
}


/********************************************/
#pragma argsused
void TMainWindow::Paint(HDC PaintDC, PAINTSTRUCT &PaintInfo)
{
   char buffer[80];
   int length;

   length = sprintf(buffer, "X = %d and Y = %d",
                    CurrPt.x, CurrPt.y);

   TextOut(PaintDC, 10, 10, buffer, length);

}

/********************************************/
int PASCAL WinMain(HINSTANCE hInstance, HINSTANCE hPrevInstance,
                   LPSTR lpCmdLine, int nCmdShow)
{

   TOwlApp ThisApp("Current Cursor Position", hInstance,
                   hPrevInstance, lpCmdLine, nCmdShow);
   ThisApp.Run();
   return ThisApp.Status;

}
```

Listing 10.8. Module definition file for CURPOS program.

```
;
; CURPOS.DEF module definition file
;
```

```
DESCRIPTION    'Display Current Mouse Position'
NAME           CURPOS
EXETYPE        WINDOWS
STUB           'WINSTUB.EXE'
HEAPSIZE       1024
STACKSIZE      8192
CODE           PRELOAD MOVEABLE DISCARDABLE
DATA           PRELOAD MOVEABLE MULTIPLE
```

The CURPOS program sets up a `WM_MOUSEMOVE` message response function. In the function, the mouse coordinates are saved, and the window client area is invalidated. A special trick is done in the `InvalidateRect` function call. You specify an update region by setting the values in a `RECT` structure. After that, only the area in the update region is cleared and then requested to be repainted. The result is a client area that does not flicker. Try moving the cursor over the text of the mouse coordinates (in the upper-left corner of the client area). Notice the cursor's annoying flash. For real proof, change the second parameter in the `InvalidateRect` function call from `rect` to `NULL`. You see the result of the entire client area being updated.

It is the `Paint` function that displays the current cursor coordinates (see Figure 10.6).

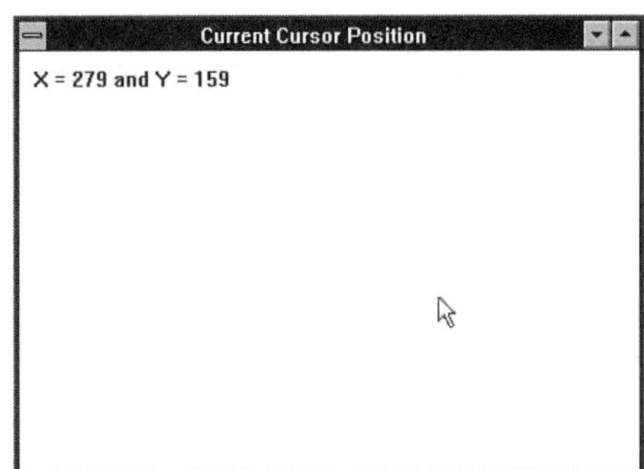

Figure 10.6.
Output of current cursor position program.

Notice, as you use the program, if you move the mouse outside the window's client area, the program no longer updates the mouse coordinates. The `WM_MOUSEMOVE` message is sent only to the window procedure when the mouse is moved within the client area of the window.

Notice also that the coordinates displayed are relative to the window. The location in the upper-left corner of the window is `0,0`. These are known as *client-area coordinates*. The x coordinate moves from left to right and becomes positive as you move to the right. The y coordinate moves from top to bottom, with the numbers becoming positive as you move down.

If you have an application in which you must catch the mouse coordinates, Windows provides routines to capture mouse input, even if the mouse is moved outside of the client area. The `SetCapture` routine forces all mouse messages to be sent to the window procedure of the window you specify in client-area coordinates. The `ReleaseCapture` routine returns mouse processing to normal.

What You Have Learned

Congratulations! You made it through Chapter 10. You are halfway through the book. I'm glad you are still with me. If you consider that you have already learned a lot about Windows programs, the fun has just begun.

This chapter covered two major methods of obtaining input in Windows. You saw how to use keyboard messages and how keyboard data can be processed in a program. In the second part of the chapter, you examined using the cursor in programs. You discovered how to obtain the coordinates of the cursor and how to change the shape of the cursor during program execution.

Chapter 11, "Working with the Graphics Device Interface," covers using graphics in your program with the Windows Graphics Device Interface (GDI).

The following topics were covered in this chapter:

- IBM-compatible computers can use several types of keyboard. The latest keyboard is the enhanced 101/102-key keyboard. It adds two function keys and duplicates keys on earlier IBM keyboards.
- The keyboard has its own microprocessor which detects when a key is pressed and sends a scan code to the computer. This is a number representing the keyboard character being pressed.

- Windows provides built-in support for keyboard keystrokes without requiring much extra effort from the programmer. Examples include processing of the system menu and use of the dialog box, accelerator keys, and menu keys.
- Your program's window procedure receives messages that correspond to the key being pressed. Every time a key is pressed, the program receives a `WM_KEYDOWN` message. When a key is released, the program receives a `WM_KEYUP` message.
- When the window procedure receives a keyboard message, several fields of the `lParam` parameter are filled in, including the repeat count, scan code, extended key flag, context code, previous key state, and transition state.
- When the window procedure receives a keyboard message, the `wParam` parameter contains a virtual key code. The virtual key code defines a standard set of keys for all keyboards that Windows operates on, now and in the future. Virtual key constants are defined in windows.h, and all begin with the prefix `VK_`.
- The window procedure also receives character codes as messages. The character code is the ASCII-equivalent character code passed to the window procedure.
- Dead characters are used for international support to add symbols that require two keystrokes, one right after another, to define the complete character.
- Character sets define which symbols are included in a group of characters. Windows includes support for the OEM character set, which supports the regular ASCII characters on IBM-type computers and the ANSI character set that contains symbols more useful in a graphical user interface such as Windows.
- Mouse input is passed to a program's window procedure as messages. Messages are defined for mouse movement and key clicks for the three mouse buttons usually found on a mouse.
- The `SetCursor` routine is used to change the current window cursor.
- The current mouse coordinates are passed with mouse messages. You can use this information to make extra use of the mouse in your programs.

11

WORKING WITH THE GDI

IN THIS CHAPTER

- What the graphics device interface (GDI) is and what its advantages are over a conventional graphics system.
- What a device context (DC) is used for, how to get a handle to one, and what the attributes of the display context are.
- How to display a single point in a window's client area using a specific color.
- Several methods of displaying text in the client area of your program.
- How to change the attributes of the display context.
- Several routines used to draw lines, both straight and curved.
- How to draw basic geometric shapes with routines that are built into the GDI.

Windows, being a graphical user interface, has (as you might expect) a rich library of routines to draw graphical output. All the text output you have seen is graphical output. In Windows, there is no such thing as a single text character, the output is all graphical. Over 50 routines are provided in the Windows application program interface for graphics device interface (GDI) functions and procedures. You learn the fundamental ones here.

This chapter looks at the routines used for graphics output to the client area of a window. You learn how to set individual points, draw text, create geometric figures, and take full advantage of color in your programs. You look at the more common graphics routines that Windows programmers use.

Overview of the GDI

The GDI is powerful because it provides both device-independent graphics operations and a rich library of display routines. The GDI is used to access video displays, printers, and plotters. This chapter looks at output on video displays only.

The major advantage when using the GDI is that it frees the programmer from having to develop device drivers (see Figure 11.1). Because Windows provides the software drivers for many output devices, programmers can focus on new features and functionality of their program rather than writing device drivers for a multitude of computers.

Figure 11.1.

The video display device setup selection.

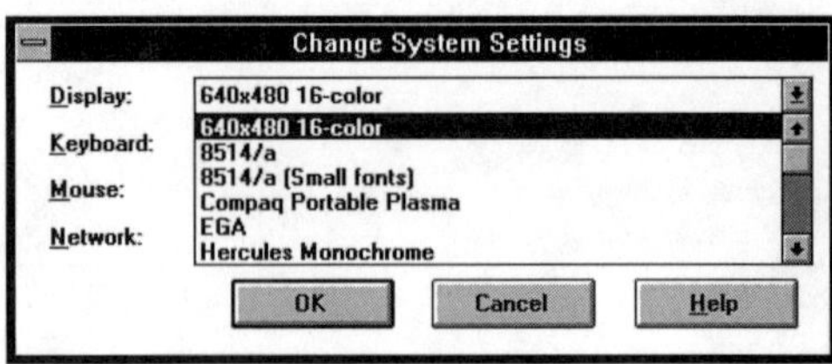

Figure 11.2 shows the flow of information from a Windows application through a GDI device context and a software device driver to the final output device. By providing software device drivers, a large number of output devices can be supported by the operating environment, both now and in the future. As new video displays are made available, the manufacturer will (hopefully) provide the necessary software device driver. This would allow a large number of software applications to use the hardware, as soon as the driver is available.

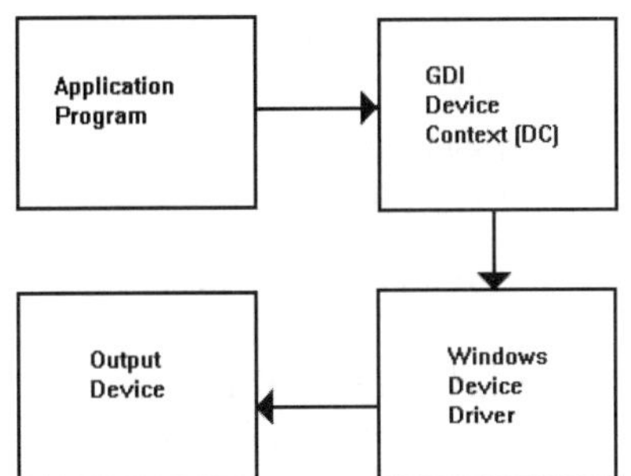

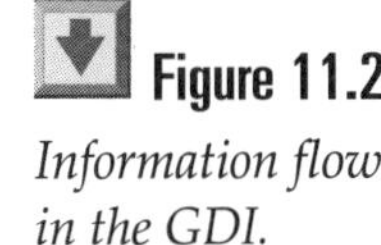

Figure 11.2.
Information flow in the GDI.

To use the GDI, an application makes calls to GDI routines. All GDI routines require a handle to a device context. With the handle to a device context, Windows can send graphics requests to the software device driver, which in turn creates visual images on the video output device.

The Device Context

When you want to output to a window, you must first request a handle to a device context. The device context specifies the characteristics and attributes of the graphics to be displayed. Device context attributes are changed by using a specific GDI routine. Table 11.1 lists the device context attributes with their default values. The rightmost column lists the GDI functions that affect or use the specified attribute.

Table 11.1. Default Attributes of the Device Context.

Attribute	*Default Value*	*GDI Routine*
Background color	white	SetBkColor
Background mode	OPAQUE	SetBKMode
Bitmap	none	CreateBitmap CreateBitmapIndirect CreateCompatibleBitmap SelectBitmap SelectObject
Brush	WHITE_BRUSH	CreateBrushIndirect CreateDIBPatternBrush CreateHatchBrush CreatePatternBrush CreateSolidBrush SelectBrush SelectObject
Brush origin	(0,0)	SetBrushOrg UnrealizeObject
Clipping region	entire client area	ExcludeClipRect IntersectClipRect OffsetClipRgn SelectClipRgn
Color palette	DEFAULT_PALETTE	CreatePalette RealizePalette SelectPalette
Current pen position	(0,0)	MoveTo
Drawing mode	R2_COPYPEN	SetROP2

Attribute	*Default Value*	*GDI Routine*
Font	SYSTEM_FONT	CreateFont CreateFontIndirect SelectFont SelectObject
Intercharacter spacing	0	SetTextCharacterExtra
Mapping Mode	MM_TEXT	SetMapMode
Pen	BLACK_PEN	CreatePen CreatePenIndirect SelectPen SelectObject
Polygon-Filling Mode	ALTERNATE	SetPolyFillMode
Stretching mode	STRETCH_ANDSCANS	SetStretchBltMode
Text color	black	SetTextColor
Viewport extent	(1,1)	SetViewPortExt
Viewport origin	(0,0)	SetViewPortOrg
Window extents	(1,1)	SetWindowExt
Window origin	(0,0)	SetWindowOrg

Not all device context attributes are used for every routine. For example, a routine that displays lines does not use the font attribute. In the same way, a routine that displays a single point on the screen does not use the bitmap attribute. When you do want to display text output, however, the device context contains the information needed to do the job. Your program doesn't have to do any work in defining fonts because it can use the default font specified in the device context.

Windows programs use several methods to get a handle to a device context. While using the ObjectWindows Library, a program's Paint method automatically receives a handle to the device context, as demonstrated here.

```
void TMainWindow::Paint(HDC PaintDC, PAINTSTRUCT &PaintInfo)
{
   RECT rect;

   GetClientRect(HWindow, &rect);

   DrawText(PaintDC, "Custom Icons and Cursors in an OWL program",
            -1, &rect,  DT_SINGLELINE ¦ DT_CENTER ¦ DT_VCENTER);
   ...
  [other program lines]
   ...
}
```

This makes it even easier to use the graphics routines. You use the handle to the display context whenever accessing GDI routines.

Using traditional C programming methods, your program's `WM_PAINT` case must use the `BeginPaint` and `EndPaint` routines to receive a handle to a device context, as follows:

```
case WM_PAINT :
{
   HDC         PaintDC;
   PAINTSTRUCT ps;

   PaintDC = BeginPaint(hWnd, &ps);

   TextOut(PaintDC, 5, 5, "Display this text", 17);
   ...
   [other program lines]
   ...
   EndPaint(hWnd, &ps);
   return 0;
}
```

Besides getting a handle to a device context, the `BeginPaint` routine also fills out the `PS` variable, which is of type `PAINTSTRUCT` that is defined in windows.h as follows:

```
typedef struct tagPAINTSTRUCT
{
    HDC         hdc;
    BOOL        fErase;
    RECT        rcPaint;
    BOOL        fRestore;
    BOOL        fIncUpdate;
    BYTE        rgbReserved[16];
} PAINTSTRUCT;
```

This variable contains a `RECT` structure indicating the area of the window that has been made invalid. Your program could analyze this data and display only the area that has been written over, thereby speeding up paint processing operations.

The `BeginPaint` and `EndPaint` routines are used only when processing the `WM_PAINT` message. The use of these two routines informs the system that your program did respond to the `WM_PAINT` message by telling the window manager the area has been validated.

Any program can obtain a handle to a device context during processing of other messages with the `GetDC` routine, as follows:

```
hDC = GetDC(hWnd);
TextOut(hDC, 5, 5, "Display this text", 17);
...
[other program lines]
...
ReleaseDC(hWnd, hDC);
```

Programs based on both the ObjectWindows Library and traditional C programs can use the `GetDC` (and corresponding `ReleaseDC`) routines to write text. It is important to always use the routines in pairs. If your program does not return the display context back to the system (using `ReleaseDC` or `EndPaint`), the limited number of display contexts (5) will be used up, and no program will be able to display any output.

Getting Device Context Capabilities

Your program can retrieve specific information about a given device context at any time. The `GetDeviceCaps` (get device capabilities) routine returns an integer value relating to the index value passed to it. Table 11.2 contains a list of the values you can obtain information about.

Table 11.2. Device parameters for GetDeviceCaps function.

Value	*Description*
DRIVERVERSION	Device driver version.
TECHNOLOGY	Device classification.
HORZSIZE	Horizontal size of display in millimeters.
VERTSIZE	Vertical size of display in millimeters.
HORZRES	Horizontal width of display in pixels.
VERTRES	Vertical width of display in pixels.
BITSPIXEL	Number of adjacent color bits per pixel.
PLANES	Number of color planes.
NUMBRUSHES	Number of brushes the device has.
NUMPENS	Number of pens the device has.
NUMMARKERS	Number of markers the device has.
NUMFONTS	Number of fonts the device has.
NUMCOLORS	Number of colors the device supports.
PDEVICESIZE	Size required for device descriptor.
CURVECAPS	Curve capabilities.
LINECAPS	Line capabilities.
POLYGONALCAPS	Polygonal capabilities.
TEXTCAPS	Text capabilities.
CLIPCAPS	Clipping capabilities.
RASTERCAPS	BitBlt capabilities.
ASPECTX	Width of a device pixel as used for line drawing.
ASPECTY	Height of device pixel as used for line drawing.

Value	Description
ASPECTXY	Length of hypotenuse.
LOGPIXELSX	Logical pixels per inch in x direction.
LOGPIXELSY	Logical pixels per inch in y direction.
SIZEPALETTE	Number of entries in physical palette.
NUMRESERVED	Number of reserved entries in palette.
COLORRES	Actual color resolution.

Although the routines encompass support for printers, plotters, and video displays, specific information can be returned by using the routine. For example,

```
hDC := GetDC(hWnd);
Result := GetDeviceCaps(hDC, HorzSize);
ReleaseDC(HWindow, hDC);
```

returns (in `Result`) the current width of the physical display in millimeters. This information can be helpful as you program for Windows. Other values that query information return a number that can be compared to constants defined in windows.h. Check the online help system in the Integrated Development Environment (IDE) for specific information on values returned by the `GetDeviceCaps` routine.

Getting to the Point

The smallest screen element you can light up is a single pixel. Listing 11.1 (POINTS.CPP) enables you to move the mouse and highlight pixels. Listing 11.2 contains the module definition file for the program. Pressing the left mouse button changes the color of the pixels. Double-clicking the left mouse button clears the window. Figure 11.3 shows several different groups of points displayed in the client area of the window.

Listing 11.1. A program to display points.

```
// POINTS.CPP - Displaying points in client area
//
// Programming Windows with Turbo C++ for Windows
// by Paul J. Perry

#define WIN31
#define STRICT

#include <owl.h>
#include <windowsx.h>


// Class Declarations

/*******************************************/
class TOwlApp : public TApplication
{
   public :
      TOwlApp (LPSTR AName, HINSTANCE hInstance, HINSTANCE
hPrevInstance, LPSTR CmdLine, int CmdShow) :
               TApplication(AName, hInstance, hPrevInstance,
               CmdLine, CmdShow) { } ;

   virtual void InitMainWindow();
};


/*******************************************/
class TMainWindow : public TWindow
{
   public :
      int ColorValue;

      TMainWindow(PTWindowsObject AParent, LPSTR ATitle);
      virtual LPSTR GetClassName();
      virtual void GetWindowClass(WNDCLASS& wndclass);
      virtual void Paint(HDC PaintDC, PAINTSTRUCT &PaintInfo);
      virtual void WMLButtonDown(TMessage& Msg)
         = [WM_FIRST + WM_LBUTTONDOWN];
      virtual void WMMouseMove(TMessage& Msg)
         = [WM_FIRST + WM_MOUSEMOVE];
      virtual void  WMLButtonDblclk(TMessage& Msg)
         = [WM_FIRST + WM_LBUTTONDBLCLK];

};
```

```
// Class Member Functions

/*******************************************/
void TOwlApp::InitMainWindow()
{
   MainWindow = new TMainWindow(NULL, Name);
}

/*******************************************/
TMainWindow::TMainWindow(PTWindowsObject AParent, LPSTR ATitle)
                         : TWindow(AParent, ATitle)
{
   Attr.W = 500;
   Attr.H = 400;
   ColorValue = 0;
}


/*******************************************/
LPSTR TMainWindow::GetClassName()
{
   return "PointsClass";
}

/*******************************************/
void TMainWindow::GetWindowClass(WNDCLASS& wndclass)
{
   TWindow::GetWindowClass(wndclass);
   wndclass.style = CS_HREDRAW ¦ CS_VREDRAW ¦ CS_DBLCLKS;

}

/*******************************************/
#pragma argsused
void TMainWindow::WMLButtonDown(TMessage& Msg)
{
   if (ColorValue >= 255)
      ColorValue = 0;

   ColorValue = ColorValue + 51;

}

/*******************************************/
#pragma argsused
void  TMainWindow::WMLButtonDblclk(TMessage& Msg)
{
```

continues

Listing 11.1. continued

```
   // Clear window
   InvalidateRect(HWindow, NULL, TRUE);
}

/*******************************************/
void TMainWindow::WMMouseMove(TMessage& Msg)
{
   HDC hDC;

   hDC = GetDC(HWindow);

   SetPixel(hDC, Msg.LP.Lo, Msg.LP.Hi,
            RGB(0, ColorValue, ColorValue));

   SetPixel(hDC, Msg.LP.Lo+1, Msg.LP.Hi+1,
            RGB(0, ColorValue, ColorValue));

   SetPixel(hDC, Msg.LP.Lo-1, Msg.LP.Hi-1,
            RGB(0, ColorValue, ColorValue));

   SetPixel(hDC, Msg.LP.Lo-1, Msg.LP.Hi+1,
            RGB(0, ColorValue, ColorValue));

   SetPixel(hDC, Msg.LP.Lo+1, Msg.LP.Hi-1,
            RGB(0, ColorValue, ColorValue));

   ReleaseDC(HWindow, hDC);

}


/*******************************************/
#pragma argsused
void TMainWindow::Paint(HDC PaintDC, PAINTSTRUCT &PaintInfo)
{
   TextOut(PaintDC, 5, 5, "Draw With the Mouse", 19);
   TextOut(PaintDC, 5, 25, "Change Colors with Left Mouse Button",
           36);
   TextOut(PaintDC, 5, 45, "Double Click Left Mouse Button to
           Clear", 39);

}


/*******************************************/
int PASCAL WinMain(HINSTANCE hInstance, HINSTANCE hPrevInstance,
                   LPSTR lpCmdLine, int nCmdShow)
```

```
{
   TOwlApp ThisApp("Display Points", hInstance,
                   hPrevInstance, lpCmdLine, nCmdShow);
   ThisApp.Run();
   return ThisApp.Status;
}
```

Listing 11.2. The module definition file for POINTS.CPP.

```
;
; POINTS.DEF module definition file
;

DESCRIPTION    'Getting To The Point'
NAME           POINTS
EXETYPE        WINDOWS
STUB           'WINSTUB.EXE'
HEAPSIZE       1024
STACKSIZE      8192
CODE           PRELOAD MOVEABLE DISCARDABLE
DATA           PRELOAD MOVEABLE MULTIPLE
```

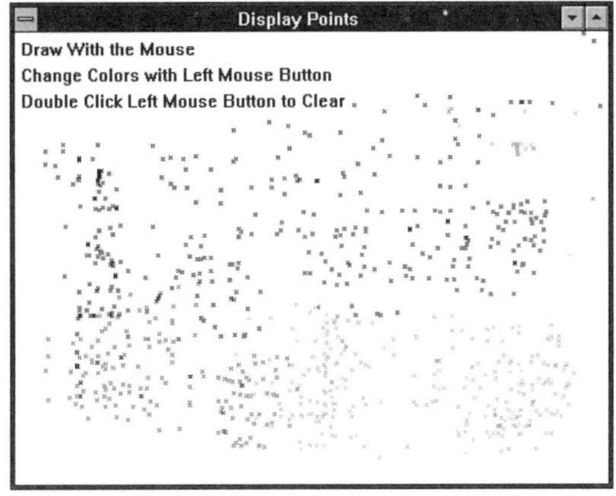

Figure 11.3.

Output for POINTS.CPP.

The `WMMouseMove` message function is executed every time the mouse is moved over the client area of the program. Each time `WMMouseMove` is executed, the current mouse cursor location has a group of pixels displayed. The program uses the `SetPixel` routine, as follows:

```
SetPixel(hDC, Msg.LP.Lo, Msg.LP.Hi,
        RGB(0, ColorValue, ColorValue));
```

This routine takes a handle to the display context, the `x` and `y` coordinates of the pixel to display, and a color value. The `x` and `y` coordinates are in client area coordinates (0,0 being the upper-left corner of the client area). The color value uses the RGB macro to return a color with different amounts of red, green, and blue. A single color value can be from 0 to 255. The combined RGB color can specify almost any color (in fact, many more colors than can be displayed on most screens at any one time).

Table 11.3 lists the most accurate RGB color values. Because RGB values are matched to the next closest one that the adapter can display, those are the only numerical values you can rely on for exact color match. To mix colors, the GDI uses a method known as dithering (described in detail later) that results in the perceived creation of new colors. The RGB color values may vary depending on the type of display to which you are outputting information.

Table 11.3. RGB color values.

RGB Value	*Color*
RGB(0,0,0)	Black
RGB(255,255,255)	White
RGB(255,0,0)	Red
RGB(0,255,0)	Green
RGB(0,0,255)	Blue
RGB(128, 128, 128)	Gray

In the POINTS.CPP program, the first color value (red) is always 0. The green and blue values change as the user clicks the mouse. Starting with black, the colors go to gray, cyan, and bright cyan. The cycle then repeats itself as the user presses the left mouse button.

To trap the double-click of the left mouse button, add a style bit to the window class, as follows:

```
void TMainWindow::GetWindowClass(WNDCLASS& wndclass)
{
   TWindow::GetWindowClass(wndclass);
   wndclass.style = CS_HREDRAW ¦ CS_VREDRAW ¦ CS_DBLCLKS;

}
```

The CS_DBLCLKS value forces Windows to check for a mouse double-click. When a double-click occurs, the `WM_LBUTTONDBLCLK` message is received. In the POINTS.CPP program, an `InvalidateRect` call forces the client area to be cleared.

Displaying the Text

Text is the fundamental method of output for many programs. Text output in Windows is different from text output in a DOS-based environment. You have already seen how your program must respond to a `WM_PAINT` message to display text (or graphics) in the client area of a window.

Using the EasyWin library, text output is accomplished with a single statement, such as:

```
#include <stdio.h>
...
printf("Text to be displayed");
...
```

This statement does not give the programmer much control over where and how the text is to be displayed. Another step a DOS programmer may use is to position the cursor and then write the text to a specific location on the screen.

Although this gives the programmer more control, programming for Windows gives more flexibility to the programmer. Text can be displayed in a number of different type styles. Chapter 16, "Even More GDI," looks at changing the characteristics of text.

The GDI provides three routines for displaying text. The functions are `TextOut`, `ExtTextOut`, and `DrawText`.

TextOut

`TextOut` is the basic method of displaying character strings in Windows. It takes a handle to a device context, the `x` and `y` position of the location to display the text, the character string, and the number of characters in the string. The routine is defined in windows.h as follows:

```
BOOL TextOut(HDC hDC, int x, int y, LPCSTR str, int length);
```

The `x` and `y` values specify the location in the client area to position the text. The default device context uses pixels as the unit by which to measure locations. Besides specifying the string, you also need to specify the length of the string as the last parameter to the function.

You can use the `TextOut` function as follows:

```
HDC hDC;
char str[] = "This text will appear in the client area";

hDC = GetDC(hWnd);

TextOut(hDC, 5, 5, str, strlen(str));

ReleaseDC(hWnd, hDC);
```

Remember to `#include` the strings.h header file in your program so that you can use the `strlen()` function. Using the `strlen()` function makes it easy to calculate the length of a string. If you prefer, you can include an integer value specifying the length of the string to display.

The `TextOut` routine (like the other text output routines) uses the default attributes specified in the device context.

ExtTextOut

The `ExtTextOut` routine is an extended version of `TextOut`. This routine adds several attributes that you can specify for displaying text. With the `ExtTextOut` routine, you can control character width, clipping, and an opaque rectangle. The routine is defined in windows.h like this:

```
BOOL ExtTextOut(HDC hDC, int x, int y, UINT options, RECT rect,
                LPCSTR str, UINT length, int spacing);
```

It takes the same parameters as the `TextOut` routine, including several additional ones that allow you to take advantage of the extra features of the routine.

The `options` parameter specifies the rectangle type. It can be either `ETO_CLIPPED` or `ETO_OPAQUE`. The `ETO_CLIPPED` constant specifies that Windows will clip text inside the specified rectangle. The `ETO_OPAQUE` value specifies that the current background color fills the rectangle.

The `rect` parameter specifies the rectangle to use for clipping or displaying a rectangle. The last parameter, `spacing`, is an array of character width values. It is used to tell the routine how to space between characters when outputting text.

To control the spacing between characters, use code such as the following:

```
int Spacing[] = {14,14,14,14,14,14,14,14,14,14,14,14,14,14,14};
char str[] = "This is a test";


ExtTextOut(PaintDC, 5, 5, 0, NULL, str,
           strlen(str), &Spacing[0]);
```

This sets the spacing between characters to 14 pixels (see Figure 11.4). You could use different values in the `Spacing` array to modify the spacing between each character.

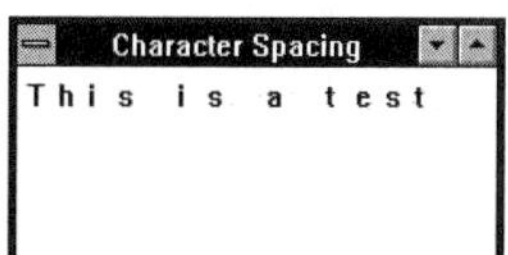

Figure 11.4.
A character spacing example.

To set a clipping region, you must specify the ETO_CLIPPED flag and the rectangle to clip to. Here is an example.

```
RECT rect;
char str[] = "This is a test";


rect.top = 6;
rect.left = 0;

rect.right = 85;
rect.bottom = 10;

ExtTextOut(PaintDC, 0, 0, ETO_CLIPPED, &rect,
           str, strlen(str), NULL);
```

This code displays only text that falls within the specified rectangle (see Figure 11.5). The left and top values are the (x,y) positions of the upper-left corner. The right and bottom values are the (x,y) values of the lower-right corner.

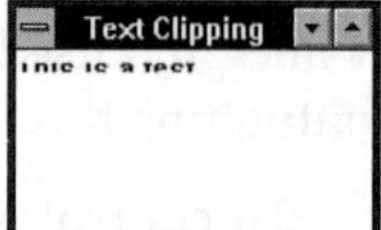

Figure 11.5.

An example of clipping.

To use the final option, an opaque rectangle, you must specify the ETO_OPAQUE flag and specify the rectangle coordinates. An example call would be:

```
RECT rect;
char str[] = "This is a test";


rect.top = 100;
rect.left = 100;

rect.right = 300;
rect.bottom = 300;

SetBkColor(PaintDC, RGB(0, 0, 255));
SetTextColor(PaintDC, RGB(255, 255, 255));

ExtTextOut(PaintDC, 150, 200, ETO_OPAQUE, &rect,
           str, strlen(str), NULL);
```

This routine sets the background color to blue and the text color to white (see Figure 11.6). After the routine displays the text, it displays a rectangle in the appropriate colors in the specified areas.

Figure 11.6.
Opaque text output.

DrawText

The `DrawText` routine is the last text output routine that is discussed in this chapter. This routine provides some advanced formatting capabilities for displaying character strings. The routine is defined in windows.h, as follows:

```
int DrawText(HDC hDC, LPCSTR str, int length, RECT rect, UINT flag);
```

As with any GDI routine, `DrawText` requires a handle to a device context as its first parameter. The next parameter is the string you want to display. When you specify the string, you can include the `&` prefix before a character to underline it. If you need to display the `&` character, include two of them, (as in `&&`). The routine takes the length of the string as the third parameter.

If you set the `length` parameter to `-1`, the routine automatically calculates the length of the string for you (you don't need to use the `strlen()` function). The `rect` parameter specifies the bounding rectangle of the text to be displayed.

The last parameter, `flag`, enables you to specify a format for the string you want to display. Table 11.4 shows the formatting constants available.

Table 11.4. DrawText style formats.

Value	*Description*
DT_TOP	Text is top-justified for single lines.
DT_LEFT	Aligns text to the left.
DT_CENTER	Centers text horizontally in rectangle.
DT_RIGHT	Aligns text to the right.
DT_VCENTER	Centers text vertically in rectangle.
DT_BOTTOM	Bottom-justified text (combine with DT_SINGLELINE).
DT_WORDBREAK	Breaks lines between words if extending past edge of rectangle.
DT_SINGLELINE	Ignores carriage returns and linefeeds.
DT_EXPANDTABS	Expands tab characters to eight characters per tab.
DT_TABSTOP	Sets tab stops.
DT_NOCLIP	Don't clip text while drawing.
DT_EXTERNALLEADING	Includes leading in line height.
DT_CALCRECT	Determines width and height of rectangle.
DT_NOPREFIX	Don't prefix characters.

Figure 11.7 shows the output of using the `DT_WORDBREAK` flag. The `Paint` method of the program has lines similar to the following:

```
RECT rect;
char str[] = "This is a test of formatting "
```

```
            "capabilities of DrawText.  "
            "This string is broken up into "
            "several lines";

rect.top = 100;
rect.left = 100;

rect.right = 400;
rect.bottom = 700;

DrawText(PaintDC, str, -1, &rect, DT_WORDBREAK);
```

The `DrawText` routine is the most versatile routine the GDI provides for outputting text. The next section explains how to change some of the device context attributes related to the routines you just looked at, as well as some new ones.

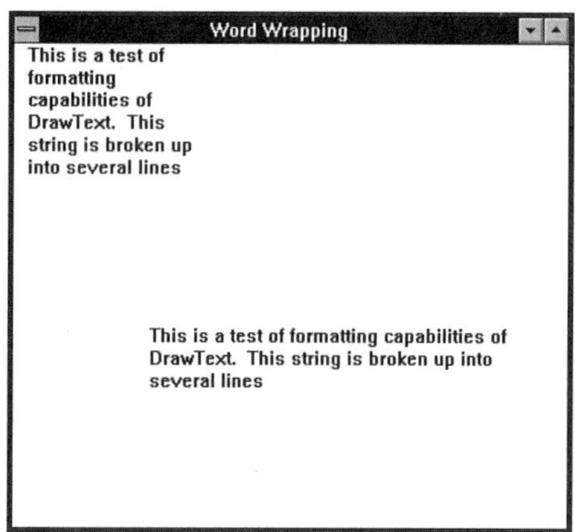

Figure 11.7.

DrawText used to display text.

Changing Device Context Attributes

As you have seen from the example programs, Windows API routines are used to change the attributes of certain display context fields. Table 11.5 lists some of the essential routines that modify device context attributes. Each of these is detailed in this section to see what they do and how they work.

Table 11.5. Device context attribute modification routines.

Routine	*Description*
SetBkColor	Sets background color.
SetTextColor	Sets text color.
SetBkMode	Sets background mode.
SetMapMode	Sets mapping mode.

Changing Colors

The `SetBkColor` function changes the current background color. It is defined in windows.h as follows:

```
COLORREF SetBkColor(HDC hDC, COLORREF color);
```

The routine takes a variable of type COLORREF. The best way to specify this value is with the `RGB` function. The `SetBkColor` routine returns the previous color which was set in the device context. Therefore, you can save this value and use it later in the program, if you need to.

The `SetTextColor` routine is valuable when using any of the text output routines you learned about earlier (`TextOut`, `ExtTextOut`, and `DrawOut`). The `SetTextColor` routine is defined similar to `SetBkColor`. The routine looks like the following:

```
COLORREF SetTextColor(HDC hDC, COLORREF color);
```

`SetTextColor` takes the handle to the device context and a color value. Again, the routine returns the previous text color that was set in the device context. Using both `SetTextColor` and `SetBkColor` enables you to set the colors that your text displayed in.

Changing Background Modes

The background mode refers to how graphics objects are displayed. The background mode defines whether the GDI should remove existing background colors on the device surface before drawing text. It also applies to brushes and nonsolid pen styles (both of which are discussed later in this chapter).

The routine is defined as follows:

```
int SetBkMode(HDC hDC, int bkMode);
```

The `bkMode` parameter specifies the background drawing mode. It can be either Opaque or Transparent. An Opaque background is filled with the current background color before the text is drawn. A Transparent background remains untouched when displaying new objects.

Changing Mapping Modes

A mapping mode refers to the units you specify when setting display coordinates. In real life, if you were to travel from your home to the supermarket, you could measure it in miles, yards, or feet. You are probably most familiar with using miles. However, if the grocery store is just around the corner, you might say that it is 100 feet away. Well, some of these same concepts creep up when working with computers.

Windows provides eight different mapping modes, or ways of measuring display items. The default mapping mode is screen pixels. In this mode, each pixel corresponds to a coordinate in the GDI. You set the mapping mode with a call to the `SetMapMode` routine. It is defined as follows:

```
int SetMapMode(HDC hDC, int MapMode);
```

The `MapMode` parameter is a constant defined in windows.h. The constants fall into one of the following groups:

- *Pixel Mode*—To use this mode you use the `MM_TEXT` identifier. It refers to the pixel mapping mode, where there is a one-to-one mapping ratio between physical pixels and GDI coordinates. Positive `x` values move to the right, and positive `y` values move down the screen.

- *Fixed Mode*—There are five fixed modes available: MM_LOMETRIC, MM_HIMETRIC, MM_LOENGLISH, MM_HIENGLISH, and MM_TWIPS. These units may be more familiar to you. Twips is a fabricated word meaning twentieth of a point. In these units, moving to the right is a positive x direction and upward is a positive y direction.
- *Isotropic Mode*—In isotropic mode, MM_ISOTROPIC, the aspect ratio and scale can be changed. It causes the scale of the horizontal and vertical dimensions to be set equivalently.
- *Anisotropic Mode*—In Anisotropic mode, MM_ANISOTROPIC, the aspect ratio and scale can be changed. This mode causes the scale of the horizontal and vertical dimensions to be set differently.

Using different mapping modes can be somewhat confusing. For the most part, this book sticks with the MM_TEXT mapping mode. After you look at some more routines for drawing graphics, you see a program that uses one of the alternate graphics mode. It is important to know about some of the flexibility provided with the GDI to change mapping modes. In graphics-intensive operations, using a different mapping mode can make programming easier.

Drawing Lines

A line is actually a set of connected points. The GDI provides routines for drawing lines, including curved lines. Before you can draw lines, you must look at an important display context attribute that describes how lines are drawn. This attribute is called a pen.

Using Pens

A pen is a display-context object that specifies how a line is drawn. Windows provides predefined (stock) pens, and you can create your own custom pens. You identify a pen with a handle. You must then select the pen into the display context.

Just as you can only write with a single pen at a time, a device context can select only a single pen at a time. The three predefined pens are `WHITE_PEN`, `BLACK_PEN`, and `NULL_PEN` (which draws transparently).

To use a pen, you must first receive a handle to a pen, using the `GetStockPen` routine. Then you select the pen (with the `SelectPen` routine), as follows:

```
HPEN hPen;

hPen = GetStockPen(WHITE_PEN);
SelectPen(PaintDC, hPen);     // White Pen now Active
```

With the handle to the pen selected, it is used for all line-drawing commands. To create new pens, you use the `CreatePen` routine. It is defined as follows:

```
HPEN CreatePen(int PenStyle, int Width, COLORREF color);
```

This routine gives you more flexibility in drawing. The `PenStyle` parameter enables you to specify a style to use for drawing lines (listed in Table 11.6). The `Width` Parameter sets the width of the pen (usually in pixels). The `Color` parameter enables you to use the RGB macro to specify a unique color.

Table 11.6. Pen styles.

Pen Style	*Description*
PS_SOLID	Solid pen style.
PS_DASH	Dashed pen style.
PS_DOT	Dotted pen style.
PS_DASHDOT	Single dash followed by dot style.
PS_DASHDOTDOT	Dash followed by two dots.
PS_NULL	No style.
PS_INSIDEFRAME	Forces line to be drawn inside shapes.

Creating a pen with the `CreatePen` function actually creates a data structure inside Windows. Before the handle to the display context is released, a program must select a stock pen into the DC and then delete the DC and the pen you created. If a program does not delete the pen, it will use up memory, possibly causing the program to crash.

To delete the pen, use the `DeletePen` routine, as follows:

```
DeletePen(hPen);
```

With an understanding of using pens, you can continue to look at the line drawing routines provided by the GDI.

Line Drawing Routines

The first line drawing routine discussed is `LineTo`. It is the most common and simplest line drawing command. This routine draws a line from the current position to the point specified in its parameters. The line is drawn with the currently selected pen.

The current position is a point value in the display context. The default value is `0,0` (the upper-left corner of the client area). It can be changed with the `MoveTo` routine. `MoveTo` takes a handle to a device context and the new `x` and `y` locations.

With the current position set, you can use the `LineTo` routine. It is defined in windows.h, as follows:

```
BOOL LineTo(HDC hDC, int x, int y);
```

After the `LineTo` function has drawn a line, it updates the value of the current position in the display context to reflect the end point of the line. You can therefore connect a series of points by making several calls to `LineTo` in a row.

The `PolyLine` function is an enhanced version of `LineTo`. Poly is a Greek derivation meaning many; this routine draws many lines with a single call. The `PolyLine` function draws a set of line segments, connecting the specified points in an array. The routine can be used in the `Paint` method of your ObjectWindows program as follows:

```
POINT Points[4];
```

```
Points[0].x = 50;
Points[0].y = 10;
Points[1].x = 250;
Points[1].y = 50;
Points[2].x = 125;
Points[2].y = 130;
Points[3].x = 50;
Points[3].y = 10;

Polyline(PaintDC, Points, sizeof(Points) / sizeof(POINT));
```

One difference with the `PolyLine` function is that it does not change the current position. However, it makes drawing a large number of points easier, because of the capability to store the points in an array.

The `LineTo` and `PolyLine` functions draw only straight lines. The `Arc` function is used to draw curved lines. It is defined as follows:

```
BOOL Arc(HDC hDC, int x1, int y1, int x2, int y2,
         int x3, int y3, int x4, int y4);
```

The center of the arc is the center of the bounding rectangle specified by the points (`x1`, `y1`) and (`x2`, `y2`). The arc starts at the point (`x3`, `y3`) and ends at the point (`x4`, `y4`).

Now that you've examined some line drawing commands, take a look at creating geometric shapes using the GDI in the next section.

Working with Shapes

Many geometric shapes are made of groups of lines. Although you can easily create a rectangle with a few calls to the `LineTo` routine, the GDI provides routines for drawing complex shapes. Figure 11.8 shows some of the shapes that were created in the Paintbrush application (which uses the GDI).

As you learned in the last section, lines use a display-context attribute called a pen. Geometric shapes use a display-context attribute called a brush. Before examining the specific geometric drawing routines, take a look at using brushes.

Figure 11.8.

Example shapes as created in Paintbrush.

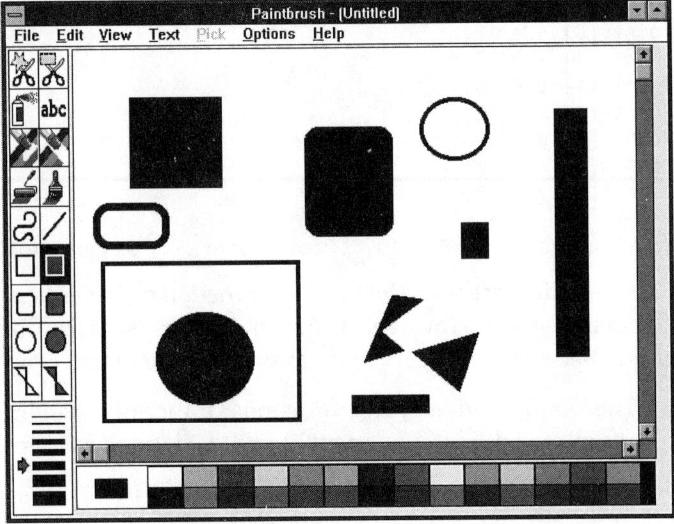

Using Brushes

A brush is another display context attribute that describes how to draw shapes. The brush describes how the interior of a shape will be displayed. Both pens and brushes are considered objects. The GDI provides several predefined or stock brushes that your program may use, as listed in Table 11.7.

Table 11.7. Predefined stock brushes.

Brush Name	*Description*
WHITE_BRUSH	White
LTGRAY_BRUSH	Light Gray
GRAY_BRUSH	Gray
DKGRAY_BRUSH	Dark Gray
BLACK_BRUSH	Black Gray
NULL_BRUSH	Transparent
HOLLOW_BRUSH	Same as Null brush

To use a different brush in your program, you must first obtain a handle to the brush and then select it as follows:

```
  HBRUSH hBrush;

  hBrush = GetStockBrush(DKGRAY_BRUSH);
  SelectBrush(PaintDC, hBrush);
...
[Brush ready to use]
...
```

Although the stock brushes are nice to have, you also can create your own custom brushes. (There are other ways to create brushes, but they are more advanced and aren't discussed here.) You can create two types of brushes: solid and hatch.

A solid brush creates a brush with a specific color value. The routine is defined as follows:

```
HBRUSH  CreateSolidBrush(COLORREF color);
```

This routine takes a single parameter, which is a color value. You usually use the `RGB` macro to return a value and specify the three color values (red, green, and blue). You learned earlier that many color values can be specified with the `RGB` function. Most monitors, however, cannot display that many colors.

In the earlier routines, it did not matter that most monitors can't display many of the colors because you were displaying a single point or a line. When displaying shapes, however, the GDI can actually *dither* color values. If you specify an available color value with the `RGB` function, it is used (for example, white, black, red, blue, and green). These are called pure colors, because they are a single value.

When dithering colors, the GDI actually mixes colors to create the appearance of a new color. For example, everybody knows that mixing red and blue creates purple. Displaying a pixel of red next to a pixel of blue on the screen and looking at it from a distance (such as 1 or 2 feet) creates the appearance of purple. The GDI includes powerful tools for creating new colors. There are some limitations to the approach, but it is workable. From this description, there is obviously no way to dither a single point.

The `CreateSolidBrush` routine can create a pen of many more colors than are usually available on a monitor. Color monitors display more colors; monochrome monitors display many more shades of gray.

There is another method you can use to create a brush—the `CreateHatchBrush` routine. It is defined in windows.h as follows:

```
HBRUSH  CreateHatchBrush(int style, COLORREF color);
```

This routine enables you to specify a color (such as `CreateSolidBrush`). You also can specify a style value that specifies a hatch pattern (listed in Table 11.8).

Table 11.8. Hatch styles.

Index Value	*Description*
HS_HORIZONTAL	Horizontal hatch pattern.
HS_VERTICAL	Vertical hatch pattern.
HS_FDIAGONAL	Upward (45 degree) hatch pattern.
HS_BDIAGONAL	Downward (45 degree) hatch pattern.
HS_CROSS	Cross mark hatch pattern.
HS_DIAGCROSS	Cross hatch (45 degree) pattern.

To use the `CreateSolidBrush` or `CreateHatchBrush` functions, you use code as follows:

```
HBRUSH hBrush;

Brush = CreateSolidBrush(RGB(25, 90, 145);
Brush = CreateHatchBrush(HS_CROSS, RGB(25, 90, 145));
```

You would then select the brush object (as demonstrated earlier) and use it to draw your figures. As you can see, the GDI allows for a great amount of flexibility in selecting brushes.

When displaying shapes, the GDI uses both the currently selected pen and the currently selected brush. The outline of the figure is drawn with the pen, and the inside of the figure is filled with the brush.

Now that you've examined brushes, you can check out the geometric shapes for which Windows includes routines.

Rectangles

To display rectangles (or boxes) use the `Rectangle` routine. It is defined in windows.h as follows:

```
BOOL    Rectangle(HDC hDC, int x1, int y1, int x2, int y2);
```

This routine takes a handle to a device context, and the coordinates of the rectangle. (`x1`, `y1`) is the upper-left corner and (`y1`, `y2`) is the lower-right corner. A related routine is the `RoundRect` routine. It draws a rectangle with rounded corners. `RoundRect` is defined as follows:

```
BOOL RoundRect(HDC hDC, int x1, int y1, int x2, int y2, int x3,
               int y2);
```

The two additional parameters `x3` and `y3` specify the width and height of the ellipse used to draw the rounded corners of the rectangle.

Polygons

A polygon is a closed figure, usually with more than four sides. The GDI provides a routine to display polygons, and it is defined as follows:

```
BOOL Polygon(HDC hDC, const POINT points, int Count);
```

To use the routine, specify an array of points to use that are connected together. If the first and last points are not the same, a line is drawn to close the figure, and the area inside is filled using the brush that is currently set in the display context.

If you have a number of polygons to draw at one time, you can use the `PolyPolygon` routine. It creates two or more polygons and is defined as follows:

```
BOOL PolyPolygon(HDC hDC, const POINT points, int pointcount,
                 int number);
```

This routine is a little trickier to use. The first parameter is your old friend the handle to the display context. The second parameter is the address of an array of vertices. The third parameter is the address of an array with the number of points in each polygon. The last parameter is the number of polygons to be drawn; it must be greater than 1.

What follows is an example of how you can use the `PolyPolygon` function:

```
POINT Points[8];
int Vertices[] = { 4, 4 };

Points[0].x = 50;
Points[0].y = 10;
Points[1].x = 250;
Points[1].y = 50;
Points[2].x = 125;
Points[2].y = 130;
Points[3].x = 50;
Points[3].y = 10;

Points[4].x = 100;
Points[4].y = 25;
Points[5].x = 300;
Points[5].y = 125;
Points[6].x = 70;
Points[6].y = 150;
Points[7].x = 100;
Points[7].y = 25;

PolyPolygon(PaintDC, Points, Vertices, sizeof(Vertices) /
sizeof(int));
```

This function creates the output shown in Figure 11.9.

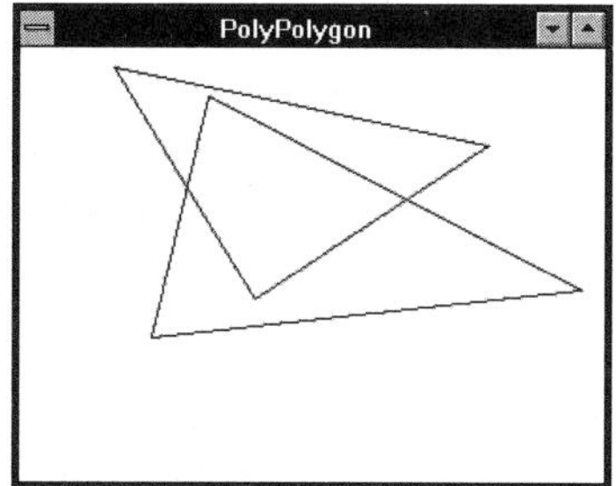

Figure 11.9.
PolyPolygon function call.

Ellipse

An ellipse is a circular shape that fits within a rectangular area. If the rectangular area is perfectly square, the figure drawn will be a perfect circle. The `Ellipse` routine is defined as follows:

```
BOOL Ellipse(HDC hDC, int x1, int y1, int x2, int y2);
```

The upper-left corner of the rectangular region is specified in the (`x1`, `y1`) parameters, and the lower-right corner of the rectangular area is specified as (`x2`, `y2`).

Pies

A pie is similar to the `Ellipse` function, except only part of the ellipse is displayed. Besides specifying an outer rectangle, you must specify the starting and ending point of the wedge you want to display. The routine is defined as follows:

```
BOOL Pie(HDC hDC, int x1, int y1, int x2, int y2,
        int x3, int y3, int x4, int y4);
```

The outer rectangle is specified by the points (`x1`, `y1`) and (`x2`, `y2`). The point at (`x3`, `y3`) is the beginning point of the wedge, and the point at (`x4`, `y4`) is the ending point of the wedge.

Putting It to Practice

Most of the GDI functions are self-explanatory and to the point. If you look at the parameters and have an idea how the shape should look, it is fairly easy to implement the function.

Now, take a look at a program that uses several of the concepts covered in this chapter. The ESCHER.CPP program (in Listing 11.3, along with module definition file in Listing 11.4) demonstrates the creation of pens, brushes, and shapes. ESCHER.CPP also shows how to use a different mapping mode. Finally, the program shows how to use a Windows timer in an ObjectWindows Library program.

Listing 11.3. ESCHER.CPP program.

```
// ESCHER.CPP - Program to display Escher's triangle in
//              a Window using Mapping Modes
//
// Programming Windows with Turbo C++ for Windows
// by Paul J. Perry

#define WIN31
#define STRICT

#define ID_TIMER 999
#define NUMBOFCOLORS 5

#include <owl.h>
#include <windowsx.h>
#include <stdlib.h>


// Class Declarations

/*********************************************/
class TOwlApp : public TApplication
{
   public :
      TOwlApp (LPSTR AName, HINSTANCE hInstance, HINSTANCE
             hPrevInstance,
         LPSTR CmdLine, int CmdShow) :
         TApplication(AName, hInstance, hPrevInstance,
                   CmdLine, CmdShow) { } ;
```

```
   virtual void InitMainWindow();
};


/*******************************************/
class TMainWindow : public TWindow
{
   public :

      int index;

      TMainWindow(PTWindowsObject AParent, LPSTR ATitle)
                  : TWindow(AParent, ATitle) { };
      virtual LPSTR GetClassName();
      virtual void GetWindowClass(WNDCLASS& wndclass);
      virtual void Paint(HDC PaintDC, PAINTSTRUCT &PaintInfo);
      virtual void SetupWindow();
      virtual void ShutDownWindow();
      virtual void WMTimer(TMessage& Msg)
         = [WM_FIRST + WM_TIMER];
};


// Class Member Functions

/*******************************************/
void TOwlApp::InitMainWindow()
{
   MainWindow = new TMainWindow(NULL, Name);
}


/*******************************************/
LPSTR TMainWindow::GetClassName()
{
   return "Escher";
}

/*******************************************/
void TMainWindow::GetWindowClass(WNDCLASS& wndclass)
{
   TWindow::GetWindowClass(wndclass);

   wndclass.hIcon = 0;     // Allow us to update it while an icon
   wndclass.hbrBackground = GetStockBrush(LTGRAY_BRUSH);

}
```

continues

Listing 11.3. continued

```
/*******************************************/
void TMainWindow::SetupWindow()
{
   if (!SetTimer(HWindow, ID_TIMER, 1000, NULL) )
   {
      MessageBox(HWindow, "Too many timers set",
           "", MB_ICONEXCLAMATION ¦ MB_OK);
      exit(1);
   }

   index = 0;

}

/*******************************************/
void TMainWindow::ShutDownWindow()
{
   KillTimer(HWindow, ID_TIMER);

   TWindow::ShutDownWindow();
}

/*******************************************/
#pragma argsused
void TMainWindow::WMTimer(TMessage& Msg)
{
   index = index%NUMBOFCOLORS;
   InvalidateRect(HWindow, NULL, TRUE);
}


/*******************************************/
#pragma argsused
void TMainWindow::Paint(HDC PaintDC, PAINTSTRUCT &PaintInfo)
{
   int   count[3] = {7,7,7};

   POINT arr[] = { {10,  183},    // bottom polygon
                {30,  218},
             {230, 218},
             {150, 80},
             {130, 115},
             {170, 183},
             {10,  183},

             {230, 218},    // right-hand polygon
```

```
            {250, 183},
            {150, 10},
            {70,  148},
                  {110, 148},
            {150, 80},
            {230, 218},

            {10,  183},    // left-hand polygon
            {170, 183},
            {150, 148},
            {70,  148},
            {150, 10},
            {110, 10},
            {10,  183} };

   COLORREF colors[NUMBOFCOLORS] =
                       { RGB(255, 0, 0),        // red
                RGB(0, 255, 0),                 // green
                RGB(0, 0, 255),                 // blue
                RGB(255, 0, 255),               // purple
                RGB(128, 128, 128) };           // gray

   RECT   rect;
   HPEN   hPen, hOldPen;
   HBRUSH hBrush, hOldBrush;

// Select a new pen in the display context
   hPen = CreatePen(PS_SOLID, 1, RGB(0,0,0));
   hOldPen = SelectPen(PaintDC, hPen);

// Select a new brush into the display context
   hBrush = CreateSolidBrush(colors[index++]);
   hOldBrush = SelectBrush(PaintDC, hBrush);

// Set the new mapping mode
   GetClientRect(HWindow, &rect);
   SetMapMode(PaintDC, MM_ISOTROPIC);
   SetWindowExt(PaintDC, 260, 228);
   SetViewportExt(PaintDC, rect.right, rect.bottom);

// draw figure and do fill
   PolyPolygon (PaintDC, arr, count, 3);

// cleanup
   SelectBrush(PaintDC, hOldBrush);
   DeleteBrush(hBrush);
```

continues

Listing 11.3. continued

```
   SelectPen(PaintDC, hOldPen);
   DeletePen(hPen);

}


/********************************************/
int PASCAL WinMain(HINSTANCE hInstance, HINSTANCE hPrevInstance,
                  LPSTR lpCmdLine, int nCmdShow)
{

   TOwlApp ThisApp("Escher's Triangle", hInstance,
                  hPrevInstance, lpCmdLine, nCmdShow);
   ThisApp.Run();
   return ThisApp.Status;

}
```

Listing 11.4. Module definition file for ESCHER program.

```
;
; ESCHER.DEF module definition file
;
DESCRIPTION    'Escher Shape Program'
NAME           ESCHER
EXETYPE        WINDOWS
STUB           'WINSTUB.EXE'
HEAPSIZE       1024
STACKSIZE      8192
CODE           PRELOAD MOVEABLE DISCARDABLE
DATA           PRELOAD MOVEABLE MULTIPLE
```

When you run the program, the output looks like Figure 11.10. If you change the size of the window, the shape takes on a new size to fit just inside the window. You can even minimize the program and the icon displays the shape. When the program is executing, the shape is updated and redisplayed in a new color each second. The program cycles between five colors (red, green, blue, purple, and dark gray) and then starts over.

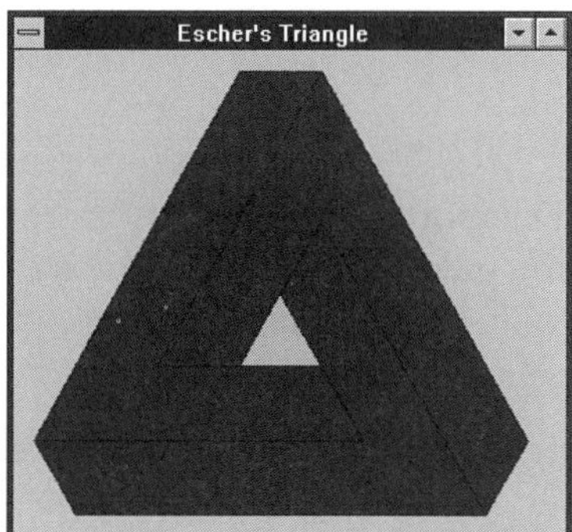

Figure 11.10.
Output of ESCHER.CPP program.

Look at each element of the program and see how it is implemented. The first and most striking item is the Escher shape (duplicated from artwork by the famous artist). The end points are stored in an integer array and then drawn using the `PolyPolygon` function. The function call looks simple enough:

```
PolyPolygon (PaintDC, arr, count, 3);
```

The `arr` array contains the end points of three polygons: the bottom, right, and left sides of the Escher. The `count` array contains the number of points in each array.

To draw the Escher shape so it fits exactly inside the window, use an alternate mapping mode, `MM_ISOTROPIC`. The `MM_ISOTROPIC` mapping mode causes the scale of the horizontal and vertical dimensions to be set equivalently. To set the mapping mode, use a single line such as this:

```
SetMapMode(PaintDC, MM_ISOTROPIC);
```

The scale is set with the `SetWindowExt` and `SetViewportExt` functions. `SetWindowExt` sets the `x` and `y` extents of the window. The call to `SetWindowExt` looks like this:

```
SetWindowExt(PaintDC, 260, 228);
```

This call informs Windows that no matter how big the window is, the x-extent goes from 0 to 260, and the y-extent goes from 0 to 228. These numbers were chosen because they are slightly larger than the Escher shape.

The `SetViewportExt` call looks like this:

```
GetClientRect(hWnd, &rect);
SetViewportExt(PaintDC, rect.right, rect.bottom);
```

This call tells Windows the extent of the viewport of the window. Therefore, every time the window size changes, you query Windows for the size of the window with the `GetClientRect` function. The viewport is then reset to the extent of the width and height of the client area of the window.

The border of the shape is specified with a pen. The call used to create a new pen is this:

```
hPen = CreatePen(PS_SOLID, 1, RGB(0,0,0));
hOldPen = SelectPen(PaintDC, hPen);
```

After the pen is created, it is selected into the display context with the `SelectPen` function. Notice, the handle to the old pen is saved (it is returned from `SelectPen`). This ensures the program can clean up after it is done.

To use different colors inside the shape, the program must create a brush. These color values are stored as COLORREF values inside an array. To create the brush, use code such as this:

```
hBrush = CreateSolidBrush(colors[index++]);
hOldBrush = SelectBrush(PaintDC, hBrush);
```

After the brush is created, it is selected into the display context, and the program saves the previously selected brush. The value of `index` is used to represent which color value to use inside the array. After `index` is used once, it is incremented.

At the end of the `Paint` member function, some clean-up work is carried out. It looks like this:

```
SelectBrush(PaintDC, hOldBrush);
DeleteBrush(hBrush);

SelectPen(PaintDC, hOldPen);
DeletePen(hPen);
```

Before the objects can be deleted, the program must first select the old brush back into the display context. The program then can safely delete the objects that were created.

That brings us to the last topic covered in the program: creating a Windows timer using the ObjectWindows Library. You saw a timer created in Chapter 6, "Working with Windows," with the program that displayed the free memory and resources available inside a program's icon. That program was written in C.

In the ObjectWindows Library, a similar method is used. The `SetupWindow` member function makes a call to `CreateTimer`. After this code is executed, the program receives `WM_TIMER` messages. Then, create a message response function for `WM_TIMER`. The body of the `WM_TIMER` function simply returns the modulus of dividing the index value by the total number of colors available. This guarantees that the program always has a number between zero and one less than the maximum number of color values available. The code looks like this:

```
void TMainWindow::WMTimer(TMessage& Msg)
{
   index = index%NUMBOFCOLORS;
   InvalidateRect(HWindow, NULL, TRUE);
}
```

At the same time, the program executes an `InvalidateRect` function, which causes Windows to redraw the client area of the program. This sends a `WM_PAINT` message to the program, and the `Paint` member function gets called to redisplay the client area.

The program is a great conversation piece. For fun, you might want to see what the `MM_ANISOTROPIC` mapping mode does. I recommend you try it so you can see how it works. To change it, all you need to do is change the call to `SetMappingMode` as follows:

```
SetMapMode(PaintDC, MM_ANISOTROPIC);
```

The difference will be that the shape of the figure changes and is distorted if the window is resized to a shape other than a square.

The program has demonstrated several techniques of GDI programming. Hopefully, by demonstrating some good coding techniques and having nice visual feedback, you will find this program enjoyable.

What You Have Learned

You have looked at a lot of new routines in this chapter. You learned how to set a single pixel on the screen. You also looked at several methods of displaying text in the client area of a window. After that, you moved to more advanced routines to display lines. You saw how pens control the attributes of line drawing and how to create straight and arced lines.

You learned that complex shapes are actually made up of several lines. You looked at some figure drawing routines. You learned how brushes (as well as pens) work to your advantage while working with these complex shapes. You found many powerful routines inside the Windows GDI.

It is time to take a deep, long breath. You have covered a lot of material. In the next section, you stand back from Windows programming concepts for a while and examine some of the programming tools that come with Turbo C++ for Windows, including Turbo Debugger for Windows (TDW) and WinSpector.

The following important points about the GDI were covered in this chapter:

- The GDI provides device-independent output by allowing software device drivers to do the actual job of outputting graphics to an output device instead of the routines doing the job.
- To use GDI routines, a program must first obtain a handle to a device context. The device context is a group of attributes that makes using the GDI functions quicker.
- In programs based on the ObjectWindows Library, the `Paint` method passes a handle to a device context. A program using traditional Windows programming methods responds to the `WM_PAINT` message and must use `BeginPaint` to get a device context and `EndPaint` to dispose of the device context.
- At any time, a program can use the GDI routines by first obtaining a handle to a device context by using `GetDC`. A program must then use `ReleaseDC` to return the handle to the device context.
- A program can use the `GetDeviceCaps` routine to query information about a device context and the device to which it is set to output.

- The `SetPixel` routine is used to light a single pixel in a window's client area.
- Text can be displayed with one of three routines: `TextOut`, `ExtTextOut`, or `DrawText`.
- `TextOut` is the basic method for outputting text. `ExtTextOut` is an extended version that enables you to specify character spacing, a clipping region, or a rectangle to be displayed. `DrawText` provides the capability of displaying formatted text.
- A pen describes attributes of drawing a line. The line drawing routines include: `LineTo`, `PolyLine`, and `Arc`.
- A brush describes the attributes relating to drawing filled figures. The routines that draw filled figures include: `Rectangle`, `Ellipse`, `Pie`, `RoundRect`, and `Polygon`.
- If your program creates any custom pens or brushes, they must be deleted when you are done using them. If not, your program uses system resources that cannot be returned to Windows unless the user restarts Windows.

12

TURBO C++ FOR WINDOWS PROGRAMMING TOOLS

IN THIS CHAPTER

- What a bug is and what types of bugs Turbo Debugger for Windows helps track.
- How to configure Turbo Debugger for Windows to run on your system.
- What the main menu options of the debugger are used for.
- How to single step and trace through your program.
- What a breakpoint is and how to set one.
- How to examine the values of variables through the debugger.
- How to trap Windows messages in the debugger.
- How to use the EasyWin library as an alternate method to debug your program.
- What WinSpector is used for and how to use it to track down problems in your code.
- How Windows help files are created.

This chapter takes a break from new Windows programming concepts and concentrates on the programming tools included with Turbo C++ for Windows. You learn how to configure and use Turbo Debugger for Windows, find what WinSpector is used for, and gain an understanding about how Help files are created in Windows.

If you are a seasoned programmer, you probably are familiar with the debugging terms in this chapter. Some of the information may be a review. Therefore, feel free to skim the information you know and move on to the information you don't. However, I have found that many people who start programming in Windows aren't familiar with the stand-alone debugger and need a little guidance.

In this chapter, you learn about some exciting tools that help you program. By the end of the chapter, I want you to have enough insight to use the tools that come with Turbo C++ for Windows to get your programs up and running faster.

About the Turbo C++ for Windows Programming Tools

Most of the tools that come with Turbo C++ for Windows are strictly for debugging your program. When you create programs of your own, you find that errors in logic start creeping into your code. This is when a debugger can help you with your programming projects.

Debugging is the process of removing bugs from your program. A *bug* is some part of your program that doesn't work properly (each part of your program that isn't working correctly is thought of as a separate bug).

The term came in existence into the bad old days when an entire room was required to store a computer. In those days, mechanical relays were used as the main switching devices inside the computer (today, integrated circuits are used). The first time the computer stopped working, engineers examined the relays and found one with a moth smashed between the electrical contacts of the relay. Appropriately, these pioneers in computers called the problem a bug. Since then, programmers have referred to programming errors as bugs.

About Debugging

Almost all programs contain errors of some type during their development process. In fact, bugs are part of computer programming. Rarely does a program run on the first try. Programmers are constantly correcting parts of their programs to make them work correctly.

There are three types of errors:

- Compile-time
- Runtime
- Logical

Compile-time errors are straightforward. They result from an error in the syntax of your program. Compile-time errors are displayed during program compilation and must be corrected before you can run the program. A debugger isn't used to correct compiler errors. They must be eliminated before you can use a debugger (a program must be compiled in order for you to debug it).

Runtime errors cause a program to terminate and produce an error message. This type of error results from incorrect error checking in your program. Sometimes runtime errors occur because a program expects the user to enter a certain type of value, but the user enters another type—for example, a string is entered when an integer value is expected. Another typical runtime error is an uninitialized variable. In this case, a variable is supposed to be set to a specific value but isn't.

With a *logical error*, a program performs differently than you expect it to. The computer always does what it is told. You may think you have told the computer a particular thing, but have inadvertently told it something else. When using a debugger, you can find what your program told the computer to do. Then, you can determine the difference between what you told it and what you want it to do. At that time, you can change the program to work as you want it to.

With Turbo Debugger for Windows, you can run your programs a line at a time and view the value of variables as the program is executed. By using the special features of the debugger, you can examine memory locations and control program flow during the execution of the program.

Using Turbo Debugger for Windows

As I mentioned, when your programs take new directions, errors in logic creep into your code. The next section in this chapter describes how you can locate and correct those errors using Turbo Debugger for Windows.

Configuring Turbo Debugger for Windows

Before starting the debugger, you must learn how to configure it.

If you are using a special super VGA video adapter, you probably need to tell Turbo Debugger for Windows about it. This is done through the TDW.INI file. This is the Turbo Debugger for Windows initialization file. It specifies video adapter options and other information related to the debugger.

WARNING

If you change any of the settings in the TDW.INI file, you must be sure only one copy of the file is presently on your system. Borland has acknowledged that the installation program erroneously installs two copies of the TDW.INI file. Therefore, be sure you keep the copy in the C:\WINDOWS subdirectory and remove the one in the C:\TCWIN\BIN subdirectory. After you do this, you should not have problems setting any of the configuration options described here.

You can load the TDW.INI file in the Integrated Development Environment (IDE) or in any other text editor you may have. The file looks something like this:

```
[TurboDebugger]
VideoDLL=
DebuggerDLL=C:\tcwin\BIN\tdwin.dll
[VideoOptions]
DebugFile=
```

```
SaveWholeScreen=no
Int2FAssist=no
IgnoreMode=no
```

The line you want to modify is the one that describes the video DLL that Turbo Debugger for Windows uses to work with your monitor. It looks like this:

```
VideoDLL=
```

Table 12.1 lists the drivers included with the package and the video adapters they work with.

Table 12.1. Turbo Debugger for Windows debugger DLLs.

Driver	*Description*
ATI.DLL	Used with VGA Wonder and XL cards.
DUAL8514.DLL	Any dual screen 8514 card.
TDVESA.DLL	Any adapter that supports VESA emulation.
TSENG.DLL	Any card based on the Tseng ET-3000 or ET-4000 chips.
S3.DLL*	Used with the Diamond Stealth card.
STB.DLL	Supports the MVP2 multiscreen video card.
SVGA.DLL*	Generic driver that works on most adapters.
ULTRA.DLL	Used with the ATI Graphics Ultra card.

**These drivers are new and don't come on the distribution disks. They must be downloaded from Borland's download BBS (408/438-9181) or from Borland's forums on CompuServe.*

Suppose you are using the ATI graphics Ultra adapter card. To tell Turbo Debugger for Windows about the adapter, you modify the TDW.INI file. The line that changes looks like this:

```
VideoDLL=c:\tcwin\bin\ultra.dll
```

Notice, you must specify the drive and path for the location of the debugger DLL.

Dual Monitor Debugging

If you have two monitors, Turbo Debugger for Windows takes advantage of both. In most cases, your main monitor is a color VGA monitor, and your second monitor is a monochrome monitor.

Turbo Debugger for Windows uses the monochrome monitor for its display, while using the color VGA monitor for your Windows display. Utilizing two monitors is a slick way to debug, because the screen doesn't switch between the debugger and Windows screens. Therefore, the time required for debugging is decreased.

Turning on Debug Information

To use the debugger, you must tell the compiler to turn on debug information. To do this, choose the Options menu, select Linker, and finally choose the Settings menu option. The Linker Settings Dialog box displays. Be sure a check mark is next to the option for Include debug information (see Figure 12.1). Press Enter or choose OK to accept the new compiler options. Setting this option instructs the compiler to include specific information in the executable file used for debugging. Also, make sure the option for including debug info in the OBJ is checked in the Options | Compiler | Advanced Code Generation dialog box.

If the Include debug information isn't set, you must recompile your program so that the debug information can be added to the executable program.

Starting the Debugger

Be sure you have a program active in the editor window you want to debug (use MINWIN.C found earlier in this book). In the IDE, you access Turbo Debugger for Windows by Choosing the Run menu and selecting Debugger (see Figure 12.2). If the program requires recompilation, the IDE takes care of it. Then, a message displays that tells you Turbo Debugger for Windows is being loaded.

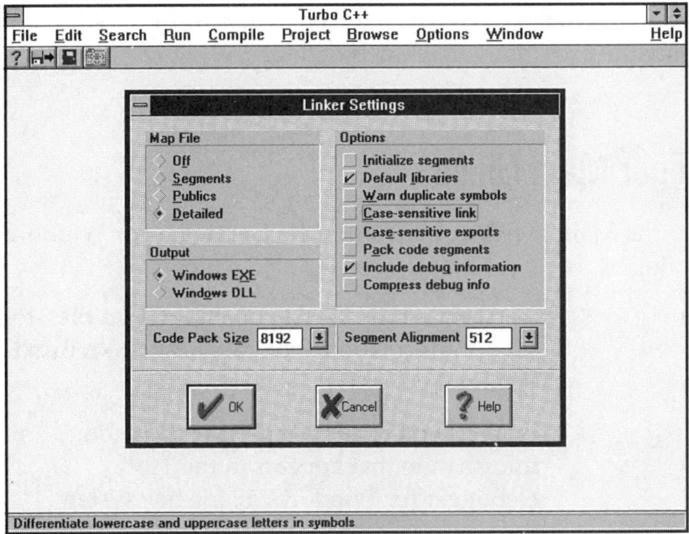

Figure 12.1.

Linker Settings dialog box.

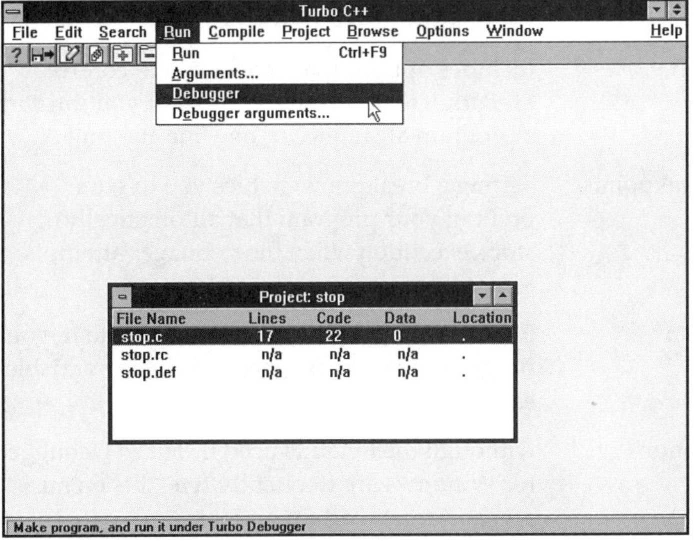

Figure 12.2.

Debugger menu option.

At first you may wonder what is happening when you start Turbo Debugger for Windows. It has some interesting characteristics. This debugger is a Windows application; however, it runs in a text-mode display. You cannot switch from the debugger by selecting the task list. You can execute only the program you are debugging.

The Debugger Main Menu

Briefly review the Main menu options in Turbo Debugger for Windows before continuing:

File	Has commands used to open different files, to report information about a file, and to return to Windows.
Edit	Enables you to copy and paste the debug information that appears in the Turbo Debugger for Windows dialog box system.
View	Enables you to view different aspects of your program, including breakpoints, watches, variables, and Windows messages.
Run	Includes options that enable you to control execution of your program so that you can run a program all at once or one line at a time.
Breakpoints	Setting a breakpoint enables you to set a point in your program that automatically stops execution when the debugger attempts to run it.
Data	Enables you to look at the value of data in your program. You can inspect and change variables easily.
Options	Although the defaults used in Turbo Debugger for Windows are frequently fine, this menu sets and resets certain options.
Window	Enables you to switch between different windows. (The Turbo Debugger for Windows desktop is similar to the IDE in that you can open multiple windows and switch between them.)

Help	Gives you online information for every menu command.

Because many of the menu options are used frequently, there are hot-key combinations that emulate those options. Table 12.2 lists the commonly used hot keys in Turbo Debugger for Windows. As individual features of the debugger are presented, the hot-key commands are introduced. If you have used Turbo Debugger for DOS, you are familiar with the operation of Turbo Debugger for Windows. Most of the hot keys are similar.

Table 12.2. The commonly used hot keys in Turbo Debugger for Windows.

Key	*Function*
F1	Displays help information.
Alt-F1	Displays last help topic.
Shift-F1	Displays help index.
F2	Sets breakpoint.
Alt-F2	Sets breakpoint address.
Ctrl-F2	Resets program to start over.
F3	Displays module list.
Alt-F3	Closes current window.
F4	Executes program to current cursor position.
Alt-F4	Reverses program flow.
Ctrl-F4	Evaluates an expression.
F5	Zooms current window to full screen size.
Alt-F5	Displays user screen.
Ctrl-F5	Moves or resizes current window.
F6	Switches to next window.
Alt-F6	Reopens last open window.

continues

Table 12.2. continued

Key	*Function*
F7	Traces into current program line.
Alt-F7	Executes a single instruction.
Ctrl-F7	Opens window to add variable to watch list.
F8	Steps into current program line.
Ctrl-F8	Toggles a breakpoint.
F9	Executes program.
F10	Set focus to Menu Bar.
Tab	Moves cursor to next window.
Arrow keys	Moves cursor in appropriate direction.
Alt-X	Quits Turbo Debugger for Windows.

Debugger Functions

To learn how to control execution of your program, use the program in Listing 12.1. It enables you to experiment with debugging features.

The program has the same functionality as the minimum C program you saw in Chapter 4, "Using the ObjectWindows Library," except some of the code is changed to demonstrate how to use the debugger.

In general, be sure you compile with debug information (as described previously) and save the file—by choosing the File menu and selecting Save—before starting Turbo Debugger for Windows.

Listing 12.1. Program for learning about the debugger.

```
// USETDW.C - Program to enable you to learn how to
//            use Turbo Debugger for Windows
//
// Programming Windows with Turbo C++ for Windows
// by Paul J. Perry

#define STRICT

#include <windowsx.h>
#include <stdlib.h>

// Function Prototypes
LRESULT CALLBACK _export MainWndProc(HWND hWnd, UINT message,
                                     WPARAM wParam, LPARAM lParam);

void InitInstance(char *ProgName, HINSTANCE hInstance);


// Global Variables
int         TimesPainted;
int         LButtonPressed;


/********************************************/
#pragma argsused
int PASCAL WinMain(HINSTANCE hInstance, HINSTANCE hPrevInstance,
                   LPSTR lpCmdParam, int nCmdShow)
{
   char        ProgName[] = "TDW Test";
   HWND        hWnd;
   MSG         msg;


// We have moved class registration into its own
//  function
   if (!hPrevInstance)
      InitInstance(ProgName, hInstance);

   hWnd = CreateWindow(ProgName, ProgName,
                       WS_OVERLAPPEDWINDOW,
                       CW_USEDEFAULT, CW_USEDEFAULT,
                       CW_USEDEFAULT, CW_USEDEFAULT,
                       NULL, NULL, hInstance, NULL);
```

continues

Listing 12.1. continued

```
   ShowWindow(hWnd, nCmdShow);
   UpdateWindow(hWnd);

   while (GetMessage(&msg, NULL, 0, 0))
   {
      TranslateMessage(&msg);
      DispatchMessage(&msg);
   }
   return msg.wParam;
}

/*******************************************/
void InitInstance(char *ProgName, HINSTANCE hInstance)
{
   WNDCLASS    wndclass;

// This will register the class

   wndclass.lpszClassName = ProgName;
   wndclass.lpfnWndProc   = (WNDPROC) MainWndProc;
   wndclass.cbClsExtra    = 0;
   wndclass.cbWndExtra    = 0;
   wndclass.hInstance     = hInstance;
   wndclass.hIcon         = LoadIcon(NULL, IDI_APPLICATION);
   wndclass.hCursor       = LoadCursor(NULL, IDC_ARROW);
   wndclass.hbrBackground = (HBRUSH) (COLOR_WINDOW + 1);
   wndclass.lpszMenuName  = NULL;
   wndclass.style         = CS_VREDRAW ¦ CS_HREDRAW;

   if (!RegisterClass(&wndclass)) exit(0);;
}



/*******************************************/
LRESULT CALLBACK _export MainWndProc(HWND hWnd, UINT message,
                                     WPARAM wParam, LPARAM lParam)
{
   switch (message)
   {
      case WM_CREATE :
      {
         TimesPainted = 0;
         LButtonPressed = 0;
         return 0;
      }
```

```
        case WM_LBUTTONDOWN :
        {
           ++LButtonPressed;
           return 0;
        }

        case WM_PAINT :
        {
           HDC         PaintDC;
           RECT        rect;
           PAINTSTRUCT ps;

           PaintDC = BeginPaint(hWnd, &ps);
           GetClientRect(hWnd, &rect);

           DrawText(PaintDC, "Example for Learning Turbo Debugger for
                    Windows", -1, &rect, DT_SINGLELINE ¦ DT_CENTER ¦
                    DT_VCENTER);

           EndPaint(hWnd, &ps);

           ++TimesPainted;
           return 0;
        }

        case WM_DESTROY :
        {
           PostQuitMessage(0);
           return 0;
        }
     }
     return DefWindowProc (hWnd, message, wParam, lParam);
}
```

When you first access the program, it appears as in Figure 12.3. Notice that the `WinMain` section of your code is displayed. An arrow marks the entry point for the program. Press F9 to execute the program, just as you do in the IDE. This action starts and executes your entire program.

After you start the program, the Windows desktop appears, and you can run the program the way you usually do. The only difference may be that it runs a little slower. This is because the debugger must trap every instruction being executed, which takes the microprocessor extra time.

Figure 12.3.

Turbo Debugger for Windows main screen.

```
 ≡  File  Edit  View  Run  Breakpoints  Data  Options  Window  Help          READY
=[■]=Module: USETDW File: ..\..\WORK\USETDW.C 26=========================1=[↑][↓]=

  /*********************************************/
  #pragma argsused
▸ int PASCAL WinMain(HINSTANCE hInstance, HINSTANCE hPrevInstance,
                     LPSTR lpCmdParam, int nCmdShow)
  {
     char         ProgName[] = "TDW Test";
     HWND         hWnd;
     MSG          msg;

  // We have moved class registration into it's own
  //  function
     if (!hPrevInstance)
        InitInstance(ProgName, hInstance);

     hWnd = CreateWindow(ProgName, ProgName,
 ─Watches────────────────────────────────────────────────────────────────2─

F1-Help F2-Bkpt F3-Mod F4-Here F5-Zoom F6-Next F7-Trace F8-Step F9-Run F10-Menu
```

After you run the program, close it in the regular manner (choose Close from the control menu or press Alt-F4). The Turbo Debugger for Windows screen reappears and displays the exit code returned by the program. In most cases, your program returns a value of `0`.

When you finish running the program, it is removed from memory. You must reset the program in memory to run it again. To reset it, press Ctrl-F2 or choose the Run menu and select the Program Reset option. Go ahead and reset the program so that you can try some of the debugging features.

Single Stepping

When you single step through a program, you execute your program one line at the time. To single step in Turbo Debugger for Windows, press F8. The screen flashes, and the arrow points to the next line of code in your program.

You can press F8 to single step through every instruction in `WinMain`. If you continue pressing F8, your program eventually executes to the window message loop. A highlight bar always signifies the current location in the program.

When tracking problems in your program, single stepping can be extremely useful. This process enables you to see exactly what instructions and in what order code is being executed.

Tracing Into

There are two methods of stepping through your program line by line. You know about the Step Over option. The other option is Trace Into, which you select by pressing F7.

At first glance, both options appear to do the same thing. They both execute a program one line at the time. The difference between the two is revealed when you start to move over a call to a user-defined function. The Trace Into option actually moves to the statement in a function and enables you to step through each statement in the function.

To try this, use F8 to single step up to the piece of code before this:

```
if (!hPrevInstance)
   InitInstance(ProgName, hInstance);
```

When you get to this code, press F7 at the call to the `InitInstance` function. Notice, the highlight bar moves to the beginning of the function, and you can view each line of the function being executed (see Figure 12.4).

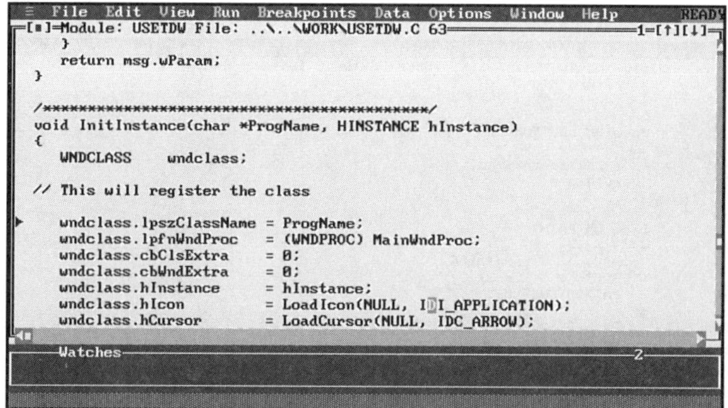

Figure 12.4.

Single stepping through the example program.

Go ahead and run the program to the end by pressing F9 and then exiting the program. Reset the program by pressing F2 and try stepping over the previous call to `InitInstance` with F8 this time. Notice, the highlight bar doesn't move to the function; rather, it moves to the next line in the program.

There are times when both methods of stepping through a program have their place. Sometimes, you want to see every line of code being executed. Other times, you don't have to see what is happening in a function, only what it returns. As you gain experience in debugging, you learn where to use which commands.

Setting Breakpoints

A breakpoint is a line in your program you set to automatically stop execution of the program during the debugging phase. When the debugger runs into a line containing a breakpoint, the program unconditionally stops and displays the highlight bar, enabling you to view the value of variables.

To set a breakpoint, move the cursor to the point in your program where you want to stop and press F2 (or choose the Debug menu and select the Toggle breakpoint option). The entire line is highlighted in red (the universal symbol for stopping—take a careful look at a stop sign the next time you speed past it) as shown in Figure 12.5.

Figure 12.5.

A breakpoint that has been set.

```
 ≡  File  Edit  View  Run  Breakpoints  Data  Options  Window  Help        READY
[■]=Module: USETDW File: ..\..\WORK\USETDW.C 104=====================1=[↑][↓]=
         return 0;
      }

      case WM_LBUTTONDOWN :
      {
         ++LButtonPressed;
         return 0;
      }

      case WM_PAINT :
      {
         HDC          PaintDC;
         RECT         rect;
         PAINTSTRUCT  ps;

►        PaintDC = BeginPaint(hWnd, &ps);
         GetClientRect(hWnd, &rect);

Watches-------------------------------------------------------------2-
Ctrl: I-Inspect W-Watch M-Module F-File P-Previous L-Line S-Search N-Next
```

After a breakpoint is set, when you execute your program by pressing Ctrl-F9 (or choosing the Run option from the Run menu), execution of the program is halted at the location of the breakpoint.

F2 works as a toggle. To turn the breakpoint off, move the cursor over a previously set breakpoint and press the same key combination. This time the red highlight disappears, and you know the breakpoint is no longer set.

Breakpoints and Window Procedures

Suppose you want to watch the code in your window procedure execute. The only way to get to it is with a breakpoint. This is because the window procedure of a program is called by Windows. Therefore, you can never step directly into the window procedure. Instead, you must set a breakpoint on the code you want to debug. The debugger comes up when that code is about to be executed. Then, you can view the values of variables (as you see next) and single step through the code.

Breakpoints and ObjectWindows Programs

You use breakpoints all the time when you are debugging your programs based on the ObjectWindows Library. This is because nearly the entire program is based on message response functions. Therefore, all the programs are called by Windows. To step through the message response function, you must set a breakpoint before you start running your program. Then, as your message response functions are called, your breakpoints cause the debugger to pop up, and you can use the other features of the debugger described here to view variables and single step through the code.

Viewing Data

Often it's nice to find the value of a variable at a certain point in a program while it's executing. You can use the `MessageBox` function to display variable values on the screen. However, this isn't always practical if you only need to view the values of variables during the debugging phase. `MessageBox` adds code and takes extra time to implement.

As you might guess, the debugger provides a way to view the values of variables. In fact, the debugger provides several ways to view variables during runtime. You can create inspector windows, display watch variables, and even evaluate program variables.

Each method of viewing data is different and is used in different cases. Inspectors open a separate window in Turbo Debugger for Windows to view data. Watches combine the values of several variables in a single Turbo Debugger for Windows window. When you evaluate a variable, you view the variable and are given a method of changing the value of the variable during program execution.

Inspectors

An inspector is a displayed window that shows the value of a variable. Although this window can be used with any type of variable, it is especially useful for structures because you can see the value of every element at once.

To display an inspector window, press Ctrl-I or choose the Inspect option from the Data menu. The Inspect Data dialog box displays, enabling you to type the name of a variable. Go ahead and type the structure name `wndclass`. A window opens that shows the value of each field in the `wndclass` data structure (see Figure 12.6).

Figure 12.6.

Inspector window for the wndclass structure.

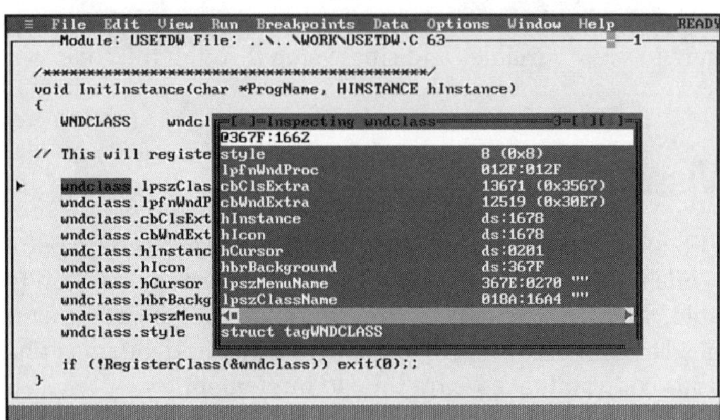

Notice, you can view only the contents of the variable when it is in scope; in this case, that means in the `InitInstance` function. Therefore, you can set a breakpoint in the function, and when the breakpoint is hit, use Ctrl-I to display the window structure field values.

You even can have an inspector window open to see the values as they change. You get a feeling of power when you have an inspector window open and, stepping through a program, see the values of variables change. You feel even better when the variables contain values you expect.

Watches

You can view multiple variables in the same window using a watch window. To set a watch variable, press Ctrl-F7, or choose the Watches menu option from the data menu and select Add Watch.

The Add Watch dialog box is displayed. This dialog box enables you to enter a variable to add to a Watch window. If a Watch window is not open, one is opened, and the variable is added to it. Figure 12.7 shows an open Watch window with three variables listed.

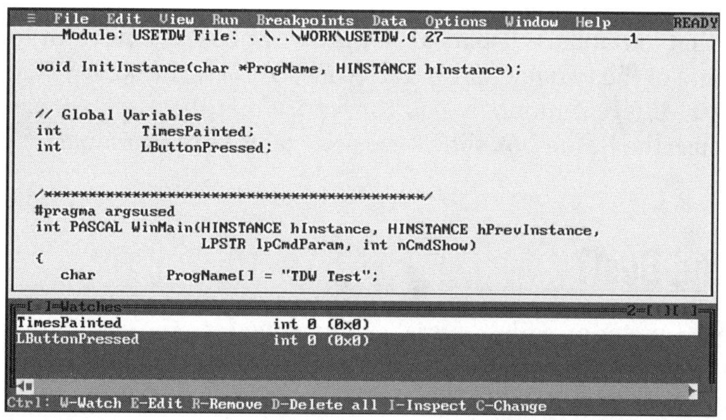

Figure 12.7.

An open Watch window.

The variable is displayed in the left of the window, followed by a colon (:) and the value (or contents) of the variable. You can add as many watch variables as you want. If you add more watches than you can view at one time, use the scroll bar on the right side of the window to view the other watch variables.

To delete a watch variable, switch to the Watch window by choosing the Window menu and selecting the Watch option. Move the highlight bar over the variable you want to remove from the window and press Delete. You always can close the Watch window by pressing Alt-F3 (or choose the Window menu and select Close).

Evaluate

Using a variable evaluation, you can view the value of a variable and change it. This feature is handy if you have an idea what is wrong in your program and think you know the correct value to give a variable. Rather than editing, recompiling, and testing the program to change the value of a variable, you can do it quickly in the debugging phase. If the change works, you can proceed to change the source code, knowing that the problem will be corrected.

To open the Evaluate and modify dialog box (see Figure 12.8), choose the Evaluate/modify option from the Data menu. This enables you to type a variable in the expression text box. As soon as you press Enter, the current value of that variable is displayed in the Result box. If you want to change the value of the variable, press Tab twice to access the New Value box and enter a different number. You can verify that the variable was modified because the Result box shows the new value of the variable.

Which Is the Best?

Although the debugger provides several ways for viewing the contents of variables, you'll soon have a feel for which situations call for which method of viewing the data. In general, a Watch window is the commonly used method for viewing program data. Inspector windows are most useful for studying data structures in detail. You utilize variable evaluation when you must modify the value of a variable.

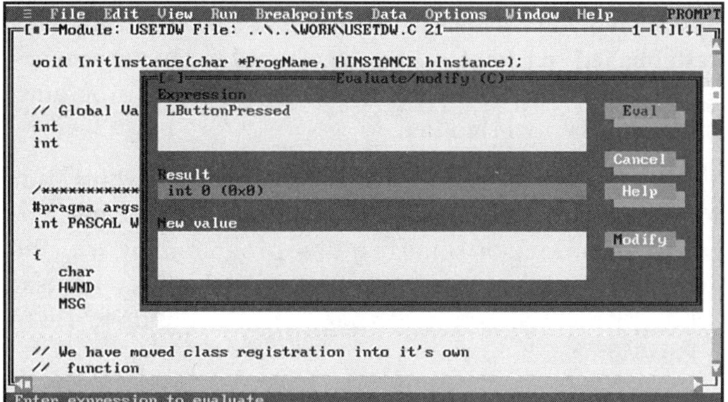

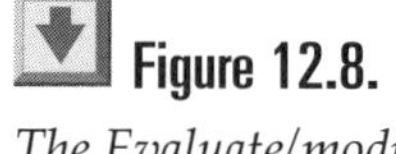

Figure 12.8.

The Evaluate/modify dialog box.

Viewing the Call Stack

The call stack shows the sequence of functions your program called to reach the function being executed. Open the call stack window by choosing the View menu and selecting the Stack option.

A listbox is displayed. It shows the functions your program called to reach the function now running, as well as the values of the parameters passed to each function. The functions are listed in reverse order. That is, the most recently called functions are at the top of the list. You always see at least one function call, and that is the `WinMain()` function.

This ends the discussion about the debugger. It is a powerful tool and has many more features than I can cover here. In fact, entire books are written just about the debugger. However, in this chapter is the knowledge you need to start using Turbo Debugger for Windows to debug your programs.

Using EasyWin to Debug Your Programs

You haven't seen the EasyWin library used since Chapter 3, "Getting Started in Windows." You might wonder why I bring it up when talking about debugging, so a little discussion first.

Although the EasyWin library is a fast way to create a program that runs in Windows, I established in Chapter 3 that you usually don't create applications based on EasyWin. After seeing some real Windows programs, you probably understand why I said that.

However, you, at times, can use the EasyWin library to debug your programs. It doesn't always work to use the stand-alone debugger. For example, you might be working on some real-time programming with the communications port, or you might not want to switch between the text screen of the debugger and the graphical screen of your Window. These are times when EasyWin can help you.

You can utilize the EasyWin library in your programs by using the `InitEasyWin` function, as follows:

```
_InitEasyWin();
```

When you put these instructions in your program, a separate EasyWin window is displayed. Now, you can use the regular `printf()` function to display the value of variables in the EasyWin window.

Using `printf()` beats having to display a floating point number in a regular window. Remember, Windows has only `TextOut`, `ExtTextOut`, and `DrawText` for displaying textual output. There is no built-in, formatted print statement.

As an example of debugging with EasyWin, take a look at the next program in Listing 12.2 (the associated module definition file is in Listing 12.3). This program is based on the ObjectWindows Library that uses the EasyWin library to display the value of a variable.

Listing 12.2. Debugging a program with the EasyWin library.

```
// EZDEBUG.CPP - Debugging a program using the
//               EasyWin library
//
// Programming Windows with Turbo C++ for Windows
// by Paul J. Perry

#define WIN31
#define STRICT
```

```
#include <owl.h>
#include <windowsx.h>

#include <stdio.h>     // for printf() function


// Class Declarations

/*******************************************/
class TOwlApp : public TApplication
{
   public :
      TOwlApp (LPSTR AName, HINSTANCE hInstance, HINSTANCE
               hPrevInstance,  LPSTR CmdLine, int CmdShow) :
               TApplication(AName, hInstance, hPrevInstance,
               CmdLine, CmdShow) { } ;

   virtual void InitMainWindow();
};


/*******************************************/
class TMainWindow : public TWindow
{
   public :
      int LButtonPressed;
      TMainWindow(PTWindowsObject AParent, LPSTR ATitle)
                  : TWindow(AParent, ATitle) { };
      virtual void SetupWindow();
      virtual void WMLButtonDown(TMessage& Msg)
         = [WM_FIRST + WM_LBUTTONDOWN];

      virtual void Paint(HDC PaintDC, PAINTSTRUCT &PaintInfo);
};

// Class Member Functions

/*******************************************/
void TOwlApp::InitMainWindow()
{
   MainWindow = new TMainWindow(NULL, Name);
}

/*******************************************/
void TMainWindow::SetupWindow()
{
```

continues

Listing 12.2. continued

```
   LButtonPressed = 0;

// Open up the EasyWin window
   _InitEasyWin();
}

/*******************************************/
#pragma argsused
void TMainWindow::WMLButtonDown(TMessage& Msg)
{
   LButtonPressed++;
// Display information to EasyWin window
   printf("Left mouse button has been pressed %d times\n",
          LButtonPressed);
}

/*******************************************/
#pragma argsused
void TMainWindow::Paint(HDC PaintDC, PAINTSTRUCT &PaintInfo)
{
   RECT rect;

   GetClientRect(HWindow, &rect);

   DrawText(PaintDC, "Click Mouse Button", -1, &rect,
            DT_SINGLELINE | DT_CENTER | DT_VCENTER);

}


/*******************************************/
int PASCAL WinMain(HINSTANCE hInstance, HINSTANCE hPrevInstance,
                   LPSTR lpCmdLine, int nCmdShow)
{

   TOwlApp ThisApp("Debugging With EasyWin", hInstance,
                   hPrevInstance, lpCmdLine, nCmdShow);
   ThisApp.Run();
   return ThisApp.Status;

}
```

Listing 12.3. Module definition file for EZDEBUG program.

```
;
;  EZDEBUG.DEF module definition file
;

DESCRIPTION    'Debugging With EasyWin'
NAME           EZDEBUG
EXETYPE        WINDOWS
STUB           'WINSTUB.EXE'
HEAPSIZE       4096
STACKSIZE      5120
CODE           PRELOAD MOVEABLE DISCARDABLE
DATA           PRELOAD MOVEABLE MULTIPLE
```

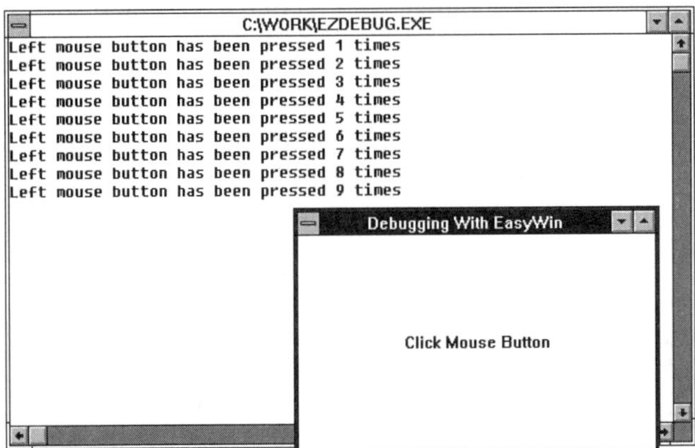

Figure 12.9.
Debugging with EasyWin.

When you execute the program, two windows are created, as shown in Figure 12.9 (one may be hiding behind the other). When you click the left mouse button in the client area of the main window, the EasyWin window displays the number of times the mouse button has been clicked. This information is stored in a variable. The value of the variable is displayed with the `printf()` function.

You can use the EasyWin library to view the value of variables in regular C programs, as well as programs based on the ObjectWindows Library. Just be sure you use the `_InitEasyWin()` function to initialize the library. If you don't, you will have linker problems.

Using WinSpector

WinSpector is a small program that runs while you are testing your program. As soon as a fatal error occurs (such as an exception 13 or a General Protection Fault), your program is aborted, and WinSpector creates a text file describing the state of your program when it crashed.

This type of debugging tool is a *postmortem* dump. The second part of the word, mortem, refers to death. Post means after. WinSpector traps your program after it dies (or crashes) and creates a log file with information about your program just before it died.

The type of information a WinSpector log can give you includes the CPU registers, an assembly language disassembly of program instructions, Windows information (version, current mode, amount of memory, and so on), and the call stack of your program.

You start WinSpector by double-clicking its icon from Program Manager. If you do much programming, as an alternative you might consider loading WinSpector every time you run Windows by adding it to the Start-up group in Program Manager. It is a small program and doesn't take much time to load.

You can set some basic options through the WinSpector Preferences dialog box (see Figure 12.10). Most of the options are self-explanatory and don't require much additional information (use the online help for complete information).

Figure 12.10.

WinSpector Preferences dialog box.

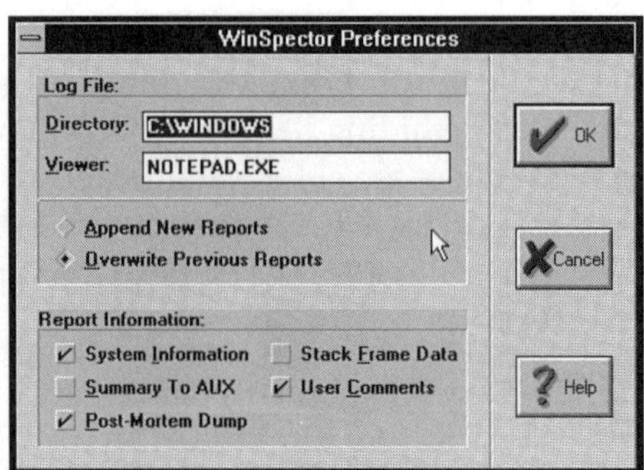

After WinSpector is loaded, minimize it to an icon. Now you can execute your program. WinSpector hides in the background like a ghost. When your program crashes, you see the customary Windows dialog box. After you choose OK (is it really OK that your program crashed?), WinSpector displays a dialog box that enables you to enter user comments. WinSpector stores the comments with its other stored information.

You can use the View Log option on the main WinSpector dialog box to display the log information that WinSpector gathered for you. It automatically brings up the Windows Notepad (or your own custom editor). Then, print the log file to a printer.

The end result is that WinSpector can help you track difficult memory corruption problems, though hopefully you won't need to use it.

The Help Compiler

Using the help compiler enables you to create help files that use the features of the Windows help engine. You can create help systems like the one used by the Turbo C++ for Windows IDE.

To create a help file, first create the text of your help file. Then run your program through the help compiler to convert it to a .HLP file. The help compiler is a command-line utility that Borland licenses from Microsoft.

Although I can't teach you about writing help files in the space available, I want to lead you in the right direction. The files that the help compiler accepts must be in a format known as Rich Text Format, or RTF. At this time, only a few word processors support RTF. One processor that supports this format is Microsoft Word for Windows.

After you create your help text file, open a DOS box. Switch to the TCWIN\BIN subdirectory to get the help compiler. Invoke the help compiler by typing HC31 and passing the name of the help file.

For full details about writing your own help files and the structure of your program, search the online help system for the key phrases "Creating Help Files." It provides details about how to structure your help files and how to link help topics with links in your program.

Writing help files is not difficult, but it can be tricky. The help system has so many features that to take advantage of them, you must really understand how the help system works. The online help does a good job of explaining how to create help files.

What You Have Learned

This chapter examined three of the additional tools in the Turbo C++ for Windows package: Turbo Debugger for Windows, WinSpector, and the Windows help compiler. Although the core of the chapter centered around debugging, you also discovered the tool used to create help files.

The following topics are covered in this chapter:

- There are three types of program errors: compile time, runtime, and logic. A debugger helps a programmer track errors in program logic.
- Turbo Debugger for Windows is a unique tool that uses a text mode-based interface. For this reason, if you use a special super VGA adapter, you may need to use a special video DLL driver.
- To debug programs at the source code level, you first must turn on the debug information. This forces the linker to include specific information in the executable file about the original source code of the program.
- The difference between the Trace Into (F7) command and the Step Over (F8) command is that Trace Into executes each line of a function, whereas Step Over executes a function as a single statement.
- A breakpoint is a line in your program you set to stop execution of your program automatically during debugging. You set a breakpoint by pressing F2 or choosing the Breakpoint menu option and specifying the Toggle breakpoint selection.

- You have three methods for viewing program variables during program execution. You can create inspectors, watches, and evaluation windows. An inspector is a window that is displayed which shows the value of a single variable. Inspector windows are used best with structure variables.
- You can use the EasyWin library to debug your Windows applications (C and C++) by including a call to the function `_InitEasyWin()` in your program. Then, use the `printf()` function for variable values to the EasyWin window.
- WinSpector is a postmortem debugging tool that outputs the state of the computer to a log file immediately before your program crashes. WinSpector usually is used to track nasty memory corruption problems.
- To add a help system to your program, use the help compiler to create context-sensitive help. You first must create a help file script in a word processor that supports RTF. Then, use the help compiler utility (HC31) to compile the RTF file in a HLP file that Windows Help engine can read directly.

13

USING DIALOG BOXES

IN THIS CHAPTER

- What dialog boxes are and how they are used.
- The 10 defined control elements found in dialog boxes.
- The differences between modal and nonmodal dialog boxes.
- How to use the predefined common dialog boxes that are part of Windows 3.1.

You have covered a great deal of information since you started examining how to program for Windows. You've seen the elements of a main overlapped window in a traditional Windows program written in both C and C++. You also saw how to use the ObjectWindows Library to simplify Windows programming using object-oriented programming techniques.

You saw Windows resources in Chapter 7, "A First Look at Resources." You learned about icons, cursors, menus, and accelerator keys. You learned how to use the Resource Workshop to view, create, and modify resources and how to use custom resources in your Windows programs.

Chapter 10, "Getting Input from the User," discussed obtaining input from the user through both the keyboard and the mouse. You saw how Windows provides built-in support for keyboard input. You also learned how to use keyboard data in your programs. When you examined the mouse cursor, you found how to change the cursor on-the-fly and how to use some of the mouse functions in the Windows applications programming interface.

This chapter takes another big step in examining Windows programming concepts by discussing dialog boxes. One of the striking elements of a graphical user environment such as Windows is dialog boxes. This chapter shows you how to use dialog boxes in your program by teaching you how to use the built-in dialog boxes that come with Windows. Chapter 14, "More About Dialog Boxes," explains how to create custom resources with the Resource Workshop.

With your knowledge about programming for Windows, using resources, and getting input, you now are ready to forge ahead and look at dialog boxes. Thus, continue your journey of Windows programming.

Dialog Boxes: Another Form of Input

Dialog boxes provide the user with a convenient way to enter data in an application program. Usually, the user responds to a menu item that has trailing ellipses ..., and a dialog box pops up. The user then can set an option, select a filename, or perform nearly any type of operation.

Dialog boxes are used to request information from the user as well as provide information to the user of the program. For example, when your program needs additional information about certain program options, a dialog box can get the information from the user.

One common dialog box that gives information is the About... option. It provides a brief copyright message and program information. Program Manager uses the About Program Manager dialog box to give information about Windows current operating mode (see Figure 13.1).

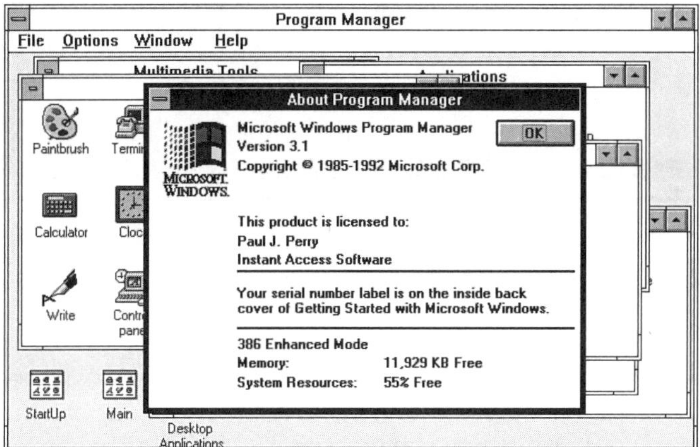

Figure 13.1.

The About Program Manager dialog box.

In Windows, a dialog box is a window that contains child windows. The child windows are dialog box controls. Windows provides 10 types of dialog box controls: pushbuttons, radio buttons, check boxes, combination boxes, static text fields, group boxes, listboxes, scroll bars, icons, and edit boxes.

Dialog boxes are another resource. They are created in the Resource Workshop dialog editor (see Figure 13.2). Dialog boxes are created separately from program source code. This makes dialog boxes easy to modify.

Figure 13.2.
Resource Workshop dialog editor.

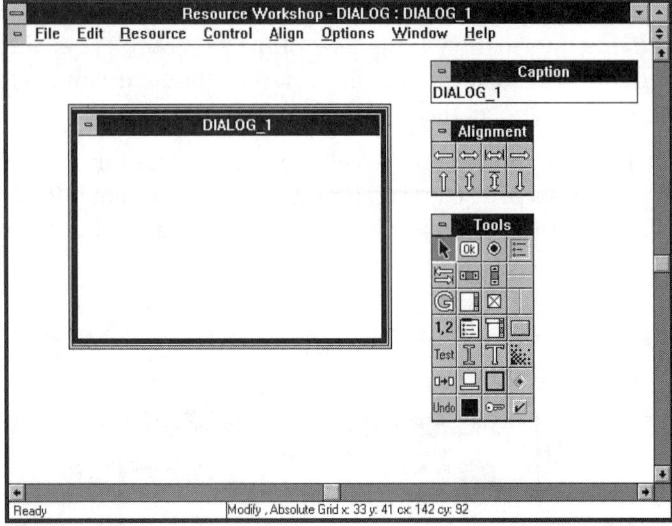

What's Your Mode?

Dialog boxes are classified in three categories. They can be modal, modeless, or system-modal. *Modal* dialog boxes don't enable the user to utilize the dialog box's parent window when that box is active. *Modeless* dialog boxes enable the user to switch between the dialog box and the program's parent window. *System-modal* dialog boxes are used in special cases to freeze every other window on the desktop until the user responds to the dialog box. System-modal dialog boxes are used in situations where disaster will strike the system if the user doesn't take immediate action.

Modal and System-Modal Dialog Boxes

The modal dialog box is the most common type of dialog box used by Windows programs (see Figure 13.3). When your program displays a modal dialog box, the user cannot switch from the dialog box to the main window (parent window) of the program. Although the user still can switch to another program running in Windows, the user must cancel the dialog box to run the main application parent window.

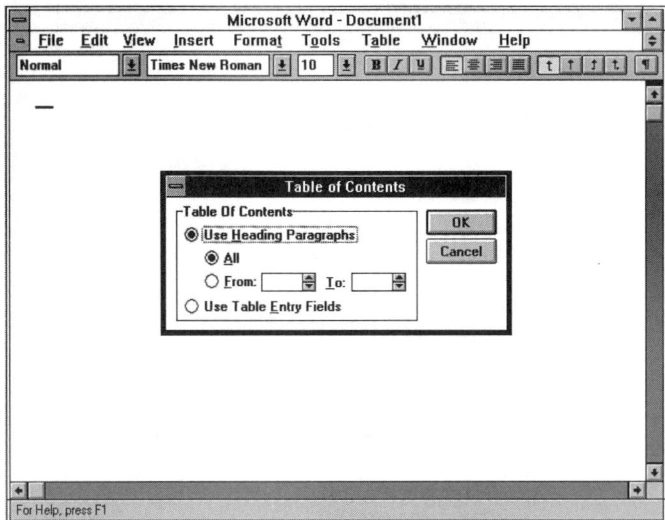

Figure 13.3.

A modal dialog box in Microsoft Word for Windows.

System-modal dialog boxes are a form of modal dialog boxes, but they do not enable the user to switch to any other window. An example of a system-modal dialog box is the one displayed when you exit Windows from Program Manager. Notice, you cannot switch from the dialog box to another window without taking some sort of action.

Use system-modal dialog boxes with caution. It isn't wise to make all your dialog boxes system-modal: one advantage of a multitasking environment like Windows is your ability to switch between executing programs. If all dialog boxes are system-modal, the multitasking advantages of Windows are defeated.

Modeless Dialog Boxes

The modeless dialog box is used when the user finds it more convenient to open the dialog box, enter data, and then switch back to the main window (see Figure 13.4) without covering the dialog box.

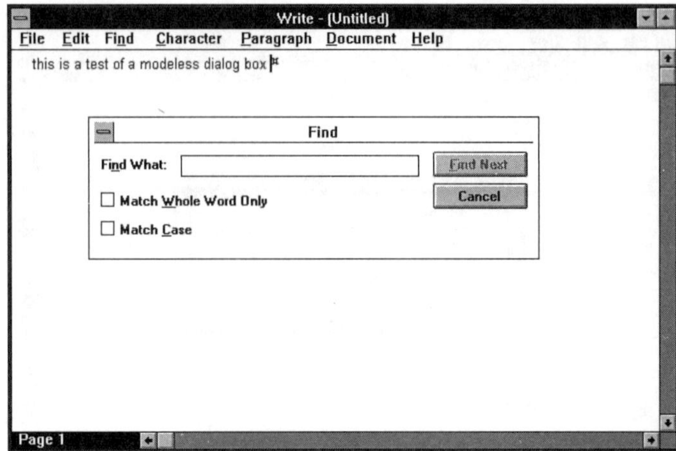

Figure 13.4.

The Find dialog box found in Windows Write.

The Find dialog box in the Windows Write program enables you to switch between the main application window and the dialog box using the mouse. When the dialog box isn't active, it loses focus, and the title bar isn't highlighted. When you use the dialog box, it regains focus, causing the title bar to be highlighted again.

Elements of Dialog Boxes

A dialog box is defined as a pop-up window. All dialog boxes consist of a combination of smaller elements (see Figure 13.5) known as control elements. The `MessageBox` routine creates a dialog box that contains text, an icon, and pushbuttons. The file dialog uses listboxes, an edit box, and pushbuttons.

There are 10 types of dialog boxes. Some are similar; others are vastly different. The control elements are as follows:

- *Pushbuttons.* Trigger an immediate action.
- *Radio Buttons.* Offer a group of options. Only one can be selected.
- *CheckBoxes.* Provide options that can be checked on or off.

- *Static Text Fields.* Provide text that doesn't change in a dialog box.
- *Group Boxes.* Enable you to group a set of controls.
- *Listboxes.* Offer the user the ability to choose an option from a list of options.
- *Combination Boxes.* Enable the user to type text and choose other items from a listbox.
- *Scroll Bars.* Enable you to prompt the user for a linear value.
- *Icons.* Enable you to enhance dialog boxes by providing visual feedback.
- *Edit Boxes.* Enable the user to enter text.

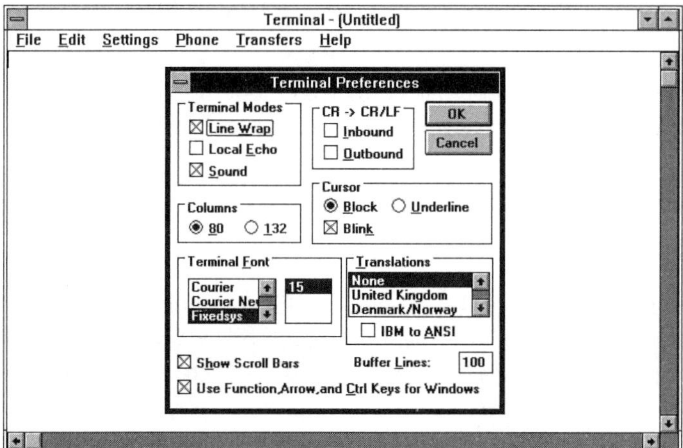

Figure 13.5.

A dialog box with control elements from the Windows Terminal.

The control elements listed previously are the ones included with Windows. You probably noticed that the control elements used by Borland in the Integrated Development Environment (IDE) (see Figure 13.6) of Turbo C++ Windows are different.

Windows is expandable, which enables you to create more elements. Borland produced their own look, the Borland Windows Custom Controls, or BWCC. Some advertisements call this appearance, the "look of chiseled steel." The exact term for these controls is *owner draw.*

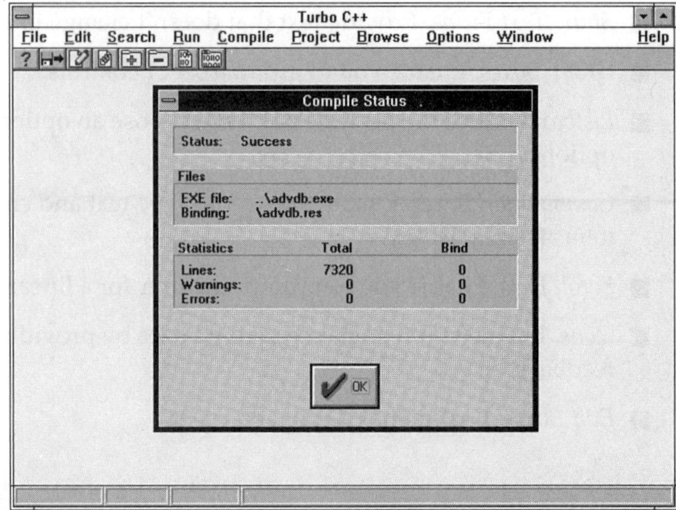

Figure 13.6.

The Compile Status dialog box in the Integrated Development Environment.

The rest of this section covers each control element. It tells you when to use them and gives you a better understanding of what they are.

Pushbuttons

Pushbuttons (command buttons) trigger an immediate action when selected by the user. There are two types of pushbuttons, standard and default. The default pushbutton has an extra thick border and is selected when the user presses Enter in the dialog box.

Nearly every dialog box has an OK and a Cancel pushbutton. These are used to accept the new dialog box settings or abort the dialog box entirely. Figure 13.7 shows an example of pushbuttons. The pushbuttons are on the right side of the dialog box.

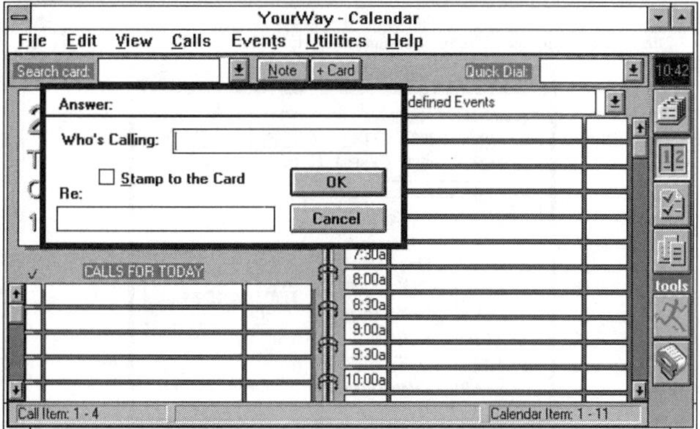

Figure 13.7.

A dialog box with pushbuttons.

Radio Buttons

Radio buttons (option buttons) appear to enable you to choose a single option from a group of options. You can select only one item at the time from the group. You change a selection by choosing a different button. The selected button contains a black circle.

Radio buttons received their name from the buttons on older car radios. On those, you could press only one button at the time to choose a station—those radios were around before digital stereos became popular.

Use a radio button when you have several options for the user to select, but only one can be selected at the time. For example, the Windows Terminal program uses radio buttons in the Communication settings dialog box (see Figure 13.8). Options currently unavailable are grayed out, and you cannot select them.

CheckBoxes

Checkboxes offer a list of options you can switch on or off. You can select as many checkbox options as are appropriate for the application being executed.

Figure 13.8.

Radio buttons used in Terminal program.

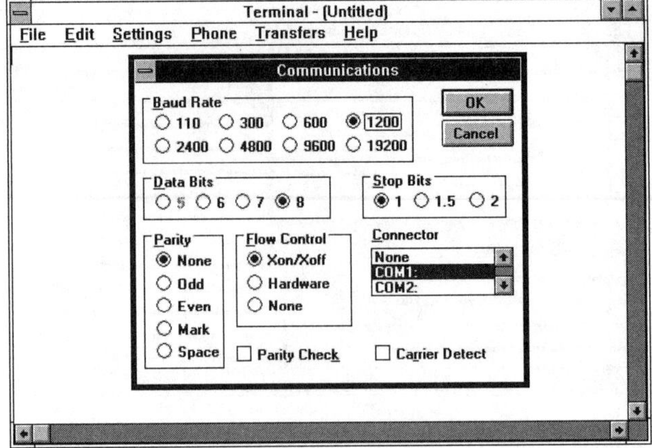

The checkbox is a small box with text, located usually to the right of the box, although text can be moved to the left. When an option in a checkbox is selected, it contains an X.

Boolean values are the best type of options to use checkboxes for. These can be checked (on) or unchecked (off). Figure 13.9 shows the checkboxes used in File Manager.

Figure 13.9.

An example of checkboxes in File Manager.

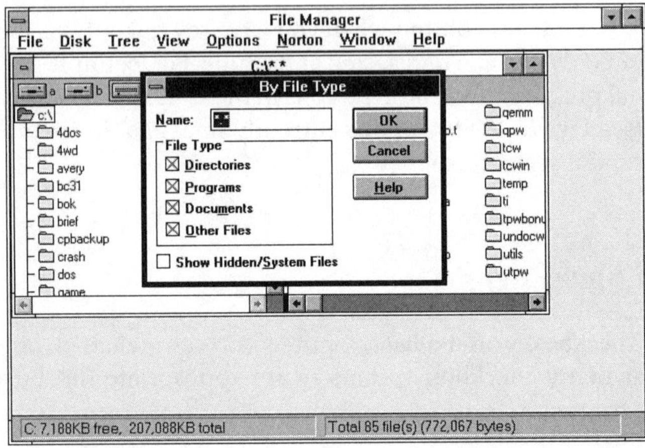

Static Text Fields

Static text fields are descriptive lines of text located in your dialog box. The fields are called static because they don't change. Most dialog boxes have static text fields, especially About boxes. The user cannot change or manipulate static text fields. They are put in the dialog box to help the user know how the box is used and how to make selections.

Group Boxes

A group box is a thick black border drawn around a set of controls. Radio buttons nearly always have a group box, to help clarify which option can be selected. Often, a group box is used with check boxes as well as other controls. However, a group box is never required. It is available to help the user understand how to use the program.

Listboxes

Listboxes provide a list of options from which the user can choose an item. If too many items are in the list to display at once, a scroll bar is displayed automatically that enables the user to browse the available options.

Listboxes are used often in Choose a File and Save File As dialog boxes, as well as any time the user has a choice from a group of items. Figure 13.10 shows a listbox used in Quattro Pro for Windows.

Combination Boxes

A combination box (combo box) appears initially as a rectangular box with the current default choice highlighted. The arrow in a square box at the right opens a list of available choices for your selection. If there are more choices than can fit in the combination box, scroll bars are provided so you can move between options.

Figure 13.10.

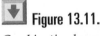

A listbox used in Quattro Pro for Windows.

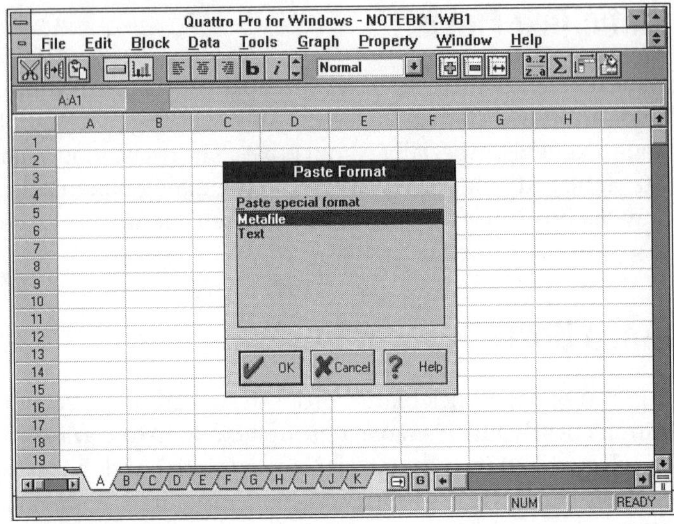

Combination boxes usually are used in dialog boxes that are too small or crowded to contain a full listbox. Microsoft Word for Windows provides combination boxes in the ribbon located at the top of the screen for the Font and Style selections (see Figure 13.11).

Figure 13.11.

Combination boxes in Word for Windows.

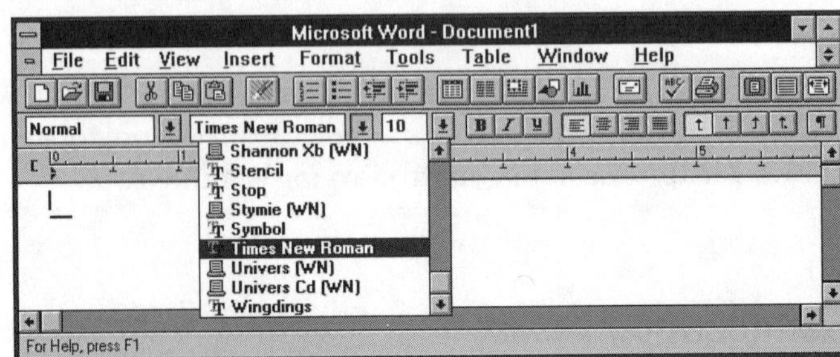

Scroll Bars

Scroll bar control elements are similar to the scroll bars that can be attached to a window. Both vertical and horizontal scroll bars can be included in a dialog box. Scroll bar control elements can be created in any width or height.

Scroll bar control elements are considered separate from listboxes or combination boxes (which may contain their own scroll bars). Figure 13.12 gives an example of a scroll bar used in the Control Panel desktop dialog box to control the cursor blink rate.

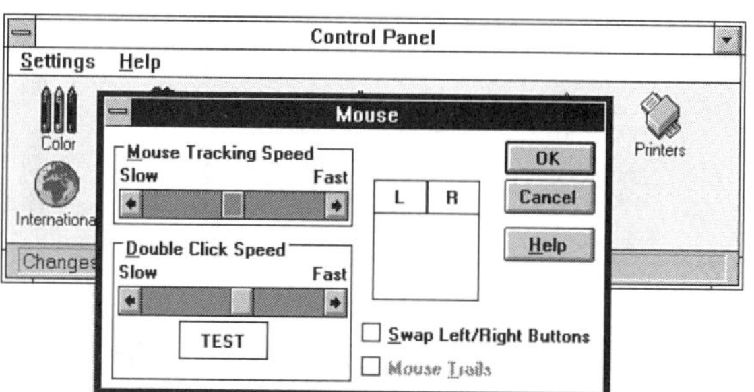

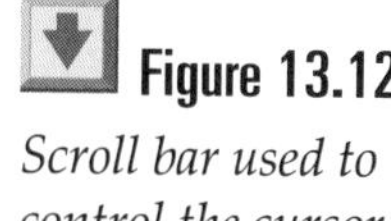

Figure 13.12.
Scroll bar used to control the cursor blink rate.

Icons

Icons are a control element primarily utilized in About dialog boxes. These are used when giving information about a program. The name given to the icon is referenced in the dialog box resource script file, and when the dialog box displays, the icon automatically appears in the dialog box.

The icon is created with the Resource Workshop icon editor, like any other icon, and can be used as the class icon for the window of your program. Figure 13.13 shows a sample of an About dialog box for Paintbrush that uses an icon.

Edit Boxes

An edit box (text box) is a rectangular box where you type information. There are single line edit boxes and multiline edit boxes. A flashing insertion point is displayed in the edit box that marks the point where the next character is displayed.

In text-based environments, the flashing point that marks the location of the next character to be entered is called a cursor. Windows calls it the caret (the cursor is used to track the position of the mouse). Figure 13.14 shows an example of a single line edit box in the Calendar program.

Figure 13.13.

The About Paintbrush dialog box.

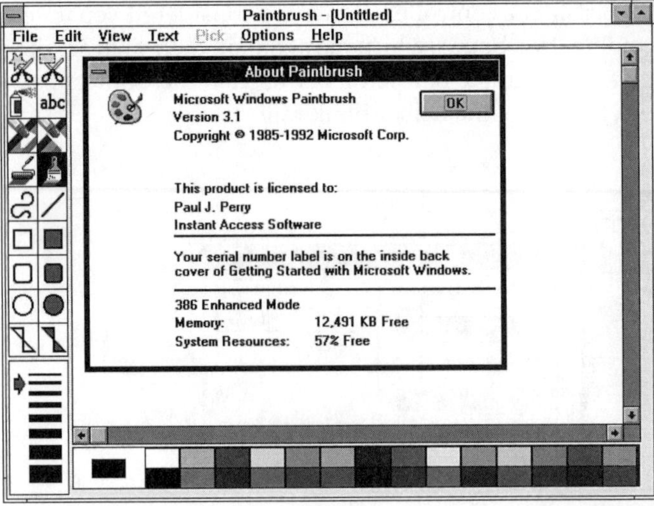

Figure 13.14.

A single line edit box in Calendar.

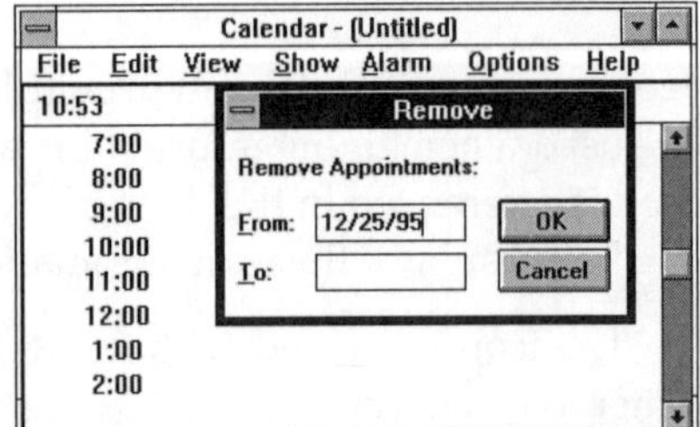

Predefined Dialog Boxes

Before you begin creating your own dialog boxes, look at some dialog boxes that are predefined. The first dialog box is the `MessageBox` routine, which is part of the Windows application programming interface. The other dialog boxes are part of the common dialogs that are new to Windows 3.1.

MessageBox

You have seen the `MessageBox` routine pop up (no pun intended) since Chapter 1, "Getting Started with Turbo C++ for Windows." It provides a convenient method of responding to user input. Any program using traditional Windows programming methods, the ObjectWindows Library, or the EasyWin library can use the `MessageBox` routine.

The exact syntax of the `MessageBox` routine follows:

```
int MessageBox(HWND hWnd, LPCSTR Text, LPCSTR Title, UINT Style);
```

The routine takes a handle to the parent window (if no parent window is present, use `NULL`), the text of the title bar, and the text to be displayed in the message box. If the Caption parameter is `NULL`, the default caption "Error" is used. The final parameter, `Style`, specifies the contents of the dialog box. It can be any combination of the values shown in Table 13.1. The style flags are combined with the C or (`|`) operator.

Table 13.1. MessageBox style flags.

Value	*Description*
MB_OK	Includes OK button.
MB_OKCANCEL	Includes OK and Cancel buttons.
MB_ABORTRETRYIGNORE	Includes Abort, Retry, and Ignore buttons.
MB_YESNOCANCEL	Includes Yes, No, and Cancel buttons.
MB_YESNO	Includes Yes and No buttons.
MB_RETRYCANCEL	Includes Retry and Cancel buttons.
MB_ICONHAND	Displays stop sign icon.

continues

Table 13.1. continued

Value	*Description*
MB_ICONQUESTION	Displays question mark icon.
MB_ICONEXCLAMATION	Displays exclamation mark icon.
MB_ICONINFORMATION	Displays lowercase "i" icon.
MB_ICONSTOP	Displays stop sign icon.
MB_DEFBUTTON1	Specifies first button as default.
MB_DEFBUTTON2	Specifies second button as default.
MB_DEFBUTTON3	Specifies third button as default.
MB_APPLMODAL	Makes message box application modal.
MB_SYSTEMMODAL	Makes message box system-modal.
MB_TASKMODAL	Makes message box task modal.

NOTE

Task modal is the same as application modal, except all top-level windows belonging to the current task are disabled when you use task modal message boxes.

Besides displaying one of five icons, you can also display several pushbuttons. So far, you have displayed only the OK button. You also can display a Cancel button with it. As a separate choice, you can display a Yes and No button or a Cancel, Abort, Retry selection of buttons. Notice, Windows uses the `MessageBox` routine internally when a disk error occurs to prompt the user for an appropriate action.

Use the final three flags in the table to specify the modality of the box. You can include only one of the three flags.

When utilizing the `MessageBox` routine, you haven't used the value returned by the function. By checking that value, you can tell which button was pressed (if multiple buttons were specified). Table 13.2 lists the constant values returned by the MessageBox routine. These values correspond to the button that was pressed.

Table 13.2. Return values of the MessageBox routine.

Value	*Description*
IDOK	OK button pressed.
IDCANCEL	Cancel button pressed.
IDABORT	Abort button pressed.
IDRETRY	Retry button pressed.
IDIGNORE	Ignore button pressed.
IDYES	Yes button pressed.
IDNO	No button pressed.

You are already familiar with using the `MessageBox`, because the first program you saw ("Hello Windows," in Chapter 1) was based on this routine. Next, take a look at the common dialogs that come with Windows 3.1.

The Common Dialog Boxes

If you've used any of the applications built into Windows 3.1, you probably noticed some similarity in the dialog boxes used between these programs. This is no mistake. In keeping with the theme of a common user interface (CUI), Windows 3.1 includes a library of common dialog boxes.

An application displays a *common dialog box* by calling a single function rather than by creating a dialog box procedure and a resource file containing a dialog box template (which you learn about in Chapter 14, "More About Dialog Boxes"). The seven common dialog boxes are color selection, font selection, file open, file save, print document/print setup, find text, and replace text.

These common dialog boxes make your life as a programmer easier. A side benefit is that they make it easier when you already know how to use the dialog box. All the code and resources for using these dialogs are a part of Windows. With the call of one function, your program can use these common dialog boxes.

Mostly, you call the dialog boxes by filling out the elements of a structure and then calling an appropriate function. The structure you must fill out and the function you call are listed in Table 13.3.

Table 13.3. The common dialog boxes and associated data structure and function calls.

Type	*Data Structure*	*API Function Call*
Select Color	CHOOSECOLOR	ChooseColor
Select Font	CHOOSEFONT	ChooseFont
File Open	OPENFILENAME	GetOpenFileName
File Save As	OPENFILENAME	GetSaveFileName
Print	PRINTDLG	PrintDlg
Find	FINDREPLACE	FindText
Replace	FINDREPLACE	ReplaceText

To use any of the common dialog boxes in your program, you must include the commdlg.h header file at the beginning of your program. This header file provides function prototypes and constant declarations necessary for using the common dialog boxes in your own programs.

Take a look at an example program to get an idea about how to use the common dialog boxes. Listing 13.1 contains the source code for a program that uses the File Open, File Save, and Choose Color dialog boxes. Listing 13.2 contains the header file for the program. Listing 13.3 contains the resource script, and Listing 13.4 contains the module definition file.

Listing 13.1. Source code for COMMFILE.C program.

```
// COMMFILE.C - Example of using the Common Dialogs
//
// Programming Windows with Turbo C++ for Windows
// by Paul J. Perry

#define STRICT

#include <windowsx.h>
#include <commdlg.h>

#include <string.h>
#include <stdio.h>

#include "commfile.h"

// Function Prototypes
LRESULT CALLBACK _export MainWndProc(HWND hWnd, UINT message,
                                     WPARAM wParam, LPARAM lParam);

void WMCommand_Handler(HWND hwnd, int id, HWND hwndCtl, UINT
                       codeNotify);
void GetFileName(HWND hWnd);
void SaveFileName(HWND hWnd);
void GetCurrentColor(HWND hWnd);

// Global Variables
char      FinalFileName[256] = "";
COLORREF  CurrentColor;

/*******************************************/
#pragma argsused
int PASCAL WinMain(HINSTANCE hInstance, HINSTANCE hPrevInstance,
                   LPSTR lpCmdParam, int nCmdShow)
{
   char        ProgName[] = "File Common Dialogs";
   HWND        hWnd;
   MSG         msg;
```

continues

Listing 13.1. continued

```
  if (!hPrevInstance)
  {
     WNDCLASS    wndclass;

     wndclass.style         = CS_VREDRAW ¦ CS_HREDRAW;
     wndclass.lpfnWndProc   = (WNDPROC) MainWndProc;
     wndclass.hInstance     = hInstance;
     wndclass.hIcon         = LoadIcon(NULL, IDI_APPLICATION);
     wndclass.hCursor       = LoadCursor(NULL, IDC_ARROW);
     wndclass.hbrBackground = (HBRUSH) (COLOR_WINDOW + 1);
     wndclass.lpszMenuName  = "MAINMENU";
     wndclass.cbClsExtra    = 0;
     wndclass.cbWndExtra    = 0;
     wndclass.lpszClassName = ProgName;

     RegisterClass(&wndclass);
  }

  hWnd = CreateWindow(ProgName, ProgName,
                      WS_OVERLAPPEDWINDOW,
                      CW_USEDEFAULT, CW_USEDEFAULT,
                      CW_USEDEFAULT, CW_USEDEFAULT,
                      NULL, NULL, hInstance, NULL);

  ShowWindow(hWnd, nCmdShow);
  UpdateWindow(hWnd);

  while (GetMessage(&msg, NULL, 0, 0))
  {
     TranslateMessage(&msg);
     DispatchMessage(&msg);
  }
  return msg.wParam;
}
/*******************************************/
void GetFileName(HWND hWnd)
{
  OPENFILENAME OpenFileName;   // Data structure for common dialog

  char Filters[] = "All Files (*.*)\0*.*\0"
                   "C++ Code (*.CPP)\0*.CPP\0"
                   "C Code (*.C)\0*.C\0"
                   "Header Files (*.H)\0*.H\0";

  // We first initialize all elements to zero
  memset(&OpenFileName, 0, sizeof(OPENFILENAME));
```

```
    // Now, we go through and initialize structure members
    OpenFileName.lpstrTitle         = "Choose a File";
    OpenFileName.hwndOwner          = hWnd;
    OpenFileName.lpstrFilter        = (LPSTR)Filters;
    OpenFileName.nFilterIndex       = 1;
    OpenFileName.lpstrFile          = (LPSTR)FinalFileName;
    OpenFileName.nMaxFile           = sizeof(FinalFileName);
    OpenFileName.Flags              = OFN_FILEMUSTEXIST | \
                                      OFN_HIDEREADONLY |  \
                                      OFN_PATHMUSTEXIST;
    OpenFileName.lpstrDefExt        = "*";
    OpenFileName.lStructSize        = sizeof(OPENFILENAME);

    // Go ahead and call dialog box function
    GetOpenFileName(&OpenFileName);
}


/*******************************************/
void SaveFileName(HWND hWnd)
{
    OPENFILENAME SaveFileName;

    char Filters[] = "All Files (*.*)\0*.*\0"
                     "C++ Code (*.CPP)\0*.CPP\0"
                     "C Code (*.C)\0*.C\0"
                     "Header Files (*.H)\0*.H\0";

    // We first initialize all elements to zero
    memset(&SaveFileName, 0, sizeof(OPENFILENAME));

    // Now we will elements of the structure
    SaveFileName.lpstrTitle         = "Save File As";
    SaveFileName.hwndOwner          = hWnd;
    SaveFileName.lpstrFilter        = (LPSTR)Filters;
    SaveFileName.nFilterIndex       = 1;
    SaveFileName.lpstrFile          = (LPSTR)FinalFileName;
    SaveFileName.nMaxFile           = sizeof(FinalFileName);
    SaveFileName.Flags              = OFN_FILEMUSTEXIST | \
                                      OFN_HIDEREADONLY |  \
                                      OFN_PATHMUSTEXIST;
    SaveFileName.lpstrDefExt        = "*";
    SaveFileName.lStructSize        = sizeof(OPENFILENAME);

    // Call the dialog function
    GetSaveFileName(&SaveFileName);
}
```

continues

Listing 13.1. continued

```
/*******************************************/
void GetCurrentColor(HWND hWnd)
{

   CHOOSECOLOR CC;
   COLORREF    CustomColors[16];

   memset(&CC, 0, sizeof(CHOOSECOLOR));

   CC.lStructSize  = sizeof(CHOOSECOLOR);
   CC.hwndOwner    = hWnd;
   CC.rgbResult    = CurrentColor;
   CC.lpCustColors = CustomColors;
   CC.Flags        = CC_RGBINIT | CC_SHOWHELP;

   ChooseColor(&CC);

   // Now assign our global variable to what was returned
   CurrentColor = CC.rgbResult;


}

/*******************************************/
#pragma argsused
void WMCommand_Handler(HWND hWnd, int id, HWND hwndCtl, UINT
                       codeNotify)
{
   switch(id)
   {
      case IDM_OPEN :
      {
         GetFileName(hWnd);
         InvalidateRect(hWnd, NULL, TRUE);
         break;

      }

      case IDM_SAVEAS :
      {
         SaveFileName(hWnd);
         InvalidateRect(hWnd, NULL, TRUE);
         break;
      }

      case IDM_EXIT :
```

```
        {
           PostQuitMessage(0);
           break;
        }

    }

}

/*******************************************/
LRESULT CALLBACK _export MainWndProc(HWND hWnd, UINT message,
                                     WPARAM wParam, LPARAM lParam)
{
   HBRUSH hBrush, hPrevBrush;

   switch (message)
   {
      case WM_PAINT :
      {
         HDC         PaintDC;
         PAINTSTRUCT ps;
         char        str[80];
         int         len;

         PaintDC = BeginPaint(hWnd, &ps);

         SetBkMode(PaintDC, TRANSPARENT);

         TextOut(PaintDC, 5, 1,
                 "Choose Menu Selection,"
                 "or press Left Mouse Button", 49);

         len = sprintf(str, "Filename is : %s", FinalFileName);
         TextOut(PaintDC, 5, 15, str, len);

         EndPaint(hWnd, &ps);
         return 0;
      }

      case WM_COMMAND :
      {
         return HANDLE_WM_COMMAND(hWnd, wParam, lParam,
                                  WMCommand_Handler);
      }

      case WM_LBUTTONUP :
      {
```

continues

Listing 13.1. continued

```
        GetCurrentColor(hWnd);

        hBrush = CreateSolidBrush(CurrentColor);

        hPrevBrush = (HBRUSH)SetClassLong(hWnd,
                          GCW_HBRBACKGROUND, (WORD)hBrush);

        DeleteBrush(hPrevBrush);

        InvalidateRect(hWnd, NULL, TRUE);
        return 0;
      }

      case WM_DESTROY :
      {
        if (hBrush)
           DeleteBrush(hBrush);

        PostQuitMessage(0);
        return 0;
      }
   }
   return DefWindowProc (hWnd, message, wParam, lParam);
}
```

Listing 13.2. Header file for COMMFILE.C program.

```
/*
 * COMMFILE.H header file
 *
 */

#define IDM_OPEN   110
#define IDM_SAVEAS 120
#define IDM_EXIT   130
```

Listing 13.3. Resource script for COMMFILE.C program.

```
#include "commfile.h"

MAINMENU MENU
BEGIN
     POPUP "&File"
     BEGIN
          MENUITEM "&Open...", IDM_OPEN
          MENUITEM "Save &As...", IDM_SAVEAS
          MENUITEM SEPARATOR
          MENUITEM "E&xit", IDM_EXIT
     END

END
```

Listing 13.4. Module definition file for COMMFILE.C program.

```
;
; COMMFILE.DEF module definition file
;


DESCRIPTION    'Common Dialog Box'
NAME           TRADITIONAL
EXETYPE        WINDOWS
STUB           'WINSTUB.EXE'
HEAPSIZE       1024
STACKSIZE      8192
CODE           PRELOAD MOVEABLE DISCARDABLE
DATA           PRELOAD MOVEABLE MULTIPLE
```

The COMMFILE.C program has two menu selections, File Open and File Save. Selecting either menu item brings the corresponding dialog box. The client area of the program's window contains the current filename. The user can click the left mouse button in the client area to select the background color of the window.

Using the File Open Dialog Box

When the user selects the File Open menu selection, the message cracker for the `WM_COMMAND` message calls the `WMCommand_Handler` function. In this function, the `GetFileName` function is called (see Figure 13.15). The `GetFileName` function is responsible for setting up the fields of the `OPENFILENAME` structure.

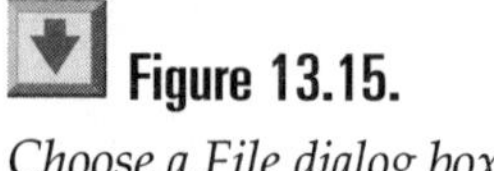
Figure 13.15.
Choose a File dialog box.

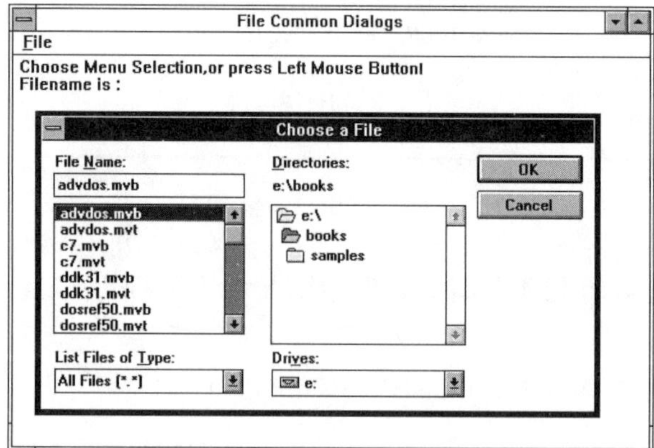

Before assigning any values, the program uses the `memset()` function to clear all of the fields to zero. This is done because the `OPENFILENAME` structure has 20 fields, and your program only uses nine of them (the others are for customization). You want to have the other structures at `NULL` (zero) values. Calling `memset()` ensures every field is set to zero.

The `lpstrTitle` field specifies the title of the dialog box. The program uses this:

```
OpenFileName.lpstrTitle = "Choose a File";
```

You can use the name of your application, the type of file you want to load, or have no title by setting it to `NULL`.

The `hwndOwner` field specifies the parent window of the dialog box. If you set this field to `NULL`, the dialog box has the desktop as its parent.

Use part of the dialog box to select the types of files to display in the file listbox. Use the lpstrFilter field to select the types of files that can be chosen. The program uses code like this:

```
char Filters[] = "All Files (*.*)\0*.*\0"
                 "C++ Code (*.CPP)\0*.CPP\0"
                 "C Code (*.C)\0*.C\0"
                 "Header Files (*.H)\0*.H\0";

OpenFileName.lpstrFilter       = (LPSTR)Filters;
```

Notice, the string you pass to the lpstrFilter field contains a terminating zero after each file type description and file specification. You must use the \0 combination to separate the filters, or the function won't process the filters correctly. The order you specify to the filter strings is the way they appear in the dialog box.

The nFilterIndex is related to the lpstrFilter field. nFilterIndex specifies the file type description that's to be selected when the dialog box starts up. Setting nFilterIndex to 1 tells it to use the first one in the list.

The lpstrFile points to a filename listed in the File Name edit control. lpstrFile is also the field that receives the full drive and pathname of the file the user selects from the dialog box. The nMaxFile field is the length of the string that receives the filename the user selects.

Use the Flags field to specify how the dialog box is supposed to work. The program uses the following flags:

```
OpenFileName.Flags = OFN_FILEMUSTEXIST ¦ \
                     OFN_HIDEREADONLY ¦  \
                     OFN_PATHMUSTEXIST;
```

The OFN_FILEMUSTEXIST flag tests the validity of the file the user selects. If the filename doesn't exist, the dialog box won't let the user select the OK button. The OFN_HIDEREADONLY flag tells the dialog box to hide the read only Checkbox. Also, the OFN_PATHMUSTEXIST flag forces the user to type valid pathnames.

The most peculiar field is the last one, lStructSize. This specifies the length of the structure in bytes. This field is filled using the sizeof(OPENFILENAME) operator to return the size of the field. The reason for passing the size of the structure is for compatibility with future versions of Windows. That is, future versions may increase the size of the field. Therefore, Windows always can keep track of the structure contents by knowing the size of the structure.

Finally, to display and open the Choose a File dialog box, call the `GetOpenFileName` with the address of the structure, as follows:

```
GetOpenFileName(&OpenFileName);
```

When the structure members are filled out, you can see how easy it is to display the dialog box.

Use the other fields of the `OPENFILENAME` structure to customize the dialog box. Although this book doesn't cover that process, you might want to check the other fields of the structure by searching for the structure name in the online help system.

Using the File Save Dialog Box

The File Save dialog box (see Figure 13.16) is similar to Choose a File. This dialog box uses the same structure types, and many of the fields are the same. In fact, the only field you may need to change is the `lpstrTitle` field, which points to the string displayed in the dialog box's title bar.

Figure 13.16.

The Save File As dialog box.

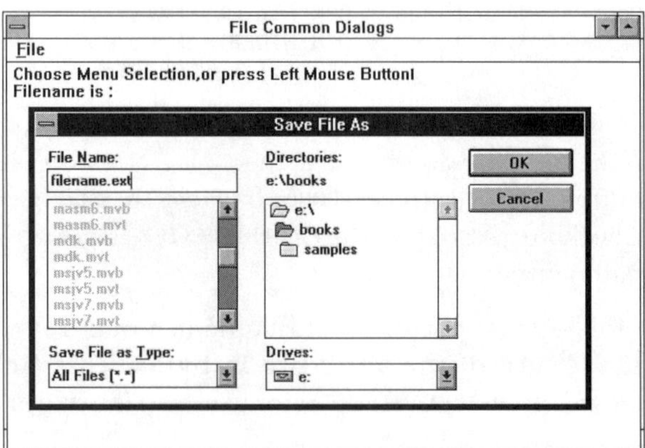

To call the Save File As dialog box, call the `GetSaveFileName` function, as follows:

```
GetSaveFileName(&SaveFileName);
```

The filename is returned in the string pointed to by the `lpstrFile` field.

Using the Choose Color Dialog Box

The Color dialog box has fewer fields to fill and is probably easier to use than the file dialog boxes. In the COMMFILE.C program, the user presses the left mouse button in the client area to show the Choose Color dialog box (see Figure 13.17).

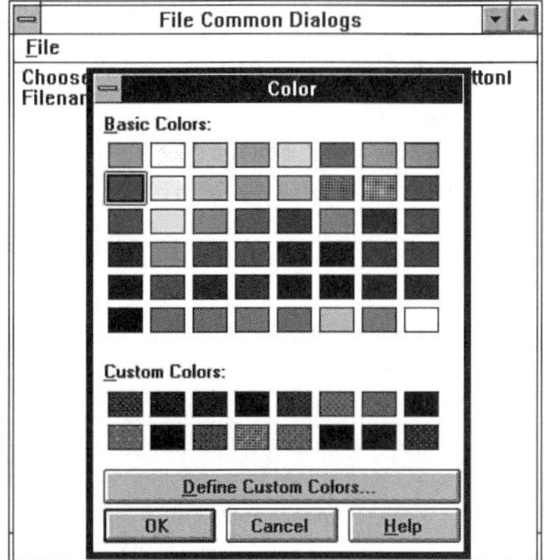

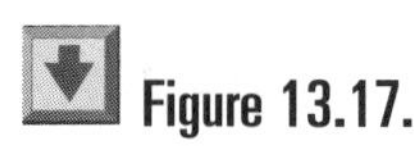

Figure 13.17.
The Color dialog box.

The new `rgbResult` field contains the RGB value of the color the user selects. You set an initial color value, which is highlighted when the dialog box is displayed.

You also can specify an array of custom colors to display in the lower-half of the dialog box. You assign this to the `lpCustColors` field of the `CHOOSECOLOR` structure. Notice, even if you don't want any custom colors selected, you still must pass a valid address of this color array.

To call the function, use code like this:

```
ChooseColor(&CC);
```

When the user selects a color, it is returned in the `rgbResult` field. The program uses this value to set the background color of the window. Recall, when you create a window class, you specify that the `hbrBackground` field identify the brush to display in the client area.

The COMMFILE program uses the value returned by the `ChooseColor` function to create a brush and then replace the class background brush with the new brush. This is done with a call to the `SetClassLong` function. Finally, after you set the background color, use a call to the `InvalidateRect` function to have the background of the client area redisplayed in the new color.

More About Common Dialogs

You will find the common dialog boxes useful in your programming. Although I won't go into the other common dialog boxes here, some of them appear later in this book in relation to other subjects. By examining the code for using the Choose a File, Save File As, and Color dialog boxes, you have a good idea about how to use the other common dialog box routines.

What You Have Learned

This chapter gave you a look at dialog boxes. You learned about the types of dialog boxes, what elements make up dialog boxes, and how to use the predefined dialog boxes that are part of Windows.

In particular, the following topics are covered in this chapter:

- Dialog boxes are another form of input in Windows that enable the user to interact with the program in a convenient manner.

- There are two types of dialog boxes, modal and modeless. When utilizing modal dialog boxes, you can't use the dialog box's parent window when the dialog box is active. Use modeless dialog boxes to switch between the dialog box and the program's parent window.
- All dialog boxes consist of a combination of smaller elements, known as control elements. There are 10 types of dialog box controls.
- The `MessageBox` routine is used to provide information to and get input from the user.
- The Common Dialogs are a set of eight dialog boxes that are part of Windows. They allow your program to use dialog boxes with little effort. The way to use common dialogs is to fill fields in a data structure and then to call the appropriate function.
- The seven common dialog boxes are color selection, font selection, file open and file save, print document, print setup, find text, and replace text.
- To use any of the common dialog boxes in your program, you must include the commdlg.h header file at the beginning of your program.

14

MORE ABOUT DIALOG BOXES

IN THIS CHAPTER

- How to use the Resource Workshop to create custom dialog boxes.
- How to create an About dialog box.
- What a dialog procedure is and how to implement one in programs written in straight C.
- How to use control elements in your custom dialog boxes.
- How to use the OWL to implement dialog boxes.
- How to use the Borland Windows Custom Controls to create the look of chiseled steel in your program.

Chapter 13, "Using Dialog Boxes," focused on what dialog boxes are, which predefined control elements can appear in a dialog box, and how to use the built-in dialog boxes already in Windows. In this chapter, you continue to examine dialog boxes. You will learn to utilize the Resource Workshop to create custom dialog boxes and you will learn the differences between processing dialog boxes in a regular C program and a program based on the ObjectWindows Library (OWL).

The Resource Workshop Dialog Box Editor

You utilize the Resource Workshop dialog box editor to create custom dialog boxes. A dialog box is generally a pop-up window that gives the user several control elements. The dialog editor enables you to include Windows predefined controls in a dialog box.

You can save dialog boxes as .RES, .RC, or .DLG files. You already know a .RES file is a binary resource file that can contain several resources. The .RC file is an ASCII resource script file. The .DLG file is an ASCII file (as the name suggests) expressly used for dialog boxes. A .DLG file has the same format as a .RC file, but a different file extension. You most commonly save the dialog boxes as .RC files and include them in the project window.

This section shows you how to use the Resource Workshop to create dialog boxes.

Starting the Dialog Editor

Start the Resource Workshop. From the main menu (see Figure 14.1), choose the File New Project option to start a new resource file. Next, select the Resource menu item and then the New option. In the dialog box that is displayed, specify the DIALOG option.

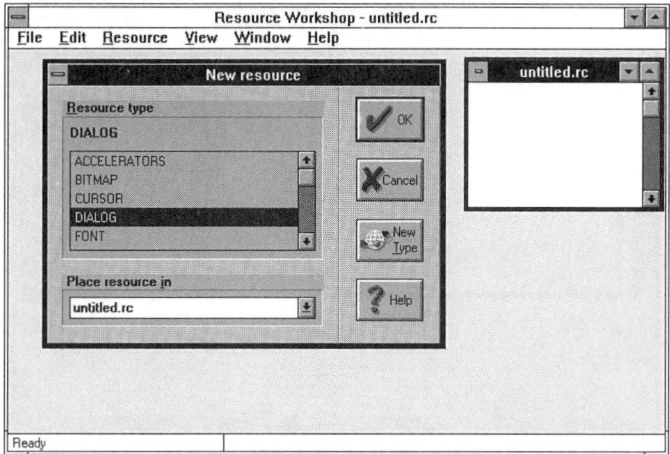

Figure 14.1.

Resource Workshop main resource selection menu.

When the dialog editor is loaded (see Figure 14.2), you see a window with several different parts. The dialog editor screen is divided into the following three sections:

- The *tools palette* enables you to place control elements in the dialog box.
- The *alignment palette* enables you to choose the alignment of control elements in a dialog box.
- The *work area* is the main section in the window. It enables you visually to construct the dialog box you want to create.

When you work with the dialog editor, run it full-screen so you can see all the tools listed in the palette area.

Using the Dialog Editor

When you start the dialog editor, a blank dialog box with the name DIALOG_1 is displayed. It's a clean slate you can work on to create your dialog box. The Control menu options enable you to select the control you want to create.

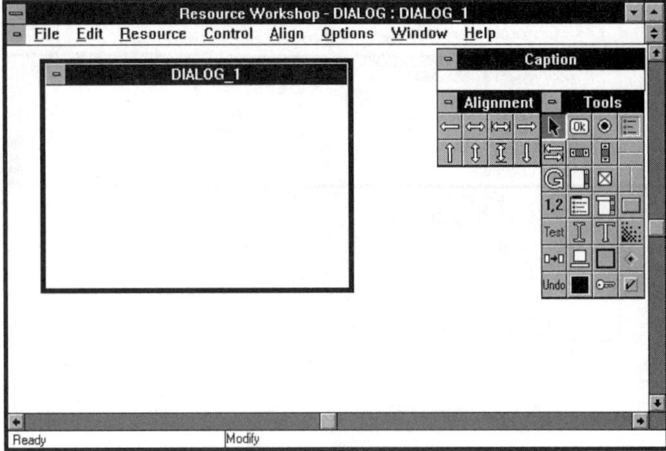

Figure 14.2.
The Dialog Editor main screen.

Creating a dialog box is easy. By choosing tools from the palette (or from the Controls menu), you specify the type of control element you want to add. You then move the cursor to the area of the sample dialog box and click on the appropriate tool. The cursor changes to a special shape, and you click anywhere in the dialog box to place the control.

To move the dialog box inside the work area, click the title bar and drag the entire dialog box. You also can change the dialog box's size. To do this, select the dialog box you're editing and move the cursor across its edges. Notice that the cursor changes to a double-pointed arrow. If you click and move the border, you change the size of the dialog box.

To change the attributes of the dialog box, double-click the top border. The Dialog attributes dialog box is displayed (see Figure 14.3). This enables you to modify the title and style of the dialog box. You can add a system menu and give most of the attributes of a normal window to the dialog box. As you begin creating dialog boxes, use the default values.

You change the attributes of a control element by double-clicking it. A dialog box is displayed that enables you to change information about the control element. The two important attributes of most elements (see Figure 14.4) are the caption (for example, what text is displayed inside the pushbutton) and the control ID, which is your reference to the control in your program.

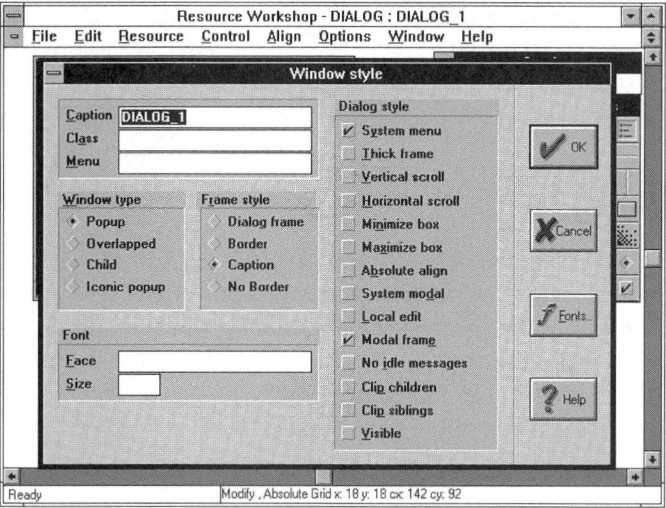

Figure 14.3.

Dialog attributes dialog box.

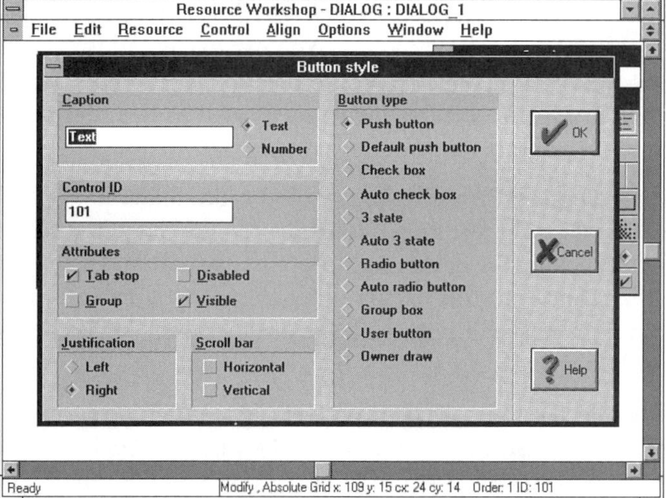

Figure 14.4.

Button-style dialog box.

You use the control ID to identify each element in the dialog box. You must give each element a unique identification number. You later utilize the control ID in your program to reference the control element. OK buttons should always receive a control ID value of 1 or the predefined constant `IDOK`. Cancel buttons should always receive a control ID value of `2` or the predefined constant `IDCANCEL`. This allows Windows to process the buttons automatically, without you writing extra code.

Creating a Dialog Box

To create a new dialog box, you choose the appropriate tool from the tools palette (as mentioned before). You then place the control element in the dialog box. After creating the control element, the tools palette automatically resets itself to the Pointer tool. You can use the right mouse button to place another control identical to the control you just placed. This makes placing many control elements of the same type easy.

With the control elements located correctly in the dialog box, you will use the alignment palette to adjust the position or size of a selected set of control elements. The controls can be aligned relative to any of the elements.

For example, if you create two pushbuttons—such as OK and Cancel—you probably want them to be the same size. You can eye it, but it's easier to let the computer perfect it for you on the first try. Two menu items enable you to align and resize control elements as well as the alignment palette on the right side of the dialog editor window.

To align several elements, you first must select more than one control element. You do that with the left mouse button and Shift. You first select a control element by clicking the item with the left mouse button. Then hold down either Shift key and continue to click other elements (not necessarily the same control type). You will notice a large outline border that covers all selected controls.

After you have selected multiple controls (see Figure 14.5), you can use the alignment palette. There are eight buttons on the alignment palette. The button pointing to the left moves controls horizontally and aligns them along the left side of the sizing frame. The button pointing to the right moves controls horizontally and aligns controls along the right side of the sizing frame.

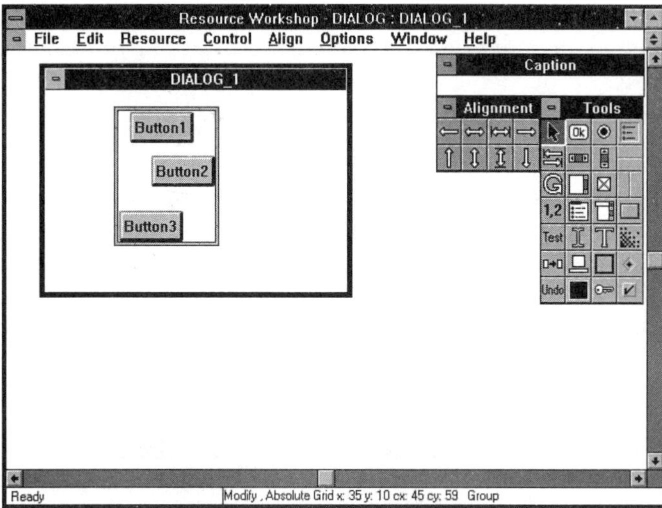

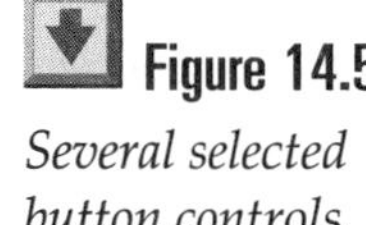

Figure 14.5.

Several selected button controls.

The button on the alignment palette with an arrow pointing up moves controls vertically and aligns them at the top of the sizing frame. The button pointing down moves controls vertically and aligns them at the bottom of the sizing frame.

The button on the alignment palette with arrows pointing left and right moves controls horizontally and centers controls in the sizing frame. The button with arrows pointing left and right with vertical lines at the end moves the sizing frame and the controls horizontally and centers them in the dialog box.

The button in the alignment palette with arrows pointing up and down moves controls vertically and centers the controls in the sizing frame. The button with arrows pointing up and down with vertical lines at the top and bottom moves the sizing frame and the controls vertically and centers them in the dialog box.

The Options menu contains important options that help you modify the dialog box. As a user moves through the elements of a dialog box, the Tab (and Shift Tab) keys move through the dialog box options, without having to use the mouse. The order in which you Tab through the control elements is important to the user. You want them to have quick and easy access to the options.

The tab order numbers are integers numbered consecutively, starting at 1 and increasing, depending on how many controls are in your dialog box. This describes the order items will be cycled through as the user presses Tab. The dialog editor enables you to change the tab order of control elements.

The default tab order is the order you first placed the control elements. To change the default order, choose the Set Order menu item from the Options menu. This displays the dialog controls as boxes with a number inside them (see Figure 14.6). The numbers refer to the tab order. As you move the mouse and click each element, the new tab order is recorded, and the numbers show the new tab order.

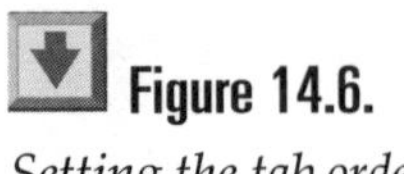

Figure 14.6.

Setting the tab order.

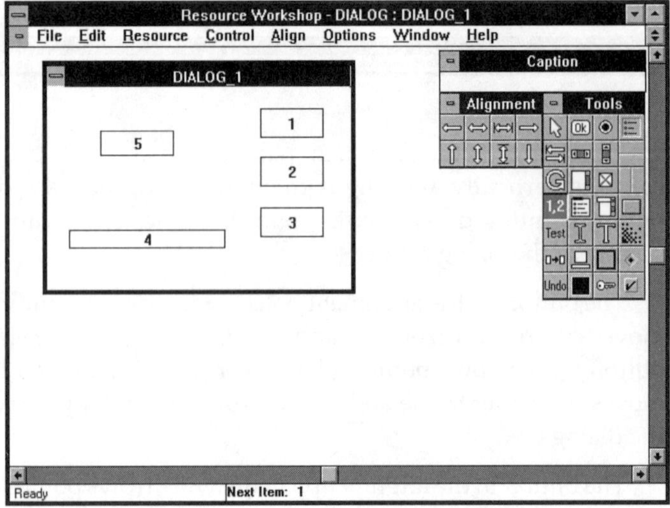

The Preferences dialog box enables you to display a number in all control elements that gives the tab order as you edit the dialog box. Choose the Options menu and select Preferences and Drawing Type to Draft to view the tab order of the controls in your dialog box.

After you create the dialog box, choose the File Save As option. Specify a filename with an appropriate extension.

Sometimes, it's handy to load the resources from an executable (EXE) file to the dialog editor and examine how they are created. This gives you an idea about how professional dialog box resources are created.

Creating an About Dialog Box

One of the most basic dialog boxes is an About dialog box. It's one of the most common dialog boxes and also the easiest to program. These dialog boxes usually give information relating to the application they're selected from. The dialog box is accessed from an About menu item on the Help menu.

Look at the code required for an About dialog box. Listing 14.1 contains the source code for the SIMPLEDB.C program. Listing 14.2 contains the resource script, and Listing 14.3 contains the module definition file. You also must create an icon (see Figure 14.7). The dialog box described in the resource script in Listing 14.2 appears in Resource Workshop in Figure 14.8.

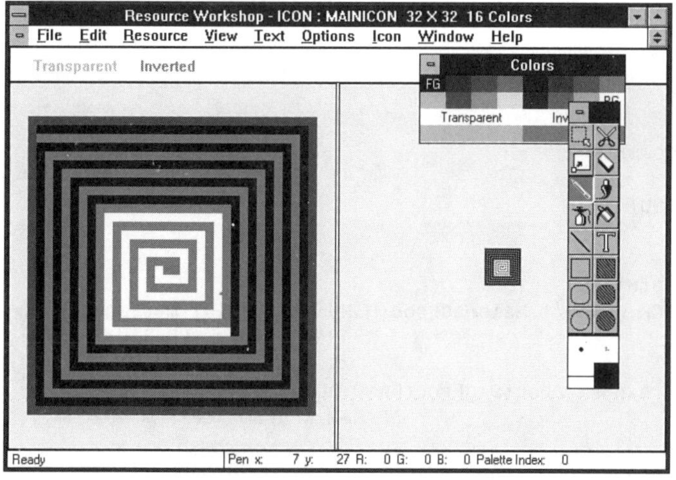

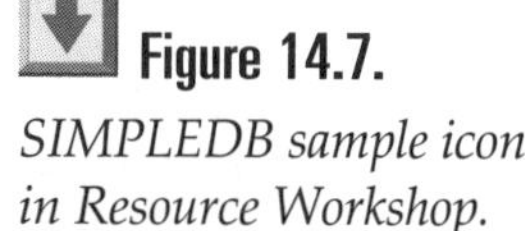

Figure 14.7.
SIMPLEDB sample icon in Resource Workshop.

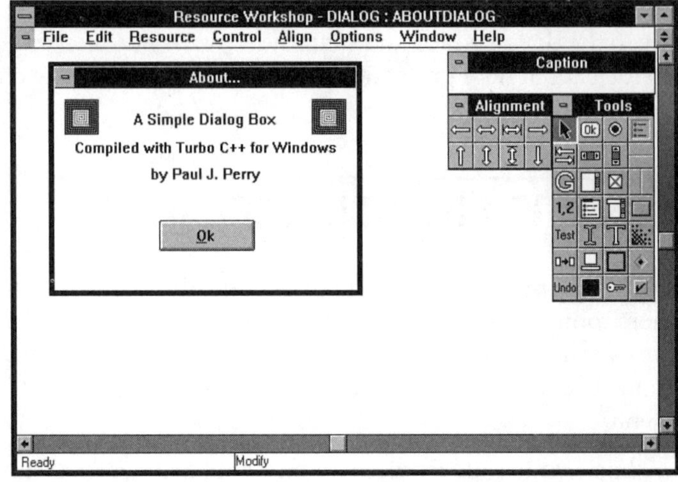

Figure 14.8. *SIMPLEDB About dialog box in Resource Workshop.*

Listing 14.1. About box demonstration program.

```
// SIMPLEDB.C - Example of a simple About dialog box
//
// Programming Windows with Turbo C++ for Windows
// by Paul J. Perry


#define STRICT

#include <windowsx.h>

#define IDM_ABOUT 10


// Function Prototypes
LRESULT CALLBACK _export MainWndProc(HWND hWnd, UINT message,
                                     WPARAM wParam, LPARAM lParam);

BOOL CALLBACK _export AboutDlgProc(HWND hDlg, UINT message,
                                   WPARAM wParam, LPARAM lParam);

void WMDlgCommand_Handler(HWND hDlg, int id, HWND hwndCtl,
                          UINT codeNotify);


// Global Variables
HINSTANCE ghInstance;
```

```
/*******************************************/
#pragma argsused
int PASCAL WinMain(HINSTANCE hInstance, HINSTANCE hPrevInstance,
                   LPSTR lpCmdParam, int nCmdShow)
{
   char         ProgName[] = "Simple About Dialog Box";
   HWND         hWnd;
   MSG          msg;
   HMENU        hMenu;


   if (!hPrevInstance)
   {
      WNDCLASS    wndclass;

      wndclass.style          = CS_VREDRAW | CS_HREDRAW;
      wndclass.lpfnWndProc    = (WNDPROC) MainWndProc;
      wndclass.hInstance      = hInstance;
      wndclass.hIcon          = LoadIcon(hInstance, "MAINICON");
      wndclass.hCursor        = LoadCursor(NULL, IDC_ARROW);
      wndclass.hbrBackground  = (HBRUSH) (COLOR_WINDOW + 1);
      wndclass.lpszMenuName   = NULL;
      wndclass.cbClsExtra     = 0;
      wndclass.cbWndExtra     = 0;
      wndclass.lpszClassName  = ProgName;

      RegisterClass(&wndclass);
   }

   ghInstance = hInstance;

   hWnd = CreateWindow(ProgName,"Simple Dialog Box",
                       WS_OVERLAPPEDWINDOW,
                       CW_USEDEFAULT, CW_USEDEFAULT,
                       CW_USEDEFAULT, CW_USEDEFAULT,
                       NULL, NULL, hInstance, NULL);

   // Get handle to system menu
   hMenu = GetSystemMenu(hWnd, FALSE);

   // Add seperator and "About..." menu option
   AppendMenu(hMenu, MF_SEPARATOR, 0, NULL);
   AppendMenu(hMenu, MF_STRING, IDM_ABOUT, "&About...");


   ShowWindow(hWnd, nCmdShow);
   UpdateWindow(hWnd);
```

continues

Listing 14.1. continued

```
   while (GetMessage(&msg, NULL, 0, 0))
   {
      TranslateMessage(&msg);
      DispatchMessage(&msg);
   }
   return msg.wParam;
}


/********************************************/
LRESULT CALLBACK _export MainWndProc(HWND hWnd, UINT message,
                                     WPARAM wParam, LPARAM lParam)
{
   switch (message)
   {
      case WM_PAINT :
      {
         HDC         PaintDC;
         RECT        rect;
         PAINTSTRUCT ps;

         PaintDC = BeginPaint(hWnd, &ps);
         GetClientRect(hWnd, &rect);

         DrawText(PaintDC, "Check System menu for About menu
                  option", -1, &rect, DT_SINGLELINE ¦ DT_CENTER ¦
                  DT_VCENTER);

      EndPaint(hWnd, &ps);
         return 0;
      }

      case WM_SYSCOMMAND :
      {
      switch(wParam)
      {
         case IDM_ABOUT :
         {
            DLGPROC AbtDlgProc;

            AbtDlgProc = (DLGPROC)MakeProcInstance
               ((FARPROC)AboutDlgProc, ghInstance);
            DialogBox(ghInstance, "ABOUTDIALOG", hWnd, AbtDlgProc);
            FreeProcInstance((FARPROC)AbtDlgProc);
            return 0;
         }
      }
```

```
        break;
        }

        case WM_DESTROY :
        {
           PostQuitMessage(0);
           return 0;
        }
    }
    return DefWindowProc (hWnd, message, wParam, lParam);
}


/*******************************************/
#pragma argsused
void WMDlgCommand_Handler(HWND hDlg, int id, HWND hwndCtl,
                          UINT codeNotify)
{
   switch(id)
   {
      case IDOK :
      case IDCANCEL :
      {
      EndDialog(hDlg, 0);
         break;
      }
   }
}

/*******************************************/
BOOL CALLBACK _export AboutDlgProc(HWND hDlg, UINT message,
                                   WPARAM wParam, LPARAM lParam)
{
   switch(message)
   {
      case WM_INITDIALOG :
      {
      return TRUE;
      }

      case WM_COMMAND :
      {
      return (BOOL)HANDLE_WM_COMMAND(hDlg, wParam, lParam,
                                     WMDlgCommand_Handler);
      }
   }

   return FALSE;
}
```

Listing 14.2. Resource script file.

```
/*
 * SIMPLEDB.RC resource script file
 *
 */

ABOUTDIALOG DIALOG 18, 18, 142, 92
STYLE DS_MODALFRAME ¦ WS_POPUP ¦ WS_CAPTION ¦ WS_SYSMENU
CAPTION "About..."
BEGIN
     PUSHBUTTON "&Ok", IDOK, 49, 60, 45, 14, WS_CHILD ¦ WS_VISIBLE
¦ WS_TABSTOP
     CTEXT "A Simple Dialog Box", -1, 0, 10, 142, 8, WS_CHILD ¦
WS_VISIBLE ¦ WS_GROUP
     CTEXT "Compiled with Turbo C++ for Windows", -1, 0, 23, 142,
8, WS_CHILD ¦ WS_VISIBLE ¦ WS_GROUP
     CTEXT "by Paul J. Perry", -1, 0, 35, 142, 8, WS_CHILD ¦
WS_VISIBLE ¦ WS_GROUP
     ICON "MAINICON", -1, 5, 5, 16, 16
     ICON "MAINICON", -1, 121, 5, 16, 16
END

MAINICON ICON "simpledb.ico"
```

Listing 14.3. Module definition file.

```
;
; SIMPLEDB.DEF module definition file
;

DESCRIPTION    'Simple About Dialog Box'
NAME           SIMPLEDB
EXETYPE        WINDOWS
STUB           'WINSTUB.EXE'
HEAPSIZE       1024
STACKSIZE      8192
CODE           PRELOAD MOVEABLE DISCARDABLE
DATA           PRELOAD MOVEABLE MULTIPLE
```

When you run the program and select the option to display a dialog box, the dialog box appears as shown in Figure 14.9. The first feature you probably will notice is how the dialog box is selected. As the client area of the program suggested, the program requires you to go to the system menu and select the About menu option. Although you can add a menu item to the resource script and then reference it from the program, I wanted to explore some new concepts.

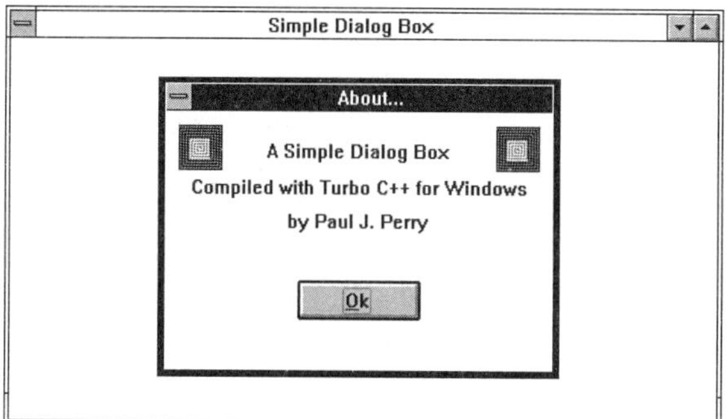

Figure 14.9.
SIMPLEDB dialog box.

To add an item to the system menu, you first must obtain a handle to the system menu. You then add items to that menu. Next, you respond to messages of type `WM_SYSCOMMAND`. To add the menu item to the system menu, you use code like this:

```
hMenu = GetSystemMenu(hWnd, FALSE);

AppendMenu(hMenu, MF_SEPARATOR, 0, NULL);
AppendMenu(hMenu, MF_STRING, IDM_ABOUT, "&About...");
```

The `AppendMenu` function adds menu items to a menu. It requires a handle to the menu as the first parameter. The first time you call it, the program appends a separator bar to the menu. The second time, the program adds the text string `"&About"`. The ampersand (`&`) denotes which character should be underlined. You must tell the `AppendMenu` function how the menu item is to be referenced. In the call, you specify an identifier for `IDM_ABOUT`. This is defined at the beginning of the program as an integer value.

Later, in the window procedure of the program, you trap the WM_SYSCOMMAND message. You then check for a wParam equal to IDM_ABOUT. You might notice this code is not forward-compatible with Windows NT. You check the wParam directly rather than use a message cracker: if the wParam isn't equal to IDM_ABOUT, you pass control to the default window procedure, and message crackers don't allow this procedure.

Finally, you allow the default window procedure to process the rest of the selections on the system menu. If you do not pass control to the default window procedure, the other system menu commands cannot be selected.

After you discover that the user does indeed want to see the About dialog box, use code such as the following to access the dialog box:

```
case IDM_ABOUT :
{
   DLGPROC AbtDlgProc;

   AbtDlgProc = (DLGPROC)MakeProcInstance((FARPROC)AboutDlgProc,
                ghInstance);
   DialogBox(ghInstance, "ABOUTDIALOG", hWnd, AbtDlgProc);
   FreeProcInstance((FARPROC)AbtDlgProc);
   return 0;
}
```

Recall, a dialog box is a window. A dialog box has its own dialog box procedure, much like the window procedure of a main window.

You use the DialogBox function to pass control to the dialog box. You must pass it the name of the dialog box (as specified in the resource script), a handle to the parent window, and a pointer to the dialog box procedure.

To call the dialog box procedure, first make a procedure instance. You do this with the MakeProcInstance function. When you make an instance of a procedure, you use resource space to store the address of the procedure. This locks the location of the dialog box procedure in memory so Windows does not relocate it. When the dialog procedure is complete, you call the FreeProcInstance function to release the memory space.

You declare the dialog box procedure similar to the window procedure. It appears as follows:

```
BOOL CALLBACK _export AboutDlgProc(HWND hDlg, UINT message,
                                   WPARAM wParam, LPARAM lParam)
```

This is almost the same as a window procedure. The only difference is the function returns a BOOL value, rather than an integer.

The body of the dialog box procedure looks like this:

```
BOOL CALLBACK _export AboutDlgProc(HWND hDlg, UINT message,
                                   WPARAM wParam, LPARAM lParam)
{
   switch(message)
   {
      case WM_INITDIALOG :
      {
           return TRUE;
      }

      case WM_COMMAND :
      {
           return (BOOL)HANDLE_WM_COMMAND(hDlg, wParam, lParam,
                                         WMDlgCommand_Handler);
      }
   }

   return FALSE;
}
```

The first message responds to the WM_INITDIALOG message. It is similar to WM_CREATE in a main window procedure because it's sent to a dialog box immediately before it is displayed. You can use it to initialize any values. However, unlike a WM_CREATE message, you must return TRUE. Notice, no default dialog box procedure is in this code; therefore, your dialog box procedure must respond to all messages.

When the user selects a control in a dialog box, Windows sends a WM_COMMAND message to the dialog box procedure. The wParam value contains the ID of the control. In your program, use a message cracker to call the WMDlgCommand_Handler function.

The WMDlgCommand_Handler function in your SIMPLEDB program responds to two values, IDOK and IDCANCEL. The code looks like this:

```
switch(id)
{
   case IDOK :
   case IDCANCEL :
```

```
    {
       EndDialog(hDlg, 0);
       break;
    }
}
```

You use the same processing for `IDOK` and `IDCANCEL`. You declare the OK button as `IDOK`. There is no cancel button in the program, but if the user presses Esc, the dialog box procedure receives an `IDCANCEL` value.

This dialog box procedure's sole operation is to end the dialog box, with a call to `EndDialog`. The dialog box automatically is removed from the screen, and control returns to the main window. That's all there is to it.

You now know how to use Resource Workshop, and you have written a program that creates a simple dialog box. Before moving to a more advanced program, look at a program based on the OWL, which uses dialog boxes.

Using the ObjectWindows Library with Dialog Boxes

Creating a dialog box in a program based on the OWL relies on creating an instance of a dialog box class. Examine how that's done. Listing 14.4 shows the source code for the program. Listings 14.5 through 14.7 are the related files required for creating the program. Figure 14.10 shows the dialog box in Resource Workshop.

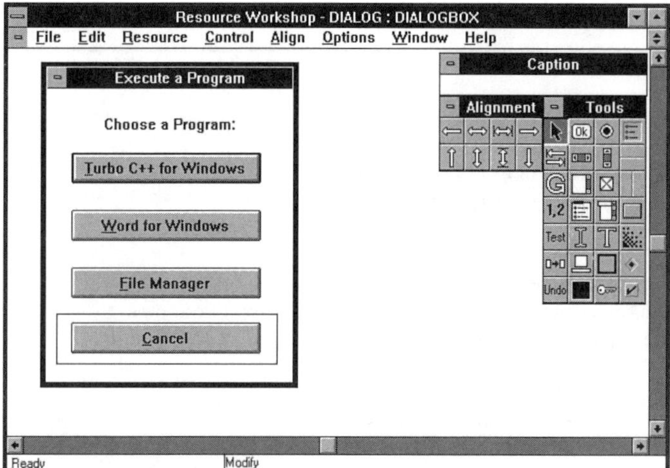

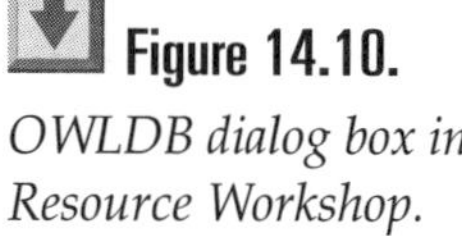

Figure 14.10.

OWLDB dialog box in Resource Workshop.

Listing 14.4. OWLDB.CPP source code.

```
// OWLDB.CPP - ObjectWindows library program which calls
//             a dialog box.
//
// Programming Windows with Turbo C++ for Windows
// by Paul J. Perry


#define WIN31
#define STRICT

#include <owl.h>
#include <dialog.h>

#include <windowsx.h>
```

continues

Listing 14.4. continued

```
#include "owldb.h"

// Class Declarations

/*******************************************/
class TOwlApp : public TApplication
{
   public :
      TOwlApp (LPSTR AName, HINSTANCE hInstance, HINSTANCE
               hPrevInstance, LPSTR CmdLine, int CmdShow) :
               TApplication(AName, hInstance, hPrevInstance,
               CmdLine, CmdShow) { } ;

   virtual void InitMainWindow();
};


/*******************************************/
class TMainWindow : public TWindow
{
   public :
      TMainWindow(PTWindowsObject AParent, LPSTR ATitle)
                    : TWindow(AParent, ATitle) { };
      virtual void Paint(HDC PaintDC, PAINTSTRUCT &PaintInfo);
      virtual LPSTR GetClassName();
      virtual void GetWindowClass(WNDCLASS& wndclass);

      virtual void CMMenuItem(TMessage &msg)
         = [CM_FIRST + IDM_MENUITEM];
};


/*******************************************/
class TDialogBox : public TDialog
{
   public :
      TDialogBox(PTWindowsObject AParent, LPSTR AName) :
      TDialog(AParent, AName) { };
      virtual void RunTCW(TMessage &msg)
      = [ID_FIRST + IDD_TCW];
      virtual void RunWinWord(TMessage &msg)
      = [ID_FIRST + IDD_WINWORD];
      virtual void RunFileMan(TMessage &msg)
         = [ID_FIRST + IDD_FILEMAN];

};
```

```
// Class Member Functions

/* ################################
   ##  TOwlApp member functions  ##
   ################################ */


/*******************************************/
void TOwlApp::InitMainWindow()
{
   MainWindow = new TMainWindow(NULL, Name);
}


/* ####################################
   ##  TMainWindow member functions  ##
   #################################### */

/*******************************************/
LPSTR TMainWindow::GetClassName()
{
   return "OwlDialog";
}

/*******************************************/
void TMainWindow::GetWindowClass(WNDCLASS& wndclass)
{
   TWindow::GetWindowClass(wndclass);

   wndclass.lpszMenuName = "MAINMENU";

}


/*******************************************/
#pragma argsused
void TMainWindow::Paint(HDC PaintDC, PAINTSTRUCT &PaintInfo)
{

   TextOut(PaintDC, 1, 1,  "Make a menu selection", 21);

}

/*******************************************/
#pragma argsused
void TMainWindow::CMMenuItem(TMessage &msg)
{
```

continues

Listing 14.4. continued

```
   GetModule()->ExecDialog(new TDialogBox(this, "DIALOGBOX"));

}

/* ####################################
   ##  TDialogBox member functions  ##
   #################################### */


/********************************************/
#pragma argsused
void TDialogBox::RunTCW(TMessage &msg)
{
   WinExec("c:\\tcwin\\bin\\tcw.exe", SW_SHOW);
}

/********************************************/
#pragma argsused
void TDialogBox::RunWinWord(TMessage &msg)
{
   WinExec("c:\\winword\\winword.exe", SW_SHOW);
}

/********************************************/
#pragma argsused
void TDialogBox::RunFileMan(TMessage &msg)
{
   WinExec("c:\\windows\\winfile.exe", SW_SHOW);
}



/* ####################################
   ##  WinMain program entry point  ##
   #################################### */

/********************************************/
int PASCAL WinMain(HINSTANCE hInstance, HINSTANCE hPrevInstance,
                   LPSTR lpCmdLine, int nCmdShow)
{

   TOwlApp ThisApp("OWL Dialog Box", hInstance,
                   hPrevInstance, lpCmdLine, nCmdShow);
   ThisApp.Run();
   return ThisApp.Status;

}
```

Listing 14.5. OWLDB.H header file.

```
/*
 * OWLDB.H header file
 *
 */

#define IDM_MENUITEM 100

#define IDD_TCW      110
#define IDD_WINWORD 120
#define IDD_FILEMAN 130
```

Listing 14.6. OWLDB.RC resource script file.

```
#include <owldb.h>

DIALOGBOX DIALOG 18, 18, 116, 133
STYLE DS_MODALFRAME ¦ WS_POPUP ¦ WS_CAPTION ¦ WS_SYSMENU
CAPTION "Execute a Program"
BEGIN
     DEFPUSHBUTTON "&Turbo C++ for Windows", IDD_TCW, 12, 29, 89,
14, WS_CHILD ¦ WS_VISIBLE ¦ WS_TABSTOP
     PUSHBUTTON "&Word for Windows", IDD_WINWORD, 12, 55, 89, 14,
WS_CHILD ¦ WS_VISIBLE ¦ WS_TABSTOP
     PUSHBUTTON "&File Manager", IDD_FILEMAN, 12, 81, 89, 14,
WS_CHILD ¦ WS_VISIBLE ¦ WS_TABSTOP
     PUSHBUTTON "&Cancel", IDCANCEL, 12, 106, 89, 14, WS_CHILD ¦
WS_VISIBLE ¦ WS_TABSTOP
     CTEXT "Choose a Program:", -1, 0, 12, 116, 8, WS_CHILD ¦
WS_VISIBLE ¦ WS_GROUP
     CONTROL "", -1, "static", SS_BLACKFRAME ¦ WS_CHILD ¦
WS_VISIBLE, 5, 102, 104, 23
END

MAINMENU MENU LOADONCALL MOVEABLE PURE DISCARDABLE
BEGIN
   MenuItem  "&Execute Program...", IDM_MENUITEM
END
```

Listing 14.7. OWLDB.DEF module definition file.

```
;
; OWLDB.DEF module definition file
;

DESCRIPTION   'OWL Dialog Box'
NAME          OWLDB
EXETYPE       WINDOWS
STUB          'WINSTUB.EXE'
HEAPSIZE      4096
STACKSIZE     5120
CODE          PRELOAD MOVEABLE DISCARDABLE
DATA          PRELOAD MOVEABLE MULTIPLE
```

When the program is running, click the Execute Program menu. The Execute a Program dialog box appears, as shown in Figure 14.11. Clicking a button that lists a program executes that program. You must have the appropriate programs on your system, and the pathnames specified in the source code must be valid.

Figure 14.11.

The Execute a Program dialog box.

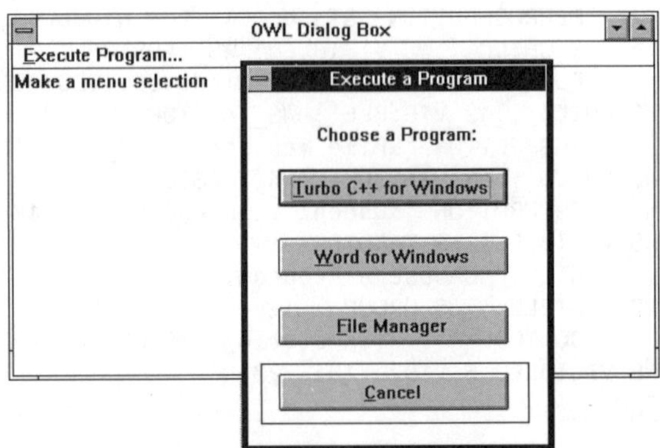

The program based on the OWL creates a message response function for the program's menu item. When the user selects the menu option, the `GetModule-> ExecDialog` function is called with a parameter of `TDialogBox`, as follows:

```
GetModule()->ExecDialog(new TDialogBox(this, "DIALOGBOX"));
```

`TDialogBox` is a class you define at the beginning of the program and derive from `TDialog`. It appears like this:

```
class TDialogBox : public TDialog
{
   public :
      TDialogBox(PTWindowsObject AParent, LPSTR AName) :
           TDialog(AParent, AName) { };
      virtual void RunTCW(TMessage &msg)
         = [ID_FIRST + IDD_TCW];
      virtual void RunWinWord(TMessage &msg)
         = [ID_FIRST + IDD_WINWORD];
      virtual void RunFileMan(TMessage &msg)
         = [ID_FIRST + IDD_FILEMAN];

};
```

You have defined a constructor and three message response functions. These message response functions respond to control elements selected in a dialog box. You refer to the dialog box control with the prefix `IDD_` (identifier to a dialog element).

After you create an instance of the dialog box procedure with the new operator, your message response functions will be executed when the related dialog box control is selected.

Each of the three message response functions use the `WinExec` function to load and run a specific program. The `WinExec` function takes two parameters. The first is the filename of the program to execute. The second parameter is how the program is to be executed. Table 14.1 lists possible values you can pass to the `WinExec` function.

Table 14.1. Values you can pass to WinExec.

Value	*Description*
`SW_HIDE`	Hides the window and passes activation to another window.
`SW_MINIMIZE`	Minimizes the specified window and activates the top-level window in the system's list.

continues

Table 14.1. continued

Value	*Description*
`SW_RESTORE`	Activates and displays a window. If the window is minimized or maximized, Windows restores it to its original size and position (same as `SW_SHOWNORMAL`).
`SW_SHOW`	Activates a window and displays it in its current size and position.
`SW_SHOWMAXIMIZED`	Activates a window and displays it as a maximized window.
`SW_SHOWMINIMIZED`	Activates a window and displays it as an icon.
`SW_SHOWMINNOACTIVE`	Displays a window as an icon. The window currently active remains active.
`SW_SHOWNA`	Displays a window in its current state. The window currently active remains active.
`SW_SHOWNOACTIVATE`	Displays a window in its most recent size and position. The window currently active remains active.
`SW_SHOWNORMAL`	Activates and displays a window. If the window is minimized or maximized, Windows restores it to its original size and position (same as `SW_RESTORE`).

You can use the `WinExec` function to execute any type of program. If it's a DOS program, a DOS box will be opened and the program will be run in it. If you pass the name of a batch file, Windows will open the DOS box and execute the batch file.

More Complex Dialog Boxes

Now that you know how to use the ObjectWindows library to process dialog boxes, consider a more advanced dialog box. This time we will go back to using C.

This program contains radio buttons, edit controls, and static text. Listing 14.8 contains the C source code for the program. Listing 14.9 contains the resource script for the file, and Listing 14.10 contains the module definition file. Figure 14.12 pictures the dialog box as shown in Resource Workshop.

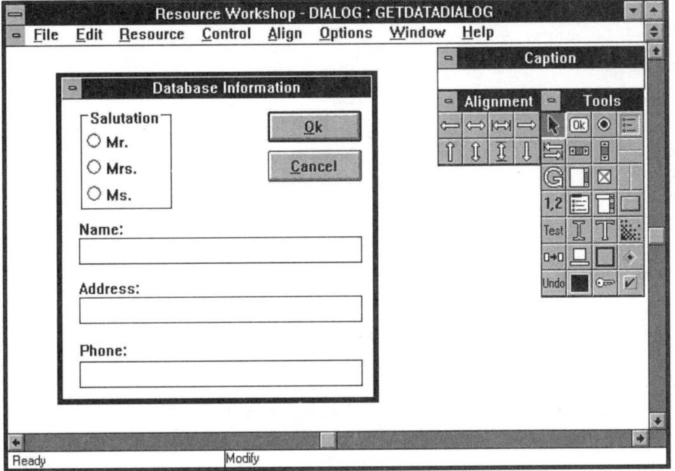

Figure 14.12.

ADVDB as displayed in Resource Workshop.

Listing 14.8. ADVDB.C source code listing.

```
// ADVDB.C - Example of an advanced dialog box
//
// Programming Windows with Turbo C++ for Windows
// by Paul J. Perry

#define STRICT
#include <windowsx.h>
#include <stdio.h>
#include <string.h>
```

continues

Listing 14.8. continued

```
#include "advdb.h"

// Function Prototypes
LRESULT CALLBACK _export MainWndProc(HWND hWnd, UINT message,
                                     WPARAM wParam, LPARAM lParam);

BOOL CALLBACK _export DlgProc(HWND hDlg, UINT message,
                              WPARAM wParam, LPARAM lParam);

void WMCommand_Handler(HWND hwnd, int id, HWND hwndCtl, UINT
                       codeNotify);

void WMDlgCommand_Handler(HWND hDlg, int id, HWND hwndCtl,
                          UINT codeNotify);


// Global Variables
HINSTANCE ghInstance;

char Salutation[SALUTLEN] = "";
char Name[NAMELEN] = "";
char Address[ADDRESSLEN] = "";
char Phone[PHONELEN] = "";

/*******************************************/
#pragma argsused
int PASCAL WinMain(HINSTANCE hInstance, HINSTANCE hPrevInstance,
                   LPSTR lpCmdParam, int nCmdShow)
{
   char        ProgName[] = "Advanced Dialog Box Demo";
   HWND        hWnd;
   MSG         msg;
   HMENU       hMenu;


   if (!hPrevInstance)
   {
      WNDCLASS    wndclass;

      wndclass.style          = CS_VREDRAW ¦ CS_HREDRAW;
      wndclass.lpfnWndProc    = (WNDPROC) MainWndProc;
      wndclass.hInstance      = hInstance;
      wndclass.hIcon          = LoadIcon(NULL, IDI_QUESTION);
      wndclass.hCursor        = LoadCursor(NULL, IDC_ARROW);
      wndclass.hbrBackground = (HBRUSH) (COLOR_WINDOW + 1);
      wndclass.lpszMenuName   = NULL;
      wndclass.cbClsExtra     = 0;
```

```
      wndclass.cbWndExtra    = 0;
      wndclass.lpszClassName = ProgName;

      RegisterClass(&wndclass);
   }

   ghInstance = hInstance;

   // Create a menu inside our program rather than from
   // a resource file template
   hMenu = CreateMenu();
   AppendMenu(hMenu, MF_STRING, IDM_GETDATA, "&Get Info...");

   hWnd = CreateWindow(ProgName,"Advanced Dialog Box Demo",
                       WS_OVERLAPPEDWINDOW,
                       CW_USEDEFAULT, CW_USEDEFAULT,
                       CW_USEDEFAULT, CW_USEDEFAULT,
                       // Notice how we reference the hMenu here
                       NULL, hMenu, hInstance, NULL);

   ShowWindow(hWnd, nCmdShow);
   UpdateWindow(hWnd);

   while (GetMessage(&msg, NULL, 0, 0))
   {
      TranslateMessage(&msg);
      DispatchMessage(&msg);
   }
   return msg.wParam;
}


/*******************************************/
#pragma argsused
void WMCommand_Handler(HWND hWnd, int id, HWND hwndCtl, UINT
                       codeNotify)
{
   if (id == IDM_GETDATA)
   {
      DLGPROC AbtDlgProc;

      AbtDlgProc = (DLGPROC)MakeProcInstance((FARPROC)DlgProc,
                    ghInstance);
      DialogBox(ghInstance, "GETDATADIALOG", hWnd, AbtDlgProc);
      FreeProcInstance((FARPROC)AbtDlgProc);
      InvalidateRect(hWnd, NULL, TRUE);
   }
}
```

continues

Listing 14.8. continued

```
/*******************************************/
LRESULT CALLBACK _export MainWndProc(HWND hWnd, UINT message,
                                     WPARAM wParam, LPARAM lParam)
{
   switch (message)
   {
      case WM_PAINT :
      {
      HDC         PaintDC;
      PAINTSTRUCT ps;
      char        buff[300];
         int         len;

         PaintDC = BeginPaint(hWnd, &ps);

      len = sprintf(buff, "Name: %s %s", Salutation, Name);
      TextOut(PaintDC, 5, 5, buff, len);

      len = sprintf(buff, "Address: %s", Address);
      TextOut(PaintDC, 5, 25, buff, len);

      len = sprintf(buff, "Phone: %s", Phone);
      TextOut(PaintDC, 5, 45, buff, len);

      EndPaint(hWnd, &ps);
         return 0;
      }

      case WM_COMMAND :
      {
      return HANDLE_WM_COMMAND(hWnd, wParam, lParam,
                               WMCommand_Handler);
      }

      case WM_DESTROY :
      {
         PostQuitMessage(0);
         return 0;
      }
   }
   return DefWindowProc (hWnd, message, wParam, lParam);
}


/*******************************************/
#pragma argsused
```

```
void WMDlgCommand_Handler(HWND hDlg, int id, HWND hwndCtl, UINT
                          codeNotify)
{
   switch(id)
   {
      case IDOK :
      {
      HWND  hCtrl;
         DWORD result;

         hCtrl = GetDlgItem(hDlg, IDD_MR);
      result = SendMessage(hCtrl, BM_GETCHECK, 0, 0L);
      if (result)
           strcpy(Salutation, "Mr.");

      hCtrl = GetDlgItem(hDlg, IDD_MRS);
      result = SendMessage(hCtrl, BM_GETCHECK, 0, 0L);
      if (result)
           strcpy(Salutation, "Mrs.");


      hCtrl = GetDlgItem(hDlg, IDD_MS);
      result = SendMessage(hCtrl, BM_GETCHECK, 0, 0L);
      if (result)
        strcpy(Salutation, "Ms.");


      // Get the text out of the edit controls
      GetDlgItemText(hDlg, IDD_NAME, Name, NAMELEN);
      GetDlgItemText(hDlg, IDD_ADDRESS, Address, ADDRESSLEN);
      GetDlgItemText(hDlg, IDD_PHONE, Phone, PHONELEN);

      // We are done getting the necessary information.
      // We can now just drop through to the processing
      //  for the IDCANCEL case.  That will end the dialog.
      }

      case IDCANCEL :
      {
      EndDialog(hDlg, 0);
      break;
      }
   }
}

/*******************************************/
BOOL CALLBACK _export DlgProc(HWND hDlg, UINT message,
                              WPARAM wParam, LPARAM lParam)
```

continues

Listing 14.8. continued

```
{
   switch(message)
   {
      case WM_INITDIALOG :
      {
      return TRUE;
      }

      case WM_COMMAND :
      {
      return (BOOL)HANDLE_WM_COMMAND(hDlg, wParam, lParam,
                                                WMDlgCommand_Handler);
      }
   }

   return FALSE;
}
```

Listing 14.9. ADVDB resource script.

```
/*
 * ADVDB.RC resource script
 *
 */

#include "advdb.h"

GETDATADIALOG DIALOG 26, 24, 146, 136
STYLE DS_MODALFRAME ¦ WS_POPUP ¦ WS_CAPTION ¦ WS_SYSMENU
CAPTION "Database Information"
BEGIN
     CONTROL "Mr.", IDD_MR, "BUTTON", BS_AUTORADIOBUTTON ¦ WS_CHILD
¦ WS_VISIBLE ¦ WS_TABSTOP, 12, 13, 28, 12
     CONTROL "Mrs.", IDD_MRS, "BUTTON", BS_AUTORADIOBUTTON ¦
WS_CHILD ¦ WS_VISIBLE ¦ WS_TABSTOP, 12, 25, 28, 12
     CONTROL "Ms.", IDD_MS, "BUTTON", BS_AUTORADIOBUTTON ¦ WS_CHILD
¦ WS_VISIBLE ¦ WS_TABSTOP, 12, 37, 28, 12
     EDITTEXT IDD_NAME, 8, 63, 133, 12
     EDITTEXT IDD_ADDRESS, 8, 90, 133, 12
     EDITTEXT IDD_PHONE, 8, 119, 133, 12
     DEFPUSHBUTTON "&Ok", IDOK, 97, 6, 44, 14, WS_CHILD ¦
```

```
WS_VISIBLE ¦ WS_TABSTOP
     PUSHBUTTON "&Cancel", IDCANCEL, 97, 24, 44, 14, WS_CHILD ¦
WS_VISIBLE ¦ WS_TABSTOP
     LTEXT "Name:", -1, 8, 55, 22, 8, WS_CHILD ¦ WS_VISIBLE ¦
WS_GROUP
     LTEXT "Address:", -1, 8, 82, 30, 8, WS_CHILD ¦ WS_VISIBLE ¦
WS_GROUP
     LTEXT "Phone:", -1, 8, 110, 30, 8, WS_CHILD ¦ WS_VISIBLE ¦
WS_GROUP
     CONTROL "Salutation", 106, "button", BS_GROUPBOX ¦ WS_CHILD ¦
WS_VISIBLE, 9, 3, 43, 47
END
```

Listing 14.10. ADVDB module definition file.

```
;
; ADVDB.DEF module definition file
;


DESCRIPTION   'Advanced Dialog Box'
NAME          ADVDB
EXETYPE       WINDOWS
STUB          'WINSTUB.EXE'
HEAPSIZE      1024
STACKSIZE     8192
CODE          PRELOAD MOVEABLE DISCARDABLE
DATA          PRELOAD MOVEABLE MULTIPLE
```

This program displays some information in the client area about a person. When the user clicks the Get Info menu item, a dialog box is displayed (see Figure 14.13) that enables the user to enter information about a person. When the dialog box is closed, the information is then updated in the program's client area.

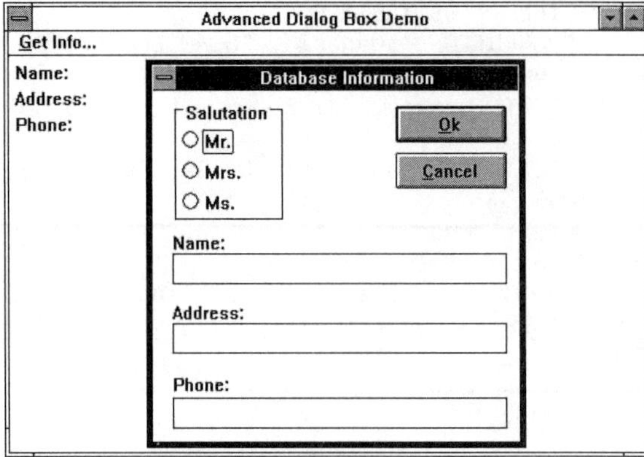

Figure 14.13.
DVDB program dialog box.

You use another method to display the menu in this program. Rather than specify the menu in the resource script, you create the menu in the program. You do this before the call to `CreateWindow`. You utilize `AppendMenu` to add a menu item. However, before you do that, use the `CreateMenu` function to return a handle to the menu. You then pass the handle to the `AppendMenu` function. It looks like this:

```
hMenu = CreateMenu();
AppendMenu(hMenu, MF_STRING, IDM_GETDATA, "&Get Info...");
```

The handle to the menu then is passed to the `CreateWindow` function:

```
hWnd = CreateWindow(ProgName,"Advanced Dialog Box Demo",
                    WS_OVERLAPPEDWINDOW,
                    CW_USEDEFAULT, CW_USEDEFAULT,
                    CW_USEDEFAULT, CW_USEDEFAULT,
                    // Notice how we reference the hMenu here
                    NULL, hMenu, hInstance, NULL);
```

This code enables you to create a menu on-the-fly in your program. Although most often you can use a menu template, the on-the-fly method enables you to add a couple of menu options without much difficulty.

The rest of the program is set up similar to the SIMPLEDB program you saw at the beginning of this chapter. There is a dialog box procedure set up, and you process `WM_COMMAND` messages in the `WMDlgCommand_Handler` function.

Several global variables to store information about a person are added. These are the following arrays:

```
char Salutation[SALUTLEN];
char Name[NAMELEN];
char Address[ADDRESSLEN];
char Phone[PHONELEN];
```

and they enable you to store specific information that the user enters into the dialog box.

Although the `WM_PAINT` processing has been modified, what's happening is clear. You are displaying the information in the client area of the screen.

Notice, the `WMDlgCommand_Handler` function has changed substantially—most importantly is the code in which you process the `IDOK` message. This message tells your program the user clicked OK. This means he is satisfied with the information entered and is ready to close the dialog box.

At this point your program receives the information from the dialog box and assigns values to the global variables based on what the user entered. With a radio button, you find whether it's selected as follows:

```
hCtrl = GetDlgItem(hDlg, IDD_MR);
result = SendMessage(hCtrl, BM_GETCHECK, 0, 0L);
if (result)
   strcpy(Salutation, "Mr.");
```

You first get a handle to the control with the `GetDlgItem` function. You must pass the handle to the dialog box and the identifier of the control. You then send the message `BM_GETCHECK` to the control with the `SendMessage` function. The `SendMessage` function returns a value in the variable result based on the message sent. If the radio button is selected, it returns a `TRUE` value. You then copy an appropriate string in the `Salutation` global variable.

To get the text from an edit control, you use the `GetDlgItemText` function. You pass a handle to the dialog box, the identifier of the edit control, the variable to receive the edit control contents, and then the maximum number of characters to copy to the buffer. The function calls look like this:

```
GetDlgItemText(hDlg, IDD_NAME, Name, NAMELEN);
GetDlgItemText(hDlg, IDD_ADDRESS, Address, ADDRESSLEN);
GetDlgItemText(hDlg, IDD_PHONE, Phone, PHONELEN);
```

The program then uses the `InvalidateRect` function to cause the `WM_PAINT` message to be processed. The result is the name information is transferred to the client area of the program.

Using the Borland Windows Custom Controls

The dialog boxes used in the Integrated Development Environment look different than all other Windows dialog boxes. This is because Borland created its own controls. These controls provide the look of chiseled steel and mimic the sharp appearance of UNIX systems running X-WINDOWS.

To use the Borland Windows Custom Controls (BWCC) in your programs, you must make the BWCC.DLL file available to Windows. It must be in the current subdirectory, the WINDOWS subdirectory, or the currently defined path. This initial step is easy to accomplish. BWCC.DLL comes with all Borland products, including Turbo Pascal for Windows, ObjectVision, and Quattro Pro for Windows.

To create a dialog box, you first must change its properties. Double-click the title bar to do that. When the Window Style dialog box is displayed, specify `bordlg` as the class. Now, press Enter to close the dialog box. When the dialog box is redisplayed, it will now contain the gray background.

You now can select the BWCC controls from the right side of the toolbar. Pushbuttons, radio buttons, and checkboxes have new controls. To create a pushbutton that contains the fancy OK or Cancel text along with the additional graphics, you must give your button a special identifier. Table 14.2 contains the identifiers.

Table 14.2. Identifier to give to Borland buttons.

Identifier	*Button Text*
`IDOK`	Ok
`IDCANCEL`	Cancel

Identifier	*Button Text*
`IDABORT`	Abort
`IDRETRY`	Retry
`IDIGNORE`	Ignore
`IDYES`	Yes
`IDNO`	No

Programming for BWCC is the same as programming regular dialog boxes, although you must include BWCC.LIB in your project to ensure that the appropriate routines are linked to your program.

Finally, rather than use the default dialog box procedure, you must call the Borland custom controls dialog box procedure. Instead of calling `DefDlgProc`, you call `BWCC DefDlgProc` to process default dialog box messages.

New MessageBox

Borland has thought of everything. They have a new version of MessageBox with the new look, BWCCMessageBox. You call it exactly as you call the regular Windows MessageBox, and it works like Windows MessageBox too.

NOTE

For complete documentation for use of the Borland Windows Custom Controls, see the file BWCCAPI.RW in the C:\TCWIN\DOC subdirectory. It contains the official information about using BWCC. At this time, Borland has not released any printed information.

What You Have Learned

This chapter examined creating custom dialog boxes. You learned to create dialog boxes in traditional C programs as well as in programs based on the ObjectWindows Library. You also learned to use the Borland Windows Custom Controls to create the look of chiseled steel in your programs.

In particular, the following topics were covered in this chapter:

- How to use the Resource Workshop to create custom dialog boxes.
- How to create an About dialog box in a C program.
- How to use dialog procedures and how they respond to Windows messages in a dialog box.
- How to use the ObjectWindows Library to implement dialog boxes.
- How to use the Borland Windows Custom Controls to create the look of chiseled steel in your program.

III ADVANCED WINDOWS PROGRAMMING

15 DYNAMIC LINK LIBRARIES

IN THIS CHAPTER

- The purpose and advantages of DLLs.
- Static linking.
- The meaning of dynamic linking.
- Recognizing DLLs that make up the Windows Application Program Interface (API).
- Using the TDUMP utility to find specific information about a program file.
- Finding how the Windows environment locates a DLL.
- How Windows manages DLLs by keeping a reference count of the number of programs currently using a DLL.
- Creating your own DLL.
- Requirements for DLL and using IMPLIBW to create an import library.
- General rules and guidelines for writing DLLs.

About Dynamic Link Libraries

DLLs play a critical role in the overall design concept of Windows programming. In fact, most of the Windows API is a set of DLLs.

Like a Windows application, a DLL is a Windows program module. It contains executable code and data that Windows loads into memory for other programs or libraries to use. Before you can examine DLLs, you first must understand the main components of program compilation and their operation.

What Is Dynamic Linking?

A good preliminary to the study of DLLs is a review of the process of compiling and linking. Every program you write in Turbo C++ for Windows undergoes a *static link* process. The program first is compiled, to convert the C and C++ instructions to machine language. Then, the program is linked with the runtime libraries, along with any other modules you specify in a project file.

The static linking process combines the routines in the libraries (such as the `strlen()` and `memset()` functions) with your compiled program code to create an executable program. The static linking process combines your program's function calls to a routine not present in the source file.

The primary advantage of static linking is that you can use it to reference a standard set of subroutines (those found in a library) to those in your program without recompiling the code or having the source code for the routines.

In static linking, the target routines found in the unit must be present at link time. They then are combined in the final .EXE file. This makes the resulting .EXE program file larger. Static linking is valuable because it makes the runtime library available to a program without having to recompile the routines every time and, most important, without requiring the source code to the routines at compile time.

The process of *dynamic linking* occurs when the program is being executed, not at compile time. Rather than include the code for the routines that a program makes calls to in the application program itself, the code is provided in a separate DLL file. The program is compiled with external references to the code in the DLL. When the program executes and it needs a routine in the DLL, Windows automatically loads the DLL and makes the routine available to the program.

The main benefits of DLLs include the following:

- Saves memory. More than one application can use the same routines in a single DLL.
- Allows change in the core routines of a program without you redistributing a new program file. If you have used a Windows program with previous releases of Windows and then used the same program in newer versions of Windows, you know the whole look and execution of the program is different. This is because the DLL files included in the new version of Windows were updated. The actual program did not change.
- Allows programs to share code and data between applications. Borland's Paradox Engine (which accesses Paradox files in a C or C++ program) includes a DLL that allows Windows programs to access database files. Multiple programs can use these routines, and only one copy of the functions ever loads into memory. If you link the routines statically, the same code would be present in several applications, thereby taking up more memory.
- Enables you to create programs based on mixed language program development. You can write a DLL in Turbo C++ for Windows and use those routines in an application written in any Windows development languages, including Turbo Pascal for Windows, Visual BASIC, Asymetrix Toolbook, Smalltalk, and even assembly language—if you are so daring.
- Provides a way to extend and customize the Windows environment. The code and data you implement in DLLs can be used by applications in the same way as the routines found in the Windows Application Program Interface (API). You can extend Windows programs such as Control Panel and File Manager by writing DLLs.

Windows System DLLs

Earlier, I mentioned that the functions that make up Windows are a group of dynamic link libraries. This is true. They are contained in several files used by the Windows system. The DLLs that make up the Windows system include the following:

- GDI.EXE. This file includes the graphics device interface routines.
- KERNAL.EXE, or KRNL286.EXE, or KRNL386.EXE. Depending on which mode you are running Windows in (Windows 3.0 real mode, standard mode, or enhanced mode), one of these three files is running. They supply the key routines used by Windows.
- USER.EXE. This contains more of the core routines used by Windows.
- COMMDLG.DLL. This provides the functions for the common dialog boxes you saw in Chapter 13, "Using Dialog Boxes."
- All driver files (including MOUSE.DRV, KEYBOARD.DRV, SOUND.DRV, COM.DRV, as well as others). These are the specialized drivers Windows uses. Printer drivers written by independent sources are also DLLs.

Although some of these files have the extension .EXE, they are still DLLs. Furthermore, if your program uses the BWCC, it uses the BWCC.DLL dynamic link library to provide these fancy looking dialog boxes.

Now that you know what DLLs are and how they are used in Windows, examine the specifics of using and creating DLLs.

Understanding Dynamic Link Libraries

A custom DLL is contained in a separate program file with an extension of .DLL. The DLL file must be present when a program that uses it runs. Windows automatically links the procedures and function calls in the program to their entry points in the DLL used by the application.

You can find detailed technical information about a .DLL file (as well as any other program file) with the TDUMP utility provided with Turbo C++ for Windows. The TDUMP utility is a DOS-based program you operate from the command line.

The program is found in the \TCWIN\BIN subdirectory in which Turbo C++ for Windows is installed. To use the program, open a DOS window and type

```
TDUMP filename
```

Be sure to include the full filename and extension of the file. The program gives detailed information about .EXE, .OBJ, .LIB, and .DLL files. Using TDUMP with any other type of file extension results in a hex dump of the file contents.

Often, the information provided is overkill. You might not understand exactly what everything means, because TDUMP tells everything about the file (sometimes too much). However, TDUMP does give important information that will help you understand what the file is used for. Try using the utility on several different files (both DOS programs and Windows applications).

Locating Dynamic Link Libraries

Windows locates a DLL by searching the same directories it searches to find an application program. It first looks in the current directory. If it does not find the DLL there, it looks in the main WINDOWS subdirectory. It then checks the Windows system directory which contains many of the system files used by Windows. As a last resort, Windows looks for a DLL in the directories listed in the PATH environment variable.

Library Reference Count

For each DLL in memory, Windows keeps a reference count that indicates the number of programs dynamically linked to the library. Windows increments the reference count when it loads an application that calls on a routine in a DLL and decrements the count when the instance terminates. If the reference count becomes zero, the DLL automatically is removed from memory.

Creating Your Own DLL

You create a DLL in Turbo C++ for Windows with two files, the source code file and a module definition file. This isn't new; almost every program you've seen so far has these two files. However, you must change some options to create a DLL.

After you create a new project for your DLL, you must specify you want to create a DLL. To do this, choose the Options menu, select Application, and then press the Windows DLL button (see Figure 15.1). These actions tell Turbo C++ for Windows you want to create a DLL. Turbo C++ for Windows then creates a file with the extension .DLL. You also should select the large memory model by selecting the Options menu, choosing Compiler, and choosing code generation.

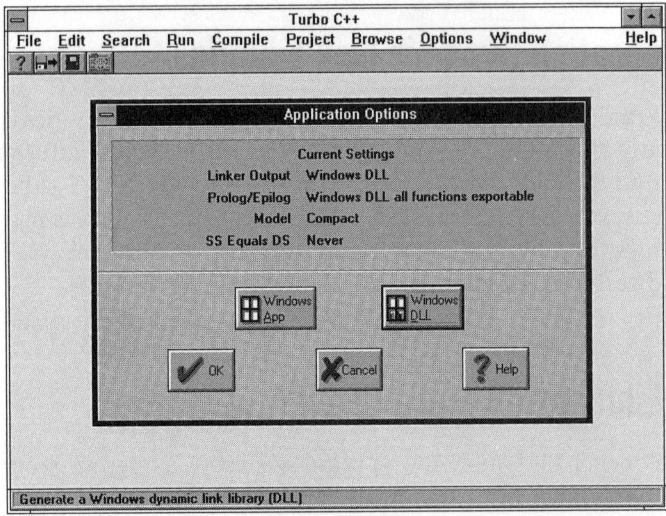

Figure 15.1.
The Application Options dialog box.

The top part of the Application Options dialog box gives certain information about the program it will create. The first line specifies whether the resulting module will be an EXE or DLL. The other information includes material about prolog and epilog code, the memory model in use, and whether SS equals DS. This last option refers to the stack segment and data segment. In a DLL, you never want SS to equal DS.

You must put several other instructions in your code for a DLL. First, consider the structure of the DLL source code file. Then, see how the module definition file is different from an application.

Structure of a DLL

Besides the functions your program calls, a DLL has two additional functions, `LibMain()` and `WEP()`. `LibMain()` is analogous to `WinMain`. The `WEP()` function stands for Windows Exit Procedure. It's called just before the DLL is unloaded from memory.

Whereas all C programs have a `main()` program entry point and all Windows programs contain a `WinMain()` program entry point, all DLLs contain a `LibMain()` function. The `LibMain()` function is called the first time the DLL is loaded. It contains any initialization code required for the DLL.

The LibMain() Function

The `LibMain()` function is passed four values, as follows:

```
int FAR PASCAL LibMain (HINSTANCE hInstance,
                        WORD wDataSeg,
                        WORD wHeapSize,
                        LPSTR lpszCmdLine)
```

Notice the function is declared `int FAR PASCAL`. It returns an integer value, is called as a far function, and uses the `Pascal` calling convention.

The first value passed to the function, `hInstance`, is the handle of the instance of the library. The second value, `wDataSeg`, is the value of the data segment register. The third value, `wHeapSize`, specifies the size of the heap, as defined later in the module definition file. The fourth value is `lpszCmdLine`.

This points to a null terminated string that specifies command-line information. This parameter is used rarely by DLLs.

In most cases, the `LibMain()` function is short and resembles this:

```
int FAR PASCAL LibMain (HINSTANCE hInstance, WORD wDataSeg,
                        WORD wHeapSize, LPSTR lpszCmdLine)
{
   if (wHeapSize > 0)
      UnlockData(0);

   return 1;
}
```

The first two lines unlock data of the library that is locked by the start-up code. The function then returns `1` if it was successfully loaded. Otherwise, it returns `0`.

The WEP() Function

The Windows exit procedure function performs clean-up for a DLL before the library is unloaded. This function is called by Windows before the DLL is unloaded.

In Windows 3.1, the `WEP()` function is optional. However, in Windows 3.0, the `WEP()` function was required. Worse yet, there were major problems associated with clean-up functions. Also, if you allocate memory in a DLL, when the DLL is unloaded, the memory is automatically freed. Therefore, it's not necessary to restore allocated memory.

Because of the problems associated with utilizing the `WEP()` function in Windows 3.0, most programs still don't make much use of that function.

The entire `WEP()` function generally is similar to this:

```
int FAR PASCAL _export WEP(int nShutDownFlag)
{
   return 1;
}
```

The variable `nShutDownFlag` specifies whether Windows is being exited entirely (in which case it contains the value `WEP_SYSTEM_EXIT`) or whether only the library is being unloaded (in which case it contains the value `WEP_FREE_DLL`).

Module Definition File

The other important file you must change when creating a DLL is the module definition file (.DEF file). The new module definition file looks something like this:

```
;
; Sample DLL module definition file
;
DESCRIPTION    'Sample DLL'
LIBRARY        SAMPDLL
EXETYPE        WINDOWS
STUB           'WINSTUB.EXE'
HEAPSIZE       0
CODE           MOVEABLE DISCARDABLE
DATA           PRELOAD MOVEABLE SINGLE
```

The line labeled `LIBRARY` replaces the line labeled `NAME` in an application. Next, you should notice that the `HEAPSIZE` is set at `0`. This is because a DLL does not have its own heap. A DLL uses either global memory or the heap of the application calling it.

Finally, the `CODE` option is set at `MOVEABLE` and `DISCARDABLE`. The DLL does not use the `PRELOAD` option, which Windows programs use.

Those are the only changes you must make to create a DLL. Next, examine the functions you put in the DLL.

Your Custom Functions

Declare any function in a DLL as `FAR PASCAL` and export it using the `_export` keyword. Here is an example from the upcoming program:

```
int FAR PASCAL _export InputBox(HWND hWndParent,
                                LPCSTR lpszTitle,
                                LPSTR Buffer,
                                int Length)
{
...
source code
...
}
```

The function returns an integer and is declared as `FAR PASCAL _export`. If you don't declare your function in this manner, your program will generate general protection (GP) errors.

Using the DLL Routines

The other aspect of creating a DLL is using the functions in the DLL from your program. To call a DLL from a program, you must create an import library. The import library is a file created with the IMPLIBW program (see Figure 15.2). The import library's main purpose is to resolve external references to particular functions. It does this by informing the Turbo C++ for Windows linker the function will be available at runtime, rather than linktime.

You run IMPLIBW by double-clicking the Import Library icon from the Turbo C++ group in Program Manager (see Figure 15.2). When the program begins, you select the File menu and choose the File Select menu item.

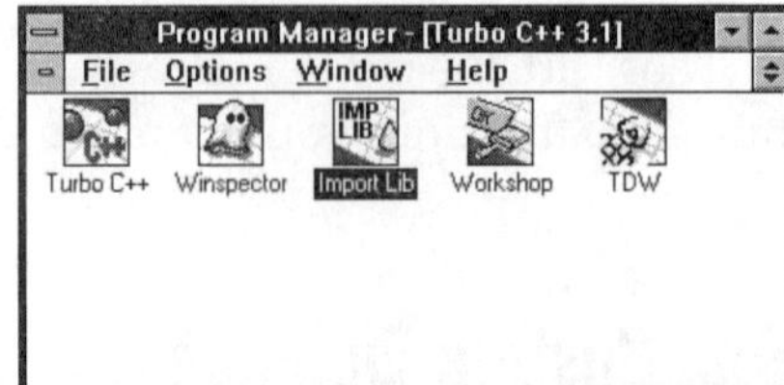

Figure 15.2.
Import library icon in Program Manager.

A dialog box is displayed that enables you to choose a DLL file. After you press OK, an import library is created (see Figure 15.3). The import library has the same base name as the DLL, but it has the file extension .LIB.

When you create your application, you must include this import library in your project. If you don't, your application won't link. You now know how to use import libraries in your programs. In Chapter 14, "More About Dialog Boxes," you learned that to use the BWCC, you must include the BWCC.LIB file in your project. BWCC.LIB is nothing more than an import library for the BWCC.DLL dynamic link library.

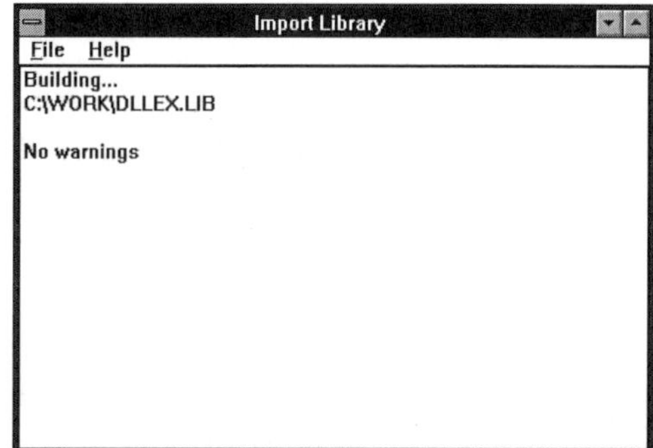

Figure 15.3.

Import library results.

Rules for Writing DLLs

The following guidelines can help you write your DLLs:

- Always use the `_export` keyword when you declare a function you expect to call from a DLL. A program still compiles without the keyword, but it does not always run correctly.
- Any variables you declare in the DLL are private to it. You cannot share global variables in the DLL with a program. The only way to transfer the data is through routines that pass them as parameters.
- A DLL can include resources such as dialog boxes and bitmaps that multiple programs can share. You include the resource in the project of the DLL the same way you include it in a program file.
- Remember, calling a routine in a DLL adds a small amount of time to executing the routine because Windows must load and link the routine as the program is executing. For routines where performance is critical, you might want to keep the routine in the main program.

A DLL Example

In Chapters 13 and 14, you saw how to use and create dialog boxes. One of the first dialog box types you learned about (in Chapter 1, "Getting Started with Turbo C++ for Windows"—wow, you sure have come a long way!) was the MessageBox function.

I don't know if you like MessageBox as much as I do, but it is a handy function. It would be nice if Windows contained several other calls that created simple dialog boxes that could be used in a variety of situations.

After brainstorming this for a time, I came up with two dialog boxes to implement in a DLL. They are InputBox and ListBox. I expect to use these in my programs almost as easily as I use MessageBox.

The InputBox Function

InputBox (see Figure 15.4) contains a single edit control that enables the user to enter a line of text.

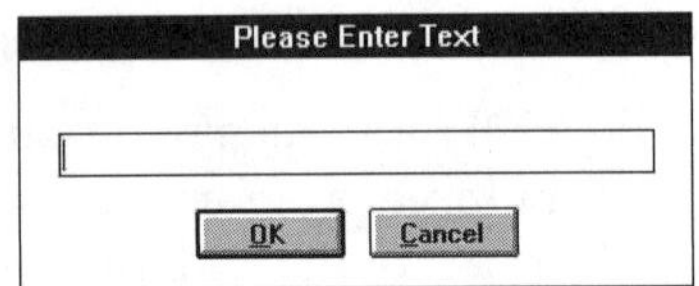

Figure 15.4.
InputBox dialog box.

The function is declared like this:

```
int InputBox(HWND hWndParent, LPCSTR lpszTitle,
             LPSTR Buffer, int Length)
```

The hWndParent parameter is a handle to the parent window. Unlike MessageBox, you cannot pass a NULL value. All dialog boxes require a handle to the window of a parent. (MessageBox must do some trickery to get around this, but that's not documented.)

The lpszTitle parameter is the address of the title to be displayed in the input box. The Buffer parameter is the address of the buffer that stores the edit line. This must be allocated before calling the function. The `Length` value is how many characters to copy into the `Buffer`.

The function returns `TRUE` if it was successful, in which case the `Buffer` will contain the text the user entered. The function returns `FALSE` if the user pressed Cancel.

The ListBox Function

`ListBox` (see Figure 15.5) contains a listbox along with two pushbuttons, OK and Cancel. It displays a listbox, fills it with items, and enables the user to select one item from the listbox.

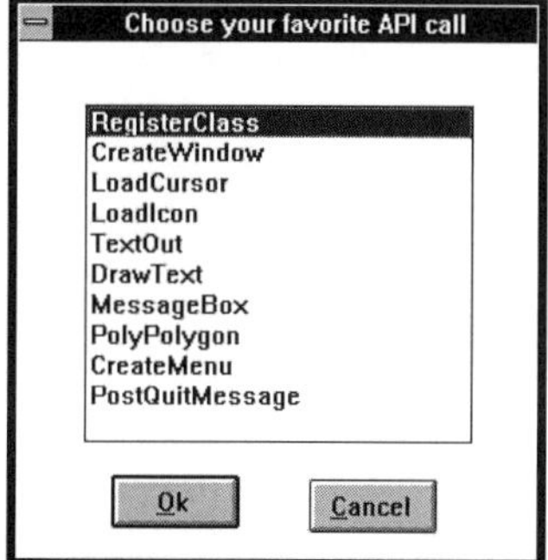

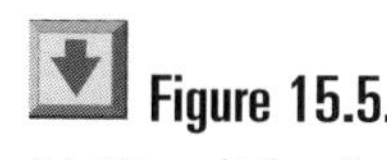

Figure 15.5.
ListBox dialog box

The function is declared like this:

```
int ListBox(HWND hWndParent, LPCSTR lpszTitle,
            char far *ItemList[])
```

The `hWndParent` value specifies the handle of the parent window. The `lpszTitle` parameter is the title to use for the `MessageBox`. Finally, the `ItemList[]` parameter is a pointer to an array of characters to fill the listbox. This array must be terminated by the `NULL` character. An example of this is the following:

```
char *list[] = { "First Item",
                 "Second Item",
```

```
                "Third Item",
                "Last Item",
                NULL };
```

It is vital that you terminate the array with the NULL value. If you don't, you will run into problems. Rather than pass another parameter that specifies how many elements are in the array, it's more efficient to terminate the array with a NULL. This uses less memory on the stack than passing an additional value specifying the number of items in the array.

Look at the code required to create this DLL. Listing 15.1 contains the C source code, Listing 15.2 contains the resource script, Listing 15.3 contains the header file, and Listing 15.4 contains the module definition file.

Listing 15.1. Example dynamic link library.

```
// DLLEX.C - Example dynamic link library
//
// Programming Windows with Turbo C++ for Windows
// by Paul J. Perry

#define STRICT

#include <windowsx.h>

#include "dllex.h"

// Data Structures
typedef struct tagXFERBUFFER1    // Used for ListBox() routine
{
   char *lpszTitle;
   char **ItemList;

} XFERBUFFER1;

typedef struct tagXFERBUFFER2   // Used for InputBox() routine
{
   char *lpszTitle;
   LPSTR lpszBuffer;
   int *length;
} XFERBUFFER2;


// Function Prototypes
```

```
BOOL FAR PASCAL _export ListBoxDlgProc(HWND hDlg, UINT message,
                        WPARAM wParam, LPARAM lParam);

BOOL FAR PASCAL _export InputBoxDlgProc(HWND hDlg, UINT message,
                        WPARAM wParam, LPARAM lParam);

void WMDlgCommand_Handler(HWND hDlg, int id,
                         HWND hwndCtl, UINT codeNotify);

int FAR PASCAL _export WEP(int nShutDownFlag);

   // The following prototypes are the functions called from
   // outside the DLL.
int FAR PASCAL _export InputBox(HWND hWndParent, LPCSTR lpszTitle,
                               LPSTR Buffer, int StrLen);

int FAR PASCAL _export ListBox(HWND hWndParent, LPCSTR lpszTitle,
                              char far *ItemList[]);


// Global Variables
HINSTANCE ghInstance;


/* ############################################
   ## These functions are required in a DLL  ##
   ############################################ */

/*******************************************/
#pragma argsused
int FAR PASCAL LibMain (HINSTANCE hInstance, WORD wDataSeg,
                        WORD wHeapSize, LPSTR lpszCmdLine)
{
   if (wHeapSize > 0)
      UnlockData(0);

   ghInstance = hInstance;

   return 1;
}

/*******************************************/
#pragma argsused
int FAR PASCAL _export WEP(int nShutDownFlag)
{
   return 1;
}
```

continues

Listing 15.1. continued

```
/* ########################################
   ##  Functions related to InputBox()  ##
   ######################################## */

/*********************************************/
int FAR PASCAL _export InputBox(HWND hWndParent, LPCSTR lpszTitle,
                                LPSTR Buffer, int Length)
{/*
    HWND   hWndParent  Handle to parent window.
    LPCSTR lpszTitle   Address of title of Input box.
    LPSTR  Buffer      Address of buffer to store edit line in
    int    Length      How many characters to copy into Buffer

    Returns: TRUE if successful,  FALSE if user pressed CANCEL */

   DLGPROC lpfnInputBoxDlgProc;
   XFERBUFFER2 XferBuffer;
   int Result;

   // Set up transfer buffer
   XferBuffer.lpszTitle = (char *) lpszTitle;
   XferBuffer.lpszBuffer = (LPSTR) Buffer;
   XferBuffer.length = &Length;

   // Call dialog box
   lpfnInputBoxDlgProc = (DLGPROC)MakeProcInstance
               ((FARPROC)InputBoxDlgProc, ghInstance);
   Result = DialogBoxParam(ghInstance, "INPUTDIALOG", hWndParent,
           lpfnInputBoxDlgProc, (LPARAM)&XferBuffer);
   FreeProcInstance((FARPROC)lpfnInputBoxDlgProc);

   return Result;

}

/*********************************************/
BOOL FAR PASCAL _export InputBoxDlgProc(HWND hDlg, UINT message,
                          WPARAM wParam, LPARAM lParam)
{
static XFERBUFFER2 *XferBuffer;

   switch(message)
   {
      case WM_INITDIALOG :
      {
```

```
      XferBuffer = (XFERBUFFER2*)lParam;

      // Set window title
      SetWindowText(hDlg, XferBuffer->lpszTitle);

      return TRUE;
      }

      case WM_COMMAND :
      {
      switch(wParam)
      {
         case IDOK :
         {
            int NumChars;

            NumChars = GetDlgItemText(hDlg, IDD_EDIT,
                                  XferBuffer->lpszBuffer,
                                  *XferBuffer->length);

            EndDialog(hDlg, NumChars);
               break;
            }

         case IDCANCEL :
         {
            EndDialog(hDlg, 0);
            break;
         }

      }

      }

   }

   return FALSE;
}


/* #####################################
   ##  Functions related to ListBox()  ##
   ##################################### */

/*******************************************/
int FAR PASCAL _export ListBox(HWND hWndParent, LPCSTR lpszTitle,
                               char far *ItemList[])
```

continues

Listing 15.1. continued

```
{ /*
    HWND   hWndParent  Handle to parent window.
    LPCSTR lpszTitle   Address of title of list box.
    LPCSTR *ItemList   Address of array of items for listbox
                 must be terminated with NULL

    Returns: The index (starting from 1) of the item selected
             Returns 0 if the user pressed cancel                */

   DLGPROC lpfnListBoxDlgProc;
   XFERBUFFER1 XferBuffer;
   int Index;

   // Setup transfer buffer
   XferBuffer.lpszTitle = (char *)lpszTitle;
   XferBuffer.ItemList  = ItemList;

   // Call dialog box
   lpfnListBoxDlgProc = (DLGPROC)MakeProcInstance
                  ((FARPROC)ListBoxDlgProc, ghInstance);
   Index = DialogBoxParam(ghInstance, "LISTBOXDIALOG", hWndParent,
                          lpfnListBoxDlgProc, (LPARAM)&XferBuffer);
   FreeProcInstance((FARPROC)lpfnListBoxDlgProc);

   // Return appropriate value
   if (Index== 0)
     return 0;     // No items selected or Cancel selected

   return ++Index;   // Index of item (starting from 1) in array
}

/*******************************************/
BOOL FAR PASCAL _export ListBoxDlgProc(HWND hDlg, UINT message,
                                  WPARAM wParam, LPARAM lParam)
{
   switch(message)
   {
      case WM_INITDIALOG :
      {
      XFERBUFFER1 *XferBuffer = (XFERBUFFER1*)lParam;
      HWND hListBox;
      int i;

      // Set window title
         SetWindowText(hDlg, XferBuffer->lpszTitle);
```

```
        // Get handle to listbox
     hListBox = GetDlgItem(hDlg, IDD_LISTBOX);

     // Fill listbox with data items
        i=0;
     while (XferBuffer->ItemList[i] != NULL)
        SendMessage(hListBox, LB_ADDSTRING, 0, (LPARAM)XferBuffer-
                    >ItemList[i++]);

     return TRUE;
     }

     case WM_COMMAND :
     {
     return (BOOL)HANDLE_WM_COMMAND(hDlg, wParam, lParam,
                                    WMDlgCommand_Handler);
     }
  }

  return FALSE;
}

/*******************************************/
#pragma argsused
void WMDlgCommand_Handler(HWND hDlg, int id, HWND hwndCtl, UINT
                          codeNotify)
{
   switch(id)
   {
      case IDD_LISTBOX :
      {
      if (codeNotify != LBN_DBLCLK)
      {
            break;
      }
      }

      case IDOK :
      {
      DWORD Index;
      HWND hListBox;

      hListBox = GetDlgItem(hDlg, IDD_LISTBOX);
      Index = SendMessage(hListBox, LB_GETCURSEL, 0, 0L);
      EndDialog(hDlg, (int)Index);
      break;
      }
```

continues

Listing 15.1. continued

```
      case IDCANCEL :
      {
      EndDialog(hDlg, 0);
      break;
      }
   }
}
```

Listing 15.2. Resource script for example DLL.

```
/*
 * DLLEX.RC resource script file
 *
 */

#include <windows.h>

#include "dllex.h"


LISTBOXDIALOG DIALOG 23, 27, 142, 136
STYLE DS_MODALFRAME ¦ WS_POPUP ¦ WS_CAPTION ¦ WS_SYSMENU
BEGIN
     LISTBOX IDD_LISTBOX, 19, 17, 105, 87
     DEFPUSHBUTTON "&Ok", IDOK, 26, 114, 35, 14, WS_CHILD ¦
WS_VISIBLE ¦ WS_TABSTOP
     PUSHBUTTON "&Cancel", IDCANCEL, 80, 115, 35, 14, WS_CHILD ¦
WS_VISIBLE ¦ WS_TABSTOP
END

INPUTDIALOG DIALOG 20, 24, 180, 64
STYLE WS_POPUP ¦ WS_CAPTION ¦ DS_SETFONT
FONT 8, "Helv"
BEGIN
     CONTROL "", IDD_EDIT, "EDIT", WS_CHILD ¦ WS_VISIBLE ¦
WS_BORDER ¦ WS_TABSTOP ¦ ES_AUTOHSCROLL, 10, 20, 160, 12
     DEFPUSHBUTTON "&OK", IDOK, 47, 42, 40, 14
     PUSHBUTTON "&Cancel", IDCANCEL, 93, 42, 40, 14
END
```

Listing 15.3. Header file for example DLL.

```
/*
 * DLLEX.H header file
 *
 */

#define IDD_LISTBOX 100

#define IDD_EDIT    200
```

Listing 15.4. Module definition file for example DLL.

```
;
; DLLEX.DEF module definition file
;

DESCRIPTION    'DLL Example'
LIBRARY        DLLEX
EXETYPE        WINDOWS
STUB           'WINSTUB.EXE'
HEAPSIZE       0
CODE           MOVEABLE DISCARDABLE
DATA           PRELOAD MOVEABLE SINGLE
```

You will want to create a project to use with these files (excluding the header file, of course) and compile it to a .DLL file.

Some tricks had to be performed to create the generic dialog boxes. You pass specific information to the dialog box procedures. For the `InputBox`, you pass the title, the address of the buffer, and the maximum number of characters to fill the buffer.

To do this, you use a different function to create the dialog box. Rather than use `DialogBox`, you utilize `DialogBoxParam`. It allows a pointer to be passed to a data item in the dialog box procedure. In this way, the `lParam` value contains a pointer to the data item when responding to the `WM_INITDIALOG` message.

What if you have more than one parameter to pass to the dialog box? For this case, you must create a structure of pointers that point to each data item you want to access from the dialog box procedure. Next, you pass a pointer to that structure with the `DialogBoxParam` function. You then can use all the pointers you want to access the dialog box procedure.

You have accomplished what you wanted. You created a DLL. However, that DLL is not too helpful unless you have a program that uses it.

Using the DLL Functions

The TSTDLL.C program in Listing 15.5 uses both the functions in the DLLEX DLL you created. It has a menu item that enables you to test both the `InputBox` and the `ListBox` functions. Listing 15.6 is the header file. Listing 15.7 is the resource script, and Listing 15.8 is the module definition file.

To link the program, you must create an import library. Use the IMPLIBW utility, as described earlier in this chapter.

Listing 15.5. Program that uses the example DLL.

```
// TSTDLL.C - Program to test DLL routines
//            Requires that the DLLEX program
//            be compiled and an import library
//            created using IMPLIBW.
//
// Programming Windows with Turbo C++ for Windows
// by Paul J. Perry


#define STRICT

#include <windowsx.h>
#include <stdio.h>

#include "tstdll.h"

// Function Prototypes
```

```
LRESULT CALLBACK _export MainWndProc(HWND hWnd, UINT message,
                         WPARAM wParam, LPARAM lParam);

void WMCommand_Handler(HWND hwnd, int id, HWND hwndCtl, UINT
                       codeNotify);


// Prototypes of functions in DLL
// usually these would appear in a header file
int FAR PASCAL ListBox(HWND hWndParent, LPCSTR lpszTitle,
                       LPCSTR *ItemList);

int FAR PASCAL InputBox(HWND hWndParent, LPSTR Title,
                        LPSTR Buffer, int Length);


/********************************************/
#pragma argsused
int PASCAL WinMain(HINSTANCE hInstance, HINSTANCE hPrevInstance,
                   LPSTR lpCmdParam, int nCmdShow)
{
   char         ProgName[] = "Test the DLL functions";
   HWND         hWnd;
   MSG          msg;


   if (!hPrevInstance)
   {
      WNDCLASS    wndclass;

      wndclass.style          = CS_VREDRAW | CS_HREDRAW;
      wndclass.lpfnWndProc    = (WNDPROC) MainWndProc;
      wndclass.hInstance      = hInstance;
      wndclass.hIcon          = LoadIcon(NULL, IDI_APPLICATION);
      wndclass.hCursor        = LoadCursor(NULL, IDC_ARROW);
      wndclass.hbrBackground = (HBRUSH) (COLOR_WINDOW + 1);
      wndclass.lpszMenuName   = "MAINMENU";
      wndclass.cbClsExtra     = 0;
      wndclass.cbWndExtra     = 0;
      wndclass.lpszClassName = ProgName;

      RegisterClass(&wndclass);
   }

   hWnd = CreateWindow(ProgName, ProgName,
                       WS_OVERLAPPEDWINDOW,
                       CW_USEDEFAULT, CW_USEDEFAULT,
```

continues

Listing 15.5. continued

```
                        CW_USEDEFAULT, CW_USEDEFAULT,
                        NULL, NULL, hInstance, NULL);

   ShowWindow(hWnd, nCmdShow);
   UpdateWindow(hWnd);

   while (GetMessage(&msg, NULL, 0, 0))
   {
      TranslateMessage(&msg);
      DispatchMessage(&msg);
   }
   return msg.wParam;
}


/*******************************************/
#pragma argsused
void WMCommand_Handler(HWND hWnd, int id, HWND hwndCtl, UINT
                        codeNotify)
{
   switch(id)
   {
      case IDM_LIST :
      {
         char *list[] = { "RegisterClass",
                          "CreateWindow",
                          "LoadCursor",
                          "LoadIcon",
                    "TextOut",
                    "DrawText",
                    "MessageBox",
                    "PolyPolygon",
                    "CreateMenu",
                          "PostQuitMessage",
                 NULL };
      char buff[255];
         int result;

      result = ListBox(hWnd, "Choose your favorite API call", list);

      sprintf(buff, "Index number = %d, message = %s",
              result, list[result-1]);

      MessageBox(hWnd, buff, "ListBox result",
                 MB_OK );
```

```
      break;

      }

      case IDM_INPUT :
      {
      char buffer[80];

      InputBox(hWnd, "Please Enter Text", buffer, 80);

      MessageBox(hWnd, buffer, "Text Entered", MB_OK);

      break;
      }

      case IDM_EXIT :
      {
      PostQuitMessage(0);
      break;
      }

   }

}

/*******************************************/
LRESULT CALLBACK _export MainWndProc(HWND hWnd, UINT message,
                                     WPARAM wParam, LPARAM lParam)
{
   switch (message)
   {
      case WM_PAINT :
      {
         HDC         PaintDC;
         RECT        rect;
         PAINTSTRUCT ps;

      PaintDC = BeginPaint(hWnd, &ps);

         GetClientRect(hWnd, &rect);

         DrawText(PaintDC, "Test DLL functions",
                  -1, &rect, DT_SINGLELINE | DT_CENTER | DT_VCENTER);

         EndPaint(hWnd, &ps);
         return 0;
      }
```

continues

Listing 15.5. continued

```
      case WM_COMMAND :
      {
      return HANDLE_WM_COMMAND(hWnd, wParam, lParam,
                               WMCommand_Handler);
      }

      case WM_DESTROY :
      {
         PostQuitMessage(0);
         return 0;
      }
   }
   return DefWindowProc (hWnd, message, wParam, lParam);
}
```

Listing 15.6. TSTDLL header file.

```
/*
 * TSTDLL.H header file
 *
 */

#define IDM_INPUT 101
#define IDM_LIST  102
#define IDM_EXIT  103
```

Listing 15.7. TSTDLL resource script.

```
/*
 * TSTDLL.RC resource script
 *
 */

#include "tstdll.h"

MAINMENU MENU
BEGIN
     POPUP "&Dialog Box"
```

```
    BEGIN
        MENUITEM "&InputBox", IDM_INPUT
        MENUITEM "&ListBox", IDM_LIST
        MENUITEM SEPARATOR
             MENUITEM "E&xit", IDM_EXIT
    END

END
```

Listing 15.8. TSTDLL module definition file.

```
;
; TSTDLL.DEF module definition file
;

DESCRIPTION   'Test the DLL'
NAME          TRADITIONAL
EXETYPE       WINDOWS
STUB          'WINSTUB.EXE'
HEAPSIZE      1024
STACKSIZE     8192
CODE          PRELOAD MOVEABLE DISCARDABLE
DATA          PRELOAD MOVEABLE MULTIPLE
```

When the program first runs, it contains a main menu. In the menu are three items. One enables you to test the `ListBox` function. Another one enables you to test the `InputBox()` function. The third one enables you to exit the program.

What You Have Learned

You covered two important Windows programming concepts in this chapter. You looked at dynamic linking and how it is used in Windows. You saw how to create your own DLLs through the creation of a library file and an import library.

This chapter examined the use of dynamic link libraries (DLL). The following important points were covered:

- A DLL is a group of routines that can be called from your Windows program. The routines are unique because the actual linking of the code is done at execution time rather than runtime.
- Static linking is the process of combining source code with library files. This creates a resulting .EXE file that contains the code for every routine used in the program.
- Dynamic linking waits until a program is executing to combine a main program's code with the routines in another file.
- The Windows application program interface is composed of DLLs, including USER.EXE, GDI.EXE, and one of the following three files: KERNAL.EXE, KRNL286.EXE, or KRNL386.EXE, as well as other driver files.
- You use the TDUMP program to return valuable information about a program or a DLL. If you use it on a DLL, you can discover what routines are included in it.
- To write a DLL in Turbo C++ for Windows, you must specify the type of application you want to create by choosing the Options menu and selecting the Application menu item and, finally, by selecting the Windows DLL button.
- You must declare any functions you want to use in a DLL as `FAR PASCAL` and the functions must be exported.
- To use the functions in a DLL, you must create an import library with the IMPLIBW utility program. The import library then should be included in the project of the application you are creating.

Dynamic Link Libraries

CHAPTER

15

16

EVEN MORE GDI

IN THIS CHAPTER

- What a metafile is, the types of metafiles available in Windows, and how to use metafiles in your programs.
- The GDI functions you cannot utilize when creating a metafile.
- The definition of fonts. You discover how TrueType fonts make programming easier and how to use different fonts in a Windows program.
- The uses of a `LOGFONT` structure's fields.
- How to use the Resource Workshop bitmap editor to create custom bitmaps.
- Find out about bitmap resources and learn how to display and manipulate a bitmap in the client area of a window.
- How to create your own splash screen, similar to the Turbo C++ for Windows Integrated Development Environment (IDE).

Chapter 11, "Working with the GDI," gave you an introduction to using the GDI. At that time, you learned how important a display context is for outputting graphics. You saw how the display context controls the overall appearance of graphical output, whether the output material is a single point, text, or a group of graphical shapes.

This chapter extends the discussion of the GDI to more advanced topics. You learn how to store a series of GDI routines in a metafile, which you can play back at a later time. After that, you see how to display text in different fonts and how to use the fonts in your programs. Finally, you learn how to create bitmaps in the Resource Workshop and use them in your programs.

Windows Metafiles

Metafiles enable you to store a series of GDI commands. Think of a metafile as a cassette tape recorder for graphics functions. You first record the commands needed to create the desired image. After you store the GDI commands in the metafile, you can play them back with a single command.

Metafiles provide a convenient method of storing graphics commands that create screen images. Metafiles are most useful when you have a specific image you want to display repeatedly in your program. Like the GDI routines, the images stored in a metafile are device independent. Therefore, you can create a metafile and output it to the video display as well as to a printer.

There are two types of metafiles in Windows. A memory metafile stores the graphics commands in a special location of memory identified by a handle. The other type of metafile is a disk-based metafile. A disk metafile saves the graphics commands in a disk file, usually identified with the extension .WMF (Windows metafile).

Memory Metafiles

Memory metafiles are the easiest to create and use. A metafile can be a maximum of 232 bytes or the largest amount of memory currently available to your program.

You follow four main steps to create a metafile. First, you create a special metafile device context with the `CreateMetafile` routine. You then use the GDI routines with the metafile device context. Finally, the metafile must be closed, at which time you receive a handle to the metafile.

To display the image, you use the `PlayMetaFile` function, passing the handle of the metafile to the function. You can play the metafile back as many times as you want. There is no limit to the number of times you can play a metafile back. For example, to create a metafile, you would use the following code:

```
HDC hMetaFileDC;
HMETAFILE hMetaFile;

hMetaFileDC = CreateMetaFile(NULL);

TextOut(hMetaFileDC, 1, 1, "Output to Metafile", 18);
llipse(hMetaFileDC, 10, 10, 200, 200);

[other GDI routines]

hMetaFile = CloseMetaFile(hMetaFileDC);
```

At this point, you can discard the handle to the metafile display context (`hMetaFileDC`). The handle to the metafile, however, is important. To play back the metafile you just created, use code such as the following:

```
PlayMetaFile(PaintDC, hMetaFile);
```

Notice, you need a handle to a display context at the time the metafile is played back. The previous example would be suitable in the `Paint` method of a program using the ObjectWindows Library, or in the `WM_PAINT` processing of a C program that uses the `BeginPaint` function to get a handle to the display context.

When the metafile is played back, it uses the attributes of the current display context. Because commands stored in a metafile rely on coordinates, the metafile is played back in exactly the same location, unless you change the viewport origin. The viewport origin specifies the location referred to as (0,0). The origin is usually the upper-left corner of the window.

To play back a metafile at a specific location, you use the following commands:

```
SetViewPortOrg(PaintDC, X, Y);
PlayMetaFile(PaintDC, hMetaFile);
```

Therefore, the point you select as (X,Y) becomes the new origin and the metafile can be played back at multiple locations. When you are done drawing the metafile, reset the viewport origin to the point (0,0) if you plan to use the original coordinate system for drawing other graphical images in your window.

Disk Metafiles

A disk metafile is better for large images, because it uses less of the Windows system memory; however, disk metafiles are slower than memory metafiles. To create a disk metafile, you must specify the disk filename to assign to the metafile when it's created, as follows:

```
hMetaFileDC := CreateMetaFile("FNAME.WMF");

TextOut(hMetaFileDC, 1, 1, "Output to Metafile", 18);
Ellipse(hMetaFileDC, 10, 10, 200, 200);
[other GDI routines]

hMetaFile := CloseMetaFile(hMetaFileDC);
```

Here, the filename of the metafile is specified in the code. As an alternative, you might use the Windows GetTempFileName function to return a temporary filename. You then delete the file when you are done using it.

After you create the disk metafile, employ the PlayMetaFile routine you used when the metafile was memory-based to play back the metafile. The same restrictions apply to viewport origins when playing back a disk metafile. A disk metafile is limited to the amount of disk space or to 232 bytes, whichever is smaller.

Metafile Routines

Not all GDI functions can be used in a metafile. The following is a list of GDI functions your application can use in a metafile:

AnimatePalette	ResizePalette
`Arc`	`RestoreDC`
`BitBlt`	`ScaleViewportExt`
`Chord`	`ScaleWindowExt`
`CreateBrushIndirect`	`SelectClipRegion`
`CreateDIBPatternBrush`	`SelectObject`
`CreateFontIndirect`	`SelectPalette`
`CreatePatternBrush`	`SetBkColor`
`CreatePenIndirect`	`SetBkMode`
`CreateRegion`	`SetDIBitsToDevice`
`DrawText`	`SetMapMode`
`Ellipse`	`SetMapperFlags`
`Escape`	`SetPixel`
`ExcludeClipRect`	`SetPolyFillMode`
`ExtTextOut`	`SetROP2`
`FloodFill`	`SetStretchBltMode`
`IntersectClipRect`	`SetTextAlign`
`LineTo`	`SetTextCharExtra`
`MoveTo`	`SetTextColor`
`OffsetClipRgn`	`SetTextJustification`
`OffsetViewportOrg`	`SetViewportExt`
`OffsetWindowOrg`	`SetViewportOrg`
`PatBlt`	`StretchBlt`
`Pie`	`StretchDIBits`
`Polygon`	`TextOut`
`Polyline`	
`PolyPolygon`	
`RealizePalette`	
`Rectangle`	

Basically, the following rules apply when you use metafiles:

- Only routines that take a handle to a device context (hDC) can be used in a metafile.

- Functions that return information cannot be used in a metafile (such as `GetDeviceCaps`).
- Those GDI functions that treat the metafile device context as if it were a real device context cannot be used (such as `ReleaseDC`, `CreateCompatibleDC`, and `DeleteDC`).

Knowing these distinctions about metafiles, look at an example program. Listing 16.1 creates a memory metafile and plays it back at every point in the program's client window area where the user clicks the left mouse button. Listing 16.2 is the module definition file.

Listing 16.1. Program to create metafiles.

```
// METAFILE.C - Example of using Windows metafiles
//
// Programming Windows with Turbo C++ for Windows
// by Paul J. Perry

#define STRICT

#include <windowsx.h>
#include <stdlib.h>
#include <stdio.h>


// Function Prototypes
LRESULT CALLBACK _export MainWndProc(HWND hWnd, UINT message,
                             WPARAM wParam, LPARAM lParam);

void WMLButtonDown_Handler(HWND hWnd, BOOL fDoubleClick,
                             int x, int y, UINT keyFlags);

int DrawCircle(HDC hDC, int x, int y, int radius);


// Structure definition
struct point
{
   int x;
   int y;
   struct point *next;
} PT;
```

```
// Global Variables
HMETAFILE hMetaFile;
struct point *first = NULL;
struct point *current;


/******************************************/
#pragma argsused
int PASCAL WinMain(HINSTANCE hInstance, HINSTANCE hPrevInstance,
                   LPSTR lpCmdParam, int nCmdShow)
{
   char        ProgName[] = "Metafile Example";
   HWND        hWnd;
   MSG         msg;


   if (!hPrevInstance)
   {
      WNDCLASS    wndclass;

      wndclass.style         = CS_VREDRAW ¦ CS_HREDRAW;
      wndclass.lpfnWndProc   = (WNDPROC) MainWndProc;
      wndclass.hInstance     = hInstance;
      wndclass.hIcon         = LoadIcon(NULL, IDI_APPLICATION);
      wndclass.hCursor       = LoadCursor(NULL, IDC_ARROW);
      wndclass.hbrBackground = (HBRUSH) (COLOR_WINDOW + 1);
      wndclass.lpszMenuName  = NULL;
      wndclass.cbClsExtra    = 0;
      wndclass.cbWndExtra    = 0;
      wndclass.lpszClassName = ProgName;

      RegisterClass(&wndclass);
   }

   hWnd = CreateWindow(ProgName,
                       "Metafile Tester - Click in Client Area",
                       WS_OVERLAPPEDWINDOW,
                       CW_USEDEFAULT, CW_USEDEFAULT,
                       CW_USEDEFAULT, CW_USEDEFAULT,
                       NULL, NULL, hInstance, NULL);

   ShowWindow(hWnd, nCmdShow);
   UpdateWindow(hWnd);

   while (GetMessage(&msg, NULL, 0, 0))
   {
```

continues

Listing 16.1. continued

```
      TranslateMessage(&msg);
      DispatchMessage(&msg);
   }
   return msg.wParam;
}

/*******************************************/
#pragma argsused
void WMLButtonDown_Handler(HWND hWnd, BOOL fDoubleClick,
                           int x, int y, UINT keyFlags)
{
   HDC hDC;
   struct point *temp;

   temp = first;

   // Store the point in a singly linked list.
   first = (struct point*) malloc(sizeof(PT));
   first->x = x;
   first->y = y;
   first->next = temp;

   // Play back the metafile next.
   hDC = GetDC(hWnd);

   SetViewportOrg(hDC, x, y);
   PlayMetaFile(hDC, hMetaFile);

   ReleaseDC(hWnd, hDC);

}

/*******************************************/
LRESULT CALLBACK _export MainWndProc(HWND hWnd, UINT message,
                                     WPARAM wParam, LPARAM lParam)
{
   switch (message)
   {
      case WM_CREATE :
      {
      HDC hMetaFileDC;
      HBRUSH hBrush, hOldBrush;

      // Start out by getting a handle to a DC which
      //   we will later associate with a metafile.
      hMetaFileDC = CreateMetaFile(NULL);
```

```
// Make sure we are using the black brush
//   and then display background rectangle.
SelectBrush(hMetaFileDC, GetStockBrush(BLACK_BRUSH));
Rectangle(hMetaFileDC, 0, 0, 50, 125);

// Display red circle.  We first need to create
//   brush, then select the brush, then draw
//   the circle.   Then, the original brush must
//   be reselected and the brush deleted.
hBrush = CreateSolidBrush(RGB(255, 0, 0));   // Red
hOldBrush = SelectBrush(hMetaFileDC, hBrush);
DrawCircle(hMetaFileDC, 25, 20, 15);
   SelectBrush(hMetaFileDC, hOldBrush);
DeleteBrush(hBrush);

// Now we create the yellow circle.  Use the same
//   logic as we did for creating the red one.
hBrush = CreateSolidBrush(RGB(255, 255, 0)); // Yellow
hOldBrush = SelectBrush(hMetaFileDC, hBrush);
DrawCircle(hMetaFileDC, 25, 60, 15);
SelectBrush(hMetaFileDC, hOldBrush);
DeleteBrush(hBrush);

// Finally, we create the green brush.
hBrush = CreateSolidBrush(RGB(0,255,0));     // Green
hOldBrush = SelectBrush(hMetaFileDC, hBrush);
DrawCircle(hMetaFileDC, 25, 100, 15);
SelectBrush(hMetaFileDC, hOldBrush);
DeleteBrush(hBrush);

// Done creating metafile.  Close the metafile
//   and get a handle to it returned.  Later,
//   we will use this handle to the metafile to
//   play it back.
hMetaFile = CloseMetaFile(hMetaFileDC);

}


case WM_PAINT :
{
   HDC PaintDC;
PAINTSTRUCT ps;

PaintDC = BeginPaint(hWnd, &ps);

current = first;
```

continues

Listing 16.1. continued

```
// Walk through the linked list in order to
//   reconstruct the contents of client area.
while (current != NULL)
{
   SetViewportOrg(PaintDC, current->x, current->y);
   PlayMetaFile(PaintDC, hMetaFile);
   current = current->next;
   }


EndPaint(hWnd, &ps);
   return 0;
}

case WM_LBUTTONDOWN :
{
return HANDLE_WM_LBUTTONDOWN(hWnd, wParam, lParam,
                              WMLButtonDown_Handler);
}

case WM_DESTROY :
{
struct point *temp;

// First, clean up after ourselves and
//   delete the metafile.
//
DeleteMetaFile(hMetaFile);

// Now, we need to free the linked list.
//   Although Windows will do this for us,
//   it is good programming style to always
//   delete any memory you allocate.
//
current = first;
while (current != NULL)
{
   temp = current->next;
   free(current);
   current = temp;
}


   PostQuitMessage(0);
   return 0;
}
```

```
   }
   return DefWindowProc (hWnd, message, wParam, lParam);
}


/*******************************************/
int DrawCircle(HDC hDC, int x, int y, int radius)
{
   int x1, x2, y1, y2;

   // Draw a circle, given the center points, and the
   //   radius.  Interestingly enough, Windows does not
   //   provide a DrawCircle() function.  Fortunately,
   //   it is easy to write our own, which just calls
   //   Windows API Ellipse() function.
   x1 = x - radius;
   y1 = y - radius;
   x2 = x + radius;
   y2 = y + radius;

   return Ellipse(hDC, x1, y1, x2, y2);
}
```

Listing 16.2. Module defintion file.

```
;
; METAFILE.DEF module definition file
;

DESCRIPTION    'Metafile Test'
NAME           METAFILE
EXETYPE        WINDOWS
STUB           'WINSTUB.EXE'
HEAPSIZE       1024
STACKSIZE      8192
CODE           PRELOAD MOVEABLE DISCARDABLE
DATA           PRELOAD MOVEABLE MULTIPLE
```

As you use the METAFILE program, when you move and click the mouse to place the image (a traffic light) in the window, you'll notice that if you resize the window, the images are all repainted (see Figure 16.1). In this book's programs that painted graphics when the user clicked the mouse buttons, the points were not saved. Thus, when the window was repainted, the images in the window were lost.

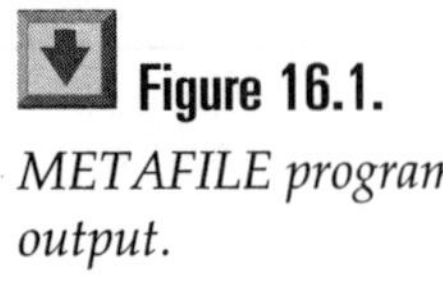
Figure 16.1.
METAFILE program output.

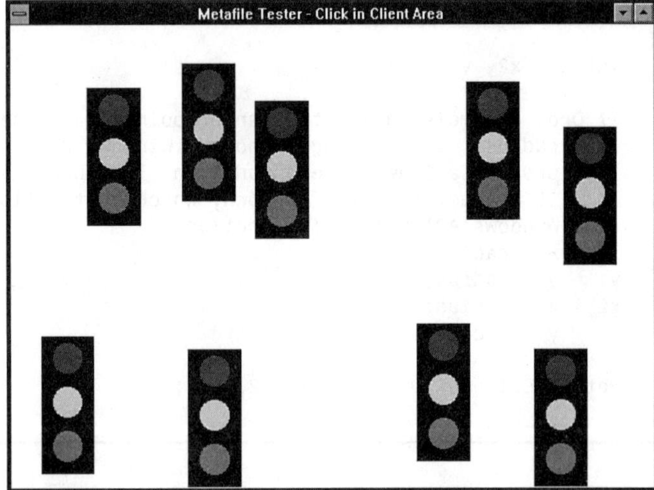

This program creates a linked list of points. Most programmers are familiar with linked lists, because they are one of the first types of data structures taught in computer science courses. In the METAFILE program, the linked list is a good type of data structure to use because there's no way to tell how many points the user might click. If the points were stored in an array, there would be an artificial limit on how many points can be used, and memory is not used efficiently if the user doesn't create the maximum number of points available.

Text and Fonts

Until now, the programs in which you have displayed text used the default Windows font. With Windows, however, you can display text in boldface and italics, modify the character size, or use an alternative typeface (see Figure 16.2). This section of the book shows how these results are created.

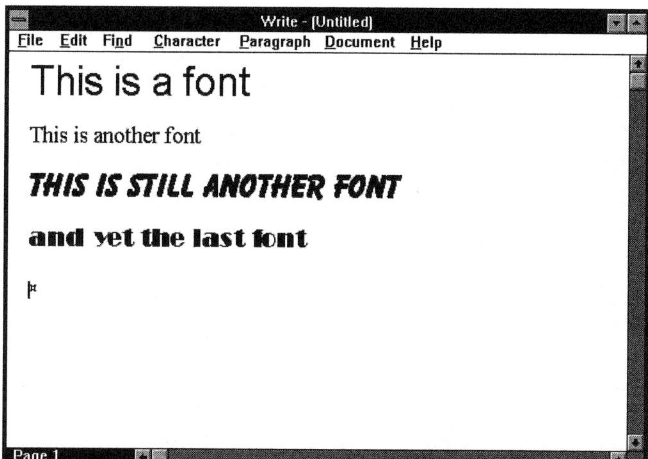

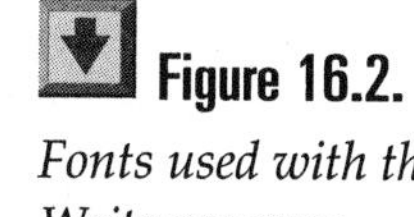

Figure 16.2.
Fonts used with the Write program.

In Chapter 11, you learned to output text to a window using the `TextOut`, `ExtTextOut`, and `DrawText` routines. You continue to use the same routines to output text; however, you learn how to modify the display context to use different fonts. As with the other display context attributes you've worked with and modified, Windows Application Program Interface (API) routines are used to modify the attributes relating to the current font in the display context.

Introduction to Fonts

The default font in the display context is the *system font*. This is a proportional font (each character is a different width) with characters in the ANSI character set. Windows uses this font when displaying text in menus, dialog boxes, and title bars.

The easiest way to write text in different fonts is to use one of the predefined stock fonts provided by Windows. The fonts are selected into the display context by first obtaining a handle to the font by calling:

```
hFont = GetStockFont(FontConstant);
```

where *FontConstant* is one of the predefined stock fonts in Table 16.1. With a handle to the font, you can select the font into the display context using

```
SelectFont(PaintDC, hFont);
```

or you can do the previous two-step process in one line of code with the following statement:

```
SelectFont(PaintDC, GetStockObject(FontConstant));
```

Remember the discussion of brushes and pens in Chapter 11. The program was capable of requesting stock pens and brushes. You used the `SelectBrush` and `SelectPen` functions to accomplish the task. When you select fonts, the process is similar.

After using the `GetStockFont` along with the `SelectFont` routine, any calls to the text output routines use the selected font.

Table 16.1. Predefined stock fonts.

Constant Name	*Description*
`OEM_FIXED_FONT`	Fixed pitch font with OEM characters.
`ANSI_FIXED_FONT`	Fixed pitch font with ANSI characters.
`ANSI_VAR_FONT`	Proportional font with ANSI characters.
`SYSTEM_FONT`	Default Font. Proportional font with ANSI characters.
`DEVICE_DEFAULT_FONT`	Font preferred by output device.
`SYSTEM_FIXED_FONT`	Fixed font with ANSI characters.

In fact, I've been holding out on you for a while. Brushes, pens, and fonts are all referred to generically as objects. Only one function selects any one of these objects in a device context. Appropriately, it is called `SelectObject`.

At this point, you probably wonder what's happening. All along, what you thought were functions aren't functions at all. The Windows API has no knowledge of any functions named `SelectBrush`, `SelectPen`, or `SelectFont`.

When you include windowsx.h in your programs, it contains macros named `SelectBrush`, `SelectPen`, and `SelectFont`. These macros call the `SelectObject` routine with the appropriate arguments. It typecasts the parameters to be appropriate for the type of object you are referring to.

The resulting code is easier to read and understand. When scanning through code, it's easier to understand what `SelectPen` refers to rather than what `SelectObject` refers to. You must be aware, however, that `SelectObject` is the function being used. If you examine much of the available Windows code, you find most of it still uses the generic `SelectObject` function call, rather than the specific macros.

Font Information

Because the size of the characters is different in each font, Windows provides several routines to obtain information about a font. Use the `GetTextMetrics` routine to find a font's character height and average width, as follows:

```
TEXTMETRIC tm;

GetTextMetrics(PaintDC, &tm)
```

You can use the `GetTextExtent` function to return the size of a line of text using the font currently selected in the display context, as follows:

```
DWORD Size;
int Height, Width;

Size = GetTextExtent(PaintDC, "Turbo C++ for Windows", 21);

Height = HIWORD(Size);
Width = LOWORD(Size);
```

This code fragment calls the `GetTextExtent` function to calculate the width and height of a string of characters passed to the routine. It returns the height in the high-ordered word, and the width in the low-ordered word.

Remember, you can use the `SetTextColor` and `SetBKColor` routines to change the color of text at any time. These routines take effect no matter what font you use.

Creating Fonts

Up to this point, you've used only the stock fonts provided with Windows. Your program can use other fonts too. This involves the use of logical fonts. A logical font is a request to Windows to create a specified font. The logical font provides a way for your program to describe the font it wants to use.

You use the `CreateFont` and `CreateFontIndirect` routines to create a logical font. The routines do exactly the same thing. The difference is `CreateFont` uses 14 parameters, whereas `CreateFontIndirect` takes a single parameter that is a record containing the same 14 values. Generally, using `CreateFontIndirect` with the logical font record is more efficient than specifying the 14 parameters separately to `CreateFont`.

The logical font (`LogFont`) record is defined in windows.h as follows:

```
typedef struct tagLOGFONT
{
    int     lfHeight;          // Average character height
    int     lfWidth;           // Average character width
    int     lfEscapement;      // Angle of text
    int     lfOrientation;     // Ignored
    int     lfWeight;          // Font weight
    BYTE    lfItalic;          // Specifies an italic font
    BYTE    lfUnderline;       // Specifies an underline font
    BYTE    lfStrikeOut;       // Specifies a strikeout font
    BYTE    lfCharSet;         // Character set of font
    BYTE    lfOutPrecision;    // Output precision
    BYTE    lfClipPrecision;   // Clipping precision
    BYTE    lfQuality;         // Font output quality
    BYTE    lfPitchAndFamily;            // Font pitch and family
    char    lfFaceName[LF_FACESIZE];     // Font's typeface
} LOGFONT;
```

The basic components of the structure are as follows:

- `lfHeight`—The average height of the characters in device units.
- `lfWidth`—The average width of the characters in device units.
- `lfEscapement`—The angle in tenths of a degree between the baseline of a character and the x-axis.
- `lfOrientation`—This value is not used and is ignored.

- `lfWeight`—The thickness of the characters. It can be any value from `0` to `1000`; however, common values are `400` for normal text and `700` for bold text.
- `lfItalic`—Set `True` for italicized text.
- `lfUnderline`—Set `True` for underlined text.
- `lfStrikeOut`—Set `True` for strikeout text.
- `lfCharSet`—Specifies the character set. Possible values include `ANSI_CHARSET`, `OEM_CHARSET`, or `SYMBOL_CHARSET`.
- `lfOutPrecision`—Defines how closely output must match the requested font.
- `lfClipPrecision`—Defines clipping precision.
- `lfQuality`—The quality of the output font. Possible values include `PROOF_QUALITY`, `DRAFT_QUALITY`, or `DEFAULT_QUALITY`.
- `lfPitchAndFamily`—Defines the pitch and style of the font. The low-order bits specify the pitch of the font and can be one of the following: `DEFAULT_PITCH`, `FIXED_PITCH`, or `VARIABLE_PITCH`.
- `lfFaceName`—This is a 32-character field for the font name. Your program can use font names to enable a user to select the font by name. Here is a list of the face names for fonts included with Windows 3.1:

Ariel	Courier
Courier New	Helvetica
Modern	Roman
Script	Symbol
System	Terminal
Tms Rmn	Times New Roman
WingDings	

To create a font, your program should set the desired fields in the logical font record and call `CreateFontIndirect`. The routine returns a handle to a font. You then use the `SelectFont` routine to make the font the one currently selected in the display context.

Remember this important point about using logical fonts: they must be deleted when your program ends. You use the `DeleteFont` function to do the job, as follows:

```
DeleteFont(hFont);
```

This call frees the memory used by the font and lets the system use it for other purposes. This is similar to deleting a pen or a brush.

It is important to remember that when you create a font, Windows returns a font that's as close as possible to the font you request. You have no guarantee, however, that it will be exactly the same one. The exception to this rule occurs when you use TrueType fonts, because the TrueType fonts exist in every size possible. Therefore, if your program uses TrueType fonts, the font created is nearly identical to the one you requested.

The Font Common Dialog

One of the common dialogs you learned about when you first looked at dialog boxes was the font selection dialog box (see Figure 16.3). The font common dialog box includes controls that enable the user to select a font, font style (such as bold, italic, or regular), a point size, and an effect (such as underline, strikeout, or a text color). One of the nice features of the dialog box is that its lower-right corner always shows the currently selected font. This gives the user visual feedback about the appearance of the font. This is an important feature of a graphical user environment such as Windows.

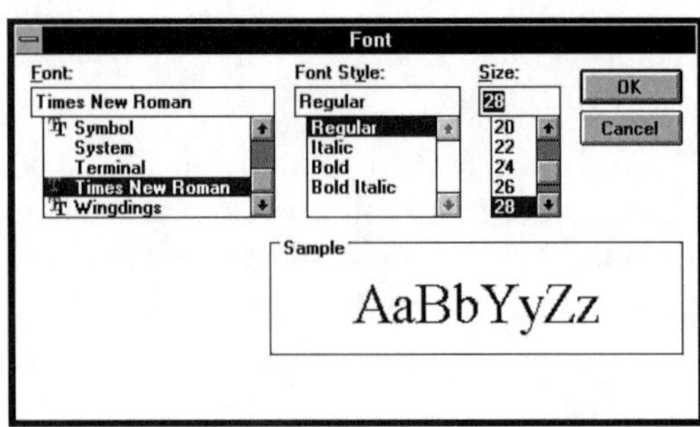

Figure 16.3.
The Choose Font common dialog box.

To use the font dialog box, an application must fill out the members of the CHOOSEFONT data structure. The program then calls the ChooseFont function. Remember to include the commdlg.h header file at the beginning of your program.

When the user makes a selection and presses OK, the lpLogFont field is filled with LOGFONT information. The program then can use the LOGFONT structure to create a font, select it into the device context, and use the text output routines to use the font.

Listing 16.3 shows an example of using the font common dialog box to select a font to display text. Listing 16.4 is the module definition file for the program.

Listing 16.3. Font demonstration program.

```
// FONT.C - Fonts demonstration program
//
// Programming Windows with Turbo C++ for Windows
// by Paul J. Perry

#define STRICT

#define IDM_FONT 100

#include <mem.h>
#include <windowsx.h>
#include <commdlg.h>


// Function Prototypes
LRESULT CALLBACK _export MainWndProc(HWND hWnd, UINT message,
                                     WPARAM wParam, LPARAM lParam);

void WMCommand_Handler(HWND hwnd, int id, HWND hwndCtl, UINT
                       codeNotify);

// Global Variables
LOGFONT CurrentFont;

/*******************************************/
#pragma argsused
int PASCAL WinMain(HINSTANCE hInstance, HINSTANCE hPrevInstance,
                   LPSTR lpCmdParam, int nCmdShow)
{
```

continues

Listing 16.3. continued

```
   char     ProgName[] = "Fonts Demo";
   HWND     hWnd;
   MSG      msg;
   HMENU    hMenu;

   if (!hPrevInstance)
   {
      WNDCLASS wndclass;

      wndclass.style         = CS_VREDRAW ¦ CS_HREDRAW;
      wndclass.lpfnWndProc   = (WNDPROC) MainWndProc;
      wndclass.hInstance     = hInstance;
      wndclass.hIcon         = LoadIcon(NULL, IDI_APPLICATION);
      wndclass.hCursor       = LoadCursor(NULL, IDC_ARROW);
      wndclass.hbrBackground = (HBRUSH) (COLOR_WINDOW + 1);
      wndclass.lpszMenuName  = NULL;
      wndclass.cbClsExtra    = 0;
      wndclass.cbWndExtra    = 0;
      wndclass.lpszClassName = ProgName;

      RegisterClass(&wndclass);
   }

   // Initialize current font to zero values.
   memset(&CurrentFont, 0, sizeof(LOGFONT));

   hMenu = CreateMenu();
   AppendMenu(hMenu, MF_STRING, IDM_FONT, "&Font...");

   hWnd = CreateWindow(ProgName, ProgName,
                       WS_OVERLAPPEDWINDOW,
                       CW_USEDEFAULT, CW_USEDEFAULT,
                       CW_USEDEFAULT, CW_USEDEFAULT,
                       NULL, hMenu, hInstance, NULL);

   ShowWindow(hWnd, nCmdShow);
   UpdateWindow(hWnd);

   while (GetMessage(&msg, NULL, 0, 0))
   {
      TranslateMessage(&msg);
      DispatchMessage(&msg);
   }
   return msg.wParam;
}
```

```
/*******************************************/
#pragma argsused
void WMCommand_Handler(HWND hWnd, int id, HWND hwndCtl, UINT
codeNotify)
{
   if (id == IDM_FONT)
   {
      CHOOSEFONT ChooseFnt;

      // Setup data structure for font common dialog

      memset(&ChooseFnt, 0, sizeof(CHOOSEFONT));

      ChooseFnt.hwndOwner    = hWnd;
      ChooseFnt.lpLogFont    = &CurrentFont;
      ChooseFnt.Flags        = CF_FORCEFONTEXIST ¦
                               \ CF_SCREENFONTS;
      ChooseFnt.nFontType    = SCREEN_FONTTYPE;
      ChooseFnt.lStructSize = sizeof(CHOOSEFONT);
      ChooseFont(&ChooseFnt);

      InvalidateRect(hWnd, NULL, TRUE);

   }
}

/*******************************************/
LRESULT CALLBACK _export MainWndProc(HWND hWnd, UINT message,
                                     WPARAM wParam, LPARAM lParam)
{
   switch (message)
   {
      case WM_PAINT :
      {
         HDC         PaintDC;
         RECT        rect;
         PAINTSTRUCT ps;
         HFONT       hFont, hOldFont;

         PaintDC = BeginPaint(hWnd, &ps);
         GetClientRect(hWnd, &rect);

         hFont = CreateFontIndirect(&CurrentFont);
         hOldFont = SelectFont(PaintDC, hFont);
```

continues

Listing 16.3. continued

```
            DrawText(PaintDC, "Now is the time for all good "
                     "Turbo C++ for Windows "
                     "Programmers to learn to use fonts",
                     -1, &rect, DT_WORDBREAK);

            SelectFont(PaintDC, hOldFont);
            DeleteFont(hFont);

            EndPaint(hWnd, &ps);
            return 0;
         }

         case WM_COMMAND :
         {
         return HANDLE_WM_COMMAND(hWnd, wParam, lParam,
                                  WMCommand_Handler);
         }

         case WM_DESTROY :
         {
            PostQuitMessage(0);
            return 0;
         }
      }
      return DefWindowProc (hWnd, message, wParam, lParam);
}
```

Listing 16.4. Module definition file.

```
;
; FONT.DEF module definition file
;

DESCRIPTION   'Font Demo'
EXETYPE       WINDOWS
STUB          'WINSTUB.EXE'
HEAPSIZE      8192
STACKSIZE     8192
CODE          PRELOAD MOVEABLE DISCARDABLE
DATA          PRELOAD MOVEABLE MULTIPLE
```

The program displays text in its main window by using the `DrawText` function (see Figure 16.4). You can choose the menu item for Fonts and select the type of font in which you want the text to be displayed. As soon as you choose a font and select OK, the dialog box closes and the text appears in the new font.

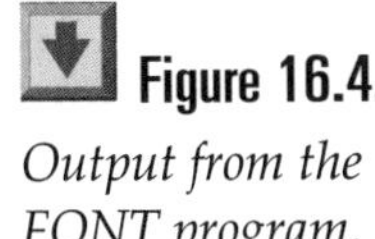

Figure 16.4.
Output from the FONT program.

Although this ends the discussion about using fonts, the topic is one of the most complex for programming in Windows. This is mainly because fonts have so many characteristics. In most cases, you don't need to use all the methods described in this section. Armed with the basic understanding of how to use fonts, you can spice up the visual effects of your Windows programs.

Using Bitmaps

I'm sure you have already seen bitmaps in a program. They are used all the time in Windows. A bitmap is binary information describing the bits that make up pixels on the screen. An application can use bitmaps to display pictures. A bitmap can be of any dimension and can consist of multiple colors.

Several bitmaps come standard with Windows (see Table 16.2) in the Windows subdirectory. You can create bitmaps in the PaintBrush application; while programming, however, use the Resource Toolkit bitmap editor to create bitmaps of different sizes. The bitmap editor gives you more control of the size of the resulting bitmap, and also enables you to work with the rest of your resources in one program.

Table 16.2. Bitmaps that come with Windows.

256color.bmp	arcade.bmp	arches.bmp	argyle.bmp	cars.bmp
castle.bmp	chess.bmp	chitz.bmp	egypt.bmp	flock.bmp
honey.bmp	leaves.bmp	marble.bmp	redbrick.bmp	rivets.bmp
squares.bmp	tartan.bmp	thatch.bmp	winlogo.bmp	zigzag.bmp

Bitmaps take the extension .BMP. You reference the .BMP file in your resource script, in the same way you reference a cursor or icon. For example, to use the bitmap named cars.bmp in your program, with the identifier `FASTCAR`, include a statement like this in your resource script (.RC file):

```
FASTCAR BITMAP "fastcar.bmp"
```

This statement associates the filename FASTCAR.BMP with the identifier `FASTCAR` in your program. The filename of the bitmap doesn't have to correspond to the identifier in any way. For example, you can use the following statement just as easily:

```
SUPERFASTCAR BITMAP "fastcar.bmp"
```

Usually, however, you want to associate descriptive identifiers with the appropriate bitmap filename.

To obtain a handle to the bitmap, you use the `LoadBitmap` function, specifying the instance of the program and the bitmap identifier. Here is an example:

```
HBITMAP hBitmap;
```

```
hBitmap = LoadBitmap(hInstance, "FASTCAR");
```

Your program now has a handle to the bitmap.

At this point, displaying a bitmap in the client area of a program becomes a little complicated. There's no function simply to display the bitmap in the client area of the window. A function such as

```
DrawBitmap(HDC hDC, HBITMAP hBitmap, int x, int y)  // Fictitious
```

would be ideal. With a function like this, you could specify the handle to the display context, the handle to the bitmap, and a starting `x` and `y` location to display the bitmap. However, no such function exists in Windows.

Instead, a program must go through a process of creating a compatible display context, selecting the bitmap into the compatible display context, copying the bitmap from one display context to the other, and then cleaning up afterwards by deleting the compatible display context and then deleting the bitmap. Examine these steps a little closer:

First, you use `LoadBitmap` to receive a handle to the bitmap.

```
hBitmap = LoadBitmap(ghInstance, "MYBITMAPNAME");
```

Next, you create a compatible display context with the statement

```
CompatDC = CreateCompatibleDC(PaintDC);
```

With a compatible display context created, you select the bitmap into it, with the following statement:

```
hOldBitmap = SelectBitmap(hCompatDC, hBitmap);
```

Finally, you use the `BitBlt`—which stands for bit block transfer—function to copy the bitmap from the source display context—the compatible DC—to the destination display context—the `PaintDC`. The statement looks something like

```
BitBlt(PaintDC, 0, 0, BitmapWidth, BitmapHeight,
       hCompatDC, 0, 0, SRCCOPY);
```

The last parameter is the raster operation (ROP) code to use for the copy. It defines how the GDI combines colors when it displays the bitmap in the destination display context. Some common values to use are in Table 16.3.

Table 16.3. Common ROP codes.

ROP Code	*Description*
`BLACKNESS`	Turns all output black.
`DSTINVERT`	Inverts the destination bitmap.
`MERGECOPY`	Combines the pattern and the source bitmap by using the Boolean AND operator.
`MERGEPAINT`	Combines the inverted source bitmap with the destination bitmap by using the Boolean OR operator.
`NOTSRCCOPY`	Copies the inverted source bitmap to the destination.
`NOTSRCERASE`	Inverts the result of combining the destination and source bitmaps by using the Boolean OR operator.
`PATCOPY`	Copies the pattern to the destination bitmap.
`PATINVERT`	Combines the destination bitmap with the pattern by using the Boolean XOR operator.
`PATPAINT`	Combines the inverted source bitmap with the pattern by using the Boolean OR operator. Combines the result of this operation with the destination bitmap by using the Boolean OR operator.
`SRCAND`	Combines pixels of the destination and source bitmaps by using the Boolean AND operator.
`SRCCOPY`	Copies the source bitmap to the destination bitmap.
`SRCERASE`	Inverts the destination bitmap and combines the result with the source bitmap by using the Boolean AND operator.
`SRCINVERT`	Combines pixels of the destination and source bitmaps by using the Boolean XOR operator.

ROP Code	*Description*
`SRCPAINT`	Combines pixels of the destination and source bitmaps by using the Boolean OR operator.
`WHITENESS`	Turns all output white.

Now that the image appears in the client area of your window, you must select the old bitmap back into the compatible display context before you can clean up. To do this, use the statement

```
SelectBitmap(hCompatDC, hOldBitmap);
```

Finally, to clean up you use the following commands:

```
DeleteDC(hCompatDC);
DeleteBitmap(hBitmap);
```

Although this may seem like a great deal of programming, consider trying to do this from inside a DOS program. Just the thought of having to work with bitmaps in a DOS program would require assembly language programming and would require much more code than is required here.

The Resource Workshop Bitmap Editor

Now that you have done the hard part of writing the code to access the bitmap, one thing is required: creating the bitmap. You use the Resource Workshop bitmap editor (what else did you expect to use?) to create bitmaps for your program.

To create a bitmap, start a new file in Resource Workshop by selecting File from the main menu and choosing the New option. When the dialog box asks for the type of file you want to create, choose a .BMP file (see Figure 16.5).

Before you start to create the bitmap, you must specify its attributes. This is done in the New Bitmap Attributes dialog box (see Figure 16.6). You specify the width and height of the bitmap in pixels, as well as how many colors the bitmap will contain. The bitmap editor appears when you enter appropriate dimensions for the bitmap. If you press Enter without specifying any values, default values are used.

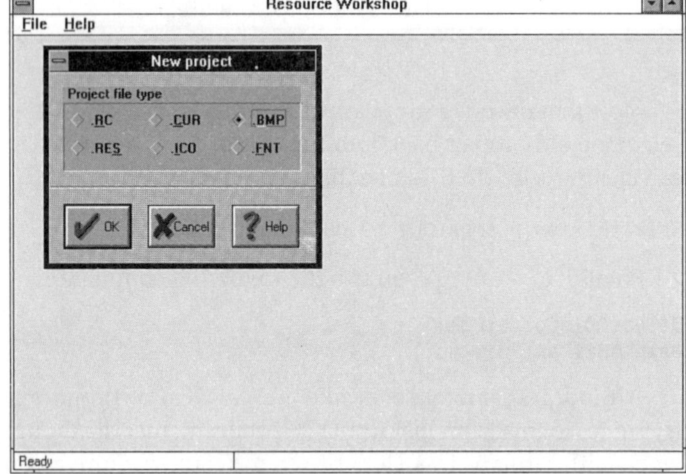

Figure 16.5.

The New project dialog box.

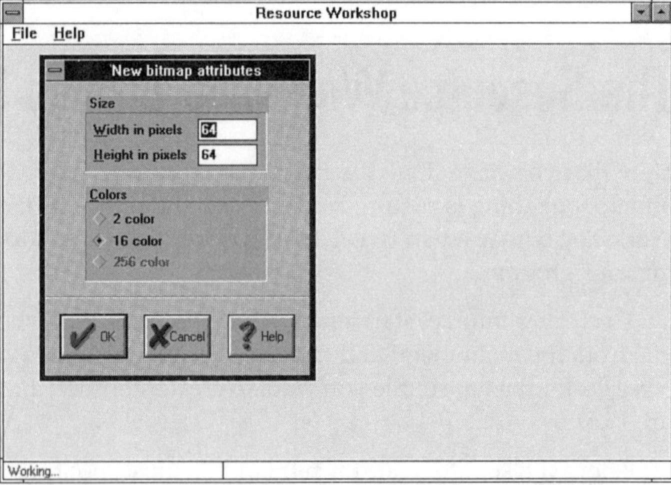

Figure 16.6.

The New bitmap attributes dialog box.

As soon as you enter appropriate attributes, the bitmap editor loads and you are ready to create your bitmap (see Figure 16.7). The bitmap editor is easy to use. It has tools similar to Windows Paintbrush that give you all the features of a paint program.

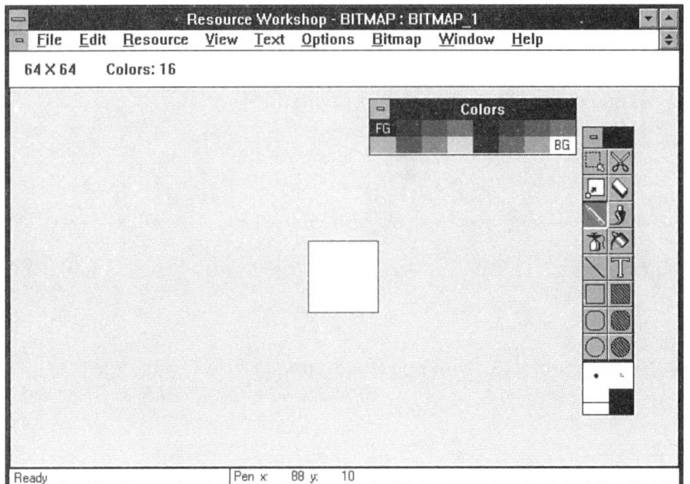

Figure 16.7.
The Resource Workshop bitmap editor.

You use the drawing tools palette on the right side of the screen along with the color palette to create your bitmap. If the bitmap is too big to be displayed in the Resource Workshop bitmap editor window, scroll bars attached to the window enable you to move into view the portion of the bitmap on which you want to work.

When you finish creating a bitmap for a program, you must choose the File menu and select Save As. At this time, you specify the filename of the bitmap. This is the filename you associate with the bitmap identifier in the resource script.

A Bitmap Example

Listing 16.5 shows a program that displays a bitmap in its client area (see Figure 16.8). Listing 16.6 contains the resource script, and Listing 16.7

contains the module definition file. To compile the program you also need a bitmap with the filename MYBITMAP.BMP.

Listing 16.5. BITMAP example program.

```
// BITMAP.C - Program to demonstrate displaying a
//             bitmap in client area of a program
//
// Programming Windows with Turbo C++ for Windows
// by Paul J. Perry


#define STRICT

#include <windowsx.h>


// Function Prototypes
LRESULT CALLBACK _export MainWndProc(HWND hWnd, UINT message,
                                     WPARAM wParam, LPARAM lParam);

// Global Variables
HINSTANCE ghInstance;


/********************************************/
#pragma argsused
int PASCAL WinMain(HINSTANCE hInstance, HINSTANCE hPrevInstance,
                   LPSTR lpCmdParam, int nCmdShow)
{
   char        ProgName[] = "Bitmap";
   HWND        hWnd;
   MSG         msg;


   if (!hPrevInstance)
   {
      WNDCLASS    wndclass;

      wndclass.style         = CS_VREDRAW ¦ CS_HREDRAW;
      wndclass.lpfnWndProc   = (WNDPROC) MainWndProc;
      wndclass.hInstance     = hInstance;
      wndclass.hIcon         = LoadIcon(NULL, IDI_APPLICATION);
      wndclass.hCursor       = LoadCursor(NULL, IDC_ARROW);
      wndclass.hbrBackground = (HBRUSH) (COLOR_WINDOW + 1);
      wndclass.lpszMenuName  = NULL;
```

```
      wndclass.cbClsExtra    = 0;
      wndclass.cbWndExtra    = 0;
      wndclass.lpszClassName = ProgName;

      RegisterClass(&wndclass);
   }

   ghInstance = hInstance;

   hWnd = CreateWindow(ProgName,"Display Bitmap Resource",
                       WS_OVERLAPPEDWINDOW,
                       CW_USEDEFAULT, CW_USEDEFAULT,
                       CW_USEDEFAULT, CW_USEDEFAULT,
                       NULL, NULL, hInstance, NULL);

   ShowWindow(hWnd, nCmdShow);
   UpdateWindow(hWnd);

   while (GetMessage(&msg, NULL, 0, 0))
   {
      TranslateMessage(&msg);
      DispatchMessage(&msg);
   }
   return msg.wParam;
}

/*******************************************/
LRESULT CALLBACK _export MainWndProc(HWND hWnd, UINT message,
                                     WPARAM wParam, LPARAM lParam)
{
   switch (message)
   {
      case WM_PAINT :
      {
         HDC          PaintDC, hCompatDC;
         RECT         rect;
         PAINTSTRUCT  ps;
         HBITMAP      hBitmap, hOldBitmap;
         BITMAP       BM;

         PaintDC = BeginPaint(hWnd, &ps);

         // Get width and height of client area
         GetClientRect(hWnd, &rect);

         // Get handle to the bitmap
         hBitmap = LoadBitmap(ghInstance, "MAINBITMAP");
```

continues

Listing 16.5. continued

```
         // Get dimensions of bitmap
         GetObject(hBitmap, sizeof(BM), &BM);

         // Create compatible display context
         hCompatDC = CreateCompatibleDC(PaintDC);

         // Select bitmap into the compataible DC
         hOldBitmap = SelectBitmap(hCompatDC, hBitmap);

         // Display bitmap in client area
         StretchBlt(PaintDC, 0, 0, rect.right, rect.bottom,
                    hCompatDC, 0, 0, BM.bmWidth, BM.bmHeight,
                    SRCCOPY);

         // De-select the bitmap
         SelectBitmap(hCompatDC, hOldBitmap);

         // Clean up after we are done
         DeleteDC(hCompatDC);
         DeleteBitmap(hBitmap);


         EndPaint(hWnd, &ps);
         return 0;
      }

      case WM_DESTROY :
      {
         PostQuitMessage(0);
         return 0;
      }
   }
   return DefWindowProc (hWnd, message, wParam, lParam);
}
```

Listing 16.6. BITMAP resource script.

```
MAINBITMAP BITMAP "mybitmap.bmp"
```

Listing 16.7. BITMAP module definition file.

```
;
; BITMAP.DEF module definition file
;

DESCRIPTION    'Bitmap Example'
NAME           BITMAP
EXETYPE        WINDOWS
STUB           'WINSTUB.EXE'
HEAPSIZE       8192
STACKSIZE      8192
CODE           PRELOAD MOVEABLE DISCARDABLE
DATA           PRELOAD MOVEABLE MULTIPLE
```

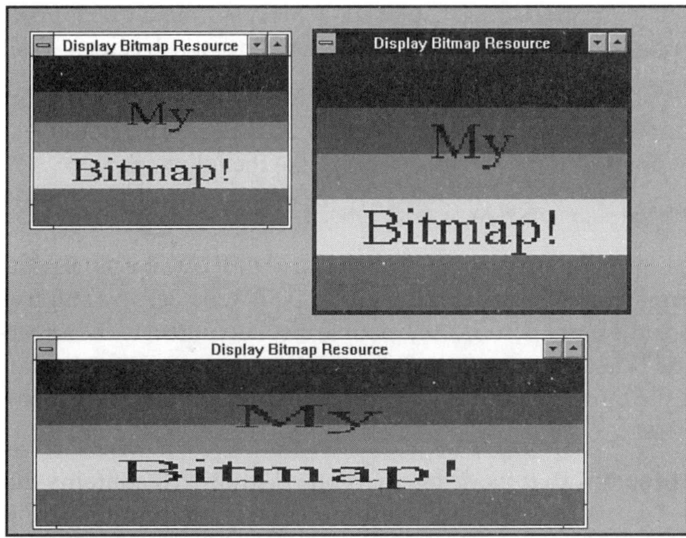

Figure 16.8.
BITMAP program output.

Notice, no matter what size the window is, the bitmap is made to fit in that area. If the client area is larger, the bitmap is displayed larger.

The most important routine in the code is the `StretchBlt` function. It is used instead of `Bitblt` to copy a bitmap. It also stretches the bitmap to fit in the destination display context. It moves a bitmap from a source rectangle to a destination rectangle, stretching or compressing the bitmap as necessary to fit the new dimensions.

Besides using the `StretchBlt` function instead of `Bitblt`, the steps you follow in the program are pretty much identical to the steps described earlier.

Creating a Splash Screen

Consider another way to use bitmaps in your programs. You have probably noticed that when you load the Turbo C++ for Windows IDE, the Turbo C++ for Windows logo is displayed in a nice bitmap. This effect is usually referred to as a splash screen.

The splash screen is a bitmap that is displayed on the screen before the main window of your program is displayed. When your main overlapped window is displayed, it overwrites the area where the splash screen was.

To display the splash screen before the main window is created, you must get a display context in `WinMain`. Instead of using `GetDC`, you use a function called `CreateDC`. The statement looks like the following:

```
hDesktopDC = CreateDC("DISPLAY", NULL, NULL, NULL);
```

This creates a handle to a display context called `DISPLAY`. It enables you to output information anywhere on the desktop. Otherwise, you still use `BitBlt` to transfer the bitmap from a compatible display context to the screen display context. That is, you load the bitmap, create a compatible display context, select the bitmap into the compatible display context, `Bitblt` the bitmap to the `DISPLAY` context, and then clean up.

Look at a program that uses this method. Listing 16.8 contains the C source code. Listing 16.9 contains the resource script, and Listing 16.10 contains the module definition file.

Listing 16.8. The SPLASH example program.

```
// SPLASH.C - Display splash screen
//
// Programming Windows with Turbo C++ for Windows
// by Paul J. Perry
```

```
#define STRICT

#include <windowsx.h>


// Function Prototypes
LRESULT CALLBACK _export MainWndProc(HWND hWnd, UINT message,
                                     WPARAM wParam, LPARAM lParam);

/*******************************************/
#pragma argsused
int PASCAL WinMain(HINSTANCE hInstance, HINSTANCE hPrevInstance,
                   LPSTR lpCmdParam, int nCmdShow)
{
   char      ProgName[] = "Display a Splash Screen";
   HWND      hWnd;
   MSG       msg;

   int       cX, cY;
   HBITMAP   hBitmap, hOldBitmap;
   HDC       hDesktopDC, hCompatDC;
   BITMAP    BM;

   if (!hPrevInstance)
   {
      WNDCLASS    wndclass;

      wndclass.style         = CS_VREDRAW | CS_HREDRAW;
      wndclass.lpfnWndProc   = (WNDPROC) MainWndProc;
      wndclass.hInstance     = hInstance;
      wndclass.hIcon         = LoadIcon(NULL, IDI_APPLICATION);
      wndclass.hCursor       = LoadCursor(NULL, IDC_ARROW);
      wndclass.hbrBackground = (HBRUSH) (COLOR_WINDOW + 1);
      wndclass.lpszMenuName  = NULL;
      wndclass.cbClsExtra    = 0;
      wndclass.cbWndExtra    = 0;
      wndclass.lpszClassName = ProgName;

      RegisterClass(&wndclass);
   }

   hWnd = CreateWindow(ProgName, ProgName,
                       WS_OVERLAPPEDWINDOW,
                       CW_USEDEFAULT, CW_USEDEFAULT,
                       CW_USEDEFAULT, CW_USEDEFAULT,
                       NULL, NULL, hInstance, NULL);
```

continues

Listing 16.8. continued

```
// The following code allows us to create a "splash screen".
//   First, get a handle to the bitmap.
hBitmap = LoadBitmap(hInstance,"SPLASH");

// Then, we nead to get a display context to the screen.
//   This allows us to display our bitmap.
hDesktopDC = CreateDC("DISPLAY", NULL, NULL, NULL);

// Get information about the bitmap.  Most importantly, we
//   want information about the width and height.
GetObject(hBitmap, sizeof(BM), &BM);

// Find out the size of the desktop.  Then calculate the center
//   of the desktop, so that the bitmap can be
//   centered correctly,
//   no matter what type of driver the user is running.
//
cX = (GetSystemMetrics(SM_CXSCREEN) / 2) - (BM.bmWidth  / 2);
cY = (GetSystemMetrics(SM_CYSCREEN) / 2) - (BM.bmHeight / 2);

// Now, it is time to copy the bitmap to the display.
//
hCompatDC = CreateCompatibleDC(hDesktopDC);

hOldBitmap = SelectBitmap(hCompatDC, hBitmap);

BitBlt(hDesktopDC, cX, cY, BM.bmWidth, BM.bmHeight,
       hCompatDC, 0, 0, SRCCOPY);

// Clean up after displaying the splash screen.
//
SelectBitmap(hCompatDC, hOldBitmap);
DeleteBitmap(hBitmap);
DeleteDC(hCompatDC);
// Done displaying DeleteDC(hDesktopDC); splash screen.


ShowWindow(hWnd, nCmdShow);
UpdateWindow(hWnd);

while (GetMessage(&msg, NULL, 0, 0))
{
   TranslateMessage(&msg);
   DispatchMessage(&msg);
}
```

```
   return msg.wParam;
}

/*******************************************/
LRESULT CALLBACK _export MainWndProc(HWND hWnd, UINT message,
                                     WPARAM wParam, LPARAM lParam)
{
   switch (message)
   {
      case WM_PAINT :
      {
         HDC         PaintDC;
      RECT        rect;
         PAINTSTRUCT ps;

         PaintDC = BeginPaint(hWnd, &ps);
         GetClientRect(hWnd, &rect);

         DrawText(PaintDC, "Did you see the splash screen?",
                  -1, &rect, DT_SINGLELINE ¦ DT_CENTER ¦ DT_VCENTER);

         EndPaint(hWnd, &ps);
         return 0;
      }

      case WM_DESTROY :
      {
         PostQuitMessage(0);
         return 0;
      }
   }
   return DefWindowProc (hWnd, message, wParam, lParam);
}
```

Listing 16.9. The SPLASH resource script.

```
SPLASH BITMAP "mybitmap.bmp"
```

Listing 16.10. The module definition file.

```
;
; SPLASH.DEF module definition file
;

DESCRIPTION    'Displaying a Splash Screen'
NAME           SPLASH
EXETYPE        WINDOWS
STUB           'WINSTUB.EXE'
HEAPSIZE       8192
STACKSIZE      8192
CODE           PRELOAD MOVEABLE DISCARDABLE
DATA           PRELOAD MOVEABLE MULTIPLE
```

The technique of a splash screen works best when you have a large program that takes a while to load. On a small program like the example, you need to keep your eyes open to see the splash screen.

Before it displays bitmap, the program also locates the center of the screen. This is better than using constants in your program. It ensures the bitmap is always displayed in the center of the screen, whether you are using a regular VGA 640x480 adapter or a super VGA in 1268x1024 resolution.

What You Have Learned

You've looked at many techniques in this chapter. You first examined metafiles and how to use them in programs. You learned how to use different fonts in your program in conjunction with the Choose Font common dialog box. You then took a look at another type of resource called a bitmap. You saw how to create bitmaps in the bitmap editor and how to use those bitmaps in your program with the `StretchBlt` routine.

Here is a summary of the topics covered in this chapter:

- A metafile is used to store a series of GDI commands and play them back later. The best use of a metafile is when you have a specific image that must be redisplayed repeatedly.

- There are two types of metafiles, memory metafiles and disk metafiles. Memory metafiles execute quicker but use more system resources. Disk-based metafiles take longer to play back, but are more permanent.
- Windows provides predefined stock fonts that your program can use at any time with the `GetStockObject` and `SelectObject` Windows routines to select the appropriate font into the current display context.
- To create a specific font, you must fill out the members of a `LOGFONT` data structure to specify exactly which font you want. You then make a request to Windows for the specified font. Windows returns a handle to a font that's as close as possible to what was originally specified. If you use the return value from the Choose Font common dialog box, you can be sure the font is available.
- A bitmap is a resource your program can use to store pictures and images.
- The Resource Workshop bitmap editor can be used to create bitmaps. You must then associate the bitmap to an identifier in your resource script before you can access the bitmap in your program.
- To use a bitmap in the program, you must go through the process of creating a compatible display context, selecting the bitmap into the compatible display context, copying the bitmap from one display context to the other (using the `BitBlt` or `StretchBlt` functions), and then cleaning up afterward by deleting the compatible display context and then deleting the bitmap.

17

USING THE MULTIPLE DOCUMENT INTERFACE

IN THIS CHAPTER

- Basic definitions relating to the MDI.
- Several examples of MDIs that you have already used.
- What a frame window is and how it relates to child windows.
- What Window classes must be registered in order to use the MDI.
- How to create the main window frame of an MDI application.
- What a modified message loop looks like in an MDI application.
- How a frame window procedure differs from that of a main overlapped window.
- What the child window procedure is used for.
- How to respond to menu commands located on the Window menu.
- How to simplify programs that use the MDI by using the ObjectWindows Library.

The Multiple Document Interface (MDI) is an interface standard that enables the user to work with multiple documents within a single application. This chapter examines how to use the MDI in your C and C++ programs. You learn about class registration, the updated message loop, and the structure of the MDI application. You also discover what objects to derive from in your programs based on the ObjectWindows Library (OWL).

About the MDI

The MDI is a standard way to write applications in which one master window holds a number of child windows. The child windows may be different documents, different views of the same documents, or different images.

One application that uses the MDI is the Turbo C++ for Windows Integrated Development Environment (IDE). (See Figure 17.1). Many other common programs also use the MDI, including Program Manager, Microsoft Word, and Quattro Pro for Windows.

For the MDI implementation in the IDE, the child windows hold a number of editor windows, project windows, and message windows all within the bounds of the main IDE window.

Figure 17.1.

The Turbo C++ for Windows MDI.

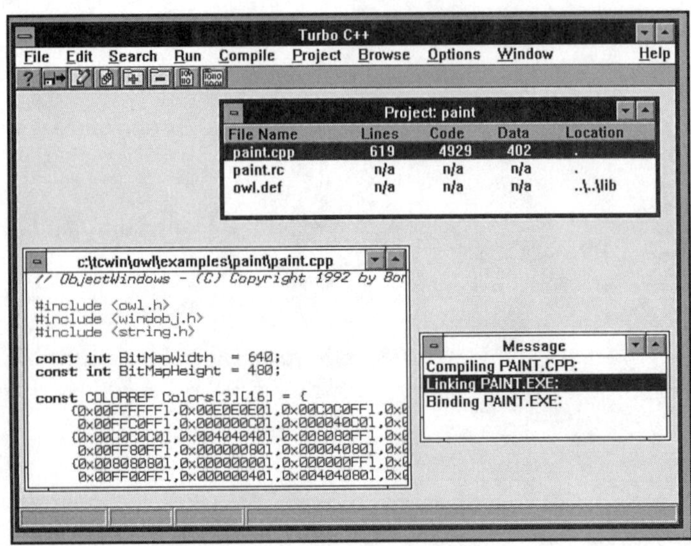

NOTE

Windows includes a handy application called System Configuration Editor (SYSEDIT.EXE). It allows you to edit the initialization files CONFIG.SYS, AUTOEXEC.BAT, WIN.INI, and SYSTEM.INI. By default, it is installed in the SYSTEM directory of Windows.

You do not see the system configuration editor in your Program Manager groups. It must be installed manually. To do so, go to the File menu and choose the New menu item. Then select the radio button for New Item. Finally, enter the filename C:\WINDOWS\SYSTEM\SYSEDIT.EXE in the Command line edit control. Press OK, and the item is added to Program Manager for future use.

Anatomy of an MDI Application

The main application window in an MDI application is called the workspace, or the frame window. The individual documents or views are displayed in separate child windows and are referred to as document windows.

The document windows also can be referred to by names that describe the contents of the windows as specified by the application using them, such as group windows (in Program Manager), directory windows (in File Manager), or spreadsheet windows (in Microsoft Excel). Figure 17.2 shows several open windows in Quattro Pro for Windows

Both the frame window and the child windows can have title bars, scroll bars, maximize and minimize buttons, and icons. One of the differences between the main window and child windows is that the child windows must remain within the boundaries of the frame window.

Figure 17.2.

The Quattro Pro for Windows MDI.

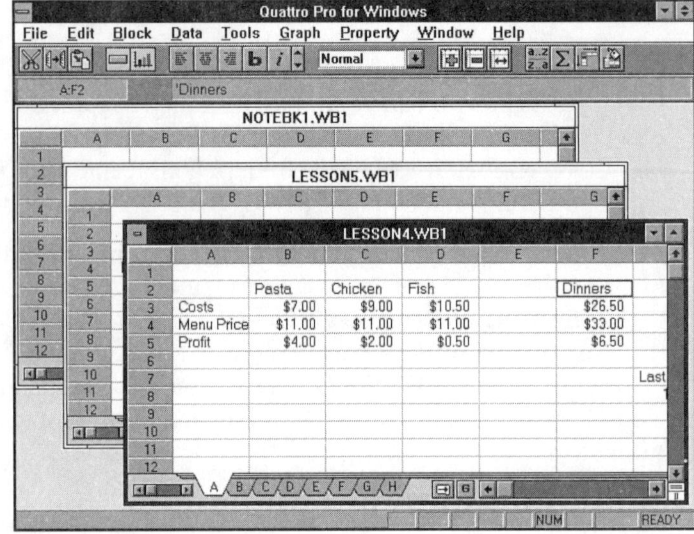

The Frame Window

The difference between a frame window and a normal main window is that the frame window's client area contains a special child known as an MDI client window. The Windows operating system controls the client window, which makes your design and coding effort easier.

To the user, the client window appears as part of the frame, and each child window appears as a separate window inside the frame window. The frame window always contains the main menu for the application.

The main window usually has a menu item called Window. It has items you can select to enable your program to display the child windows in a tiled (see Figure 17.3) and cascaded (see Figure 17.4) fashion. You also can arrange the icons so they appear in a row at the lower-left corner of the application (see Figure 17.5). Finally, the Window menu grows each time a child window is created, enabling the user to make a specific child window active instantly.

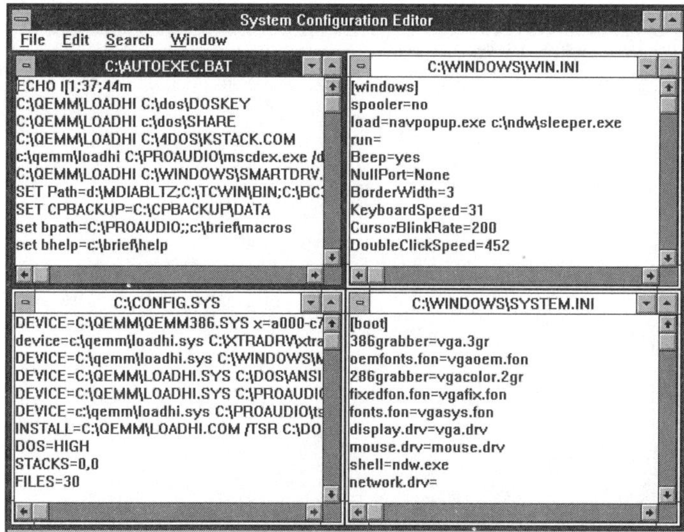

Figure 17.3.

The child windows of System Editor tiled.

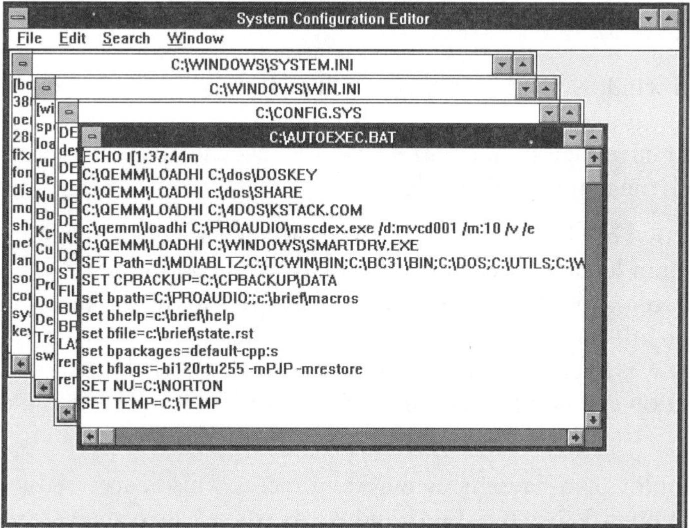

Figure 17.4.

The child windows of System Editor cascaded.

Figure 17.5.

The icons of System Editor arranged in a row.

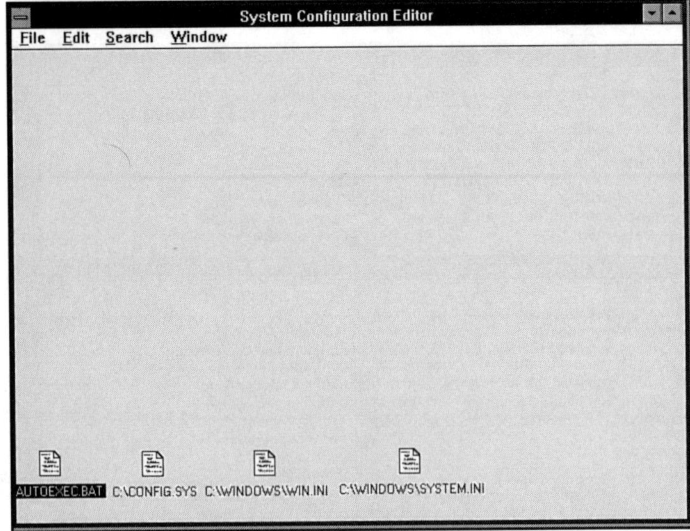

The Child Windows

Only one child window is active at any one time. It is indicated by a highlighted title bar and appears in front of all other child windows. Child windows don't have their own menu. They must use the menu selections associated with the main frame window.

Child windows can be minimized. In that case, they appear as a unique icon at the bottom-left corner of the frame window. A child window usually uses a different icon than the main application. If the child window is maximized, the title bar of the child window disappears, and the name of the child window is appended to the application name in the main title bar. The restore button appears directly below the restore button for the frame window.

A child window can have its own system menu. This is accessed by pressing Alt-hyphen. When the child window is restored, its system menu appears below the main system menu for the application. To close a child window, you press Ctrl-F4. Ctrl-F6 is used to switch between child windows in the main frame window.

Now that you understand the important components of a program that uses the MDI, examine the basic steps involved in actually creating a program that utilizes the MDI.

Creating an MDI Application

The initialization section of `WinMain` is one area of difference between programs that use the MDI and regular Windows applications. Although the process is similar, the MDI requires your application to set certain values in the window's class structure. You must also register a class for both the main window and any child windows in the program.

Additionally, your program must handle the menu items associated with the child windows (Tile, Cascade, and Arrange icons, and to Close all). Coding these menu commands are not too difficult because Windows provides messages you can send to carry out the associated task. Your program just needs to trap the menu command and then send the appropriate message.

Window Class Registration

There are a minimum of two window classes that must be registered. First, the MDI frame must be registered. This class is similar to any other main window class. The second class that must be registered is the window class used for child windows in the MDI.

An application can have more than one window class for MDI child windows if there's more than one type of document available in the application. Then, a child window class must be registered for each document type.

There are several differences between the window class for child windows and normal windows. The class structure for child windows differs from the class structure for normal windows in the following ways:

- An icon is necessary for the class structure. The user can minimize a child window as though it is a normal application. To demonstrate, you can use the built-in `IDI_APPLICATION` icon; however, in a full application, you want to use a custom icon referenced in your resource script.
- Always set the menu name to `NULL`. The MDI does not require child windows to have their own menus.

- The class structure may leave extra bytes available in the window structure. This allows the application to associate related data, such as a filename with a particular child window.

As in a regular Windows program, applications usually register the window classes only if they are the first instance of the program being executed. Here is an example of the class registration for a typical MDI application:

```
if (!hPrevInstance)
{
   WNDCLASS    wndclass;

   // Setup class information for frame window class
   wndclass.style          = CS_VREDRAW ¦ CS_HREDRAW;
   wndclass.lpfnWndProc    = (WNDPROC) FrameWndProc;
   wndclass.hInstance      = hInstance;
   wndclass.hIcon          = LoadIcon(NULL, IDI_APPLICATION);
   wndclass.hCursor        = LoadCursor(NULL, IDC_ARROW);
   wndclass.hbrBackground = (HBRUSH) (COLOR_WINDOW + 1);
   wndclass.lpszMenuName  = "MAINMENU";
   wndclass.cbClsExtra    = 0;
   wndclass.cbWndExtra    = 0;
   wndclass.lpszClassName = szFrame;

   RegisterClass(&wndclass);  // Register frame class

   // Setup class information for MDI child window class
   wndclass.style          = CS_VREDRAW ¦ CS_HREDRAW;
   wndclass.lpfnWndProc    = (WNDPROC) MDIChildWndProc;
   wndclass.hIcon          = LoadIcon(NULL, IDI_APPLICATION);
   wndclass.hCursor        = LoadCursor(NULL, IDC_ARROW);
   wndclass.hbrBackground = (HBRUSH) (COLOR_WINDOW + 1);
   wndclass.lpszMenuName  = NULL;
   wndclass.cbClsExtra    = 0;
   wndclass.cbWndExtra    = sizeof(LOCALHANDLE);
   wndclass.lpszClassName = szChild;

   RegisterClass(&wndclass);  // Register MDI child class

}
```

Notice, two classes are registered. The first one is the frame window class. Compare this to the main overlapped window in a normal Windows application. The second class is the child window class. If your program has several different types of child windows, a class must be registered for each one.

Creating the Windows

When your application has registered the appropriate window classes, you can create its windows. As always, you use the CreateWindow function to create the frame window. Next, you create the child windows. Your program creates a single child window when it is first started.

You must also create the client window. This usually is done in response to the WM_CREATE message. The client window is created with the CreateWindow function. You specify MDICLIENT as the client window's class name. It is a class preregistered by Windows to provide client window processing capabilities.

When you create the client window, set the last parameter of lParam to point to a CLIENTCREATESTRUCT data structure. It contains two fields. The first is a handle to the menu that has the child window names added to it (usually the Window menu). The other parameter is the identifier to give to the first MDI child window created.

This is how you can create the client window for your program:

```
CLIENTCREATESTRUCT ccs;

ccs.hWindowMenu  = GetSubMenu(GetMenu(hWnd), 1); // "Window" menu

ccs.idFirstChild = ID_FIRSTCHILD;

hMDIClientWnd = CreateWindow("MDICLIENT", NULL,
                WS_CHILD ¦ WS_CLIPCHILDREN ¦ WS_VISIBLE,
                0, 0, 0, 0, hWnd, 0, ghInstance,
                (LPSTR)&ccs);

ShowWindow(hMDIClientWnd, SW_SHOW);
```

One of the elements of the CLIENTCREATESTRUCT is a handle to the Window menu. This information must be passed to Windows, because as new child windows are created, a menu option is added (by Windows) to the Window menu. This option enables the user to immediately make the specified child window active.

You can pass any valid menu handle to the structure member. However, the Microsoft guidelines for the MDI specify that the Window menu is to list the currently open child windows.

Modifying the Main Message Loop

The main message loops for programs based on the MDI and for regular Windows applications are quite similar. However, there are some differences.

A program based on the MDI uses the `TranslateMDISysAccel` function to translate child window accelerator keys. This allows the processing of the child window's system menu. The following sample shows what the new message looks like in a MDI application:

```
while (GetMessage(&msg, NULL, 0, 0))
{
   if(!TranslateMDISysAccel(hMDIClientWnd, &msg))
   {
      TranslateMessage(&msg);
      DispatchMessage(&msg);
   }
}
```

The Frame Window Procedure

A regular Windows program usually has at least one main window procedure. The frame window procedure replaces this in a program based on the MDI.

The window procedure for a program based on the MDI passes all messages to the `DefFrameProc()` function. This is different from regular Windows programs, which pass messages to the default window procedure, or `DefWindowProc`.

The `DefFrameProc()` function handles the `WM_SIZE` messages by resizing the client window to fit in the new client area of the frame window. It also takes care of responding to the `WM_SETFOCUS` message by setting the focus to the active child window.

The Child Window Procedure

The child window procedure handles processing messages associated with the child window. There is usually one child window procedure for each type of child window class in your application.

Messages you do not process in the child window procedure must be passed to the `DefMDIChildProc()` default child window procedure. This handles all the messages in a default manner, similar to `DefWindowProc()`.

Child Window Creation

Child windows usually are created in response to the user selecting a menu item and are created differently than most windows.

Rather than use the `CreateWindow` function, you send a `WM_MDICREATE` message to the client window. The `lParam` parameter of this message is set a far pointer to a `MDICREATESTRUCT` data structure. This structure contains fields that enable you to specify information about the child windows.

When you fill out the `MDICREATESTRUCT` data members, you specify the class name, the instance of the application creating the child windows, the location within the frame window, and the style of the child windows.

The following example shows how to create child windows in a program that uses the MDI:

```
HWND hWnd;
MDICREATESTRUCT mcs;

mcs.szClass  = szChild;
mcs.hOwner   = ghInstance;
mcs.x        = CW_USEDEFAULT;
mcs.y        = CW_USEDEFAULT;
mcs.cx       = CW_USEDEFAULT;
mcs.cy       = CW_USEDEFAULT;
mcs.style    = CS_VREDRAW ¦ CS_HREDRAW;
```

```
hWnd = (HWND)SendMessage(hMDIClientWnd, WM_MDICREATE, 0,
                         (LONG)(LPMDICREATESTRUCT)&mcs);

ShowWindow(hWnd, SW_SHOW);
```

Notice that you can specify certain window creation attributes, including the class name, the beginning x and y coordinates, the width (cx), the height (cy), and the window style.

Closing All Child Windows

To destroy a child window, you use the WM_MDIDESTROY message. You must specify the child window's hWnd so that the system can tell which window to destroy.

You can use code such as this:

```
SendMessage(hMDIClientWnd, WM_MDIDESTROY, (WORD)hWndTemp, 0L);
```

If you want to close all the open child windows, you must create a while loop that looks for any child windows that may still be open. It then closes each window. The following code fragment shows an example of how this can be done:

```
hWndTemp = GetWindow(hMDIClientWnd, GW_CHILD);

while (hWndTemp)
{
   hWndTemp = GetWindow(hMDIClientWnd, GW_CHILD);

      while(hWndTemp && GetWindow(hWndTemp, GW_OWNER))
         hWndTemp = GetWindow(hWndTemp, GW_HWNDNEXT);

      if (hWndTemp)
         SendMessage(hMDIClientWnd, WM_MDIDESTROY, (WORD)hWndTemp,
                 0L);
      else
         break;
}
```

Responding to the Windows Menu Item

The Windows interface design guide states that programs based on the MDI have a main menu item titled Window. It provides commands that enable the user to rearrange child windows. Different styles in which child windows can be rearranged include cascading, tiling, and aligning icons.

Windows provides messages that make processing these menu items easy. Table 17.1 shows the Windows message, along with the menu item the user selects to carry out the specified functionality.

Table 17.1. Windows arrangement of menu items and associated messages.

Message	*Menu Command*
WM_MDITITLE	Window | Tile
WM_MDICASCADE	Window | Cascade
WM_MDIICONARRANGE	Window | Arrange Icons

Using the messages is just a matter of sending the appropriate message to the client window. An example of arranging icons follows:

```
case IDM_ARRANGE :
{
   SendMessage(hMDIClientWnd, WM_MDIICONARRANGE, 0, 0L);
   break;
}
```

It's nice that the designers of Windows decided to add these messages. It makes it a lot easier to implement the MDI when some of the major functionality is taken care of.

Now that you have gone through all the elements of a program that uses the MDI, look at an example program. Listing 17.1 is the C source code for such a program. Listing 17.2 is the resource script for the program. Listing 17.3 is the module definition file, and Listing 17.4 is the header file. Figure 17.6 shows the output of the program.

Listing 17.1. Example MDI program.

```
// MINMDI.C - Minimum Windows MDI C Program
//
// Programming Windows with Turbo C++ for Windows
// by Paul J. Perry

#define STRICT

#include <windowsx.h>

#include "minmdi.h"

// Function Prototypes
LRESULT CALLBACK _export FrameWndProc(HWND hWnd, UINT message,
                           WPARAM wParam, LPARAM lParam);

LRESULT CALLBACK _export MDIChildWndProc(HWND hWnd, UINT message,
                           WPARAM wParam, LPARAM lParam);

HWND FAR PASCAL MakeNewChild (char *pName);

void CloseAllChildren(void);

void WMCommand_Handler(HWND hwnd, int id, HWND hwndCtl, UINT
                       codeNotify);


// Global Variables
HINSTANCE ghInstance;

char szFrame[] = "frame";
char szChild[] = "child";

HWND hFrameWnd = NULL;
HWND hMDIClientWnd = NULL;
HMENU hFrameMenu;



/*******************************************/
#pragma argsused
int PASCAL WinMain(HINSTANCE hInstance, HINSTANCE hPrevInstance,
                   LPSTR lpCmdParam, int nCmdShow)
{
   MSG         msg;

   ghInstance = hInstance;
```

```
if (!hPrevInstance)
{
   WNDCLASS    wndclass;

   // Setup class information for frame window class
   wndclass.style          = CS_VREDRAW ¦ CS_HREDRAW;
   wndclass.lpfnWndProc    = (WNDPROC) FrameWndProc;
   wndclass.hInstance      = hInstance;
   wndclass.hIcon          = LoadIcon(NULL, IDI_APPLICATION);
   wndclass.hCursor        = LoadCursor(NULL, IDC_ARROW);
   wndclass.hbrBackground  = (HBRUSH) (COLOR_WINDOW + 1);
   wndclass.lpszMenuName   = "MAINMENU";
   wndclass.cbClsExtra     = 0;
   wndclass.cbWndExtra     = 0;
   wndclass.lpszClassName  = szFrame;

   RegisterClass(&wndclass);  // Register frame class

   // Setup class information for MDI child window class
   wndclass.style          = CS_VREDRAW ¦ CS_HREDRAW;
   wndclass.lpfnWndProc    = (WNDPROC) MDIChildWndProc;
   wndclass.hIcon          = LoadIcon(NULL, IDI_APPLICATION);
   wndclass.hCursor        = LoadCursor(NULL, IDC_ARROW);
   wndclass.hbrBackground  = (HBRUSH) (COLOR_WINDOW + 1);
   wndclass.lpszMenuName   = NULL;
   wndclass.cbClsExtra     = 0;
   wndclass.cbWndExtra     = sizeof(LOCALHANDLE);
   wndclass.lpszClassName  = szChild;

   RegisterClass(&wndclass);  // Register MDI child class

}

// Create frame window
hFrameWnd = CreateWindow(szFrame, "MDI Demo Program",
                         WS_OVERLAPPEDWINDOW ¦ WS_CLIPCHILDREN,
                         CW_USEDEFAULT, CW_USEDEFAULT,
                         CW_USEDEFAULT, CW_USEDEFAULT,
                         NULL, NULL, hInstance, NULL);


// Create initial child window
if (hFrameWnd && hMDIClientWnd)
{
   ShowWindow(hFrameWnd, nCmdShow);
   UpdateWindow(hFrameWnd);
   MakeNewChild("First Window");
}
```

continues

Listing 17.1. continued

```
   // Message loop has been modified
   while (GetMessage(&msg, NULL, 0, 0))
   {
      if(!TranslateMDISysAccel(hMDIClientWnd, &msg))
      {
         TranslateMessage(&msg);
         DispatchMessage(&msg);
      }
   }

   return msg.wParam;
}

/*******************************************/
LRESULT CALLBACK _export FrameWndProc(HWND hWnd, UINT message,
                                      WPARAM wParam, LPARAM lParam)
{
   switch (message)
   {
      case WM_CREATE :
      {
         CLIENTCREATESTRUCT ccs;

         // Must create client window first.
         //
         // The first item points to the menu which will
         // have the child menu titles added to it.
         ccs.hWindowMenu  = GetSubMenu(GetMenu(hWnd), 1);
         // The next item, is the identifier to give to
         // the first child window.
         ccs.idFirstChild = IDM_WINDOWCHILD;

         // Create the client window.
         hMDIClientWnd = CreateWindow("MDICLIENT", NULL,
                              WS_CHILD | WS_CLIPCHILDREN |
                              WS_VISIBLE, 0, 0, 0, 0, hWnd, 0,
                              ghInstance, (LPSTR)&ccs);

         ShowWindow(hMDIClientWnd, SW_SHOW);

         return 0;
      }

      case WM_COMMAND :
      {
```

```
            return HANDLE_WM_COMMAND(hWnd, wParam, lParam,
                                    WMCommand_Handler);
        }

        case WM_CLOSE :
        {
            DestroyWindow(hWnd);
            return 0;
        }

        case WM_DESTROY :
        {
            PostQuitMessage(0);
            return 0;
        }
    }

    // Use the default frame handler rather than
    // the default window procedure.
    return DefFrameProc (hWnd, hMDIClientWnd, message, wParam,
                         lParam);
}

/*******************************************/
#pragma argsused
void WMCommand_Handler(HWND hWnd, int id, HWND hwndCtl, UINT
                       codeNotify)
{

    // Most of the menu commands can be taken care of by
    // windows by sending messages to the client window.
    //
    switch(id)
    {
        case IDM_NEW:        // Display another MDI child window
        {
            MakeNewChild("Another Window");
            break;
        }

        case IDM_EXIT :      // Exit program
        {
            SendMessage(hWnd, WM_CLOSE, 0, 0L);
            break;
        }

        case IDM_TILE :      // Tile child windows
        {
```

continues

Listing 17.1. continued

```
            SendMessage(hMDIClientWnd, WM_MDITILE, 0, 0L);
            break;
         }

         case IDM_CASCADE :    // Cascade child windows
         {
            SendMessage(hMDIClientWnd, WM_MDICASCADE, 0, 0L);
            break;
         }

         case IDM_ARRANGE :    // Arrange icons at bottom of
         {                     // frame window.
            SendMessage(hMDIClientWnd, WM_MDIICONARRANGE, 0, 0L);
            break;

         }

         case IDM_CLOSEALL :  // Close all the child windows.
         {
            CloseAllChildren();
            break;
         }

         // If we don't use the WM_COMMAND messages, we must
         // pass them on to the default frame procedure.
         //
         default :
         {
            DefFrameProc(hWnd, hMDIClientWnd, WM_COMMAND, id, 0L);
         }

      }
}


/*******************************************/
LRESULT CALLBACK _export MDIChildWndProc(HWND hWnd, UINT message,
                           WPARAM wParam, LPARAM lParam)
{
   // This is the window procedure for the MDI child
   // windows.  Any functionality for each child
   // would be added in this function.
   //
   switch(message)
   {
```

```
      case WM_PAINT :
      {
         HDC PaintDC;
         PAINTSTRUCT ps;

         PaintDC = BeginPaint(hWnd, &ps);

         TextOut(PaintDC, 5, 5, "MDI Child Window", 16);

         EndPaint(hWnd, &ps);

         return 0;
      }
   }

   return DefMDIChildProc(hWnd, message, wParam, lParam);
}


/*******************************************/
HWND FAR PASCAL MakeNewChild (char *pName)
{
   HWND hWnd;
   MDICREATESTRUCT mcs;

   // This function creates a new child window.

   if (!pName)
      mcs.szTitle = "No Title";
   else
      mcs.szTitle = (LPSTR)pName;

   mcs.szClass  = szChild;
   mcs.hOwner   = ghInstance;
   mcs.x        = CW_USEDEFAULT;
   mcs.y        = CW_USEDEFAULT;
   mcs.cx       = CW_USEDEFAULT;
   mcs.cy       = CW_USEDEFAULT;
   mcs.style    = CS_VREDRAW ¦ CS_HREDRAW;

   hWnd = (HWND)SendMessage(hMDIClientWnd, WM_MDICREATE, 0,
                         (LONG)(LPMDICREATESTRUCT)&mcs);

   ShowWindow(hWnd, SW_SHOW);

   return hWnd;

}
```

continues

Listing 17.1. continued

```
/*******************************************/
void CloseAllChildren(void)
{
   HWND hWndTemp;

   // This function cycles through all the child
   // MDI windows and closes them.
   //
   hWndTemp = GetWindow(hMDIClientWnd, GW_CHILD);

   while (hWndTemp)
   {
      hWndTemp = GetWindow(hMDIClientWnd, GW_CHILD);

      while(hWndTemp && GetWindow(hWndTemp, GW_OWNER))
         hWndTemp = GetWindow(hWndTemp, GW_HWNDNEXT);

      if (hWndTemp)
         SendMessage(hMDIClientWnd, WM_MDIDESTROY, (WORD)hWndTemp,
                     0L);
      else
         break;
   }

}
```

Listing 17.2. Resource script for MDI example.

```
/*
 * MINMDI.RC resource script file
 *
 */

#include "minmdi.h"

MAINMENU MENU
BEGIN
     POPUP "&File"
     BEGIN
          MENUITEM "&New Window", IDM_NEW
          MENUITEM SEPARATOR
          MENUITEM "E&xit", IDM_EXIT
     END
```

```
    POPUP "&Window"
    BEGIN
        MENUITEM "&Cascade, IDM_CASCADE
        MENUITEM "&Tile, IDM_TILE
        MENUITEM "Arrange &Icons", IDM_ARRANGE
        MENUITEM "Close &All", IDM_CLOSEALL
    END
END
```

Listing 17.3. Module definition file for MDI example.

```
;
; MINMDI.DEF module definition file
;

DESCRIPTION   'Minimum MDI Application'
NAME          MINMDI
EXETYPE       WINDOWS
STUB          'WINSTUB.EXE'
HEAPSIZE      1024
STACKSIZE     8192
CODE          PRELOAD MOVEABLE DISCARDABLE
DATA          PRELOAD MOVEABLE MULTIPLE
```

Listing 17.4. Header file for MDI example program.

```
/*
 * MINMDI.H header file
 *
 */

#define IDM_NEW  100
#define IDM_EXIT 110

#define IDM_CASCADE  120
#define IDM_TILE     130
#define IDM_ARRANGE  140
#define IDM_CLOSEALL 150

#define IDM_WINDOWCHILD 200
```

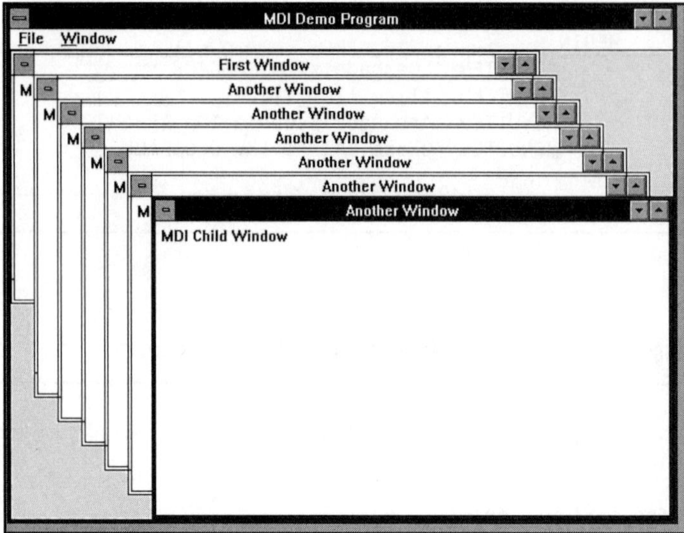

Figure 17.6.
The example MDI program.

This program demonstrates the basic functionality built in the MDI application. The user can create multiple child windows by choosing the New Window menu item. After multiple child windows have been opened, the options in the Windows menu enable the user to manipulate the size and location of the child windows.

Now that you know how to write a basic application that uses the MDI in C, examine how it's done in OWL. When a program is based on the OWL, implementation of the MDI is easier. The OWL encapsulates much of the functionality of the MDI for you, reducing your work as a programmer.

OWL and the MDI

Creating a program based on the MDI is much easier when you use the OWL. Because the OWL handles a great deal of the internals of creating the client windows for you, it simplifies programming the MDI.

Programs based on the OWL that are to use the MDI must include the mdi.h header file at the beginning of the program. The statement looks like this:

```
#include <mdi.h>
```

Your OWL program creates three classes. You still have a class derived from the `TApplication` class. The frame window is derived from the `TMDIFrame` class. Child windows are derived from the `TWindow` class.

Creating Child Windows

To create a new child window, you only need to use the `MakeWindow` member function. Here is an example:

```
MakeWindow(new TChildMDIWindow(this, "Child Window"));
```

The child window has its own class. Thus, you can do all the regular window processing for the MDI.

Menu Items and OWL

Most menu items for MDI programs are automatically processed for you. You don't have to write a line of code to process them. You only have to create a resource script that contains appropriate menu items and then give them the correct identifiers. Include owlrc.h in the resource script to declare the proper identifiers. The resource script in Listing 17.6 gives you an idea about how to name the menu items.

Listing 17.5 shows an example of using the OWL to create a program based on the MDI. Listing 17.6 contains the resource script, and Listing 17.7 contains the module definition file. As you can tell, using the OWL simplifies coding.

Listing 17.5. Source code for OWL MDI demo.

```
// OWLMDI.CPP - Example MDI application using ObjectWindows Library
//
// Programming Windows with Turbo C++ for Windows
// by Paul J. Perry

#define WIN31
#define STRICT

#include <owl.h>
#include <mdi.h>
#include <windowsx.h>


// Class Declarations

/*******************************************/
class TOwlApp : public TApplication
{
   public :
      TOwlApp (LPSTR AName, HINSTANCE hInstance, HINSTANCE
               hPrevInstance, LPSTR CmdLine, int CmdShow) :
               TApplication(AName, hInstance, hPrevInstance,
               CmdLine, CmdShow) { } ;

   virtual void InitMainWindow();
};


/*******************************************/
class TChildMDIWindow : public TWindow
{
   public :
      TChildMDIWindow(PTWindowsObject AParent, LPSTR ATitle)
                      : TWindow(AParent, ATitle) { };
      virtual void Paint(HDC PaintDC, PAINTSTRUCT &PaintInfo);
};

/*******************************************/
class TMDIFrameWindow : public TMDIFrame
{
   public :
      TMDIFrameWindow(LPSTR ATitle, LPSTR MenuName);
      virtual PTWindowsObject CreateChild();
      virtual BOOL CloseChildren();
};
```

```
// Class Member Functions

/*################################
  ##  TOwlApp member functions  ##
  ################################*/

/*******************************************/
void TOwlApp::InitMainWindow()
{
   MainWindow = new TMDIFrameWindow(NULL, "MAINMENU");
}


/*########################################
  ##  TChildMDIWindow member functions  ##
  ########################################*/

/*******************************************/
#pragma argsused
void TChildMDIWindow::Paint(HDC PaintDC, PAINTSTRUCT &PaintInfo)
{

   TextOut(PaintDC, 5, 5,  "Client Window", 13);

}


/*######################################
  ## TMDIFrameWindow member functions ##
  ######################################*/

TMDIFrameWindow::TMDIFrameWindow(LPSTR ATitle, LPSTR MenuName) :
   TMDIFrame(ATitle, MenuName)
{
   // Specify which menu to add child window list to
   ChildMenuPos = 1;

}


/*******************************************/
PTWindowsObject TMDIFrameWindow::CreateChild()
{
   return GetApplication()->MakeWindow(new TChildMDIWindow
       (this, "Child Window"));
}
```

continues

Listing 17.5. continued

```
/*******************************************/
BOOL TMDIFrameWindow::CloseChildren()
{
   BOOL result;

   result = TMDIFrame::CloseChildren();

   return result;
}


/*####################################
  ##  WinMain program entry point  ##
  ####################################*/

/*******************************************/
int PASCAL WinMain(HINSTANCE hInstance, HINSTANCE hPrevInstance,
                   LPSTR lpCmdLine, int nCmdShow)
{

   TOwlApp ThisApp("ObjectWindows Library Program", hInstance,
                   hPrevInstance, lpCmdLine, nCmdShow);
   ThisApp.Run();
   return ThisApp.Status;

}
```

Listing 17.6. Resource script for OWL MDI demo.

```
/*
 * OWLMDI resource script
 *
 */

#include <windows.h>
#include <owlrc.h>

MAINMENU MENU LOADONCALL MOVEABLE PURE DISCARDABLE
BEGIN
   POPUP "&File"
   BEGIN
```

```
      MENUITEM "New", CM_CREATECHILD
      MENUITEM "E&xit", CM_EXIT
   END
   POPUP "&Window"
   BEGIN
      MENUITEM "&Cascade", CM_CASCADECHILDREN
      MENUITEM "&Tile", CM_TILECHILDREN
      MENUITEM "Arrange &Icons", CM_ARRANGEICONS
      MENUITEM "Close &All", CM_CLOSECHILDREN
   END
END
```

Listing 17.7. Module definition file for OWL MDI demo.

```
;
;  OWLMDI.DEF module definition file
;

DESCRIPTION    'OWL MDI Demo'
NAME           MINOWL
EXETYPE        WINDOWS
STUB           'WINSTUB.EXE'
HEAPSIZE       4096
STACKSIZE      5120
CODE           PRELOAD MOVEABLE DISCARDABLE
DATA           PRELOAD MOVEABLE MULTIPLE
```

The MDI requires more effort to implement. However, the results you can achieve certainly elevate the functionality of your application.

What You Have Learned

This chapter covered the MDI. You learned what the MDI is, how it works, and how to implement it in both C and C++ (using the OWL). The following topics were covered in this chapter:

- The MDI is a standard that enables the user to work with multiple documents within a single application.
- Commercial examples of programs that use the MDI include the Turbo C++ for Windows IDE, Program Manager, Quattro Pro for Windows, and the System Configuration editor.
- The main application window of an MDI application is the frame window. The individual documents are child windows.
- Both the frame window and child windows must have a Window class registered for them. This usually is done in the `WinMain` section of your program.
- The frame window procedure passes all unhandled messages to the `DefFrameProc()`. This is similar to passing unhandled messages in the main window procedure to the `DefWindowProc()` function.
- The menu items associated with the Windows menu can be carried out by sending messages to the client window with an associated identifier.
- Programs written with the OWL and based on the MDI must include the mdi.h header file at the beginning of the program. The resource script for these programs must include the owlrc.h header file to declare menu identifiers.
- ObjectWindows programs that use the MDI derive classes from `TApplication`, `TMDIFrame`, and `TWindow`.
- To create new child Windows, a program uses the `MakeWindow` member function.

18

USING THE CLIPBOARD

IN THIS CHAPTER

- The clipboard data formats available with Windows.
- How to copy and paste text to and from the clipboard.
- How to use the clipboard with other types of data, including metafiles and bitmaps.

The final chapters of this book cover data interchange between applications. One of the principal advantages of Windows is its ability to share data between programs. In any multitasking environment, there is a need to transfer data between applications. You are already aware of Dynamic Link Libraries (DLLs). However, DLLs don't provide a method for data interchange the user can control. This chapter looks at writing programs that use the Windows clipboard.

The primary means of transferring data between applications in Windows is the clipboard. You copy information from your program in the clipboard. You then start another program and paste the clipboard contents in it. The information can be among other types, ASCII text data, Windows graphical metafiles, or bitmaps. This process of data interchange is largely controlled by the user.

This chapter looks at copying and pasting text and graphics in the clipboard. As usual, you learn about the concepts involved and see sample programs that explain the concepts presented.

Using the Clipboard

Most programs that use the clipboard include a top-level menu selection labeled Edit. Under it, three items are in a pop-up menu item: Cut, Copy, and Paste. Frequently, accelerator keys are associated with these menu selections as well.

To copy or cut objects to the clipboard, the user first must select the desired item. To do this, the user uses the keyboard, pressing Shift or dragging the mouse cursor over the desired item. The Cut menu option deletes the currently selected object and puts it in the clipboard. The Copy menu option copies the selected object to the clipboard without deleting it. The Paste menu option does not require an object to be selected first. It copies the contents of the clipboard to the data area of the program.

About the Clipboard

The clipboard is actually an area of your computer's memory that Windows uses to store text or graphics images copied from a Windows application. After you store data in the clipboard, you can switch to another application and paste the data in it.

Windows provides a Clipboard Viewer (CLIPBRD.EXE). Don't confuse this program with where the clipboard data is stored. The Clipboard Viewer only displays the current contents of the clipboard (see Figure 18.1). It does not act as the actual location where the clipboard data is stored.

Figure 18.1.
Windows Clipboard Viewer program.

The location where the data is stored can be different every time you use the clipboard. Windows uses a global memory object to store the clipboard contents. Your program requests a handle to the global memory and passes it to Windows when defining the clipboard data.

The clipboard supports several data formats. Your program must specify what type of data to send to the clipboard. You specify the data type with a constant beginning with the letters `CF_` (clipboard format). The following formats are available:

- `CF_TEXT`—An ASCII character string in the ANSI character set. The end of each line is signified with a line-feed character. This is the simplest form of clipboard data.
- `CF_BITMAP`—A Windows 2-compatible bitmap image that is usually device-dependent.

- CF_METAFILEPICT—A metafile picture. This is a combination of a metafile (see Chapter 16, "Even More GDI") and additional information about how the metafile is played back.
- CF_SYLK—Data using Microsoft's "Symbolic Link" format. This is a format used to transfer data between Excel and other programs.
- CF_DIF—Data in Lotus Corporation's "Data Interchange Format." Use this to transfer spreadsheet data.
- CF_TIFF—Transfers graphical images in the "Tagged Image File Format" devised by Microsoft, Aldus Corporation, and Hewlett Packard.
- CF_OEMTEXT—Data that uses the OEM character set. This is similar to CF_TEXT.
- CF_DIB—This is a Windows 3-compatible bitmap image that is usually device-independent.
- CF_PALETTE—A color palette usually used in combination with CF_DIB to transfer information about the colors in the bitmap.

In addition to these predefined clipboard formats, an application can register its own clipboard format. However, custom clipboard formats might not be supported by other applications, making the clipboard contents difficult to use from other programs.

Transferring Text to the Clipboard

To transfer text data to the clipboard, your application follows these steps:

1. Copy the text string to Windows global memory.
2. Open the clipboard.
3. Empty the current clipboard contents.
4. Set the new data format in the clipboard.
5. Close the clipboard.

To copy the string to global memory, use the `GlobalAlloc` API routine to allocate the memory, as follows:

```
hGlobalString = GlobalAlloc(GMEM_MOVEABLE, Length+1);
```

This routine allocates global memory and returns a handle to the string. The memory must be specified as moveable with the `GMEM_MOVEABLE` constant.

You then lock the memory, so it won't be relocated. You do this using the `GlobalLock` routine, as follows:

```
PtrGlobalStr = GlobalLock(hGlobalString);
```

To copy a local string to the global memory, you can use code such as this:

```
for (n=0; n < len; n++)
   *lpMem++ = EditText[n];
```

At this point, you must unlock the memory, so if Windows needs to, it can be moved around. Do this with the `GlobalUnlock` routine, as follows:

```
GlobalUnlock(hGlobalString);
```

You now are ready to start using the clipboard-specific commands. To open and empty the clipboard, you use the following commands:

```
OpenClipboard(hWnd);
EmptyClipboard();
```

You can now pass the handle to the global memory along with the identifier for the type of item being put in the clipboard (`CF_ IDENTIFIER`) and then close the clipboard, as follows:

```
SetClipboardData(CF_TEXT, hGlobalString);
CloseClipboard();
```

While putting text in the clipboard, you must use the `OpenClipboard` and `CloseClipboard` functions during processing of the same message. It is wrong to open the clipboard and then pass control back to Windows. If this happens, another application cannot access the clipboard.

After you call the `SetClipboardData` routine, you must not make use of the handle to the global string. The memory block now belongs to the clipboard. If your program modifies it, the whole concept of the clipboard (a static place to store data) is ruined.

Getting Text out of the Clipboard

Now that you know how to put text in the clipboard, look at how you get text out of the clipboard. Again, you must follow several steps while pasting text from the clipboard:

1. Open the clipboard.
2. Find out whether the clipboard format you need is currently available.
3. Get the clipboard data from the clipboard and copy it to a local variable.
4. Close the clipboard.

To open the clipboard, use the following command:

```
OpenClipboard(hWnd);
```

To find whether the type of data you need is currently available, call the `IsClipboardFormatAvailable` routine along with the clipboard format you want to retrieve. If the format is available, the routine returns a `True` value, as follows:

```
IsAvailable = IsClipboardFormatAvailable(CF_TEXT);
```

To obtain the data from the clipboard, use the `GetClipboardData`, as follows:

```
hGlobalStr = GetClipboardData(CF_TEXT);
```

If the routine returns a `True` value, you can copy the handle to the global clipboard data to a separate location (you don't want to modify the clipboard). One method for doing this is as follows:

```
GlobalStrSize = GlobalSize(hGlobalStr);
PtrGlobalStr = GlobalLock(hGlobalStr);
for (n=o: n< len: ntt)
   *lpMem++ = EditText[n]
GlobalUnlock(hGlobalStr);
```

This method retrieves a global string from Windows and copies the clipboard text to the global memory area. It uses the same method as discussed earlier in locking and unlocking the memory being referenced.

A Clipboard Example

The following program (CLIPTXT.CPP) enables you to copy text to the clipboard and get text from the clipboard to display in the client area of the program. Listing 18.1 contains the source code for the program. Listing 18.2 contains the resource script for the program. Listing 18.3 contains the header file, and Listing 18.4 contains the module definition file.

Listing 18.1. Example program for using text with the clipboard.

```
// CLIPTXT.CPP - Shows how to Copy and Paste text in Clipboard
//
// Programming Windows with Turbo C++ for Windows
// by Paul J. Perry

#define WIN31
#define STRICT

#include <inputdia.h>
#include <string.h>
#include <owl.h>
#include <windowsx.h>

#include "cliptxt.h"

/****************************************/
class TMyApp : public TApplication
{
   public:
      TMyApp(LPSTR AName, HINSTANCE hInstance,
             HINSTANCE hPrevInstance, LPSTR lpCmdLine,
             int nCmdShow)
             :TApplication(AName, hInstance, hPrevInstance,
lpCmdLine, nCmdShow) { };
      virtual void InitMainWindow();
};

/****************************************/
_CLASSDEF(TMyWindow)
class TMyWindow : public TWindow
{
   public:
```

continues

Listing 18.1. continued

```
      LPSTR lpStr;  // string which has been copied from clipboard
      TMyWindow(LPSTR ATitle);
      virtual void Copy(RTMessage Msg)
        = [CM_FIRST + CM_COPY];
      virtual void Paste(RTMessage Msg)
        = [CM_FIRST + CM_PASTE];
      virtual void View(RTMessage Msg)
        = [CM_FIRST + CM_VIEW];
      virtual void Paint(HDC PaintDC, PAINTSTRUCT &PaintInfo);
};

/****************************************/
TMyWindow::TMyWindow(LPSTR ATitle) : TWindow(NULL, ATitle)
{
   AssignMenu("MAINMENU");
}  lpStr=Null;

/****************************************/
void TMyWindow::Copy(RTMessage)
{
   char   EditText[79];
   HANDLE hGlobalMem;
   LPSTR  lpMem;
   int    n, len;

   strcpy(EditText, "");

   if (GetApplication()->ExecDialog(new TInputDialog(this,
       "Copy Text", "Type something",EditText,
       sizeof(EditText))) == IDOK);
   {
      // first allocate memory and lock it in place
      len = strlen(EditText);

      hGlobalMem = GlobalAlloc(GHND, (DWORD) len + 1);
      lpMem = (LPSTR)GlobalLock(hGlobalMem);

      // Copy the character string to the global memory
      for (n=0; n < len; n++)
         *lpMem++ = EditText[n];

      GlobalUnlock(hGlobalMem);

      if (OpenClipboard(HWindow))
      {
      EmptyClipboard();
```

```
      SetClipboardData(CF_TEXT, hGlobalMem);
      CloseClipboard();
      }
   }

}

/****************************************/
void TMyWindow::Paste(RTMessage)
{
   HANDLE   hCBMem;
   HANDLE   hMyGlobalMem;
   LPSTR    lpClipMem;

   if (!IsClipboardFormatAvailable(CF_TEXT))
   {
      MessageBox(HWindow,"TEXT not available in Clipboard",
                 "Message", MB_OK ¦ MB_ICONASTERISK);
      return;
   }

   if (OpenClipboard (HWindow) )
   {
      hCBMem = GetClipboardData(CF_TEXT);  // Get handle to CB mem

      // allocate our own global memory to copy CB data to
      hMyGlobalMem = GlobalAlloc (GHND, GlobalSize(hCBMem));

      // get the actual memory referenced by the handles
      lpStr = (LPSTR)GlobalLock(hMyGlobalMem);
      lpClipMem = (LPSTR)GlobalLock(hCBMem);

      lstrcpy(lpStr, lpClipMem);  // Copy CB data to our string

      GlobalUnlock(hMyGlobalMem);   // Unlock Memory
      GlobalUnlock(hCBMem);

      CloseClipboard();
      InvalidateRect(HWindow, NULL, TRUE);
   }
}

/****************************************/
void TMyWindow::View(RTMessage)
{
   WinExec("CLIPBRD.EXE", SW_SHOW);
}
```

continues

Listing 18.1. continued

```
/****************************************/
#pragma argsused
void TMyWindow::Paint(HDC PaintDC, PAINTSTRUCT _FAR & PaintInfo)
{
   RECT rect;

   GetClientRect(HWindow, &rect);

   DrawText(PaintDC, lpStr, -1, &rect, DT_LEFT);

}

/****************************************/
void TMyApp::InitMainWindow()
{
   MainWindow = new TMyWindow(Name);
}

/****************************************/
#pragma argsused
int PASCAL WinMain(HINSTANCE hInstance, HINSTANCE hPrevInstance,
                   LPSTR lpCmdLine, int nCmdShow)
{
   TMyApp MyApp("Clipboard Example", hInstance, hPrevInstance,
                lpCmdLine, nCmdShow);
   MyApp.Run();
   return MyApp.Status;
}
```

Listing 18.2. Resource script.

```
/*
 * CLIPTXT.RC resource script
 *
 */

#include <owlrc.h>
#include <inputdia.dlg>

#include "cliptxt.h"
```

```
MAINMENU MENU
BEGIN
     POPUP "&Edit"
     BEGIN
          MENUITEM "&Copy", CM_COPY
          MENUITEM "&Paste", CM_PASTE
          MENUITEM SEPARATOR
          MENUITEM "&View Clipboard", CM_VIEW
     END

END
```

Listing 18.3. Header file.

```
/*
 * CLIPTXT.H header file
 *
 */

#define CM_COPY  101
#define CM_PASTE 102
#define CM_VIEW  103
```

Listing 18.4. Module definition file.

```
;
;  CLIPTXT.DEF module definition file
;

NAME        ClipText
DESCRIPTION  'Clipboard Example'
EXETYPE      WINDOWS
CODE         PRELOAD MOVEABLE DISCARDABLE
DATA         PRELOAD MOVEABLE MULTIPLE
HEAPSIZE     4096
STACKSIZE    5120
```

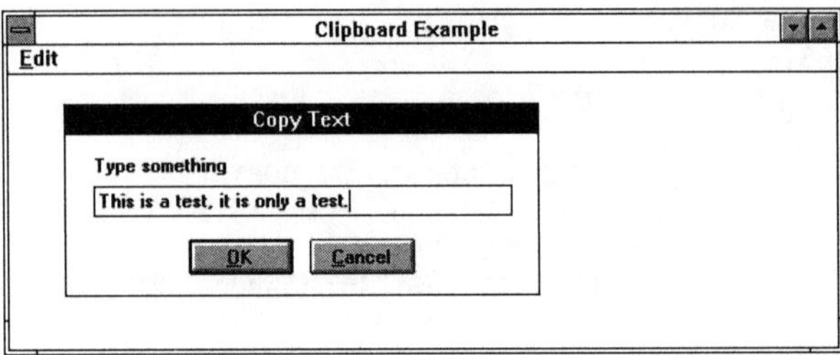

Figure 18.2.
CLIPTXT demonstration program.

Figure 18.2 shows the CLIPTXT program as it is being executed. The program is based on the ObjectWindows library (OWL). As you run the program, notice the familiar dialog box displayed.

When text is entered to be stored in the clipboard, an Input Dialog is used. It looks like the one designed in Chapter 15, "Dynamic Link Libraries." The idea behind the one developed in Chapter 15 was borrowed from a similar object that is available in the OWL. Look at it and see how it's used.

Using OWL Input Dialogs

The OWL provides a stock dialog box, referred to as an input dialog. It is a simple predefined dialog box that prompts the user for a single line of text. It includes OK and Cancel command buttons. The input dialog is a modal dialog box; therefore, you cannot switch to the main window of your program when it is used.

To use the input dialog, you must include the inputdia.h header file in your source code, as follows:

```
#include <inputdia.h>
```

You must also include the resource template in your resource script, with a line such as the following:

```
#include <inputdia.dlg>
```

To use the input dialog, you create an instance of the object by calling the new operator. You specify the string to use for the title bar and another string that is displayed inside the dialog box. Using the input dialog is easy. Create an instance of the `TInputDialog` dialog like this:

```
GetApplication()->ExecDialog(new TInputDialog(this,
             "Copy Text", "Type something",EditText,
             sizeof(EditText)));
```

When the user presses OK, the string the user entered is returned in the `EditText` buffer. Most of the time, you will want to test the return value to be sure the user clicked OK, rather than Cancel.

The ObjectWindows input dialog is available only to programs written for the OWL. If you want to use an input dialog in your C programs, use the example from Chapter 16.

The Clipboard and Metafiles

Using metafiles with the clipboard is a bit trickier than when using text. Although the steps are the same, you must set the values of a data structure describing the metafile. You first declare a structure of type `LPMETAFILEPICT`, as follows:

```
LPMETAFILEPICT    lpMFP;
```

After you finish allocating memory for the metafile, set the four fields of the structure. They specify the mapping mode, the `x` and `y` extents, and the handle to the metafile. An example of doing this is:

```
lpMFP->mm   = MM_TEXT;  // Mapping mode
lpMFP->xExt = 1;        // x-extent
lpMFP->yExt = 1;        // y-extent
lpMFP->hMF  = hMetaFile;// handle to the metafile
```

Listing 18.5 shows the source code of an example program for copying and pasting metafiles with the clipboard. Listing 18.6 is the header file, Listing 18.7 is the resource script, and Listing 18.8 is the module definition file. Figure 18.3 shows the output of the program.

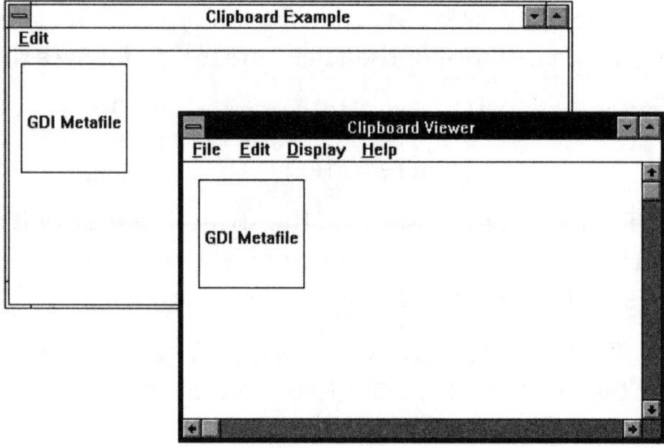

Figure 18.3.
CLIPMTF example program.

Listing 18.5. Example program to cut and paste metafiles.

```
// CLIPMTF.CPP - Copying and pasting metafiles to/from the clipboard
//
//
// Programming Windows with Turbo C++ for Windows
// by Paul J. Perry


#define WIN31
#define STRICT

#include <owl.h>
#include <inputdia.h>
#include <string.h>
#include <windowsx.h>

#include "clipmtf.h"

/*****************************************/
class TMyApp : public TApplication
{
   public:
      TMyApp(LPSTR AName, HINSTANCE hInstance, HINSTANCE
             hPrevInstance,
             LPSTR lpCmdLine, int nCmdShow)
             : TApplication(AName, hInstance, hPrevInstance,
lpCmdLine, nCmdShow) {};
   virtual void InitMainWindow();
};
```

```
/******************************************/
class TMyWindow : public TWindow
{
   public:
      HMETAFILE       hMetaFile;        // handle to a metafile
      BOOL            mfavail;          // Is Metafile available?
      LPMETAFILEPICT  lpMFP, lpMFP2;    // Two structures of
                                           METAFILEPICT

      TMyWindow(LPSTR ATitle);
      virtual void Copy(RTMessage Msg)
        = [CM_FIRST + CM_COPY];
      virtual void Paste(RTMessage Msg)
        = [CM_FIRST + CM_PASTE];
      virtual void View(RTMessage Msg)
        = [CM_FIRST + CM_VIEW];
      virtual void Paint(HDC PaintDC, PAINTSTRUCT &PaintInfo);
};

/******************************************/
TMyWindow::TMyWindow(LPSTR ATitle) : TWindow(NULL, ATitle)
{
   mfavail = FALSE;
   AssignMenu("MAINMENU");
}

/******************************************/
void TMyWindow::Copy(RTMessage)
{
   HDC                hdcMeta;
   GLOBALHANDLE    hGlobalMem;


   // First, create a memory metafile
   hdcMeta = CreateMetaFile(NULL);

   // Put some commands into the metafile
   Rectangle(hdcMeta, 10, 10, 100, 100);
   TextOut(hdcMeta,15, 50, "GDI Metafile", 12);

   // end creation of metafile
   hMetaFile = CloseMetaFile(hdcMeta);

   // Now, allocate global memory for a structure of METAFILEPICT
   hGlobalMem = GlobalAlloc(GHND, (DWORD) sizeof (METAFILEPICT));
   lpMFP = (LPMETAFILEPICT) GlobalLock(hGlobalMem);
```

continues

Listing 18.5. continued

```
   // Set the fields of the METAFILEPICT structure and unlock
   memory
   lpMFP->mm   = MM_TEXT;
   lpMFP->xExt = 1;
   lpMFP->yExt = 1;
   lpMFP->hMF  = hMetaFile;
   GlobalUnlock(hGlobalMem);

   // Finally, we transfer the global memory block to the clipboard
   if (OpenClipboard(HWindow));
   {
      EmptyClipboard();
      SetClipboardData(CF_METAFILEPICT, hGlobalMem);
      CloseClipboard();
   }

}

/****************************************/
void TMyWindow::Paste(RTMessage)
{
   GLOBALHANDLE hClipBoardMem;
   HANDLE       hMem;


   // Make sure a metafile is actually available in the clipboard
   if (!IsClipboardFormatAvailable(CF_METAFILEPICT))
   {
      MessageBox(HWindow,"Metafile not available in Clipboard",
                 NULL, MB_OK ¦ MB_ICONASTERISK);
      return;
   }

   // We know a metafile exists, go ahead and retrieve the
   METAFILEPICT
   if (OpenClipboard (HWindow) )
   {
      // Get handle to METAFILEPICT structure and lock it
      hClipBoardMem = GetClipboardData(CF_METAFILEPICT);
      lpMFP = (LPMETAFILEPICT) GlobalLock(hClipBoardMem);

      // Allocate local memory for a copy of the METAFILEPICT
      structure
      hMem = GlobalAlloc(LHND, sizeof(METAFILEPICT));
      lpMFP2 = (LPMETAFILEPICT) GlobalLock(hMem);
```

```
      // Assign members of METAFILEPICT structure to local memory
      lpMFP2->mm   = lpMFP->mm;
      lpMFP2->xExt = lpMFP->xExt;
      lpMFP2->yExt = lpMFP->yExt;
      lpMFP2->hMF  = lpMFP->hMF;

      // Give the global memory back to Windows
      GlobalUnlock(hClipBoardMem);

      // All done, close the clipboard
      CloseClipboard();

      // A METAFILEPICT is now available.  Go display it in Paint
      function.
      mfavail = TRUE;
      InvalidateRect(HWindow, NULL, TRUE);
   }

}

/****************************************/
void TMyWindow::View(RTMessage)
{
   WinExec("CLIPBRD.EXE", SW_SHOW);
}

/****************************************/
#pragma argsused
void TMyWindow::Paint(HDC PaintDC, PAINTSTRUCT &PaintInfo)
{
   RECT rect;

   GetClientRect(HWindow, &rect);

   if (!mfavail)
   {
      DrawText(PaintDC, "Select Paste menu item to get clipboard
               contents", -1, &rect, DT_LEFT);
   }
   else
   {
      PlayMetaFile(PaintDC, lpMFP2->hMF);
   }
}

/****************************************/
void TMyApp::InitMainWindow()
```

continues

Listing 18.5. continued

```
{
   MainWindow = new TMyWindow(Name);
}

/****************************************/
int PASCAL WinMain(HINSTANCE hInstance, HINSTANCE hPrevInstance,
                   LPSTR lpCmdLine, int nCmdShow)
{
   TMyApp MyApp("Clipboard Example", hInstance, hPrevInstance,
                lpCmdLine, nCmdShow);
   MyApp.Run();
   return MyApp.Status;
}
```

Listing 18.6. Header file for CLIPMTF program.

```
/*
 * CLIPMTF.H header file
 *
 */

#define CM_COPY  101
#define CM_PASTE 102
#define CM_VIEW  103
```

Listing 18.7. Resource script for CLIPMTF program.

```
/*
 * CLPIMTF.RC resource script
 *
 */

#include <owlrc.h>
#include <inputdia.dlg>

#include "clipmtf.h"
```

```
MAINMENU MENU
BEGIN
     POPUP "&Edit"
     BEGIN
          MENUITEM "&Copy Metafile", CM_COPY
          MENUITEM "&Paste Metafile", CM_PASTE
          MENUITEM SEPARATOR
          MENUITEM "&View Clipboard", CM_VIEW
     END

END
```

Listing 18.8. Module definition file for CLIPMTF program.

```
;
; CLIPMTF.DEF module definition file
;

NAME          CLIPMTF
DESCRIPTION   'Clipboard Example'
EXETYPE       WINDOWS
CODE          PRELOAD MOVEABLE DISCARDABLE
DATA          PRELOAD MOVEABLE MULTIPLE
HEAPSIZE      4096
STACKSIZE     5120
```

The Clipboard and Bitmaps

When transferring bitmaps to the clipboard, you first must load the bitmap and obtain a handle to the bitmap, using the `LoadBitmap` function. You can use code such as this:

```
hBMP = LoadBitmap(hInstance, "BITMAPNAME");
```

Then, in your call to `SetClipboardData`, specify the `CF_BITMAP` identifier along with the handle to the bitmap.

Listings 18.9 through 18.12 show how to use bitmaps with the clipboard in your programs. Figure 18.4 shows the output of the CLIPBMP program.

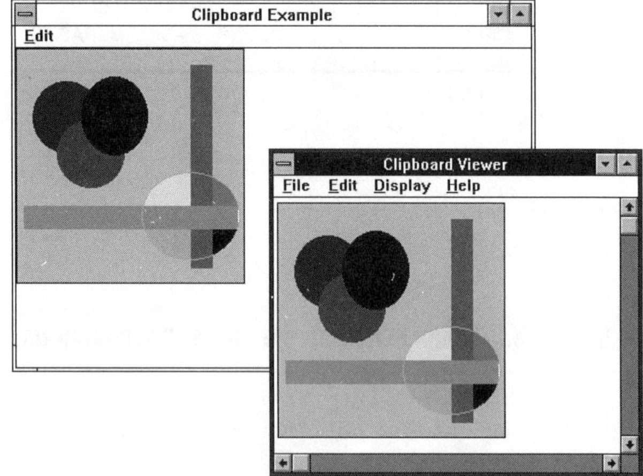

Figure 18.4. *CLIPBMP example program.*

Listing 18.9. CLIPBMP example program.

```
// CLIPBMP.CPP - Copying and Pasting bitmaps to/from clipboard
//
// Programming Windows with Turbo C++ for Windows
// by Paul J. Perry

#define WIN31
#define STRICT

#include <owl.h>
#include <windowsx.h>

#include <inputdia.h>
#include <string.h>


#include "clipbmp.h"
```

```
/****************************************/
class TMyApp : public TApplication
{
   public:
      TMyApp(LPSTR AName, HINSTANCE hInstance,
             HINSTANCE hPrevInstance,
             LPSTR lpCmdLine, int nCmdShow)
             : TApplication(AName, hInstance, hPrevInstance,
lpCmdLine, nCmdShow) {};
      virtual void InitMainWindow();
};

/****************************************/
_CLASSDEF(TMyWindow)
class TMyWindow : public TWindow
{
   public:
      HBITMAP hBitmap;
      BOOL bmpavail;

      TMyWindow(LPSTR ATitle);
      virtual void Copy(RTMessage Msg)
        = [CM_FIRST + CM_COPY];
      virtual void Paste(RTMessage Msg)
        = [CM_FIRST + CM_PASTE];
      virtual void View(RTMessage Msg)
        = [CM_FIRST + CM_VIEW];
      virtual void Paint(HDC PaintDC, PAINTSTRUCT &PaintInfo);
};


/****************************************/
TMyWindow::TMyWindow(LPSTR ATitle) : TWindow(NULL, ATitle)
{
   bmpavail = FALSE;
   AssignMenu("MAINMENU");
}

/****************************************/
void TMyWindow::Copy(RTMessage)
{
   HANDLE hBMP;

   // First, get handle to clipboard resource
   //
   hBMP = LoadBitmap(GetApplication()->hInstance,
                     MAKEINTRESOURCE(MAINBITMAP));
```

continues

Listing 18.9. continued

```
   if (OpenClipboard(HWindow))
   {
      EmptyClipboard();                       // Clear out clipboard
      SetClipboardData(CF_BITMAP, hBMP);      // Pass handle to clip
                                                 board
      CloseClipboard();                       // Must close it when
                                                 done
   }

}

/****************************************/
void TMyWindow::Paste(RTMessage)
{
   // If a bitmap is not available, tell the user
   //
   if (!IsClipboardFormatAvailable(CF_BITMAP))
   {
      MessageBox(HWindow,"BITMAP not available in Clipboard",
                 NULL, MB_OK ¦ MB_ICONASTERISK);
      return;
   }

   if (OpenClipboard(HWindow))                   // Get access
   {
      hBitmap = (HBITMAP)GetClipboardData(CF_BITMAP);

      CloseClipboard();                          // Always close it
      bmpavail = TRUE;
      InvalidateRect(HWindow, NULL, TRUE);       // Go display bitmap
   }
}

/****************************************/
void TMyWindow::View(RTMessage)
{
   WinExec("CLIPBRD.EXE", SW_SHOW);
}


/****************************************/
#pragma argsused
void TMyWindow::Paint(HDC PaintDC, PAINTSTRUCT &PaintInfo)
{
   HDC hdcMem;    // Handle to a memory display context
   BITMAP bmp;    // Bitmap structure
```

```
    if (bmpavail) // Do this only if the user has selected Paste
    {
       hdcMem = CreateCompatibleDC(PaintDC);
       SelectObject(hdcMem, hBitmap); // move bitmap into memory DC
       GetObject(hBitmap, sizeof(BITMAP), (LPSTR) &bmp);

       BitBlt(PaintDC, 0, 0, bmp.bmWidth, bmp.bmHeight,
              hdcMem, 0, 0, SRCCOPY);

       DeleteDC(hdcMem);    // Delete memory display context
    }

}

/*****************************************/
void TMyApp::InitMainWindow()
{
   MainWindow = new TMyWindow(Name);
}

/*****************************************/
int PASCAL WinMain(HINSTANCE hInstance, HINSTANCE hPrevInstance,
                   LPSTR lpCmdLine, int nCmdShow)
{
   TMyApp MyApp("Clipboard Example", hInstance, hPrevInstance,
                lpCmdLine, nCmdShow);
   MyApp.Run();
   return MyApp.Status;
}
```

Listing 18.10. Header file for CLIPBMP program.

```
/*
 * CLIPBMP.H header file
 *
 */

#define CM_COPY  101
#define CM_PASTE 102
#define CM_VIEW  103

#define MAINBITMAP 200
```

Listing 18.11. Resource script for CLIPBMP file.

```
/*
 * CLIPBMP.RC resource script
 *
 */

#include <owlrc.h>
#include <clipbmp.h>
#include <inputdia.dlg>

#include "clipbmp.h"

MAINMENU MENU
BEGIN
     POPUP "&Edit"
     BEGIN
          MENUITEM "&Copy Bitmap", CM_COPY
          MENUITEM "&Paste Bitmap", CM_PASTE
          MENUITEM SEPARATOR
          MENUITEM "&View Clipboard", CM_VIEW
     END

END

MAINBITMAP BITMAP clipbmp.bmp
```

Listing 18.12. Module definition file for CLIPBMP file.

```
;
; CLIPBMP.DEF module definition file
;

DESCRIPTION    'Clipboard Example'
NAME           CLIPBMP
EXETYPE        WINDOWS
STUB           'WINSTUB.EXE'
HEAPSIZE       1024
STACKSIZE      8192
CODE           PRELOAD MOVEABLE DISCARDABLE
DATA           PRELOAD MOVEABLE MULTIPLE
```

What You Have Learned

This chapter looked at using the clipboard to transfer data between programs. You learned the concept behind the Windows clipboard, and you saw how to transfer text, metafiles, and bitmaps with it.

The following topics were covered in this chapter:

- The clipboard is a type of data exchange in Windows that is controlled by the user.
- The clipboard is an area in memory that a program can access. The CLIPBRD.EXE program that comes with Windows is a clipboard viewer and not the actual location where the clipboard data is stored.
- Nine different clipboard formats are available for Windows applications. They are identified with the `CF_` prefix (clipboard format). The most common clipboard formats are `CF_text`, `CF_METAFILEPICT`, and `CF_BITMAP`.
- Windows stores clipboard data in global memory. This is memory that Windows controls and makes available to running applications.
- Five steps are followed to transfer text to the clipboard: first, the program must copy a string to Windows global memory; second, it opens the clipboard; third, the current clipboard contents must be emptied; fourth, the format of the clipboard data must be set; and fifth, the clipboard must be closed.
- Four steps are followed to get text from the clipboard: first, the clipboard must be opened; second, you must find whether the clipboard format you need is available; third, you get the clipboard data from the clipboard and copy it to local memory; and fourth, your program must close the clipboard.
- When your program opens and closes the clipboard, it must be done within the same function. If you leave the clipboard open between processing different Windows messages, the clipboard is not available to other applications.

- Transferring a metafile through the clipboard first requires filling out the data members of the LPMETAFILEPIC structure and passing the structure to the clipboard routines.
- Transferring a bitmap through the clipboard requires you to get a handle to the clipboard and then pass the handle of the clipboard to Windows when you specify the CF_BITMAP format.

19

DYNAMIC DATA EXCHANGE

IN THIS CHAPTER

■

What is meant by the dynamic data exchange (DDE) standard and practical examples of uses for DDE.

■

Definitions related to DDE, including client, server, conversation, hot links, and warm links.

■

The messages associated with DDE and their uses.

■

How to use DDE to communicate with Program Manager.

■

What the DDE Management Library (DDEML) is and how to use it.

■

The new functions available in the DDEML.

■

How to initialize the DDEML with your specific callback function.

The next type of data interchange you examine is Dynamic Data Exchange (DDE). DDE allows Windows applications to communicate transparently with the user. Using DDE, you can link data between your program and other commercial Windows applications without intervention by the user.

Dynamic Data Exchange

DDE is a standard for Windows applications to exchange data and invoke macro commands between applications. DDE is a method of application-driven data transfer. That is, the application decides what data to transfer and when to transfer it.

Windows has a message-based framework. Therefore, passing messages between applications is the most appropriate method of transferring information. Remember, though, Windows messages contain only two parameters, `wParam` and `lParam`. To implement DDE, a standard has been devised for the parameters to refer to other pieces of data that can be exchanged between programs.

You will learn about the basics of DDE and the new Microsoft standard for DDE, the Dynamic Data Exchange Management Library (DDEML). However, to understand the management library, you must be familiar with DDE basics.

Uses for DDE

Data transfer between applications is one of the most important aspects of using a multitasking operating system. Possible uses for Windows DDE include the following:

- Link a spreadsheet graph to a word processing document. Anytime the data changes in the spreadsheet, the graph in the word processor is updated to show the new data points.
- Use a Windows communication program that receives stock market quotations by phone for specific predefined stocks and transfer

them to a spreadsheet. The prices are transferred automatically to a spreadsheet every time the stock prices are received. Also, the stock prices can be analyzed and the appropriate reports created in the spreadsheet.

- Combine database information in a word processing document to create form letters that are printed automatically. With DDE, the whole process can be done in the database, starting with the query for names matching a specific criteria.
- Enable a batch-language application to receive commands from other programs to carry out specific tasks. Any number of commands can be created and handled by programs that use the DDE specification of the batch language.
- Enable an installation program to communicate with the system to initialize Program Manager groups and items.

Clearly, DDE offers many exciting capabilities. Data transfer between programs is an important element of most commercial programs currently on the market.

The subject of DDE is complicated. Like other concepts in Windows programming, many pages could be written about it. Nevertheless, this chapter gives you enough information to understand how to use DDE in your programs. The goal is to write an installation program that links with Program Manager to set up group icons. For more information, I recommend *Windows Programmer's Guide to OLE/DDE* by Jeffrey Clark.

Basic Definitions

For an application to use DDE, the program must be written specifically to respond to DDE messages. The programs must cooperate to share the data.

Two applications sharing data through DDE are in a *conversation.* A conversation is a logical connection between two applications. In this conversation, the two applications alternately transmit data to each other. The application that starts the conversation is the *client* application. The application responding to the client is the *server* application.

NOTE

Don't confuse the terms server and client with those used in a networking environment. When discussing Windows DDE, the client and server are two separate programs, not parts of a computer system designed to share data.

The client always initiates a conversation; therefore, the server must be running before a client program attempts to initiate the conversation.

Permanent Data Links

After a conversation has begun, the client program can establish a permanent data link with the server. There are two kinds of permanent data links, warm and hot. A *warm link* enables the server to notify the client that the value of a data item has changed, but the server does not send the data value to the client until the client requests it. In a *hot link,* the server sends the changed value immediately to the client.

Specification of Exchanged Data

The data exchanged between applications is referred to in a three-level hierarchy of application name, topic, and item. At the highest level is the application name, next is the conversation topic, and finally the data item name.

The *application name* is usually the name of the server application. More than one application name can be active at any one time. For example, Borland ObjectVision uses the application name VISION. Microsoft Excel uses the application name Excel. Table 19.1 lists common application names for several commercial programs.

Table 19.1. DDE server application names for common programs.

Application	*Server Name*
Ami Pro	amipro
Crosstalk	xtalk
DynaComm	dynacomm
Microsoft Excel	excel
Borland ObjectVision	vision
Polaris Packrat	packrat
Asymetrix ToolBook	toolbook
Microsoft Word for Windows	winword

The *conversation topic* is a general classification of data. The topic is usually different depending on the type of program involved in the data exchange. A word processing program might use a document name as a topic. A spreadsheet might use the filename of the spreadsheet as the topic.

The *data item* is the information exchanged between the applications. The item can be text, graphics, or numbers. The client and server must use the same application name and topic when referring to the data item. This allows multiple conversations at the same time.

DDE Messages

The DDE.H header file defines nine messages for programmers using DDE. All DDE conversations are conducted by passing certain messages between the client and the server program. Each DDE message is prefixed with the `WM_DDE_` identifier, as follows:

- `WM_DDE_INITIATE`. Sent by the client to a server to initiate a conversation. The message is sent by the client program to ask whether a currently active program can supply the client with information.

- WM_DDE_TERMINATE. Ends the DDE conversation previously established with the WM_DDE_INITIATE message sent by either the client or the server.
- WM_DDE_ACK. Acknowledges receipt of a DDE message. It is sent in response to all messages. The message provides a positive or negative acknowledgment of the receipt of a message.
- WM_DDE_REQUEST. Requests a one-time data transfer from the server application.
- WM_DDE_ADVISE. Allows for the establishment of a permanent data link by requesting the server application to supply an update of a data item when it changes.
- WM_DDE_UNADVISE. Terminates a permanent data link.
- WM_DDE_DATA. Transfers a data item value from the server to the client application.
- WM_DDE_POKE. Transfers data from the client to the server application.
- WM_DDE_EXECUTE. Requests a server application to execute a specific command.

Using DDE

In the DDE, atoms are an important process of exchanging messages. An *atom* is an integer equated to a character string. Windows keeps a table to the current atoms. The table stores an atom value and associates it with a character string. An application can add or delete atoms from the atom table.

Initiating the Conversation

To start the DDE, the WM_DDE_INITIATE message is sent by a client to all potential servers currently running. If the client already has the handle to the window of the server application, it can specify the handle of that window; if not, you use -1 as the window handle. Your program uses the SendMessage routine, as follows:

```
SendMessage(hWnd(-1), WM_DDE_INITIATE, hWindow, lParam);
```

Servers reply to the client by using the SendMessage routine with the WM_DDE_ACK message.

Transferring an Item

After the DDE conversation has been established, the client can obtain the value of a data item from the server by issuing the WM_DDE_REQUEST message. To obtain an item from the server, the client sends the server a WM_DDE_REQUEST message specifying the desired item and format, as follows:

```
PostMessage(hServerWindow, WM_DDE_REQUEST, hClientWindow,
                          MakeLong(CF_TEXT, atomItem))
```

This example specifies a clipboard format of CF_TEXT. The server is responsible for deleting the item atom.

Terminating the Conversation

If the client wants to terminate a specific data link, the client sends the server a WM_DDE_UNADVISE message, as follows:

```
PostMessage(hServerWindow, WM_DDE_UNADVISE, hClientWindow, 0);
```

The server checks whether the client currently has a link to the specific item in the conversation. The server responds with a WM_DDE_ACK message, and the conversation is terminated.

Talking to Program Manager

Program Manager is a DDE server. It features a command-string interface that allows other applications to create, display, and delete groups. The following list describes the commands recognized by Program Manager:

- CreateGroup(GroupName,[GroupPath]). Instructs Program Manager to create a new group window.

- `AddItem(CmdLine[Name[IconPath[IconIndex[,xPos, yPos]]]])`. Adds a new program item to the active group.
- `DeleteGroup(GroupName)`. Deletes a group, including all contents and associated data files.
- `ShowGroup(GroupName, ShowCommand)`. Instructs program manager to change the appearance of a group window.
- `ExitProgManager(SaveState)`. Tells Program Manager to quit and (optionally) save its current state.

The Program PROGTALK.CPP in the TCWIN\OWL\EXAMPLES\PROGTALK directory has an example of adding groups to Program Manager by using DDE. The program you write is based on the DDEML. You might want to examine PROGTALK to see how the same kind of actions are carried out in a program based solely on regular DDE.

Two programs can establish a DDE link only if they agree on the meanings of the name, topic, and item. Therefore, for Windows applications you create that use DDE, include detailed information about how to link with the program.

The Dynamic Data Exchange Management Library

The dynamic data exchange management library (DDEML) is a set of routines for simplifying DDE. Rather than have two programs process DDE to transfer messages between each other, the DDEML acts as a middleman. Applications call DDEML functions that, in turn, exchange data between programs (see Figure 19.1).

Standard DDE:

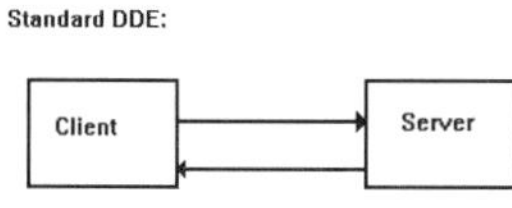

Figure 19.1.

Difference between DDE and DDEML.

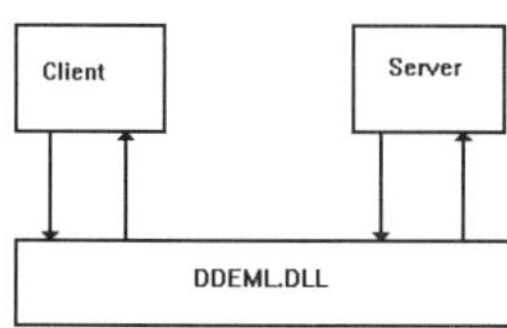

The DDEML is a dynamic link library that simplifies sending, posting, and receiving DDE messages. The DDEML is new for Windows 3.1 and did not exist in Windows 3.0. However, if the user has the DDEML.DLL file available at runtime, the DDEML can be used with Windows 3.0. Also, Windows 3.0's real mode was intended as a method of compatibility with Windows 2.0 applications, and the DDEML doesn't run under real mode.

The DDEML defines 27 functions that support both server and client transactions (see Table 19.2). Notice, all the functions start with the letters `Dde`. Although there are 27 functions, most programs do not use all of them.

Table 19.2. Dynamic data exchange management library API functions.

Function	*Description*
`DdeAbandonTransaction`	Abandons an asynchronous transaction.
`DdeAccessData`	Accesses a DDEML global memory object.
`DdeAddData`	Adds data to a DDEML global memory object.
`DdeClientTransaction`	Begins a DDEML data transaction.

continues

Table 19.2. continued

Function	*Description*
`DdeCmpStringHandles`	Compares two DDEML string handles.
`DdeConnect`	Establishes a conversation with a server application.
`DdeConnectList`	Establishes multiple DDEML conversations.
`DdeCreateDataHandle`	Creates a DDEML data handle.
`DdeCreateStringHandle`	Creates a DDEML string handle.
`DdeDisconnect`	Terminates a DDEML conversation.
`DdeDisconnectList`	Destroys a DDEML conversation list.
`DdeEnableCallback`	Enables or disables one or more DDEML conversations.
`DdeFreeDataHandle`	Frees a global memory object.
`DdeFreeStringHandle`	Frees a DDEML string handle.
`DdeGetData`	Copies data from a global memory object to a buffer.
`DdeGetLastError`	Returns an error value set by a DDEML function.
`DdeInitialize`	Registers an application with the DDEML.
`DdeKeepStringHandle`	Increments the usage count for a string handle.
`DdeNameService`	Registers or unregisters a service name.
`DdePostAdvise`	Prompts a server to send advise data to a client.

Function	*Description*
`DdeQueryConvInfo`	Retrieves information about a DDEML conversation.
`DdeQueryNextServer`	Obtains the next handle in a DDEML conversation list.
`DdeQueryString`	Copies string-handle text to a buffer.
`DdeReconnect`	Reestablishes a DDEML conversation.
`DdeSetUserHandle`	Associates a user-defined handle with a transaction.
`DdeUnaccessData`	Frees a DDEML global memory object.
`DdeUninitialize`	Frees DDEML resources associated with an application.

Using DDEML

In some ways, programming an application that uses the DDEML is similar to programming a regular DDE application. All the regular terms regarding client, server, application, name, and item are the same. However, in other ways, utilizing the DDEML is different. When using the DDEML, API functions are called, rather then sending messages between applications. A program also must include the DDEML.H header file at the beginning of the source code to include prototypes for the functions.

Applications written with the DDEML can be one of three types: *client, server,* and *monitor*. Client and server applications are the most common types. Client applications request data or services from a server application. A monitor application can be used for debugging when analysis of the messages being passed between applications is required.

With the DDEML, an application identifies the data and services that client applications request by using service names, topic names, and item names. A service name is a string a client application uses to establish a conversation with a server application. A service name is equivalent to an application name with regular DDE.

A program can have multiple servers that accept the same service name. To eliminate this ambiguity, topic names and item names make the service unique. Topic names and item names are also strings. This combination of topic names and item names allows a client application to exchange data and services with a server application.

The DDEML Callback Function

One of the conventions of the DDEML is the requirement of a callback function. This callback function receives messages pertaining only to the DDE. You must define the DDEML callback function like this:

```
HDDEDATA FAR PASCAL _export DdeCallBackProc(UINT iType, UINT iFmt,
HCONV hConv, HSZ hsz1, HSZ hsz2, HDDEDATA hData, DWORD Data1,
DWORD Data2)
```

You can name the function whatever you want. A brief description of the parameters are in Table 19.3.

Table 19.3. DDEML callback function parameters.

Parameter	*Description*
`iType`	Transaction type.
`iFmt`	Clipboard data format.
`hConv`	Conversation handle.
`hsz1`	Handle for first string.
`hsz2`	Handle for a second string.

Parameter	Description
`hData`	Global memory object handle.
`Data1`	Transaction-specific data.
`Data2`	Transaction-specific data.

When an application uses the DDEML, it must first register the callback function with the DDEML. This is done with the `DdeInitilize` function. A call to this function only registers an application with the DDEML. It does not start a conversation.

When your program calls `DdeInitialize`, it supplies a pointer to the callback function. This is obtained with the `MakeProcInstance` function, as follows:

```
fnDdeCallBack = MakeProcInstance((FARPROC)DdeCallBackProc,
                                 ghInstance);

result = DdeInitialize(&idInst, (PFNCALLBACK)fnDdeCallBack,
                     APPCLASS_STANDARD | APPCMD_CLIENTONLY, 0L);
```

After calling the `DdeInitialize` function, your program should check the return value. If an invalid value is returned, the program should give a warning. Here is an example:

```
if (result)
{
   MessageBox(hWnd, "Unable to initialize", "ProgName",
              MB_ICONEXCLAMATION | MB_OK);
   return FALSE;
}
```

To connect with another application, the client program calls the `DdeConnect` function. The function takes the `ID` instance (returned from the `DdeInitialize` function), the service, and the topic, as follows:

```
hConv = DdeConnect(idInst, hszService, hszTopic,
                   (PCONVCONTEXT) NULL);
if (hConv == NULL)
{
   MessageBox(hWnd, "Error connecting with DDE", NULL, MB_OK);
   return;
}
```

The service and topic are string handles. They must be created from the DdeCreateStringHandle function like this:

```
hszService = DdeCreateStringHandle(idInst,"PROGMAN" ,CP_WINANSI);
hszTopic = DdeCreateStringHandle(idInst,"PROGMAN", CP_WINANSI);
```

Notice, the hszService and hszTopic variables are, in turn, passed to the DdeConnect function.

DDEML Transactions

After a conversation has been established, client applications issue transactions by calling the DdeClientTransaction function. The function has the following prototype:

```
HDDEDATA DdeClientTransaction(void FAR* pData, DWORD cbData,
        HCONV hConv, HSZ hszItem, UINT wFmt, UINT wType,
        DWORD dwTimeout, DWORD FAR* pdwResult);
```

The parameters with a brief description are listed in Table 19.4.

Table 19.4. DdeClientTransaction( ) parameters.

Parameter	*Description*
lpvData	Address of data to pass to server.
cbData	Length of data.
hConv	Handle of conversation.
hszItem	Handle of item-name string.
uFmt	Clipboard data format.
uType	Transaction type.
uTimeout	Time-out duration.
lpuResult	Points to transaction result.

The lpvData and cbDataLen parameters specify a data handle and the length of the data. The hszItem parameter is the item name for the transaction. The wFmt parameter is the clipboard format of the data item.

The dwTimeOut parameter specifies the maximum length of time, in milliseconds, the client waits for a response from the server application in a synchronous transaction. Set this parameter to TIMEOUT_ASYNC for *asynchronous transactions*. Asynchronous transactions allow a client application to issue multiple transactions without waiting for the server to process the transaction. When a client application issues a synchronous transaction, it enters a loop where the program can process user input. It, however, cannot issue another DDE request until DdeClientTransaction returns.

The uType parameter specifies the transaction type. The client application can poke data to a server application by specifying the transaction type XTYP_POKE in the DdeClientTransaction function.

The XTYP_EXECUTE transaction type requests a server application to execute a command string. The format of the command string depends on the server. The DDEML sends the XTYP_EXECUTE transaction to the server application's callback function. The server can access the data through the DdeAccessData function. The client should check the lpdwResult parameter when the DdeClientTransaction function returns to be sure the transaction was successful. If the lpdwResult flag is DDE_FBUSY, the client can issue the transaction later in the conversation.

A client application can specify a transaction type of XTYP_REQUEST. In this case, the DDEML requests data from the specified server application for the client application. If the server application can render the data item, it returns a handle to the data item. The DDEML passes the data handle as the return value from the DdeClientTransaction function.

Client applications can establish links to a server application by using the XTYP_ADVSTART transaction. To create a warm link, the client application combines XTYP_ADVSTART with the XTYP_NODATA flag.

When a client application wants to end an advise loop, it posts an XTYP_ADVSTOP transaction type using the DdeClientTransaction function.

Ending the Transaction

Before your program ends, it should call the `DdeUninitialize` function when it no longer needs the DDEML. An application should call `DdeUninitialize` after DDE has ended and after its message loop has terminated.

A DDEML Example

Now that you have examined how a regular DDE and the DDEML work, you are ready for an example. Listing 19.1 contains a client DDEML program to interact with Program Manager. It is written in C and uses the DDEML to carry out DDE. Listing 19.2 contains the header file; Listing 19.3 contains the resource script; and Listing 19.4 contains the module definition file.

Listing 19.1. Demonstration DDEML program.

```
// DDEMLDMO.C - Dynamic Data Exchange Management Library
//              demonstration program
//
// Programming Windows with Turbo C++ for Windows
// by Paul J. Perry


#define STRICT

#include <windowsx.h>
#include <ddeml.h>

#include "ddemldmo.h"


// Function Prototypes
LRESULT CALLBACK _export MainWndProc(HWND hWnd, UINT message,
                                   WPARAM wParam, LPARAM lParam);

HDDEDATA FAR PASCAL _export DdeCallBackProc(UINT iType, UINT iFmt,
                              HCONV hConv, HSZ hs1, HSZ hsz2,
                              HDDEDATA hData, DWORD Data1,
                              DWORD Data2);
```

```
void WMCommand_Handler(HWND hwnd, int id, HWND hwndCtl, UINT
                       codeNotify);

void PaintGradiantBackground(HWND hWnd, HDC hDC, int Steps);

// Global Variables
char        ProgName[]   = "DDEML Demo";
FARPROC     fnDdeCallBack;
DWORD       result;
HINSTANCE   ghInstance;
HCONV       hConv        = NULL;
HSZ         hszService, hszTopic, hszItem;
HDDEDATA    hData;
DWORD       idInst = 0L;


/*******************************************/
#pragma argsused
int PASCAL WinMain(HINSTANCE hInstance, HINSTANCE hPrevInstance,
                   LPSTR lpCmdParam, int nCmdShow)
{
   HWND     hWnd;
   MSG      msg;

   if (!hPrevInstance)
   {
      WNDCLASS    wndclass;

      wndclass.style         = CS_VREDRAW | CS_HREDRAW;
      wndclass.lpfnWndProc   = (WNDPROC) MainWndProc;
      wndclass.hInstance     = hInstance;
      wndclass.hIcon         = LoadIcon(NULL, IDI_APPLICATION);
      wndclass.hCursor       = LoadCursor(NULL, IDC_ARROW);
      wndclass.hbrBackground = GetStockBrush(BLACK_BRUSH);
      wndclass.lpszMenuName  = "MAINMENU";
      wndclass.cbClsExtra    = 0;
      wndclass.cbWndExtra    = 0;
      wndclass.lpszClassName = ProgName;

      RegisterClass(&wndclass);
   }

   ghInstance = hInstance;

   hWnd = CreateWindow(ProgName, ProgName,
                       WS_OVERLAPPEDWINDOW,
                       CW_USEDEFAULT, CW_USEDEFAULT,
                       CW_USEDEFAULT, CW_USEDEFAULT,
                       NULL, NULL, hInstance, NULL);
```

continues

Listing 19.1. continued

```
   ShowWindow(hWnd, nCmdShow);
   UpdateWindow(hWnd);


   while (GetMessage(&msg, NULL, 0, 0))
   {
      TranslateMessage(&msg);
      DispatchMessage(&msg);
   }
   return msg.wParam;
}

/*******************************************/
#pragma argsused
HDDEDATA FAR PASCAL _export DdeCallBackProc(UINT iType, UINT iFmt,
                             HCONV hConv, HSZ hs1, HSZ hsz2,
                             HDDEDATA hData, DWORD Data1, DWORD
                             Data2)
{
   switch (iType)
   {
      case XTYP_DISCONNECT :
      {
         MessageBox(NULL, "Server forced disconncect", NULL, MB_OK
                    | MB_ICONSTOP);

      }

      case XTYP_ERROR:
         break;

      case XTYP_XACT_COMPLETE:
         break;


   }

   return ((HDDEDATA) NULL);

}

/*******************************************/
#pragma argsused
void WMCommand_Handler(HWND hWnd, int id, HWND hwndCtl, UINT
                       codeNotify)
{
```

```
switch (id)
{
   case IDM_EXIT :
   {
   SendMessage(hWnd, WM_DESTROY, 0, 0L);
   }

   case IDM_GO :
   {
   char Cmd1[] = "[CreateGroup(Group Name)]";
   char Cmd2[] = "[AddItem(Dummy Item)]";
   char Cmd3[] = "[AddItem(c:\DDEMLDMO.EXE,DDEML Demo)]";

      // Create string handles
   hszService = DdeCreateStringHandle(idInst,"PROGMAN",
                                      CP_WINANSI);
   hszTopic = DdeCreateStringHandle(idInst,"PROGMAN",
                                    CP_WINANSI);
   hszItem = DdeCreateStringHandle(idInst, NULL,CP_WINANSI);

      // Make DDE connection
   hConv = DdeConnect(idInst, hszService, hszTopic,
                      (PCONVCONTEXT) NULL);
   if (hConv == NULL)
   {
      MessageBox(hWnd, "Error connecting with DDE", NULL,
                 MB_OK);
      return;
   }

   // Send messages to ProgMan
      //   First, send CreateGroup command.
   hData = DdeCreateDataHandle(idInst, &Cmd1,
             sizeof(Cmd1), 0L, hszItem, CF_TEXT, 0);

   if (hData != NULL)
      hData = DdeClientTransaction((LPBYTE)hData, -1, hConv,
        hszItem, CF_TEXT, XTYP_EXECUTE, 1000, &result);

   // Next, send AddItem command to create
      //    a dummy item name.
   hData = DdeCreateDataHandle(idInst, &Cmd2,
             sizeof(Cmd2), 0L, hszItem, CF_TEXT, 0);

   if (hData != NULL)
      hData = DdeClientTransaction((LPBYTE)hData, -1, hConv,
        hszItem, CF_TEXT, XTYP_EXECUTE, 1000, &result);
```

continues

Listing 19.1. continued

```
      // Now, send AddItem command to create
         //    the programs name
      hData = DdeCreateDataHandle(idInst, &Cmd3,
                sizeof(Cmd3), 0L, hszItem, CF_TEXT, 0);

      if (hData != NULL)
         hData = DdeClientTransaction((LPBYTE)hData, -1, hConv,
           hszItem, CF_TEXT, XTYP_EXECUTE, 1000, &result);


      // Remove DDE connection
      DdeDisconnect(hConv);


      }

   }
}

/*******************************************/
LRESULT CALLBACK _export MainWndProc(HWND hWnd, UINT message,
                                     WPARAM wParam, LPARAM lParam)
{
   switch (message)
   {
      case WM_CREATE :
      {
      fnDdeCallBack = MakeProcInstance((FARPROC)DdeCallBackProc,
      ghInstance);

      result = DdeInitialize(&idInst, (PFNCALLBACK)fnDdeCallBack,
                     APPCLASS_STANDARD | APPCMD_CLIENTONLY, 0L);
      if (result)
      {
         MessageBox(hWnd, "Unable to initialize", ProgName,
                     MB_ICONEXCLAMATION | MB_OK);
                     DestroyWindow(hWnd);
                     return FALSE;
      }

      }

      case WM_PAINT :
      {
         HDC         PaintDC;
```

```
    RECT        rect;
    PAINTSTRUCT ps;

       PaintDC = BeginPaint(hWnd, &ps);
    GetClientRect(hWnd, &rect);

       // Display the "fancy" background
    PaintGradiantBackground(hWnd, PaintDC, 32);

       // We don't want the output to look ugly
    SetBkMode(PaintDC, TRANSPARENT);

    // Make sure the text will be displayed in white
    SetTextColor(PaintDC, RGB(255, 255, 255));

    DrawText(PaintDC, "Example DDEML Program to "
             "Communicate with ProgMan",
             -1, &rect, DT_SINGLELINE ¦ DT_CENTER ¦
             DT_VCENTER);

       EndPaint(hWnd, &ps);
       return 0;
    }

    case WM_COMMAND :
    {
    return HANDLE_WM_COMMAND(hWnd, wParam, lParam,
                             WMCommand_Handler);
    }


    case WM_DESTROY :
    {
    FreeProcInstance(fnDdeCallBack);
       DdeUninitialize(idInst);

       PostQuitMessage(0);
       return 0;
    }
  }

  return DefWindowProc (hWnd, message, wParam, lParam);
}


/*******************************************/
void PaintGradiantBackground(HWND hWnd, HDC hDC, int Steps)
{
```

continues

```
   int     i, colorinc, Stepsize;
   RECT    rect, rect2;
   HBRUSH  hBrush;

   GetClientRect(hWnd, &rect);

   rect2.left  = 0;
   rect2.right = rect.right;

   Stepsize = (rect.bottom/Steps) + 1;

   colorinc = 255 / (Steps);

   // Create and display the colors
   for (i=0; i<=Steps; i++)
   {
      hBrush = CreateSolidBrush(RGB(0, 0, i*colorinc));
      rect2.top = rect.top + i * Stepsize;
      rect2.bottom = rect.top + (i+1)*Stepsize;

      FillRect(hDC, &rect2, hBrush);
      DeleteBrush(hBrush);
   }

}
```

Listing 19.2. DDEMLDMO header file.

```
/*
 * DDEMLDMO.Hheader file
 *
 */


#define IDM_GO   100
#define IDM_EXIT 110
```

Listing 19.3. DDEMLDMO resource script.

```
/*
 * Dynamic data exchange management library demo
 *
 */

#include "ddemldmo.h"

MAINMENU MENU
BEGIN
     POPUP "&File"
     BEGIN
          MENUITEM "E&xit", IDM_EXIT
     END

     POPUP "&Install"
     BEGIN
          MENUITEM "&Go", IDM_GO
     END

END
```

Listing 19.4. DDEMLDMO module definition file.

```
;
; DDEMLDMO.DEF module definition file
;

DESCRIPTION    'DDEML Demo'
NAME           DDEMLDMO
EXETYPE        WINDOWS
STUB           'WINSTUB.EXE'
HEAPSIZE       1024
STACKSIZE      8192
CODE           PRELOAD MOVEABLE DISCARDABLE
DATA           PRELOAD MOVEABLE MULTIPLE
```

When you run the DDEMLDMO program, a menu item is displayed that enables you to start the install procedure (see Figure 19.2). When you choose the Install menu option and select Go, a transaction is started with Program Manager. A new group is added with two items (see Figure 19.3). One is an item for the DDEMLDMO program, and the other is an extra icon that points to nothing. Because you don't specify an icon, Program Manager assigns the item a default icon.

Figure 19.2.

DDEMLDMO program's main window.

Figure 19.3.

Program Manager with new group.

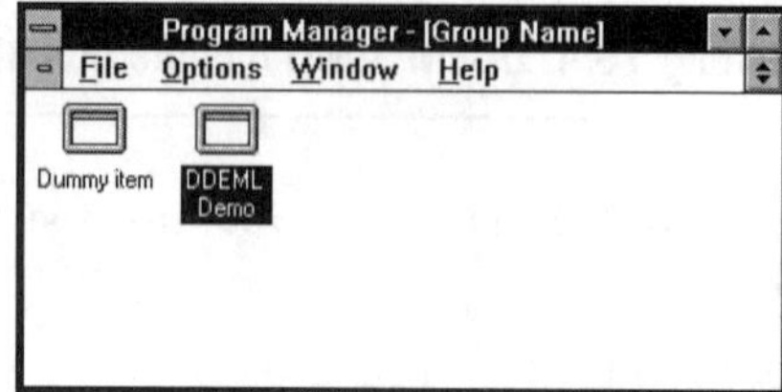

A New Background Color

As a side note, you might notice the background window for the DDEMLDMO program looks a little different than other programs in this book. The background uses a gradient fill that gradually changes from black at the top of the window to dark blue at the bottom.

The following function accomplishes this effect:

```
void PaintGradiantBackground(HWND hWnd, HDC hDC, int Steps)
{
   int     i, colorinc, Stepsize;
   RECT    rect, rect2;
   HBRUSH  hBrush;

   GetClientRect(hWnd, &rect);

   rect2.left  = 0;
   rect2.right = rect.right;

   Stepsize = (rect.bottom/Steps) + 1;

   colorinc = 255 / (Steps);

   // Create and display the colors
   for (i=0; i<=Steps; i++)
   {
      hBrush = CreateSolidBrush(RGB(0, 0, i*colorinc));
      rect2.top = rect.top + i * Stepsize;
      rect2.bottom = rect.top + (i+1)*Stepsize;

      FillRect(hDC, &rect2, hBrush);
      DeleteBrush(hBrush);
   }

}
```

The function takes a number that specifies the number of lines of color to use in the window. It then enters a loop in which a brush is created with a specified color. The `FillRect()` function is used to display a rectangle of color starting at the top of the window. As the loop is executed, the entire window is colored with the gradient fill color.

What You Have Learned

This chapter covered the topic of dynamic data exchange. Besides regular dynamic data exchange (which is based on messages) the dynamic data exchange management library was discussed. In particular, the following topics are covered:

- Dynamic data exchange is a devised standard of messages used to transfer information between cooperating applications.
- Two programs transferring information with dynamic data exchange are engaged in a conversation.
- The application that starts the conversation is the client application. The program that responds to the client is the server application.
- A permanent data link between two applications can be characterized in one of two types. A warm link allows a server to notify the client that a value of a data item has changed, but the server does not send the data value to the client until the client requests it. In a hot link, the server sends the changed value immediately to the client application.
- The data exchanged between applications is stored in a three-level hierarchy. The application name is the name of the server application. The conversation topic is a general classification of data. The data item is the information exchanged between applications.
- There are nine special Windows messages defined for dynamic data exchange. They all start with the `WM_DDE_` prefix and require you to include the DDE.H header file in your program to declare them.
- To send the dynamic data exchange messages to other applications, use the `SendMessage` and `PostMessage` API routines.
- Program Manager includes several dynamic data exchange commands for adding, deleting, and displaying program groups. An installation program can use these commands to create Program Manager groups for a newly installed application automatically.
- The dynamic data exchange management library is a group of functions in the DDEML.DLL dynamic link library that simplifies sending, posting, and receiving dynamic data exchange messages.
- The dynamic data exchange management library comes as part of Windows 3.1 and requires that a program be running in Windows standard or enhanced operating modes.

- The dynamic data exchange management library declares 27 new API functions. To use them in your program, you must include the DDEML.H header file.

20
PUTTING IT ALL TOGETHER

IN THIS CHAPTER

- Using a custom icon in a program.
- Handling main menu options.
- Processing mouse messages.
- Creating and using dialog boxes.
- Manipulating bitmaps.
- Creating a SpeedBar.
- Creating a help screen.

This chapter is a little different from the other chapters in this book. No new topics are discussed, and you don't learn about any new programming tools. This chapter's purpose is to show you how to use what you have learned to create a large Windows program. Although the program doesn't stack up with the code required for a major application such as a commercial spreadsheet or a word processor, it does give you a good idea about tying concepts together.

About the Program

When you first glance at a graphical image in Windows, it might be difficult to tell how the image was created. For example, if you look at the Borland Windows Custom Controls (you know, the "look of chiseled steel"), it can be difficult to tell how the effect was created. Actually, if a program has a gray background and you display a white line on the top and left sides and, at the same time, display a black line on the right and bottom sides, you get a three-dimensional effect.

The program presented here, called Magnify, is a tool for magnifying portions of the screen (see Figure 20.1). It is easy to use. Choose a magnification factor and then click the mouse cursor in the client area of the program. Now, drag the cursor about the screen. The client area of the program is filled with the area surrounding the mouse cursor.

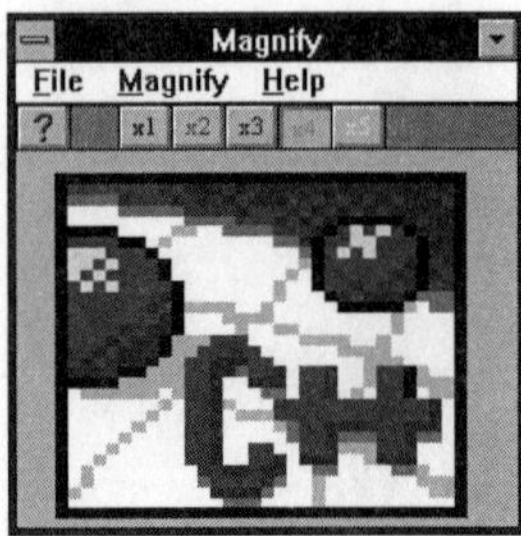

Figure 20.1.
Using the Magnify program.

The program is based on the ObjectWindows Library and is made up of three .CPP source code modules, three header files, a resource script, a module definition file, an icon, and six bitmaps (one for each SpeedBar button). Table 20.1 lists the files to include in the project, along with a brief description. Notice the use of the BWCC.LIB import library, which is included with Turbo C++ for Windows and usually is found in the C:\TCWIN\LIB subdirectory. Table 20.2 lists the header files used in the program (remember, header files aren't included in the project). Table 20.3 lists the graphical resources required for the program (these are referenced in the resource script).

Table 20.1. Files that must be included in the Magnify project (PRJ) file.

File	*Description*
magmain.cpp	Main entry point for the program.
magwnd.cpp	Handles main window processing.
magspeed.cpp	Handles processing of the SpeedBar.
magnify.rc	Resource script that contains menus and dialog box templates, as well as references to icons and bitmaps.
magnify.def	Module definition file.
bwcc.lib	Import library for Borland Windows Custom Controls.

Table 20.2. Magnify header files.

File	*Description*
magnify.h	Declares classes used throughout the program.
magmenus.h	Defines menu identifiers.
maglobal.h	Global variable declarations.

Table 20.3. Graphical images used in Magnify program.

File	*Description*
magnify.ico	Program's main icon.
times1.bmp	Bitmap for x1 SpeedBar button.
times2.bmp	Bitmap for x2 SpeedBar button.
times3.bmp	Bitmap for x3 SpeedBar button.
times4.bmp	Bitmap for x4 SpeedBar button.
times5.bmp	Bitmap for x5 SpeedBar button.
helpbmp.bmp	Bitmap for help SpeedBar button.

Program Preliminaries

The magnify.h header file declares the classes for the program. Three classes are declared, one derived from `TApplication` and two derived from `TWindow`. The class derived from `TApplication`, called `TOwlApp`, takes care of application specific processing. `TMainWindow` is derived from `TWindow` and provides processing for the main window of the program. `TSpeedBarWindow` also is derived from `TWindow` and provides support for processing the SpeedBar, which is a separate window.

The magmain.cpp module is rather small. It contains some global variable initialization, the constructor for `TOwlApp`, and the `WinMain` program entry point.

Main Window Processing

The main window is processed in the magwnd.cpp module. It contains code for processing main menu commands and mouse movements and for painting the client area. The `TMainWindow` constructor sets the initial size of the window. The `GetWindowClass` member function initializes the class members and sets initial attributes for the window.

Responding to the Main Menu

Message response functions are declared in the `TMainWindow` class and respond to the menu commands. The File menu simply contains an Exit option that allows the user to shut down the program. The Magnify option is one way to select a magnification factor (the other being the SpeedBar). A check mark next to the menu item notifies the user of the currently selected magnification factor.

When a magnification factor is selected through the menus, it calls a function in the `SpeedBarWindow` class to check the menu item and to display the button on the SpeedBar so it appears "pressed in." This design choice allows the code for selecting the magnification factor to appear in only one place.

The Help menu item gives access to an Information menu item and an About box. The Information box (see Figure 20.2) is a `MessageBox` with multiple lines. The "`\n`" character is used to specify a line-feed in the message box.

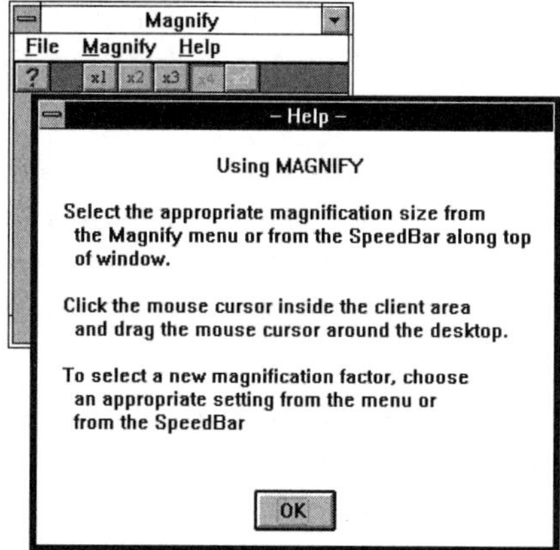

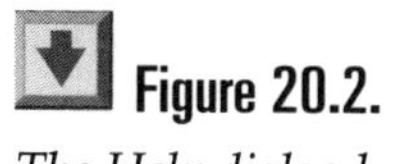

Figure 20.2.

The Help dialog box.

The About box uses the Borland Windows Custom Controls to display a brief title and copyright message. The dialog box contains the program's icons and several lines of static text (see Figure 20.3).

Figure 20.3.
The About dialog box.

Responding to the Mouse

When the user clicks the left mouse button in the client area of the program, the `WMLButtonDown` function is executed. The `SetCapture` API function is called immediately. This directs Windows to send all mouse messages to the currently active window, even if the mouse cursor moves outside the client area. The `DrawMouseRect` function is called to display the rectangular square around the mouse cursor. This designates the area being magnified in the client area.

The `DrawMouseRect` function creates a display context for the screen (similar to when you created a splash screen in Chapter 16, "Even More GDI"). This function sets the drawing mode to `R2_NOT`. The `Polyline` function displays the rectangle.

When the rectangle is drawn, the `R2_NOT` drawing mode displays without losing what is under the square. `R2_NOT` draws the rectangle over the same location a second time, so the rectangle disappears, and whatever was there before appears untouched. This is important because the program should not leave trails on the screen.

As the user moves the mouse, the `WMMouseMove` message response function is called. It first draws the rectangle around the cursor (to make it disappear). `WMMouseMove` then draws the rectangle at the new mouse location. The `StretchBlt` function is used to copy the area around the cursor to the client area.

Finally, when the user releases the mouse, the `WMLButtonUp` function is called. It uses the `ReleaseCapture` API function to cause mouse messages to be sent to the window the mouse is moved over, reversing the results of the `SetCursor` function.

SpeedBar Processing

In the `SetupWindows` member function of `TMainWindow`, an instance of `TSpeedBarWindow` is created. The idea is to force the SpeedBar window to be displayed beneath the menu of the main window. Therefore, the `TSpeedBarWindow` constructor sets the initial location of the window below the menu bar of the program. The style of the SpeedBar Window is set to `WS_CHILD ¦ WS_VISIBLE ¦ WS_BORDER`. Thus, it is a child window with a border and is initially displayed.

The `Paint` member function takes care of displaying the SpeedBar bitmaps in the appropriate locations by calling the `DisplayButton` member function to paint a specified bitmap at a specific location in the SpeedBar window.

Because the SpeedBar buttons contain graphical images, regular Windows buttons cannot be used. Instead, the program does all processing of SpeedBar buttons. That is, the program must paint the button's image, detect the click of the mouse button, decide which button the user wanted to select, and then paint the selected button.

The program uses two types of buttons. The Help button works similarly to a regular button. You press it, it appears "pressed in;" you let go, and the button appears as normal. On the other hand, the buttons used for the magnification factor stay pressed in. This visually enables the user to know which magnification factor is selected.

The SpeedBar class includes a `WMLButtonDown` message response function. This checks the coordinates of the mouse and displays the button for the area in the SpeedBar for which the mouse button has been pressed. You notice different processing for the Help button than for the other buttons, because of its different style.

The `WMLButtonUp` function takes care of displaying the Help button in its default location. The magnification buttons don't require any processing for this, because they work differently than the Help buttons.

The Code

The source code for the program follows. Listing 20.1 contains magmain.cpp. Listing 20.2 contains magwnd.cpp. Listing 20.3 contains magspeed.cpp. Listing 20.4 contains magnify.h. Listing 20.5 contains magmenus.h. Listing 20.6 contains maglobal.h. Listing 20.7 contains magnify.rc, and Listing 20.8 contains magnify.def. The graphical resources are not in this chapter, but you find them on the included diskette.

Listing 20.1. MAGMAIN.CPP main Magnify program module.

```
// MAGMAIN.CPP  main module for MAGNIFY program
//
// (c) 1992 Paul J. Perry
//


#include "magnify.h"

// Global variables

int SpeedBarHeight = 21;
int SpeedBarButtonWidth  = 24;
int MagFactor = 5;
BOOL But_H_Displayed = FALSE;
int PrevMagfactor;
int Xsize;
int Ysize;


/*---------------------------------
   TOwlApp Class Member Functions
---------------------------------*/
```

```
/*******************************************/
void TOwlApp::InitMainWindow()
{
   MainWindow = new TMainWindow(NULL, Name);
}


/*--------------------------------
    WinMain Program Entry Point
--------------------------------*/
/*******************************************/
int PASCAL WinMain(HINSTANCE hInstance, HINSTANCE hPrevInstance,
                   LPSTR lpCmdLine, int nCmdShow)
{

   TOwlApp ThisApp("Magnify", hInstance, hPrevInstance,
                   lpCmdLine, nCmdShow);
   ThisApp.Run();
   return ThisApp.Status;

}
```

Listing 20.2. MAGWND.CPP code for processing main window.

```
// MAGWND.CPP member functions for main window of
//            MAGNIFY program
//
// (c) 1992 Paul J. Perry
//

#include <bwcc.h>

#include "magnify.h"
#include "maglobal.h"


// Class data member initialization

BOOL TMainWindow::Capturing = FALSE;
BOOL TMainWindow::SavedScreen = FALSE;

POINT TMainWindow::PrevBeginPoint = { 0, 0 };
POINT TMainWindow::PrevEndPoint = { 0, 0 };
```

continues

Listing 20.2. continued

```
POINT TMainWindow::BeginPoint = { 0, 0 };
POINT TMainWindow::EndPoint = { 0, 0 };


/*--------------------------------------
    TMainWindow Class Member Functions
--------------------------------------*/

/********************************************/
TMainWindow::TMainWindow(PTWindowsObject AParent, LPSTR ATitle)
            : TWindow(AParent, ATitle)
{
   // Set initial size of window
   Attr.W = 190;
   Attr.H = 190;
}



/********************************************/
LPSTR TMainWindow::GetClassName()
{
   return "MagnifyClass";
}

/********************************************/
void TMainWindow::GetWindowClass(WNDCLASS& wndclass)
{
   TWindow::GetWindowClass(wndclass);

   // Set new values for window class
   wndclass.hIcon = LoadIcon(GetApplication()->hInstance,
                             "MAGICON");
   wndclass.lpszMenuName = "MAINMENU";

   Attr.Style = WS_OVERLAPPED ¦ WS_CAPTION ¦ WS_SYSMENU ¦
   WS_THICKFRAME ¦ WS_MINIMIZEBOX;
}


/********************************************/
void TMainWindow::SetupWindow()
{
```

```
    // Create a compatible DC for saving Window contents when
    //    minimized
    HDC hDC = GetDC(HWindow);
    hMemDC = CreateCompatibleDC(hDC);
    ReleaseDC(HWindow, hDC);

    SpeedBarWindow = new TSpeedBarWindow(this, NULL);
    GetApplication()->MakeWindow(SpeedBarWindow);
}

/*******************************************/
void TMainWindow::ShutDownWindow()
{
    TWindowsObject::ShutDownWindow();
}

/*******************************************/
void TMainWindow::DrawMouseRect(POINT UpperLeft,
                    POINT LowerRight)
{
    POINT PointList[5];

    HDC hDC = CreateDC("DISPLAY", NULL, NULL, NULL);

    SetROP2(hDC, R2_NOT);

    ClientToScreen(HWindow, &UpperLeft);
    ClientToScreen(HWindow, &LowerRight);

    PointList[0].x = UpperLeft.x;
    PointList[0].y = UpperLeft.y;
    PointList[1].x = LowerRight.x;
    PointList[1].y = UpperLeft.y;
    PointList[2].x = LowerRight.x;
    PointList[2].y = LowerRight.y;
    PointList[3].x = UpperLeft.x;
    PointList[3].y = LowerRight.y;
    PointList[4].x = UpperLeft.x;
    PointList[4].y = UpperLeft.y;

    // Display box around mouse cursor as the user moves the
    //    mouse outside of the client area.
    Polyline(hDC, PointList, sizeof(PointList) / sizeof(POINT));

    DeleteDC(hDC);
}
```

continues

Listing 20.2. continued

```
/*******************************************/
void TMainWindow::WMLButtonDown(RTMessage Msg)
{
   SetCapture(HWindow);
   Capturing = TRUE;

   BeginPoint.x = LOWORD(Msg.LParam) - Xsize;
   BeginPoint.y = HIWORD(Msg.LParam) - Ysize;
   EndPoint.x   = LOWORD(Msg.LParam) + Xsize;
   EndPoint.y   = HIWORD(Msg.LParam) + Ysize;

   DrawMouseRect(BeginPoint, EndPoint);

   PrevBeginPoint = BeginPoint;
   PrevEndPoint = EndPoint;
}

/*******************************************/
void TMainWindow::WMMouseMove(RTMessage Msg)
{
   HDC hDC;
   RECT rect;

   if (Capturing)
   {
      BeginPoint.x = LOWORD(Msg.LParam) - Xsize;
      BeginPoint.y = HIWORD(Msg.LParam) - Ysize;
      EndPoint.x   = LOWORD(Msg.LParam) + Xsize;
      EndPoint.y   = HIWORD(Msg.LParam) + Ysize;

      // Erase rectangle drawn during WM_LBUTTONDOWN message
      DrawMouseRect(PrevBeginPoint, PrevEndPoint);

      // Draw new rectangle
      DrawMouseRect(BeginPoint, EndPoint);

      // Transfer mouse rectangle box contents to client window
      hDC = GetDC(HWindow);
      GetClientRect(HWindow, &rect);
      StretchBlt(hDC, 0, 0+SpeedBarHeight, rect.right, rect.bottom,
                 hDC,
           BeginPoint.x+1, BeginPoint.y+1,
           EndPoint.x - BeginPoint.x-1,
           EndPoint.y - BeginPoint.y-1, SRCCOPY);
      ReleaseDC(HWindow, hDC);
```

```
      PrevBeginPoint = BeginPoint;
      PrevEndPoint = EndPoint;
   }
}

/*******************************************/
#pragma argsused
void TMainWindow::WMLButtonUp(RTMessage Msg)
{
   ReleaseCapture();
   Capturing = FALSE;

   DrawMouseRect(BeginPoint, EndPoint);

   BeginPoint.x = 0;
   BeginPoint.y = 0;
   EndPoint.x = 0;
   EndPoint.y = 0;

   PrevBeginPoint.x = 0;
   PrevBeginPoint.y = 0;
   PrevEndPoint.x = 0;
   PrevEndPoint.y = 0;

}

/*******************************************/
#pragma argsused
void TMainWindow::WMActivateApp(RTMessage Msg)
{
   HBITMAP hOldBM;


   if ( !(BOOL)Msg.WParam)
   {
      GetClientRect(HWindow, &BMrect);
      HDC hDC = GetDC(HWindow);

      hBitmap = CreateCompatibleBitmap(hDC, BMrect.right,
                                       BMrect.bottom);
      hOldBM = SelectBitmap(hMemDC, hBitmap);

      BitBlt(hMemDC, 0, 0, BMrect.right, BMrect.bottom, hDC, 0, 0,
             SRCCOPY);
      SelectBitmap(hMemDC, hOldBM);
      DeleteBitmap(hBitmap);
      SavedScreen = TRUE;
```

continues

Listing 20.2. continued

```
      ReleaseDC(HWindow, hDC);
   }

}

/*******************************************/
#pragma argsused
void TMainWindow::Paint(HDC PaintDC, PAINTSTRUCT &PaintInfo)
{
   if (SavedScreen)
   {
      RECT rect;
      GetClientRect(HWindow, &rect);
      StretchBlt(PaintDC, 0, 0, rect.right, rect.bottom,
           hMemDC, 0, 0, BMrect.right, BMrect.bottom, SRCCOPY);
      SavedScreen = TRUE;
   }

}

/*******************************************/
#pragma argsused
void TMainWindow::ExitProgram(RTMessage Msg)
{
   PostQuitMessage(0);
}

/*******************************************/
#pragma argsused
void TMainWindow::AboutProgram(RTMessage Msg)
{
   TDialog *PAbout;

   PAbout = new TDialog(this, "ABOUTDIALOG");
   GetApplication()->ExecDialog(PAbout);

}

/*******************************************/
#pragma argsused
void TMainWindow::Help(RTMessage Msg)
{
   MessageBox(HWindow,
   "                              Using MAGNIFY\n\n"
   " Select the appropriate magnification size from\n"
```

```
    "   the Magnify menu or from the SpeedBar along top\n"
    "   of window.\n"
    "\n"
    " Click the mouse cursor inside the client area\n"
    "   and drag the mouse cursor around the desktop.\n"
    "\n"
    " To select a new magnification factor, choose\n"
    "   an appropriate setting from the menu or\n"
    "   from the SpeedBar\n",

    "-- Help --", MB_OK);

}

/*******************************************/
#pragma argsused
void TMainWindow::TimesOne(RTMessage Msg)
{
   SpeedBarWindow->SetMagnificationButton(1);
}

/*******************************************/
#pragma argsused
void TMainWindow::TimesTwo(RTMessage Msg)
{
   SpeedBarWindow->SetMagnificationButton(2);
}

/*******************************************/
#pragma argsused
void TMainWindow::TimesThree(RTMessage Msg)
{
   SpeedBarWindow->SetMagnificationButton(3);
}

/*******************************************/
#pragma argsused
void TMainWindow::TimesFour(RTMessage Msg)
{
   SpeedBarWindow->SetMagnificationButton(4);
}

/*******************************************/
#pragma argsused
void TMainWindow::TimesFive(RTMessage Msg)
{
   SpeedBarWindow->SetMagnificationButton(5);
}
```

Listing 20.3. MAGSPEED.CPP code for processing the SpeedBar.

```
//  MAGSPEED.CPP module which processes the speedbar for
//                MAGNIFY application
//
// (c) 1992 Paul J. Perry
//

#include "magnify.h"
#include "maglobal.h"
#include "magmenus.h"

/*-----------------------------------------------
    TSpeedBarWindow Class Member Functions
-----------------------------------------------*/

/*********************************************/
TSpeedBarWindow::TSpeedBarWindow(PTWindowsObject AParent, LPSTR
                                  ATitle)
             : TWindow(AParent, ATitle)
{
   Attr.Style = WS_CHILD ¦ WS_VISIBLE ¦ WS_BORDER;
   Attr.X = 0;
   Attr.Y = 0;
   Attr.W = 999;
   Attr.H = SpeedBarHeight;
}

/*********************************************/
void TSpeedBarWindow::GetWindowClass(WNDCLASS& wndclass)
{
   TWindow::GetWindowClass(wndclass);
   wndclass.hbrBackground = (HBRUSH)LTGRAY_BRUSH;
}

/*********************************************/
LPSTR TSpeedBarWindow::GetClassName()
{
   return "SpeedBarWindow";
}

/*********************************************/
void TSpeedBarWindow::SetMagnificationButton(int Factor)
{

/*
 * Set the rectangle size which the cursor will turn to when you
 * drag out of the client area.  Factor should be between 1 and 5.
```

```
 *
 */

   RECT  rect;
   HDC   hDC = GetDC(HWindow);
   HMENU hMenu = GetMenu( ((PTMainWindow)Parent)->HWindow);


   GetClientRect(HWindow, &rect);

   if (PrevMagFactor)
   {
      switch(PrevMagFactor)
      {
      case 1 :
      {
         DisplayButton(hDC, SpeedBarButtonWidth*2, "TIMES1BMP");
         CheckMenuItem(hMenu, IDM_TIMESONE, MF_UNCHECKED);
            break;
         }

      case 2 :
      {
         DisplayButton(hDC, SpeedBarButtonWidth*3+1, "TIMES2BMP");
         CheckMenuItem(hMenu, IDM_TIMESTWO, MF_UNCHECKED);
            break;
         }

      case 3 :
      {
         DisplayButton(hDC, SpeedBarButtonWidth*4+2, "TIMES3BMP");
         CheckMenuItem(hMenu, IDM_TIMESTHREE, MF_UNCHECKED);
            break;
         }

      case 4 :
      {
         DisplayButton(hDC, SpeedBarButtonWidth*5+3, "TIMES4BMP");
         CheckMenuItem(hMenu, IDM_TIMESFOUR, MF_UNCHECKED);
            break;
         }

      case 5 :
      {
         DisplayButton(hDC, SpeedBarButtonWidth*6+4, "TIMES5BMP");
         CheckMenuItem(hMenu, IDM_TIMESFIVE, MF_UNCHECKED);
            break;
      }
```

continues

Listing 20.3. continued

```
      }
   }

   switch(Factor)
   {
      case 1 :
      {
      Xsize = (rect.right/10);
      Ysize = (rect.bottom*4);
      DisplayPushedButton(hDC, SpeedBarButtonWidth*2, "TIMES1BMP");
      PrevMagFactor = Factor;
      MagFactor = Factor;
      CheckMenuItem(hMenu, IDM_TIMESONE, MF_CHECKED);
      break;
      }

      case 2 :
      {
      Xsize = 60; // (rect.right)/4;
      Ysize = 60; // (rect.bottom)/4;
      DisplayPushedButton(hDC, SpeedBarButtonWidth*3+1, "TIMES2BMP");
      PrevMagFactor = Factor;
      MagFactor = Factor;
      CheckMenuItem(hMenu, IDM_TIMESTWO, MF_CHECKED);
      break;
      }

      case 3 :
      {
      Xsize = 40; // (rect.right)/8;
         Ysize = 40; // (rect.bottom)/8;
      DisplayPushedButton(hDC, SpeedBarButtonWidth*4+2, "TIMES3BMP");
      PrevMagFactor = Factor;
      MagFactor = Factor;
      CheckMenuItem(hMenu, IDM_TIMESTHREE, MF_CHECKED);
      break;
      }

      case 4 :
      {
      Xsize = 20; // (rect.right)/16;
         Ysize = 20; // (rect.bottom)/16;
```

```
        DisplayPushedButton(hDC, SpeedBarButtonWidth*5+3, "TIMES4BMP");
        PrevMagFactor = Factor;
        MagFactor = Factor;
        CheckMenuItem(hMenu, IDM_TIMESFOUR, MF_CHECKED);
        break;
        }

        case 5 :
        {
        Xsize = 10;  // (rect.right)/32;
           Ysize = 10; // (rect.bottom)/32;
        DisplayPushedButton(hDC, SpeedBarButtonWidth*6+4, "TIMES5BMP");
        PrevMagFactor = Factor;
        MagFactor = Factor;
        CheckMenuItem(hMenu, IDM_TIMESFIVE, MF_CHECKED);
        break;
        }
    }
    ReleaseDC(HWindow, hDC);

}

/*******************************************/
BOOL TSpeedBarWindow::DisplayButton(HDC PaintDC, int Distance,
                                    LPCSTR lpszBitmap)
{
/*
 * Display a button in the Speedbar Window
 *
 * Parameters:
 *
 *    int Distance - Distance from the left of the scroll bar to
 *              show the button.  This is specified in pixels.
 *
 *    LPCSTR lpszBitmap - The name of the bitmap resource
 *
 */

   RECT       rect;
   HBITMAP    hOldBM;

   HDC        MemDC      = CreateCompatibleDC(PaintDC);
   HINSTANCE  hInstance  = GetApplication()->hInstance;
```

continues

Listing 20.3. continued

```
   // Give the entire location of the button a dark gray background
   rect.left   = Distance;
   rect.top    = 0;
   rect.right  = Distance + SpeedBarButtonWidth;
   rect.bottom = SpeedBarHeight;
   FillRect(PaintDC, &rect, GetStockBrush(GRAY_BRUSH));

   // Draw black line to separate right side of button
   SelectPen(PaintDC, GetStockPen(BLACK_PEN));
   MoveTo(PaintDC, Distance+22+2, 0);
   LineTo(PaintDC, Distance+22+2, SpeedBarHeight);

   // Draw white lines on left and top sides of button
   SelectPen(PaintDC, GetStockPen(WHITE_PEN));
   MoveTo(PaintDC, Distance, 23);
   LineTo(PaintDC, Distance, 0);
   LineTo(PaintDC, Distance+22, 0);

   HBITMAP hBM = LoadBitmap(hInstance, lpszBitmap);

   hOldBM = SelectBitmap(MemDC, hBM);
   BitBlt(PaintDC, Distance+1, 1, 21, 16, MemDC,
       0, 0, SRCCOPY);

   // Cleanup now that we are done using the bitmap
   SelectBitmap(MemDC, hOldBM);

   DeleteBitmap(hBM);

   DeleteDC(MemDC);
   return TRUE;
}

/*******************************************/
BOOL TSpeedBarWindow::DisplayPushedButton(HDC PaintDC, int Distance,
                                          LPCSTR lpszBitmap)
{
   RECT        rect;
   HBITMAP     hOldBM;

   HDC         hMemDC     = CreateCompatibleDC(PaintDC);
   HINSTANCE   hInstance = GetApplication()->hInstance;

   // Draw black line to separate right side of button
   SelectPen(PaintDC, GetStockPen(BLACK_PEN));
   MoveTo(PaintDC, Distance+22+2, 0);
```

```
   LineTo(PaintDC, Distance+22+2, SpeedBarHeight);


   // Redraw dark gray background for button
   rect.left   = Distance;
   rect.top    = 0;
   rect.right  = Distance + SpeedBarButtonWidth;
   rect.bottom = SpeedBarHeight;
   FillRect(PaintDC, &rect, GetStockBrush(GRAY_BRUSH));


   rect.left   = Distance+2;
   rect.top    = 2;
   rect.right  = Distance + SpeedBarButtonWidth;
   rect.bottom = SpeedBarHeight+1;
   FillRect(PaintDC, &rect, GetStockBrush(LTGRAY_BRUSH));

   HBITMAP hBM = LoadBitmap(hInstance, lpszBitmap);


   hOldBM = SelectBitmap(hMemDC, hBM);
   BitBlt(PaintDC, Distance+1+1, 1+1, 23, 18, hMemDC,
       0, 0, SRCCOPY);

   // Cleanup after we are done processing bitmap
   SelectBitmap(hMemDC, hOldBM);

   DeleteDC(hMemDC);
   DeleteBitmap(hBM);

   return TRUE;
}


/*********************************************/
void TSpeedBarWindow::WMLButtonDown(RTMessage Msg)
{
   int x = LOWORD(Msg.LParam);

   SetCapture(HWindow);

   if (x <= SpeedBarButtonWidth)
   {
      HDC hDC = GetDC(HWindow);
      DisplayPushedButton(hDC, 0, "HELPBMP");
      But_H_Displayed = TRUE;
      ReleaseDC(HWindow, hDC);
   }
```

continues

Listing 20.3. continued

```
   // Times 1
   if ( (x<SpeedBarButtonWidth*3) && (x>SpeedBarButtonWidth*2) )
   {
      SetMagnificationButton(1);
   }

   // Times 2
   if ( (x<SpeedBarButtonWidth*4) && (x>SpeedBarButtonWidth*3) )
   {
      SetMagnificationButton(2);
   }

   // Times 3
   if ( (x<SpeedBarButtonWidth*5) && (x>SpeedBarButtonWidth*4) )
   {
      SetMagnificationButton(3);
   }

   // Times 4
   if ( (x<SpeedBarButtonWidth*6) && (x>SpeedBarButtonWidth*5) )
   {
      SetMagnificationButton(4);
   }

   // Times 5
   if ( (x<SpeedBarButtonWidth*7) && (x>SpeedBarButtonWidth*6) )
   {
      SetMagnificationButton(5);
   }

}

/*******************************************/
#pragma argsused
void TSpeedBarWindow::WMLButtonUp(RTMessage Msg)
{

   if (But_H_Displayed)
   {
      HDC hDC = GetDC(HWindow);
      DisplayButton(hDC, 0, "HELPBMP");
      ReleaseDC(HWindow, hDC);
      But_H_Displayed = FALSE;
      ((PTMainWindow)Parent)->Help(Msg);

   }
```

```
   ReleaseCapture();
}

/*******************************************/
#pragma argsused
void TSpeedBarWindow::Paint(HDC PaintDC, PAINTSTRUCT &PaintInfo)
{
   // Display buttons in speedbar
   DisplayButton(PaintDC, 0, "HELPBMP");

   SelectPen(PaintDC, GetStockPen(BLACK_PEN));
   MoveTo(PaintDC, SpeedBarButtonWidth*2-1, 0);
   LineTo(PaintDC, SpeedBarButtonWidth*2-1, SpeedBarHeight);

   DisplayButton(PaintDC, SpeedBarButtonWidth*2, "TIMES1BMP");
   DisplayButton(PaintDC, SpeedBarButtonWidth*3+1, "TIMES2BMP");
   DisplayButton(PaintDC, SpeedBarButtonWidth*4+2, "TIMES3BMP");
   DisplayButton(PaintDC, SpeedBarButtonWidth*5+3, "TIMES4BMP");
   DisplayButton(PaintDC, SpeedBarButtonWidth*6+4, "TIMES5BMP");

   SetMagnificationButton(MagFactor);
}
```

Listing 20.4. The magnify.h header file declares program classes.

```
//
//  MAGNIFY.H header file
//
// (c) 1992 Paul J. Perry
//

#define WIN31
#define STRICT

#include <owl.h>
#include <windowsx.h>

#include "magmenus.h"

// Class Declarations

/*******************************************/
class TOwlApp : public TApplication
{
```

continues

Listing 20.4. continued

```
   public :
      TOwlApp (LPSTR AName, HINSTANCE hInstance, HINSTANCE
             hPrevInstance,
          LPSTR CmdLine, int CmdShow) :
          TApplication(AName, hInstance, hPrevInstance,
                       CmdLine, CmdShow) { } ;

   virtual void InitMainWindow();
};

/********************************************/
_CLASSDEF(TSpeedBarWindow)
class TSpeedBarWindow : public TWindow
{
   public :
      TSpeedBarWindow(PTWindowsObject AParent, LPSTR ATitle);

      BOOL DisplayButton(HDC PaintDC, int Distance, LPCSTR
                         lpszBitmap);
      BOOL DisplayPushedButton(HDC PaintDC, int Distance,
                               LPCSTR lpszBitmap);
      void SetMagnificationButton(int Factor);

      virtual LPSTR GetClassName();
      virtual void GetWindowClass(WNDCLASS& wndclass);
      virtual void Paint(HDC PaintDC, PAINTSTRUCT &PaintInfo);
      virtual void WMLButtonDown(RTMessage Msg)
     = [WM_FIRST + WM_LBUTTONDOWN];
      virtual void WMLButtonUp(RTMessage Msg)
     = [WM_FIRST + WM_LBUTTONUP];
};


/********************************************/
_CLASSDEF(TMainWindow)
class TMainWindow : public TWindow
{
   public :
      static BOOL  Capturing;
      static BOOL  SavedScreen;
      static POINT PrevBeginPoint, PrevEndPoint;
      static POINT BeginPoint, EndPoint;
```

```
    HBITMAP          hBitmap;
    RECT             BMrect;
    HDC              hMemDC;
    PTSpeedBarWindow SpeedBarWindow;

    TMainWindow(PTWindowsObject AParent, LPSTR ATitle);

    void DrawMouseRect(POINT UpperLeft, POINT LowerRight);

    virtual void Paint(HDC PaintDC, PAINTSTRUCT &PaintInfo);
    virtual void SetupWindow();
    virtual void ShutDownWindow();
    virtual LPSTR GetClassName();
    virtual void GetWindowClass(WNDCLASS& wndclass);

    // WM_ Window message response functions
    virtual void WMLButtonDown(RTMessage Msg)
   = [WM_FIRST + WM_LBUTTONDOWN];
    virtual void WMMouseMove(RTMessage Msg)
   = [WM_FIRST + WM_MOUSEMOVE];
    virtual void WMLButtonUp(RTMessage Msg)
   = [WM_FIRST + WM_LBUTTONUP];
    virtual void WMActivateApp(RTMessage Msg)
   = [WM_FIRST + WM_ACTIVATEAPP];

    // Menu message response functions
    virtual void ExitProgram(RTMessage Msg)
   = [CM_FIRST + IDM_FILEEXIT];
    virtual void AboutProgram(RTMessage Msg)
   = [CM_FIRST + IDM_HELPABOUT];
    virtual void Help(RTMessage Msg)
   = [CM_FIRST + IDM_HELPINFO];
    virtual void TimesOne(RTMessage Msg)
   = [CM_FIRST + IDM_TIMESONE];
    virtual void TimesTwo(RTMessage Msg)
   = [CM_FIRST + IDM_TIMESTWO];
    virtual void TimesThree(RTMessage Msg)
   = [CM_FIRST + IDM_TIMESTHREE];
    virtual void TimesFour(RTMessage Msg)
   = [CM_FIRST + IDM_TIMESFOUR];
    virtual void TimesFive(RTMessage Msg)
   = [CM_FIRST + IDM_TIMESFIVE];

};
```

Listing 20.5. The magmenus.h contains menu definitions.

```
//
// MAGMENUS.H header file
//
// (c) 1992 Paul J. Perry

#define IDM_FILEEXIT    101
#define IDM_TIMESONE    102
#define IDM_TIMESTWO    103
#define IDM_TIMESTHREE  104
#define IDM_TIMESFOUR   105
#define IDM_TIMESFIVE   106
#define IDM_HELPINFO    107
#define IDM_HELPABOUT   108
```

Listing 20.6. The maglobal.h declares global variables.

```
//
// MAGLOBAL.H - Header file to declare global variables
//
// (c) 1992 Paul J. Perry


// Global Variables

extern int SpeedBarHeight;
extern int SpeedBarButtonWidth;
extern int MagFactor;
extern int Xsize;
extern int Ysize;
extern BOOL But_H_Displayed;
extern int PrevMagFactor;
```

Listing 20.7. MAGNIFY.RC resource script.

```
/*
 * MAGNIFY.RC resource script
 *
 * (c) 1992 Paul J. Perry
```

```
 *
 */

#include "magmenus.h"

MAGICON ICON "magnify.ico"

HELPBMP   BITMAP "helpbmp.bmp"
TIMES1BMP BITMAP "times1.bmp"
TIMES2BMP BITMAP "times2.bmp"
TIMES3BMP BITMAP "times3.bmp"
TIMES4BMP BITMAP "times4.bmp"
TIMES5BMP BITMAP "times5.bmp"


MAINMENU MENU
BEGIN
     POPUP "&File"
     BEGIN
          MENUITEM "E&xit", IDM_FILEEXIT
     END

     POPUP "&Magnify"
     BEGIN
          MENUITEM "x&1", IDM_TIMESONE
          MENUITEM "x&2", IDM_TIMESTWO
          MENUITEM "x&3", IDM_TIMESTHREE
          MENUITEM "x&4", IDM_TIMESFOUR
          MENUITEM "x&5", IDM_TIMESFIVE, CHECKED
     END

     POPUP "&Help"
     BEGIN
          MENUITEM "&Information", IDM_HELPINFO
          MENUITEM SEPARATOR
          MENUITEM "&About", IDM_HELPABOUT
     END

END

ABOUTDIALOG DIALOG 19, 22, 125, 68
STYLE DS_MODALFRAME | WS_POPUP | WS_CAPTION | WS_SYSMENU
CLASS "bordlg"
FONT 10, "Times New Roman"
BEGIN
     CONTROL "", 101, "BorShade", 1 | WS_CHILD | WS_VISIBLE, 4, 6,
     117, 32
```

continues

Listing 20.7. continued

```
     CONTROL "Button", IDOK, "BorBtn", BS_PUSHBUTTON | WS_CHILD |
        WS_VISIBLE | WS_TABSTOP, 47, 44, 32, 20
     CTEXT "Magnify", -1, 36, 8, 83, 8, WS_CHILD | WS_VISIBLE |
        WS_GROUP
     CTEXT "by Paul J. Perry", -1, 35, 20, 84, 8, WS_CHILD |
        WS_VISIBLE | WS_GROUP
     ICON "MAGICON", -1, 12, 10, 18, 17, WS_CHILD | WS_VISIBLE
     CONTROL "", 102, "BorShade", 2 | WS_CHILD | WS_VISIBLE, 2, 42,
        121, 1
     CONTROL "", 102, "BorShade", 2 | WS_CHILD | WS_VISIBLE, 2, 2,
        121, 1
END
```

Listing 20.8. MAGNIFY.DEF module definition file.

```
;
; MAGNIFY.DEF module definition file
; (c) 1992 Paul J. Perry

DESCRIPTION    'Magnify'
NAME           TRADITIONAL
EXETYPE        WINDOWS
STUB           'WINSTUB.EXE'
HEAPSIZE       4096
STACKSIZE      5120
CODE           PRELOAD MOVEABLE DISCARDABLE
DATA           PRELOAD MOVEABLE MULTIPLE
```

Epilogue

As you come to the end of this book, I truly hope you've gotten something out of it. You have learned about Windows programming and how to write programs for Windows. I want to congratulate you on making it to the end of the book. Many readers might make it through the first couple of chapters and set the book aside, saving it for a rainy day.

You'll always have more to learn (Windows NT, OLE, and so on), but you have a firm basis for learning about what is to come. I have enjoyed writing this book and hope you have enjoyed reading it. If you have any comments or suggestions, I'd like to hear from you. Please send a letter to:

Paul J. Perry
Turbo C++ for Windows Programming for Beginners
P.O. Box 66841
Scotts Valley, CA 95067

A VIRTUAL KEY CODES

The following list shows the symbolic constant names, hexadecimal values, and descriptive information for the Windows virtual key codes. The codes are in numeric order.

Table A.1. Virtual key codes.

Name	*Hex Value*	*IBM Keyboard Key*
VK_LBUTTON	01	Left mouse button
VK_RBUTTON	02	Right mouse button
VK_CANCEL	03	Ctrl-Break
VK_MBUTTON	04	
VK_BACK	08	Backspace
VK_TAB	09	Tab
VK_CLEAR	0C	Numeric keypad 5 with Num Lock Off
VK_RETURN	0D	Enter
VK_SHIFT	10	Shift
VK_CONTROL	11	Ctrl
VK_MENU	12	Alt
VK_PAUSE	13	Pause
VK_CAPITAL	14	Caps Lock
VK_ESCAPE	1B	Esc
VK_SPACE	20	Spacebar
VK_PRIOR	21	Page Up
VK_NEXT	22	Page Down
VK_END	23	End
VK_HOME	24	Home
VK_LEFT	25	Left arrow

Name	Hex Value	IBM Keyboard Key
VK_UP	26	Up arrow
VK_RIGHT	27	Right arrow
VK_DOWN	28	Down arrow
VK_SELECT	29	
VK_PRINT	2A	
VK_EXECUTE	2B	
VK_SNAPSHOT	2C	Print screen
VK_INSERT	2D	Ins
VK_DELETE	2E	Del
VK_HELP	2F	
VK_0	30	0
VK_1	31	1
VK_2	32	2
VK_3	33	3
VK_4	34	4
VK_5	35	5
VK_6	36	6
VK_7	37	7
VK_8	38	8
VK_9	39	9
VK_A	41	A
VK_B	42	B
VK_C	43	C
VK_D	44	D
VK_E	45	E

continues

Table A.1. continued

Name	*Hex Value*	*IBM Keyboard Key*
VK_F	46	F
VK_G	47	G
VK_H	48	H
VK_I	49	I
VK_J	4A	J
VK_K	4B	K
VK_L	4C	L
VK_M	4D	M
VK_N	4E	N
VK_O	4F	O
VK_P	50	P
VK_Q	51	Q
VK_R	52	R
VK_S	53	S
VK_T	54	T
VK_U	55	U
VK_V	56	V
VK_W	57	W
VK_X	58	X
VK_Y	59	Y
VK_Z	5A	Z
VK_NUMPAD0	60	Numeric keypad 0 with Num Lock on
VK_NUMPAD1	61	Numeric keypad 1 with Num Lock on
VK_NUMPAD2	62	Numeric keypad 2 with Num Lock on

Name	Hex Value	IBM Keyboard Key
VK_NUMPAD3	63	Numeric keypad 3 with Num Lock on
VK_NUMPAD4	64	Numeric keypad 4 with Num Lock on
VK_NUMPAD5	65	Numeric keypad 5 with Num Lock on
VK_NUMPAD6	66	Numeric keypad 6 with Num Lock on
VK_NUMPAD7	67	Numeric keypad 7 with Num Lock on
VK_NUMPAD8	68	Numeric keypad 8 with Num Lock on
VK_NUMPAD9	69	Numeric keypad 9 with Num Lock on
VK_MULTIPLY	6A	Numeric keypad *
VK_ADD	6B	Numeric keypad +
VK_SEPARATOR	6C	
VK_SUBTRACT	6D	Numeric keypad -
VK_DECIMAL	6E	Numeric keypad .
VK_DIVIDE	6F	Numeric keypad /
VK_F1	70	Function key F1
VK_F2	71	Function key F2
VK_F3	72	Function key F3
VK_F4	73	Function key F4
VK_F5	74	Function key F5
VK_F6	75	Function key F6
VK_F7	76	Function key F7
VK_F8	77	Function key F8
VK_F9	78	Function key F9
VK_F10	79	Function key F10
VK_F11	7A	Function key F11
VK_F12	7B	Function key F12

continues

Table A.1. continued

Name	*Hex Value*	*IBM Keyboard Key*
VK_F13	7C	
VK_F14	7D	
VK_F15	7E	
VK_F16	7F	
VK_NUMLOCK	90	Num Lock

B ASCII CODES

This appendix shows the ASCII (American Standard Code for Information and Interchange) character code values in hex and decimal. The original ASCII character set is composed of only the first 127 characters which are composed of a 7-bit value. The additional codes (128 to 255) are called the IBM extended ASCII character set because they are stored in 8 bits (one full byte).

Dec X_{10}	*Hex* X_{16}	*Binary* X_2	*ASCII Character*
000	00	0000 0000	null
001	01	0000 0001	☺
002	02	0000 0010	☻
003	03	0000 0011	♥
004	04	0000 0100	♦
005	05	0000 0101	♣
006	06	0000 0110	♠
007	07	0000 0111	•
008	08	0000 1000	◘
009	09	0000 1001	○
010	0A	0000 1010	◙
011	0B	0000 1011	♂
012	0C	0000 1100	♀
013	0D	0000 1101	♪
014	0E	0000 1110	♫
015	0F	0000 1111	☼
016	10	0001 0000	►

Dec X_{10}	Hex X_{16}	Binary X_2	ASCII Character
017	11	0001 0001	◄
018	12	0001 0010	↕
019	13	0001 0011	!!
020	14	0001 0100	¶
021	15	0001 0101	§
022	16	0001 0110	–
023	17	0001 0111	↨
024	18	0001 1000	↑
025	19	0001 1001	↓
026	1A	0001 1010	→
027	1B	0001 1011	←
028	1C	0001 1100	FS
029	1D	0001 1101	GS
030	1E	0001 1110	RS
031	1F	0001 1111	US
032	20	0010 0000	SP
033	21	0010 0001	!
034	22	0010 0010	"
035	23	0010 0011	#
036	24	0010 0100	$
037	25	0010 0101	%
038	26	0010 0110	&
039	27	0010 0111	'
040	28	0010 1000	(
041	29	0010 1001	)
042	2A	0010 1010	*
043	2B	0010 1011	+
044	2C	0010 1100	,
045	2D	0010 1101	-
046	2E	0010 1110	.
047	2F	0010 1111	/

Dec X_{10}	*Hex* X_{16}	*Binary* X_2	*ASCII Character*
048	30	0011 0000	0
049	31	0011 0001	1
050	32	0011 0010	2
051	33	0011 0011	3
052	34	0011 0100	4
053	35	0011 0101	5
054	36	0011 0110	6
055	37	0011 0111	7
056	38	0011 1000	8
057	39	0011 1001	9
058	3A	0011 1010	:
059	3B	0011 1011	;
060	3C	0011 1100	<
061	3D	0011 1101	=
062	3E	0011 1110	>
063	3F	0011 1111	?
064	40	0100 0000	@
065	41	0100 0001	A
066	42	0100 0010	B
067	43	0100 0011	C
068	44	0100 0100	D
069	45	0100 0101	E
070	46	0100 0110	F
071	47	0100 0111	G
072	48	0100 1000	H
073	49	0100 1001	I
074	4A	0100 1010	J
075	4B	0100 1011	K
076	4C	0100 1100	L
077	4D	0100 1101	M
078	4E	0100 1110	N

Dec X_{10}	Hex X_{16}	Binary X_2	ASCII Character
079	4F	0100 1111	O
080	50	0101 0000	P
081	51	0101 0001	Q
082	52	0101 0010	R
083	53	0101 0011	S
084	54	0101 0100	T
085	55	0101 0101	U
086	56	0101 0110	V
087	57	0101 0111	W
088	58	0101 1000	X
089	59	0101 1001	Y
090	5A	0101 1010	Z
091	5B	0101 1011	[
092	5C	0101 1100	\
093	5D	0101 1101	]
094	5E	0101 1110	^
095	5F	0101 1111	_
096	60	0110 0000	`
097	61	0110 0001	a
098	62	0110 0010	b
099	63	0110 0011	c
100	64	0110 0100	d
101	65	0110 0101	e
102	66	0110 0110	f
103	67	0110 0111	g
104	68	0110 1000	h
105	69	0110 1001	i
106	6A	0110 1010	j
107	6B	0110 1011	k
108	6C	0110 1100	l
109	6D	0110 1101	m

Dec X_{10}	*Hex* X_{16}	*Binary* X_2	*ASCII Character*
110	6E	0110 1110	n
111	6F	0110 1111	o
112	70	0111 0000	p
113	71	0111 0001	q
114	72	0111 0010	r
115	73	0111 0011	s
116	74	0111 0100	t
117	75	0111 0101	u
118	76	0111 0110	v
119	77	0111 0111	w
120	78	0111 1000	x
121	79	0111 1001	y
122	7A	0111 1010	z
123	7B	0111 1011	{
124	7C	0111 1100	¦
125	7D	0111 1101	}
126	7E	0111 1110	~
127	7F	0111 1111	DEL
128	80	1000 0000	Ç
129	81	1000 0001	ü
130	82	1000 0010	é
131	83	1000 0011	â
132	84	1000 0100	ä
133	85	1000 0101	à
134	86	1000 0110	å
135	87	1000 0111	ç
136	88	1000 1000	ê
137	89	1000 1001	ë
138	8A	1000 1010	è
139	8B	1000 1011	ï
140	8C	1000 1100	î

Dec X_{10}	*Hex* X_{16}	*Binary* X_2	*ASCII Character*
141	8D	1000 1101	ì
142	8E	1000 1110	Ä
143	8F	1000 1111	Å
144	90	1001 0000	É
145	91	1001 0001	æ
146	92	1001 0010	Æ
147	93	1001 0011	ô
148	94	1001 0100	ö
149	95	1001 0101	ò
150	96	1001 0110	û
151	97	1001 0111	ù
152	98	1001 1000	ÿ
153	99	1001 1001	Ö
154	9A	1001 1010	Ü
155	9B	1001 1011	¢
156	9C	1001 1100	£
157	9D	1001 1101	¥
158	9E	1001 1110	Pt
159	9F	1001 1111	ƒ
160	A0	1010 0000	á
161	A1	1010 0001	í
162	A2	1010 0010	ó
163	A3	1010 0011	ú
164	A4	1010 0100	ñ
165	A5	1010 0101	Ñ
166	A6	1010 0110	ª
167	A7	1010 0111	º
168	A8	1010 1000	¿
169	A9	1010 1001	⌐
170	AA	1010 1010	¬
171	AB	1010 1011	½

Dec X_{10}	Hex X_{16}	Binary X_{2}	ASCII Character
172	AC	1010 1100	¼
173	AD	1010 1101	¡
174	AE	1010 1110	«
175	AF	1010 1111	»
176	B0	1011 0000	░
177	B1	1011 0001	▒
178	B2	1011 0010	▓
179	B3	1011 0011	│
180	B4	1011 0100	┤
181	B5	1011 0101	╡
182	B6	1011 0110	╢
183	B7	1011 0111	╖
184	B8	1011 1000	╕
185	B9	1011 1001	╣
186	BA	1011 1010	║
187	BB	1011 1011	╗
188	BC	1011 1100	╝
189	BD	1011 1101	╜
190	BE	1011 1110	╛
191	BF	1011 1111	┐
192	C0	1100 0000	└
193	C1	1100 0001	┴
194	C2	1100 0010	┬
195	C3	1100 0011	├
196	C4	1100 0100	─
197	C5	1100 0101	┼
198	C6	1100 0110	╞
199	C7	1100 0111	╟
200	C8	1100 1000	╚
201	C9	1100 1001	╔
202	CA	1100 1010	╩

Dec X_{10}	Hex X_{16}	Binary X_2	ASCII Character
203	CB	1100 1011	╦
204	CC	1100 1100	╠
205	CD	1100 1101	═
206	CE	1100 1110	╬
207	CF	1100 1111	╧
208	D0	1101 0000	╨
209	D1	1101 0001	╤
210	D2	1101 0010	╥
211	D3	1101 0011	╙
212	D4	1101 0100	╘
213	D5	1101 0101	╒
214	D6	1101 0110	╓
215	D7	1101 0111	╫
216	D8	1101 1000	╪
217	D9	1101 1001	┘
218	DA	1101 1010	┌
219	DB	1101 1011	█
220	DC	1101 1100	▄
221	DD	1101 1101	▌
222	DE	1101 1110	▐
223	DF	1101 1111	▀
224	E0	1110 0000	α
225	E1	1110 0001	β
226	E2	1110 0010	Γ
227	E3	1110 0011	π
228	E4	1110 0100	Σ
229	E5	1110 0101	σ
230	E6	1110 0110	µ
231	E7	1110 0111	τ
232	E8	1110 1000	Φ
233	E9	1110 1001	θ

Dec X_{10}	*Hex* X_{16}	*Binary* X_2	*ASCII Character*
234	EA	1110 1010	Ω
235	EB	1110 1011	δ
236	EC	1110 1100	∞
237	ED	1110 1101	ø
238	EE	1110 1110	∈
239	EF	1110 1111	∩
240	F0	1111 0000	≡
241	F1	1111 0001	±
242	F2	1111 0010	≥
243	F3	1111 0011	≤
244	F4	1111 0100	⌠
245	F5	1111 0101	⌡
246	F6	1111 0110	÷
247	F7	1111 0111	≈
248	F8	1111 1000	°
249	F9	1111 1001	•
250	FA	1111 1010	·
251	FB	1111 1011	√
252	FC	1111 1100	η
253	FD	1111 1101	²
254	FE	1111 1110	■
255	FF	1111 1111	

BIBLIOGRAPHY

The following is a partial list of other books you may be interested in obtaining for additional information about programming for Windows. Although this is not any type of endorsement for these books, they are ones I have found helpful.

Programming Windows 3.1, by Charles Petzold. Microsoft Press.

This was the first book written about programming for Windows. It is considered by many the "bible" of Windows programming. Although it does not cover the ObjectWindows Library, no serious Windows programmer should be without this book.

Windows 3.1: A Developer's Guide, by Jeffrey M. Richter. M&T Books.

A great book to have when you want to learn about some of the more advanced elements of programming for Windows. Topics include: installation programs, setting up printers, special dialog box techniques, and many other goodies. As you create more advanced programs, you will probably want to read this book.

The Waite Group's Windows API Bible, by James L. Conger. Waite Group Press.

Includes 30 chapters (and over 1,000 pages) that describe every Windows API function available. Although the book does not cover Windows 3.1-specific information, this is a good book to have. What I like the most is that for every Windows API function, the author provides a short code example that demonstrates exactly how the function is used.

Windows Programmer's Guide to OLE/DDE, by Jeffrey Clark. Sams Publishing.

A great book that focuses entirely on DDE, DDEML, and OLE. Although somewhat technical, this is a good book to have if you are working with any of these types of interapplication communications. The first half of the book covers DDE/DDEML and the second half covers OLE. Although the book does not use any Borland language tools, most of the examples can be recompiled with only minor modifications, and the Windows API function calls will all be the same.

Windows Programmer's Guide to ObjectWindows Library, by Namir Shammas. Sams Publishing.

If you want to program exclusively with the ObjectWindows Library, this is the book you will want to read. It covers the ObjectWindows Library extensively. You learn about most of the classes that come with OWL and how to use them. Many example programs are included with this book.

Windows API Guides, Volumes 1–4, by Microsoft Press.

These four books document every function, message, and file format that Microsoft makes available to developers. Although these books are rather expensive, they contain valuable information and are required material for a serious Windows developer. As a note, most of the information in these books is the same information available in the online help system of Turbo C++ for Windows. Also, Borland has API reference books that include the same information; however, their typeface is smaller and they have been reorganized so they fit into three volumes. Borland charges considerably less for their manuals but they are only available from Borland.

INDEX

Symbols

A

B

C

D

E

F

G

H

I

J-K

L

M

N

O

P

R

S

T

U

V

W

X-Y-Z

Installing The Floppy Disk

The software included with this book is stored in a compressed form. You cannot use the software without first installing it on your hard drive.

Note: To install the files, you'll need at least 1.2 megabytes of free space on your hard drive.

1. From a DOS prompt, set your default drive to the drive that contains the installation diskette.
2. Type **INSTALL *drive*** (where *drive* is the drive letter of your hard drive), and press Enter.

This will install all the files to a directory called \TURBO! on your hard drive.

- Program code from the book is located in individual subdirectories for each chapter. For example, the code from Chapter 14 is in \TURBO!\CHAP14.
- The files for the Control Palette demo are located in \TURBO!\DEMO. You must execute the INSTALL program in this directory before you can use this application.

What's On The Disk

The disk included with this book contains:

- The program code discussed in the book.
- A demonstration of Blaise Computing's *Control Palette*, a collection of controls, a custom dialog class, and other Windows elements for building sophisticated and attractive user interfaces.
- WEDL (Windows Enhanced Dialog Library), a collection of functions for Windows programmers that makes dialog box data entry dramatically easier.